MY LIFE

RICHARD WAGNER

MY LIFE

BY

RICHARD WAGNER

38340

Authorized Translation

TUDOR PUBLISHING COMPANY
NEW YORK   MCMXXXVI

PREFACE

THE contents of these volumes have been written down directly from my dictation, over a period of several years, by my friend and wife, who wished me to tell her the story of my life. It was the desire of both of us that these details of my life should be accessible to our family and to our sincere and trusted friends; and we decided therefore, in order to provide against a possible destruction of the one manuscript, to have a small number of copies printed at our own expense. As the value of this autobiography consists in its unadorned veracity, which, under the circumstances, is its only justification, therefore my statements had to be accompanied by precise names and dates; hence there could be no question of their publication until some time after my death, should interest in them still survive in our descendants, and on that point I intend leaving directions in my will.

If, on the other hand, we do not refuse certain intimate friends a sight of these papers now, it is that, relying on their genuine interest in the contents, we are confident that they will not pass on their knowledge to any who do not share their feelings in the matter.

RICHARD WAGNER.

CONTENTS

PART I. 1813–1842

PART II. 1842–1850 (DRESDEN)

CONTENTS

Part III. 1850–1861

Part IV. 1861–1864

MY LIFE

MY LIFE

PART I

1813–1842

I was born at Leipzig on the 22nd of May 1813, in a room on the second floor of the ' Red and White Lion,' and two days later was baptized at St. Thomas's Church, and christened Wilhelm Richard.

My father, Friedrich Wagner, was at the time of my birth a clerk in the police service at Leipzig, and hoped to get the post of Chief Constable in that town, but he died in the October of that same year. His death was partly due to the great exertions imposed upon him by the stress of police work during the war troubles and the battle of Leipzig, and partly to the fact that he fell a victim to the nervous fever which was raging at that time. As regards his father's position in life, I learnt later that he had held a small civil appointment as toll collector at the Ranstädt Gate, but had distinguished himself from those in the same station by giving his two sons a superior education, my father, Friedrich, studying law, and the younger son, Adolph, theology.

My uncle subsequently exercised no small influence on my development; we shall meet him again at a critical turning-point in the story of my youth.

My father, whom I had lost so early, was, as I discovered afterwards, a great lover of poetry and literature in general, and possessed in particular an almost passionate affection for the drama, which was at that time much in vogue among the educated classes. My mother told me, among other things, that he took her to Lauchstädt for the first performance of the *Braut von Messina,* and that on the promenade he pointed out Schiller and Goethe to her, and reproved her warmly for never having heard of these great men. He is said to have been not altogether free from a gallant interest in actresses. My mother used to complain jokingly that she often had to keep lunch waiting for him while he was paying court to a certain famous actress of the day.[1] When she scolded him, he vowed that he had been delayed by papers that had to be attended to, and as a proof of his assertion pointed to his fingers, which were supposed to be stained with ink, but on closer inspection were found to be quite clean. His great fondness for the theatre was further shown by his choice of the actor, Ludwig Geyer, as one of his intimate friends. Although his choice of this friend was no doubt mainly due to his love for the theatre, he at the same time introduced into his family the noblest of benefactors; for this modest artist, prompted by a warm interest in the lot of his friend's large family, so unexpectedly left destitute, devoted the remainder of his life to making strenuous efforts to maintain and educate the orphans. Even when the police official was spending his evenings at the theatre, the worthy actor generally filled his place in the family circle, and it seems had frequently to appease my mother, who, rightly or wrongly, complained of the frivolity of her husband.

How deeply the homeless artist, hard pressed by life and tossed to and fro, longed to feel himself at home in a sympathetic family circle, was proved by the fact that a year after his friend's death he married his widow, and from that time forward became a most loving father to the seven children that had been left behind.

In this onerous undertaking he was favoured by an unexpected improvement in his position, for he obtained a remunerative, respectable, and permanent engagement, as a character actor, at the newly established Court Theatre in Dresden. His talent for painting, which had already helped him to earn a livelihood when forced by extreme poverty to break off his university studies, again stood him in good stead in his position at Dresden. True, he complained even more than his critics that he had been kept from a regular and systematic study of this art, yet his extraordinary aptitude, for portrait painting in particular, secured him such important commissions that he unfortunately exhausted his strength prematurely by his

[1] Madame Hartwig.

twofold exertions as painter and actor. Once, when he was invited to Munich to fulfil a temporary engagement at the Court Theatre, he received, through the distinguished recommendation of the Saxon Court, such pressing commissions from the Bavarian Court for portraits of the royal family that he thought it wise to cancel his contract altogether. He also had a turn for poetry. Besides fragments — often in very dainty verse — he wrote several comedies, one of which, *Der Bethlehemitische Kindermord*, in rhymed Alexandrines, was often performed; it was published and received the warmest praise from Goethe.

This excellent man, under whose care our family moved to Dresden when I was two years old, and by whom my mother had another daughter, Cecilia, now also took my education in hand with the greatest care and affection. He wished to adopt me altogether, and accordingly, when I was sent to my first school, he gave me his own name, so that till the age of fourteen I was known to my Dresden schoolfellows as Richard Geyer; and it was not until some years after my stepfather's death, and on my family's return to Leipzig, the home of my own kith and kin, that I resumed the name of Wagner.

The earliest recollections of my childhood are associated with my stepfather, and passed from him to the theatre. I well remember that he would have liked to see me develop a talent for painting; and his studio, with the easel and the pictures upon it, did not fail to impress me. I remember in particular that I tried, with a childish love of imitation, to copy a portrait of King Frederick Augustus of Saxony; but when this simple daubing had to give place to a serious study of drawing, I could not stand it, possibly because I was discouraged by the pedantic technique of my teacher, a cousin of mine, who was rather a bore. At one time during my early boyhood I became so weak after some childish ailment that my mother told me later she used almost to wish me dead, for it seemed as though I should never get well. However, my subsequent good health apparently astonished my parents. I afterwards learnt the noble part played by my excellent stepfather on this occasion also; he never gave way to despair, in spite of the cares and troubles of so large a family, but remained patient throughout, and never lost the hope of pulling me through safely.

My imagination at this time was deeply impressed by my acquaintance with the theatre, with which I was brought into contact, not only as a childish spectator from the mysterious stagebox, with its access to the stage, and by visits to the wardrobe with its fantastic costumes, wigs and other disguises, but also by taking a part in the performances myself. After I had been filled with fear by seeing my father play the villain's part in such tragedies as *Die Waise und der Mörder, Die beiden Galeerensklaven,* I occasionally took part in comedy. I remember that I appeared in *Der Weinberg an der Elbe,* a piece specially written to welcome the King of Saxony on his return from captivity, with music by the conductor, C. M. von Weber. In this I figured in a *tableau vivant* as an angel, sewn up in tights with wings on my back, in a graceful pose which I had laboriously practised. I also remember on this occasion being given a big iced cake, which I was assured the King had intended for me personally. Lastly, I can recall taking a child's part in which I had a few words to speak in Kotzebue's *Menschenhass und Reue,*[1] which furnished me with an excuse at school for not having learnt my lessons. I said I had too much to do, as I had to learn by heart an important part in *Den Menschen ausser der Reihe.*[2]

On the other hand, to show how seriously my father regarded my education, when I was six years old he took me to a clergyman in the country at Possendorf, near Dresden, where I was to be given a sound and healthy training with other boys of my own class. In the evening, the vicar, whose name was Wetzel, used to tell us the story of Robinson Crusoe, and discuss it with us in a highly instructive manner. I was, moreover, much impressed by a biography of Mozart which was read aloud; and the newspaper accounts and monthly reports of the events of the Greek War of Independence stirred my imagination deeply. My love for Greece, which afterwards made me turn with enthusiasm to the mythology and history of ancient Hellas, was thus the natural outcome of the intense and painful interest I took in the

[1] 'Misanthropy and Remorse.'

[2] 'The Man out of the Rank or Row.' In the German this is a simple phonetic corruption of Kotzebue's title, which might easily occur to a child who had only heard, and not read, that title. — EDITOR.

events of this period. In after years the story of the struggle
of the Greeks against the Persians always revived my impressions of this modern revolt of Greece against the Turks.

One day, when I had been in this country home scarcely a
year, a messenger came from town to ask the vicar to take me
to my parents' house in Dresden, as my father was dying.

We did the three hours' journey on foot; and as I was very
exhausted when I arrived, I scarcely understood why my
mother was crying. The next day I was taken to my father's
bedside; the extreme weakness with which he spoke to me,
combined with all the precautions taken in the last desperate
treatment of his complaint — acute hydrothorax — made the
whole scene appear like a dream to me, and I think I was too
frightened and surprised to cry.

In the next room my mother asked me to show her what I
could play on the piano, wisely hoping to divert my father's
thoughts by the sound. I played *Ueb' immer Treu' und
Redlichkeit,* and my father said to her, ' Is it possible he
has musical talent ? '

In the early hours of the next morning my mother came
into the great night nursery, and, standing by the bedside of
each of us in turn, told us, with sobs, that our father was dead,
and gave us each a message with his blessing. To me she
said, ' He hoped to make something of you.'

In the afternoon my schoolmaster, Wetzel, came to take
me back to the country. We walked the whole way to Possendorf, arriving at nightfall. On the way I asked him many
questions about the stars, of which he gave me my first intelligent idea.

A week later my stepfather's brother arrived from Eisleben
for the funeral. He promised, as far as he was able, to support
the family, which was now once more destitute, and undertook
to provide for my future education.

I took leave of my companions and of the kind-hearted
clergyman, and it was for his funeral that I paid my next visit
to Possendorf a few years later. I did not go to the place
again till long afterwards, when I visited it on an excursion
such as I often made, far into the country, at the time when I
was conducting the orchestra in Dresden. I was much grieved

not to find the old parsonage still there, but in its place a more
pretentious modern structure, which so turned me against the
locality, that thenceforward my excursions were always made
in another direction.

This time my uncle brought me back to Dresden in the
carriage. I found my mother and sister in the deepest mourning, and remember being received for the first time with a
tenderness not usual in our family; and I noticed that the same
tenderness marked our leavetaking, when, a few days later,
my uncle took me with him to Eisleben.

This uncle, who was a younger brother of my stepfather,
had settled there as a goldsmith, and Julius, one of my elder
brothers, had already been apprenticed to him. Our old
grandmother also lived with this bachelor son, and as it was
evident that she could not live long, she was not informed of
the death of her eldest son, which I, too, was bidden to keep
to myself. The servant carefully removed the crape from my
coat, telling me she would keep it until my grandmother died,
which was likely to be soon.

I was now often called upon to tell her about my father, and
it was no great difficulty for me to keep the secret of his death,
as I had scarcely realised it myself. She lived in a dark back
room looking out upon a narrow courtyard, and took a great
delight in watching the robins that fluttered freely about her,
and for which she always kept fresh green boughs by the
stove. When some of these robins were killed by the cat, I
managed to catch others for her in the neighbourhood, which
pleased her very much, and, in return, she kept me tidy and
clean. Her death, as had been expected, took place before
long, and the crape that had been put away was now openly
worn in Eisleben.

The back room, with its robins and green branches, now
knew me no more, but I soon made myself at home with a
soap-boiler's family, to whom the house belonged, and became
popular with them on account of the stories I told them.

I was sent to a private school kept by a man called Weiss,
who left an impression of gravity and dignity upon my mind.

Towards the end of the fifties I was greatly moved at reading
in a musical paper the account of a concert at Eisleben, con-

sisting of parts of *Tannhäuser,* at which my former master, who had not forgotten his young pupil, had been present. The little old town with Luther's house, and the numberless memorials it contained of his stay there, has often, in later days, come back to me in dreams. I have always wished to revisit it and verify the clearness of my recollections, but, strange to say, it has never been my fate to do so. We lived in the market-place, where I was often entertained by strange sights, such, for instance, as performances by a troupe of acrobats, in which a man walked a rope stretched from tower to tower across the square, an achievement which long inspired me with a passion for such feats of daring. Indeed, I got so far as to walk a rope fairly easily myself with the help of a balancing-pole. I had made the rope out of cords twisted together and stretched across the courtyard, and even now I still feel a desire to gratify my acrobatic instincts. The thing that attracted me most, however, was the brass band of a Hussar regiment quartered at Eisleben. It often played a certain piece which had just come out, and which was making a great sensation, I mean the ' Huntsmen's Chorus ' out of the *Freischütz,* that had been recently performed at the Opera in Berlin. My uncle and brother asked me eagerly about its composer, Weber, whom I must have seen at my parents' house in Dresden, when he was conductor of the orchestra there.

About the same time the *Jungfernkranz* was zealously played and sung by some friends who lived near us. These two pieces cured me of my weakness for the ' Ypsilanti ' Waltz, which till that time I had regarded as the most wonderful of compositions.

I have recollections of frequent tussles with the town boys, who were constantly mocking at me for my ' square ' cap ; and I remember, too, that I was very fond of rambles of adventure among the rocky banks of the Unstrut.

My uncle's marriage late in life, and the starting of his new home, brought about a marked alteration in his relations to my family.

After a lapse of a year I was taken by him to Leipzig, and handed over for some days to the Wagners, my own father's relatives, consisting of my uncle Adolph and his sister

Friederike Wagner. This extraordinarily interesting man, whose influence afterwards became ever more stimulating to me, now for the first time brought himself and his singular environment into my life.

He and my aunt were very close friends of Jeannette Thomé, a queer old maid who shared with them a large house in the market-place, in which, if I am not mistaken, the Electoral family of Saxony had, ever since the days of Augustus the Strong, hired and furnished the two principal storeys for their own use whenever they were in Leipzig.

So far as I know, Jeannette Thomé really owned the second storey, of which she inhabited only a modest apartment looking out on the courtyard. As, however, the King merely occupied the hired rooms for a few days in the year, Jeannette and her circle generally made use of his splendid apartments, and one of these staterooms was made into a bedroom for me.

The decorations and fittings of these rooms also dated from the days of Augustus the Strong. They were luxurious with heavy silk and rich rococo furniture, all of which were much soiled with age. As a matter of fact, I was delighted by these large strange rooms, looking out upon the bustling Leipzig market-place, where I loved above all to watch the students in the crowd making their way along in their old-fashioned ' Club ' attire, and filling up the whole width of the street.

There was only one portion of the decorations of the rooms that I thoroughly disliked, and this consisted of the various portraits, but particularly those of high-born dames in hooped petticoats, with youthful faces and powdered hair. These appeared to me exactly like ghosts, who, when I was alone in the room, seemed to come back to life, and filled me with the most abject fear. To sleep alone in this distant chamber, in that old-fashioned bed of state, beneath those unearthly pictures, was a constant terror to me. It is true I tried to hide my fear from my aunt when she lighted me to bed in the evening with her candle, but never a night passed in which I was not a prey to the most horrible ghostly visions, my dread of which would leave me in a bath of perspiration.

The personality of the three chief occupants of this storey was admirably adapted to materialise the ghostly impressions of the house into a reality that resembled some strange fairy-tale.

Jeannette Thomé was very small and stout; she wore a fair Titus wig, and seemed to hug to herself the consciousness of vanished beauty. My aunt, her faithful friend and guardian, who was also an old maid, was remarkable for the height and extreme leanness of her person. The oddity of her otherwise very pleasant face was increased by an exceedingly pointed chin.

My uncle Adolph had chosen as his permanent study a dark room in the courtyard. There it was that I saw him for the first time, surrounded by a great wilderness of books, and attired in an unpretentious indoor costume, the most striking feature of which was a tall, pointed felt cap, such as I had seen worn by the clown who belonged to the troupe of rope-dancers at Eisleben. A great love of independence had driven him to this strange retreat. He had been originally destined for the Church, but he soon gave that up, in order to devote himself entirely to philological studies. But as he had the greatest dislike of acting as a professor and teacher in a regular post, he soon tried to make a meagre livelihood by literary work. He had certain social gifts, and especially a fine tenor voice, and appears in his youth to have been welcome as a man of letters among a fairly wide circle of friends at Leipzig.

On a trip to Jena, during which he and a companion seem to have found their way into various musical and oratorical associations, he paid a visit to Schiller. With this object in view, he had come armed with a request from the management of the Leipzig Theatre, who wanted to secure the rights of *Wallenstein*, which was just finished. He told me later of the magic impression made upon him by Schiller, with his tall slight figure and irresistibly attractive blue eyes. His only complaint was that, owing to a well-meant trick played on him by his friend, he had been placed in a most trying position; for the latter had managed to send Schiller a small volume of Adolph Wagner's poems in advance.

The young poet was much embarrassed to hear Schiller address him in flattering terms on the subject of his poetry, but was convinced that the great man was merely encouraging him out of kindness. Afterwards he devoted himself entirely to philological studies — one of his best-known publications in that department being his *Parnasso Italiano,* which he dedicated to Goethe in an Italian poem. True, I have heard experts say that the latter was written in unusually pompous Italian; but Goethe sent him a letter full of praise, as well as a silver cup from his own household plate. The impression that I, as a boy of eight, conceived of Adolph Wagner, amid the surroundings of his own home, was that he was a peculiarly puzzling character.

I soon had to leave the influence of this environment and was brought back to my people at Dresden. Meanwhile my family, under the guidance of my bereaved mother, had been obliged to settle down as well as they could under the circumstances. My eldest brother Albert, who originally intended to study medicine, had, upon the advice of Weber, who had much admired his beautiful tenor voice, started his theatrical career in Breslau. My second sister Louisa soon followed his example, and became an actress. My eldest sister Rosalie had obtained an excellent engagement at the Dresden Court Theatre, and the younger members of the family all looked up to her; for she was now the main support of our poor sorrowing mother. My family still occupied the same comfortable home which my father had made for them. Some of the spare rooms were occasionally let to strangers, and Spohr was among those who at one time lodged with us. Thanks to her great energy, and to help received from various sources (among which the continued generosity of the Court, out of respect to the memory of my late stepfather, must not be forgotten), my mother managed so well in making both ends meet, that even my education did not suffer.

After it had been decided that my sister Clara, owing to her exceedingly beautiful voice, should also go on the stage, my mother took the greatest care to prevent me from developing any taste whatever for the theatre. She never ceased to reproach herself for having consented to the theatrical career of my eldest brother, and as my second brother showed no greater talents than those which were useful to him as a goldsmith, it was now her chief desire to see some progress made towards the fulfilment of the hopes and wishes of my stepfather, ' who hoped to make something of me.' On the completion of my eighth year I was sent to the Kreuz Grammar School in Dresden, where it was hoped I would study! There I was placed at the bottom of the lowest class, and started my education under the most unassuming auspices.

My mother noted with much interest the slightest signs I might show of a growing love and ability for my work. She herself, though not highly educated, always created a lasting impression on all who really learnt to know her, and displayed a peculiar combination of practical domestic efficiency and keen intellectual animation. She never gave one of her children any definite information concerning her antecedents. She came from Weissenfels, and admitted that her parents had been bakers [1] there. Even in regard to her maiden name she always spoke with some embarrassment, and intimated that it was ' Perthes,' though, as we afterwards ascertained, it was in reality ' Bertz.' Strange to say, she had been placed in a high-class boarding-school in Leipzig, where she had enjoyed the advantage of the care and interest of one of ' her father's influential friends,' to whom she afterwards referred as being a Weimar prince who had been very kind to her family in Weissenfels. Her education in that establishment seems to have been interrupted on account of the sudden death of this ' friend.' She became acquainted with my father at a very early age, and married him in the first bloom of her youth, he also being very young, though he already held an appointment. Her chief characteristics seem to have been a keen sense of humour and an amiable temper, so we need not suppose that it was merely a sense of duty towards the family of a departed comrade that afterwards induced the admirable Ludwig Geyer to enter into matrimony with her when she was no longer youthful, but rather that he was impelled to that step by a sincere and warm regard for the widow of his friend. A portrait of her, painted by Geyer during the lifetime of my father, gives one a very favourable impression of what she must have been. Even from the time when my recollection of her is quite distinct, she always had to wear a cap owing to some slight affection of the head, so that I have no recollection of her as

---

[1] According to more recent information — mill-owners.

a young and pretty mother. Her trying position at the head of a numerous family (of which I was the seventh surviving member), the difficulty of obtaining the wherewithal to rear them, and of keeping up appearances on very limited resources, did not conduce to evolve that tender sweetness and solicitude which are usually associated with motherhood. I hardly ever recollect her having fondled me. Indeed, demonstrations of affection were not common in our family, although a certain impetuous, almost passionate and boisterous manner always characterised our dealings. This being so, it naturally seemed to me quite a great event when one night I, fretful with sleepiness, looked up at her with tearful eyes as she was taking me to bed, and saw her gaze back at me proudly and fondly, and speak of me to a visitor then present with a certain amount of tenderness.

What struck me more particularly about her was the strange enthusiasm and almost pathetic manner with which she spoke of the great and of the beautiful in Art. Under this heading, however, she would never have let me suppose that she included dramatic art, but only Poetry, Music, and Painting. Consequently, she often even threatened me with her curse should I ever express a desire to go on the stage. Moreover, she was very religiously inclined. With intense fervour she would often give us long sermons about God and the divine quality in man, during which, now and again, suddenly lowering her voice in a rather funny way, she would interrupt herself in order to rebuke one of us. After the death of our stepfather she used to assemble us all round her bed every morning, when one of us would read out a hymn or a part of the Church service from the prayer-book before she took her coffee. Sometimes the choice of the part to be read was hardly appropriate, as, for instance, when my sister Clara on one occasion thoughtlessly read the 'Prayer to be said in time of War,' and delivered it with so much expression that my mother interrupted her, saying: 'Oh, stop! Good gracious me! Things are not quite so bad as that. There's no war on at present!'

In spite of our limited means we had lively and — as they appeared to my boyish imagination — even brilliant evening parties sometimes. After the death of my stepfather, who, thanks to his success as a portrait painter, in the later years of his life had raised his income to what for those days was a really decent total, many agreeable acquaintances of very good social position whom he had made during this flourishing period still remained on friendly terms with us, and would occasionally join us at our evening gatherings. Amongst those who came were the members of the Court Theatre, who at that time gave very charming and highly entertaining parties of their own, which, on my return to Dresden later on, I found had been altogether given up.

Very delightful, too, were the picnics arranged between us and our friends at some of the beautiful spots around Dresden, for these excursions were always brightened by a certain artistic spirit and general good cheer. I remember one such outing we arranged to Loschwitz, where we made a kind of gypsy camp, in which Carl Maria von Weber played his part in the character of cook. At home we also had some music. My sister Rosalie played the piano, and Clara was beginning to sing. Of the various theatrical performances we organised in those early days, often after elaborate preparation, with the view of amusing ourselves on the birthdays of our elders, I can hardly remember one, save a parody on the romantic play of *Sappho,* by Grillparzer, in which I took part as one of the singers in the crowd that preceded Phaon's triumphal car. I endeavoured to revive these memories by means of a fine puppet show, which I found among the effects of my late stepfather, and for which he himself had painted some beautiful scenery. It was my intention to surprise my people by means of a brilliant performance on this little stage. After I had very clumsily made several puppets, and had provided them with a scanty wardrobe made from cuttings of material purloined from my sisters, I started to compose a chivalric drama, in which I proposed to rehearse my puppets. When I had drafted the first scene, my sisters happened to discover the MS. and literally laughed it to scorn, and, to my great annoyance, for a long time afterwards they chaffed me by repeating one particular sentence which I had put into the mouth of the heroine, and which was — *Ich höre schon den Ritter trabsen* (' I hear his knightly footsteps falling ').

I now returned with renewed ardour to the theatre, with which, even at this time, my family was in close touch. *Der Freischütz* in particular appealed very strongly to my imagination, mainly on account of its ghostly theme. The emotions of terror and the dread of ghosts formed quite an important factor in the development of my mind. From my earliest childhood certain mysterious and uncanny things exercised an enormous influence over me. If I were left alone in a room for long, I remember that, when gazing at lifeless objects such as pieces of furniture, and concentrating my attention upon them, I would suddenly shriek out with fright, because they seemed to me alive. Even during the latest years of my boyhood, not a night passed without my waking out of some ghostly dream and uttering the most frightful shrieks, which subsided only at the sound of some human voice. The most severe rebuke or even chastisement seemed to me at those times no more than a blessed release. None of my brothers or sisters would sleep anywhere near me. They put me to sleep as far as possible away from the others, without thinking that my cries for help would only be louder and longer; but in the end they got used even to this nightly disturbance.

In connection with this childish terror, what attracted me so strongly to the theatre — by which I mean also the stage, the rooms behind the scenes, and the dressing-rooms — was not so much the desire for entertainment and amusement such as that which impels the present-day theatre-goers, but the fascinating pleasure of finding myself in an entirely different atmosphere, in a world that was purely fantastic and often gruesomely attractive. Thus to me a scene, even a wing, representing a bush, or some costume or characteristic part of it, seemed to come from another world, to be in some way as attractive as an apparition, and I felt that contact with it might serve as a lever to lift me from the dull reality of daily routine to that delightful region of spirits. Everything connected with a theatrical performance had for me the charm of mystery, it both bewitched and fascinated me, and while I was trying, with the help of a few playmates, to imitate the performance of *Der Freischütz,* and to devote myself energetically to reproducing the needful costumes and masks in my

grotesque style of painting, the more elegant contents of my
sisters' wardrobes, in the beautifying of which I had often
seen the family occupied, exercised a subtle charm over my
imagination; nay, my heart would beat madly at the very
touch of one of their dresses.

In spite of the fact that, as I already mentioned, our family
was not given to outward manifestations of affection, yet the
fact that I was brought up entirely among feminine surroundings must necessarily have influenced the development of the
sensitive side of my nature. Perhaps it was precisely because
my immediate circle was generally rough and impetuous, that
the opposite characteristics of womanhood, especially such as
were connected with the imaginary world of the theatre,
created a feeling of such tender longing in me.

Luckily these fantastic humours, merging from the gruesome
into the mawkish, were counteracted and balanced by more
serious influences undergone at school at the hands of my
teachers and schoolfellows. Even there, it was chiefly the
weird that aroused my keenest interest. I can hardly judge
whether I had what would be called a good head for study. I
think that, in general, what I really liked I was soon able to
grasp without much effort, whereas I hardly exerted myself
at all in the study of subjects that were uncongenial. This
characteristic was most marked in regard to arithmetic and,
later on, mathematics. In neither of these subjects did I
ever succeed in bringing my mind seriously to bear upon the
tasks that were set me. In the matter of the Classics, too, I
paid only just as much attention as was absolutely necessary
to enable me to get a grasp of them; for I was stimulated by
the desire to reproduce them to myself dramatically. In this
way Greek particularly attracted me, because the stories from
Greek mythology so seized upon my fancy that I tried to
imagine their heroes as speaking to me in their native tongue,
so as to satisfy my longing for complete familiarity with them.
In these circumstances it will be readily understood that the
grammar of the language seemed to me merely a tiresome
obstacle, and bv no means in itself an interesting branch of
knowledge.

The fact that my study of languages was never very thorough,

perhaps best explains the fact that I was afterwards so ready
to cease troubling about them altogether. Not until much
later did this study really begin to interest me again, and that
was only when I learnt to understand its physiological and
philosophical side, as it was revealed to our modern Germanists
by the pioneer work of Jakob Grimm. Then, when it was
too late to apply myself thoroughly to a study which at last
I had learned to appreciate, I regretted that this newer conception of the study of languages had not yet found acceptance
in our colleges when I was younger.

Nevertheless, by my successes in philological work I managed
to attract the attention of a young teacher at the Kreuz
Grammar School, a Master of Arts named Sillig, who proved
very helpful to me. He often permitted me to visit him and
show him my work, consisting of metric translations and a few
original poems, and he always seemed very pleased with my
efforts in recitation. What he thought of me may best be
judged perhaps from the fact that he made me, as a boy of
about twelve, recite not only ' Hector's Farewell ' from the
Iliad, but even Hamlet's celebrated monologue. On one
occasion, when I was in the fourth form of the school, one of
my schoolfellows, a boy named Starke, suddenly fell dead, and
the tragic event aroused so much' sympathy, that not only did
the whole school attend the funeral, but the headmaster also
ordered that a poem should be written in commemoration of
the ceremony, and that this poem should be published. Of the
various poems submitted, among which there was one by myself, prepared very hurriedly, none seemed to the master
worthy of the honour which he had promised, and he therefore announced his intention of substituting one of his own
speeches in the place of our rejected attempts. Much distressed by this decision, I quickly sought out Professor Sillig,
with the view of urging him to intervene on behalf of my poem.
We thereupon went through it together. Its well-constructed
and well-rhymed verses, written in stanzas of eight lines,
determined him to revise the whole of it carefully. Much
of its imagery was bombastic, and far beyond the conception
of a boy of my age. I recollect that in one part I had drawn
extensively from the monologue in Addison's *Cato,* spoken

by Cato just before his suicide. I had met with this passage in an English grammar, and it had made a deep impression upon me. The words: ' The stars shall fade away, the sun himself grow dim with age, and nature sink in years,' which, at all events, were a direct plagiarism, made Sillig laugh — a thing at which I was a little offended. However, I felt very grateful to him, for, thanks to the care and rapidity with which he cleared my poem of these extravagances, it was eventually accepted by the headmaster, printed, and widely circulated.

The effect of this success was extraordinary, both on my schoolfellows and on my own family. My mother devoutly folded her hands in thankfulness, and in my own mind my vocation seemed quite a settled thing. It was clear, beyond the possibility of a doubt, that I was destined to be a poet. Professor Sillig wished me to compose a grand epic, and suggested as a subject ' The Battle of Parnassus,' as described by Pausanias. His reasons for this choice were based upon the legend related by Pausanias, viz., that in the second century B.C. the Muses from Parnassus aided the combined Greek armies against the destructive invasion of the Gauls by provoking a panic among the latter. I actually began my heroic poem in hexameter verse, but could not get through the first canto.

Not being far enough advanced in the language to understand the Greek tragedies thoroughly in the original, my own attempts to construct a tragedy in the Greek form were greatly influenced by the fact that quite by accident I came across August Apel's clever imitation of this style in his striking poems ' Polyïdos ' and ' Aitolier.' For my theme I selected the death of Ulysses, from a fable of Hyginus, according to which the aged hero is killed by his son, the offspring of his union with Calypso. But I did not get very far with this work either, before I gave it up.

My mind became so bent upon this sort of thing, that duller studies naturally ceased to interest me. The mythology, legends, and, at last, the history of Greece alone attracted me.

I was fond of life, merry with my companions, and always ready for a joke or an adventure. Moreover, I was constantly forming friendships, almost passionate in their ardour, with

one or the other of my comrades, and in choosing my
associates I was mainly influenced by the extent to which
my new acquaintance appealed to my eccentric imagination. At one time it would be poetising and versifying that
decided my choice of a friend; at another, theatrical enterprises,
while now and then it would be a longing for rambling and
mischief.

Furthermore, when I reached my thirteenth year, a great
change came over our family affairs. My sister Rosalie, who
had become the chief support of our household, obtained an
advantageous engagement at the theatre in Prague, whither
mother and children removed in 1826, thus giving up the
Dresden home altogether. I was left behind in Dresden, so
that I might continue to attend the Kreuz Grammar School
until I was ready to go up to the university. I was therefore
sent to board and lodge with a family named Böhme, whose
sons I had known at school, and in whose house I already felt
quite at home. With my residence in this somewhat rough,
poor, and not particularly well-conducted family, my years of
dissipation began. I no longer enjoyed the quiet retirement
necessary for work, nor the gentle, spiritual influence of my
sisters' companionship. On the contrary, I was plunged into
a busy, restless life, full of rough horseplay and of quarrels.
Nevertheless, it was there that I began to experience the
influence of the gentler sex in a manner hitherto unknown
to me, as the grown-up daughters of the family and their
friends often filled the scanty and narrow rooms of the house.
Indeed, my first recollections of boyish love date from this
period. I remember a very beautiful young girl, whose name,
if I am not mistaken, was Amalie Hoffmann, coming to call at
the house one Sunday. She was charmingly dressed, and her
appearance as she came into the room literally struck me
dumb with amazement. On other occasions I recollect pretending to be too helplessly sleepy to move, so that I might be
carried up to bed by the girls, that being, as they thought, the
only remedy for my condition. And I repeated this, because
I found, to my surprise, that their attention under these
circumstances brought me into closer and more gratifying
proximity with them.

The most important event during this year of separation from my family was, however, a short visit I paid to them in Prague. In the middle of the winter my mother came to Dresden, and took me back with her to Prague for a week. Her way of travelling was quite unique. To the end of her days she preferred the more dangerous mode of travelling in a hackney carriage to the quicker journey by mail-coach, so that we spent three whole days in the bitter cold on the road from Dresden to Prague. The journey over the Bohemian mountains often seemed to be beset with the greatest dangers, but happily we survived our thrilling adventures and at last arrived in Prague, where I was suddenly plunged into entirely new surroundings.

For a long time the thought of leaving Saxony on another visit to Bohemia, and especially Prague, had had quite a romantic attraction for me. The foreign nationality, the broken German of the people, the peculiar headgear of the women, the native wines, the harp-girls and musicians, and finally, the ever present signs of Catholicism, its numerous chapels and shrines, all produced on me a strangely exhilarating impression. This was probably due to my craze for everything theatrical and spectacular, as distinguished from simple bourgeois customs. Above all, the antique splendour and beauty of the incomparable city of Prague became indelibly stamped on my fancy. Even in my own family surroundings I found attractions to which I had hitherto been a stranger. For instance, my sister Ottilie, only two years older than myself, had won the devoted friendship of a noble family, that of Count Pachta, two of whose daughters, Jenny and Auguste, who had long been famed as the leading beauties of Prague, had become fondly attached to her. To me, such people and such a connection were something quite novel and enchanting. Besides these, certain beaux esprits of Prague, among them W. Marsano, a strikingly handsome and charming man, were frequent visitors at our house. They often earnestly discussed the tales of Hoffmann, which at that date were comparatively new, and had created some sensation. It was now that I made my first though rather superficial acquaintance with this romantic visionary, and so received a stimulus which influenced me for many years even to the point of infatuation, and gave me very peculiar ideas of the world.

In the following spring, 1827, I repeated this journey from Dresden to Prague, but this time on foot, and accompanied by my friend Rudolf Böhme. Our tour was full of adventure. We got to within an hour of Teplitz the first night, and next day we had to get a lift in a wagon, as we had walked our feet sore; yet this only took us as far as Lowositz, as our funds had quite run out. Under a scorching sun, hungry and half-fainting, we wandered along bypaths through absolutely unknown country, until at sundown we happened to reach the main road just as an elegant travelling coach came in sight. I humbled my pride so far as to pretend I was a travelling journeyman, and begged the distinguished travellers for alms, while my friend timidly hid himself in the ditch by the roadside. Luckily we decided to seek shelter for the night in an inn, where we took counsel whether we should spend the alms just received on a supper or a bed. We decided for the supper, proposing to spend the night under the open sky. While we were refreshing ourselves, a strange-looking wayfarer entered. He wore a black velvet skull-cap, to which a metal lyre was attached like a cockade, and on his back he bore a harp. Very cheerfully he set down his instrument, made himself comfortable, and called for a good meal. He intended to stay the night, and to continue his way next day to Prague, where he lived, and whither he was returning from Hanover.

My good spirits and courage were stimulated by the jovial manners of this merry fellow, who constantly repeated his favourite motto, ' non plus ultra.' We soon struck up an acquaintance, and in return for my confidence, the strolling player's attitude to me was one of almost touching sympathy. It was agreed that we should continue our journey together next day on foot. He lent me two twenty-kreutzer pieces (about ninepence), and allowed me to write my Prague address in his pocket-book. I was highly delighted at this personal success. My harpist grew extravagantly merry; a good deal of Czernosek wine was drunk; he sang and played on his harp like a madman, continually reiterating his ' non plus ultra,' till at last, overcome with wine, he fell down on the straw, which had been spread out on the floor for our common bed. When the sun once more peeped in, we could not rouse him, and we had to make up our minds to set off in the freshness of the early morning without him, feeling convinced that the sturdy fellow would overtake us during the day. But it was in vain that we looked out for him on the road and during our subsequent stay in Prague. Indeed, it was not until several weeks later that the extraordinary fellow turned up at my mother's, not so much to collect payment of his loan, as to inquire about the welfare of the young friend to whom that loan had been made.

The remainder of our journey was very fatiguing, and the joy I felt when I at last beheld Prague from the summit of a hill, at about an hour's distance, simply beggars description. Approaching the suburbs, we were for the second time met by a splendid carriage, from which my sister Ottilie's two lovely friends called out to me in astonishment. They had recognised me immediately, in spite of my terribly sunburnt face, blue linen blouse, and bright red cotton cap. Overwhelmed with shame, and with my heart beating like mad, I could hardly utter a word, and hurried away to my mother's to attend at once to the restoration of my sunburnt complexion. To this task I devoted two whole days, during which I swathed my face in parsley poultices; and not till then did I seek the pleasures of society. When, on the return journey, I looked back once more on Prague from the same hilltop, I burst into tears, flung myself on the earth, and for a long time could not be induced by my astonished companion to pursue the journey. I was downcast for the rest of the way, and we arrived home in Dresden without any further adventures.

During the same year I again gratified my fancy for long excursions on foot by joining a numerous company of grammar school boys, consisting of pupils of several classes and of various ages, who had decided to spend their summer holidays in a tour to Leipzig. This journey also stands out among the memories of my youth, by reason of the strong impressions it left behind. The characteristic feature of our party was that we all aped the student, by behaving and dressing extravagantly in the most approved student fashion. After going as far as Meissen on the market-boat, our path lay off the main road, through villages with which I was as yet unfamiliar. We spent the night in the vast barn of a village inn, and our adventures were of the wildest description. There we saw a large marionette show, with almost life-sized figures. Our entire party settled themselves in the auditorium, where their presence was a source of some anxiety to the managers, who had only reckoned on an audience of peasants. *Genovefa* was the play given. The ceaseless silly jests, and constant interpolations and jeering interruptions, in which our corps of embryo-students indulged, finally aroused the anger even of the peasants, who had come prepared to weep. I believe I was the only one of our party who was pained by these impertinences, and in spite of involuntary laughter at some of my comrades' jokes, I not only defended the play itself, but also its original, simple-minded audience. A popular catch-phrase which occurred in the piece has ever since remained stamped on my memory. ' Golo ' instructs the inevitable Kaspar that, when the Count Palatine returns home, he must ' tickle him behind, so that he should feel it in front ' (*hinten zu kitzeln, dass er es vorne fühle*). Kaspar conveys Golo's order verbatim to the Count, and the latter reproaches the unmasked rogue in the following terms, uttered with the greatest pathos: ' O Golo, Golo! thou hast told Kaspar to tickle me behind, so that I shall feel it in front ! '

From Grimma our party rode into Leipzig in open carriages, but not until we had first carefully removed all the outward emblems of the undergraduate, lest the local students we were likely to meet might make us rue our presumption.

Since my first visit, when I was eight years old, I had only once returned to Leipzig, and then for a very brief stay, and under circumstances very similar to those of the earlier visit. I now renewed my fantastic impressions of the Thomé house, but this time, owing to my more advanced education, I looked forward to more intelligent intercourse with my uncle Adolph. An opening for this was soon provided by my joyous astonishment on learning that a bookcase in the large anteroom, containing a goodly collection of books, was my property, having been left me by my father. I went through the books with my uncle, selected at once a number of Latin authors in the handsome Zweibrück edition, along with sundry attractive looking works of poetry and *belles-lettres*, and arranged for them to be sent to Dresden. During this visit I was very much interested in the life of the students. In addition to my impressions of the theatre and of Prague, now came those of the so-called swaggering undergraduate. A great change had taken place in this class. When, as a lad of eight, I had my first glimpse of students, their long hair, their old German costume with the black velvet skull-cap and the shirt collar turned back from the bare neck, had quite taken my fancy. But since that time the old student 'associations' which affected this fashion had disappeared in the face of police prosecutions. On the other hand, the national student clubs, no less peculiar to Germans, had become conspicuous. These clubs adopted, more or less, the fashion of the day, but with some little exaggeration. Albeit, their dress was clearly distinguishable from that of other classes, owing to its picturesqueness, and especially its display of the various club-colours. The ' Comment,' that compendium of pedantic rules of conduct for the preservation of a defiant and exclusive *esprit de corps*, as opposed to the bourgeois classes, had its fantastic side, just as the most philistine peculiarities of the Germans have, if you probe them deeply enough. To me it represented the idea of emancipation from the yoke of school and family. The longing to become a student coincided unfortunately with my growing dislike for drier studies and with my ever-increasing fondness for cultivating romantic poetry. The results of this soon showed themselves in my resolute attempts to make a change.

At the time of my confirmation, at Easter, 1827, I had considerable doubt about this ceremony, and I already felt a serious falling off of my reverence for religious observances. The boy who, not many years before, had gazed with agonised sympathy on the altarpiece in the Kreuz Kirche (Church of the Holy Cross), and had yearned with ecstatic fervour to hang upon the Cross in place of the Saviour, had now so far lost his veneration for the clergyman, whose preparatory confirmation classes he attended, as to be quite ready to make fun of him, and even to join with his comrades in withholding part of his class fees, and spending the money in sweets. How

matters stood with me spiritually was revealed to me, almost
to my horror, at the Communion service, when I walked in
procession with my fellow-communicants to the altar to the
sound of organ and choir. The shudder with which I received
the Bread and Wine was so ineffaceably stamped on my memory,
that I never again partook of the Communion, lest I should do
so with levity. To avoid this was all the easier for me, seeing
that among Protestants such participation is not compulsory.

I soon, however, seized, or rather created, an opportunity
of forcing a breach with the Kreuz Grammar School, and thus
compelled my family to let me go to Leipzig. In self-defence
against what I considered an unjust punishment with which I
was threatened by the assistant headmaster, Baumgarten-
Crusius, for whom I otherwise had great respect, I asked to be
discharged immediately from the school on the ground of sudden
summons to join my family in Leipzig. I had already left the
Böhme household three months before, and now lived alone in
a small garret, where I was waited on by the widow of a court
plate-washer, who at every meal served up the familiar thin
Saxon coffee as almost my sole nourishment. In this attic I did
little else but write verses. Here, too, I formed the first outlines of that stupendous tragedy which afterwards filled my
family with such consternation. The irregular habits I acquired through this premature domestic independence induced
my anxious mother to consent very readily to my removal to
Leipzig, the more so as a part of our scattered family had
already migrated there.

My longing for Leipzig, originally aroused by the fantastic
impressions I had gained there, and later by my enthusiasm
for a student's life, had recently been still further stimulated.
I had seen scarcely anything of my sister Louisa, at that time
a girl of about twenty-two, as she had gone to the theatre of
Breslau shortly after our stepfather's death. Quite recently
she had been in Dresden for a few days on her way to Leipzig,
having accepted an engagement at the theatre there. This
meeting with my almost unknown sister, her hearty manifestations of joy at seeing me again, as well as her sprightly,
merry disposition, quite won my heart. To live with her
seemed an alluring prospect, especially as my mother and

Ottilie had joined her for a while. For the first time a sister had treated me with some tenderness. When at last I reached Leipzig at Christmas in the same year (1827), and there found my mother with Ottilie and Cecilia (my half-sister), I fancied myself in heaven. Great changes, however, had already taken place. Louisa was betrothed to a respected and well-to-do bookseller, Friedrich Brockhaus. This gathering together of the relatives of the penniless bride-elect did not seem to trouble her remarkably kind-hearted fiancé. But my sister may have become uneasy on the subject, for she soon gave me to understand that she was not taking it quite in good part. Her desire to secure an entrée into the higher social circles of bourgeois life naturally produced a marked change in her manner, at one time so full of fun, and of this I gradually became so keenly sensible that finally we were estranged for a time. Moreover, I unfortunately gave her good cause to reprove my conduct. After I got to Leipzig I quite gave up my studies and all regular school work, probably owing to the arbitrary and pedantic system in vogue at the school there.

In Leipzig there were two higher-class schools, one called St. Thomas's School, and the other, and the more modern, St. Nicholas's School. The latter at that time enjoyed a better reputation than the former; so there I had to go. But the council of teachers before whom I appeared for my entrance examination at the New Year (1828) thought fit to maintain the dignity of their school by placing me for a time in the upper third form, whereas at the Kreuz Grammar School in Dresden I had been in the second form. My disgust at having to lay aside my Homer — from which I had already made written translations of twelve songs — and take up the lighter Greek prose writers was indescribable. It hurt my feelings so deeply, and so influenced my behaviour, that I never made a friend of any teacher in the school. The unsympathetic treatment I met with made me all the more obstinate, and various other circumstances in my position only added to this feeling. While student life, as I saw it day by day, inspired me ever more and more with its rebellious spirit, I unexpectedly met with another cause for despising the dry monotony of

school régime. I refer to the influence of my uncle, Adolph
Wagner, which, though he was long unconscious of it, went a
long way towards moulding the growing stripling that I then
was.

The fact that my romantic tastes were not based solely on
a tendency to superficial amusement was shown by my ardent
attachment to this learned relative. In his manner and conversation he was certainly very attractive; the many-sidedness
of his knowledge, which embraced not only philology but also
philosophy and general poetic literature, rendered intercourse
with him a most entertaining pastime, as all those who knew
him used to admit. On the other hand, the fact that he was
denied the gift of writing with equal charm, or clearness, was
a singular defect which seriously lessened his influence upon
the literary world, and, in fact, often made him appear ridiculous, as in a written argument he would perpetrate the most
pompous and involved sentences. This weakness could not
have alarmed me, because in the hazy period of my youth the
more incomprehensible any literary extravagance was, the more
I admired it; besides which, I had more experience of his
conversation than of his writings. He also seemed to find
pleasure in associating with the lad who could listen with so
much heart and soul. Yet unfortunately, possibly in the
fervour of his discourses, of which he was not a little proud,
he forgot that their substance, as well as their form, was far
above my youthful powers of comprehension. I called daily
to accompany him on his constitutional walk beyond the city
gates, and I shrewdly suspect that we often provoked the
smiles of those passers-by who overheard the profound and
often earnest discussions between us. The subjects generally
ranged over everything serious or sublime throughout the
whole realm of knowledge. I took the most enthusiastic
interest in his copious library, and tasted eagerly of almost
all branches of literature. without really grounding myself
in any one of them.

My uncle was delighted to find in me a very willing listener
to his recital of classic tragedies. He had made a translation
of Œdipus, and, according to his intimate friend Tieck, justly
flattered himself on being an excellent reader.

I remember once, when he was sitting at his desk reading out a Greek tragedy to me, it did not annoy him when I fell fast asleep, and he afterwards pretended he had not noticed it. I was also induced to spend my evenings with him, owing to the friendly and genial hospitality his wife showed me. A very great change had come over my uncle's life since my first acquaintance with him at Jeannette Thomé's. The home which he, together with his sister Friederike, had found in his friend's house seemed, as time went on, to have brought in its train duties that were irksome. As his literary work assured him a modest income, he eventually deemed it more in accordance with his dignity to make a home of his own. A friend of his, of the same age as himself, the sister of the æsthete Wendt of Leipzig, who afterwards became famous, was chosen by him to keep house for him. Without saying a word to Jeannette, instead of going for his usual afternoon walk he went to the church with his chosen bride, and got through the marriage ceremonies as quickly as possible; and it was only on his return that he informed us he was leaving, and would have his things removed that very day. He managed to meet the consternation, perhaps also the reproaches, of his elderly friend with quiet composure; and to the end of his life he continued his regular daily visits to ' Mam'selle Thomé,' who at times would coyly pretend to sulk. It was only poor Friederike who seemed obliged at times to atone for her brother's sudden unfaithfulness.

What attracted me in my uncle most strongly was his blunt contempt of the modern pedantry in State, Church, and School, to which he gave vent with some humour. Despite the great moderation of his usual views on life, he yet produced on me the effect of a thorough free-thinker. I was highly delighted by his contempt for the pedantry of the schools. Once, when I had come into serious conflict with all the teachers of the Nicolai School, and the rector of the school had approached my uncle, as the only male representative of my family, with a serious complaint about my behaviour, my uncle asked me during a stroll round the town, with a calm smile as though he were speaking to one of his own age, what I had been up to with the people at school. I explained the whole affair to

him, and described the punishment to which I had been
subjected, and which seemed to me unjust. He pacified me,
and exhorted me to be patient, telling me to comfort myself
with the Spanish proverb, *un rey no puede morír,* which he
explained as meaning that the ruler of a school must of
necessity always be in the right.

He could not, of course, help noticing, to his alarm, the
effect upon me of this kind of conversation, which I was far
too young to appreciate. Although it annoyed me one day,
when I wanted to begin reading Gœthe's *Faust,* to hear him
say quietly that I was too young to understand it, yet, according to my thinking, his other conversations about our own
great poets, and even about Shakespeare and Dante, had made
me so familiar with these sublime figures that I had now for
some time been secretly busy working out the great tragedy
I had already conceived in Dresden. Since my trouble at
school I had devoted all my energies, which ought by rights
to have been exclusively directed to my school duties, to the
accomplishment of this task. In this secret work I had only
one confidante, my sister Ottilie, who now lived with me at
my mother's. I can remember the misgivings and alarm
which the first confidential communication of my great poetic
enterprise aroused in my good sister; yet she affectionately
suffered the tortures I sometimes inflicted on her by reciting
to her in secret, but not without emotion, portions of my
work as it progressed. Once, when I was reciting to her one
of the most gruesome scenes, a heavy thunderstorm came on.
When the lightning flashed quite close to us, and the thunder
rolled, my sister felt bound to implore me to stop; but she
soon found it was hopeless, and continued to endure it with
touching devotion.

But a more significant storm was brewing on the horizon
of my life. My neglect of school reached such a point that it
could not but lead to a rupture. Whilst my dear mother had
no presentiment of this, I awaited the catastrophe with longing
rather than with fear.

In order to meet this crisis with dignity I at length decided
to surprise my family by disclosing to them the secret of my
tragedy, which was now completed. They were to be informed

of this great event by my uncle. I thought I could rely upon his hearty recognition of my vocation as a great poet on account of the deep harmony between us on all other questions of life, science, and art. I therefore sent him my voluminous manuscript, with a long letter which I thought would please him immensely. In this I communicated to him first my ideas with regard to the St. Nicholas's School, and then my firm determination from that time forward not to allow any mere school pedantry to check my free development. But the event turned out very different from what I had expected. It was a great shock to them. My uncle, quite conscious that he had been indiscreet, paid a visit to my mother and brother-in-law, in order to report the misfortune that had befallen the family, reproaching himself for the fact that his influence over me had not always, perhaps, been for my good. To me he wrote a serious letter of discouragement; and to this day I cannot understand why he showed so small a sense of humour in understanding my bad behaviour. To my surprise he merely said that he reproached himself for having corrupted me by conversations unsuited to my years, but he made no attempt to explain to me good-naturedly the error of my ways.

The crime this boy of fifteen had committed was, as I said before, to have written a great tragedy, entitled *Leubald und Adelaïde*. The manuscript of this drama has unfortunately been lost, but I can still see it clearly in my mind's eye. The handwriting was most affected, and the backward-sloping tall letters with which I had aimed at giving it an air of distinction had already been compared by one of my teachers to Persian hieroglyphics. In this composition I had constructed a drama in which I had drawn largely upon Shakespeare's *Hamlet*, *King Lear*, and *Macbeth*, and Goethe's *Götz von Berlichingen*. The plot was really based on a modification of *Hamlet*, the difference consisting in the fact that my hero is so completely carried away by the appearance of the ghost of his father, who has been murdered under similar circumstances, and demands vengeance, that he is driven to fearful deeds of violence; and, with a series of murders on his conscience, he eventually goes mad. Leubald, whose character is a mixture of Hamlet and Harry

Hotspur, had promised his father's ghost to wipe from the face
of the earth the whole race of Roderick, as the ruthless murderer
of the best of fathers was named. After having slain Roderick
himself in mortal combat, and subsequently all his sons and
other relations who supported him, there was only one obstacle
that prevented Leubald from fulfilling the dearest wish of his
heart, which was to be united in death with the shade of his
father: a child of Roderick's was still alive. During the
storming of his castle the murderer's daughter had been carried
away into safety by a faithful suitor, whom she, however,
detested. I had an irresistible impulse to call this maiden
'Adelaïde.' As even at that early age I was a great enthusiast
for everything really German, I can only account for the obviously un-German name of my heroine by my infatuation
for Beethoven's Adelaïde, whose tender refrain seemed to me
the symbol of all loving appeals. The course of my drama was
now characterised by the strange delays which took place in
the accomplishment of this last murder of vengeance, the chief
obstacle to which lay in the sudden passionate love which arose
between Leubald and Adelaïde. I succeeded in representing
the birth and avowal of this love by means of extraordinary
adventures. Adelaïde was once more stolen away by a robber-
knight from the lover who had been sheltering her. After
Leubald had thereupon sacrificed the lover and all his relations,
he hastened to the robber's castle, driven thither less by a
thirst for blood than by a longing for death. For this reason
he regrets his inability to storm the robber's castle forthwith,
because it is well defended, and, moreover, night is fast falling;
he is therefore obliged to pitch his tent. After raving for a
while he sinks down for the first time exhausted, but being
urged, like his prototype Hamlet, by the spirit of his father to
complete his vow of vengeance, he himself suddenly falls into
the power of the enemy during a night assault. In the subter-
ranean dungeons of the castle he meets Roderick's daughter
for the first time. She is a prisoner like himself, and is craftily
devising flight. Under circumstances in which she produces
on him the impression of a heavenly vision, she makes her
appearance before him. They fall in love, and fly together
into the wilderness, where they realise that they are deadly

enemies. The incipient insanity which was already noticeable
in Leubald breaks out more violently after this discovery,
and everything that can be done to intensify it is contributed
by the ghost of his father, which continually comes between
the advances of the lovers. But this ghost is not the only
disturber of the conciliating love of Leubald and Adelaïde.
The ghost of Roderick also appears, and according to the
method followed by Shakespeare in *Richard III.*, he is joined
by the ghosts of all the other members of Adelaïde's family
whom Leubald has slain. From the incessant importunities
of these ghosts Leubald seeks to free himself by means of
sorcery, and calls to his aid a rascal named Flamming. One
of *Macbeth's* witches is summoned to lay the ghosts; as she
is unable to do this efficiently, the furious Leubald sends her
also to the devil; but with her dying breath she despatches
the whole crowd of spirits who serve her to join the ghosts of
those already pursuing him. Leubald, tormented beyond
endurance, and now at last raving mad, turns against his
beloved, who is the apparent cause of all his misery. He stabs
her in his fury; then finding himself suddenly at peace, he
sinks his head into her lap, and accepts her last caresses as her
life-blood streams over his own dying body.

I had not omitted the smallest detail that could give this
plot its proper colouring, and had drawn on all my knowledge
of the tales of the old knights, and my acquaintance with *Lear*
and *Macbeth,* to furnish my drama with the most vivid situations. But one of the chief characteristics of its poetical form
I took from the pathetic, humorous, and powerful language of
Shakespeare. The boldness of my grandiloquent and bombastic expressions roused my uncle Adolph's alarm and astonishment. He was unable to understand how I could have
selected and used with inconceivable exaggeration precisely
the most extravagant forms of speech to be found in *Lear* and
Götz von Berlichingen. Nevertheless, even after everybody had
deafened me with their laments over my lost time and perverted talents, I was still conscious of a wonderful secret solace
in the face of the calamity that had befallen me. I knew, a
fact that no one else could know, namely, that my work could
only be rightly judged when set to the music which I had

resolved to write for it, and which I intended to start composing
immediately.

I must now explain my position with respect to music hitherto.
For this purpose I must go back to my earliest attempts in
the art. In my family two of my sisters were musical; the
elder one, Rosalie, played the piano, without, however, displaying any marked talent. Clara was more gifted; in
addition to a great deal of musical feeling, and a fine rich
touch on the piano, she possessed a particularly sympathetic
voice, the development of which was so premature and remarkable that, under the tuition of Mieksch, her singing master,
who was famous at that time, she was apparently ready for
the rôle of a prima donna as early as her sixteenth year, and
made her début at Dresden in Italian opera as 'Cenerentola'
in Rossini's opera of that name. Incidentally I may remark
that this premature development proved injurious to Clara's
voice, and was detrimental to her whole career. As I have
said, music was represented in our family by these two sisters.
It was chiefly owing to Clara's career that the musical conductor C. M. von Weber often came to our house. His visits
were varied by those of the great male-soprano Sassaroli; and
in addition to these two representatives of German and Italian
music, we also had the company of Mieksch, her singing master.
It was on these occasions that I as a child first heard German
and Italian music discussed, and learnt that any one who
wished to ingratiate himself with the Court must show a preference for Italian music, a fact which led to very practical results
in our family council. Clara's talent, while her voice was still
sound, was the object of competition between the representatives of Italian and German opera. I can remember quite
distinctly that from the very beginning I declared myself in
favour of German opera; my choice was determined by the
tremendous impression made on me by the two figures of
Sassaroli and Weber. The Italian male-soprano, a huge pot-
bellied giant, horrified me with his high effeminate voice, his
astonishing volubility, and his incessant screeching laughter.
In spite of his boundless good-nature and amiability, particularly to my family, I took an uncanny dislike to him. On
account of this dreadful person, the sound of Italian, either

spoken or sung, seemed to my ears almost diabolical; and when, in consequence of my poor sister's misfortune, I heard them often talking about Italian intrigues and cabals, I conceived so strong a dislike for everything connected with this nation that even in much later years I used to feel myself carried away by an impulse of utter detestation and abhorrence.

The less frequent visits of Weber, on the other hand, seemed to have produced upon me those first sympathetic impressions which I have never since lost. In contrast to Sassaroli's repulsive figure, Weber's really refined, delicate, and intellectual appearance excited my ecstatic admiration. His narrow face and finely-cut features, his vivacious though often half-closed eyes, captivated and thrilled me; whilst even the bad limp with which he walked, and which I often noticed from our windows when the master was making his way home past our house from the fatiguing rehearsals, stamped the great musician in my imagination as an exceptional and almost superhuman being. When, as a boy of nine, my mother introduced me to him, and he asked me what I was going to be, whether I wanted perhaps to be a musician, my mother told him that, though I was indeed quite mad on *Freischütz,* yet she had as yet seen nothing in me which indicated any musical talent.

This showed correct observation on my mother's part; nothing had made so great an impression on me as the music of *Freischütz,* and I tried in every possible way to procure a repetition of the impressions I had received from it, but, strange to say, least of all by the study of music itself. Instead of this, I contented myself with hearing bits from *Freischütz* played by my sisters. Yet my passion for it gradually grew so strong that I can remember taking a particular fancy for a young man called Spiess, chiefly because he could play the overture to *Freischütz,* which I used to ask him to do whenever I met him. It was chiefly the introduction to this overture which at last led me to attempt, without ever having received any instruction on the piano, to play this piece in my own peculiar way, for, oddly enough, I was the only child in our family who had not been given music lessons. This was probably due to my mother's anxiety to keep me away from any artistic interests of this kind in case they might arouse in me a longing for the theatre.

When I was about twelve years old, however, my mother engaged a tutor for me named Humann, from whom I received regular music lessons, though only of a very mediocre description. As soon as I had acquired a very imperfect knowledge of fingering I begged to be allowed to play overtures in the form of duets, always keeping Weber as the goal of my ambition. When at length I had got so far as to be able to play the overture to *Freischütz* myself, though in a very faulty manner, I felt the object of my study had been attained, and I had no inclination to devote any further attention to perfecting my technique.

Yet I had attained this much: I was no longer dependent for music on the playing of others; from this time forth I used to try and play, albeit very imperfectly, everything I wanted to know. I also tried Mozart's *Don Juan,* but was unable to get any pleasure out of it, mainly because the Italian text in the arrangement for the piano placed the music in a frivolous light in my eyes, and much in it seemed to me trivial and unmanly. (I can remember that when my sister used to sing Zerlinen's ariette, *Batti, batti, ben Masetto,* the music repelled me, as it seemed so mawkish and effeminate.)

On the other hand, my bent for music grew stronger and stronger, and I now tried to possess myself of my favourite pieces by making my own copies. I can remember the hesitation with which my mother for the first time gave me the money to buy the scored paper on which I copied out Weber's *Lützow's Jagd,* which was the first piece of music I transcribed.

Music was still a secondary occupation with me when the news of Weber's death and the longing to learn his music to *Oberon* fanned my enthusiasm into flame again. This received fresh impetus from the afternoon concerts in the Grosser Garten at Dresden, where I often heard my favourite music played by Zillmann's Town Band, as I thought, exceedingly well. The mysterious joy I felt in hearing an orchestra play quite close to me still remains one of my most pleasant memories. The mere tuning up of the instruments put me in a state of mystic excitement; even the striking of fifths on the violin seemed to me like a greeting from the spirit world — which, I may mention incidentally, had a very real meaning for me. When I was still almost a baby, the sound of these fifths, which has always excited me, was closely associated in my mind with ghosts and spirits. I remember that even much later in life I could never pass the small palace of Prince Anthony, at the end of the Ostra Allee in Dresden, without a shudder; for it was there I had first heard the sound of a violin, a very common experience to me afterwards. It was close by me, and seemed to my ears to come from the stone figures with which this palace is adorned, some of which are provided with musical instruments. When I took up my post as musical conductor at Dresden, and had to pay my official visit to Morgenroth, the President of the Concert Committee, an elderly gentleman who lived for many years opposite that princely palace, it seemed odd to find that the player of fifths who had so strongly impressed my musical fancy as a boy was anything but a supernatural spectre. And when I saw the well-known picture in which a skeleton plays on his violin to an old man on his deathbed, the ghostly character of those very notes impressed itself with particular force upon my childish imagination. When at last, as a young man, I used to listen to the Zillmann Orchestra in the Grosser Garten almost every afternoon, one may imagine the rapturous thrill with which I drew in all the chaotic variety of sound that I heard as the orchestra tuned up: the long drawn A of the oboe, which seemed like a call from the dead to rouse the other instruments, never failed to raise all my nerves to a feverish pitch of tension, and when the swelling C in the overture to *Freischütz* told me that I had stepped, as it were with both feet, right into the magic realm of awe. Any one who had been watching me at that moment could hardly have failed to see the state I was in, and this in spite of the fact that I was such a bad performer on the piano.

Another work also exercised a great fascination over me, namely, the overture to *Fidelio* in E major, the introduction to which affected me deeply. I asked my sisters about Beethoven, and learned that the news of his death had just arrived. Obsessed as I still was by the terrible grief caused

by Weber's death, this fresh loss, due to the decease of this
great master of melody, who had only just entered my life,
filled me with strange anguish, a feeling nearly akin to my
childish dread of the ghostly fifths on the violin. It was now
Beethoven's music that I longed to know more thoroughly;
I came to Leipzig, and found his music to *Egmont* on the piano
at my sister Louisa's. After that I tried to get hold of his
sonatas. At last, at a concert at the Gewandthaus, I heard
one of the master's symphonies for the first time; it was the
Symphony in A major. The effect on me was indescribable.
To this must be added the impression produced on me by
Beethoven's features, which I saw in the lithographs that
were circulated everywhere at that time, and by the fact that
he was deaf, and lived a quiet secluded life. I soon conceived
an image of him in my mind as a sublime and unique supernatural being, with whom none could compare. This image
was associated in my brain with that of Shakespeare; in ecstatic dreams I met both of them, saw and spoke to them, and
on awakening found myself bathed in tears.

It was at this time that I came across Mozart's *Requiem*,
which formed the starting-point of my enthusiastic absorption
in the works of that master. His second finale to *Don Juan*
inspired me to include him in my spirit world.

I was now filled with a desire to compose, as I had before
been to write verse. I had, however, in this case to master
the technique of an entirely separate and complicated subject.
This presented greater difficulties than I had met with in
writing verse, which came to me fairly easily. It was these
difficulties that drove me to adopt a career which bore some
resemblance to that of a professional musician, whose future
distinction would be to win the titles of Conductor and Writer
of Opera.

I now wanted to set *Leubald und Adelaïde* to music,
similar to that which Beethoven wrote to Goethe's *Egmont;*
the various ghosts from the spirit world, who were each to
display different characteristics, were to borrow their own dis-
tinctive colouring from appropriate musical accompaniment.
In order to acquire the necessary technique of composition
quickly I studied Logier's *Methode des Generalbasses*, a work

which was specially recommended to me at a musical lending library as a suitable text-book from which this art might be easily mastered. I have distinct recollections that the financial difficulties with which I was continually harassed throughout my life began at this time. I borrowed Logier's book on the weekly payment system, in the fond hope of having to pay for it only during a few weeks out of the savings of my weekly pocket-money. But the weeks ran on into months, and I was still unable to compose as well as I wished. Mr. Frederick Wieck, whose daughter afterwards married Robert Schumann, was at that time the proprietor of that lending library. He kept sending me troublesome reminders of the debt I owed him; and when my bill had almost reached the price of Logier's book I had to make a clean breast of the matter to my family, who thus not only learnt of my financial difficulties in general, but also of my latest transgression into the domain of music, from which, of course, at the very most, they expected nothing better than a repetition of *Leubald und Adelaïde*.

There was great consternation at home; my mother, sister, and brother-in-law, with anxious faces, discussed how my studies should be superintended in future, to prevent my having any further opportunity for transgressing in this way. No one, however, yet knew the real state of affairs at school, and they hoped I would soon see the error of my ways in this case as I had in my former craze for poetry.

But other domestic changes were taking place which necessitated my being for some little time alone in our house at Leipzig during the summer of 1829, when I was left entirely to my own devices. It was during this period that my passion for music rose to an extraordinary degree. I had secretly been taking lessons in harmony from G. Müller, afterwards organist at Altenburg, an excellent musician belonging to the Leipzig orchestra. Although the payment of these lessons was also destined to get me into hot water at home later on, I could not even make up to my teacher for the delay in the payment of his fees by giving him the pleasure of watching me improve in my studies. His teaching and exercises soon filled me with the greatest disgust, as to my mind it all seemed so dry. For me music was a spirit, a noble and mystic monster, and any attempt to regulate it seemed to lower it in my eyes. I gathered much more congenial instruction about it from Hoffmann's *Phantasiestücken* than from my Leipzig orchestra player; and now came the time when I really lived and breathed in Hoffmann's artistic atmosphere of ghosts and spirits. With my head quite full of Kreissler, Krespel, and other musical spectres from my favourite author, I imagined that I had at last found in real life a creature who resembled them: this ideal musician in whom for a time I fancied I had discovered a second Kreissler was a man called Flachs. He was a tall, exceedingly thin man, with a very narrow head and an extraordinary way of walking, moving, and speaking, whom I had seen at all those open-air concerts which formed my principal source of musical education. He was always with the members of the orchestra, speaking exceedingly quickly, first to one and then the other; for they all knew him, and seemed to like him. The fact that they were making fun of him I only learned, to my great confusion, much later. I remember having noticed this strange figure from my earliest days in Dresden, and I gathered from the conversations which I overheard that he was indeed well known to all Dresden musicians. This circumstance alone was sufficient to make me take a great interest in him; but the point about him which attracted me more than anything was the manner in which he listened to the various items in the programme: he used to give peculiar, convulsive nods of his head, and blow out his cheeks as though with sighs. All this I regarded as a sign of spiritual ecstasy. I noticed, moreover, that he was quite alone, that he belonged to no party, and paid no attention to anything in the garden save the music; whereupon my identification of this curious being with the conductor Kreissler seemed quite natural. I was determined to make his acquaintance, and I succeeded in doing so. Who shall describe my delight when, on going to call on him at his rooms for the first time, I found innumerable bundles of scores! I had as yet never seen a score. It is true I discovered, to my regret, that he possessed nothing either by Beethoven, Mozart, or Weber; in fact, nothing but immense quantities of works, masses, and cantatas by composers such as Staerkel, Stamitz, Steibelt, etc., all of whom

were entirely unknown to me. Yet Flachs was able to tell me
so much that was good about them that the respect which I
felt for scores in general helped me to overcome my regret at
not finding anything by my beloved masters. It is true I
learnt later that poor Flachs had only come into the possession
of these particular scores through unscrupulous dealers, who
had traded on his weakness of intellect and palmed off this
worthless music on him for large sums of money. At all events,
they were scores, and that was quite enough for me. Flachs
and I became most intimate; we were always seen going about
together — I, a lanky boy of sixteen, and this weird, shaky
flaxpole. The doors of my deserted home were often opened
for this strange guest, who made me play my compositions to
him while he ate bread and cheese. In return, he once
arranged one of my airs for wind instruments, and, to my
astonishment, it was actually accepted and played by the band
in Kintschy's Swiss Châlet. That this man had not the
smallest capacity to teach me anything never once occurred
to me; I was so firmly convinced of his originality that there
was no need for him to prove it further than by listening
patiently to my enthusiastic outpourings. But as, in course
of time, several of his own friends joined us, I could not help
noticing that the worthy Flachs was regarded by them all as
a half-witted fool. At first this merely pained me, but a
strange incident unexpectedly occurred which converted me to
the general opinion about him. Flachs was a man of some
means, and had fallen into the toils of a young lady of dubious
character who he believed was deeply in love with him. One
day, without warning, I found his house closed to me, and
discovered, to my astonishment, that jealousy was the cause.
The unexpected discovery of this liaison, which was my first
experience of such a case, filled me with a strange horror. My
friend suddenly appeared to me even more mad than he really
was. I felt so ashamed of my persistent blindness that for
some time to come I never went to any of the garden concerts
for fear I should meet my sham Kreissler.

By this time I had composed my first Sonata in D minor.
I had also begun a pastoral play, and had worked it out in
what I felt sure must be an entirely unprecedented way.

I chose Goethe's *Laune der Verliebten* as a model for the form and plot of my work. I scarcely even drafted out the libretto, however, but worked it out at the same time as the music and orchestration, so that, while I was writing out one page of the score, I had not even thought out the words for the next page. I remember distinctly that following this extraordinary method, although I had not acquired the slightest knowledge about writing for instruments, I actually worked out a fairly long passage which finally resolved itself into a scene for three female voices followed by the air for the tenor. My bent for writing for the orchestra was so strong that I procured a score of *Don Juan*, and set to work on what I then considered a very careful orchestration of a fairly long air for soprano. I also wrote a quartette in D major after I had myself sufficiently mastered the alto for the viola, my ignorance of which had caused me great difficulty only a short time before, when I was studying a quartette by Haydn.

Armed with these works, I set out in the summer on my first journey as a musician. My sister Clara, who was married to the singer Wolfram, had an engagement at the theatre at Magdeburg, whither, in characteristic fashion, I set forth upon my adventure on foot.

My short stay with my relations provided me with many experiences of musical life. It was there that I met a new freak, whose influence upon me I have never been able to forget. He was a musical conductor of the name of Kühnlein, a most extraordinary person. Already advanced in years, delicate and, unfortunately, given to drink, this man nevertheless impressed one by something striking and vigorous in his expression. His chief characteristics were an enthusiastic worship of Mozart and a passionate depreciation of Weber. He had read only one book — Goethe's *Faust* — and in this work there was not a page in which he had not underlined some passage, and made some remark in praise of Mozart or in disparagement of Weber. It was to this man that my brother-in-law confided the compositions which I had brought with me in order to learn his opinion of my abilities. One evening, as we were sitting comfortably in an inn, old Kühnlein came in, and approached us with a friendly, though serious manner.

I thought I read good news in his features, but when my
brother-in-law asked him what he thought of my work, he
answered quietly and calmly, ' There is not a single good note
in it!' My brother-in-law, who was accustomed to Kühnlein's
eccentricity, gave a loud laugh which reassured me somewhat.
It was impossible to get any advice or coherent reasons for his
opinion out of Kühnlein; he merely renewed his abuse of
Weber and made some references to Mozart which, nevertheless, made a deep impression upon me, as Kühnlein's language
was always very heated and emphatic.

On the other hand, this visit brought me a great treasure,
which was responsible for leading me in a very different direction from that advised by Kühnlein. This was the score of
Beethoven's great Quartette in E flat major, which had only
been fairly recently published, and of which my brother-in-law
had a copy made for me. Richer in experience, and in the
possession of this treasure, I returned to Leipzig to the nursery
of my queer musical studies. But my family had now returned
with my sister Rosalie, and I could no longer keep secret from
them the fact that my connection with the school had been
entirely suspended, for a notice was found saying that I had
not attended the school for the last six months. As a complaint addressed by the rector to my uncle about me had not
received adequate attention, the school authorities had apparently made no further attempts to exercise any supervision
over me, which I had indeed rendered quite impossible by
absenting myself altogether.

A fresh council of war was held in the family to discuss
what was to be done with me. As I laid particular stress on
my bent for music, my relations thought that I ought, at any
rate, to learn one instrument thoroughly. My brother-in-law,
Brockhaus, proposed to send me to Hummel, at Weimar, to
be trained as a pianist, but as I loudly protested that by
' music ' I meant ' composing,' and not ' playing an instrument,' they gave way, and decided to let me have regular
lessons in harmony from Müller, the very musician from whom
I had had instruction on the sly some little while before, and
who had not yet been paid. In return for this I promised
faithfully to go back to work conscientiously at St. Nicholas's

School. I soon grew tired of both. I could brook no control, and this unfortunately applied to my musical instruction as well. The dry study of harmony disgusted me more and more, though I continued to conceive fantasias, sonatas, and overtures, and work them out by myself. On the other hand, I was spurred on by ambition to show what I could do at school if I liked. When the Upper School boys were set the task of writing a poem, I composed a chorus in Greek, on the recent War of Liberation. I can well imagine that this Greek poem had about as much resemblance to a real Greek oration and poetry, as the sonatas and overtures I used to compose at that time had to thoroughly professional music. My attempt was scornfully rejected as a piece of impudence. After that I have no further recollections of my school. My continued attendance was a pure sacrifice on my side, made out of consideration for my family: I did not pay the slightest attention to what was taught in the lessons, but secretly occupied myself all the while with reading any book that happened to attract me.

As my musical instruction also did me no good, I continued in my wilful process of self-education by copying out the scores of my beloved masters, and in so doing acquired a neat handwriting, which in later years has often been admired. I believe my copies of the C minor Symphony and the Ninth Symphony by Beethoven are still preserved as souvenirs.

Beethoven's Ninth Symphony became the mystical goal of all my strange thoughts and desires about music. I was first attracted to it by the opinion prevalent among musicians, not only in Leipzig but elsewhere, that this work had been written by Beethoven when he was already half mad. It was considered the *non plus ultra* of all that was fantastic and incomprehensible, and this was quite enough to rouse in me a passionate desire to study this mysterious work. At the very first glance at the score, of which I obtained possession with such difficulty, I felt irresistibly attracted by the long-sustained pure fifths with which the first phrase opens: these chords, which, as I related above, had played such a supernatural part in my childish impressions of music, seemed in this case to form the spiritual keynote of my own life. This, I thought, must surely contain the secret of all secrets, and accordingly the first thing to be done was to make the score my own by a process of laborious copying. I well remember that on one occasion the sudden appearance of the dawn made such an uncanny impression on my excited nerves that I jumped into bed with a scream as though I had seen a ghost. The symphony at that time had not yet been arranged for the piano; it had found so little favour that the publisher did not feel inclined to run the risk of producing it. I set to work at it, and actually composed a complete piano solo, which I tried to play to myself. I sent my work to Schott, the publisher of the score, at Mainz. I received in reply a letter saying ' that the publishers had not yet decided to issue the Ninth Symphony for the piano, but that they would gladly keep my laborious work,' and offered me remuneration in the shape of the score of the great *Missa Solemnis* in D, which I accepted with great pleasure.

In addition to this work I practised the violin for some time, as my harmony master very rightly considered that some knowledge of the practical working of this instrument was indispensable for any one who had the intention of composing for the orchestra. My mother, indeed, paid the violinist Sipp (who was still playing in the Leipzig orchestra in 1865) eight thalers for a violin (I do not know what became of it), with which for quite three months I must have inflicted unutterable torture upon my mother and sister by practising in my tiny little room. I got so far as to play certain Variations in F sharp by Mayseder, but only reached the second or third. After that I have no further recollections of this practising, in which my family fortunately had very good reasons of their own for not encouraging me.

But the time now arrived when my interest in the theatre again took a passionate hold upon me. A new company had been formed in my birthplace under very good auspices. The Board of Management of the Court Theatre at Dresden had taken over the management of the Leipzig theatre for three years. My sister Rosalie was a member of the company, and through her I could always gain admittance to the performances; and that which in my childhood had been merely the interest aroused by a strange spirit of curiosity now became a more deep-seated and conscious passion.

Julius Cæsar, Macbeth, Hamlet, the plays of Schiller, and to crown all, Goethe's *Faust,* excited and stirred me deeply. The Opera was giving the first performances of Marschner's *Vampir* and *Templer und Jüdin.* The Italian company arrived from Dresden, and fascinated the Leipzig audience by their consummate mastery of their art. Even I was almost carried away by the enthusiasm with which the town was overwhelmed, into forgetting the boyish impressions which Signor Sassaroli had stamped upon my mind, when another miracle — which also came to us from Dresden — suddenly gave a new direction to my artistic feelings and exercised a decisive influence over my whole life. This consisted of a special performance given by Wilhelmine Schröder-Devrient, who at that time was at the zenith of her artistic career, young, beautiful, and ardent, and whose like I have never again seen on the stage. She made her appearance in *Fidelio.*

If I look back on my life as a whole, I can find no event that produced so profound an impression upon me. Any one who can remember that wonderful woman at this period of her life must to some extent have experienced the almost satanic ardour which the intensely human art of this incomparable actress poured into his veins. After the performance I rushed to a friend's house and wrote a short note to the singer, in which I briefly told her that from that moment my life had acquired its true significance, and that if in days to come she should ever hear my name praised in the world of Art, she must remember that she had that evening made me what I then swore it was my destiny to become. This note I left at her hotel, and ran out into the night as if I were mad. In the year 1842, when I went to Dresden to make my début with *Rienzi,* I paid several visits to the kind-hearted singer, who startled me on one occasion by repeating this letter word for word. It seemed to have made an impression on her too, as she had actually kept it.

At this point I feel myself obliged to acknowledge that the great confusion which now began to prevail in my life, and particularly in my studies, was due to the inordinate effect this artistic interpretation had upon me. I did not know where to turn, or how to set about producing something myself which might place me in direct contact with the impression I had received, while everything that could not be brought into touch with it seemed to me so shallow and meaningless that I could not possibly trouble myself with it. I should have liked to compose a work worthy of a Schröder-Devrient; but as this was quite beyond my power, in my headlong despair I let all artistic endeavour slide, and as my work was also utterly insufficient to absorb me, I flung myself recklessly into the life of the moment in the company of strangely chosen associates, and indulged in all kinds of youthful excesses.

I now entered into all the dissipations of raw manhood, the outward ugliness and inward emptiness of which make me marvel to this day. My intercourse with those of my own age had always been the result of pure chance. I cannot remember that any special inclination or attraction determined me in the choice of my young friends. While I can honestly say that I was never in a position to stand aloof out of envy from any one who was specially gifted, I can only explain my indifference in the choice of my associates by the fact that through inexperience regarding the sort of companionship that would be of advantage to me, I cared only to have some one who would accompany me in my excursions, and to whom I could pour out my feelings to my heart's content without caring what effect it might have upon him. The result of this was that after a stream of confidences to which my own excitement was the only response, I at length reached the point when I turned and looked at my friend; to my astonishment I generally found that there was no question of response at all, and as soon as I set my heart on drawing something from him in return, and urged him to confide in me, when he really had nothing to tell, the connection usually came to an end and left no trace on my life. In a certain sense my strange relationship with Flachs was typical of the great majority of my ties in after-life. Consequently, as no lasting personal bond of friendship ever found its way into my life, it is easy to understand how delight in the dissipations of student life could become

a passion of some duration, because in it individual intercourse
is entirely replaced by a common circle of acquaintances. In
the midst of rowdyism and ragging of the most foolish description I remained quite alone, and it is quite possible that
these frivolities formed a protecting hedge round my inmost
soul, which needed time to grow to its natural strength and not
be weakened by reaching maturity too soon.

My life seemed to break up in all directions; I had to leave
St. Nicholas's School at Easter 1830, as I was too deeply in disgrace with the staff of masters ever to hope for any promotion
in the University from that quarter. It was now determined
that I should study privately for six months and then go to
St. Thomas's School, where I should be in fresh surroundings
and be able to work up and qualify in a short time for the
University. My uncle Adolph, with whom I was constantly
renewing my friendship, and who also encouraged me about
my music and exercised a good influence over me in that respect, in spite of the utter degradation of my life at that time,
kept arousing in me an ever fresh desire for scientific studies.
I took private lessons in Greek from a scholar, and read
Sophocles with him. For a time I hoped this noble poet would
again inspire me to get a real hold on the language, but the
hope was vain. I had not chosen the right teacher, and,
moreover, his sitting-room in which we pursued our studies
looked out on a tanyard, the repulsive odour of which affected
my nerves so strongly that I became thoroughly disgusted
both with Sophocles and Greek. My brother-in-law, Brockhaus, who wanted to put me in the way of earning some pocket-
money, gave me the correcting of the proof-sheets of a new
edition he was bringing out of Becker's *Universal History*,
revised by Löbell. This gave me a reason for improving by
private study the superficial general instruction on every subject which is given at school, and I thus acquired the valuable
knowledge which I was destined to have in later life of most
of the branches of learning so uninterestingly taught in class.
I must not forget to mention that, to a certain extent, the attraction exercised over me by this first closer study of history
was due to the fact that it brought me in eightpence a sheet,
and I thus found myself in one of the rarest positions in my life,

actually earning money; yet I should be doing myself an injustice if I did not bear in mind the vivid impressions I now for the first time received upon turning my serious attention to those periods of history with which I had hitherto had a very superficial acquaintance. All I recollect about my school days in this connection is that I was attracted by the classical period of Greek history; Marathon, Salamis, and Thermopylae composed the canon of all that interested me in the subject. Now for the first time I made an intimate acquaintance with the Middle Ages and the French Revolution, as my work in correcting dealt precisely with the two volumes which contained these two periods. I remember in particular that the description of the Revolution filled me with sincere hatred for its heroes; unfamiliar as I was with the previous history of France, my human sympathy was horrified by the cruelty of the men of that day, and this purely human impulse remained so strong in me that I remember how even quite recently it cost me a real struggle to give any weight to the true political significance of those acts of violence.

How great, then, was my astonishment when one day the current political events of the time enabled me, as it were, to gain a personal experience of the sort of national upheavals with which I had come into distant contact in the course of my proof-correcting. The special editions of the *Leipzig Gazette* brought us the news of the July Revolution in Paris. The King of France had been driven from his throne; Lafayette, who a moment before had seemed a myth to me, was again riding through a cheering crowd in the streets of Paris; the Swiss Guards had once more been butchered in the Tuileries, and a new King knew no better way of commending himself to the populace than by declaring himself the embodiment of the Republic. Suddenly to become conscious of living at a time in which such things took place could not fail to have a startling effect on a boy of seventeen. The world as a historic phenomenon began from that day in my eyes, and naturally my sympathies were wholly on the side of the Revolution, which I regarded in the light of a heroic popular struggle crowned with victory, and free from the blemish of the terrible excesses that stained the first French Revolution. As the whole of Europe, including some of the German states, was soon plunged more or less violently into rebellion, I remained for some time in a feverish state of suspense, and now first turned my attention to the causes of these upheavals, which I regarded as struggles of the young and hopeful against the old and effete portion of mankind. Saxony also did not remain unscathed; in Dresden it came to actual fighting in the streets, which immediately produced a political change in the shape of the proclamation of the regency of the future King Frederick, and the granting of a constitution. This event filled me with such enthusiasm that I composed a political overture, the prelude of which depicted dark oppression in the midst of which a strain was at last heard under which, to make my meaning clearer, I wrote the words *Friedrich und Freiheit;* this strain was intended to develop gradually and majestically into the fullest triumph, which I hoped shortly to see successfully performed at one of the Leipzig Garden Concerts.

However, before I was able to develop my politico-musical conceptions further, disorders broke out in Leipzig itself which summoned me from the precincts of Art to take a direct share in national life. National life in Leipzig at this time meant nothing more than antagonism between the students and the police, the latter being the arch-enemy upon whom the youthful love of liberty vented itself. Some students had been arrested in a street broil who were now to be rescued. The undergraduates, who had been restless for some days, assembled one evening in the Market Place and the Clubs, mustered together, and made a ring round their leaders. The whole proceeding was marked by a certain measured solemnity, which impressed me deeply. They sang *Gaudeamus igitur,* formed up into column, and picking up from the crowd any young men who sympathised with them, marched gravely and resolutely from the Market Place to the University buildings, to open the cells and set free the students who had been arrested. My heart beat fast as I marched with them to this 'Taking of the Bastille,' but things did not turn out as we expected, for in the courtyard of the Paulinum the solemn procession was stopped by Rector Krug, who had come down to meet it with his grey head bared; his assurance that the captives had already been released at his request was greeted with a thundering cheer, and the matter seemed at an end.

But the tense expectation of a revolution had grown too great not to demand some sacrifice. A summons was suddenly spread calling us to a notorious alley in order to exercise popular justice upon a hated magistrate who, it was rumoured, had unlawfully taken under his protection a certain house of ill-fame in that quarter. When I reached the spot with the tail-end of the crowd, I found the house had been broken into and all sorts of violence had been committed. I recall with horror the intoxicating effect this unreasoning fury had upon me, and cannot deny that without the slightest personal provocation I shared, like one possessed, in the frantic on-slaught of the undergraduates, who madly shattered furniture and crockery to bits. I do not believe that the ostensible motive for this outrage, which, it is true, was to be found in a fact that was a grave menace to public morality, had any weight with me whatever; on the contrary, it was the purely devilish fury of these popular outbursts that drew me, too, like a madman into their vortex.

The fact that such fits of fury are not quick to abate, but, in accordance with certain natural laws, reach their proper conclusion only after they have degenerated into frenzy, I was to learn in my own person. Scarcely did the summons ring out for us to march to another resort of the same kind than I too found myself in the tide which set towards the opposite end of the town. There the same exploits were re-peated, and the most ludicrous outrages perpetrated. I can-not remember that the enjoyment of alcoholic drinks con-tributed to the intoxication of myself and my immediate fellows. I only know that I finally got into the state that usually suc-ceeds a debauch, and upon waking next morning, as if from a hideous nightmare, had to convince myself that I had really taken part in the events of the previous night by a trophy I possessed in the shape of a tattered red curtain, which I had brought home as a token of my prowess. The thought that people generally, and my own family in particular, were wont to put a lenient construction upon youthful escapades was a great comfort to me; outbursts of this kind on the part of the young were regarded as righteous indignation against really serious scandals, and there was no need for me to be afraid of owning up to having taken part in such excesses.

The dangerous example, however, which had been set by the undergraduates incited the lower classes and the mob to similar excesses on the following nights, against employers and any who were obnoxious to them. The matter at once assumed a more serious complexion; property was threatened, and a conflict between rich and poor stood grinning at our doors. As there were no soldiers in the town, and the police were thoroughly disorganised, the students were called in as a protection against the lower orders. An undergraduate's hour of glory now began, such as I could only have thirsted for in my schoolboy dreams. The student became the tutelar deity of Leipzig, called on by the authorities to arm and band together in defence of property, and the same young men who two days before had yielded to a rage for destruction, now mustered in the University courtyard. The proscribed names of the students' clubs and unions were shouted by the mouths of town councillors and chief constables in order to summon curiously equipped undergraduates, who thereupon, in simple mediæval array of war, scattered throughout the town, occupied the guard-rooms at the gates, provided sentinels for the grounds of various wealthy merchants, and, as occasion demanded, took places which seemed threatened, more especially inns, under their permanent protection.

Though, unluckily, I was not yet a member of their body, I anticipated the delights of academic citizenship by half-impudent, half-obsequious solicitation of the leaders of the students whom I honoured most. I had the good fortune to recommend myself particularly to these ' cocks of the walk,' as they were styled, on account of my relationship to Brockhaus, in whose grounds the main body of these champions were encamped for some time. My brother-in-law was among those who had been seriously threatened, and it was only owing to really great presence of mind and assurance that he succeeded in saving his printing works, and especially his steam presses, which were the chief object of attack, from destruction. To protect his property against further assault, detachments of

students were told off to his grounds as well; the excellent
entertainment which the generous master of the house offered
his jovial guardians in his pleasant summer-house enticed the
pick of the students to him. My brother-in-law was for several weeks guarded day and night against possible attacks
by the populace, and on this occasion, as the mediator of a
flowing hospitality, I celebrated among the most famous
' bloods ' of the University the true saturnalia of my scholarly
ambition.

For a still longer period the guarding of the gates was
entrusted to the students; the unheard-of splendour which
accordingly became associated with this post drew fresh as-
pirants to the spot from far and near. Every day huge char-
tered vehicles discharged at the Halle Gate whole bands of
the boldest sons of learning from Halle, Jena, Göttingen, and
the remotest regions. They got down close to the guards at
the gate, and for several weeks never set foot in an inn or any
other dwelling; they lived at the expense of the Council, drew
vouchers on the police for food and drink, and knew but one
care, that the possibility of a general quieting of men's minds
would make their opportune guardianship superfluous. I never
missed a day on guard or a night either, alas! trying to impress on my family the urgent need for my personal endurance. Of course, the quieter and really studious spirits among
us soon resigned these duties, and only the flower of the flock
of undergraduates remained so staunch that it became difficult
for the authorities to relieve them of their task. I held out
to the very last, and succeeded in making most astonishing
friends for my age. Many of the most audacious remained
in Leipzig even when there was no guard duty to fulfil, and
peopled the place for some time with champions of an extraordinarily desperate and dissipated type, who had been repeatedly sent down from various universities for rowdyism
or debt, and who now, thanks to the exceptional circumstances
of the day, found a refuge in Leipzig, where at first they had
been received with open arms by the general enthusiasm of
their comrades.

In the presence of all these phenomena I felt as if I were
surrounded by the results of an earthquake which had upset

the usual order of things. My brother-in-law, Friedrich Brockhaus, who could justly taunt the former authorities of the
place with their inability to maintain peace and order, was
carried away by the current of a formidable movement of opposition. He made a daring speech at the Guildhall before
their worships the Town Council, which brought him popularity, and he was appointed second-in-command of the newly
constituted Leipzig Municipal Guard. This body at length
ousted my adored students from the guard-rooms of the town
gates, and we no longer had the right of stopping travellers
and inspecting their passes. On the other hand, I flattered
myself that I might regard my new position as a boy citizen
as equivalent to that of the French National Guard, and my
brother-in-law, Brockhaus, as a Saxon Lafayette, which, at
all events, succeeded in furnishing my soaring excitement with
a healthy stimulant. I now began to read the papers and
cultivate politics enthusiastically; however, the social intercourse of the civic world did not attract me sufficiently to
make me false to my beloved academic associates. I followed
them faithfully from the guard-rooms to the ordinary bars,
where their splendour as men of the literary world now sought
retirement.

My chief ambition was to become one of them as soon as
possible. This, however, could only be accomplished by being
again entered at a grammar school. St. Thomas's, whose headmaster was a feeble old man, was the place where my wishes
could be most speedily attained.

I joined the school in the autumn of 1830 simply with the
intention of qualifying myself for the Leaving Examination
by merely nominal attendance there. The chief thing in connection with it was that I and friends of the same bent succeeded in establishing a sham students' association called the
Freshman's Club. It was formed with all possible pedantry,
the institution of the ' Comment ' was introduced, fencing-
practice and sword-bouts were held, and an inaugural meeting
to which several prominent students were invited, and at which
I presided as ' Vice ' in white buckskin trousers and great
jack-boots, gave me a foretaste of the delights awaiting me as
a full-blown son of the Muses.

The masters of St. Thomas's, however, were not quite so ready to fall in with my aspirations to studentship; at the end of the half-year they were of the opinion that I had not given a thought to their institution, and nothing could persuade them that I had earned a title to academic citizenship by any acquisition of knowledge. Some sort of decision was necessary, so I accordingly informed my family that I had made up my mind not to study for a profession at the University, but to become a musician. There was nothing to prevent me matriculating as 'Studiosus Musicae,' and, without therefore troubling myself about the pedantries of the authorities at St. Thomas's, I defiantly quitted that seat af learning from which I had derived small profit, and presented myself forthwith to the rector of the University, whose acquaintance I had made on the evening of the riot, to be enrolled as a student of music. This was accordingly done without further ado, on the payment of the usual fees.

I was in a great hurry about it, for in a week the Easter vacation would begin, and the 'men' would go down from Leipzig, when it would be impossible to be elected member of a club until the vacation was over, and to stay all those weeks at home in Leipzig without having the right to wear the coveted colours seemed to me unendurable torture. Straight from the rector's presence I ran like a wounded animal to the fencing school, to present myself for admission to the Saxon Club, showing my card of matriculation. I attained my object, I could wear the colours of the Saxonia, which was in the fashion at that time, and in great request because it numbered so many delightful members in its ranks.

The strangest fate was to befall me in this Easter vacation, during which I was really the only remaining representative of the Saxon Club in Leipzig. In the beginning this club consisted chiefly of men of good family as well as the better class elements of the student world; all of them were members of highly placed and well-to-do families in Saxony in general, and in particular from the capital, Dresden, and spent their vacation at their respective homes. There remained in Leipzig during the vacations only those wandering students who had no homes, and for whom in reality it was always or never holiday time. Among these a separate club had arisen of daring and desperate young reprobates who had found a last refuge, as I said, at Leipzig in the glorious period I have recorded. I had already made the personal acquaintance of these swashbucklers, who pleased my fancy greatly, when they were guarding the Brockhaus grounds. Although the regular duration of a university course did not exceed three years, most of these men had never left their universities for six or seven years.

I was particularly fascinated by a man called Gebhardt, who was endowed with extraordinary physical beauty and strength, and whose slim heroic figure towered head and shoulders above all his companions. When he walked down the street arm-in-arm with two of the strongest of his comrades, he used suddenly to take it into his head, by an easy movement of his arm, to lift his friends high in the air and flutter along in this way as though he had a pair of human wings. When a cab was going along the streets at a sharp trot, he would seize a spoke of the wheel with one hand and force it to pull up. Nobody ever told him that he was stupid because they were afraid of his strength, hence his limitations were scarcely noticed. His redoubtable strength, combined with a temperate disposition, lent him a majestic dignity which placed him above the level of an ordinary mortal. He had come to Leipzig from Mecklenburg in the company of a certain Degelow, who was as powerful and adroit, though by no means of such gigantic proportions, as his friend, and whose chief attraction lay in his great vivacity and animated features. He had led a wild and dissipated life in which play, drink, passionate love affairs, and constant and prompt duelling had rung the changes. Ceremonious politeness, an ironic and pedantic coldness, which testified to bold self-confidence, combined with a very hot temper, formed the chief characteristics of this personage and natures akin to his. Degelow's wildness and passion were lent a curious diabolical charm by the possession of a malicious humour which he often turned against himself, whereas towards others he exercised a certain chivalrous tenderness.

These two extraordinary men were joined by others who

possessed all the qualities essential to a reckless life, together with real and headstrong valour. One of them, named Stelzer, a regular Berserker out of the Nibelungenlied, who was nick-named Lope, was in his twentieth term. While these men openly and consciously belonged to a world doomed to destruc-tion, and all their actions and escapades could only be explained by the hypothesis that they all believed that inevitable ruin was imminent, I made in their company the acquaintance of a certain Schröter, who particularly attracted me by his cor-dial disposition, pleasant Hanoverian accent, and refined wit. He was not one of the regular young dare-devils, towards whom he adopted a calm observant attitude, while they were all fond of him and glad to see him. I made a real friend of this Schröter, although he was much older than I was. Through him I became acquainted with the works and poems of H. Heine, and from him I acquired a certain neat and saucy wit, and I was quite ready to surrender myself to his agreeable influence in the hope of improving my outward bearing. It was his company in particular that I sought every day; in the afternoon I generally met him in the Rosenthal or Kintschy's Châlet, though always in the presence of those wonderful Goths who excited at once my alarm and admiration.

They all belonged to university clubs which were on hostile terms with the one of which I was a member. What this hos-tility between the various clubs meant only those can judge who are familiar with the tone prevalent among them in those days. The mere sight of hostile colours sufficed to infuriate these men, who otherwise were kind and gentle, provided they had taken the slightest drop too much. At all events, as long as the old stagers were sober they would look with good-natured complacency at a slight young fellow like me in the hostile colours moving among them so amicably. Those colours I wore in my own peculiar fashion. I had made use of the brief week during which my club was still in Leipzig to become the possessor of a splendid ' Saxon ' cap, richly embroidered with silver, and worn by a man called Müller, who was after-wards a prominent constable at Dresden. I had been seized with such a violent craving for this cap that I managed to buy it from him, as he wanted money to go home. In spite of this remarkable cap I was, as I have said, welcome in the den of this band of rowdies: my friend Schröter saw to that. It was only when the grog, which was the principal beverage of these wild spirits, began to work that I used to notice curious glances and overhear doubtful speeches, the significance of which was for some time hidden from me by the dizziness in which my own senses were plunged by this baneful drink.

As I was inevitably bound on this account to be mixed up in quarrels for some time to come, it afforded me a great satisfaction that my first fight, as a matter of fact, arose from an incident more creditable to me than those provocations which I had left half unnoticed. One day Degelow came up to Schröter and me in a wine-bar that we often frequented, and in quite a friendly manner confessed to us confidentially his liking for a young and very pretty actress whose talent Schröter disputed. Degelow rejoined that this was as it might be, but that, for his part, he regarded the young lady as the most respectable woman in the theatre. I at once asked him if he considered my sister's reputation was not as good. According to students' notions it was impossible for Degelow, who doubtless had not the remotest intention of being insulting, to give me any assurance further than to say that he certainly did not think my sister had an inferior reputation, but that, nevertheless, he meant to abide by his assertion concerning the young lady he had mentioned. Hereupon followed without delay the usual challenge, opening with the words, 'You're an ass,' which sounded almost ridiculous to my own ears when I said them to this seasoned swashbuckler.

I remember that Degelow too gasped with astonishment, and lightning seemed to flash from his eyes; but he controlled himself in the presence of my friend, and proceeded to observe the usual formalities of a challenge, and chose broadswords (*krumme Säbel*) as the weapons for the fight. The event made a great stir among our companions, but I saw less reason than before to abstain from my usual intercourse with them. Only I became more strict about the behaviour of the swashbucklers, and for several days no evening passed without producing a challenge between me and some formidable bully, until at last Count Solms, the only member of my club who had returned to Leipzig as yet, visited me as though he were an intimate friend and inquired into what had occurred. He applauded my conduct, but advised me not to wear my colours until the return of our comrades from the vacation, and to keep away from the bad company into which I had ventured. Fortunately I had not long to wait; university life soon began again, and the fencing ground was filled. The unenviable position, in which, in student phrase, I was suspended with a half-dozen of the most terrible swordsmen, earned me a glorious reputation among the 'freshmen' and 'juniors,' and even among the older 'champions' of the Saxonia.

My seconds were duly arranged, the dates for the various duels on hand settled, and by the care of my seniors the needful time was secured for me to acquire some sort of skill in fencing. The light heart with which I awaited the fate which threatened me in at least one of the impending encounters I myself could not understand at the time; on the other hand, the way in which that fate preserved me from the consequences of my rashness seems truly miraculous in my eyes to this day, and worthy of further description.

The preparations for a duel included obtaining some experience of these encounters by being present at several of them. We freshmen attained this object by what is called 'carrying duty,' that is to say, we were entrusted with the rapiers of the corps (precious weapons of honour belonging to the association), and had to take them first to the grinder and thence to the scene of encounter, a proceeding which was attended with some danger, as it had to be done surreptitiously, since duelling was forbidden by law; in return we acquired the right of assisting as spectators at the impending engagements.

When I had earned this honour, the meeting-place chosen for the duel I was to watch was the billiard-room of an inn in the Burgstrasse; the table had been moved to one side, and on it the authorised spectators took their places. Among them I stood up with a beating heart to watch the dangerous encounters between those doughty champions. I was told on this occasion of the story of one of my friends (a Jew named Levy, but known as Lippert), who on this very floor had given

so much ground before his antagonist that the door had to
be opened for him, and he fell back through it down the steps
into the street, still believing he was engaged in the duel.
When several bouts had been finished, two men came on to
the ' pitch,' Tempel, the president of the *Markomanen*, and a
certain Wohlfart, an old stager, already in his fourteenth half-
year of study, with whom I also was booked for an encounter
later on. When this was the case, a man was not allowed to
watch, in order that the weak points of the duellist might not
be betrayed to his future opponent. Wohlfart was accordingly
asked by my chiefs whether he wanted me removed; whereupon he replied with calm contempt, ' Let them leave the
little freshman there, in God's name! ' Thus I became an eye-
witness of the disablement of a swordsman who nevertheless
showed himself so experienced and skilful on the occasion that
I might well have become alarmed for the issue of my future
encounter with him. His gigantic opponent cut the artery
of his right arm, which at once ended the fight; the surgeon
declared that Wohlfart would not be able to hold a sword
again for years, under which circumstances my proposed meeting with him was at once cancelled. I do not deny that this
incident cheered my soul.

Shortly afterwards the first general reunion of our club was
held at the Green Tap. These gatherings are regular hot-
beds for the production of duels. Here I brought upon myself
a new encounter with one Tischer, but learned at the same time
that I had been relieved of two of my most formidable previous
engagements of the kind by the disappearance of my opponents,
both of whom had escaped on account of debt and left no trace
behind them. The only one of whom I could hear anything
was the terrible Stelzer, surnamed Lope. This fellow had
taken advantage of the passing of Polish refugees, who had
at that time already been driven over the frontier and were
making their way through Germany to France, to disguise
himself as an ill-starred champion of freedom, and he subsequently found his way to the Foreign Legion in Algeria. On
the way home from the gathering, Degelow, whom I was to
meet in a few weeks, proposed a ' truce.' This was a device
which, if it was accepted, as it was in this case, enabled the

future combatants to entertain and talk to one another, which was otherwise most strictly forbidden. We wandered back to the town arm-in-arm; with chivalrous tenderness my interesting and formidable opponent declared that he was delighted at the prospect of crossing swords with me in a few weeks' time; that he regarded it as an honour and a pleasure, as he was fond of me and respected me for my valorous conduct. Seldom has any personal success flattered me more. We embraced, and amid protestations which, owing to a certain dignity about them, acquired a significance I can never forget, we parted. He informed me that he must first pay a visit to Jena, where he had an appointment to fight a duel. A week later the news of his death reached Leipzig; he had been mortally wounded in the duel at Jena.

I felt as if I were living in a dream, out of which I was aroused by the announcement of my encounter with Tischer. Though he was a first-rate and vigorous fighter, he had been chosen by our chiefs for my first passage of arms because he was fairly short. In spite of being unable to feel any great confidence in my hastily acquired and little practised skill in fencing, I looked forward to this my first duel with a light heart. Although it was against the rules, I never dreamed of telling the authorities that I was suffering from a slight rash which I had caught at that time, and which I was informed made wounds so dangerous that if it were reported it would postpone the meeting, in spite of the fact that I was modest enough to be prepared for wounds. I was sent for at ten in the morning, and left home smiling to think what my mother and sisters would say if in a few hours I were brought back in the alarming state I anticipated. My chief, Herr v. Schönfeld, was a pleasant, quiet sort of man, who lived on the marsh. When I reached his house, he leant out of the window with his pipe in his mouth, and greeted me with the words: 'You can go home, my lad, it is all off; Tischer is in hospital.' When I got upstairs I found several 'leading men' assembled, from whom I learned that Tischer had got very drunk the night before, and had in consequence laid himself open to the most outrageous treatment by the inhabitants of a house of ill-fame. He was terribly hurt, and had been taken by the police in the first instance to the hospital. This inevitably meant rustication, and, above all, expulsion from the academic association to which he belonged.

I cannot clearly recall the incidents that removed from Leipzig the few remaining fire-eaters to whom I had pledged myself since that fatal vacation-time; I only know that this side of my fame as a student yielded to another. We celebrated the 'freshmen's gathering,' to which all those who could manage it drove a four-in-hand in a long procession through the town. After the president of the club had profoundly moved me with his sudden and yet prolonged solemnity, I conceived the desire to be among the very last to return home from the outing. Accordingly I stayed away three days and three nights, and spent the time chiefly in gambling, a pastime which from the first night of our festivity cast its devilish snares around me. Some half-dozen of the smartest club members chanced to be together at early dawn in the Jolly Peasant, and forthwith formed the nucleus of a gambling club, which was reinforced during the day by recruits coming back from the town. Members came to see whether we were still at it, members also went away, but I with the original six held out for days and nights without faltering.

The desire that first prompted me to take part in the play was the wish to win enough for my score (two thalers): this I succeeded in doing, and thereupon I was inspired with the hope of being able to settle all the debts I had made at that time by my winnings at play. Just as I had hoped to learn composition most quickly by Logier's method, but had found myself hampered in my object for a long period by unexpected difficulties, so my plan for speedily improving my financial position was likewise doomed to disappointment. To win was not such an easy matter, and for some three months I was such a victim to the rage for gambling that no other passion was able to exercise the slightest influence over my mind.

Neither the *Fechtboden* (where the students' fights were practised), nor the beer-house, nor the actual scene of the fights, ever saw my face again. In my lamentable position I racked my brains all day to devise ways and means of getting the money wherewith to gamble at night. In vain did my poor mother try everything in her power to induce me not to come home so late at night, although she had no idea of the real nature of my debauches: after I had left the house in the afternoon I never returned till dawn the next day, and I reached my room (which was at some distance from the others) by climbing over the gate, for my mother had refused to give me a latch-key.

In despair over my ill-luck, my passion for gambling grew into a veritable mania, and I no longer felt any inclination for those things which at one time had lured me to student life. I became absolutely indifferent to the opinion of my former companions and avoided them entirely; I now lost myself in the smaller gambling dens of Leipzig, where only the very scum of the students congregated. Insensible to any feeling of self-respect, I bore even the contempt of my sister Rosalie; both she and my mother hardly ever deigning to cast a glance at the young libertine whom they only saw at rare intervals, looking deadly pale and worn out: my ever-growing despair made me at last resort to foolhardiness as the only means of forcing hostile fate to my side. It suddenly struck me that only by dint of big stakes could I make big profits. To this end I decided to make use of my mother's pension, of which I was trustee of a fairly large sum. That night I lost everything I had with me except one thaler: the excitement with which I staked that last coin on a card was an experience hitherto quite strange to my young life. As I had had nothing to eat, I was obliged repeatedly to leave the gambling table owing to sickness. With this last thaler I staked my life, for my return to my home was, of course, out of the question. Already I saw myself in the grey dawn, a prodigal son, fleeing from all I held dear, through forest and field towards the unknown. My mood of despair had gained so strong a hold upon me that, when my card won, I immediately placed all the money on a fresh stake, and repeated this experiment until I had won quite a considerable amount. From that moment my luck grew continuously. I gained such confidence that I risked the most hazardous stakes: for suddenly it dawned upon me that this was destined to be my last day with the cards. My good fortune now became so obvious that the bank thought it wise to close. Not only had I won back all the money I had lost, but I had won enough to pay off all my debts as well. My sensations during the whole of this process were of the most sacred nature: I felt as if God and His angels were standing by my side and were whispering words of warning and of consolation into my ears.

Once more I climbed over the gate of my home in the early hours of the morning, this time to sleep peacefully and soundly and to awake very late, strengthened and as though born again.

No sense of shame deterred me from telling my mother, to whom I presented her money, the whole truth about this decisive night. I voluntarily confessed my sin in having utilised her pension, sparing no detail. She folded her hands and thanked God for His mercy, and forthwith regarded me as saved, believing it impossible for me ever to commit such a crime again.

And, truth to tell, gambling had lost all fascination for me from that moment. The world, in which I had moved like one demented, suddenly seemed stripped of all interest or attraction. My rage for gambling had already made me quite indifferent to the usual student's vanities, and when I was freed from this passion also, I suddenly found myself face to face with an entirely new world.

To this world I belonged henceforth: it was the world of real and serious musical study, to which I now devoted myself heart and soul.

Even during this wild period of my life, my musical development had not been entirely at a standstill; on the contrary, it daily became plainer that music was the only direction towards which my mental tendencies had a marked bent. Only I had got quite out of the habit of musical study. Even now it seems incredible that I managed to find time in those days to finish quite a substantial amount of composition. I have but the faintest recollection of an Overture in C major ($\frac{6}{8}$ time), and of a Sonata in B flat major arranged as a duet; the latter pleased my sister Ottilie, who played it with me, so much that I arranged it for orchestra. But another work of this period, an Overture in B flat major, left an indelible impression on my mind on account of an incident connected with it. This composition, in fact, was the outcome of my study of Beethoven's Ninth Symphony in about the same degree as *Leubald und Adelaïde* was the result of my study of Shakespeare. I had made a special point of bringing out the mystic meaning in the orchestra, which I divided into three distinctly different and opposite elements. I wanted to make the characteristic nature of these elements clear to the score reader the moment he looked at it by a striking display of colour, and only the fact that I could not get any green ink made this picturesque idea impossible. I employed black ink for the brass instruments alone, the strings were to have red and the wind green ink. This extraordinary score I gave for perusal to Heinrich Dorn, who was at that time musical director of the Leipzig theatre. He was very young, and impressed me as being a very clever musician and a witty man of the world, whom the Leipzig public made much of.

Nevertheless, I have never been able to understand how he could have granted my request to produce this overture.

Some time afterwards I was rather inclined to believe with others, who knew how much he enjoyed a good joke, that he intended to treat himself to a little fun. At the time, however, he vowed that he thought the work interesting, and maintained that if it were only brought out as a hitherto unknown work by Beethoven, the public would receive it with respect, though without understanding.

It was the Christmas of the fateful year 1830; as usual, there would be no performance at the theatre on Christmas Eve, but instead a concert for the poor had been organised, which received but scant support. The first item on the programme was called by the exciting title ' New Overture ' — nothing more! I had surreptitiously listened to the rehearsal with some misgiving. I was very much impressed by the coolness with which Dorn fenced with the apparent confusion which the members of the orchestra showed with regard to this mysterious composition. The principal theme of the Allegro was contained in four bars; after every fourth bar, however, a fifth bar had been inserted, which had nothing to

do with the melody, and which was announced by a loud bang
on the kettle-drum on the second beat. As this drum-beat
stood out alone, the drummer, who continually thought he
was making a mistake, got confused, and did not give the right
sharpness to the accent as prescribed by the score. Listening
from my hidden corner, and frightened at my original intention,
this accidentally different rendering did not displease me. To
my genuine annoyance, however, Dorn called the drummer
to the front and insisted on his playing the accents with the
prescribed sharpness. When, after the rehearsal, I told the
musical director of my misgivings about this important fact,
I could not get him to promise a milder interpretation of the
fatal drum-beat; he stuck to it that the thing would sound
very well as it was. In spite of this assurance my restlessness
grew, and I had not the courage to introduce myself to my
friends in advance as the author of the ' New Overture.'

My sister Ottilie, who had already been forced to survive
the secret readings of *Leubald und Adelaïde*, was the only
person willing to come with me to hear my work. It was
Christmas Eve, and there was to be the usual Christmas tree,
presents, etc., at my brother-in-law's, Friedrich Brockhaus,
and both of us naturally wanted to be there. My sister, in
particular, who lived there, had a good deal to do with the
arrangements, and could only get away for a short while, and
that with great difficulty; our amiable relation accordingly
had the carriage ready for her so that she might get back more
quickly. I made use of this opportunity to inaugurate, as it
were, my entrée into the musical world in a festive manner.
The carriage drew up in front of the theatre. Ottilie went into
my brother-in-law's box, which forced me to try and find a
seat in the pit. I had forgotten to buy a ticket, and was refused admission by the man at the door. Suddenly the tuning
up of the orchestra grew louder and louder, and I thought I
should have to miss the beginning of my work. In my anxiety
I revealed myself to the man at the door as the composer of
the ' New Overture,' and in this way succeeded in passing
without a ticket. I pushed my way through to one of the first
rows of the pit, and sat down in terrible anxiety.

The Overture began: after the theme of the ' black ' bras-

instruments had made itself heard with great emphasis, the
'red' Allegro theme started, in which, as I have already
mentioned, every fifth bar was interrupted by the drum-beat
from the 'black' world. What kind of effect the 'green'
theme of the wind instruments, which joined in afterwards,
produced upon the listeners, and what they must have thought
when 'black,' 'red,' and 'green' themes became intermingled,
has always remained a mystery to me, for the fatal drum-beat,
brutally hammered out, entirely deprived me of my senses,
especially as this prolonged and continually recurring effect
now began to rouse, not only the attention, but the merriment
of the audience. I heard my neighbours calculating the return
of this effect; knowing the absolute correctness of their
calculation, I suffered ten thousand torments, and became
almost unconscious. At last I awoke from my nightmare
when the Overture, to which I had disdained to give what
I considered a trite ending, came to a standstill most
unexpectedly.

No phantoms like those in Hoffmann's *Tales* could have
succeeded in producing the extraordinary state in which I came
to my senses on noticing the astonishment of the audience at
the end of the performance. I heard no exclamations of disapproval, no hissing, no remarks, not even laughter; all I saw
was intense astonishment at such a strange occurrence, which
impressed them, as it did me, like a horrible nightmare. The
worst moment, however, came when I had to leave the pit
and take my sister home. To get up and pass through the
people in the pit was horrible indeed. Nothing, however,
equalled the pain of coming face to face with the man at the
door; the strange look he gave me haunted me ever afterwards, and for a considerable time I avoided the pit of the
Leipzig theatre.

My next step was to find my sister, who had gone through
the whole sad experience with infinite pity; in silence we
drove home to be present at a brilliant family festivity, which
contrasted with grim irony with the gloom of my bewilderment.

In spite of it all I tried to believe in myself, and thought I
could find comfort in my overture to the *Braut von Messina,*
which I believed to be a better work than the fatal one I had

just heard. A reinstatement, however, was out of the question, for the directors of the Leipzig theatre regarded me for a long time as a very doubtful person, in spite of Dorn's friendship. It is true that I still tried my hand at sketching out compositions to Goethe's *Faust,* some of which have been preserved to this day: but soon my wild student's life resumed its sway and drowned the last remnant of serious musical study in me.

I now began to imagine that because I had become a student I ought to attend the University lectures. From Traugott Krug, who was well known to me on account of his having suppressed the student's revolt, I tried to learn the first principles of philosophy; a single lesson sufficed to make me give this up. Two or three times, however, I attended the lectures on æsthetics given by one of the younger professors, a man called Weiss. This perseverance was due to the interest which Weiss immediately aroused in me. When I made his acquaintance at my uncle Adolph's house, Weiss had just translated the metaphysics of Aristotle, and, if I am not mistaken, dedicated them in a controversial spirit to Hegel.

On this occasion I had listened to the conversation of these two men on philosophy and philosophers, which made a tremendous impression on me. I remember that Weiss was an absent-minded man, with a hasty and abrupt manner of speaking; he had an interesting and pensive expression which impressed me immensely. I recollect how, on being accused of a want of clearness in his writing and style, he justified himself by saying that the deep problems of the human mind could not in any case be solved by the mob. This maxim, which struck me as being very plausible, I at once accepted as the principle for all my future writing. I remember that my eldest brother Albert, to whom I once had to write for my mother, grew so disgusted with my letter and style that he said he thought I must be going mad.

In spite of my hopes that Weiss's lectures would do me much good, I was not capable of continuing to attend them, as my desires in those days drove me to anything but the study of æsthetics. Nevertheless, my mother's anxiety at this time on my behalf made me try to take up music again. As Müller, the teacher under whom I had studied till that time, had not been able to inspire me with a permanent love of study, it was necessary to discover whether another teacher might not be better able to induce me to do serious work.

Theodor Weinlich, who was choirmaster and musical director at St. Thomas's Church, held at that time this important and ancient post which was afterwards occupied by Schicht, and before him by no less a person than Sebastian Bach. By education he belonged to the old Italian school of music, and had studied in Bologna under Pater Martini. He had made a name for himself in this art by his vocal compositions, in which his fine manner of treating the parts was much praised. He himself told me one day that a Leipzig publisher had offered him a very substantial fee if he would write for his firm another book of vocal exercises similar to the one which had proved so profitable to his first publisher. Weinlich told him that he had not got any exercises of the kind ready at the moment, but offered him instead a new Mass, which the publisher refused with the words: ' Let him who got the meat gnaw the bones.' The modesty with which Weinlich told me this little story showed how excellent a man he was. As he was in a very bad and weak state of health when my mother introduced me to him, he at first refused to take me as a pupil. But, after having resisted all persuasions, he at last took pity on my musical education, which, as he soon discovered from a fugue which I had brought with me, was exceedingly faulty. He accordingly promised to teach me, on condition that I should give up all attempts at composing for six months, and follow his instructions implicitly. To the first part of my promise I remained faithful, thanks to the vast vortex of dissipation into which my life as a student had drawn me.

When, however, I had to occupy myself for any length of time with nothing but four-part harmony exercises in strictly rigorous style, it was not only the student in me, but also the composer of so many overtures and sonatas, that was thoroughly disgusted. Weinlich, too, had his grievances against me, and decided to give me up.

During this period I came to the crisis of my life, which led to the catastrophe of that terrible evening at the gambling den. But an even greater blow than this fearful experience awaited me when Weinlich decided not to have anything more to do with me. Deeply humiliated and miserable, I besought the gentle old man, whom I loved dearly, to forgive me, and I promised him from that moment to work with unflagging energy. One morning at seven o'clock Weinlich sent for me to begin the rough sketch for a fugue; he devoted the whole morning to me, following my work bar by bar with the greatest attention, and giving me his valuable advice. At twelve o'clock he dismissed me with the instruction to perfect and finish the sketch by filling in the remaining parts at home.

When I brought him the fugue finished, he handed me his own treatment of the same theme for comparison. This common task of fugue writing established between me and my good-natured teacher the tenderest of ties, for, from that moment, we both enjoyed the lessons. I was astonished how quickly the time flew. In eight weeks I had not only gone through a number of the most intricate fugues, but had also waded through all kinds of difficult evolutions in counterpoint, when one day, on bringing him an extremely elaborate double fugue, he took my breath away by telling me that after this there was nothing left for him to teach me.

As I was not aware of any great effort on my part, I often wondered whether I had really become a well-equipped musician. Weinlich himself did not seem to attach much importance to what he had taught me: he said, 'Probably you will never write fugues or canons; but what you have mastered is Independence: you can now stand alone and rely upon having a fine technique at your fingers' ends if you should want it.'

The principal result of his influence over me was certainly the growing love of clearness and fluency to which he had trained me. I had already had to write the above-mentioned fugue for ordinary voices; my feeling for the melodious and vocal had in this way been awakened. In order to keep me strictly under his calming and friendly influence, he had at the same time given me a sonata to write which, as a proof of my friendship for him, I had to build up on strictly harmonic and thematic lines, for which he recommended me a very early and childlike sonata by Pleyel as a model.

Those who had only recently heard my Overture must, indeed, have wondered how I ever wrote this sonata, which has been published through the indiscretion of Messrs. Breitkopf and Härtel (to reward me for my abstemiousness Weinlich induced them to publish this poor composition). From that moment he gave me a free hand. To begin with I was allowed to compose a Fantasia for the pianoforte (in F sharp minor) which I wrote in a quite informal style by treating the melody in recitative form; this gave me intense satisfaction because it won me praise from Weinlich.

Soon afterwards I wrote three overtures which all met with his entire approval. In the following winter (1831–1832) I succeeded in getting the first of them, in D minor, performed at one of the Gewandhaus concerts.

At that time a very simple and homely tone reigned supreme in this institution. The instrumental works were not conducted by what we call ' a conductor of the orchestra,' but were simply played to the audience by the *leader* of the orchestra. As soon as the singing began, Pohlenz took his place at the conductor's desk; he belonged to the type of fat and pleasant musical directors, and was a great favourite with the Leipzig public. He used to come on the platform with a very important-looking blue baton in his hand.

One of the strangest events which occurred at that time was the yearly production of the Ninth Symphony of Beethoven; after the first three movements had been played straight through like a Haydn symphony, as well as the orchestra could manage it, Pohlenz, instead of having to conduct a vocal quartette, a cantata, or an Italian aria, took his place at the desk to undertake this highly complicated instrumental work, with its particularly enigmatical and incoherent opening, one of the most difficult tasks that could possibly be found for a musical conductor. I shall never forget the impression produced upon me at the first rehearsal by the anxiously and carefully played 3/4 time, and the way in which the wild shrieks of the trumpet (with which this movement begins) resulted in the most extraordinary confusion of sound.

He had evidently chosen this tempo in order, in some way, to manage the recitative of the double basses; but it was utterly hopeless. Pohlenz was in a bath of perspiration, the recitative did not come off, and I really began to think that Beethoven must have written nonsense; the double bass player, Temmler, a faithful veteran of the orchestra, prevailed upon Pohlenz at last, in rather coarse and energetic language, to put down the baton, and in this way the recitative really proceeded properly. All the same, I felt at this time that I had come to the humble conclusion, in a way I can hardly explain, that this extraordinary work was still beyond my comprehension. For a long time I gave up brooding over this composition, and I turned my thoughts with simple longing towards a clearer and calmer musical form.

My study of counterpoint had taught me to appreciate, above all, Mozart's light and flowing treatment of the most difficult technical problems, and the last movement of his great Symphony in C major in particular served me as example for my own work. My D minor Overture, which clearly showed the influence of Beethoven's *Coriolanus* Overture, had been favourably received by the public; my mother began to have faith in me again, and I started at once on a second overture (in C major), which really ended with a ' Fugato ' that did more credit to my new model than I had ever hoped to accomplish.

This overture, also, was soon afterwards performed at a recital given by the favourite singer, Mlle. Palazzesi (of the Dresden Italian Opera). Before this I had already introduced it at a concert given by a private musical society called ' Euterpe', when I had conducted it myself.

I remember the strange impression I received from a remark that my mother made on that occasion; as a matter of fact this work, which was written in a counterpoint style, without any real passion or emotion, had produced a strange effect upon her. She gave vent to her astonishment by warmly praising the *Egmont* Overture, which was played at the same concert, maintaining that ' this kind of music was after all more fascinating than any stupid fugue.'

At this time I also wrote (as my third opus) an overture to Raupach's drama, *König Enzio,* in which again Beethoven's influence made itself even more strongly felt. My sister Rosalie succeeded in getting it performed at the theatre before the play; for the sake of prudence they did not announce it on the programme the first time. Dorn conducted it, and as the performance went off all right, and the public showed no dissatisfaction, my overture was played with my full name on the programme several times during the run of the above-mentioned drama.

After this I tried my hand at a big Symphony (in C major); in this work I showed what I had learnt by using the influence of my study of Beethoven and Mozart towards the achievement of a really pleasant and intelligible work, in which the fugue was again present at the end, while the themes of the various movements were so constructed that they could be played consecutively.

Nevertheless, the passionate and bold element of the *Sinfonia Eroica* was distinctly discernible, especially in the first movement. The slow movement, on the contrary, contained reminiscences of my former musical mysticism. A kind of repeated interrogative exclamation of the minor third merging into the fifth connected in my mind this work (which I had finished with the utmost effort at clearness) with my very earliest period of boyish sentimentality.

When, in the following year, I called on Friedrich Rochlitz, at that time the 'Nestor' of the musical æsthetes in Leipzig, and president of the Gewandhaus, I prevailed upon him to promise me a performance of my work. As he had been given my score for perusal before seeing me, he was quite astonished to find that I was a very young man, for the character of my music had prepared him to see a much older and more experienced musician. Before this performance took place many things happened which I must first mention, as they were of great importance to my life.

My short and stormy career as a student had drowned in me not only all longing for further development, but also all interest in intellectual and spiritual pursuits. Although, as I have pointed out, I had never alienated myself entirely from music, my revived interest in politics aroused my first real disgust for my senseless student's life, which soon left no deeper traces on my mind than the remembrance of a terrible nightmare.

The Polish War of Independence against Russian supremacy filled me with growing enthusiasm. The victories which the Poles obtained for a short period during May, 1831, aroused my enthusiastic admiration: it seemed to me as though the world had, by some miracle, been created anew. As a contrast to this, the news of the battle of Ostrolenka made it appear as if the end of the world had come. To my astonishment, my boon companions scoffed at me when I commented upon some of these events; the terrible lack of all fellow-feeling and comradeship amongst the students struck me very forcibly. Any kind of enthusiasm had to be smothered or turned into pedantic bravado, which showed itself in the form of affectation and indifference. To get drunk with deliberate cold-bloodedness, without even a glimpse of humour, was reckoned almost as brave a feat as duelling. Not until much later did I understand the far nobler spirit which animated the lower classes in Germany in comparison with the sadly degenerate state of the University students. In those days I felt terribly indignant at the insulting remarks which I brought upon myself when I deplored the battle of Ostrolenka.

To my honour be it said, that these and similar impressions helped to make me give up my low associates. During my studies with Weinlich the only little dissipation I allowed myself was my daily evening visit to Kintschy, the confectioner in the Klostergasse, where I passionately devoured the latest newspapers. Here I found many men who held the same political views as myself, and I specially loved to listen to the eager political discussions of some of the old men who frequented the place. The literary journals, too, began to interest me; I read a great deal, but was not very particular in my choice. Nevertheless, I now began to appreciate intelligence and wit, whereas before only the grotesque and the fantastic had had any attraction for me.

My interest in the issue of the Polish war, however, remained paramount. I felt the siege and capture of Warsaw as a personal calamity. My excitement when the remains of the Polish army began to pass through Leipzig on their way to France was indescribable, and I shall never forget the impression produced upon me by the first batch of these unfortunate soldiers on the occasion of their being quartered at the Green Shield, a public-house in the Meat Market. Much as this depressed me, I was soon roused to a high pitch of enthusiasm, for in the lounge of the Leipzig Gewandhaus, where that night Beethoven's C minor Symphony was being played, a group of heroic figures, the principal leaders of the Polish revolution, excited my admiration. I felt more particularly attracted by Count Vincenz Tyszkiéwitcz, a man of exceptionally powerful physique and noble appearance, who impressed me by his dignified and aristocratic manner and his quiet self-reliance — qualities with which I had not met before. When I saw a man of such kingly bearing in a tight-fitting coat and red velvet cap, I at once realised my foolishness in ever having worshipped the ludicrously dressed up little heroes of our students' world. I was delighted to meet this gentleman again at the house of my brother-in-law, Friedrich Brockhaus, where I saw him frequently.

My brother-in-law had the greatest pity and sympathy for the Polish rebels, and was the president of a committee whose task it was to look after their interests, and for a long time he made many personal sacrifices for their cause.

The Brockhaus establishment now became tremendously attractive to me. Around Count Vincenz Tyszkiéwitcz, who remained the lodestar of this small Polish world, gathered a great many other wealthy exiles, amongst whom I chiefly remember a cavalry captain of the name of Bansemer, a man of unlimited kindness, but of a rather frivolous nature; he possessed a marvellous team of four horses which he drove at such breakneck speed as to cause great annoyance to the people of Leipzig. Another man of importance with whom I remember dining was General Bem, whose artillery had made such a gallant stand at Ostrolenka.

Many other exiles passed through this hospitable house, some of whom impressed us by their melancholy, warlike bearing, others by their refined behaviour. Vincenz Tyszkiéwitcz, however, remained my ideal of a true man, and I loved him with a profound adoration. He, too, began to be interested in me; I used to call upon him nearly every day, and was sometimes present at a sort of martial feast, from which he often withdrew in order to be able to open his heart to me about the anxieties which oppressed him. He had, in fact, received absolutely no news of the whereabouts of his wife and little son since they separated at Volhynien. Besides this, he was under the shadow of a great sorrow which drew all sympathetic natures to him. To my sister Louise he had confided the terrible calamity that had once befallen him. He had been married before, and while staying with his wife in one of his lonely castles, in the dead of night he had seen a ghostly apparition at the window of his bedroom. Hearing his name called several times, he had taken up a revolver to protect himself from possible danger, and had shot his own wife, who had had the eccentric idea of teasing him by pretending to be a ghost. I had the pleasure of sharing his joy on hearing that his family was safe. His wife joined him in Leipzig with their beautiful boy, Janusz. I felt sorry not to be able to feel the same sympathy for this lady as I did for her husband; perhaps one of the reasons of my antipathy was the obvious and conspicuous way in which she made herself up, by means of which the poor woman probably tried to hide how much her beauty had suffered through the terrible strain of the past events. She soon went back to Galicia to try and save what she could of their property, and also to provide her husband with a pass from the Austrian Government, by means of which he could follow her.

Then came the third of May. Eighteen of the Poles who were still in Leipzig met together at a festive dinner in a hotel outside the town; on this day was to be celebrated the first anniversary of the third of May, so dear to the memory of the Poles. Only the chiefs of the Leipzig Polish Committee received invitations, and as a special favour I also was asked. I shall never forget that occasion. The dinner became an orgy; throughout the evening a brass band from the town played Polish folksongs, and these were sung by the whole company, led by a Lithuanian called Zan, in a manner now triumphant and now mournful. The beautiful ' Third of May ' song more particularly drew forth a positive uproar of enthusiasm. Tears and shouts of joy grew into a terrible tumult; the excited men grouped themselves on the grass swearing eternal friendship in the most extravagant terms, for which the word 'Oiczisna' (Fatherland) provided the principal theme, until at last night threw her veil over this wild debauch.

That evening afterwards served me as the theme for an orchestral composition (in the form of an overture) named *Polonia;* I shall recount the fate of this work later on. My friend Tyszkiéwitcz's passport now arrived, and he made up his mind to go back to Galicia *via* Brünn, although his friends considered it was very rash of him to do so. I very much wanted to see something of the world, and Tyszkiéwitcz's offer to take me with him, induced my mother to consent to my going to Vienna, a place that I had long wished to visit. I took with me the scores of my three overtures which had already been performed, and also that of my great symphony as yet unproduced, and had a grand time with my Polish patron, who took me in his luxurious travelling-coach as far as the capital of Moravia. During a short stop at Dresden the exiles of all classes gave our beloved Count a friendly farewell dinner in Pirna, at which the champagne flowed freely, while the health was drunk of the future ' Dictator of Poland.'

At last we separated at Brünn, from which place I continued my journey to Vienna by coach. During the afternoon and night, which I was obliged to spend in Brünn by myself, I went through terrible agonies from fear of the cholera which, as I unexpectedly heard, had broken out in this place. There I was all alone in a strange place, my faithful friend just departed, and on hearing of the epidemic I felt as if a malicious demon had caught me in his snare in order to annihilate me. I did not betray my terror to the people in the hotel, but when I was shown into a very lonely wing of the house and left by myself in this wilderness, I hid myself in bed with my clothes on, and lived once again through all the horrors of ghost stories as I had done in my boyhood. The cholera stood before me like a living thing; I could see and touch it; it lay in my bed and embraced me. My limbs turned to ice, I felt frozen to the very marrow. Whether I was awake or asleep I never knew; I only remember how astonished I was when, on awakening, I felt thoroughly well and healthy.

At last I arrived in Vienna, where I escaped the epidemic

which had penetrated as far as that town. It was midsummer of the year 1832. Owing to the introductions I had with me, I found myself very much at home in this lively city, in which I made a pleasant stay of six weeks. As my sojourn, however, had no really practical purpose, my mother looked upon the cost of this holiday, short as it seemed, as an unnecessary extravagance on my part. I visited the theatres, heard Strauss, made excursions, and altogether had a very good time. I am afraid I contracted a few debts as well, which I paid off later on when I was conductor of the Dresden orchestra. I had received very pleasant impressions of musical and theatrical life, and for a long time Vienna lived in my memory as the acme of that extraordinarily productive spirit peculiar to its people. I enjoyed most of all the performances at the *Theater an der Wien,* at which they were acting a grotesque fairy play called *Die Abenteuer Fortunat's zu Wasser und zu Land,* in, which a cab was called on the shores of the Black Sea and which made a tremendous impression on me. About the music I was more doubtful. A young friend of mine took me with immense pride to a performance of Gluck's *Iphigenia in Tauris,* which was made doubly attractive by a first-rate cast including Wild, Stäudigl and Binder: I must confess that on the whole I was bored by this work, but I did not dare say so. My ideas of Gluck had attained gigantic proportions from my reading of Hoffmann's well-known *Phantasies;* my anticipation of this work therefore, which I had not studied yet, had led me to expect a treatment full of overpowering dramatic force. It is possible that Schröder-Devrient's acting in *Fidelio* had taught me to judge everything by her exalted standard.

With the greatest trouble I worked myself up to some kind of enthusiasm for the great scene between Orestes and the Furies. I hoped against hope that I should be able to admire the remainder of the opera. I began to understand the Viennese taste, however, when I saw how great a favourite the opera *Zampa* became with the public, both at the Kärnthner Thor and at the Josephstadt. Both theatres competed vigorously in the production of this popular work, and although the public had seemed mad about *Iphigenia,* nothing equalled their enthusiasm for *Zampa.* No sooner had they left the Josephstadt Theatre in the greatest ecstasies about *Zampa* than they proceeded to the public-house called the Sträusslein. Here they were immediately greeted by the strains of selections from *Zampa* which drove the audience to feverish excitement. I shall never forget the extraordinary playing of Johann Strauss, who put equal enthusiasm into everything he played, and very often made the audience almost frantic with delight.

At the beginning of a new waltz this demon of the Viennese musical spirit shook like a Pythian priestess on the tripod, and veritable groans of ecstasy (which, without doubt, were more due to his music than to the drinks in which the audience had indulged) raised their worship for the magic violinist to almost bewildering heights of frenzy.

The hot summer air of Vienna was absolutely impregnated with *Zampa* and Strauss. A very poor students' rehearsal at the Conservatoire, at which they performed a Mass by Cherubini, seemed to me like an alms paid begrudgingly to the study of classical music. At the same rehearsal one of the professors, to whom I was introduced, tried to make the students play my Overture in D minor (the one already performed in Leipzig). I do not know what his opinion was, nor that of the students, with regard to this attempt; I only know they soon gave it up.

On the whole I had wandered into doubtful musical bypaths; and I now withdrew from this first educational visit to a great European art centre in order to start on a cheap, but long and monotonous return journey to Bohemia, by stage-coach. My next move was a visit to the house of Count Pachta, of whom I had pleasant recollections from my boyhood days. His estate, Pravonin, was about eight miles from Prague. Received in the kindest possible way by the old gentleman and his beautiful daughters, I enjoyed his delightful hospitality until late into the autumn. A youth of nineteen, as I then was, with a fast-growing beard (for which my sisters had already prepared the young ladies by letter), the continual and close intimacy with such kind and pretty girls could hardly fail to make a strong impression on my imagination. Jenny, the elder of the two, was slim, with black hair, blue eyes, and wonderfully noble features; the younger one, Auguste, was a little smaller, and stouter, with a magnificent complexion, fair hair, and brown eyes. The natural and sisterly manner with which both girls treated me and conversed with me did not blind me to the fact that I was expected to fall in love with one or the other of them. It amused them to see how embarrassed I got in my efforts to choose between them, and consequently they teased me tremendously.

Unfortunately, I did not act judiciously with regard to the daughters of my host: in spite of their homely education, they belonged to a very aristocratic house, and consequently hesitated between the hope of marrying men of eminent position in their own sphere, and the necessity of choosing husbands amongst the higher middle classes, who could afford to keep them in comfort. The shockingly poor, almost mediæval, education of the Austrian so-called cavalier, made me rather despise the latter; the girls, too, had suffered from the same lack of proper training. I soon noticed with disgust how little they knew about things artistic, and how much value they attached to superficial things. However much I might try to interest them in those higher pursuits which had become necessary to me, they were incapable of appreciating them. I advocated a complete change from the bad library novels, which represented their only reading, from the Italian operatic arias, sung by Auguste, and, last but not least, from the horsy, insipid cavaliers, who paid their court to both Jenny and her sister in the most coarse and offensive manner. My zeal in this latter respect soon gave rise to great unpleasantness. I became hard and insulting, harangued them about the French Revolution, and begged them with fatherly admonitions ' for the love of heaven ' to be content with well-educated middle-class men, and give up those impertinent suitors who could only harm their reputation. The indignation provoked by my friendly advice I often had to ward off with the harshest retorts. I never apologised, but tried by dint of real or feigned jealousy to get our friendship back on the old footing. In this way, undecided, half in love and half angry, one cold November day I said good-bye to these pretty children. I soon met the whole family again at Prague, where I made a long sojourn, without, however, staying at the Count's residence.

My stay at Prague was to be of great musical importance to me. I knew the director of the Conservatoire, Dionys Weber, who promised to bring my symphony before the public; I also spent much of my time with an actor called Moritz, to whom, as an old friend of our family, I had been recommended, and there I made the acquaintance of the young musician Kittl.

Moritz, who noticed that not a day passed but what I went to the much-feared chief of the Conservatoire upon some pressing musical business, once despatched me with an improvised parody on Schiller's *Bürgschaft:* —

> *Zu Dionys dem Direktor schlich*
> *Wagner, die Partitur im Gewande;*
> *Ihn schlugen die Schüler im Bande:*
> *' Was wolltest du mit den Noten sprich? '*
> *Entgegnet ihm finster der Wütherich:*
> *' Die Stadt vom schlechten Geschmacke befreien!*
> *Das sollst du in den Rezensionen bereuen.'* [1]

Truly I had to deal with a kind of ' Dionysius the Tyrant.' A man who did not acknowledge Beethoven's genius beyond his Second Symphony, a man who looked upon the *Eroica* as the acme of bad taste on the master's part; who praised Mozart alone, and next to him tolerated only Lindpaintner: such a man was not easy to approach, and I had to learn the art of making use of tyrants for one's own purposes. I dissimulated; I pretended to be struck by the novelty of his ideas, never contradicted him, and, to point out the similarity of our standpoints, I referred him to the end fugue in my Overture and in my Symphony (both in C major), which I had only succeeded in making what they were through having studied Mozart. My reward soon followed: Dionys set to work to study my orchestral creations with almost youthful energy.

[1] To Dionys, the Director, crept
Wagner, the score in his pocket;
The students arrested him forthwith:
' What do'st thou with that music, say? '
Thus asked him the angry tyrant:
' To free the town from taste too vile!
For this the critics will make thee suffer.'

The students of the Conservatoire were compelled to practise with the greatest exactitude my new symphony under his dry and terribly noisy baton. In the presence of several of my friends, amongst whom was also the dear old Count Pachta in his capacity of President of the Conservatoire Committee, we actually held a first performance of the greatest work that I had written up to that date.

During these musical successes I went on with my love-making in the attractive house of Count Pachta, under the most curious circumstances. A confectioner of the name of Hascha was my rival. He was a tall, lanky young man who, like most Bohemians, had taken up music as a hobby; he played the accompaniments to Auguste's songs, and naturally fell in love with her. Like myself, he hated the frequent visits of the cavaliers, which seemed to be quite the custom in this city; but while my displeasure expressed itself in humour, his showed itself in gloomy melancholy. This mood made him behave boorishly in public: for instance, one evening, when the chandelier was to be lighted for the reception of one of these gentlemen, he ran his head purposely against this orna-ment and broke it. The festive illumination was thus rendered impossible; the Countess was furious, and Hascha had to leave the house never to return.

I well remember that the first time I was conscious of any feelings of love, these manifested themselves as pangs of jealousy, which had, however, nothing to do with real love: this happened one evening when I called at the house. The Countess kept me by her side in an ante-room, while the girls, beautifully dressed and gay, flirted in the reception-room with those hateful young noblemen. All I had ever read in Hoffmann's *Tales* of certain demoniacal intrigues, which until that moment had been obscure to me, now became really tangible facts, and I left Prague with an obviously unjust and exagger-ated opinion of those things and those people, through whom I had suddenly been dragged into an unknown world of elementary passions.

On the other hand I had gained by my stay at Pravonin: I had written poetry as well as musical compositions. My musical work was a setting of *Glockentöne,* a poem by the friend of my youth, Theodor Apel. I had already written an aria for soprano which had been performed the winter before at one of the theatre concerts. But my new work was decidedly the first vocal piece I had written with real inspiration; generally speaking, I suppose it owed its characteristics to the influence of Beethoven's *Liederkreis:* all the same, the impression that it has left on my mind is that it was absolutely part of myself, and pervaded by a delicate sentimentality which was brought into relief by the dreaminess of the accompaniment. My poetical efforts lay in the direction of a sketch of a tragi-operatic subject, which I finished in its entirety in Prague under the title of *Die Hochzeit* ('The Wedding'). I wrote it without anybody's knowledge, and this was no easy matter, seeing that I could not write in my chilly little hotel-room, and had therefore to go to the house of Moritz, where I generally spent my mornings. I remember how I used quickly to hide my manuscript behind the sofa as soon as I heard my host's footsteps.

An extraordinary episode was connected with the plot of this work.

Already years ago I had come across a tragic story, whilst perusing Büsching's book on chivalry, the like of which I have never since read. A lady of noble birth had been assaulted one night by a man who secretly cherished a passionate love for her, and in the struggle to defend her honour superhuman strength was given her to fling him into the courtyard below. The mystery of his death remained unexplained until the day of his solemn obsequies, when the lady herself, who attended them and was kneeling in solemn prayer, suddenly fell forward and expired. The mysterious strength of this profound and passionate story made an indelible impression upon my mind. Fascinated, moreover, by the peculiar treatment of similar phenomena in Hoffmann's *Tales,* I sketched a novel in which musical mysticism, which I still loved so deeply, played an important part. The action was supposed to take place on the estate of a rich patron of the fine arts: a young couple was going to be married, and had invited the friend of the bridegroom, an interesting but melancholy and mysterious young man, to their wedding. Intimately connected with the whole affair was a strange old organist. The mystic relations which gradually developed between the old musician, the melancholy young man and the bride, were to grow out of the unravelment of certain intricate events, in a somewhat similar manner to that of the mediæval story above related. Here was the same idea: the young man mysteriously killed, the equally strange sudden death of his friend's bride, and the old organist found dead on his bench after the playing of an impressive requiem, the last chord of which was inordinately prolonged as if it never would end.

I never finished this novel: but as I wanted to write the libretto for an opera, I took up the theme again in its original shape, and built on this (as far as the principal features went) the following dramatic plot: —

Two great houses had lived in enmity, and had at last decided to end the family feud. The aged head of one of these houses invited the son of his former enemy to the wedding of his daughter with one of his faithful partisans. The wedding feast is thus used as an opportunity for reconciling the two families. Whilst the guests are full of the suspicion and fear of treachery, their young leader falls violently in love with the bride of his newly found ally. His tragic glance deeply affects her; the festive escort accompanies her to the bridal chamber, where she is to await her beloved; leaning against her tower-window she sees the same passionate eyes fixed on her, and realises that she is face to face with a tragedy.

When he penetrates into her chamber, and embraces her with frantic passion, she pushes him backwards towards the balcony, and throws him over the parapet into the abyss, from whence his mutilated remains are dragged by his companions. They at once arm themselves against the presumed treachery, and call for vengeance; tumult and confusion fill the courtyard: the interrupted wedding feast threatens to end in a night of slaughter. The venerable head of the house at last succeeds in averting the catastrophe. Messengers are sent to bear the tidings of the mysterious calamity to the relatives of the victim: the corpse itself shall be the medium of reconciliation, for, in the presence of the different generations of the suspected family, Providence itself shall decide which of its members has been guilty of treason. During the preparations for the obsequies the bride shows signs of approaching madness; she flies from her bridegroom, refuses to be united to him, and locks herself up in her tower-chamber. Only when, at night, the gloomy though gorgeous ceremony commences, does she appear at the head of her women to be present at the burial service, the gruesome solemnity of which is interrupted by the news of the approach of hostile forces and then by the armed attack of the kinsmen of the murdered man. When the avengers of the presumed treachery penetrate into the chapel and call upon the murderer to declare himself, the horrified lord of the manor points towards his daughter who, turning away from her bridegroom, falls lifeless by the coffin of her victim. This nocturnal drama, through which ran reminiscences of *Leubald und Adelaïde* (the work of my far-off boyhood), I wrote in the darkest vein, but in a more polished and more noble style, disdaining all light-effects, and especially all operatic embellishments. Tender passages occurred here and there all the same, and Weinlich, to whom I had already shown the beginning of my work on my return to Leipzig, praised me for the clearness and good vocal quality of the introduction I had composed to the first act; this was an Adagio for a vocal septette, in which I had tried to express the reconciliation of the hostile families, together with the emotions of the wedded couple and the sinister passion of the secret lover. My principal object was, all the same, to win my sister Rosalie's approval. My poem, however, did not find favour in her eyes: she missed all that which I had purposely avoided, insisted on the ornamentation and development of the simple situation, and desired more brightness generally. I made up my mind in an instant: I took the manuscript, and without a suggestion of ill-temper, destroyed it there and then. This action had nothing whatever to do with wounded vanity. It was prompted merely by my desire honestly to prove to my sister how little I thought of my own work and how much I cared for her opinion. She was held in great and loving esteem by my mother and by the rest of our family, for she was their principal breadwinner: the important salary she earned as an actress constituted nearly the whole income out of which my mother had to defray the household expenses. For the sake of her profession she enjoyed many advantages at home. Her part of the house had been specially arranged so that she should have all the necessary comfort and peace for her studies; on marketing days, when the others had to put up with the simplest fare, she had to have the same dainty food as usual. But more than any of these things did her charming gravity and her refined way of speaking place her above the younger children. She was thoughtful and gentle and never joined us in our rather loud conversation. Of course, I had been the one member of the family who had caused the greatest anxieties both to my mother and to my motherly sister, and during my life as a student the strained relations between us had made a terrible impression on me. When therefore they tried to believe in me again, and once more showed some interest in my work, I was full of gratitude and happiness. The thought of getting this sister to look kindly upon my aspirations, and even to expect great things of me, had become a special stimulus to my ambition. Under these circumstances a tender and almost sentimental relationship grew up between Rosalie and myself, which in its purity and sincerity could vie with the noblest form of friendship between man and woman. This was principally due to her exceptional individuality. She had not any real talent, at least not for acting, which had often been considered stagey and unnatural. Nevertheless she was much appreciated owing to her charming appearance as well as to her pure and dignified womanliness, and I remember many tokens of esteem which she received in those days. All the same, none of these advances ever seemed to lead to the prospect of a marriage, and year by year went by without bringing her hopes of a suitable match — a fact which to me appeared quite unaccountable. From time to time I thought I noticed that Rosalie suffered from this state of affairs. I remember one evening when, believing herself to be alone, I heard her sobbing and moaning; I stole away unnoticed, but her grief made such an impression upon me that from that moment I vowed to bring some joy into her life, principally by making a name for myself. Not without reason had our stepfather Geyer given my gentle sister the nickname of ' Geistchen ' (little spirit). for if her

talent as an actress was not great, her imagination and her love of
art and of all high and noble things were perhaps, on that account alone, all the greater. From her lips I had first heard
expressions of admiration and delight concerning those subjects
which became dear to me later on, and she moved amongst a
circle of serious and interesting people who loved the higher
things of life without this attitude ever degenerating into
affectation.

On my return from my long journey I was introduced to
Heinrich Laube, whom my sister had added to her list of intimate friends. It was at the time when the after-effects of the
July revolution were beginning to make themselves felt amongst
the younger men of intellect in Germany, and of these Laube
was one of the most conspicuous. As a young man he came
from Silesia to Leipzig, his principal object being to try and
form connections in this publishing centre which might be of
use to him in Paris, whither he was going, and from which place
Börne also made a sensation amongst us by his letters. On
this occasion Laube was present at a representation of a play
by Ludwig Robert, *Die Macht der Verhältnisse* (' The Power of
Circumstances '). This induced him to write a criticism for
the Leipzig *Tageblatt,* which made such a sensation through
its terse and lively style that he was at once offered, in addition
to other literary work, the post of editor of *Die elegante Welt.*
In our house he was looked upon as a genius; his curt and often
biting manner of speaking, which seemed to exclude all attempt
at poetic expression, made him appear both original and daring:
his sense of justice, his sincerity and fearless bluntness made
one respect his character, hardened as it had been in youth by
great adversity. On me he had a very inspiring effect, and I
was very much astonished to find that he thought so much
of me as to write a flattering notice about my talent in his
paper after hearing the first performance of my symphony.

This performance took place in the beginning of the year
1833 at the Leipzig Schneider-Herberge. It was, by the bye,
in this dignified old hall that the society ' Euterpe ' held its
concerts! The place was dirty, narrow, and poorly lighted,
and it was here that my work was introduced to the Leipzig
public for the first time, and by means of an orchestra that

interpreted it simply disgracefully. I can only think of that evening as a gruesome nightmare; and my astonishment was therefore all the greater at seeing the important notice which Laube wrote about the performance. Full of hope, I therefore looked forward to a performance of the same work at the Gewandhaus concert, which followed soon after, and which came off brilliantly in every way. It was well received and well spoken of in all the papers; of real malice there was not a trace — on the contrary, several notices were encouraging, and Laube, who had quickly become celebrated, confided to me that he was going to offer me a libretto for an opera, which he had first written for Meyerbeer. This staggered me somewhat, for I was not in the least prepared to pose as a poet, and my only idea was to write a real plot for an opera. As to the precise manner, however, in which such a book had to be written, I already had a very definite and instinctive notion, and I was strengthened in the certainty of my own feelings in the matter when Laube now explained the nature of his plot to me. He told me that he wanted to arrange nothing less than *Kosziusko* into a libretto for grand opera! Once again I had qualms, for I felt at once that Laube had a mistaken idea about the character of a dramatic subject. When I inquired into the real action of the play, Laube was astonished that I should expect more than the story of the Polish hero, whose life was crowded with incident; in any case, he thought there was quite sufficient action in it to describe the unhappy fate of a whole nation. Of course the usual heroine was not missing; she was a Polish girl who had a love affair with a Russian; and in this way some sentimental situations were also to be found in the plot. Without a moment's delay I assured my sister Rosalie that I would not set this story to music: she agreed with me, and begged me only to postpone my answer to Laube. My journey to Würzburg was of great help to me in this respect, for it was easier to write my decision to Laube than to announce it to him personally. He accepted the slight rebuff with good grace, but he never forgave me, either then or afterwards, for writing my own words!

When he heard what subject I had preferred to his brilliant political poem, he made no effort to conceal his contempt for my choice. I had borrowed the plot from a dramatic fairy-tale by Gozzi, *La Donna Serpente,* and called it *Die Feen* ('The Fairies'). The names of my heroes I chose from different Ossian and similar poems: my prince was called Arindal; he was loved by a fairy called Ada, who held him under her spell and kept him in fairyland, away from his realm, until his faithful friends at last found him and induced him to return, for his country was going to rack and ruin, and even its capital had fallen into the enemy's hands. The loving fairy herself sends the prince back to his country; for the oracle has decreed that she shall lay upon her lover the severest of tasks. Only by performing this task triumphantly can he make it possible for her to leave the immortal world of fairies in order to share the fate of her earthly lover, as his wife. In a moment of deepest despair about the state of his country, the fairy queen appears to him and purposely destroys his faith in her by deeds of the most cruel and inexplicable nature. Driven mad by a thousand fears, Arindal begins to imagine that all the time he has been dealing with a wicked sorceress, and tries to escape the fatal spell by pronouncing a curse upon Ada. Wild with sorrow, the unhappy fairy sinks down, and reveals their mutual fate to the lover, now lost to her for ever, and tells him that, as a punishment for having disobeyed the decree of Fate, she is doomed to be turned into stone (in Gozzi's version she becomes a serpent). Immediately afterwards it appears that all the catastrophes which the fairy had prophesied were but deceptions: victory over the enemy as well as the growing prosperity and welfare of the kingdom now follow in quick succession: Ada is taken away by the Fates, and Arindal, a raving madman, remains behind alone. The terrible sufferings of his madness do not, however, satisfy the Fates: to bring about his utter ruin they appear before the repentant man and invite him to follow them to the nether world, on the pretext of enabling him to free Ada from the spell. Through the treacherous promises of the wicked fairies Arindal's madness grows into sublime exaltation; and one of his household magicians, a faithful friend, having in the meantime equipped him with magic weapons and charms, he now follows the traitresses. The latter cannot get over their astonishment when they see how

Arindal overcomes one after the other of the monsters of the
infernal regions: only when they arrive at the vault in which
they show him the stone in human shape do they recover their
hope of vanquishing the valiant prince, for, unless he can
break the charm which binds Ada, he must share her fate and
be doomed to remain a stone for ever. Arindal, who until
then has been using the dagger and the shield given him by
the friendly magician, now makes use of an instrument — a
lyre — which he has brought with him, and the meaning of
which he had not yet understood. To the sounds of this
instrument he now expresses his plaintive moans, his remorse,
and his overpowering longing for his enchanted queen. The
stone is moved by the magic of his love: the beloved one is
released. Fairyland with all its marvels opens its portals, and
the mortal learns that, owing to his former inconstancy, Ada
has lost the right to become his wife on earth, but that her
beloved, through his great and magic power, has earned the
right to live for ever by her side in fairyland.

Although I had written *Die Hochzeit* in the darkest vein,
without operatic embellishments, I painted this subject with
the utmost colour and variety. In contrast to the lovers out
of fairyland I depicted a more ordinary couple, and I even
introduced a third pair that belonged to the coarser and more
comical servant world. I purposely went to no pains in the
matter of the poetic diction and the verse. My idea was not
to encourage my former hopes of making a name as a poet;
I was now really a 'musician' and a 'composer,' and wished
to write a decent opera libretto simply because I was sure
that nobody else could write one for me; the reason being that
such a book is something quite unique and cannot be written
either by a poet or by a mere man of letters. With the intention
of setting this libretto to music, I left Leipzig in January, 1833,
to stay in Würzburg with my eldest brother Albert, who at
the time held an appointment at the theatre. It now seemed
necessary for me to begin to apply my musical knowledge to
a practical purpose, and to this end my brother had promised
to help me in getting some kind of post at the small Würzburg
theatre. I travelled by post to Bamberg via Hof, and in Bamberg I stayed a few days in the company of a young man

called Schunke, who from a player on the horn had become an actor. With the greatest interest I learned the story of Caspar Hauser, who at that time was very well known, and who (if I am not mistaken) was pointed out to me. In addition to this, I admired the peculiar costumes of the market-women, thought with much interest of Hoffmann's stay at this place, and of how it had led to the writing of his *Tales,* and resumed my journey (to Würzburg) with a man called Hauderer, and suffered miserably from the cold all the way.

My brother Albert, who was almost a new acquaintance to me, did his best to make me feel at home in his not over luxurious establishment. He was pleased to find me less mad than he had expected me to be from a certain letter with which I had succeeded in frightening him some time previously, and he really managed to procure me an exceptional occupation as choir-master at the theatre, for which I received the monthly fee of ten guilders. The remainder of the winter was devoted to the serious study of the duties required of a musical director: in a very short time I had to tackle two new grand operas, namely, Marschner's *Vampir* and Meyerbeer's *Robert der Teufel,* in both of which the chorus played a considerable part. At first I felt absolutely like a beginner, and had to start on *Camilla von Paër,* the score of which was utterly unknown to me. I still remember that I felt I was doing a thing which I had no right to undertake: I felt quite an amateur at the work. Soon, however, Marschner's score interested me sufficiently to make the labour seem worth my while. The score of *Robert* was a great disappointment to me: from the newspapers I had expected plenty of originality and novelty; I could find no trace of either in this transparent work, and an opera with a finale like that of the second act could not be named in the same breath with any of my favourite works. The only thing that impressed me was the unearthly keyed trumpet which, in the last act, represented the voice of the mother's ghost.

It was remarkable to observe the æsthetic demoralisation into which I now fell through having daily to deal with such a work. I gradually lost my dislike for this shallow and exceedingly uninteresting composition (a dislike I shared with many

German musicians) in the growing interest which I was compelled to take in its interpretation; and thus it happened that the insipidness and affectation of the commonplace melodies ceased to concern me save from the standpoint of their capability of eliciting applause or the reverse. As, moreover, my future career as musical conductor was at stake, my brother, who was very anxious on my behalf, looked favourably on this lack of classical obstinacy on my part, and thus the ground was gradually prepared for that decline in my classical taste which was destined to last some considerable time.

All the same, this did not occur before I had given some proof of my great inexperience in the lighter style of writing. My brother wanted to introduce a ' Cavatine ' from the *Piraten,* by Bellini, into the same composer's opera, *Straniera;* the score was not to be had, and he entrusted me with the instrumentation of this work. From the piano score alone I could not possibly detect the heavy and noisy instrumentation of the ritornelles and intermezzi which, musically, were so very thin; the composer of a great C major Symphony with an end fugue could only help himself out of the difficulty by the use of a few flutes and clarinets playing in thirds. At the rehearsal the ' Cavatine ' sounded so frightfully thin and shallow that my brother made me serious reproaches about the waste of copying expenses. But I had my revenge: to the tenor aria of ' Aubry ' in Marschner's *Vampir* I added an Allegro, for which I also wrote the words.

My work succeeded splendidly, and earned the praise of both the public and my brother. In a similar German style I wrote the music to my *Feen* in the course of the year 1833. My brother and his wife left Würzburg after Easter in order to avail themselves of several invitations at friends' houses; I stayed behind with the children — three little girls of tender years — which placed me in the extraordinary position of a responsible guardian, a post for which I was not in the least suited at that time of my life. My time was divided between my work and pleasure, and in consequence I neglected my charges. Amongst the friends I made there, Alexander Müller had much influence over me; he was a good musician and pianist, and I used to listen for hours to his improvisations on given themes — an accomplishment in which he so greatly excelled, that I could not fail to be impressed. With him and some other friends, amongst whom was also Valentin Hamm, I often made excursions in the neighbourhood, on which occasions the Bavarian beer and the Frankish wine were wont to fly. Valentin Hamm was a grotesque individual, who entertained us often with his excellent violin playing; he had an enormous stretch on the piano, for he could reach an interval of a twelfth. *Der Letzte Hieb*, a public beer-garden situated on a pleasant height, was a daily witness of my fits of wild and often enthusiastic boisterousness; never once during those mild summer nights did I return to my charges without having waxed enthusiastic over art and the world in general. I also remember a wicked trick which has always remained a blot in my memory. Amongst my friends was a fair and very enthusiastic Swabian called Fröhlich, with whom I had exchanged my score of the C minor Symphony for his, which he had copied out with his own hand. This very gentle, but rather irritable young man had taken such a violent dislike to one André, whose malicious face I also detested, that he declared that this person spoilt his evenings for him, merely by being in the same room with him. The unfortunate object of his hatred tried all the same to meet us whenever he could : friction ensued, but André would insist upon aggravating us. One evening Fröhlich lost patience. After some insulting retort, he tried to chase him from our table by striking him with a stick : the result was a fight in which Frölich's friends felt they must take part, though they all seemed to do so with some reluctance. A mad longing to join the fray also took possession of me. With the others I helped in knocking our poor victim about, and I even heard the sound of one terrible blow which I struck André on the head, whilst he fixed his eyes on me in bewilderment.

I relate this incident to atone for a sin which has weighed very heavily on my conscience ever since. I can compare this sad experience only with one out of my earliest boyhood days, namely the drowning of some puppies in a shallow pool behind my uncle's house in Eisleben. Even to this day I cannot think of the slow death of these poor little creatures without horror. I have never quite forgotten some of my thoughtless and reckless actions; for the sorrows of others, and in particular those of animals, have always affected me deeply to the extent of filling me with a disgust of life.

My first love affair stands out in strong contrast against these recollections. It was only natural that one of the young chorus ladies with whom I had to practise daily should know how to attract my attentions. Therese Ringelmann, the daughter of a grave-digger, thanks to her beautiful soprano voice, led me to believe that I could make a great singer of her. After I told her of this ambitious scheme, she paid much attention to her appearance, and dressed elegantly for the rehearsals, and a row of white pearls which she wound through her hair specially fascinated me. During the summer holidays I gave Therese regular lessons in singing, according to a method which has always remained a mystery to me ever since. I also called on her very often at her house, where, fortunately, I never met her unpleasant father, but always her mother and her sisters. We also met in the public gardens, but false vanity always kept me from telling my friends of our relations. I do not know whether the fault lay with her lowly birth, her lack of education, or my own doubt about the sincerity of my affections; but in any case when, in addition to the fact that I had my reasons for being jealous, they also tried to urge me to a formal engagement, this love affair came quietly to an end.

An infinitely more genuine affair was my love for Friederike Galvani, the daughter of a mechanic, who was undoubtedly of Italian origin. She was very musical, and had a lovely voice; my brother had patronised her and helped her to a début at his theatre, which test she stood brilliantly. She was rather small, but had large dark eyes and a sweet disposition. The first oboist of the orchestra, a good fellow as well as a clever musician, was thoroughly devoted to her. He was looked upon as her *fiancé*, but, owing to some incident in his past, he was not allowed to visit at her parents' house, and the marriage was not to take place for a long time yet. When the autumn of my year in Würzburg drew near, I received an invitation from friends to be present at a country wedding at a little distance from Würzburg; the oboist and his *fiancée* had also been invited. It was a jolly, though primitive affair; we drank and danced, and I even tried my hand at violin playing, but I must have forgotten it badly, for even with the second violin I could not manage to satisfy the other musicians. But my success with Friederike was all the greater; we danced like mad through the many couples of peasants until at one moment we got so excited that, losing all self-control, we embraced each other while her real lover was playing the dance music. For the first time in my life I began to feel a flattering sensation of self-respect when Friederike's *fiancé*, on seeing how we two flirted, accepted the situation with good grace, if not without some sadness. I had never had the chance of thinking that I could make a favourable impression on any young girl. I never imagined myself good-looking, neither had I ever thought it possible that I could attract the attention of pretty girls.

On the other hand, I had gradually acquired a certain self-reliance in mixing with men of my own age. Owing to the exceptional vivacity and innate susceptibility of my nature — qualities which were brought home to me in my relations with members of my circle — I gradually became conscious of a certain power of transporting or bewildering my more indolent companions.

From my poor oboist's silent self-control on becoming aware of the ardent advances of his betrothed towards me, I acquired, as I have said, the first suggestion of the fact that I might count for something, not only among men, but also among women. The Frankish wine helped to bring about a state of ever greater confusion, and under the cover of its influence I at length declared myself, quite openly, to be Friederike's lover. Ever so far into the night, in fact, when day was already breaking, we set off home together to Würzburg in an open wagon. This was the crowning triumph of my delightful adventure; for while all the others, including, in the end, the jealous oboist, slept off their debauch in the face of the dawning day, I, with my cheek against Friederike's, and listening to the warbling of the larks, watched the coming of the rising sun.

On the following day we had scarcely any idea of what had

happened. A certain sense of shame, which was not unbecoming, held us aloof from one another: and yet I easily won access to Friederike's family, and from that time forward was daily a welcome guest, when for some hours I would linger in unconcealed intimate intercourse with the same domestic circle from which the unhappy betrothed remained excluded. No word was ever mentioned of this last connection; never once did it even dawn upon Friederike to effect any change in the state of affairs, and it seemed to strike no one that I ought, so to speak, to take the *fiancé's* place. The confiding manner in which I was received by all, and especially by the girl herself, was exactly similar to one of Nature's great processes, as, for instance, when spring steps in and winter passes silently away. Not one of them ever considered the material consequences of the change, and this is precisely the most charming and flattering feature of this first youthful love affair, which was never to degenerate into an attitude which might give rise to suspicion or concern. These relations ended only with my departure from Würzburg, which was marked by the most touching and most tearful leavetaking.

For some time, although I kept up no correspondence, the memory of this episode remained firmly imprinted on my mind. Two years later, while making a rapid journey through the old district, I once more visited Friederike: the poor child approached me utterly shamefaced. Her oboist was still her lover, and though his position rendered marriage impossible, the unfortunate young woman had become a mother. I have heard nothing more of her since.

Amid all this traffic of love I worked hard at my opera, and, thanks to the loving sympathy of my sister Rosalie, I was able to find the necessary good spirits for the task. When at the commencement of the summer my earnings as a conductor came to an end, this same sister again made it her business loyally to provide me with ample pocket-money, so that I might devote myself solely to the completion of my work, without troubling about anything or being a burden to any one. At a much later date I came across a letter of mine written to Rosalie in those days, which were full of a tender, almost adoring love for that noble creature.

When the winter was at hand my brother returned, and the theatre reopened. Truth to tell, I did not again become connected with it, but acquired a position, which was even more prominent, in the concerts of the Musical Society in which I produced my great overture in C major, my symphony, and eventually portions of my new opera as well. An amateur with a splendid voice, Mademoiselle Friedel, sang the great aria from *Ada*. In addition to this, a trio was given which, in one of its passages, had such a moving effect upon my brother, who took part in it, that, to his astonishment, as he himself admitted, he completely lost his cue on account of it.

By Christmas my work had come to an end, my score was written out complete with the most laudable neatness, and now I was to return to Leipzig for the New Year, in order to get my opera accepted by the theatre there. On the way home I visited Nuremberg, where I stayed a week with my sister Clara and with her husband, who were engaged at the theatre there. I well remember how happy and comfortable I felt during this pleasant visit to the very same relatives who a few years previously, when I had stayed with them at Magdeburg, had been upset by my resolve to adopt music as a calling. Now I had become a real musician, had written a grand opera, and had already brought out many things without coming to grief. The sense of all this was a great joy to me, while it was no less flattering to my relatives, who could not fail to see that the supposed misfortune had in the end proved to my advantage. I was in a jolly mood and quite unrestrained — a state of mind which was very largely the result not only of my brother-in-law's cheerful and sociable household, but also of the pleasant tavern life of the place. In a much more confident and elated spirit I returned to Leipzig, where I was able to lay the three huge volumes of my score before my highly delighted mother and sister.

Just then my family was the richer for the return of my brother Julius from his long wanderings. He had worked a good while in Paris as a goldsmith, and had now set up for himself in that capacity in Leipzig. He too, like the rest, was eager to hear something out of my opera, which, to be sure, was not so easy, as I entirely lacked the gift of playing anything of the sort in an easy and intelligible way. Only when I was able to work myself into a state of absolute ecstasy was it possible for me to render something with any effect. Rosalie knew that I meant it to draw a sort of declaration of love from her; but I have never felt certain whether the embrace and the sisterly kiss which were awarded me after I had sung my great aria from *Ada*, were bestowed on me from real emotion or rather out of affectionate regard. On the other hand, the zeal with which she urged my opera on the director of the theatre, Ringelhardt, the conductor and the manager was unmistakable, and she did it so effectually that she obtained their consent for its performance, and that very speedily. I was particularly interested to learn that the management immediately showed themselves eager to try to settle the matter of the costumes for my drama: but I was astonished to hear that the choice was in favour of oriental attire, whereas I had intended, by the names I had selected, to suggest a northern character for the setting. But it was precisely these names which they found unsuitable, as fairy personages are not seen in the North, but only in the East; while apart from this, the original by Gozzi, which formed the basis of the work, undoubtedly bore an oriental character. It was with the utmost indignation that I opposed the insufferable turban and caftan style of dress, and vehemently advocated the knightly garb worn in the early years of the Middle Ages. I then had to come to a thorough understanding with the conductor, Stegmayer, on the subject of my score. He was a remarkable, short, fat man, with fair curly hair, and an exceptionally jovial disposition; he was, however, very hard to bring to a point. When over our wine we always arrived at an understanding very quickly, but as soon as we sat at the piano, I had to listen to the most extraordinary objections concerning the trend of which I was for some time extremely puzzled. As the matter was much delayed by this vacillation, I put myself into closer communication with the stage manager of the opera, Hauser, who at that time was much appreciated as a singer and patron of art by the people of Leipzig.

With this man, too, I had the strangest experiences: he who had captivated the audiences of Leipzig, more especially with his impersonation of the barber and the Englishman in

Fra Diavolo, suddenly revealed himself in his own house as the most fanatical adherent of the most old-fashioned music. I listened with astonishment to the scarcely veiled contempt with which he treated even Mozart, and the only thing he seemed to regret was that we had no operas by Sebastian Bach. After he had explained to me that dramatic music had not actually been written yet, and that properly speaking Gluck alone had shown any ability for it, he proceeded to what seemed an exhaustive examination of my own opera, concerning which all I had wished to hear from him was whether it was fit to be performed. Instead of this, however, his object seemed to be to point out the failure of my purpose in every number. I sweated blood under the unparalleled torture of going through my work with this man; and I told my mother and sister of my grave depression. All these delays had already succeeded in making it impossible to perform my opera at the date originally fixed, and now it was postponed until August of the current year (1834).

An incident which I shall never forget inspired me with fresh courage. Old Bierey, an experienced and excellent musician, and in his day a successful composer, who, thanks more particularly to his long practice as a conductor at the Breslau theatre, had acquired a perfectly practical knowledge of such things, was then living at Leipzig, and was a good friend of my people. My mother and sister begged him to give his opinion about the fitness of my opera for the stage, and I duly submitted the score to him. I cannot say how deeply affected and impressed I was to see this old gentleman appear one day among my relatives, and to hear him declare with genuine enthusiasm that he simply could not understand how so young a man could have composed such a score. His remarks concerning the greatness which he had recognised in my talent were really irresistible, and positively amazed me. When asked whether he considered the work presentable and calculated to produce an effect, he declared his only regret was that he was no longer at the head of a theatre, because, had he been, he would have thought himself extremely lucky to secure such a man as myself permanently for his enterprise. At this announcement my family was overcome with joy, and their feelings were all the more justified seeing that, as they all knew, Bierey was by no means an amiable romancer, but a practical musician well seasoned by a life full of experience. The delay was now borne with better spirits, and for a long time I was able to wait hopefully for what the future might bring. Among other things, I now began to enjoy the company of a new friend in the person of Laube, who at that time, although I had not set his *Kosziusko* to music, was at the zenith of his fame. The first portion of his novel, *Young Europe,* the form of which was epistolary, had appeared, and had a most stimulating effect on me, more particularly in conjunction with all the youthful hopefulness which at that time pulsated in my veins. Though his teaching was essentially only a repetition of that in Heinse's *Ardinghello,* the forces that then surged in young breasts were given full and eloquent expression. The guiding spirit of this tendency was followed in literary criticism, which was aimed mainly at the supposed or actual incapacity of the semi-classical occupants of our various literary thrones. Without the slightest mercy the pedants,[1] among whom Tieck for one was numbered, were treated as sheer encumbrances and hindrances to the rise of a new literature. That which led to a remarkable revulsion of my feelings with regard to those German composers who hitherto had been admired and respected, was partly the influence of these critical skirmishes, and the luring sprightliness of their tone; but mainly the impression made by a fresh visit of Schröder-Devrient to Leipzig, when her rendering of Romeo in Bellini's *Romeo and Juliet* carried every one by storm. The effect of it was not to be compared with anything that had been witnessed theretofore. To see the daring, romantic figure of the youthful lover against a background of such obviously shallow and empty music prompted one, at all events, to meditate doubtfully upon the cause of the great lack of effect in solid German music as it had been applied hitherto to the drama. Without for the moment plunging too deeply into this meditation, I allowed myself to be borne along with the current of my youthful feelings, then roused to ardour, and turned involuntarily to the task of working off all that brooding seriousness

---

[1] *Zöpfe* in the German text. — TRANSLATOR.

which in my earlier years had driven me to such pathetic
mysticism.

What Pohlenz had not done by his conducting of the Ninth
Symphony, what the Vienna Conservatoire, Dionys Weber, and
many other clumsy performances (which had led me to regard
classical music as absolutely colourless) had not fully accomplished, was achieved by the inconceivable charm of the most
unclassical Italian music, thanks to the wonderful, thrilling,
and entrancing impersonation of Romeo by Schröder-Devrient.
What effect such powerful, and as regards their causes, incomprehensible, effects had upon my opinion was shown in the
frivolous way in which I was able to contrive a short criticism
of Weber's *Euryanthe* for the *Elegante Zeitung*. This opera
had been performed by the Leipzig company shortly before the
appearance of Schröder-Devrient: cold and colourless performers, among whom the singer in the title-rôle, appearing in
the wilderness with the full sleeves which were then the pink
of fashion, is still a disagreeable memory. Very laboriously,
and without verve, but simply with the object of satisfying the
demands of classical rules, this company did its utmost to dispel
even the enthusiastic impressions of Weber's music which I
had formed in my youth. I did not know what answer to
make to a brother critic of Laube's, when he pointed out to me
the laboured character of this operatic performance, as soon as
he was able to contrast it with the entrancing effect of that
Romeo evening. Here I found myself confronted with a
problem, the solving of which I was just at that time disposed
to take as easily as possible, and displayed my courage by
discarding all prejudice, and that daringly, in the short criticism just mentioned in which I simply scoffed at *Euryanthe*.
Just as I had had my season of wild oat sowing as a student, so
now I boldly rushed into the same courses in the development
of my artistic taste.

It was May, and beautiful spring weather, and a pleasure
trip that I now undertook with a friend into the promised land
of my youthful romance, Bohemia, was destined to bring the
unrestrained ' Young-European ' mood in me to full maturity.
This friend was Theodor Apel. I had known him a long while,
and had always felt particularly flattered by the fact that I

had won his hearty affection; for, as the son of the gifted master of metre and imitator of Greek forms of poetry, August Apel, I felt that admiring deference for him which I had never yet been able to bestow upon the descendant of a famous man. Being well-to-do and of a good family, his friendship gave me such opportunities of coming into touch with the easy circumstances of the upper classes as were not of frequent occurrence in my station of life. While my mother, for instance, regarded my association with this highly respectable family with great satisfaction, I for my part was extremely gratified at the thought of the cordiality with which I was received in such circles.

Apel's earnest wish was to become a poet, and I took it for granted that he had all that was needed for such a calling; above all, what seemed to me so important, the complete freedom that his considerable fortune assured him by liberating him from all need of earning his living or of adopting a profession for a livelihood. Strange to say, his mother, who on the death of his distinguished father had married a Leipzig lawyer, was very anxious about the vocation he should choose, and wished her son to make a fine career in the law, as she was not at all disposed to favour his poetical gifts. And it was to her attempts to convert me to her view, in order that by my influence I might avert the calamity of a second poet in the family, in the person of the son, that I owed the specially friendly relations that obtained between herself and me. All her suggestions succeeded in doing, however, was to stimulate me, even more than my own favourable opinion of his talent could, to confirm my friend in his desire to be a poet, and thus to support him in his rebellious attitude towards his family.

He was not displeased at this. As he was also studying music and composed quite nicely, I succeeded in being on terms of the greatest intimacy with him. The fact that he had spent the very year in which I had sunk into the lowest depths of undergraduate madness, studying at Heidelberg and not at Leipzig, had kept him unsullied by any share in my strange excesses, and when we now met again at Leipzig, in the spring of 1834, the only thing that we still had in common was the æsthetic aspiration of our lives, which we now strove by way

of experiment to divert into the direction of the enjoyment
of life. Gladly would we have flung ourselves into lively adventures if only the conditions of our environment and of
the whole middle-class world in which we lived had in any way
admitted of such things. Despite all the promptings of our instincts, however, we got no further than planning this excursion
to Bohemia. At all events, it was something that we made the
journey not by the post, but in our own carriage, and our
genuine pleasure continued to lie in the fact that at Teplitz,
for instance, we daily took long drives in a fine carriage. When
in the evening we had supped off trout at the Wilhelmsburg,
drunk good Czernosek wine with Bilin water, and duly excited
ourselves over Hoffmann, Beethoven, Shakespeare, Heinse's
Ardinghello, and other matters, and then, with our limbs comfortably outstretched in our elegant carriage, drove back in
the summer twilight to the ' King of Prussia,' where we occupied the large balcony-room on the first floor, we felt that
we had spent the day like young gods, and for sheer exuberance
could think of nothing better to do than to indulge in the most
frightful quarrels which, especially when the windows were
open, would collect numbers of alarmed listeners in the square
before the inn.

One fine morning I stole away from my friend in order to
take my breakfast alone at the ' Schlackenburg,' and also to
seize an opportunity of jotting down the plan of a new operatic
composition in my note-book. With this end in view, I had
mastered the subject of Shakespeare's *Measure for Measure*,
which, in accordance with my present mood, I soon transformed pretty freely into a libretto entitled *Liebesverbot. Young
Europe* and *Ardinghello*, and the strange frame of mind into
which I had fallen with regard to classical operatic music,
furnished me with the keynote of my conception, which was
directed more particularly against puritanical hypocrisy, and
which thus tended boldly to exalt ' unrestrained sensuality.'
I took care to understand the grave Shakespearean theme only
in this sense. I could see only the gloomy strait-laced viceroy,
his heart aflame with the most passionate love for the beautiful
novice, who, while she beseeches him to pardon her brother
condemned to death for illicit love, at the same time kindles

the most dangerous fire in the stubborn Puritan's breast by infecting him with the lovely warmth of her human emotion.

The fact that these powerful features are so richly developed in Shakespeare's creation only in order that, in the end, they may be weighed all the more gravely in the scales of justice, was no concern of mine: all I cared about was to expose the sinfulness of hypocrisy and the unnaturalness of such cruel moral censure. Thus I completely dropped *Measure for Measure*, and made the hypocrite be brought to justice only by the avenging power of love. I transferred the theme from the fabulous city of Vienna to the capital of sunny Sicily, in which a German viceroy, indignant at the inconceivably loose morals of the people, attempts to introduce a puritanical reform, and comes miserably to grief over it. *Die Stumme von Portici* probably contributed to some extent to this theme, as did also certain memories of *Die Sizilianische Vesper*. When I remember that at last even the gentle Sicilian Bellini constituted a factor in this composition, I cannot, to be sure, help smiling at the strange medley in which the most extraordinary misunderstandings here took shape.

This remained for the present a mere draft. Studies from life destined for my work were first to be carried out on this delightful excursion to Bohemia. I led my friend in triumph to Prague, in the hope of securing the same impressions for him which had stirred me so profoundly when I was there. We met my fair friends in the city itself; for, owing to the death of old Count Pachta, material changes had taken place in the family, and the surviving daughters no longer went to Pravonin. My behaviour was full of arrogance, and by means of it I doubtless wished to vent a certain capricious lust of revenge for the feelings of bitterness with which I had taken leave of this circle some years previously. My friend was well received. The changed family circumstances forced the charming girls ever more and more imperatively to come to some decision as to their future, and a wealthy bourgeois, though not exactly in trade himself, but in possession of ample means, seemed to the anxious mother, at all events, a good adviser. Without either showing or feeling any malice in the matter, I expressed my pleasure at the sight of the strange confusion

caused by Theodor's introduction into the family by the mer-
riest and wildest jests: for my only intercourse with the ladies
consisted purely of jokes and friendly chaff. They could not
understand how it was that I had altered so strangely. There
was no longer any of that love of wrangling, that rage for
instructing, and that zeal in converting in me which formerly
they had found so irritating. But at the same time not a
sensible word could I be made to utter, and they who were now
wanting to talk over many things seriously could get nothing
out of me save the wildest tomfoolery. As on this occasion,
in my character of an uncaged bird, I boldly allowed myself
many a liberty against which they felt themselves powerless,
my exuberant spirits were excited all the more when my friend,
who was led away by my example, tried to imitate me — a
thing they took in very bad part from him.

Only once was there any attempt at seriousness between us:
I was sitting at the piano, and was listening to my companion,
who was telling the ladies that in a conversation at the hotel I
had found occasion to express myself most warmly to some
one who appeared to be surprised on hearing of the domestic
and industrious qualities of my lady friends. I was deeply
moved when, as the outcome of my companion's remarks, I
gathered what unpleasant experiences the poor things had
already been through: for what seemed to me a very natural
action on my part, appeared to fill them with unexpected
pleasure. Jenny, for instance, came up to me and hugged me
with great warmth. By general consent I was now granted
the right of behaving with almost studied rudeness, and I
replied even to Jenny's warm outburst only with my usual
banter.

In our hotel, the ' Black Horse,' which was so famous in
those days, I found the playground in which I was able to
carry the mischievous spirit not exhausted at the Pachta's house
to the point of recklessness. Out of the most accidental material in table and travelling guests we succeeded in gathering a company around us which allowed us, until far into the
night, to lead it into the most inconceivable follies. To all
this I was incited more particularly by the personality of a
very timid and undersized business man from Frankfort *on*

the Oder, who longed to seem of a daring disposition; and his presence stimulated me, if only owing to the remarkable chance it gave me of coming into contact with some one who was at home in Frankfort ' on the Oder.' Any one who knows how things then stood in Austria can form some idea of my recklessness when I say that I once went so far as to cause our symposium in the public room to bellow the *Marseillaise* out loud into the night. Therefore, when after this heroic exploit was over, and while I was undressing, I clambered on the outer ledges of the windows from one room to the other on the second floor, I naturally horrified those who did not know of the love of acrobatic feats which I had cultivated in my earliest boyhood.

Even if I had exposed myself without fear to such dangers, I was soon sobered down next morning by a summons from the police. When, in addition to this, I recalled the singing of the *Marseillaise,* I was filled with the gravest fears. After having been detained at the station a long time, owing to a strange misunderstanding, the upshot of it was that the inspector who was told off to examine me found that there was not sufficient time left for a serious hearing, and, to my great relief, I was allowed to go after replying to a few harmless questions concerning the intended length of my stay. Nevertheless, we thought it advisable not to yield to the temptation of playing any more pranks beneath the spread wings of the double eagle.

By means of a circuitous route into which we were led by our insatiable longing for adventures — adventures which, as a matter of fact, occurred only in our imagination, and which to all intents and purposes were but modest diversions on the road — we at length got back to Leipzig. And with this return home the really cheerful period of my life as a youth definitely closed. If, up to that time, I had not been free from serious errors and moments of passion, it was only now that care cast its first shadow across my path.

My family had anxiously awaited my return in order to inform me that the post of conductor had been offered to me by the Magdeburg Theatre Company. This company during the current summer month was performing at a watering place called Lauchstädt. The manager could not get on with an incompetent conductor that had been sent to him, and in his extremity had applied to Leipzig in the hope of getting a substitute forthwith. Stegmayer, the conductor, who had no inclination to practise my score *Feen* during the hot summer weather, as he had promised to do, promptly recommended me for the post, and in that way really managed to shake off a very troublesome tormentor. For although, on the one hand, I really desired to be able to abandon myself freely and without restraint to the torrent of adventures that constitute the artist's life, yet a longing for independence, which could be won only by my earning my own living, had been greatly strengthened in me by the state of my affairs. Albeit, I had the feeling that a solid basis for the gratification of this desire was not to be laid in Lauchstädt; nor did I find it easy to assist the plot concocted against the production of my *Feen*. I therefore determined to make a preliminary visit to the place just to see how things stood.

This little watering-place had, in the days of Goethe and Schiller, acquired a very wide reputation. Its wooden theatre had been built according to the design of the former, and the first performance of the *Braut von Messina* had been given there. But although I repeated all this to myself, the place made me feel rather doubtful. I asked for the house of the director of the theatre. He proved to be out, but a small dirty boy, his son, was told to take me to the theatre to find ' Papa.' Papa, however, met us on the way. He was an elderly man; he wore a dressing-gown, and on his head a cap. His delight at greeting me was interrupted by complaints about a serious indisposition, for which his son was to fetch him a cordial from a shop close by. Before despatching the boy on this errand he pressed a real silver penny into his hand with a certain ostentation which was obviously for my benefit. This person was Heinrich Bethmann, surviving husband of the famous actress of that name, who, having lived in the heyday of the German stage, had won the favour of the King of Prussia; and won it so lastingly, that long after her death it had continued to be extended to her spouse. He always drew a nice pension from the Prussian court, and permanently enjoyed its support without ever being able to forfeit its protection by his irregular and dissipated ways.

At the time of which I am speaking he had sunk to his lowest, owing to continued theatre management. His speech and manners revealed the sugary refinement of a bygone day, while all that he did and everything about him testified to the most shameful neglect. He took me back to his house, where he presented me to his second wife, who, crippled in one foot, lay on an extraordinary couch while an elderly bass, concerning whose excessive devotion Bethmann had already complained to me quite openly, smoked his pipe beside her. From there the director took me to his stage manager, who lived in the same house.

With the latter, who was just engaged in a consultation about the repertory with the theatre attendant, a toothless old skeleton, he left me to settle the necessary arrangements. As soon as Bethmann had gone, Schmale, the stage manager, shrugged his shoulders and smiled, assuring me that that was just the way of the director, to put everything on his back and trouble himself about nothing. There he had been sitting for over an hour, discussing with Kröge what should be put on next Sunday: it was all very well his starting *Don Juan,* but how could he get a rehearsal carried out, when the Merseburg town bandsmen, who formed the orchestra, would not come over on Saturday to rehearse?

All the time Schmale kept reaching out through the open window to a cherry tree from which he picked and persistently ate the fruit, ejecting the stones with a disagreeable noise. Now it was this last circumstance in particular which decided me; for, strange to say, I have an innate aversion from fruit. I informed the stage manager that he need not trouble at all about *Don Juan* for Sunday, since for my part, if they had reckoned on my making my first appearance at this performance, I must anyhow disappoint the director, as I had no choice but to return at once to Leipzig, where I had to put my affairs in order. This polite manner of tendering my absolute refusal to accept the appointment — a conclusion I had quickly arrived at in my own mind — forced me to practise some dissimulation, and made it necessary for me to appear as if I really had some other purpose in coming to Lauchstädt. This pretence in itself was quite unnecessary, seeing that I was quite determined never to return there again.

People offered to help me in finding a lodging, and a young actor whom I had chanced to know at Würzburg undertook to be my guide in the matter. While he was taking me to the best lodging he knew, he told me that presently he would do me the kindness of making me the housemate of the prettiest and nicest girl to be found in the place at the time. She was the junior lead of the company, Mademoiselle Minna Planer, of whom doubtless I had already heard.

As luck would have it, the promised damsel met us at the door of the house in question. Her appearance and bearing formed the most striking contrast possible to all the unpleasant impressions of the theatre which it had been my lot to receive on this fateful morning. Looking very charming and fresh, the young actress's general manner and movements were full of a certain majesty and grave assurance which lent an agreeable and captivating air of dignity to her otherwise pleasant expression. Her scrupulously clean and tidy dress completed the startling effect of the unexpected encounter. After I had been introduced to her in the hall as the new conductor, and after she had done regarding with astonishment the stranger who seemed so young for such a title, she recommended me kindly to the landlady of the house, and begged that I might be well looked after; whereupon she walked proudly and serenely across the street to her rehearsal.

I engaged a room on the spot, agreed to *Don Juan* for Sunday, regretted greatly that I had not brought my luggage with me from Leipzig, and hastened to return thither as quickly as possible in order to get back to Lauchstädt all the sooner. The die was cast. The serious side of life at once confronted me in the form of significant experiences. At Leipzig I had to take a furtive leave of Laube. At the instance of Prussia he had been warned off Saxon soil, and he half guessed at the meaning which was to be attached to this move. The time of undisguised reaction against the Liberal movement of the early 'thirties had set in: the fact that Laube was concerned in no sort of political work, but had devoted himself merely to literary activity, always aiming simply at æsthetic objects, made the action of the police quite incomprehensible to us for the time being. The disgusting ambiguity with which the Leipzig authorities answered all his questions as to the cause of his expulsion soon gave him the strongest suspicions as to what their intentions towards him actually were.

Leipzig, as the scene of his literary labours, being inestimably precious, it mattered greatly to him to keep within reach of it. My friend Apel owned a fine estate on Prussian soil, within but a few hours' distance of Leipzig, and we conceived the wish of seeing Laube hospitably harboured there. My friend, who without infringing the legal stipulations was in a position to give the persecuted man a place of refuge, immediately assented, and with great readiness, to our desire, but confessed to us next day, after having communicated with his family, that he thought he might incur some unpleasantnesses if he entertained Laube. At this the latter smiled, and in a manner I shall never forget, though I have noticed in the course of my life that the expression which I then saw in his face was one which has often flitted over my own features. He took his leave, and in a short time we heard that he had been arrested, owing to having undertaken fresh proceedings against former members of the Burschenschaft (Students' League), and had been lodged in the municipal prison at Berlin. I had thus had two experiences which weighed me down like lead, so I packed my scanty portmanteau, took leave of my mother and sister, and, with a stout heart, started on my career as a conductor.

In order to be able to look upon the little room under Minna's lodging as my new home, I was forced also to make the best of Bethmann's theatrical enterprise. As a matter of fact, a performance of *Don Juan* was given at once, for the director, who prided himself on being a connoisseur of things artistic, suggested that opera to me as one with which it would be wise for an aspiring young artist, of a good family, to make his début. Despite the fact that, apart from some of my own instrumental compositions, I had never yet conducted, and least of all in opera, the rehearsal and the performance went off fairly well. Only once or twice did discrepancies appear in the recitative of Donna Anna; yet this did not involve me in any kind of hostility, and when I took my place unabashed and calm for the production of *Lumpaci Vagabundus,* which I had practised very thoroughly, the people generally seemed to have gained full confidence in the theatre's new acquisition.

The fact that I submitted without bitterness and even with some cheerfulness to this unworthy use of my musical talent, was due less to my taste being at this period, as I called it, in its salad days, than to my intercourse with Minna Planer, who was employed in that magic trifle as the Amorous Fairy. Indeed, in the midst of this dust-cloud of frivolity and vulgarity, she always seemed very much like a fairy, the reasons of whose descent into this giddy whirl, which of a truth seemed neither to carry her away nor even to affect her, remained an absolute mystery. For while I could discover nothing in the opera singers save the familiar stage caricatures and grimaces, this fair actress differed wholly from those about her in her unaffected soberness and dainty modesty, as also in the absence of all theatrical pretence and stiltedness. There was only one young man whom I could place beside Minna on the ground of qualities like those I recognised in her. This fellow was Friedrich Schmitt, who had only just adopted the stage as a career in the hope of making a ' hit ' in opera, to which, as the possessor of an excellent tenor voice, he felt himself called. He too differed from the rest of the company, especially in the earnestness which he brought to bear upon his studies and his work in general: the soulful manly pitch of his chest voice, his clear, noble enunciation and intelligent rendering of his words, have always remained as standards in my memory. Owing to the fact that he was wholly devoid of theatrical talent, and acted clumsily and awkwardly, a check was soon put to his progress, but he always remained dear to me as a clever and original man of trustworthy and upright character — my only associate.

But my dealings with my kind housemate soon became a cherished habit, while she returned the ingenuously impetuous advances of the conductor of one-and-twenty with a certain tolerant astonishment which, remote as it was from all coquetry and ulterior motives, soon made familiar and friendly intercourse possible with her. When, one evening, I returned late to my ground-floor room, by climbing through the window, for I had no latch-key, the noise of my entry brought Minna to her window just over mine. Standing on my window ledge I begged her to allow me to bid her good-night once more. She had not the slightest objection to this, but declared it must be done from the window, as she always had her door locked by the people of the house, and nobody could get in that way. She kindly facilitated the handshake by leaning far out of her window, so that I could take her hand as I stood on my ledge. When later on I had an attack of erysipelas, from which I often suffered, and with my face all swollen and frightfully distorted concealed myself from the world in my gloomy room, Minna visited me repeatedly, nursed me, and assured me that my distorted features did not matter in the least. On recovering, I paid her a visit and complained of a rash that had remained round my mouth, and which seemed so unpleasant that I apologised for showing it to her. This also she made light of. Then I inferred she would not give me a kiss, whereupon she at once gave me practical proof that she did not shrink from that either.

This was all done with a friendly serenity and composure that had something almost motherly about it, and it was free from all suggestion of frivolity or of heartlessness. In a few weeks the company had to leave Lauchstädt to proceed to Rudolstadt and fulfil a special engagement there. I was particularly anxious to make this journey, which in those days was an arduous undertaking, in Minna's company, and if only I had succeeded in getting my well-earned salary duly paid by Bethmann, nothing would have hindered the fulfilment of my wish. But in this matter I encountered exceptional difficulties, which in the course of eventful years grew in chronic fashion into the strangest of ailments. Even at Lauchstädt I had discovered that there was only one man who drew his salary in full, namely the bass Kneisel, whom I had seen smoking his pipe beside the couch of the director's lame wife. I was assured that if I cared greatly about getting some of my wages from time to time, I could obtain this favour only by paying court to Mme. Bethmann. This time I preferred once more to appeal to my family for help, and therefore travelled to Rudolstadt through Leipzig, where, to the sad astonishment of my mother, I had to replenish my coffer with the necessary supplies. On the way to Leipzig I had travelled with Apel through his estate, he having fetched me from Lauchstädt for the purpose. His arrival was fixed in my memory by a noisy banquet which my wealthy friend gave at the hotel in my honour. It was on this occasion that I and one of the other guests succeeded in completely destroying a huge, massively built Dutch-tile stove, such as we had in our room at the inn. Next morning none of us could understand how it had happened.

It was on this journey to Rudolstadt that I first passed through Weimar, where on a rainy day I strolled with curiosity, but without emotion, towards Goethe's house. I had pictured something rather different, and thought I should experience livelier impressions from the active theatre life of Rudolstadt, to which I felt strongly attracted. In spite of the fact that I was not to be conductor myself, this post having been entrusted to the leader of the royal orchestra, who had been specially engaged for our performances, yet I was so fully occupied with rehearsals for the many operas and musical comedies required to regale the frivolous public of the principality that I found no leisure for excursions into the charming regions of this little land. In addition to these severe and ill-paid labours, two passions held me chained during the six weeks of my stay in Rudolstadt. These were, first, a longing to write the libretto of *Liebesverbot;* and secondly, my growing attachment to Minna. It is true, I sketched out a musical composition about this time, a symphony in E major, whose first movement (¾ time) I completed as a separate piece. As regards style and design, this work was suggested by Beethoven's Seventh and Eighth Symphonies, and, so far as I can remember, I should have had no need to be ashamed of it, had I been able to complete it, or keep the part I had actually finished. But I had already begun at this time to form the opinion that, to produce anything fresh and truly noteworthy in the realm of symphony, and according to Beethoven's methods, was an impossibility. Whereas opera, to which I felt inwardly drawn, though I had no real example I wished to copy, presented itself to my mind in varied and alluring shapes as a most fascinating form of art. Thus, amid manifold and passionate agitations, and in the few leisure hours which were left to me, I completed the greater part of my operatic poem, taking infinitely more pains, both as regards words and versification, than with the text of my earlier *Feen*. Moreover, I found myself possessed of incomparably greater assurance in the arrangement and partial invention of situations than when writing that earlier work.

On the other hand, I now began for the first time to experience the cares and worries of a lover's jealousy. A change, to me inexplicable, manifested itself in Minna's hitherto unaffected and gentle manner towards me. It appears that my artless solicitations for her favour, by which at that time I meant nothing serious, and in which a man of the world would merely have seen the exuberance of a youthful and easily satisfied infatuation, had given rise to certain remarks and comments upon the popular actress. I was astonished to learn, first from her reserved manner, and later from her own lips, that she felt compelled to inquire into the seriousness of my intentions, and to consider their consequences. She was at that time, as I had already discovered, on very intimate terms with a young nobleman, whose acquaintance I first made in Lauchstädt, where he used to visit her. I had already realised on that occasion that he was unfeignedly and cordially attached to her; in fact, in the circle of her friends she was regarded as engaged to Herr von O., although it was obvious that marriage was out of the question, as the young lover was quite without means, and owing to the high standing of his family it was essential that he should sacrifice himself to a marriage of convenience, both on account of his social position and of the career which he would have to adopt. During this stay at Rudolstadt Minna appears to have gathered certain information on this point which troubled and depressed her, thus rendering her more inclined to treat my impetuous attempts at courtship with cool reserve.

After mature deliberation I recognised that, in any case, *Young Europe, Ardinghello,* and *Liebesverbot* could not be produced at Rudolstadt; but it was a very different matter for the *Fee Amorosa*, with its merry theatrical mood, and an *Ehrlicher Bürger Kind* to seek a decent livelihood. Therefore, greatly discouraged, I proceeded to accentuate the more extravagant situations of my *Liebesverbot* by rioting with a few comrades in the sausage-scented atmosphere of the Rudolstadt Vogelwiese. At this time my troubles again brought me more or less into contact with the vice of gambling, although on this occasion it only cast temporary fetters about me in the very harmless form of the dice and roulette-tables out on the open market-place.

We were looking forward to the time when we should leave Rudolstadt for the half-yearly winter season at the capital, Magdeburg, mainly because I should there resume my place at the head of the orchestra, and might in any case count on a better reward for my musical efforts. But before returning to Magdeburg I had to endure a trying interval at Bernburg, where Bethmann, the director, in addition to his other undertakings, had also promised sundry theatrical performances. During our brief stay in the town I had to arrange for the presentation, with a mere fraction of the company, of several operas, which were again to be conducted by the royal conductor of the place. But in addition to these professional labours, I had to endure such a meagre, ill-provided and grievously farcical existence as was enough to disgust me, if not for ever, at any rate for the time being, with the wretched profession of a theatrical conductor. Yet I survived even this, and Magdeburg was destined to lead me eventually to the real glory of my adopted profession.

The sensation of sitting in command at the very conductor's desk from which, not many years before, the great master Kühnlein had so moved the perplexed young enthusiast by the weighty wisdom of his musical directorship, was not without its charm for me, and, indeed, I very quickly succeeded in obtaining perfect confidence in conducting an orchestra. I was soon a *persona grata* with the excellent musicians of the orchestra. Their splendid combination in spirited overtures, which, especially towards the finale, I generally took at an unheard-of speed, often earned for us all the intoxicating applause of the public. The achievements of my fiery and often exuberant zeal won me recognition from the singers, and were greeted by the audience with rapturous appreciation. As in Magdeburg, at least in those days, the art of theatrical criticism was but slightly developed, this universal satisfaction was a great encouragement, and at the end of the first three months of my Magdeburg conductorship I felt sustained by the flattering and comforting assurance that I was one of the bigwigs of opera. Under these circumstances, Schmale, the stage manager, who has been my good friend ever since, proposed a special gala performance for New Year's Day, which he felt sure would be a triumph. I was to compose the necessary music. This was very speedily done; a rousing overture, several melodramas and choruses were all greeted with enthusiasm, and brought us such ample applause that we repeated the performance with great success, although such repetitions after the actual gala day were quite contrary to usage.

With the new year (1835) there came a decisive turning-point in my life. After the rupture between Minna and myself at Rudolstadt, we had been to some extent lost to one another; but our friendship was resumed on our meeting again in Magdeburg; this time, however, it remained cool and purposely indifferent. When she first appeared in the town, a year before, her beauty had attracted considerable notice, and I now learned that she was the object of great attention from several young noblemen, and had shown herself not unmoved by the compliment implied by their visits. Although her reputation, thanks to her absolute discretion and self-respect, remained beyond reproach, my objection to her receiving such attentions grew very strong, owing possibly, in some degree, to the memory of the sorrows I had endured in Pachta's house in Prague. Although Minna assured me that the conduct of these gentlemen was much more discreet and decent than that of theatre-goers of the bourgeois class, and especially than that of certain young musical conductors, she never succeeded in soothing the bitterness and insistence with which I protested against her acceptance of such attentions. So we spent three unhappy months in ever-increasing estrangement, and at the same time, in half-frantic despair, I pretended to be fond of the most undesirable associates, and acted in every way with such blatant levity that Minna, as she told me afterwards, was filled with the deepest anxiety and solicitude concerning me. Moreover, as the ladies of the opera company were not slow to pay court to their youthful conductor, and especially as one young woman, whose reputation was not spotless, openly set her cap at me, this anxiety of Minna's seems at last to have culminated in a definite decision. I hit upon the idea of treating the *élite* of our opera company to oysters and punch in my own room on New Year's Eve. The married couples were invited, and then came the question whether Fräulein Planer would consent to take part in such a festivity. She accepted quite ingenuously, and presented herself, as neatly and becomingly dressed as ever, in my bachelor apartments, where things soon grew pretty lively. I had already warned my landlord that we were not likely to be very quiet, and reassured him as to any possible damage to his furniture. What the champagne failed to accomplish, the punch eventually succeeded in doing; all the restraints of petty conventionality, which the company usually endeavoured to observe, were cast aside, giving place to an unreserved demeanour all round, to which no one objected. And then it was that Minna's queenly dignity distinguished her from all her companions. She never lost her self-respect; and whilst no one ventured to take the slightest liberty with her, every one very clearly recognised the simple candour with which she responded to my kindly and solicitous attentions. They could not fail to see that the link existing between us was not to be compared to any ordinary *liaison,* and we had the satisfaction of seeing the flighty young lady who had so openly angled for me fall into a fit over the discovery.

From that time onward I remained permanently on the best of terms with Minna. I do not believe that she ever felt any sort of passion or genuine love for me, or, indeed, that she was capable of such a thing, and I can therefore only describe her feeling for me as one of heartfelt goodwill, and the sincerest desire for my success and prosperity, inspired as she was with the kindest sympathy, and genuine delight at, and admiration for, my talents. All this at last became part of her nature. She obviously had a very favourable opinion of my abilities, though she was surprised at the rapidity of my success. My eccentric nature, which she knew so well how to humour pleasantly by her gentleness, stimulated her to the continual exercise of the power, so flattering to her own vanity, and without ever betraying any desire or ardour herself, she never met my impetuous advances with coldness.

At the Magdeburg theatre I had already made the acquaintance of a very interesting woman called Mme. Haas. She was an actress, no longer in her first youth, and played so-called ' chaperone's parts.' This lady won my sympathy by telling me she had been friendly ever since her youth with Laube, in whose destiny she continued to take a heartfelt and cordial interest. She was clever, but far from happy, and an unprepossessing exterior, which with the lapse of years grew more uninviting, did not tend to make her any happier. She lived in meagre circumstances, with one child, and appeared to remember her better days with a bitter grief. My first visit to her was paid merely to inquire after Laube's fate, but I soon became a frequent and familiar caller. As she and Minna speedily became fast friends, we three often spent pleasant evenings talking together. But when, later on, a certain jealousy manifested itself on the part of the elder woman towards the younger, our confidential relations were more or less disturbed, for it particularly grieved me to hear Minna's talents and mental gifts criticised by the other. One evening I had promised Minna to have tea with her and Mme. Haas, but I had thoughtlessly promised to go to a whist party first. This engagement I purposely prolonged, much as it wearied me, in the deliberate hope that her companion — who had already grown irksome to me — might have left before my arrival. The only way in which I could do this was by drinking hard, so that I had the very unusual experience of rising from a sober whist party in a completely fuddled condition, into which I had imperceptibly fallen, and in which I refused to believe. This incredulity deluded me into keeping my engagement for tea, although it was so late. To my intense disgust the elder woman was still there when I arrived, and her presence at once had the effect of rousing my tipsiness to a violent outbreak; for she seemed astonished at my rowdy and unseemly behaviour, and made several remarks upon it intended for jokes, whereupon I scoffed at her in the coarsest manner, so that she immediately left the house in high dudgeon. I had still sense enough to be conscious of Minna's astonished laughter at my outrageous conduct. As soon as she realised, however, that my condition was such as to render my removal impossible without great commotion, she rapidly formed a resolution which must indeed have cost her an effort, though it was carried out with the utmost calmness and good-humour. She did all she could for me, and procured me the necessary relief, and when I sank into a heavy slumber, unhesitatingly resigned her own bed to my use. There I slept until awakened by the wonderful grey of dawn. On recognising where I was, I at once realised and grew ever more convinced of the fact that this morning's sunrise marked the starting-point of an infinitely momentous period of my life. The demon of care had at last entered into my existence.

Without any light-hearted jests, without gaiety or joking of any description, we breakfasted quietly and decorously together, and at an hour when, in view of the compromising circumstances of the previous evening, we could set out without attracting undue notice, I set off with Minna for a long walk beyond the city gates. Then we parted, and from that day forward freely and openly gratified our desires as an acknowledged pair of lovers.

The peculiar direction which my musical activities had gradually taken continued to receive ever fresh impetus, not only from the successes, but also from the disasters which about this time befell my efforts. I produced the overture to my *Feen* with very satisfactory results at a concert given by the Logengesellschaft, and thereby earned considerable applause. On the other hand, news came from Leipzig confirming the shabby action of the directors of the theatre in that place with regard to the promised presentation of this opera. But, happily for me, I had begun the music for my *Liebesverbot*, an occupation which so absorbed my thoughts that I lost all interest in the earlier work, and abstained with proud indifference from all further effort to secure its performance in Leipzig. The success of its overture alone amply repaid me for the composition of my first opera.

Meanwhile, in spite of numerous other distractions, I found
time, during the brief six months of this theatrical season in
Magdeburg, to complete a large portion of my new opera, besides doing other work. I ventured to introduce two duets
from it at a concert given in the theatre, and their reception
encouraged me to proceed hopefully with the rest of the opera.

During the second half of this season my friend Apel came
to sun himself enthusiastically in the splendour of my musical
directorship. He had written a drama, *Columbus*, which I
recommended to our management for production. This was a
peculiarly easy favour to win, as Apel volunteered to have a
new scene, representing the Alhambra, painted at his own
expense. Besides this, he proposed to effect many welcome
improvements in the condition of the actors taking part in his
play; for, owing to the continued preference displayed by the
directress for Kneisel, the bass, they had all suffered very much
from uncertainty about their wages. The piece itself appeared
to me to contain much that was good. It described the difficulties and struggles of the great navigator before he set sail
on his first voyage of discovery. The drama ended with the
momentous departure of his ships from the harbour of Palos,
an episode whose results are known to all the world. At my
desire Apel submitted his play to my uncle Adolph, and even
in his critical opinion it was remarkable for its lively and
characteristic popular scenes. On the other hand, a love romance, which he had woven into the plot, struck me as unnecessary and dull. In addition to a brief chorus for some
Moors who were expelled from Granada, to be sung on their
departure from the familiar home country, and a short orchestral
piece by way of conclusion, I also dashed off an overture for
my friend's play. I sketched out the complete draft of this
one evening at Minna's house, while Apel was left free to talk
to her as much and as loudly as he liked. The effect this composition was calculated to produce rested on a fundamental
idea which was quite simple, yet startling in its development.
Unfortunately I worked it out rather hurriedly. In not very
carefully chosen phrasing the orchestra was to represent the
ocean, and, as far as might be, the ship upon it. A forcible,
pathetically yearning and aspiring theme was the only com-

prehensible idea amid the swirl of enveloping sound. When the whole had been repeated, there was a sudden jump to a different theme in extreme *pianissimo,* accompanied by the swelling vibrations of the first violins, which was intended to represent a Fata Morgana. I had secured three pairs of trumpets in different keys, in order to produce this exquisite, gradually dawning and seductive theme with the utmost niceties of shade and variety of modulation. This was intended to represent the land of desire towards which the hero's eyes are turned, and whose shores seem continually to rise before him only to sink elusively beneath the waves, until at last they soar in very deed above the western horizon, the crown of all his toil and search, and stand clearly and unmistakably revealed to all the sailors, a vast continent of the future. My six trumpets were now to combine in one key, in order that the theme assigned to them might re-echo in glorious jubilation. Familiar as I was with the excellence of the Prussian regimental trumpeters, I could rely upon a startling effect, especially in this concluding passage. My overture astonished every one, and was tumultuously applauded. The play itself, however, was acted without dignity. A conceited comedian, named Ludwig Meyer, completely ruined the title part, for which he excused himself on the ground that, having to act as stage manager also, he had been unable to commit his lines to memory. Nevertheless, he managed to enrich his wardrobe with several splendid costumes at Apel's expense, wearing them, as Columbus, one after the other. At all events, Apel had lived to see a play of his own actually performed, and although this was never repeated, yet it afforded me an oppor-tunity of increasing my personal popularity with the people of Magdeburg, as the overture was several times repeated at concerts by special request.

But the chief event of this theatrical season occurred towards its close. I induced Mme. Schröder-Devrient, who was staying in Leipzig, to come to us for a few special performances, when, on two occasions, I had the great satisfaction and stimulating experience of myself conducting the operas in which she sang, and thus entering into immediate artistic collaboration with her. She appeared as Desdemona and Romeo. In the latter rôle particularly she surpassed herself, and kindled a fresh flame in my breast. This visit brought us also into closer personal contact. So kindly disposed and sympathetic did she show herself towards me, that she even volunteered to lend me her services at a concert which I proposed to give for my own benefit, although this would necessitate her returning after a brief absence. Under circumstances so auspicious I could only expect the best possible results from my concert, and in my situation at that time its proceeds were a matter of vital importance to me. My scanty salary from the Magdeburg opera company had become altogether illusory, being paid only in small and irregular instalments, so that I could see but one way of meeting my daily expenses. These included frequent entertainment of a large circle of friends, consisting of singers and players, and the situation had become unpleasantly accentuated by no small number of debts. True, I did not know their exact amount; but reckoned that I could at least form an advantageous, if indefinite, estimate of the sum to be realized by my concert, whereby the two unknown quantities might balance each other. I therefore consoled my creditors with the tale of these fabulous receipts, which were to pay them all in full the day after the concert. I even went so far as to invite them to come and be paid at the hotel to which I had moved at the close of the season.

And, indeed, there was nothing unreasonable in my counting on the highest imaginable receipts, when supported by so great and popular a singer, who, moreover, was returning to Magdeburg on purpose for the event. I consequently acted with reckless prodigality as regards cost, launching out into all manner of musical extravagance, such as engaging an excellent and much larger orchestra, and arranging many rehearsals. Unfortunately for me, however, nobody would believe that such a famous actress, whose time was so precious, would really return again to please a little Magdeburg conductor. My pompous announcement of her appearance was almost universally regarded as a deceitful manœuvre, and people took offence at the high prices charged for seats. The result was that the hall was only very scantily filled, a fact which particularly grieved me on account of my generous patroness. Her

promise I had never doubted. Punctually on the day appointed
she reappeared to support me, and now had the painful and unaccustomed experience of performing before a small audience.
Fortunately, she treated the matter with great good-humour
(which, I learned later, was prompted by other motives, not
personally concerning me). Among several pieces she sang
Beethoven's *Adelaïde* most exquisitely, wherein, to my own
astonishment, I accompanied her on the piano. But, alas! another and more unexpected mishap befell my concert, through
our unfortunate selection of pieces. Owing to the excessive
reverberation of the saloon in the Hotel ' The City of London,'
the noise was unbearable. My Columbus *Overture*, with its six
trumpets, had early in the evening filled the audience with terror; and now, at the end, came Beethoven's *Schlacht bei Vit-
toria*, for which, in enthusiastic expectation of limitless receipts,
I had provided every imaginable orchestral luxury. The firing
of cannon and musketry was organised with the utmost elaboration, on both the French and English sides, by means of specially
constructed and costly apparatus; while trumpets and bugles
had been doubled and trebled. Then began a battle, such as
has seldom been more cruelly fought in a concert-room. The
orchestra flung itself, so to speak, upon the scanty audience
with such an overwhelming superiority of numbers that the
latter speedily gave up all thought of resistance and literally
took to flight. Mme. Schröder-Devrient had kindly taken a
front seat, that she might hear the concert to an end. Much
as she may have been inured to terrors of this kind, this was
more than she could stand, even out of friendship for me.
When, therefore, the English made a fresh desperate assault
upon the French position, she took to flight, almost wringing
her hands. Her action became the signal for a panic-stricken
stampede. Every one rushed out; and Wellington's victory was
finally celebrated in a confidential outburst between myself and
the orchestra alone. Thus ended this wonderful musical festival.
Schröder-Devrient at once departed, deeply regretting the ill-
success of her well-meant effort, and kindly left me to my fate.

After seeking comfort in the arms of my sorrowing sweetheart, and attempting to nerve myself for the morrow's battle,
which did not seem likely to end in a victorious symphony, I

returned next morning to the hotel. I found I could only reach
my rooms by running the gauntlet between long rows of men
and women in double file, who had all been specially invited
thither for the settlement of their respective affairs. Reserving
the right to select individuals from among my visitors for
separate interview, I first of all led in the second trumpeter
of the orchestra, whose duty it had been to look after the cash
and the music. From his account I learned that, owing to the
high fees which, in my generous enthusiasm, I had promised to
the orchestra, a few more shillings and sixpences would still
have to come out of my own pocket to meet these charges
alone. When this was settled, the position of affairs was plain.
The next person I invited to come in was Mme. Gottschalk, a
trustworthy Jewess, with whom I wanted to come to some arrangement respecting the present crisis. She perceived at once
that more than ordinary help was required in this case, but
did not doubt that I should be able to obtain it from my
opulent connections in Leipzig. She undertook, therefore, to
appease the other creditors with tranquillising assurances, and
railed, or pretended to rail, against their indecent conduct with
great vigour. Thus at last we succeeded, though not without
some difficulty, in making the corridor outside my door once
more passable.

The theatrical season was now over, our company on the
point of dissolution, and I myself free from my appointment.
But meanwhile the unhappy director of our theatre had passed
from a state of chronic to one of acute bankruptcy. He paid
with paper money, that is to say, with whole sheets of box-
tickets for performances which he guaranteed should take place.
By dint of great craft Minna managed to extract some profit
even from these singular treasury-bonds. She was living at
this time most frugally and economically. Moreover, as the
dramatic company still continued its efforts on behalf of its
members — only the opera troupe having been dissolved — she
remained at the theatre. Thus, when I started out on my
compulsory return to Leipzig, she saw me off with hearty good-
wishes for our speedy reunion, promising to spend the next
holidays in visiting her parents in Dresden, on which occasion
she hoped also to look me up in Leipzig.

Thus it came about that early in May I once more went home to my own folk, in order that after this abortive first attempt at civic independence, I might finally lift the load of debt with which my efforts in Magdeburg had burdened me. An intelligent brown poodle faithfully accompanied me, and was entrusted to my family for food and entertainment as the only visible property I had acquired. Nevertheless, my mother and Rosalie succeeded in founding good hopes for my future career upon the bare fact of my being able to conduct an orchestra. To me, on the other hand, the thought of returning once more to my former life with my family was very discomfiting. My relation to Minna in particular spurred me on to resume my interrupted career as speedily as possible. The great change which had come over me in this respect was more apparent than ever when Minna spent a few days with me in Leipzig on her way home. Her familiar and genial presence proclaimed that my days of parental dependence were past and gone. We discussed the renewal of my Magdeburg engagement, and I promised her an early visit in Dresden. I obtained permission from my mother and sister to invite her one evening to tea, and in this way I introduced her to my family. Rosalie saw at once how matters stood with me, but made no further use of the discovery than to tease me about being in love. To her the affair did not appear dangerous; but to me things wore a very different aspect, for this love-lorn attachment was entirely in keeping with my independent spirit, and my ambition to win myself a place in the world of art.

My distaste for Leipzig itself was furthermore strengthened by a change which occurred there at this time in the realm of music. At the very time that I, in Magdeburg, was attempting to make my reputation as a musical conductor by thoughtless submission to the frivolous taste of the day, Mendelssohn-Bartholdy was conducting the Gewandhaus concerts, and inaugurating a momentous epoch for himself and the musical taste of Leipzig. His influence had put an end to the simple ingenuousness with which the Leipzig public had hitherto judged the productions of its sociable subscription concerts. Through the influence of my good old friend Pohlenz, who was not yet altogether laid on the shelf, I managed to produce my

Columbus Overture at a benefit concert given by the favourite
young singer, Livia Gerhart. But, to my amazement, I found
that the taste of the musical public in Leipzig had been given
a different bent, which not even my rapturously applauded
overture, with its brilliant combination of six trumpets, could
influence. This experience deepened my dislike of everything
approaching a classical tone, in which sentiment I found myself
in complete accord with honest Pohlenz, who sighed good-
naturedly over the downfall of the good old times.

Arrangements for a musical festival at Dessau, under Friedrich Schneider's conductorship, offered me a welcome chance
of quitting Leipzig. For this journey, which could be performed on foot in seven hours, I had to procure a passport
for eight days. This document was destined to play an important part in my life for many years to come; for on several
occasions and in various European countries it was the only
paper I possessed to prove my identity. In fact, owing to
my evasion of military duty in Saxony, I never again succeeded
in obtaining a regular pass until I was appointed musical
conductor in Dresden. I derived very little artistic pleasure
or benefit of any kind from this occasion; on the contrary,
it gave a fresh impetus to my hatred of the classical. I heard
Beethoven's Symphony in C minor conducted by a man whose
physiognomy, resembling that of a drunken satyr, filled me
with unconquerable disgust. In spite of an interminable row
of contrabassi, with which a conductor usually coquettes at
musical festivals, his performance was so expressionless and
inane that I turned away in disgust as from an alarming and
repulsive problem, and desisted from all attempts to explain the
impassable gulf which, as I again perceived, yawned between
my own vivid and imaginative conception of this work and
the only living presentations of it which I had ever heard.
But for the present my tormented spirits were cheered and
calmed by hearing the classical Schneider's oratorio *Absalom*
rendered as an absolute burlesque.

It was in Dessau that Minna had made her first début on the
stage, and while there I heard her spoken of by frivolous young
men in the tone usual in such circles when discussing young
and beautiful actresses. My eagerness in contradicting this

chatter and confounding the scandalmongers revealed to me more clearly than ever the strength of the passion which drew me to her.

I therefore returned to Leipzig without calling on my relatives, and there procured means for an immediate journey to Dresden. On the way (the journey was still performed by express coach) I met Minna, accompanied by one of her sisters, already on the way back to Magdeburg. Promptly procuring a posting ticket for the return journey to Leipzig, I actually set off thither with my dear girl; but by the time we reached the next station I had succeeded in persuading her to turn back with me to Dresden. By this time the mail-coach was far ahead of us, and we had to travel by special post-chaise. This lively bustling to and fro seemed to astonish the two girls, and put them into high spirits. The extravagance of my conduct had evidently roused them to the expectation of adventures, and it now behoved me to fulfil this expectation. Procuring from a Dresden acquaintance the necessary cash, I conducted my two lady friends through the Saxon Alps, where we spent several right merry days of innocent and youthful gaiety. Only once was this disturbed by a passing fit of jealousy on my part, for which, indeed, there was no occasion, but which fed itself in my heart on a nervous apprehension of the future, and upon the experience I had already gained of womenkind. Yet, despite this blot, our excursion still lingers in my memory as the sweetest and almost sole remembrance of unalloyed happiness in the whole of my life as a young man. One evening in particular stands out in bright relief, during which we sat together almost all night at the wateringplace of Schandau in glorious summer weather. Indeed, my subsequent long and anxious connection with Minna, interwoven as it was with the most painful and bitter vicissitudes, has often appeared to me as a persistently prolonged expiation of the brief and harmless enjoyment of those few days.

After accompanying Minna to Leipzig, whence she continued her journey to Magdeburg, I presented myself to my family, but told them nothing of my Dresden excursion. I now braced my energies, as though under the stern compulsion of a strange and deep sense of duty, to the task of making such arrangements as would speedily restore me to my dear one's side. To this end a fresh engagement had to be negotiated with Director Bethmann for the coming winter season. Unable to await the conclusion of our contract in Leipzig, I availed myself of Laube's presence at the baths in Kösen, near Naumburg, to pay him a visit. Laube had only recently been discharged from the Berlin municipal gaol, after a tormenting inquisition of nearly a year's duration. On giving his parole not to leave the country until the verdict had been given, he had been permitted to retire to Kösen, from which place he, one evening, paid us a secret visit in Leipzig. I can still call his woebegone appearance to mind. He seemed hopelessly resigned, though he spoke cheerfully with regard to all his earlier dreams of better things; and owing to my own worries at that time about the critical state of my affairs, this impression still remains one of my saddest and most painful recollections. While at Kösen I showed him a good many of the verses for my *Liebesverbot,* and although he spoke coldly of my presumption in wishing to write my own libretto, I was slightly encouraged by his appreciation of my work.

Meanwhile I impatiently awaited letters from Magdeburg. Not that I had any doubt as to the renewal of my engagement; on the contrary, I had every reason to regard myself as a good acquisition for Bethmann; but I felt as though nothing which tended to bring me nearer to Minna could move fast enough. As soon as I received the necessary tidings, I hurried away to make all needful arrangements on the spot for ensuring a magnificent success in the coming Magdeburg operatic season.

Through the tireless munificence of the King of Prussia fresh and final assistance had been granted to our perennially bankrupt theatrical director. His Majesty had assigned a not inconsiderable sum to a committee consisting of substantial Magdeburg citizens, as a subsidy to be expended on the theatre under Bethmann's management. What this meant, and the respect with which I thereupon regarded the artistic conditions of Magdeburg, may be best imagined if one remembers the neglected and forlorn surroundings amid which such provincial theatres usually drag out their lives. I offered at once to undertake a long journey in search of good operatic singers. I said

I would find the means for this at my own risk, and the only guarantee I demanded from the management for eventual reimbursement was that they should assign me the proceeds of a future benefit performance. This offer was gladly accepted, and in pompous tones the director furnished me with the necessary powers, and moreover gave me his parting blessing. During this brief interval I lived once more in intimate communion with Minna — who now had her mother with her — and then took fresh leave of her for my venturesome enterprise.

But when I got to Leipzig I found it by no means easy to procure the funds, so confidently counted on when in Magdeburg, for the expenses of my projected journey. The glamour of the royal protection of Prussia for our theatrical undertaking, which I portrayed in the liveliest colours to my good brother-in-law Brockhaus, quite failed to dazzle him, and it was at the cost of great pains and humiliation that I finally got my ship of discovery under weigh.

I was naturally drawn first of all to my old wonderland of Bohemia. There I merely touched at Prague and, without visiting my lovely lady friends, I hurried forward so that I might first sample the opera company then playing for the season at Karlsbad. Impatient to discover as many talents as I could as soon as possible, so as not to exhaust my funds to no purpose, I attended a performance of *La Dame Blanche,* sincerely hoping to find the whole performance first class. But not until much later did I fully realise how wretched was the quality of all these singers. I selected one of them, a bass named Gräf, who was singing Gaveston. When in due course he made his début at Magdeburg, he provoked so much well-founded dissatisfaction, that I could not find a word to say in reply to the mockery which this acquisition brought upon me.

But the small success with which the real object of my tour was attended was counterbalanced by the pleasantness of the journey itself. The trip through Eger, over the Fichtel mountains, and the entry into Bayreuth, gloriously illuminated by the setting sun, have remained happy memories to this day.

My next goal was Nuremberg, where my sister Clara and her husband were acting, and from whom I might reckon on sound information as to the object of my search. It was particularly

nice to be hospitably received in my sister's house, where I
hoped to revive my somewhat exhausted means of travel.
In this hope I reckoned chiefly upon the sale of a snuff-box
presented to me by a friend, which I had secret reasons to
suppose was made of platinum. To this I could add a gold
signet-ring, given me by my friend Apel for composing the
overture to his *Columbus*. The value of the snuff-box unfortunately proved to be entirely imaginary; but by pawning
these two jewels, the only ones I had left, I hoped to provide
myself with the bare necessaries for continuing my journey
to Frankfort. It was to this place and the Rhine district
that the information I had gathered led me to direct my steps.
Before leaving I persuaded my sister and brother-in-law to
accept engagements in Magdeburg; but I still lacked a first
tenor and a soprano, whom hitherto I had altogether failed
to discover.

My stay in Nuremberg was most agreeably prolonged
through a renewed meeting with Schröder-Devrient, who just
at that time was fulfilling a short engagement in that town.
Meeting her again was like seeing the clouds disperse, which,
since our last meeting, had darkened my artistic horizon.

The Nuremberg operatic company had a very limited repertoire. Besides *Fidelio* they could produce nothing save
Die Schweizerfamilie, a fact about which this great singer
complained, as this was one of her first parts sung in early
youth, for which she was hardly any longer suited, and which,
in addition, she had played *ad nauseam*. I also looked forward
to the performance of *Die Schweizerfamilie* with misgivings,
and even with anxiety, for I feared lest this tame opera and the
old-fashioned sentimental part of Emmeline would weaken
the great impression the public, as well as myself, had formed
up to that moment of the work of this sublime artist.
Imagine, therefore, how deeply moved and astonished I was,
on the evening of the performance, to find that it was in this
very part that I first realised the truly transcendental genius
of this extraordinary woman. That anything so great as
her interpretation of the character of the Swiss maiden could
not be handed down to posterity as a monument for all time
can only be looked upon as one of the most sublime sacrifices

demanded by dramatic art, and as one of its highest manifestations. When, therefore, such phenomena appear, we cannot
hold them in too great reverence, nor look upon them as too
sacred.

Apart from all these new experiences which were to become
of so much value to my whole life and to my artistic development, the impressions I received at Nuremberg, though they
were apparently trivial in their origin, left such indelible traces
on my mind, that they revived within me later on, though
in quite a different and novel form.

My brother-in-law, Wolfram, was a great favourite with the
Nuremberg theatrical world; he was witty and sociable, and
as such made himself much liked in theatrical circles. On this
occasion I received singularly delightful proofs of the spirit
of extravagant gaiety manifested on these evenings at the inn,
in which I also took part. A master carpenter, named Lauermann, a little thick-set man, no longer young, of comical
appearance and gifted only with the roughest dialect, was
pointed out to me in one of the inns visited by our friends as
one of those oddities who involuntarily contributed most to
the amusement of the local wags. Lauermann, it seems, imagined himself an excellent singer, and as a result of this presumption, evinced interest only in those in whom he thought
he recognised a like talent. In spite of the fact that, owing
to this singular peculiarity, he became the butt of constant
jest and scornful mockery, he never failed to appear every
evening among his laughter-loving persecutors. So often had
he been laughed at and hurt by their scorn, that it became
very difficult to persuade him to give a display of his artistic
skill, and this at last could only be effected by artfully devised traps, so laid as to appeal to his vanity. My arrival
as an unknown stranger was utilised for a manœuvre of this
kind. How poor was the opinion they held of the unfortunate
mastersinger's judgment was revealed when, to my great
amazement, my brother-in-law introduced me to him as the
great Italian singer, Lablache. To his credit I must confess
that Lauermann surveyed me for a long time with incredulous
distrust, and commented with cautious suspicion on my juvenile
appearance, but especially on the evidently tenor character

of my voice. But the whole art of these tavern associates and
their principal enjoyment consisted in leading this poor enthusiast to believe the incredible, a task on which they spared neither
time nor pains.

My brother-in-law succeeded in making the carpenter believe that I, while receiving fabulous sums for my performances, wished by a singular act of dissimulation, and by
visiting public inns, to withdraw from the general public; and
that, moreover, when it came to a meeting between ' Lauermann ' and ' Lablache,' the only real interest could be to hear
Lauermann and not Lablache, seeing that the former had nothing to learn from the latter, but only Lablache from him. So
singular was the conflict between incredulity, on the one hand,
and keenly excited vanity on the other, that finally the poor
carpenter became really attractive to me. I began to play the
rôle assigned me with all the skill I could command, and after
a couple of hours, which were relieved by the strangest antics,
we at last gained our end. The wondrous mortal, whose flashing eyes had long been fixed on me in the greatest excitement,
worked his muscles in the peculiarly fantastic fashion which
we are accustomed to associate with a music-making automa-
ton, the mechanism of which has been duly wound up: his
lips quivered, his teeth gnashed, his eyes rolled convulsively,
until finally there broke forth, in a hoarse oily voice, an uncommonly trivial street-ballad. Its delivery, accompanied by a
regular movement of his outstretched thumbs behind the ears,
and during which his fat face glowed the brightest red, was unhappily greeted with a wild burst of laughter from all present,
which excited the unlucky master to the most furious wrath.
With studied cruelty this wrath was greeted by those, who
until then had shamelessly flattered him, with the most extravagant mockery, until the poor wretch at last absolutely foamed
with rage.

As he was leaving the inn amid a hail of curses from his
infamous friends, an impulse of genuine pity prompted me
to follow him, that I might beg his forgiveness and seek in
some way to pacify him, a task all the more difficult since he
was especially bitter against me as the latest of his enemies,
and the one who had so deeply deceived his eager hope of

hearing the genuine Lablache. Nevertheless, I succeeded in stopping him on the threshold; and now the riotous company silently entered into an extraordinary conspiracy to induce Lauermann to sing again that very evening. How they managed this I can as little remember as I can call to mind the effect of the spirituous liquors I imbibed. In any case, I suspect that drink must eventually have been the means of subduing Lauermann, just as it also rendered my own recollections of the wonderful events of that prolonged evening at the inn extremely vague. After Lauermann had for the second time suffered the same mockery, the whole company felt itself bound to accompany the unhappy man to his home. They carried him thither in a wheelbarrow, which they found outside the house, and in this he arrived, in triumph, at his own door, in one of those marvellous narrow alleys peculiar to the old city. Frau Lauermann, who was aroused from slumber to receive her husband, enabled us, by her torrent of curses, to form some idea of the nature of their marital and domestic relations. Mockery of her husband's vocal talents was with her also a familiar theme; but to this she now added the most dreadful reproaches for the worthless scamps who, by encouraging him in this delusion, kept him from profitably following his trade, and even led him to such scenes as the present one. Thereupon the pride of the suffering mastersinger reasserted itself; for while his wife painfully assisted him to mount the stairs, he harshly denied her right to sit in judgment upon his vocal gifts, and sternly ordered her to be silent. But even now this wonderful night-adventure was by no means over. The entire swarm moved once more in the direction of the inn. Before the house, however, we found a number of fellows congregated, among them several workmen, against whom, owing to police regulations as to closing hours, the doors were shut. But the regular guests of the house, who were of our party, and who were on terms of old friendship with the host, thought that it was nevertheless permissible and possible to demand entrance. The host was troubled at having to bar his door against friends, whose voices he recognised; yet it was necessary to prevent the new arrivals from forcing a way in with them. Out of this situation a mighty confusion arose, which,

what with shouting and clamour and an inexplicable growth in
the number of the disputants, soon assumed a truly demoniacal
character. It seemed to me as though in a few moments the
whole town would break into a tumult, and I thought I should
once more have to witness a revolution, the real origin of which
no man could comprehend. Then suddenly I heard some one
fall, and, as though by magic, the whole mass scattered in
every direction. One of the regular guests, who was familiar
with an ancient Nuremberg boxing trick, desiring to put an
end to the interminable riot and to cut his way home through
the crowd, gave one of the noisiest shouters a blow with his
fist between the eyes, laying him senseless on the ground,
though without seriously injuring him. And this it was that
so speedily broke up the whole throng. Within little more
than a minute of the most violent uproar of hundreds of human
voices, my brother-in-law and I were able to stroll arm-in-arm
through the moonlit streets, quietly jesting and laughing, on
our way home; and then it was that, to my amazement and
relief, he informed me that he was accustomed to this sort of
life every evening.

At last, however, it became necessary seriously to attend
to the purpose of my journey. Only in passing did I touch at
Würzburg for a day. I remember nothing of the meeting
with my relations and acquaintance beyond the melancholy
visit to Friederike Galvani already mentioned. On reaching
Frankfort I was obliged to seek at once the shelter of a decent
hotel, in order to await there the result of my solicitations for
subsidies from the directorate of the Magdeburg theatre. My
hopes of securing the real stars of our operatic undertaking
were formed with a view to a season at Wiesbaden, where, I
was told, a good operatic company was on the point of dissolution. I found it extremely difficult to arrange the short
journey thither; yet I managed to be present at a rehearsal
of *Robert der Teufel,* in which the tenor Freimüller distinguished himself. I interviewed him at once, and found him
willing to entertain my proposals for Magdeburg. We concluded the necessary agreement, and I then returned with all
speed to my headquarters, the Weidenbusch Hotel in Frankfort.
There I had to spend another anxious week, during which I

waited in vain for the necessary travelling expenses to arrive
from Magdeburg. To kill time I had recourse, among other
things, to a large red pocket-book which I carried about with me
in my portmanteau, and in which I entered, with exact details
of dates, etc., notes for my future biography — the selfsame
book which now lies before me to freshen my memory, and
which I have ever since added to at various periods of my
life, without leaving any gaps. Through the neglect of the
Magdeburg managers my situation, which was already serious,
became literally desperate, when I made an acquisition in
Frankfort which gave me almost more pleasure than I was able
to bear. I had been present at a production of the *Zauberflöte*
under the direction of Guhr, then wonderfully renowned as ' a
conductor of genius,' and was agreeably surprised at the truly
excellent quality of the company. It was, of course, useless to
think of luring one of the leading stars into my net; on the
other hand, I saw clearly enough that the youthful Fräulein
Limbach, who sang the ' first boy's ' part, possessed a desirable
talent. She accepted my offer of an engagement, and, indeed,
seemed so anxious to be rid of her Frankfort engagement that
she resolved to escape from it surreptitiously. She revealed
her plans to me, and begged me to assist her in carrying them
out; for, inasmuch as the directors might get wind of the affair,
there was no time to lose. At all events, the young lady assumed that I had abundant credit, supplied for my official
business journey by the Magdeburg theatre committee, whose
praises I had so diligently sung. But already I had been compelled to pledge my scanty travelling gear in order to provide
for my own departure. To this point I had persuaded the host,
but now found him by no means inclined to advance me the
additional funds needed for carrying off a young singer. To
cloak the bad behaviour of my directors I was compelled to invent some tale of misfortune, and to leave the astonished and
indignant young lady behind. Heartily ashamed of this adventure, I travelled through rain and storm via Leipzig, where
I picked up my brown poodle, and reaching Magdeburg,
there resumed my work as musical director on the 1st of
September.

The result of my business labours gave me but little joy.

The director, it is true, proved triumphantly that he had sent five whole golden louis to my address in Frankfort, and that my tenor and the youthful lady-singer had also been provided with proper contracts, but not with the fares and advances demanded. Neither of them came; only the basso Gräf arrived with pedantic punctuality from Karlsbad, and immediately provoked the chaff of our theatrical wags. He sang at a rehearsal of the *Schweizerfamilie* with such a schoolmasterly drone that I completely lost my composure. The arrival of my excellent brother-in-law Wolfram with my sister Clara was of more advantage for musical comedy than for grand opera, and caused me considerable trouble into the bargain; for, being honest folk and used to decent living, they speedily perceived that, in spite of royal protection, the condition of the theatre was but very insecure, as was natural under so unscrupulous a management as that of Bethmann, and recognised with alarm that they had seriously compromised their family position. My courage had already begun to sink when a happy chance brought us a young woman, Mme. Pollert (*née* Zeibig), who was passing through Magdeburg with her husband, an actor, in order to fulfil a special engagement in that town; she was gifted with a beautiful voice, was a talented singer, and well suited for the chief rôles. Necessity had at last driven the directors to action, and at the eleventh hour they sent for the tenor Freimüller. But I was particularly gratified when the love which had arisen between him and young Limbach in Frankfort enabled the enterprising tenor to carry away this singer, to whom I had behaved so miserably. Both arrived radiant with joy. Along with them we engaged Mme. Pollert, who, in spite of her pretentiousness, met with favour from the public. A well-trained and musically competent baritone, Herr Krug, afterwards the conductor of a choir in Karlsruhe, had also been discovered, so that all at once I stood at the head of a really good operatic company, among which the basso Gräf could be fitted in only with great difficulty, by being kept as much as possible in the background. We succeeded quickly with a series of operatic performances which were by no means ordinary, and our repertory included everything of this nature that had ever been written for the theatre. I was particularly pleased with the presentation of Spohr's *Jessonda,* which was truly not without sublimity, and raised us high in the esteem of all cultured lovers of music. I was untiring in my endeavours to discover some means of elevating our performances above the usual level of excellence compatible with the meagre resources of provincial theatres. I persistently fell foul of the director Bethmann by strengthening my orchestra, which he had to pay; but, on the other hand, I won his complete goodwill by strengthening the chorus and the theatre music, which cost him nothing, and which lent such splendour to our presentations that subscriptions and audiences increased enormously. For instance, I secured the regimental band, and also the military singers, who in the Prussian army are admirably organised, and who assisted in our performances in return for free passes to the gallery granted to their relatives. Thus I managed to furnish with the utmost completeness the specially strong orchestral accompaniment demanded by the score of Bellini's *Norma,* and was able to dispose of a body of male voices for the impressive unison portion of the male chorus in the introduction of that work such as even the greatest theatres could rarely command. In later years I was able to assure Auber, whom I often met over an ice in Tortoni's café in Paris, that in his *Lestocq* I had been able to render the part of the mutinous soldiery, when seduced into conspiracy, with an absolutely full number of voices, a fact for which he thanked me with astonishment and delight.

Amid such circumstances of encouragement the composition of my *Liebesverbot* made rapid strides towards completion. I intended the presentation of this piece for the benefit performance which had been promised me as a means of defraying my expenses, and I worked hard in the hope of improving my reputation, and at the same time of accomplishing something by no means less desirable, and that was the betterment of my financial position. Even the few hours which I could snatch from business to spend at Minna's side were devoted with unexampled zeal to the completion of my score. My diligence moved even Minna's mother, who looked with some uneasiness upon our love affair. She had remained over the summer on a visit to her daughter, and managed

the house for her. Owing to her interference a new and
urgent anxiety had entered into our relations, which pressed for
serious settlement. It was natural that we should begin to
think of what it was all going to lead to. I must confess that
the idea of marriage, especially in view of my youth, filled me
with dismay, and without indeed reflecting on the matter, or
seriously weighing its pros and cons, a naïve and instinctive
feeling prevented me even from considering the possibility of a
step which would have such serious consequences upon my whole
life. Moreover, our modest circumstances were in so alarming
and uncertain a state that even Minna declared that she was
more anxious to see these improved than to get me to marry her.
But she was also driven to think of herself, and that promptly,
for trouble arose with regard to her own position in the Magdeburg theatre. There she had met with a rival in her own
speciality, and as this woman's husband became chief stage
manager, and consequently had supreme power, she grew to be
a source of great danger. Seeing, therefore, that at this very
moment Minna received advantageous offers from the managers of the Königstadt theatre in Berlin, then doing a splendid
business, she seized the opportunity to break off her connection
with the Magdeburg theatre, and thus plunged me, whom she
did not appear to consider in the matter, into the depths of
despair. I could not hinder Minna from going to Berlin to
fulfil a special engagement there, although this was not in
accordance with her agreement, and so she departed, leaving
me behind, overcome with grief and doubt as to the meaning
of her conduct. At last, mad with passion, I wrote to her
urging her to return, and the better to move her and not to
separate her fate from my own, I proposed to her in a strictly
formal manner, and hinted at the hope of early marriage.
About the same time my brother-in-law, Wolfram, having
quarrelled with the director Bethmann and cancelled his
contract with him, also went to the Königstadt theatre to
fulfil a special engagement. My good sister Clara, who had
remained behind for a while amid the somewhat unpleasant
conditions of Magdeburg, soon perceived the anxious and
troubled temper in which her otherwise cheerful brother was
rapidly consuming himself. One day she thought it advisable

to show me a letter from her husband, with news from Berlin, and especially concerning Minna, in which he earnestly deplored my passion for this girl, who was acting quite unworthily of me. As she lodged at his hotel, he was able to observe that not only the company she kept, but also her own conduct, were perfectly scandalous. The extraordinary impression which this dreadful communication made upon me decided me to abandon the reserve I had hitherto shown towards my relatives with regard to my love affairs. I wrote to my brother-in-law in Berlin, telling him how matters stood with me, and that my plans greatly depended on Minna, and further, how extremely important it was for me to learn from him the indubitable truth concerning her of whom he had sent so evil an account. From my brother-in-law, usually so dry and given to joking, I received a reply which filled my heart to overflowing again. He confessed that he had accused Minna too hastily, and regretted that he had allowed idle chatter to influence him in founding a charge, which, on investigation, had proved to be altogether groundless and unjust; he declared, moreover, that on nearer acquaintance and conversation with her he had been so fully convinced of the genuineness and uprightness of her character, that he hoped with all his heart that I might see my way to marry her. And now a storm raged in my heart. I implored Minna to return at once, and was glad to learn that, for her part, she was not inclined to renew her engagement at the Berlin theatre, as she had now acquired a more intimate knowledge of the life there, and found it too frivolous. All that remained, then, was for me to facilitate the resumption of her Magdeburg engagement. To this end, therefore, at a meeting of the theatre committee, I attacked the director and his detested stage manager with such energy, and defended Minna against the wrong done her by them both with such passion and fervour, that the other members, astonished at the frank confession of my affection, yielded to my wishes without any further ado. And now I set off by extra post in the depth of night and in dreadful winter weather to meet my returning sweetheart. I greeted her with tears of deepest joy, and led her back in triumph to her cosy Magdeburg home, already become so dear to me.

Meanwhile, as our two lives, thus severed for a while, were being drawn more and more closely together, I finished the score of my *Liebesverbot* about New Year 1836. For the development of my future plans I depended not a little upon the success of this work; and Minna herself seemed not disinclined to yield to my hopes in this respect. We had reason to be concerned as to how matters would pan out for us at the beginning of the spring, for this season is always a bad one in which to start such precarious theatrical enterprises. In spite of royal support and the participation of the theatre committee in the general management of the theatre, our worthy director's state of perennial bankruptcy suffered no alteration, and it seemed as if his theatrical undertaking could not possibly last much longer in any form. Nevertheless, with the help of the really first-rate company of singers at my disposal, the production of my opera was to mark a complete change in my unsatisfactory circumstances. With the view of recovering the travelling expenses I had incurred during the previous summer, I was entitled to a benefit performance. I naturally fixed this for the presentation of my own work, and did my utmost so that this favour granted me by the directors should prove as inexpensive to them as possible. As they would nevertheless be compelled to incur some expense in the production of the new opera, I agreed that the proceeds of the first presentation should be left to them, while I should claim only those of the second. I did not consider it altogether unsatisfactory that the time for the rehearsals was postponed until the very end of the season, for it was reasonable to suppose that our company, which was often greeted with unusual applause, would receive special attention and favour from the public during its concluding performances. Unfortunately, however, contrary to our expectations, we never reached the proper close of this season, which had been fixed for the end of April; for already in March, owing to irregularity in the payment of salaries, the most popular members of the company, having found better employment elsewhere, tendered their resignations to the management, and the director, who was unable to raise the necessary cash, was compelled to bow to the inevitable. Now, indeed, my spirits sank, for it seemed more than doubtful whether my *Liebesverbot* would ever be produced at all. I owed it entirely to the warm affection felt for me personally by all members of the opera company, that the singers consented not only to remain until the end of March, but also to undertake the toil of studying and rehearsing my opera, a task which, considering the very limited time, promised to be extremely arduous. In the event of our having to give two representations, the time at our disposal was so very short that, for all the rehearsals, we had but ten days before us. And since we were concerned not with a light comedy or farce, but with a grand opera, and one which, in spite of the trifling character of its music, contained numerous and powerful concerted passages, the undertaking might have been regarded almost as foolhardy. Nevertheless, I built my hopes upon the extraordinary exertions which the singers so willingly made in order to please me; for they studied continuously, morning, noon, and night. But seeing that, in spite of all this, it was quite impossible to attain to perfection, especially in the matter of words, in the case of every one of these harassed performers, I reckoned further on my own acquired skill as conductor to achieve the final miracle of success. The peculiar ability I possessed of helping the singers and of making them, in spite of much uncertainty, seem to flow smoothly onwards, was clearly demonstrated in our orchestral rehearsals, in which, by dint of constant prompting, loud singing with the performers and vigorous directions as to necessary action, I got the whole thing to run so easily that it seemed quite possible that the performance might be a reasonable success after all. Unfortunately, we did not consider that in front of the public all these drastic methods of moving the dramatic and musical machinery would be restricted to the movements of my baton and to my facial expression. As a matter of fact the singers, and especially the men, were so extraordinarily uncertain that from beginning to end their embarrassment crippled the effectiveness of every one of their parts. Freimüller, the tenor, whose memory was most defective, sought to patch up the lively and emotional character of his badly learned rôle of the madcap Luzio by means of routine work

learned in *Fra Diavolo* and *Zampa,* and especially by the aid
of an enormously thick, brightly coloured and fluttering plume
of feathers. Consequently, as the directors failed to have the
book of words printed in time, it was impossible to blame the
public for being in doubt as to the main outlines of the story,
seeing that they had only the sung words to guide them. With
the exception of a few portions played by the lady singers,
which were favourably received, the whole performance, which
I had made to depend largely upon bold, energetic action
and speech, remained but a musical shadow-play, to which
the orchestra contributed its own inexplicable effusions, sometimes with exaggerated noise. As characteristic of the treatment of my tone-colour, I may mention that the band-master
of a Prussian military band, who, by the bye, had been well
pleased with the performance, felt it incumbent upon him to
give me some well-meant hints for my future guidance, as to
the manipulation of the Turkish drum. Before I relate the
further history of this wonderful work of my youth, I will
pause a moment briefly to describe its character, and especially
its poetical elements.

Shakespeare's play, which I kept throughout in mind as the
foundation of my story, was worked out in the following
manner: —

An unnamed king of Sicily leaves his country, as I suggest,
for a journey to Naples, and hands over to the Regent appointed — whom I simply call Friedrich, with the view of
making him appear as German as possible — full authority to
exercise all the royal power in order to effect a complete reform in the social habits of his capital, which had provoked
the indignation of the Council. At the opening of the play
we see the servants of the public authority busily employed
either in shutting up or in pulling down the houses of popular
amusement in a suburb of Palermo, and in carrying off the
inmates, including hosts and servants, as prisoners. The populace oppose this first step, and much scuffling ensues. In
the thickest of the throng the chief of the sbirri, Brighella
(basso-buffo), after a preliminary roll of drums for silence,
reads out the Regent's proclamation, according to which the acts
just performed are declared to be directed towards establishing

a higher moral tone in the manners and customs of the people.
A general outburst of scorn and a mocking chorus meets this
announcement. Luzio, a young nobleman and juvenile scape-
grace (tenor), seems inclined to thrust himself forward as
leader of the mob, and at once finds an occasion for playing
a more active part in the cause of the oppressed people on
discovering his friend Claudio (also a tenor) being led away
to prison. From him he learns that, in pursuance of some
musty old law unearthed by Friedrich, he is to suffer the
penalty of death for a certain love escapade in which he is
involved. His sweetheart, union with whom had been prevented by the enmity of their parents, has borne him a child.
Friedrich's puritanical zeal joins cause with the parents'
hatred; he fears the worst, and sees no way of escape save
through mercy, provided his sister Isabella may be able, by
her entreaties, to melt the Regent's hard heart. Claudio implores his friend at once to seek out Isabella in the convent of
the Sisters of St. Elizabeth, which she has recently entered as
novice. There, between the quiet walls of the convent, we first
meet this sister, in confidential intercourse with her friend
Marianne, also a novice. Marianne reveals to her friend, from
whom she has long been parted, the unhappy fate which has
brought her to the place. Under vows of eternal fidelity she had
been persuaded to a secret *liaison* with a man of high rank.
But finally, when in extreme need she found herself not only
forsaken, but threatened by her betrayer, she discovered him
to be the mightiest man in the state, none other than the
King's Regent himself. Isabella's indignation finds vent in
impassioned words, and is only pacified by her determination
to forsake a world in which so vile a crime can go unpunished.
— When now Luzio brings her tidings of her own brother's
fate, her disgust at her brother's misconduct is turned at once
to scorn for the villainy of the hypocritical Regent, who pre-
sumes so cruelly to punish the comparatively venial offence
of her brother, which, at least, was not stained by treachery.
Her violent outburst imprudently reveals her to Luzio in a
seductive aspect; smitten with sudden love, he urges her to
quit the convent for ever and to accept his hand. She con-
trives to check his boldness, but resolves at once to avail herself

of his escort to the Regent's court of justice. — Here the trial scene is prepared, and I introduce it by a burlesque hearing of several persons charged by the sbirro captain with offences against morality. The earnestness of the situation becomes more marked when the gloomy form of Friedrich strides through the inrushing and unruly crowd, commanding silence, and he himself undertakes the hearing of Claudio's case in the sternest manner possible. The implacable judge is already on the point of pronouncing sentence when Isabella enters, and requests, before them all, a private interview with the Regent. In this interview she behaves with noble moderation towards the dreaded, yet despised man before her, and appeals at first only to his mildness and mercy. His interruptions merely serve to stimulate her ardour: she speaks of her brother's offence in melting accents, and implores forgiveness for so human and by no means unpardonable a crime. Seeing the effect of her moving appeal, she continues with increasing ardour to plead with the judge's hard and unresponsive heart, which can certainly not have remained untouched by sentiments such as those which had actuated her brother, and she calls upon his memory of these to support her desperate plea for pity. At last the ice of his heart is broken. Friedrich, deeply stirred by Isabella's beauty, can no longer contain himself, and promises to grant her petition at the price of her own love. Scarcely has she become aware of the unexpected effect of her words when, filled with indignation at such incredible villainy, she cries to the people through doors and windows to come in, that she may unmask the hypocrite before the world. The crowd is already rushing tumultuously into the hall of judgment, when, by a few significant hints, Friedrich, with frantic energy, succeeds in making Isabella realise the impossibility of her plan. He would simply deny her charge, boldly pretend that his offer was merely made to test her, and would doubtless be readily believed so soon as it became only a question of rebutting a charge of lightly making love to her. Isabella, ashamed and confounded, recognises the madness of her first step, and gnashes her teeth in silent despair. While then Friedrich once more announces his stern resolve to the people, and pronounces sentence on the prisoner, it suddenly occurs to Isabella, spurred by the painful recollection of Marianne's fate, that what she has failed to procure by open means she might possibly obtain by craft. This thought suffices to dispel her sorrow, and to fill her with utmost gaiety. Turning to her sorrowing brother, her agitated friends, and the perplexed crowd, she assures them all that she is ready to provide them with the most amusing of adventures. She declares that the carnival festivities, which the Regent has just strictly forbidden, are to be celebrated this year with unusual licence; for this dreaded ruler only pretends to be so cruel, in order the more pleasantly to astonish them by himself taking a merry part in all that he has just forbidden. They all believe that she has gone mad, and Friedrich in particular reproves her incomprehensible folly with passionate severity. But a few words on her part suffice to transport the Regent himself with ecstasy; for in a whisper she promises to grant his desire, and that on the following night she will send him such a message as shall ensure his happiness. — And so ends the first act in a whirl of excitement.

We learn the nature of the heroine's hastily formed plan at the beginning of the second act, in which she visits her brother in his cell, with the object of discovering whether he is worthy of rescue. She reveals Friedrich's shameful proposal to him, and asks if he would wish to save his life at the price of his sister's dishonour. Then follow Claudio's fury and fervent declaration of his readiness to die; whereupon, bidding farewell to his sister, at least for this life, he makes her the bearer of the most tender messages to the dear girl whom he leaves behind. After this, sinking into a softer mood, the unhappy man declines from a state of melancholy to one of weakness. Isabella, who had already determined to inform him of his rescue, hesitates in dismay when she sees him fall in this way from the heights of noble enthusiasm to a muttered confession of a love of life still as strong as ever, and even to a stammering query as to whether the suggested price of his salvation is altogether impossible. Disgusted, she springs to her feet, thrusts the unworthy man from her, and declares that to the shame of his death he has further added her most hearty contempt. After having handed him over again to his gaoler, her mood once more changes swiftly to one of wanton gaiety. True, she resolves to punish the waverer by leaving him for a time in uncertainty as to his fate; but stands firm by her resolve to rid the world of the abominable seducer who dared to dictate laws to his fellow-men. She tells Marianne that she must take her place at the nocturnal rendezvous, at which Friedrich so treacherously expected to meet her (Isabella), and sends Friedrich an invitation to this meeting. In order to entangle the latter even more deeply in ruin, she stipulates that he must come disguised and masked, and fixes the rendezvous in one of those pleasure resorts which he has just suppressed. To the madcap Luzio, whom she also desires to punish for his saucy suggestion to a novice, she relates the story of Friedrich's proposal, and her pretended intention of complying, from sheer necessity, with his desires. This she does in a fashion so incomprehensively light-hearted that the otherwise frivolous man, first dumb with amazement, ultimately yields to a fit of desperate rage. He swears that, even if the noble maiden herself can endure such shame, he will himself strive by every means in his power to avert it, and would prefer to set all Palermo on fire and in tumult rather than allow such a thing to happen. And, indeed, he arranges things in such a manner that on the appointed evening all his friends and acquaintances assemble at the end of the Corso, as though for the opening of the prohibited carnival procession. At nightfall, as things are beginning to grow wild and merry, Luzio appears, and sings an extravagant carnival song, with the refrain:

> Who joins us not in frolic jest
> Shall have a dagger in his breast;

by which means he seeks to stir the crowd to bloody revolt. When a band of sbirri approaches, under Brighella's leadership, to scatter the gay throng, the mutinous project seems on the point of being accomplished. But for the present Luzio prefers to yield, and to scatter about the neighbourhood, as he must first of all win the real leader of their enterprise: for here was the spot which Isabella had mischievously revealed to him as the place of her pretended meeting with the Regent. For the latter Luzio therefore lies in wait. Recognising him

in an elaborate disguise, he blocks his way, and as Friedrich
violently breaks loose, is on the point of following him with
shouts and drawn sword, when, on a sign from Isabella, who is
hidden among some bushes, he is himself stopped and led away.
Isabella then advances, rejoicing in the thought of having
restored the betrayed Marianne to her faithless spouse. Believing that she holds in her hand the promised pardon for her
brother, she is just on the point of abandoning all thought of
further vengeance when, breaking the seal, to her intense horror
she recognises by the light of a torch that the paper contains
but a still more severe order of execution, which, owing to
her desire not to disclose to her brother the fact of his pardon,
a mere chance had now delivered into her hand, through the
agency of the bribed gaoler. After a hard fight with the
tempestuous passion of love, and recognising his helplessness
against this enemy of his peace, Friedrich has in fact already
resolved to face his ruin, even though as a criminal, yet still
as a man of honour. An hour on Isabella's breast, and then —
his own death by the same law whose implacable severity shall
also claim Claudio's life. Isabella, perceiving in this conduct
only a further proof of the hypocrite's villainy, breaks out once
more into a tempest of agonised despair. Upon her cry for
immediate revolt against the scoundrelly tyrant, the people
collect together and form a motley and passionate crowd.
Luzio, who also returns, counsels the people with stinging
bitterness to pay no heed to the woman's fury; he points out
that she is only tricking them, as she has already tricked him
— for he still believes in her shameless infidelity. Fresh confusion; increased despair of Isabella; suddenly from the background comes the burlesque cry of Brighella for help, who,
himself suffering from the pangs of jealousy, has by mistake
arrested the masked Regent, and thus led to the latter's discovery. Friedrich is recognised, and Marianne, trembling on
his breast, is also unmasked. Amazement, indignation! Cries
of joy burst forth all round; the needful explanations are
quickly given, and Friedrich sullenly demands to be set before
the judgment-seat of the returning King. Claudio, released
from prison by the jubilant populace, informs him that the
sentence of death for crimes of love is not intended for all

times; messengers arrive to announce the unexpected arrival
in harbour of the King; it is resolved to march in full masked
procession to meet the beloved Prince, and joyously to pay
him homage, all being convinced that he will heartily rejoice
to see how ill the gloomy puritanism of Germany is suited to
his hot-blooded Sicily. Of him it is said:

> Your merry festals please him more
> Than gloomy laws or legal lore.

Friedrich, with his freshly affianced wife, Marianne, must lead
the procession, followed by Luzio and the novice, who is for
ever lost to the convent.

These spirited and, in many respects, boldly devised scenes
I had clothed in suitable language and carefully written verse,
which had already been noticed by Laube. The police at first
took exception to the title of the work, which, had I not
changed it, would have led to the complete failure of my plans
for its presentation. It was the week before Easter, and the
theatre was consequently forbidden to produce jolly, or at least
frivolous, plays during this period. Luckily the magistrate,
with whom I had to treat concerning the matter, did not show
any inclination to examine the libretto himself; and when I
assured him that it was modelled upon a very serious play of
Shakespeare's, the authorities contented themselves merely with
changing the somewhat startling title. *Die Novize von Palermo,*
which was the new title, had nothing suspicious about it, and
was therefore approved as correct without further scruple. I
fared quite otherwise in Leipzig, where I attempted to introduce this work in the place of my *Feen,* when the latter was
withdrawn. The director, Ringelhardt, whom I sought to
win over to my cause by assigning the part of Marianne to his
daughter, then making her début in opera, chose to reject my
work on the apparently very reasonable grounds that the
tendency of the theme displeased him. He assured me that,
even if the Leipzig magistrates had consented to its production
— a fact concerning which his high esteem for that body led
him to have serious doubts — he himself, as a conscientious
father, could certainly not permit his daughter to take part
in it.

Strange to say, I suffered nothing from the suspicious nature of the libretto of my opera on the occasion of its production in Magdeburg; for, as I have said, thanks to the unintelligible manner in which it was produced, the story remained a complete mystery to the public. This circumstance, and the fact that no opposition had been raised on the ground of its *tendency*, made a second performance possible, and as nobody seemed to care one way or the other, no objections were raised. Feeling sure that my opera had made no impression, and had left the public completely undecided about its merits, I reckoned that, in view of this being the farewell performance of our opera company, we should have good, not to say large, takings. Consequently I did not hesitate to charge ' full ' prices for admittance. I cannot rightly judge whether, up to the commencement of the overture, any people had taken their places in the auditorium; but about a quarter of an hour before the time fixed for beginning, I saw only Mme. Gottschalk and her husband, and, curiously enough, a Polish Jew in full dress, seated in the stalls. Despite this, I was still hoping for an increase in the audience, when suddenly the most incredible commotion occurred behind the scenes. Herr Pollert, the husband of my prima donna (who was acting Isabella), was assaulting Schreiber, the second tenor, a very young and handsome man taking the part of Claudio, and against whom the injured husband had for some time been nursing a secret rancour born of jealousy. It appeared that the singer's husband, who had surveyed the theatre from behind the drop-scene with me, had satisfied himself as to the style of the audience, and decided that the longed-for hour was at hand when, without injuring the operatic enterprise, he could wreak vengeance on his wife's lover. Claudio was so severely used by him that the unfortunate fellow had to seek refuge in the dressing-room, his face covered with blood. Isabella was told of this, and rushed despairingly to her raging spouse, only to be so soundly cuffed by him that she went into convulsions. The confusion that ensued amongst the company soon knew no bounds: they took sides in the quarrel, and little was wanting for it to turn into a general fight, as everybody seemed to regard this unhappy evening as particularly favourable for the paying off of any old scores and supposed insults. This much was clear, that the couple suffering from the effects of Herr Pollert's conjugal resentment were unfit to appear that evening. The manager was sent before the drop-scene to inform the small and strangely assorted audience gathered in the theatre that, owing to unforeseen circumstances, the representation would not take place.

This was the end of my career as director and composer in Magdeburg, which in the beginning had seemed so full of promise and had been started at the cost of considerable sacrifice. The serenity of art now gave way completely before the stern realities of life. My position gave food for meditation, and the outlook was not a cheerful one. All the hopes that I and Minna had founded upon the success of my work had been utterly destroyed. My creditors, who had been appeased by the anticipation of the expected harvest, lost faith in my talents, and now counted solely on obtaining bodily possession of me, which they endeavoured to do by speedily instituting legal proceedings. Now that every time I came home I found a summons nailed to my door, my little dwelling in the *Breiter Weg* became unbearable; I avoided going there, especially since my brown poodle, who had hitherto enlivened this retreat, had vanished, leaving no trace. This I looked upon as a bad sign, indicating my complete downfall.

At this time Minna, with her truly comforting assurance and firmness of bearing, was a tower of strength to me and the one thing I had left to fall back upon. Always full of resource, she had first of all provided for her own future, and was on the point of signing a not unfavourable contract with the directors of the theatre at Königsberg in Prussia. It was now a question of finding me an appointment in the same place as musical conductor; this post was already filled. The Königsberg director, however, gathering from our correspondence that Minna's acceptance of the engagement depended upon the possibility of my being taken on at the same theatre, held out the prospect of an approaching vacancy, and expressed his willingness to allow it to be filled by me. On the strength of this assurance it was decided that Minna should go on to Königsberg and pave the way for my arrival there.

Ere these plans could be carried out, we had still to spend a time of dreadful and acute anxiety, which I shall never forget, within the walls of Magdeburg. It is true I made one more personal attempt in Leipzig to improve my position, on which occasion I entered into the transactions mentioned above with the director of the theatre regarding my new opera. But I soon realised that it was out of the question for me to remain in my native town, and in the disquieting proximity of my family, from which I was restlessly anxious to get away. My excitability and depression were noticed by my relations. My mother entreated me, whatever else I might decide to do, on no account to be drawn into marriage while still so young. To this I made no reply. When I took my leave, Rosalie accompanied me to the head of the stairs. I spoke of returning as soon as I had attended to certain important business matters, and wanted to wish her a hurried good-bye: she grasped my hand, and gazing into my face, exclaimed, " God alone knows when I shall see you again! ' This cut me to the heart, and I felt conscience-stricken. The fact that she was expressing the presentiment she felt of her early death I only realised when, barely two years later, without having seen her again, I received the news that she had died very suddenly.

I spent a few more weeks with Minna in the strictest retirement in Magdeburg: she endeavoured to the best of her ability to relieve the embarrassment of my position. In view of our approaching separation, and the length of time we might be parted, I hardly left her side, our only relaxation being the walks we took together round the outskirts of the town. Anxious forebodings weighed upon us; the May sun which lit the sad streets of Magdeburg, as if in mockery of our forlorn condition, was one day more clouded over than I have ever seen it since, and filled me with a positive dread. On our way home from one of these walks, as we were approaching the bridge crossing the Elbe, we caught sight of a man flinging himself from it into the water beneath. We ran to the bank, called for help, and persuaded a miller, whose mill was situated on the river, to hold out a rake to the drowning man, who was being swept in his direction by the current. With indescribable anxiety we waited for the decisive moment — saw the sinking man stretch out his hands towards the rake, but he failed to grasp it, and at the same moment disappeared under the mill, never to be seen again. On the morning that I accompanied Minna to the stage-coach to bid her a most sorrowful farewell, the whole population was pouring from one of the gateways of the town towards a big field, to witness the execution of a man condemned to be put to death on the wheel ' from below.' [1] The culprit was a soldier who had murdered his sweetheart in a fit of jealousy. When, later in the day, I sat down to my last dinner at the inn, I heard the dreadful details of the Prussian mode of execution being discussed on all sides. A young magistrate, who was a great lover of music, told us about a conversation he had had with the executioner, who had been procured from Halle, and with whom he had discussed the most humane method of hastening the death of the victim; in telling us about him, he recalled the elegant dress and manners of this ill-omened person with a shudder.

These were the last impressions I carried away from the scene of my first artistic efforts and of my attempts at earning an independent livelihood. Often since then on my departure from places where I had expected to find prosperity, and to which I knew I should never return, those impressions have recurred to my mind with singular persistence. I have always had much the same feelings upon leaving any place where I had stayed in the hope of improving my position.

Thus I arrived in Berlin for the first time on the 18th May, 1836, and made acquaintance with the peculiar features of that pretentious royal capital. While my position was an uncertain one, I sought a modest shelter at the Crown Prince in the Königstrasse, where Minna had stayed a few months before. I found a friend on whom I could rely when I came across Laube again, who, while awaiting his verdict, was

---

[1] *Durch das Rad von unten.* The punishment of the wheel was usually inflicted upon murderers, incendiaries, highwaymen and church robbers. There were two methods of inflicting this: (1) ' from above downwards ' (*von oben nach unten*), in which the condemned man was despatched instantly owing to his neck getting broken from the start; and (2) ' from below upwards ' (*von unten nach oben*), which is the method referred to above, and in which all the limbs of the victim were broken previous to his body being actually twisted through the spokes of the wheel. — EDITOR.

busying himself with private and literary work in Berlin.
He was much interested in the fate of my work *Liebesverbot*,
and advised me to turn my present situation to account for
the purpose of obtaining the production of this opera at the
Königstadt theatre.   This theatre was under the direction
of one of the most curious creatures in Berlin: he was called
'Cerf,' and the title of *Commissionsrath* had been conferred
upon him by the King of Prussia.   To account for the favours
bestowed upon him by royalty, many reasons of a not very
edifying nature were circulated.   Through this royal patronage
he had succeeded in extending considerably the privileges
already enjoyed by the suburban theatre.   The decline of grand
opera at the Theatre Royal had brought light opera, which
was performed with great success at the Königstadt theatre,
into public favour.   The director, puffed up by success, openly
laboured under the delusion that he was the right man in the
right place, and expressed his entire agreement with those
who declared that one could only expect a theatre to be successfully managed by common and uneducated men, and
continued to cling to his blissful and boundless state of
ignorance in the most amusing manner.   Relying absolutely
upon his own insight, he had assumed an entirely dictatorial
attitude towards the officially appointed artists of his theatre,
and allowed himself to deal with them according to his likes
and dislikes.   I seemed destined to be favoured by this mode
of procedure: at my very first visit Cerf expressed his satisfaction with me, but wished to make use of me as a 'tenor.'
He offered no objection whatever to my request for the production of my opera, but, on the contrary, promised to have it
staged immediately.   He seemed particularly anxious to appoint
me conductor of the orchestra.   As he was on the point of
changing his operatic company, he foresaw that his present
conductor, Gläser, the composer of *Adlershorst,* would hinder
his plans by taking the part of the older singers: he was therefore anxious to have me associated with his theatre, that he
might have some one to support him who was favourably disposed towards the new singers.

   All this sounded so plausible, that I could scarcely be blamed
for believing that the wheel of fortune had taken a favourable

turn for me, and for feeling a sense of lightheartedness at the thought of such rosy prospects. I had scarcely allowed myself the few modifications in my manner of living which these improved circumstances seemed to justify, ere it was made clear to me that my hopes were built upon sand. I was filled with positive dread when I soon fully realised how nearly Cerf had come to defrauding me, merely it would seem for his own amusement. After the manner of despots, he had given his favours personally and autocratically; the withdrawal and annulment of his promises, however, he made known to me through his servants and secretaries, thus placing his strange conduct towards me in the light of the inevitable result of his dependence upon officialdom.

As Cerf wished to rid himself of me without even offering me compensation, I was obliged to try to come to some understanding regarding all that had been definitely arranged between us, and this with the very people against whom he had previously warned me and had wanted me to side with him. The conductor, stage manager, secretary, etc., had to make it clear to me that my wishes could not be satisfied, and that the director owed me no compensation whatever for the time he had made me waste while awaiting the fulfilment of his promises. This unpleasant experience has been a source of pain to me ever since.

Owing to all this my position was very much worse than it had been before. Minna wrote to me frequently from Königsberg, but she had nothing encouraging to tell me with regard to my hopes in that direction. The director of the theatre there seemed unable to come to any clear understanding with his conductor, a circumstance which I was afterwards able to understand, but which at the time appeared to me inexplicable, and made my chance of obtaining the coveted appointment seem exceedingly remote. It seemed certain, however, that the post would be vacant in the autumn, and as I was drifting about aimlessly in Berlin and refused for a moment to entertain the thought of returning to Leipzig, I snatched at this faint hope, and in imagination soared above the Berlin quicksands to the safety of the harbour on the Baltic.

I only succeeded in doing so, however, after I had struggled through difficult and s erious inward conflicts to which my relations with Minna gave rise. An incomprehensible feature in the character of this otherwise apparently simple-minded woman had thrown my young heart into a turmoil. A good-natured, well-to-do tradesman of Jewish extraction, named Schwabe, who till that time had been established in Magdeburg, made friendly advances to me in Berlin, and I soon discovered that his sympathy was chiefly due to the passionate interest which he had conceived for Minna. It afterwards became clear to me that an intimacy had existed between this man and Minna, which in itself could hardly be considered as a breach of faith towards me, since it had ended in a decided repulse of my rival's courtship in my favour. But the fact of this episode having been kept so secret that I had not had the faintest idea of it before, and also the suspicion I could not avoid harbouring that Minna's comfortable circumstances were in part due to this man's friendship, filled me with gloomy misgivings. But as I have said, although I could find no real cause to complain of infidelity, I was distracted and alarmed, and was at last driven to the half-desperate resolve of regaining my balance in this respect by obtaining complete possession of Minna. It seemed to me as though my stability as a citizen as well as my professional success would be assured by a recognised union with Minna. The two years spent in the theatrical world had, in fact, kept me in a constant state of distraction, of which in my heart of hearts I was most painfully conscious. I realised vaguely that I was on the wrong path; I longed for peace and quiet, and hoped to find these most effectually by getting married, and so putting an end to the state of things that had become the source of so much anxiety to me.

It was not surprising that Laube noticed by my untidy, passionate, and wasted appearance that something unusual was amiss with me. It was only in his company, which I always found comforting, that I gained the only impressions of Berlin which compensated me in any way for my misfortunes. The most important artistic experience I had, came to me through the performance of *Ferdinand Cortez,* conducted by Spontini himself, the spirit of which astonished me more than anything I had ever heard before. Though the actual production, especially as regards the chief characters, who as a whole could not be regarded as belonging to the flower of Berlin opera, left me unmoved, and though the effect never reached a point that could be even distantly compared to that produced upon me by Schröder-Devrient, yet the exceptional precision, fire, and richly organised rendering of the whole was new to me. I gained a fresh insight into the peculiar dignity of big theatrical representations, which in their several parts could, by well-accentuated rhythm, be made to attain the highest pinnacle of art. This extraordinarily distinct impression took a drastic hold of me, and above all served to guide me in my conception of *Rienzi,* so that, speaking from an artistic point of view, Berlin may be said to have left its traces on my development.

For the present, however, my chief concern was to extricate myself from my extremely helpless position. I was determined to turn my steps to Königsberg, and communicated my decision, and the hopes founded upon it, to Laube. This excellent friend, without further inquiry, made a point of exerting his energies to free me from my present state of despair, and to help me to reach my next destination, an object which, through the assistance of several of his friends, he succeeded in accomplishing. When he said good-bye to me, Laube with sympathetic foresight warned me, should I succeed in my desired career of musical conductor, not to allow myself to be entangled in the shallowness of stage life, and advised me, after fatiguing rehearsals, instead of going to my sweetheart, to take a serious book in hand, in order that my greater gifts might not go uncultivated. I did not tell him that by taking an early and decisive step in this direction I intended to protect myself effectually against the dangers of theatrical intrigues. On the 7th of July, therefore, I started on what was at that time an extremely troublesome and fatiguing journey to the distant town of Königsberg.

It seemed to me as though I were leaving the world, as I travelled on day after day through the desert marches. Then followed a sad and humiliating impression of Königsberg, where, in one of the poorest-looking suburbs, Tragheim, near the theatre, and in a lane such as one would expect to find in a village, I found the ugly house in which Minna lodged. The friendly and quiet kindness of manner, however, which was peculiar to her, soon made me feel at home. She was popular at the theatre, and was respected by the managers and actors, a fact which seemed to augur well for her betrothed, the part I was now openly to assume.

Though as yet there seemed no distinct prospect of my getting the appointment I had come for, yet we agreed that I could hold out a little longer, and that the matter would certainly be arranged in the end. This was also the opinion of the eccentric Abraham Möller, a worthy citizen of Königsberg, who was devoted to the theatre, and who took a very friendly interest in Minna, and finally also in me. This man, who was already well advanced in life, belonged to the type of theatre lovers now probably completely extinct in Germany, but of whom so much is recorded in the history of actors of earlier times. One could not spend an hour in the company of this man, who at one time had gone in for the most reckless speculations, without having to listen to his account of the glory of the stage in former times, described in most lively terms. As a man of means he had at one time made the acquaintance of nearly all the great actors and actresses of his day, and had even known how to win their friendship. Through too great a liberality he unfortunately found himself in reduced circumstances, and was now obliged to procure the means to satisfy his craving for the theatre and his desire to protect those belonging to it by entering into all kinds of strange business transactions, in which, without running any real risk, he felt there was something to be gained. He was accordingly only able to afford the theatre a very meagre support, but one which was quite in keeping with its decrepit condition.

This strange man, of whom the theatre director, Anton Hübsch, stood to a certain extent in awe, undertook to procure me my appointment. The only circumstance against me was the fact that Louis Schubert, the famous musician whom I had known from very early times as the first violoncellist of the Magdeburg orchestra, had come to Königsberg from Riga, where the theatre had been closed for a time, and where he had left his wife, in order to fill the post of musical conductor here until the new theatre in Riga was opened, and he could return. The reopening of the Riga theatre, which had already been fixed for the Easter of this year, had been postponed, and he was now anxious not to leave Königsberg. Since Schubert was a thorough master in his art, and since his choosing to remain or go depended entirely on circumstances over which he had no control, the theatre director found himself in the embarrassing position of having to secure some one who would be willing to wait to enter upon his appointment till Schubert's business called him away. Consequently a young musical conductor who was anxious to remain in Königsberg at any price could but be heartily welcomed as a reserve and substitute in case of emergency. Indeed, the director declared himself willing to give me a small retaining fee till the time should arrive for my definite entrance upon my duties.

Schubert, on the contrary, was furious at my arrival; there was no longer any necessity for his speedy return to Riga, since the reopening of the theatre there had been postponed indefinitely. Moreover, he had a special interest in remaining in Königsberg, as he had conceived a passion for the prima donna there, which considerably lessened his desire to return to his wife. So at the last moment he clung to his Königsberg post with great eagerness, regarded me as his deadly enemy, and, spurred on by his instinct of self-preservation, used every means in his power to make my stay in Königsberg, and the already painful position I occupied while awaiting his departure, a veritable hell to me.

While in Magdeburg I had been on the friendliest footing with both musicians and singers, and had been shown the greatest consideration by the public, I here found I had to defend myself on all sides against the most mortifying ill-will. This hostility towards me, which soon made itself apparent, contributed in no small degree to make me feel as though in coming to Königsberg I had gone into exile. In spite of my eagerness, I realised that under the circumstances my marriage with Minna would prove a hazardous undertaking. At the beginning of August the company went to Memel for a time, to open the summer season there, and I followed Minna a few days later. We went most of the way by sea, and crossed the

Kurische Haff in a sailing vessel in bad weather with the wind against us — one of the most melancholy crossings I have ever experienced. As we passed the thin strip of sand that divides this bay from the Baltic Sea, the castle of Runsitten, where Hoffmann laid the scene of one of his most gruesome tales (*Das Majorat*), was pointed out to me. The fact that in this desolate neighbourhood, of all places in the world, I should after so long a lapse of time be once more brought in contact with the fantastic impressions of my youth, had a singular and depressing effect on my mind. The unhappy sojourn in Memel, the lamentable rôle I played there, everything in short, contributed to make me find my only consolation in Minna, who, after all, was the cause of my having placed myself in this unpleasant position. Our friend Abraham followed us from Königsberg and did all kinds of queer things to promote my interests, and was obviously anxious to put the director and conductor at variance with each other. One day Schubert, in consequence of a dispute with Hübsch on the previous night, actually declared himself too unwell to attend a rehearsal of *Euryanthe,* in order to force the manager to summon me suddenly to take his place. In doing this my rival maliciously hoped that as I was totally unprepared to conduct this difficult opera, which was seldom played, I would expose my incapacity in a manner most welcome to his hostile intentions. Although I had never really had a score of *Euryanthe* before me, his wish was so little gratified, that he elected to get well for the representation in order to conduct it himself, which he would not have done if it had been found necessary to cancel the performance on account of my incompetence. In this wretched position, vexed in mind, exposed to the severe climate, which even on summer evenings struck me as horribly cold, and occupied merely in warding off the most painful troubles of life, my time, as far as any professional advancement was concerned, was completely lost. At last, on our return to Königsberg, and particularly under the guardianship of Möller, the question as to what was to be done was more earnestly considered. Finally, Minna and I were offered a fairly good engagement in Danzig, through the influence of my brother-in-law Wolfram and his wife, who had gone there.

Möller seized this opportunity to induce the director Hübsch,
who was anxious not to lose Minna, to sign a contract including
us both, and by which it was understood that under any
circumstances I should be officially appointed as conductor at
his theatre from the following Easter. Moreover, for our
wedding, a benefit performance was promised, for which we
chose *Die Stumme von Portici,* to be conducted by me in person.
For, as Möller remarked, it was absolutely necessary for us to
get married, and to have a due celebration of the event; there
was no getting out of it. Minna made no objection, and all
my past endeavours and resolutions seemed to prove that my
one desire was to take anchor in the haven of matrimony. In
spite of this, however, a strange conflict was going on within
me at this time. I had become sufficiently intimate with
Minna's life and character to realise the wide difference between
our two natures as fully as the important step I was about to
take necessitated; but my powers of judgment were not yet
sufficiently matured.

My future wife was the child of poor parents, natives of
Oederan in the Erzgebirge in Saxony. Her father was no
ordinary man; he possessed enormous vitality, but in his old
age showed traces of some feebleness of mind. In his young days
he had been a trumpeter in Saxony, and in this capacity had
taken part in a campaign against the French, and had also been
present at the battle of Wagram. He afterwards became a
mechanic, and took up the trade of manufacturing cards for
carding wool, and as he invented an improvement in the process of their production, he is said to have made a very good
business of it for some time. A rich manufacturer of Chemnitz
once gave him a large order to be delivered at the end of the
year: the children, whose pliable fingers had already proved
serviceable in this respect, had to work hard day and night,
and in return the father promised them an exceptionally happy
Christmas, as he expected to get a large sum of money. When
the longed-for time arrived, however, he received the announcement of his client's bankruptcy. The goods that had already
been delivered were lost, and the material that remained on
his hands there was no prospect of selling. The family never
succeeded in recovering from the state of confusion into which

this misfortune had thrown them; they went to Dresden, where the father hoped to find remunerative employment as a skilled mechanic, especially in the manufacture of pianos, of which he supplied separate parts. He also brought away with him a large quantity of the fine wire which had been destined for the manufacture of the cards, and which he hoped to be able to sell at a profit. The ten-year-old Minna was commissioned to sell separate lots of it to the milliners for making flowers. She would set out with a heavy basketful of wire, and had such a gift for persuading people to buy that she soon disposed of the whole supply to the best advantage. From this time the desire was awakened in her to be of active use to her impoverished family, and to earn her own living as soon as possible, in order not to be a burden on her parents. As she grew up and developed into a strikingly beautiful woman, she attracted the attention of men at a very early age. A certain Herr von Einsiedel fell passionately in love with her, and took advantage of the inexperienced young girl when she was off her guard. Her family was thrown into the utmost consternation, and only her mother and elder sister could be told of the terrible position in which Minna found herself. Her father, from whose anger the worst consequences were to be feared, was never informed that his barely seventeen-year-old daughter had become a mother, and under conditions that had threatened her life, had given birth to a girl. Minna, who could obtain no redress from her seducer, now felt doubly called upon to earn her own livelihood and leave her father's house. Through the influence of friends, she had been brought into contact with an amateur theatrical society: while acting in a performance given there, she attracted the notice of members of the Royal Court Theatre, and in particular drew the attention of the director of the Dessau Court Theatre, who was present, and who immediately offered her an engagement. She gladly caught at this way of escape from her trying position, as it opened up the possibility of a brilliant stage career, and of some day being able to provide amply for her family. She had not the slightest passion for the stage, and utterly devoid as she was of any levity or coquetry, she merely saw in a theatrical career the means of earning a quick, and possibly even a rich, livelihood. Without any artistic training, the theatre merely meant for her the company of actors and actresses. Whether she pleased or not seemed of importance in her eyes only in so far as it affected her realisation of a comfortable independence. To use all the means at her disposal to assure this end seemed to her as necessary as it is for a tradesman to expose his goods to the best advantage.

The friendship of the director, manager, and favourite members of the theatre she regarded as indispensable, whilst those frequenters of the theatre who, through their criticism or taste, influenced the public, and thus also had weight with the management, she recognised as beings upon whom the attainment of her most fervent desires depended. Never to make enemies of them appeared so natural and so necessary that, in order to maintain her popularity, she was prepared to sacrifice even her self-respect. She had in this way created for herself a certain peculiar code of behaviour, that on the one hand prompted her to avoid scandals, but on the other hand found excuses even for making herself conspicuous as long as she herself knew that she was doing nothing wrong. Hence arose a mixture of inconsistencies, the questionable sense of which she was incapable of grasping. It was clearly impossible for her not to lose all real sense of delicacy; she showed, however, a sense of the fitness of things, which made her have regard to what was considered proper, though she could not understand that mere appearances were a mockery when they only served to cloak the absence of a real sense of delicacy. As she was without idealism, she had no artistic feeling; neither did she possess any talent for acting, and her power of pleasing was due entirely to her charming appearance. Whether in time routine would have made her become a good actress it is impossible for me to say. The strange power she exercised over me from the very first was in no wise due to the fact that I regarded her in any way as the embodiment of my ideal; on the contrary, she attracted me by the soberness and seriousness of her character, which supplemented what I felt to be wanting in my own, and afforded me the support that in my wanderings after the ideal I knew to be necessary for me.

I had soon accustomed myself never to betray my craving

after the ideal before Minna: unable to account for this even
to myself, I always made a point of avoiding the subject by
passing it over with a laugh and a joke; but, on this account,
it was all the more natural for me to feel qualms when fears
arose in my mind as to her really possessing the qualities to
which I had attributed her superiority over me. Her strange
tolerance with regard to certain familiarities and even importunities on the part of patrons of the theatre, directed even
against her person, hurt me considerably; and on my reproaching her for this, I was driven to despair by her assuming an
injured expression as though I had insulted her. It was quite
by chance that I came across Schwabe's letters, and thus gained
an astonishing insight into her intimacy with that man, of
which she had left me in ignorance, and allowed me to gain
my first knowledge during my stay in Berlin. All my latent
jealousy, all my inmost doubts concerning Minna's character,
found vent in my sudden determination to leave the girl at
once. There was a violent scene between us, which was
typical of all our subsequent altercations. I had obviously
gone too far in treating a woman who was not passionately in
love with me, as if I had a real right over her; for, after
all, she had merely yielded to my importunity, and in no
way belonged to me. To add to my perplexity, Minna only
needed to remind me that from a worldly point of view she
had refused very good offers in order to give way to the impetuosity of a penniless young man, whose talent had not yet been
put to any real test, and to whom she had nevertheless shown
sympathy and kindness.

What she could least forgive in me was the raging vehemence with which I spoke, and by which she felt so insulted, that
upon realising to what excesses I had gone, there was nothing
I could do but try and pacify her by owning myself in the
wrong, and begging her forgiveness. Such was the end of this
and all subsequent scenes, outwardly, at least, always to her
advantage. But peace was undermined for ever, and by the
frequent recurrence of such quarrels, Minna's character underwent a considerable change. Just as in later times she became
perplexed by what she considered my incomprehensible conception of art and its proportions, which upset her ideas about

everything connected with it, so now she grew more and more confused by my greater delicacy in regard to morality, which was very different from hers, especially as in many other respects I displayed a freedom of opinion which she could neither comprehend nor approve.

A feeling of passionate resentment was accordingly roused in her otherwise tranquil disposition. It was not surprising that this resentment increased as the years went on, and manifested itself in a manner characteristic of a girl sprung from the lower middle class, in whom mere superficial polish had taken the place of any true culture. The real torment of our subsequent life together lay in the fact that, owing to her violence, I had lost the last support I had hitherto found in her exceptionally sweet disposition. At that time I was filled only with a dim foreboding of the fateful step I was taking in marrying her. Her agreeable and soothing qualities still had such a beneficial effect upon me, that with the frivolity natural to me, as well as the obstinacy with which I met all opposition, I silenced the inner voice that darkly foreboded disaster.

Since my journey to Königsberg I had broken off all communication with my family, that is to say, with my mother and Rosalie, and I told no one of the step I had decided to take. Under my old friend Möller's audacious guidance I overcame all the legal difficulties that stood in the way of our union. According to Prussian law, a man who has reached his majority no longer requires his parents' consent to his marriage: but since, according to this same provision, I was not yet of age, I had recourse to the law of Saxony, to which country I belonged by birth, and by whose regulations I had already attained my majority at the age of twenty-one. Our banns had to be published at the place where we had been living during the past year, and this formality was carried out in Magdeburg without any further objections being raised. As Minna's parents had given their consent, the only thing that still remained to be done to make everything quite in order was for us to go together to the clergyman of the parish of Tragheim. This proved a strange enough visit. It took place the morning preceding the performance to be given for our benefit, in which Minna had chosen the pantomimic rôle of Fenella; her costume was not ready yet, and there was still a great deal to be done. The rainy cold November weather made us feel out of humour, when, to add to our vexation, we were kept standing in the hall of the vicarage for an unreasonable time. Then an altercation arose between us which speedily led to such bitter vituperation that we were just on the point of separating and going each our own way, when the clergyman opened the door. Not a little embarrassed at having surprised us in the act of quarrelling, he invited us in. We were obliged to put a good face on the matter, however; and the absurdity of the situation so tickled our sense of humour that we laughed; the parson was appeased, and the wedding fixed for eleven o'clock the next morning.

Another fruitful source of irritation, which often led to the outbreak of violent quarrelling between us, was the arrangement of our future home, in the interior comfort and beauty of which I hoped to find a guarantee of happiness. The economical ideas of my bride filled me with impatience. I was determined that the inauguration of a series of prosperous years which I saw before me must be celebrated by a correspondingly comfortable home. Furniture, household utensils, and all necessaries were obtained on credit, to be paid for by instalment. There was, of course, no question of a dowry, a wedding outfit, or any of the things that are generally considered indispensable to a well-founded establishment. Our witnesses and guests were drawn from the company of actors accidentally brought together by their engagement at the Königsberg theatre. My friend Möller made us a present of a silver sugar-basin, which was supplemented by a silver cake-basket from another stage friend, a peculiar and, as far as I can remember, rather interesting young man named Ernst Castell. The benefit performance of the *Die Stumme von Portici,* which I conducted with great enthusiasm, went off well, and brought us in as large a sum as we had counted upon. After spending the rest of the day before our wedding very quietly, as we were tired out after our return from the theatre, I took up my abode for the first time in our new home. Not wishing to use the bridal bed, decorated for the occasion, I lay down on a hard sofa, without even sufficient covering on me, and froze valiantly while awaiting the happiness of the following day. I was pleasantly excited the next morning by the arrival of Minna's belongings, packed in boxes and baskets. The weather, too, had quite cleared up, and the sun was shining brightly; only our sitting-room refused to get properly warm, which for some time drew down Minna's reproaches upon my head for my supposed carelessness in not having seen to the heating arrangements. At last I dressed myself in my new suit, a dark blue frock-coat with gold buttons. The carriage drove up, and I set out to fetch my bride. The bright sky had put us all in good spirits, and in the best of humour I met Minna, who was dressed in a splendid gown chosen by me. She greeted me with sincere cordiality and pleasure shining from her eyes; and taking the fine weather as a good omen, we started off for what now seemed to us a most cheerful wedding. We enjoyed the satisfaction of seeing the church as over-crowded as if a brilliant theatrical representation were being given; it was quite a difficult matter to make our way to the altar, where a group no less worldly than the rest, con-sisting of our witnesses, dressed in all their theatrical finery, were assembled to receive us. There was not one real friend amongst all those present, for even our strange old friend Möller was absent, because no suitable partner had been found for him. I was not for a single moment insensible to the chilling frivolity of the congregation, who seemed to impart their tone to the whole ceremony. I listened like one in a dream to the nuptial address of the parson, who, I was afterwards told, had had a share in producing the spirit of bigotry which at this time was so prevalent in Königs-berg, and which exercised such a disquieting influence on its population.

A few days later I was told that a rumour had got about the town that I had taken action against the parson for some gross insults contained in his sermon; I did not quite see what was meant, but supposed that the exaggerated report arose from a passage in his address which I in my excitement had misunderstood. The preacher, in speaking of the dark days, of which we were to expect our share, bade us look to an unknown friend, and I glanced up inquiringly for further particulars of this mysterious and influential patron who chose so strange a way of announcing himself. Reproachfully, and with peculiar emphasis, the pastor then pronounced the name of this unknown friend: Jesus. Now I was not in any way insulted by this, as people imagined, but was simply disappointed; at the same time, I thought that such exhortations were probably usual in nuptial addresses.

But, on the whole, I was so absent-minded during this ceremony, which was double Dutch to me, that when the parson held out the closed prayer-book for us to place our wedding rings upon, Minna had to nudge me forcibly to make me follow her example.

At that moment I saw, as clearly as in a vision, my whole being divided into two cross-currents that dragged me in different directions; the upper one faced the sun and carried me onward like a dreamer, whilst the lower one held my nature captive, a prey to some inexplicable fear. The extraordinary levity with which I chased away the conviction which kept forcing itself upon me, that I was committing a twofold sin, was amply accounted for by the really genuine affection with which I looked upon the young girl whose truly exceptional character (so rare in the environment in which she had been placed) led her thus to bind herself to a young man without any means of support. It was eleven o'clock on the morning of the 24th of November, 1836, and I was twenty-three and a half.

On the way home from church, and afterwards, my good spirits rose superior to all my doubts.

Minna at once took upon herself the duty of receiving and entertaining her guests. The table was spread, and a rich feast, at which Abraham Möller, the energetic promoter of our marriage, also took part, although he had been rather put out by his exclusion from the church ceremony, made up for the coldness of the room, which for a long time refused to get warm, to the great distress of the young hostess.

Everything went off in the usual uneventful way. Nevertheless, I retained my good spirits till the next morning, when I had to present myself at the magistrate's court to meet the demands of my creditors, which had been forwarded to me from Magdeburg to Königsburg.

My friend Möller, whom I had retained for my defence, had foolishly advised me to meet my creditors' demands by pleading infancy according to the law of Prussia, at all events until actual assistance for the settlement of the claims could be obtained.

The magistrate, to whom I stated this plea as I had been advised, was astonished, being probably well aware of my marriage on the previous day, which could only have taken place on the production of documentary proof of my majority. I naturally only gained a brief respite by this manœuvre, and the troubles which beset me for a long time afterwards had their origin on the first day of my marriage.

During the period when I held no appointment at the theatre I suffered various humiliations. Nevertheless, I thought it wise to make the most of my leisure in the interests of my art, and I finished a few pieces, among which was a grand overture on *Rule Britannia*.

When I was still in Berlin I had written the overture entitled *Polonia,* which has already been mentioned in connection with the Polish festival. *Rule Britannia* was a further and deliberate step in the direction of mass effects; at the close a strong military band was to be added to the already over-full orchestra, and I intended to have the whole thing performed at the Musical Festival in Königsberg in the summer.

To these two overtures I added a supplement — an overture entitled *Napoleon.* The point to which I devoted my chief attention was the selection of the means for producing certain effects, and I carefully considered whether I should express the annihilating stroke of fate that befell the French Emperor in Russia by a beat on the tom-tom or not. I believe it was to a great extent my scruples about the introduction of this beat that prevented me from carrying out my plan just then.

On the other hand, the conclusions which I had reached regarding the ill-success of *Liebesverbot* resulted in an operatic sketch in which the demands made on the chorus and the staff of singers should be more in proportion to the known capacity of the local company, as this small theatre was the only one at my disposal.

A quaint tale from the *Arabian Nights* suggested the very

subject for a light work of this description, the title of which, if I remember rightly, was *Männerlist grösser als Frauenlist* (' Man outwits Woman ').

I transplanted the story from Bagdad to a modern setting. A young goldsmith offends the pride of a young woman by placing the above motto on the sign over his shop; deeply veiled, she steps into his shop and asks him, as he displays such excellent taste in his work, to express his opinion on her own physical charms; he begins with her feet and her hands, and finally, noticing his confusion, she removes the veil from her face. The jeweller is carried away by her beauty, whereupon she complains to him that her father, who has always kept her in the strictest seclusion, describes her to all her suitors as an ugly monster, his object being, she imagines, simply to keep her dowry. The young man swears that he will not be frightened off by these foolish objections, should the father raise them against his suit. No sooner said than done. The daughter of this peculiar old gentleman is promised to the unsuspecting jeweller, and is brought to her bridegroom as soon as he has signed the contract. He then sees that the father has indeed spoken the truth, the real daughter being a perfect scarecrow. The beautiful lady returns to the bridegroom to gloat over his desperation, and promises to release him from his terrible marriage if he will remove the motto from his signboard. At this point I departed from the original, and continued as follows: The enraged jeweller is on the point of tearing down his unfortunate signboard when a curious apparition leads him to pause in the act. He sees a bear-leader in the street making his clumsy beast dance, in whom the luckless lover recognises at a glance his own father, from whom he has been parted by a hard fate.

He suppresses any sign of emotion, for in a flash a scheme occurs to him by which he can utilise this discovery to free himself from the hated marriage with the daughter of the proud old aristocrat.

He instructs the bear-leader to come that evening to the garden where the solemn betrothal is to take place in the presence of the invited guests.

He then explains to his young enemy that he wishes to leave

the signboard up for the time being, as he still hopes to prove the truth of the motto.

After the marriage contract, in which the young man arrogates to himself all kinds of fictitious titles of nobility, has been read to the assembled company (composed, say, of the *élite* of the noble immigrants at the time of the French Revolution), there is heard suddenly the pipe of the bear-leader, who enters the garden with his prancing beast. Angered by this trivial diversion, the astonished company become indignant when the bridegroom, giving free vent to his feelings, throws himself with tears of joy into the arms of the bear-leader and loudly proclaims him as his long-lost father. The consternation of the company becomes even greater, however, when the bear itself embraces the man they supposed to be of noble birth, for the beast is no less a person than his own brother in the flesh who, on the death of the real bear, had donned its skin, thus enabling the poverty-stricken pair to continue to earn their livelihood in the only way left to them. This public disclosure of the bridegroom's lowly origin at once dissolves the marriage, and the young woman, declaring herself outwitted by man, offers her hand in compensation to the released jeweller.

To this unassuming subject I gave the title of the *Glückliche Bärenfamilie,* and provided it with a dialogue which afterwards met with Holtei's highest approval.

I was about to begin the music for it in a new light French style, but the seriousness of my position, which grew more and more acute, prevented further progress in my work.

In this respect my strained relations with the conductor of the theatre were still a constant source of trouble. With neither the opportunity nor the means to defend myself, I had to submit to being maligned and rendered an object of suspicion on all sides by my rival, who remained master of the field. The object of this was to disgust me with the idea of taking up my appointment as musical conductor, for which the contract had been signed for Easter. Though I did not lose my self-confidence, I suffered keenly from the indignity and the depressing effect of this prolonged strain.

When at last, at the beginning of April, the moment arrived

for the musical conductor Schubert to resign, and for me to take over the whole charge, he had the melancholy satisfaction of knowing that not only was the standing of the opera seriously weakened by the departure of the prima donna, but that there was good reason to doubt whether the theatre could be carried on at all. This month of Lent, which was such a bad time in Germany for all similar theatrical enterprises, decimated the Königsberg audience with the rest. The director took the greatest trouble imaginable to fill up the gaps in the staff of the opera by means of engaging strangers temporarily, and by new acquisitions, and in this my personality and unflagging activity were of real service; I devoted all my energy to buoying up by word and deed the tattered ship of the theatre, in which I now had a hand for the first time.

For a long time I had to try and keep cool under the most violent treatment by a clique of students, among whom my predecessor had raised up enemies for me; and by the unerring certainty of my conducting I had to overcome the initial opposition of the orchestra, which had been set against me.

After laboriously laying the foundation of personal respect, I was now forced to realise that the business methods of the director, Hübsch, had already involved too great a sacrifice to permit the theatre to make its way against the unfavourableness of the season, and in May he admitted to me that he had come to the point of being obliged to close the theatre.

By summoning up all my eloquence, and by making suggestions which promised a happy issue, I was able to induce him to persevere; nevertheless, this was only possible by making demands on the loyalty of his company, who were asked to forego part of their salaries for a time. This aroused general bitterness on the part of the uninitiated, and I found myself in the curious position of being forced to place the director in a favourable light to those who were hard hit by these measures, while I myself and my position were affected in such a manner that my situation became daily more unendurable under the accumulation of intolerable difficulties taking their root in my past.

But though I did not even then lose courage, Minna, who as my wife was robbed of all that she had a right to expect, found this turn of fate quite unbearable. The hidden canker of our married life which, even before our marriage, had caused me the most terrible anxiety and led to violent scenes, reached its full growth under these sad conditions. The less I was able to maintain the standard of comfort due to our position by working and making the most of my talents, the more did Minna, to my insufferable shame, consider it necessary to take this burden upon herself by making the most of her personal popularity. The discovery of similar condescensions — as I used to call them — on Minna's part, had repeatedly led to revolting scenes, and only her peculiar conception of her professional position and the needs it involved had made a charitable interpretation possible.

I was absolutely unable to bring my young wife to see my point of view, or to make her realise my own wounded feelings on these occasions, while the unrestrained violence of my speech and behaviour made an understanding once and for all impossible. These scenes frequently sent my wife into convulsions of so alarming a nature that, as will easily be realised, the satisfaction of reconciling her once more was all that remained to me. Certain it was that our mutual attitude became more and more incomprehensible and inexplicable to us both.

These quarrels, which now became more frequent and more distressing, may have gone far to diminish the strength of any affection which Minna was able to give me, but I had no idea that she was only waiting for a favourable opportunity to come to a desperate decision.

To fill the place of tenor in our company, I had summoned Friedrich Schmitt to Königsberg, a friend of my first year in Magdeburg, to whom allusion has already been made. He was sincerely devoted to me, and helped me as much as possible in overcoming the dangers which threatened the prosperity of the theatre as well as my own position.

The necessity of being on friendly terms with the public made me much less reserved and cautious in making new acquaintances, especially when in his company.

A rich merchant, of the name of Dietrich, had recently constituted himself a patron of the theatre, and especially of

the women. With due deference to the men with whom they
were connected, he used to invite the pick of these ladies to
dinner at his house, and affected, on these occasions, the well-
to-do Englishman, which was the beau-ideal for German
merchants, especially in the manufacturing towns of the
north.

I had shown my annoyance at the acceptance of the invitation, sent to us among the rest, at first simply because his looks
were repugnant to me. Minna considered this very unjust.
Anyhow, I set my face decidedly against continuing our
acquaintance with this man, and although Minna did not
insist on receiving him, my conduct towards the intruder was
the cause of angry scenes between us.

One day Friedrich Schmitt considered it his duty to inform
me that this Herr Dietrich had spoken of me at a public dinner
in such a manner as to lead every one to suppose that he had
a suspicious intimacy with my wife. I felt obliged to suspect
Minna of having, in some way unknown to me, told the fellow
about my conduct towards her, as well as about our precarious
position.

Accompanied by Schmitt, I called this dangerous person to
account on the subject in his own home. At first this only
led to the usual denials. Afterwards, however, he sent secret
communications to Minna concerning the interview, thus providing her with a supposed new grievance against me in the
form of my inconsiderate treatment of her.

Our relations now reached a critical stage, and on certain
points we preserved silence.

At the same time — it was towards the end of May, 1837 —
the business affairs of the theatre had reached the crisis above
mentioned, when the management was obliged to fall back
on the self-sacrificing co-operation of the staff to assure the
continuance of the undertaking. As I have said before, my
own position at the end of a year so disastrous to my welfare
was seriously affected by this; nevertheless, there seemed to
be no alternative for me but to face these difficulties patiently,
and relying on the faithful Friedrich Schmitt, but ignoring
Minna, I began to take the necessary steps for making my
post at Königsberg secure. This, as well as the arduous part

I took in the business of the theatre, kept me so busy and so
much away from home, that I was not able to pay any particular attention to Minna's silence and reserve.

On the morning of the 31st of May I took leave of Minna,
expecting to be detained till late in the afternoon by rehearsals
and business matters. With my entire approval she had for
some time been accustomed to have her daughter Nathalie,
who was supposed by every one to be her youngest sister, to
stay with her.

As I was about to wish them my usual quiet good-bye, the
two women rushed after me to the door and embraced me
passionately, Minna as well as her daughter bursting into tears.
I was alarmed, and asked the meaning of this excitement, but
could get no answer from them, and I was obliged to leave
them and ponder alone over their peculiar conduct, of the
reason for which I had not even the faintest idea.

I arrived home late in the afternoon, worn out by my exertions and worries, dead-tired, pale and hungry, and was
surprised to find the table not laid and Minna not at home,
the maid telling me that she had not yet returned from her
walk with Nathalie.

I waited patiently, sinking down exhausted at the work-
table, which I absent-mindedly opened. To my intense astonishment it was empty. Horror-struck, I sprang up and
went to the wardrobe, and realised at once that Minna had
left the house; her departure had been so cunningly planned
that even the maid was unaware of it.

With death in my soul I dashed out of the house to investi-
gate the cause of Minna's disappearance.

Old Möller, by his practical sagacity, very soon found out
that Dietrich, his personal enemy, had left Königsberg in the
direction of Berlin by the special coach in the morning.

This horrible fact stood staring me in the face.

I had now to try and overtake the fugitives. With the
lavish use of money this might have been possible, but funds
were lacking, and had, in part, to be laboriously collected.

On Möller's advice I took the silver wedding presents with
me in case of emergency, and after the lapse of a few terrible
hours went off, also by special coach, with my distressed old

friend. We hoped to overtake the ordinary mail-coach, which had started a short time before, as it was probable that Minna would also continue her journey in this, at a safe distance from Königsberg.

This proved impossible, and when next morning at break of day we arrived in Elbing, we found our money exhausted by the lavish use of the express coach, and were compelled to return; we discovered, moreover, that even by using the ordinary coach we should be obliged to pawn the sugar-basin and cake-dish.

This return journey to Königsberg rightly remains one of the saddest memories of my youth. Of course, I did not for a moment entertain the idea of remaining in the place; my one thought was how I could best get away. Hemmed in between the law-suits of my Magdeburg creditors and the Königsberg tradesmen, who had claims on me for the payment by instalment of my domestic accounts, my departure could only be carried out in secrecy. For this very reason, too, it was necessary for me to raise money, particularly for the long journey from Königsberg to Dresden, whither I determined to go in quest of my wife, and these matters detained me for two long and terrible days.

I received no news whatever from Minna; from Möller I ascertained that she had gone to Dresden, and that Dietrich had only accompanied her for a short distance on the excuse of helping her in a friendly way.

I succeeded in assuring myself that she really only wished to get away from a position that filled her with desperation, and for this purpose had accepted the assistance of a man who sympathised with her, and that she was for the present seeking rest and shelter with her parents. My first indignation at the event accordingly subsided to such an extent that I gradually acquired more sympathy for her in her despair, and began to reproach myself both for my conduct and for having brought unhappiness on her.

I became so convinced of the correctness of this view during the tedious journey to Dresden via Berlin, which I eventually undertook on the 3rd of June, that when at last I found Minna at the humble abode of her parents, I was really quite unable to express anything but repentence and heartbroken sympathy.

It was quite true that Minna thought herself badly treated by me, and declared that she had only been forced to take this desperate step by brooding over our impossible position, to which she thought me both blind and deaf. Her parents were not pleased to see me: the painfully excited condition of their daughter seemed to afford sufficient justification for her complaints against me. Whether my own sufferings, my hasty pursuit, and the heartfelt expression of my grief made any favourable impression on her, I can really hardly say, as her manner towards me was very confused and, to a certain extent, incomprehensible. Still she was impressed when I told her that there was a good prospect of my obtaining the post of musical conductor at Riga, where a new theatre was about to be opened under the most favourable conditions. I felt that I must not press for new resolutions concerning the regulation of our future relations just then, but must strive the more earnestly to lay a better foundation for them. Consequently, after spending a fearful week with my wife under the most painful conditions, I went to Berlin, there to sign my agreement with the new director of the Riga theatre. I obtained the appointment on fairly favourable terms which, I saw, would enable me to keep house in such a style that Minna could retire from the theatre altogether. By this means she would be in a position to spare me all humiliation and anxiety.

On returning to Dresden, I found that Minna was ready to lend a willing ear to my proposed plans, and I succeeded in inducing her to leave her parents' house, which was very cramped for us, and to establish herself in the country at Blasewitz, near Dresden, to await our removal to Riga. We found modest lodgings at an inn on the Elbe, in the farmyard of which I had often played as a child. Here Minna's frame of mind really seemed to be improving. She had begged me not to press her too hard, and I spared her as much as possible. After a few weeks I thought I might consider the period of uneasiness past, but was surprised to find the situation growing worse again without any apparent reason. Minna then told me of some advantageous offers she had received from different theatres, and astonished me one day by announcing her intention of taking a short pleasure trip with a girl friend and her family. As I felt obliged to avoid putting any restraint upon her, I offered no objection to the execution of this project, which entailed a week's separation, but accompanied her back to her parents myself, promising to await her return quietly at Blasewitz. A few days later her eldest sister called to ask me for the written permission required to make out a passport for my wife. This alarmed me, and I went to Dresden to ask her parents what their daughter was about. There, to my surprise, I met with a very unpleasant reception; they reproached me coarsely for my behaviour to Minna, whom they said I could not even manage to support, and when I only replied by asking for information as to the whereabouts of my wife, and about her plans for the future, I was put off with improbable statements. Tormented by the sharpest forebodings, and understanding nothing of what had occurred, I went back to the village, where I found a letter from Königsberg, from Möller, which poured light on all my misery. Herr Dietrich had gone to Dresden, and I was told the name of the hotel at which he was staying. The terrible illumination thrown by this communication upon Minna's conduct showed me in a flash what to do. I hurried into town to make the necessary inquiries at the hotel mentioned, and found that the man in question had been there, but had moved on again. He had vanished, and Minna too! I now knew enough to demand of the Fates why, at such an early age, they had sent me this terrible experience which, as it seemed to me, had poisoned my whole existence.

I sought consolation for my boundless grief in the society of my sister Ottilie and her husband, Hermann Brockhaus, an excellent fellow to whom she had been married for some years. They were then living at their pretty summer villa in the lovely Grosser Garten, near Dresden. I had looked them up at once the first time I went to Dresden, but as I had not at that time the slightest idea of how things were going to turn out, I had told them nothing, and had seen but little of them. Now I was moved to break my obstinate silence, and unfold to them the cause of my misery, with but few reservations.

For the first time I was in a position gratefully to appreciate the advantages of family intercourse, and of the direct and disinterested intimacy between blood relations. Explanations were hardly necessary, and as brother and sister we found ourselves as closely linked now as we had been when we were children. We arrived at a complete understanding without having to explain what we meant; I was unhappy, she was happy; consolation and help followed as a matter of course.

This was the sister to whom I once had read *Leubald und Adelaïde* in a thunderstorm; the sister who had listened, filled with astonishment and sympathy, to that eventful performance of my first overture on Christmas Eve, and whom I now found married to one of the kindest of men, Hermann Brockhaus, who soon earned a reputation for himself as an expert in oriental languages. He was the youngest brother of my elder brother-in-law, Friedrich Brockhaus. Their union was blessed by two children; their comfortable means favoured a life free from care, and when I made my daily pilgrimage from Blasewitz to the famous Grosser Garten, it was like stepping from a desert into paradise to enter their house (one of the popular villas), knowing that I would invariably find a welcome in this happy family circle. Not only was my spirit soothed and benefited by intercourse with my sister, but my creative instincts, which had long lain dormant, were stimulated afresh by the society of my brilliant and learned brother-in-law. It was brought home to me, without in any way hurting my feelings, that my early marriage, excusable as it may have been, was yet an error to be retrieved, and my mind regained sufficient elasticity to compose some sketches, designed this time not merely to meet the requirements of the theatre as I knew it. During the last wretched days I had spent with Minna at Blasewitz, I had read Bulwer Lytton's novel, *Rienzi;* during my convalescence in the bosom of my sympathetic family, I now worked out the scheme for a grand opera under the inspiration of this book. Though obliged for the present to return to the limitations of a small theatre, I tried from this time onwards to aim at enlarging my sphere of action. I sent my overture, *Rule Britannia,* to the Philharmonic Society in London, and tried to get into communication with Scribe in Paris about a setting for H. König's novel, *Die Hohe Braut,* which I had sketched out.

Thus I spent the remainder of this summer of ever-happy memory. At the end of August I had to leave for Riga to take up my new appointment. Although I knew that my sister Rosalie had shortly before married the man of her choice, Professor Oswald Marbach of Leipzig, I avoided that city, probably with the foolish notion of sparing myself any humiliation, and went straight to Berlin, where I had to receive certain additional instructions from my future director, and also to obtain my passport. There I met a younger sister of Minna's, Amalie Planer, a singer with a pretty voice, who had joined our opera company at Magdeburg for a short time. My report of Minna quite overwhelmed this exceedingly kind-hearted girl. We went to a performance of *Fidelio* together, during which she, like myself, burst into tears and sobs. Refreshed by the sympathetic impression I had received, I went by way of Schwerin, where I was disappointed in my hopes of finding traces of Minna, to Lübeck, to wait for a merchant ship going to Riga. We had set sail for Travemünde when an unfavourable wind set in, and held up our departure for a week: I had to spend this disagreeable time in a miserable ship's tavern. Thrown on my own resources I tried, amongst other things, to read *Till Eulenspiegel,* and this popular book first gave me the idea of a real German comic opera. Long afterwards, when I was composing the words for my *Junger Siegfried,* I remember having many vivid recollections of this melancholy sojourn in Travemünde and my reading of *Till Eulenspiegel.* After a voyage of four days we at last reached port at Bolderaa. I was conscious of a peculiar thrill on coming into contact with Russian officials, whom I had instinctively detested since the days of my sympathy with the Poles as a boy. It seemed to me as if the harbour police must read enthusiasm for the Poles in my face, and would send me to Siberia on the spot, and I was the more agreeably surprised, on reaching Riga, to find myself surrounded by the familiar German element which, above all, pervaded everything connected with the theatre.

After my unfortunate experiences in connection with the

conditions of small German stages, the way in which this newly opened theatre was run had at first a calming effect on my mind. A society had been formed by a number of well-to-do theatre-goers and rich business men to raise, by voluntary subscription, sufficient money to provide the sort of management they regarded as ideal with a solid foundation. The director they appointed was Karl von Holtei, a fairly popular dramatic writer, who enjoyed a certain reputation in the theatrical world. This man's ideas about the stage represented a special tendency, which was at that time on the decline. He possessed, in addition to his remarkable social gifts, an extraordinary acquaintance with all the principal people connected with the theatre during the past twenty years, and belonged to a society called *Die Liebenswürdigen Libertins* ('The Amiable Libertines'). This was a set of young would-be wits, who looked upon the stage as a playground licensed by the public for the display of their mad pranks, from which the middle class held aloof, while people of culture were steadily losing all interest in the theatre under these hopeless conditions.

Holtei's wife had in former days been a popular actress at the Königstadt theatre in Berlin, and it was here, at the time when Henriette Sontag raised it to the height of its fame, that Holtei's style had been formed. The production there of his melodrama *Leonore* (founded on Bürger's ballad) had in particular earned him a wide reputation as a writer for the stage, besides which he produced some *Liederspiele,* and among them one, entitled *Der Alte Feldherr,* became fairly popular. His invitation to Riga had been particularly welcome, as it bid fair to gratify his craving to absorb himself completely in the life of the stage; he hoped, in this out-of-the-way place, to indulge his passion without restraint. His peculiar familiarity of manner, his inexhaustible store of amusing small talk, and his airy way of doing business, gave him a remarkable hold on the tradespeople of Riga, who wished for nothing better than such entertainment as he was able to give them. They provided him liberally with all the necessary means and treated him in every respect with entire confidence. Under his auspices my own engagement had been very easily secured. Surly old pedants he would have none of, favouring young men

on the score of their youth alone. As far as I myself was
concerned, it was enough for him to know that I belonged to
a family which he knew and liked, and hearing, moreover, of
my fervent devotion to modern Italian and French music in
particular, he decided that I was the very man for him. He
had the whole shoal of Bellini's, Donizetti's, Adam's, and
Auber's operatic scores copied out, and I was to give the good
people of Riga the benefit of them with all possible speed.

The first time I visited Holtei I met an old Leipzig acquaintance, Heinrich Dorn, my former mentor, who now held the permanent municipal appointment of choir-master at the church
and music-teacher in the schools. He was pleased to find his
curious pupil transformed into a practical opera conductor of
independent position, and no less surprised to see the eccentric
worshipper of Beethoven changed into an ardent champion of
Bellini and Adam. He took me home to his summer residence,
which was built, according to Riga phraseology, ' in the fields,'
that is literally, on the sand. While I was giving him some
account of the experiences through which I had passed, I grew
conscious of the strangely deserted look of the place. Feeling
frightened and homeless, my initial uneasiness gradually developed into a passionate longing to escape from all the whirl of
theatrical life which had wooed me to such inhospitable regions.
This uneasy mood was fast dispelling the flippancy which at
Magdeburg had led to my being dragged down to the level
of the most worthless stage society, and had also conduced to
spoil my musical taste. It also contained the germs of a new
tendency which developed during the period of my activity
at Riga, brought me more and more out of touch with the
theatre, thereby causing Director Holtei all the annoyance
which inevitably attends disappointment.

For some time, however, I found no difficulty in making the
best of a bad bargain. We were obliged to open the theatre
before the company was complete. To make this possible, we
gave a performance of a short comic opera by C. Blum, called
Marie, Max und Michel. For this work I composed an additional air for a song which Holtei had written for the bass
singer, Günther; it consisted of a sentimental introduction and
a gay military rondo, and was very much appreciated. Later on,

I introduced another additional song into the *Schweizerfamilie,*
to be sung by another bass singer, Scheibler; it was of a devo-
tional character, and pleased not only the public, but myself,
and showed signs of the upheaval which was gradually taking
place in my musical development. I was entrusted with the
composition of a tune for a National Hymn written by Brakel
in honour of the Tsar Nicholas's birthday. I tried to give it
as far as possible the right colouring for a despotic patriarchal
monarch, and once again I achieved some fame, for it was sung
for several successive years on that particular day. Holtei
tried to persuade me to write a bright, gay comic opera, or
rather a musical play, to be performed by our company just
as it stood. I looked up the libretto of my *Glückliche Bärenfamilie,* and found Holtei very well disposed towards it (as I
have stated elsewhere); but when I unearthed the little music
which I had already composed for it, I was overcome with disgust at this way of writing; whereupon I made a present of the
book to my clumsy, good-natured friend, Löbmann, my right-
hand man in the orchestra, and never gave it another thought
from that day to this. I managed, however, to get to work on
the libretto of *Rienzi,* which I had sketched out at Blasewitz.
I developed it from every point of view, on so extravagant a
scale, that with this work I deliberately cut off all possibility
of being tempted by circumstances to produce it anywhere but
on one of the largest stages in Europe.

But while this helped to strengthen my endeavour to escape
from all the petty degradations of stage life, new complications
arose which affected me more and more seriously, and offered
further opposition to my aims. The prima donna engaged by
Holtei had failed us, and we were therefore without a singer
for grand opera. Under the circumstances, Holtei joyfully
agreed to my proposal to ask Amalie, Minna's sister (who was
glad to accept an engagement that brought her near me), to
come to Riga at once. In her answer to me from Dresden,
where she was then living, she informed me of Minna's return
to her parents, and of her present miserable condition owing to
a severe illness. I naturally took this piece of news very coolly,
for what I had heard about Minna since she left me for the last
time had forced me to authorise my old friend at Königsberg

to take steps to procure a divorce. It was certain that Minna had stayed for some time at a hotel in Hamburg with that ill-omened man, Herr Dietrich, and that she had spread abroad the story of our separation so unreservedly that the theatrical world in particular had discussed it in a manner that was positively insulting to me. I simply informed Amalie of this, and requested her to spare me any further news of her sister.

Hereupon Minna herself appealed to me, and wrote me a positively heartrending letter, in which she openly confessed her infidelity. She declared that she had been driven to it by despair, but that the great trouble she had thus brought upon herself having taught her a lesson, all she now wished was to return to the right path. Taking everything into account, I concluded that she had been deceived in the character of her seducer, and the knowledge of her terrible position had placed her both morally and physically in a most lamentable con-dition, in which, now ill and wretched, she turned to me again to acknowledge her guilt, crave my forgiveness, and assure me, in spite of all, that she had now become fully aware of her love for me. Never before had I heard such sentiments from Minna, nor was I ever to hear the same from her again, save on one touching occasion many years later, when similar outpourings moved and affected me in the same way as this particular letter had done. In reply I told her that there should never again be any mention between us of what had occurred, for which I took upon myself the chief blame; and I can pride myself on having carried out this resolution to the letter.

When her sister's engagement was satisfactorily settled, I at once invited Minna to come to Riga with her. Both gladly accepted my invitation, and arrived from Dresden at my new home on 19th October, wintry weather having already set in. With much regret I perceived that Minna's health had really suffered, and therefore did all in my power to provide her with all the domestic comforts and quiet she needed. This pre-sented difficulties, for my modest income as a conductor was all I had at my disposal, and we were both firmly determined not to let Minna go on the stage again. On the other hand, the carrying out of this resolve, in view of the financial incon-

venience it entailed, produced strange complications, the nature
of which was only revealed to me later, when startling developments divulged the real moral character of the manager Holtei.
For the present I had to let people think that I was jealous of
my wife. I bore patiently with the general belief that I had
good reasons to be so, and rejoiced meanwhile at the restoration of our peaceful married life, and especially at the sight of
our humble home, which we made as comfortable as our means
would allow, and in the keeping of which Minna's domestic
talents came strongly to the fore. As we were still childless,
and were obliged as a rule to enlist the help of a dog in order
to give life to the domestic hearth, we once lighted upon the
eccentric idea of trying our luck with a young wolf which was
brought into the house as a tiny cub. When we found, however, that this experiment did not increase the comfort of our
home life, we gave him up after he had been with us a few
weeks. We fared better with sister Amalie; for she, with her
good-nature and simple homely ways, did much to make up
for the absence of children for a time. The two sisters, neither
of whom had had any real education, often returned playfully
to the ways of their childhood. When they sang children's
duets, Minna, though she had had no musical training, always
managed very cleverly to sing seconds, and afterwards, as we
sat at our evening meal, eating Russian salad, salt salmon from
the Dwina, or fresh Russian caviare, we were all three very
cheerful and happy far away in our northern home.

Amalie's beautiful voice and real vocal talent at first won
for her a very favourable reception with the public, a fact
which did us all a great deal of good. Being, however, very
short, and having no very great gift for acting, the scope of
her powers was very limited, and as she was soon surpassed
by more successful competitors, it was a real stroke of good
luck for her that a young officer in the Russian army, then
Captain, now General, Carl von Meck, fell head over ears in
love with the simple girl, and married her a year later. The
unfortunate part of this engagement, however, was that it
caused many difficulties, and brought the first cloud over our
ménage à trois. For, after a while, the two sisters quarrelled
bitterly, and I had the very unpleasant experience of living

for a whole year in the same house with two relatives who neither saw nor spoke to each other.

We spent the winter at the beginning of 1838 in a very small dingy dwelling in the old town; it was not till the spring that we moved into a pleasanter house in the more salubrious Petersburg suburb, where, in spite of the sisterly breach before referred to, we led a fairly bright and cheerful life, as we were often able to entertain many of our friends and acquaintances in a simple though pleasant fashion. In addition to members of the stage I knew a few people in the town, and we received and visited the family of Dorn, the musical director, with whom I became quite intimate. But it was the second musical director, Franz Löbmann, a very worthy though not a very gifted man, who became most faithfully attached to me. However, I did not cultivate many acquaintances in wider circles, and they grew fewer as the ruling passion of my life grew steadily stronger; so that when, later on, I left Riga, after spending nearly two years there, I departed almost as a stranger, and with as much indifference as I had left Magdeburg and Königsberg. What, however, specially embittered my departure was a series of experiences of a particularly disagreeable nature, which firmly determined me to cut myself off entirely from the necessity of mixing with any people like those I had met with in my previous attempts to create a position for myself at the theatre.

Yet it was only gradually that I became quite conscious of all this. At first, under the safe guidance of my renewed wedded happiness, which had for a time been so disturbed in its early days, I felt distinctly better than I had before in all my professional work. The fact that the material position of the theatrical undertaking was assured exercised a healthy influence on the performances. The theatre itself was cooped up in a very narrow space; there was as little room for scenic display on its tiny stage as there was accommodation for rich musical effects in the cramped orchestra. In both directions the strictest limits were imposed, yet I contrived to introduce considerable reinforcements into an orchestra which was really only calculated for a string quartette, two first and two second violins, two violas, and one 'cello. These successful exertions of mine were the first cause of the dislike Holtei evinced towards me later on. After this we were able to get good concerted music for the opera. I found the thorough study of Méhul's opera, *Joseph in Aegypten*, very stimulating. Its noble and simple style, added to the touching effect of the music, which quite carries one away, did much towards effecting a favourable change in my taste, till then warped by my connection with the theatre.

It was most gratifying to feel my former serious taste again aroused by really good dramatic performances. I specially remember a production of *King Lear*, which I followed with the greatest interest, not only at the actual performances, but at all the rehearsals as well. Yet these educative impressions tended to make me feel ever more and more dissatisfied with my work at the theatre. On the one hand, the members of the company became gradually more distasteful to me, and on the other I was growing discontented with the management. With regard to the staff of the theatre, I very soon found out the hollowness, vanity, and the impudent selfishness of this uncultured and undisciplined class of people, for I had now lost my former liking for the Bohemian life that had such an attraction for me at Magdeburg. Before long there were but a few members of our company with whom I had not quarrelled, thanks to one or the other of these drawbacks. But my saddest experience was, that in such disputes, into which in fact I was led simply by my zeal for the artistic success of the performances as a whole, not only did I receive no support from Holtei, the director, but I actually made him my enemy. He even declared publicly that our theatre had become far too respectable for his taste, and tried to convince me that good theatrical performances could not be given by a strait-laced company.

In his opinion the idea of the dignity of theatrical art was pedantic nonsense, and he thought light serio-comic vaudeville the only class of performance worth considering. Serious opera, rich musical *ensemble*, was his particular aversion, and my demands for this irritated him so that he met them only with scorn and indignant refusals. Of the strange connection between this artistic bias and his taste in the domain of morality I was also to become aware, to my horror, in due course. For the present I felt so repelled by the declaration of his artistic antipathies, as to let my dislike for the theatre as a profession steadily grow upon me. I still took pleasure in some good performances which I was able to get up, under favourable circumstances, at the larger theatre at Mitau, to where the company went for a time in the early part of the summer. Yet it was while I was there, spending most of my time reading Bulwer Lytton's novels, that I made a secret resolve to try hard to free myself from all connection with the only branch of theatrical art which had so far been open to me.

The composition of my *Rienzi,* the text of which I had finished in the early days of my sojourn in Riga, was destined to bridge me over to the glorious world for which I had longed so intensely. I had laid aside the completion of my *Glückliche Bärenfamilie,* for the simple reason that the lighter character of this piece would have thrown me more into contact with the very theatrical people I most despised. My greatest consolation now was to prepare *Rienzi* with such an utter disregard of the means which were available there for its production, that my desire to produce it would force me out of the narrow confines of this puny theatrical circle to seek a fresh connection with one of the larger theatres. It was after our return from Mitau, in the middle of the summer of 1838, that I set to work on this composition, and by so doing roused myself to a state of enthusiasm which, considering my position, was nothing less than desperate dare-devilry. All to whom I confided my plan perceived at once, on the mere mention of my subject, that I was preparing to break away from my present position, in which there could be no possibility of producing my work, and I was looked upon as light-headed and fit only for an asylum.

To all my acquaintances my procedure seemed stupid and reckless. Even the former patron of my peculiar Leipzig overture thought it impracticable and eccentric, seeing that I had again turned my back on light opera. He expressed this opinion very freely in the *Neue Zeitschrift für Musik,* in a report of a concert I had given towards the end of the previous winter, and openly ridiculed the Magdeburg *Columbus* Overture and the *Rule Britannia* Overture previously mentioned. I myself had not taken any pleasure in the performance of either of these overtures, as my predilection for cornets, strongly marked in both these overtures, again played me a sorry trick, as I had evidently expected too much of our Riga musicians, and had to endure all kinds of disappointment on the occasion of the performance. As a complete contrast to my extravagant setting of *Rienzi,* this same director, H. Dorn, had set to work to write an opera in which he had most carefully borne in mind the conditions obtaining at the Riga theatre. *Der Schöffe von Paris,* an historical operetta of the period of the siege of Paris by Joan of Arc, was practised and performed by us to the complete satisfaction of the composer. However, the success of this work gave me no reason for abandoning my project to complete my *Rienzi,* and I was secretly pleased to find that I could regard this success without a trace of envy. Though animated by no feeling of rivalry, I gradually gave up associating with the Riga artists, confining myself chiefly to the performance of the duties I had undertaken, and worked away at the two first acts of my big opera without troubling myself at all whether I should ever get so far as to see it produced.

The serious and bitter experiences I had had so early in life had done much to guide me towards that intensely earnest side of my nature that had manifested itself in my earliest youth. The effect of these bitter experiences was now to be still further emphasised by other sad impressions. Not long after Minna had rejoined me, I received from home the news of the death of my sister Rosalie. It was the first time in my life that I had experienced the passing away of one near and dear to me. The death of this sister struck me as a most cruel and significant blow of fate; it was out of love and respect for her that I had turned away so resolutely from my youthful excesses, and it was to gain her sympathy that I had devoted special thought and care to my first great works. When the passions and cares of life had come upon me and driven me away from my home, it was she who had read deep down into my sorely stricken heart, and who had bidden me that anxious farewell on my departure from Leipzig. At the time of my disappearance, when the news of my wilful marriage and of my consequent unfortunate position reached my family, it was she who, as my mother informed me later, never lost her faith in me, but who always cherished the hope that I would one day reach the full development of my capabilities and make a genuine success of my life.

Now, at the news of her death, and illuminated by the recollection of that one impressive farewell, as by a flash of lightning I saw the immense value my relations with this sister had been to me, and I did not fully realise the extent of her influence until later on, when, after my first striking successes, my mother tearfully lamented that Rosalie had not lived to witness them. It really did me good to be again in communication with my family. My mother and sisters had had news of my doings somehow or other, and I was deeply touched, in the letters which I was now receiving from them, to hear no reproaches anent my headstrong and apparently heartless behaviour, but only sympathy and heartfelt solicitude. My family had also received favourable reports about my wife's good qualities, a fact about which I was particularly glad, as I was thus spared the difficulties of defending her questionable behaviour to me, which I should have been at pains to excuse. This produced a salutary calm in my soul, which had so recently been a prey to the worst anxieties. All that had driven me with such passionate haste to an improvident and premature marriage, all that had consequently weighed on me so ruinously, now seemed set at rest, leaving peace in its stead. And although the ordinary cares of life still pressed on me for many years, often in a most vexatious and troublesome form, yet the anxieties attendant on my ardent youthful wishes were in a manner subdued and calm. From thence forward till the attainment of my professional independence, all my life's struggles could be directed entirely towards that more ideal aim which, from the time of the conception of my *Rienzi,* was to be my only guide through life.

It was only later that I first realised the real character of my life in Riga, from the utterance of one of its inhabitants, who was astonished to learn of the success of a man of whose importance, during the whole of his two years' sojourn in the small capital of Livonia, nothing had been known. Thrown entirely on my own resources, I was a stranger to every one. As I mentioned before, I kept aloof from all the theatre folk, in consequence of my increasing dislike of them, and therefore, when at the end of March, 1839, at the close of my second winter there, I was given my dismissal by the management, although this occurrence surprised me for other reasons, yet I felt fully reconciled to this compulsory change in my life. The reasons which led to this dismissal were, however, of such a nature that I could only regard it as one of the most disagreeable experiences of my life. Once, when I was lying dangerously ill, I heard of Holtei's real feelings towards me. I had caught a severe cold in the depth of winter at a theatrical rehearsal, and it at once assumed a serious character, owing to the fact that my nerves were in a state of constant irritation from the continual annoyance and vexatious worry caused by the contemptible character of the theatrical management. It was just at the time when a special performance of the opera *Norma* was to be given by our company in Mitau. Holtei insisted on my getting up from a sick-bed to make this wintry journey, and thus to expose myself to the danger of seriously increasing my cold in the icy theatre at Mitau. Typhoid fever was the consequence, and this pulled me down to such an extent that Holtei, who heard of my condition, is said to have remarked at the theatre that I should probably never conduct again, and that, to all intents and purposes, ' I was on my last legs.' It was to a splendid homœopathic physician, Dr. Prutzer, that I owed my recovery and my life. Not long after that Holtei left our theatre and Riga for ever; his occupation there, with ' the far too respectable conditions,' as he expressed it, had become intolerable to him. In addition, however, circumstances had arisen in his domestic life (which had been much affected by the death of his wife) which seemed to make him consider a complete break with Riga eminently desirable. But to my astonishment I now first became aware that I too had unconsciously been a sufferer from the troubles he had brought upon himself. When Holtei's successor in the management — Joseph Hoffmann the singer — informed me that his predecessor had made it a condition to his taking over the post that he should enter into the same engagement that Holtei had made with the conductor Dorn for the post which I had hitherto filled, and my reappointment had therefore been made an

impossibility, my wife met my astonishment at this news by
giving me the reason, of which for some considerable time past
she had been well aware, namely, Holtei's special dislike of
us both. When I was afterwards informed by Minna of what
had happened — she having purposely kept it from me all this
time, so as not to cause bad feeling between me and my director — a ghastly light was thrown upon the whole affair. I
did indeed remember perfectly how, soon after Minna's arrival
in Riga, I had been particularly pressed by Holtei not to prevent my wife's engagement at the theatre. I asked him to
talk things quietly over with her, so that he might see that
Minna's unwillingness rested on a mutual understanding, and
not on any jealousy on my part. I had intentionally given him
the time when I was engaged at the theatre on rehearsals for
the necessary discussions with my wife. At the end of these
meetings I had, on my return, often found Minna in a very
excited condition, and at length she declared emphatically that
under no circumstances would she accept the engagement offered by Holtei. I had also noticed in Minna's demeanour
towards me a strange anxiety to know why I was not unwilling
to allow Holtei to try to persuade her. Now that the catastrophe had occurred, I learned that Holtei had in fact used
these interviews for making improper advances to my wife,
the nature of which I only realised with difficulty on further
acquaintance with this man's peculiarities, and after having
heard of other instances of a similar nature. I then discovered
that Holtei considered it an advantage to get himself talked
about in connection with pretty women, in order thus to divert
the attention of the public from other conduct even more dis-
reputable. After this Minna was exceedingly indignant at
Holtei, who, finding his own suit rejected, appeared as the
medium for another suitor, on whose behalf he urged that he
would think none the worse of her for rejecting him, a grey-
haired and penniless man, but at the same time advocated the
suit of Brandenburg, a very wealthy and handsome young
merchant. His fierce indignation at this double repulse, his
humiliation at having revealed his real nature to no purpose,
seems, to judge from Minna's observations, to have been exceedingly great. I now understood too well that his frequent and

profoundly contemptuous sallies against respectable actors and actresses had not been mere spirited exaggerations, but that he had probably often had to complain of being put thoroughly to shame on this account.

The fact that the playing of such criminal parts as the one he had had in view with my wife was unable to divert the ever-increasing attention of the outside world from his vicious and dissolute habits, does not seem to have escaped him; for those behind the scenes told me candidly that it was owing to the fear of very unpleasant revelations that he had suddenly decided to give up his position at Riga altogether. Even in much later years I heard about Holtei's bitter dislike of me, a dislike which showed itself, among other things, in his denunciation of *The Music of the Future*,[1] and of its tendency to jeopardise the simplicity of pure sentiment. I have previously mentioned that he displayed so much personal animosity against me during the latter part of the time we were together in Riga that he vented his hostility upon me in every possible way. Up to that time I had felt inclined to ascribe it to the divergence of our respective views on artistic points.

To my dismay I now became aware that personal considerations alone were at the bottom of all this, and I blushed to realise that by my former unreserved confidence in a man whom I thought was absolutely honest, I had based my knowledge of human nature on such very weak foundations. But still greater was my disappointment when I discovered the real character of my friend H. Dorn. During the whole time of our intercourse at Riga, he, who formerly treated me more like a good-natured elder brother, had become my most confidential friend. We saw and visited each other almost daily, very frequently in our respective homes. I kept not a single secret from him, and the performance of his *Schöffe von Paris* under my direction was as successful as if it had been under his own. Now, when I heard that my post had been given to him, I felt obliged to ask him about it, in order to learn whether there was any mistake on his part as to my intention regarding the position I had hitherto held. But from his letter in reply

[1] *Zukunftsmusik* is a pamphlet revealing some of Wagner's artistic aims and aspirations, written 1860–61. — EDITOR.

I could clearly see that Dorn had really made use of Holtei's dislike for me to extract from him, before his departure, an arrangement which was both binding on his successor and also in his (Dorn's) own favour. As my friend he ought to have known that he could benefit by this agreement only in the event of my resigning my appointment in Riga, because in our confidential conversations, which continued to the end, he always carefully refrained from touching on the possibility of my going away or remaining. In fact, he declared that Holtei had distinctly told him he would on no account re-engage me, as I could not get on with the singers. He added that after this one could not take it amiss if he, who had been inspired with fresh enthusiasm for the theatre by the success of his *Schöffe von Paris*, had seized and turned to his own advantage the chance offered to him. Moreover, he had gathered from my confidential communications that I was very awkwardly situated, and that, owing to my small salary having been cut down by Holtei from the very beginning, I was in a very precarious position on account of the demands of my creditors in Königsberg and Magdeburg. It appeared that these people had employed against me a lawyer, who was a friend of Dorn's, and that, consequently, he had come to the conclusion that I would not be able to remain in Riga. Therefore, even as my friend, he had felt his conscience quite clear in accepting Holtei's proposal.

In order not to leave him in the complacent enjoyment of this self-deception, I put it clearly before him that he could not be ignorant of the fact that a higher salary had been promised to me for the third year of my contract; and that, by the establishment of orchestral concerts, which had already made a favourable start, I now saw my way to getting free from those long-standing debts, having already overcome the difficulties of the removal and settling down. I also asked him how he would act if I saw it was to my own interest to retain my post, and to call on him to resign his agreement with Holtei, who, as a matter of fact, after his departure from Riga, had withdrawn his alleged reason for my dismissal. To this I received no answer, nor have I had one up to the present day; but, on the other hand, in 1865, I was astonished to see

Dorn enter my house in Munich unannounced, and when to his joy I recognised him, he stepped up to me with a gesture which clearly showed his intention of embracing me. Although I managed to evade this, yet I soon saw the difficulty of preventing him from addressing me with the familiar form of 'thou,' as the attempt to do so would have necessitated explanations that would have been a useless addition to all my worries just then; for it was the time when my *Tristan* was being produced.

Such a man was Heinrich Dorn. Although, after the failure of three operas, he had retired in disgust from the theatre to devote himself exclusively to the commercial side of music, yet the success of his opera, *Der Schöffe von Paris,* in Riga helped him back to a permanent place among the dramatic musicians of Germany. But to this position he was first dragged from obscurity, across the bridge of infidelity to his friend, and by the aid of virtue in the person of Director Holtei, thanks to a magnanimous oversight on the part of Franz Listz. The preference of King Friedrich Wilhelm IV. for church scenes contributed to secure him eventually his important position at the greatest lyric theatre in Germany, the Royal Opera of Berlin. For he was prompted far less by his devotion to the dramatic muse than by his desire to secure a good position in some important German city, when, as already hinted, through Liszt's recommendation he was appointed musical director of Cologne Cathedral. During a fête connected with the building of the cathedral he managed, as a musician, so to work upon the Prussian monarch's religious feelings, that he was appointed to the dignified post of musical conductor at the Royal Theatre, in which capacity he long continued to do honour to German dramatic music in conjunction with Wilhelm Taubert.

I must give J. Hoffmann, who from this time forward was the manager of the Riga theatre, the credit of having felt the treachery practised upon me very deeply indeed. He told me that his contract with Dorn bound him only for one year, and that the moment the twelve months had elapsed he wished to come to a fresh agreement with me. As soon as this was known, my patrons in Riga came forward with offers of teaching engagements and arrangements for sundry concerts, by way of compensating me for the year's salary which I should lose by being away from my work as a conductor. Though I was much gratified by these offers, yet, as I have already pointed out, the longing to break loose from the kind of theatrical life which I had experienced up to that time so possessed me that I resolutely seized this chance of abandoning my former vocation for an entirely new one. Not without some shrewdness, I played upon my wife's indignation at the treachery I had suffered, in order to make her fall in with my eccentric notion of going to Paris. Already in my conception of *Rienzi* I had dreamed of the most magnificent theatrical conditions, but now, without halting at any intermediate stations, my one desire was to reach the very heart of all European grand opera. While still in Magdeburg I had made H. König's romance, *Die Hohe Braut,* the subject of a grand opera in five acts, and in the most luxurious French style. After the scenic draft of this opera, which had been translated into French, was completely worked out, I sent it from Königsberg to Scribe in Paris. With this manuscript I sent a letter to the famous operatic poet, in which I suggested that he might make use of my plot, on condition that he would secure me the composition of the music for the Paris Opera House. To convince him of my ability to compose Parisian operatic music, I also sent him the score of my *Liebesverbot.* At the same time I wrote to Meyerbeer, informing him of my plans, and begging him to support me. I was not at all disheartened at receiving no reply, for I was content to know that now at last ' I was in communication with Paris.' When, therefore, I started out upon my daring journey from Riga, I seemed to have a comparatively serious object in view, and my Paris projects no longer struck me as being altogether in the air. In addition to this I now heard that my youngest sister, Cecilia, had become betrothed to a certain Eduard Avenarius, an employee of the Brockhaus book-selling firm, and that he had undertaken the management of their Paris branch. To him I applied for news of Scribe, and for an answer to the application I had made to that gentleman some years previously. Avenarius called on Scribe, and from him received an acknowledgment of the receipt of my earlier communication. Scribe also showed that he had some recollection of the subject itself; for he said that, so far as he could remember, there was a *joueuse de harpe* in the piece, who was ill-treated by her brother. The fact that this merely incidental item had alone remained in his memory led me to conclude that he had not extended his acquaintance with the piece beyond the first act, in which the item in question occurs. When, moreover, I heard that he had nothing to say in regard to my score, except that he had had portions of it played over to him by a pupil of the Conservatoire, I really could not flatter myself that he had entered into definite and conscious relations with me. And yet I had palpable evidence in a letter of his to Avenarius, which the latter forwarded to me, that Scribe had actually occupied himself with my work, and that I was indeed in communication with him, and this letter of Scribe's made such an impression upon my wife, who was by no means inclined to be sanguine, that she gradually overcame her apprehensions in regard to the Paris adventure. At last it was fixed and settled that on the expiry of my second year's contract in Riga (that is to say, in the coming summer, 1839), we should journey direct from Riga to Paris, in order that I might try my luck there as a composer of opera.

The production of my *Rienzi* now began to assume greater importance. The composition of its second act was finished before we started, and into this I wove a heroic ballet of extravagant dimensions. It was now imperative that I should speedily acquire a knowledge of French, a language which, during my classical studies at the Grammar School, I had contemptuously laid aside. As there were only four weeks in which to recover the time I had lost, I engaged an excellent French master. But as I soon realised that I could achieve but little in so short a time, I utilised the hours of the lessons in order to obtain from him, under the pretence of receiving instruction, an idiomatic translation of my *Rienzi* libretto. This I wrote with red ink on such parts of the score as were finished, so that on reaching Paris I might immediately submit my half-finished opera to French judges of art.

Everything now seemed to be carefully prepared for my

departure, and all that remained to be done was to raise the necessary funds for my undertaking. But in this respect the outlook was bad. The sale of our modest household furniture, the proceeds of a benefit concert, and my meagre savings only sufficed to satisfy the importunate demands of my creditors in Magdeburg and Königsberg. I knew that if I were to devote all my cash to this purpose, there would not be a farthing left. Some way out of the fix must be found, and this our old Königsberg friend, Abraham Möller, suggested in his usual flippant and obscure manner. Just at this critical moment he paid us a second visit to Riga. I acquainted him with the difficulties of our position, and all the obstacles which stood in the way of my resolve to go to Paris. In his habitual laconical way he counselled me to reserve all my savings for our journey, and to settle with my creditors when my Parisian successes had provided the necessary means. To help us in carrying out this plan, he offered to convey us in his carriage across the Russian frontier at top speed to an East Prussian port. We should have to cross the Russian frontier without passports, as these had been already impounded by our foreign creditors. He assured us that we should find it quite simple to carry out this very hazardous expedition, and declared that he had a friend on a Prussian estate close to the frontier who would render us very effective assistance. My eagerness to escape at any price from my previous circumstances, and to enter with all possible speed upon the wider field, in which I hoped very soon to realise my ambition, blinded me to all the unpleasantnesses which the execution of his proposal must entail. Director Hoffmann, who considered himself bound to serve me to the utmost of his ability, facilitated my departure by allowing me to leave some months before the expiration of my engagement. After continuing to conduct the operatic portion of the Mitau theatrical season through the month of June, we secretly started in a special coach hired by Möller and under his protection. The goal of our journey was Paris, but many unheard-of hardships were in store for us before we were to reach that city.

The sense of contentment involuntarily aroused by our passage through the fruitful Courland in the luxuriant month of July, and by the sweet illusion that now at last I had cut myself loose from a hateful existence, to enter upon a new and boundless path of fortune, was disturbed from its very outset by the miserable inconveniences occasioned by the presence of a huge Newfoundland dog called Robber. This beautiful creature, originally the property of a Riga merchant, had, contrary to the nature of his race, become devotedly attached to me. After I had left Riga, and during my long stay in Mitau, Robber incessantly besieged my empty house, and so touched the hearts of my landlord and the neighbours by his fidelity, that they sent the dog after me by the conductor of the coach to Mitau, where I greeted him with genuine effusion, and swore that, in spite of all difficulties, I would never part with him again. Whatever might happen, the dog must go with us to Paris. And yet, even to get him into the carriage proved almost impossible. All my endeavours to find him a place in or about the vehicle were in vain, and, to my great grief, I had to watch the huge northern beast, with his shaggy coat, gallop all day long in the blazing sun beside the carriage. At last, moved to pity by his exhaustion, and unable to bear the sight any longer, I hit upon a most ingenious plan for bringing the great animal with us into the carriage, where, in spite of its being full to overflowing, he was just able to find room.

On the evening of the second day we reached the Russo-Prussian frontier. Möller's evident anxiety as to whether we should be able to cross it safely showed us plainly that the matter was one of some danger. His good friend from the other side duly turned up with a small carriage, as arranged, and in this conveyance drove Minna, myself, and Robber through by-paths to a certain point, whence he led us on foot to a house of exceedingly suspicious exterior, where, after handing us over to a guide, he left us. There we had to wait until sundown, and had ample leisure in which to realise that we were in a smugglers' drinking den, which gradually became filled to suffocation with Polish Jews of most forbidding aspect.

At last we were summoned to follow our guide. A few hundred feet away, on the slope of a hill, lay the ditch which runs the whole length of the Russian frontier, watched continu-

ally and at very narrow intervals by Cossacks. Our chance
was to utilise the few moments after the relief of the watch,
during which the sentinels were elsewhere engaged. We had,
therefore, to run at full speed down the hill, scramble through
the ditch, and then hurry along until we were beyond the
range of the soldiers' guns; for the Cossacks were bound in
case of discovery to fire upon us even on the other side of the
ditch. In spite of my almost passionate anxiety for Minna,
I had observed with singular pleasure the intelligent behaviour
of Robber, who, as though conscious of the danger, silently
kept close to our side, and entirely dispelled my fear that he
would give trouble during our dangerous passage. At last our
trusted helpmeet reappeared, and was so delighted that he
hugged us all in his arms. Then, placing us once more in his
carriage, he drove us to the inn of the Prussian frontier village,
where my friend Möller, positively sick with anxiety, leaped
sobbing and rejoicing out of bed to greet us.

It was only now that I began to realise the danger to which
I had exposed, not only myself, but also my poor Minna, and
the folly of which I had been guilty through my ignorance of
the terrible difficulties of secretly crossing the frontier — difficulties concerning which Möller had foolishly allowed me to
remain in ignorance.

I was simply at a loss to convey to my poor exhausted wife
how extremely I regretted the whole affair.

And yet the difficulties we had just overcome were but the
prelude to the calamities incidental to this adventurous journey
which had such a decisive influence on my life. The following
day, when, with courage renewed, we drove through the rich
plain of Tilsit to Arnau, near Königsberg, we decided, as the
next stage of our journey, to proceed from the Prussian harbour
of Pillau by sailing vessel to London. Our principal reason for
this was the consideration of the dog we had with us. It was
the easiest way to take him. To convey him by coach from
Königsberg to Paris was out of the question, and railways were
unknown. But another consideration was our budget; the
whole result of my desperate efforts amounted to not quite
one hundred ducats, which were to cover not only the journey
to Paris, but our expenses there until I should have earned

something. Therefore, after a few days' rest in the inn at Arnau, we drove to the little seaport town of Pillau, again accompanied by Möller, in one of the ordinary local conveyances, which was not much better than a wagon. In order to avoid Königsberg, we passed through the smaller villages and over bad roads. Even this short distance was not to be covered without accident. The clumsy conveyance upset in a farmyard, and Minna was so severely indisposed by the accident, owing to an internal shock, that I had to drag her — with the greatest difficulty, as she was quite helpless — to a peasant's house. The people were surly and dirty, and the night we spent there was a painful one for the poor sufferer. A delay of several days occurred before the departure of the Pillau vessel, but this was welcome as a respite to allow of Minna's recovery. Finally, as the captain was to take us without a passport, our going on board was accompanied by exceptional difficulties. We had to contrive to slip past the harbour watch to our vessel in a small boat before daybreak. Once on board, we still had the troublesome task of hauling Robber up the steep side of the vessel without attracting attention, and after that to conceal ourselves at once below deck, in order to escape the notice of officials visiting the ship before its departure. The anchor was weighed, and at last, as the land faded gradually out of sight, we thought we could breathe freely and feel at ease.

We were on board a merchant vessel of the smallest type. She was called the *Thetis;* a bust of the nymph was erected in the bows, and she carried a crew of seven men, including the captain. With good weather, such as was to be expected in summer, the journey to London was estimated to take eight days. However, before we had left the Baltic, we were delayed by a prolonged calm. I made use of the time to improve my knowledge of French by the study of a novel, *La Dernière Aldini,* by George Sand. We also derived some entertainment from associating with the crew. There was an elderly and peculiarly taciturn sailor named Koske, whom we observed carefully because Robber, who was usually so friendly, had taken an irreconcilable dislike to him. Oddly enough, this fact was to add in some degree to our troubles in the hour of danger. After seven days' sailing we were no further than

Copenhagen, where, without leaving the vessel, we seized an opportunity of making our very spare diet on board more bearable by various purchases of food and drink. In good spirits we sailed past the beautiful castle of Elsinore, the sight of which brought me into immediate touch with my youthful impressions of *Hamlet*. We were sailing all unsuspecting through the Cattegat to the Skagerack, when the wind, which had at first been merely unfavourable, and had forced us to a process of weary tacking, changed on the second day to a violent storm. For twenty-four hours we had to struggle against it under disadvantages which were quite new to us. In the captain's painfully narrow cabin, in which one of us was without a proper berth, we were a prey to sea-sickness and endless alarms. Unfortunately, the brandy cask, at which the crew fortified themselves during their strenuous work, was let into a hollow under the seat on which I lay at full length. Now it happened to be Koske who came most frequently in search of the refreshment which was such a nuisance to me, and this in spite of the fact that on each occasion he had to encounter Robber in mortal combat. The dog flew at him with renewed rage each time he came climbing down the narrow steps. I was thus compelled to make efforts which, in my state of complete exhaustion from sea-sickness, rendered my condition every time more critical. At last, on 27th July, the captain was compelled by the violence of the west wind to seek a harbour on the Norwegian coast. And how relieved I was to behold that far-reaching rocky coast, towards which we were being driven at such speed! A Norwegian pilot came to meet us in a small boat, and, with experienced hand, assumed control of the *Thetis*, whereupon in a very short time I was to have one of the most marvellous and most beautiful impressions of my life. What I had taken to be a continuous line of cliffs turned out on our approach to be a series of separate rocks projecting from the sea. Having sailed past them, we perceived that we were surrounded, not only in front and at the sides, but also at our back, by these reefs, which closed in behind us so near together that they seemed to form a single chain of rocks. At the same time the hurricane was so broken by the rocks in our rear that the further we sailed through this

ever-changing labyrinth of projecting rocks, the calmer the
sea became, until at last the vessel's progress was perfectly
smooth and quiet as we entered one of those long sea-roads
running through a giant ravine — for such the Norwegian
fjords appeared to me.

A feeling of indescribable content came over me when the
enormous granite walls echoed the hail of the crew as they cast
anchor and furled the sails. The sharp rhythm of this call
clung to me like an omen of good cheer, and shaped itself
presently into the theme of the seamen's song in my *Fliegender Holländer*. The idea of this opera was, even at that
time, ever present in my mind, and it now took on a definite
poetic and musical colour under the influence of my recent impressions. Well, our next move was to go on shore. I learned
that the little fishing village at which we landed was called Sand-
wike, and was situated a few miles away from the much larger
town of Arendal. We were allowed to put up at the hospitable
house of a certain ship's captain, who was then away at sea, and
here we were able to take the rest we so much needed, as the
unabated violence of the wind in the open detained us there
two days. On 31st July the captain insisted on leaving, despite the pilot's warning. We had been on board the *Thetis*
a few hours, and were in the act of eating a lobster for the
first time in our lives, when the captain and the sailors began
to swear violently at the pilot, whom I could see at the helm,
rigid with fear, striving to avoid a reef — barely visible above
the water — towards which our ship was being driven. Great
was our terror at this violent tumult, for we naturally thought
ourselves in the most extreme danger. The vessel did actually
receive a severe shock, which, to my vivid imagination, seemed
like the splitting up of the whole ship. Fortunately, however,
it transpired that only the side of our vessel had fouled the
reef, and there was no immediate danger. Nevertheless, the
captain deemed it necessary to steer for a harbour to have the
vessel examined, and we returned to the coast and anchored
at another point. The captain then offered to take us in a small
boat with two sailors to Tromsond, a town of some importance
situated at a few hours' distance, where he had to invite the
harbour officials to examine his ship. This again proved a most

attractive and impressive excursion. The view of one fjord in particular, which extended far inland, worked on my imagination like some unknown, awe-inspiring desert. This impression was intensified, during a long walk from Tromsond up to the plateau, by the terribly depressing effect of the dun moors, bare of tree or shrub, boasting only a covering of scanty moss, which stretch away to the horizon, and merge imperceptibly into the gloomy sky. It was long after dark when we returned from this trip in our little boat, and my wife was very anxious. The next morning (1st August), reassured as to the condition of the vessel, and the wind favouring us, we were able to go to sea without further hindrance.

After four days' calm sailing a strong north wind arose, which drove us at uncommon speed in the right direction. We began to think ourselves nearly at the end of our journey when, on 6th August, the wind changed, and the storm began to rage with unheard-of violence. On the 7th, a Wednesday, at half-past two in the afternoon, we thought ourselves in imminent danger of death. It was not the terrible force with which the vessel was hurled up and down, entirely at the mercy of this sea monster, which appeared now as a fathomless abyss, now as a steep mountain peak, that filled me with mortal dread; my premonition of some terrible crisis was aroused by the despondency of the crew, whose malignant glances seemed superstitiously to point to us as the cause of the threatening disaster. Ignorant of the trifling occasion for the secrecy of our journey, the thought may have occurred to them that our need of escape had arisen from suspicious or even criminal circumstances. The captain himself seemed, in his extreme distress, to regret having taken us on board; for we had evidently brought him ill-luck on this familiar passage — usually a rapid and uncomplicated one, especially in summer. At this particular moment there raged, beside the tempest on the water, a furious thunderstorm overhead, and Minna expressed the fervent wish to be struck by lightning with me rather than to sink, living, into the fearful flood. She even begged me to bind her to me, so that we might not be parted as we sank. Yet another night was spent amid these incessant terrors, which only our extreme exhaustion helped to mitigate.

The following day the storm had subsided; the wind remained unfavourable, but was mild. The captain now tried to find our bearings by means of his astronomical instruments. He complained of the sky, which had been overcast so many days, swore that he would give much for a single glimpse of the sun or the stars, and did not conceal the uneasiness he felt at not being able to indicate our whereabouts with certainty. He consoled himself, however, by following a ship which was sailing some knots ahead in the same direction, and whose movements he observed closely through the telescope. Suddenly he sprang up in great alarm, and gave a vehement order to change our course. He had seen the ship in front go aground on a sand-bank, from which, he asserted, she could not extricate herself; for he now realised that we were near the most dangerous part of the belt of sand-banks bordering the Dutch coast for a considerable distance. By dint of very skilful sailing, we were enabled to keep the opposite course towards the English coast, which we in fact sighted on the evening of 9th August, in the neighbourhood of Southwold. I felt new life come into me when I saw in the far distance the English pilots racing for our ship. As competition is free among pilots on the English coast, they come out as far as possible to meet incoming vessels, even when the risks are very great.

The winner in our case was a powerful grey-haired man, who, after much vain battling with the seething waves, which tossed his light boat away from our ship at each attempt, at last succeeded in boarding the *Thetis*. (Our poor, hardly-used boat still bore the name, although the wooden figure-head of our patron nymph had been hurled into the sea during our first storm in the Cattegat — an ill-omened incident in the eyes of the crew.) We were filled with pious gratitude when this quiet English sailor, whose hands were torn and bleeding from his repeated efforts to catch the rope thrown to him on his approach, took over the rudder. His whole personality impressed us most agreeably, and he seemed to us the absolute guarantee of a speedy deliverance from our terrible afflictions. We rejoiced too soon, however, for we still had before us the perilous passage through the sand-banks off the English coast, where, as I was assured, nearly four hundred ships are wrecked on an average every year. We were fully twenty-four hours (from the evening of the 10th to the 11th of August) amid these sandbanks, fighting a westerly gale, which hindered our progress so seriously that we only reached the mouth of the Thames on the evening of the 12th of August. My wife had, up to that point, been so nervously affected by the innumerable danger signals, consisting chiefly of small guardships painted bright red and provided with bells on account of the fog, that she could not close her eyes, day or night, for the excitement of watching for them and pointing them out to the sailors. I, on the contrary, found these heralds of human proximity and deliverance so consoling that, despite Minna's reproaches, I indulged in a long refreshing sleep. Now that we were anchored in the mouth of the Thames, waiting for daybreak, I found myself in the best of spirits; I dressed, washed, and even shaved myself up on deck near the mast, while Minna and the whole exhausted crew were wrapped in deep slumber. And with deepening interest I watched the growing signs of life in this famous estuary. Our desire for a complete release from our detested confinement led us, after we had sailed a little way up, to hasten our arrival in London by going on board a passing steamer at Gravesend. As we neared the capital, our astonishment steadily increased at the number of ships of all sorts that filled the river, the houses, the streets, the famous docks, and other maritime constructions which lined the banks. When at last we reached London Bridge, this incredibly crowded centre of the greatest city in the world, and set foot on land after our terrible three weeks' voyage, a pleasurable sensation of giddiness overcame us as our legs carried us staggering through the deafening uproar. Robber seemed to be similarly affected, for he whisked round the corners like a mad thing, and threatened to get lost every other minute. But we soon sought safety in a cab, which took us, on our captain's recommendation, to the Horseshoe Tavern, near the Tower, and here we had to make our plans for the conquest of this giant metropolis.

The neighbourhood in which we found ourselves was such that we decided to leave it with all possible haste. A very friendly little hunchbacked Jew from Hamburg suggested

better quarters in the West End, and I remember vividly our
drive there, in one of the tiny narrow cabs then in use, the
journey lasting fully an hour. They were built to carry two
people, who had to sit facing each other, and we therefore had
to lay our big dog crosswise from window to window. The
sights we saw from our whimsical nook surpassed anything
we had imagined, and we arrived at our boarding-house in
Old Compton Street agreeably stimulated by the life and the
overwhelming size of the great city. Although at the age of
twelve I had made what I supposed to be a translation of a
monologue from Shakespeare's *Romeo and Juliet*, I found my
knowledge of English quite inadequate when it came to conversing with the landlady of the King's Arms. But the good
dame's social condition as a sea-captain's widow led her to think
she could talk French to me, and her attempts made me wonder
which of us knew least of that language. And then a most
disturbing incident occurred — we missed Robber, who must
have run away at the door instead of following us into the house.
Our distress at having lost our good dog after having brought
him all the way there with such difficulty occupied us exclusively during the first two hours we spent in this new home
on land. We kept constant watch at the window until, of a
sudden, we joyfully recognised Robber strolling unconcernedly
towards the house from a side street. Afterwards we learned
that our truant had wandered as far as Oxford Street in search
of adventures, and I have always considered his amazing
return to a house which he had not even entered as a strong
proof of the absolute certainty of the animal's instincts in the
matter of memory.

We now had time to realise the tiresome after-effects of the
voyage. The continuous swaying of the floor and our clumsy
efforts to keep from falling we found fairly entertaining; but
when we came to take our well-earned rest in the huge English
double bed, and found that that too rocked up and down, it
became quite unbearable. Every time we closed our eyes we
sank into frightful abysses, and, springing up again, cried out
for help. It seemed as if that terrible voyage would go on
to the end of our lives. Added to this we felt miserably sick;
for, after the atrocious food on board, we had been only too

ready to partake, with less discretion than relish, of tastier fare.

We were so exhausted by all these trials that we forgot to consider what was, after all, the vital question — the probable result in hard cash. Indeed, the marvels of the great city proved so fascinating, that we started off in a cab, for all the world as if we were on a pleasure trip, to follow up a plan I had sketched on my map of London. In our wonder and delight at what we saw, we quite forgot all we had gone through. Costly as it proved, I considered our week's stay justified in view of Minna's need of rest in the first place, and secondly, the excellent opportunity it afforded me of making acquaintances in the musical world. During my last visit to Dresden I had sent *Rule Britannia*, the overture composed at Königsberg, to Sir John Smart, president of the Philharmonic Society. It is true he had never acknowledged it, but I felt it the more incumbent on me to bring him to task about it. I therefore spent some days trying to find out where he lived, wondering meanwhile in which language I should have to make myself understood, but as the result of my inquiries I discovered that Smart was not in London at all. I next persuaded myself that it would be a good thing to look up Bulwer Lytton, and to come to an understanding about the operatic performance of his novel, *Rienzi*, which I had dramatised. Having been told, on the continent, that Bulwer was a member of Parliament, I went to the House, after a few days, to inquire on the spot. My total ignorance of the English language stood me in good stead here, and I was treated with unexpected consideration; for, as none of the lower officials in that vast building could make out what I wanted, I was sent, step by step, to one high dignitary after the other, until at last I was introduced to a distinguished-looking man, who came out of a large hall as we passed, as an entirely unintelligible individual. (Minna was with me all the time; only Robber had been left behind at the King's Arms.) He asked me very civilly what I wanted, in French, and seemed favourably impressed when I inquired for the celebrated author. He was obliged to tell me, however, that he was not in London. I went on to ask whether I could not be admitted to a debate, but was told that, in consequence of the old Houses of Parliament having been burnt down, they were using temporary premises where the space was so limited that only a few favoured visitors could procure cards of admittance. But on my pressing more urgently he relented, and shortly after opened a door leading direct into the strangers' seats in the House of Lords. It seemed reasonable to conclude from this that our friend was a lord in person. I was immensely interested to see and hear the Premier, Lord Melbourne, and Brougham (who seemed to me to take a very active part in the proceedings, prompting Melbourne several times, as I thought), and the Duke of Wellington, who looked so comfortable in his grey beaver hat, with his hands diving deep into his trousers pockets, and who made his speech in so conversational a tone that I lost my feeling of excessive awe. He had a curious way, too, of accenting his points of special emphasis by shaking his whole body. I was also much interested in Lord Lyndhurst, Brougham's particular enemy, and was amazed to see Brougham go across several times to sit down coolly beside him, apparently with a view to prompting even his opponent. The matter in hand was, as I learned afterwards from the papers, the discussion of measures to be taken against the Portuguese Government to ensure the passing of the Anti-Slavery Bill. The Bishop of London, who was one of the speakers on this occasion, was the only one of these gentlemen whose voice and manner seemed to me stiff or unnatural, but possibly I was prejudiced by my dislike of parsons generally.

After this pleasing adventure I imagined I had exhausted the attractions of London for the present, for although I could not gain admittance to the Lower House, my untiring friend, whom I came across again as I went out, showed me the room where the Commons sat, explained as much as was necessary, and gave me a sight of the Speaker's woolsack, and of his mace lying hidden under the table. He also gave me such careful details of various things that I felt I knew all there was to know about the capital of Great Britain. I had not the smallest intention of going to the Italian opera, possibly because I imagined the prices to be too ruinous. We thoroughly explored all the principal streets, often tiring ourselves out; we shuddered through a ghastly London Sunday, and wound up with a train trip (our very first) to Gravesend Park, in the company of the captain of the *Thetis*. On the 20th of August we crossed over to France by steamer, arriving the same evening at Boulogne-sur-mer, where we took leave of the sea with the fervent desire never to go on it again.

We were both of us secretly convinced that we should meet with disappointments in Paris, and it was partly on that account that we decided to spend a few weeks at or near Boulogne. It was, in any case, too early in the season to find the various important people whom I proposed to see, in town; on the other hand, it seemed to me a most fortunate circumstance that Meyerbeer should happen to be at Boulogne. Also, I had the instrumentation of part of the second act of *Rienzi* to finish, and was bent on having at least half of the work ready to show on my arrival in the costly French capital. We therefore set out to find less expensive accommodation in the country round Boulogne. Beginning with the immediate neighbourhood, our search ended in our taking two practically unfurnished rooms in the detached house of a rural wine merchant's, situated on the main road to Paris at half an hour's distance from Boulogne. We next provided scanty but adequate furniture, and in bringing our wits to bear upon this matter Minna particularly distinguished herself. Besides a bed and two chairs, we dug up a table, which, after I had cleared away my *Rienzi* papers, served for our meals, which we had to prepare at our own fireside.

While we were here I made my first call on Meyerbeer. I had often read in the papers of his proverbial amiability, and bore him no ill-will for not replying to my letter. My favourable opinion was soon to be confirmed, however, by his kind reception of me. The impression he made was good in every respect, particularly as regards his appearance. The years had not yet given his features the flabby look which sooner or later mars most Jewish faces, and the fine formation of his brow round about the eyes gave him an expression of countenance that inspired confidence. He did not seem in the least inclined to depreciate my intention of trying my luck in Paris as a

composer of opera; he allowed me to read him my libretto for
Rienzi, and really listened up to the end of the third act. He
kept the two acts that were complete, saying that he wished
to look them over, and assured me, when I again called on him,
of his whole-hearted interest in my work. Be this as it may,
it annoyed me somewhat that he should again and again fall
back on praising my minute handwriting, an accomplishment
he considered especially Saxonian. He promised to give me
letters of recommendation to Duponchel, the manager of the
Opera House, and to Habeneck, the conductor. I now felt
that I had good cause to extol my good fortune which, after
many vicissitudes, had sent me precisely to this particular
spot in France. What better fortune could have befallen me
than to secure, in so short a time, the sympathetic interest of
the most famous composer of French opera! Meyerbeer took
me to see Moscheles, who was then in Boulogne, and also
Fräulein Blahedka, a celebrated virtuoso whose name I had
known for many years. I spent a few informal musical evenings at both houses, and thus came into close touch with musical
celebrities, an experience quite new to me.

I had written to my future brother-in-law, Avernarius, in
Paris, to ask him to find us suitable accommodations, and we
started on our journey thither on 16th September in the diligence, my efforts to hoist Robber on to the top being attended
by the usual difficulties.

My first impression of Paris proved disappointing in view
of the great expectations I had cherished of that city; after
London it seemed to me narrow and confined. I had imagined
the famous boulevards to be much vaster, for instance, and was
really annoyed, when the huge coach put us down in the Rue
de la Juissienne, to think that I should first set foot on Parisian
soil in such a wretched little alley. Neither did the Rue
Richelieu, where my brother-in-law had his book-shop, seem
imposing after the streets in the west end of London. As for
the *chambre garnie,* which had been engaged for me in the Rue
de la Tonnellerie, one of the narrow side-streets which link the
Rue St. Honoré with the Marché des Innocents, I felt positively
degraded at having to take up my abode there. I needed all
the consolation that could be derived from an inscription,

placed under a bust of Molière, which read: *maison où naquit Molière*, to raise my courage after the mean impression the house had first made upon me. The room, which had been prepared for us on the fourth floor, was small but cheerful, decently furnished, and inexpensive. From the windows we could see the frightful bustle in the market below, which became more and more alarming as we watched it, and I wondered what we were doing in such a quarter.

Shortly after this, Avenarius had to go to Leipzig to bring home his bride, my youngest sister Cecilia, after the wedding in that city. Before leaving, he gave me an introduction to his only musical acquaintance, a German holding an appointment in the music department of the *Bibliothèque Royale*, named E. G. Anders, who lost no time in looking us up in Molière's house. He was, as I soon discovered, a man of very unusual character, and, little as he was able to help me, he left an affecting and ineffaceable impression on my memory. He was a bachelor in the fifties, whose reverses had driven him to the sad necessity of earning a living in Paris entirely without assistance. He had fallen back on the extraordinary bibliographical knowledge which, especially in reference to music, it had been his hobby to acquire in the days of his prosperity. His real name he never told me, wishing to guard the secret of that, as of his misfortunes, until after his death. For the time being he told me only that he was known as Anders, was of noble descent, and had held property on the Rhine, but that he had lost everything owing to the villainous betrayal of his gullibility and good-nature. The only thing he had managed to save was his very considerable library, the size of which I was able to estimate for myself. It filled every wall of his small dwelling. Even here in Paris he soon complained of bitter enemies; for, in spite of having come furnished with an introduction to influential people, he still held the inferior position of an employee in the library. In spite of his long service there and his great learning, he had to see really ignorant men promoted over his head. I discovered afterwards that the real reason lay in his unbusinesslike methods, and the effeminacy consequent on the delicate way in which he had been nutured in early life, which made him incapable of developing the energy necessary for his work. On a miserable pittance of fifteen hundred francs a year, he led a weary existence, full of anxiety. With nothing in view but a lonely old age, and the probability of dying in a hospital, it seemed as if our society put new life into him; for though we were poverty-stricken, we looked forward boldly and hopefully to the future. My vivacity and invincible energy filled him with hopes of my success, and from this time forward he took a most tender and unselfish part in furthering my interests. Although he was a contributor to the *Gazette Musicale*, edited by Moritz Schlesinger, he had never succeeded in making his influence felt there in the slightest degree. He had none of the versatility of a journalist, and the editors entrusted him with little besides the preparation of bibliographical notes. Oddly enough, it was with this unworldly and least resourceful of men that I had to discuss my plan for the conquest of Paris, that is, of musical Paris, which is made up of all the most questionable characters imaginable. The result was practically always the same; we merely encouraged each other in the hope that some unforeseen stroke of luck would help my cause.

To assist us in these discussions Anders called in his friend and housemate Lehrs, a philologist, my acquaintance with whom was soon to develop into one of the most beautiful friendships of my life. Lehrs was the younger brother of a famous scholar at Königsberg. He had left there to come to Paris some years before, with the object of gaining an independent position by his philological work. This he preferred, in spite of the attendant difficulties, to a post as teacher with a salary which only in Germany could be considered sufficient for a scholar's wants. He soon obtained work from Didot, the bookseller, as assistant editor of a large edition of Greek classics, but the editor traded on his poverty, and was much more concerned about the success of his enterprise than about the condition of his poor collaborator. Lehrs had therefore perpetually to struggle against poverty, but he preserved an even temper, and showed himself in every way a model of disinterestedness and self-sacrifice. At first he looked upon me only as a man in need of advice, and incidentally a fellow-sufferer in Paris; for he had no knowledge of music, and had no particular interest in it. We soon became so intimate that I had him dropping in nearly every evening with Anders, Lehrs being extremely useful to his friend, whose unsteadiness in walking obliged him to use an umbrella and a walking-stick as crutches. He was also nervous in crossing crowded thorough-fares, and particularly so at night; while he always liked to make Lehrs cross my threshold in front of him to distract the attention of Robber, of whom he stood in obvious terror. Our usually good-natured dog became positively suspicious of this visitor, and soon adopted towards him the same aggressive attitude which he had shown to the sailor Koske on board the *Thetis*. The two men lived at an *hôtel garni* in Rue de Seine. They complained greatly of their landlady, who appropriated so much of their income that they were entirely in her power. Anders had for years been trying to assert his independence by leaving her, without being able to carry out his plan. We soon threw off mutually every shred of disguise as to the present state of our finances, so that, although the two house-holds were actually separated, our common troubles gave us all the intimacy of one united family.

The various ways by which I might obtain recognition in Paris formed the chief topic of our discussions at that time. Our hopes were at first centred on Meyerbeer's promised letters of introduction. Duponchel, the director of the Opera, did actually see me at his office, where, fixing a monocle in his right eye, he read through Meyerbeer's letter without betraying the least emotion, having no doubt opened similar communi-cations from the composer many times before. I went away, and never heard another word from him. The elderly con-ductor, Habeneck, on the other hand, took an interest in my work that was not merely polite, and acceded to my request to have something of mine played at one of the orchestral practises at the Conservatoire as soon as he should have leisure. I had, unfortunately, no short instrumental piece that seemed suitable except my queer *Columbus* Overture, which I considered the most effective of all that had emanated from my pen. It had been received with great applause on the occasion of its per-formance in the theatre at Magdeburg, with the assistance of the valiant trumpeters from the Prussian garrison. I gave

Habeneck the score and parts, and was able to report to our committee at home that I had now one enterprise on foot.

I gave up the attempt to try and see Scribe on the mere ground of our having had some correspondence, for my friends had made it clear to me, in the light of their own experience, that it was out of the question to expect this exceptionally busy author to occupy himself seriously with a young and unknown musician. Anders was able to introduce me to another acquaintance, however, a certain M. Dumersan. This grey-haired gentleman had written some hundred vaudeville pieces, and would have been glad to see one of them performed as an opera on a larger scale before his death. He had no idea of standing on his dignity as an author, and was quite willing to undertake the translation of an existing libretto into French verse. We therefore entrusted him with the writing of my *Liebesverbot*, with a view to a performance at the Théâtre de la Renaissance, as it was then called. (It was the third existing theatre for lyric drama, the performances being given in the new Salle Ventadour, which had been rebuilt after its destruction by fire.) On the understanding that it was to be a literal translation, he at once turned the three numbers of my opera, for which I hoped to secure a hearing, into neat French verse. Besides this, he asked me to compose a chorus for a vaudeville entitled *La Descente de la Courtille,* which was to be played at the Variétés during the carnival.

This was a second opening. My friends now strongly advised me to write something small in the way of songs, which I could offer to popular singers for concert purposes. Both Lehrs and Anders produced words for these. Anders brought a very innocent *Dors, mon enfant,* written by a young poet of his acquaintance; this was the first thing I composed to a French text. It was so successful that, when I had tried it over softly several times on the piano, my wife, who was in bed, called out to me that it was heavenly for sending one to sleep. I also set *L'Attente* from Hugo's *Orientales,* and Ronsard's song, *Mignonne,* to music. I have no reason to be ashamed of these small pieces, which I published subsequently as a musical supplement to *Europa* (Lewald's publication) in 1841.

I next stumbled on the idea of writing a grand bass aria with a chorus, for Lablache to introduce into his part of Orovist in Bellini's *Norma*. Lehrs had to hunt up an Italian political refugee to get the text out of him. This was done, and I produced an effective composition à la Bellini (which still exists among my manuscripts), and went off at once to offer it to Lablache.

The friendly Moor, who received me in the great singer's anteroom, insisted upon admitting me straight into his master's presence without announcing me. As I had anticipated some difficulty in getting near such a celebrity, I had written my request, as I thought this would be simpler than explaining verbally.

The black servant's pleasant manner made me feel very uncomfortable; I entrusted my score and letter to him to give to Lablache, without taking any notice of his kindly astonishment at my refusal of his repeated invitation to go into his master's room and have an interview, and I left the house hurriedly, intending to call for my answer in a few days. When I came back Lablache received me most kindly, and assured me that my aria was excellent, though it was impossible to introduce it into Bellini's opera after the latter had already been performed so very often. My relapse into the domain of Bellini's style, of which I had been guilty through the writing of this aria, was therefore useless to me, and I soon became convinced of the fruitlessness of my efforts in that direction. I saw that I should need personal introductions to various singers in order to ensure the production of one of my other compositions.

When Meyerbeer at last arrived in Paris, therefore, I was delighted. He was not in the least astonished at the lack of success of his letters of introduction; on the contrary, he made use of this opportunity to impress upon me how difficult it was to get on in Paris, and how necessary it was for me to look out for less pretentious work. With this object he introduced me to Maurice Schlesinger, and leaving me at the mercy of that monstrous person, went back to Germany.

At first Schlesinger did not know what to do with me; the acquaintances I made through him (of whom the chief was the violinist Panofka) led to nothing, and I therefore returned to my advisory board at home, through whose influence I had recently received an order to compose the music to the *Two Grenadiers*, by Heine, translated by a Parisian professor. I wrote this song for baritone, and was very pleased with the result; on Ander's advice I now tried to find singers for my new compositions. Mme. Pauline Viardot, on whom I first called, went through my songs with me. She was very amiable, and praised them, but did not see why *she* should sing them. I went through the same experience with a Mme. Widmann, a grand contralto, who sang my *Dors, mon enfant* with great feeling; all the same she had no further use for my composition. A certain M. Dupont, third tenor at the grand opera, tried my setting of the Ronsard poem, but declared that the language in which it was written was no longer palatable to the Paris public. M. Geraldy, a favourite concert singer and teacher, who allowed me to call and see him frequently, told me that the *Two Grenadiers* was impossible, for the simple reason that the accompaniment at the end of the song, which I had modelled upon the *Marseillaise*, could only be sung in the streets of Paris to the accompaniment of cannons and gunshots. Habeneck was the only person who fulfilled his promise to conduct my *Columbus* Overture at one of the rehearsals for the benefit of Anders and myself. As, however, there was no question of producing this work even at one of the celebrated Conservatoire concerts, I saw clearly that the old gentleman was only moved by kindness and a desire to encourage me. It could not lead to anything further, and I myself was convinced that this extremely superficial work of my young days could only give the orchestra a wrong impression of my talents. However, these rehearsals, to my surprise, made such an unexpected impression on me in other ways that they exercised a decisive influence in the crisis of my artistic development. This was due to the fact that I listened repeatedly to Beethoven's Ninth Symphony, which, by dint of untiring practice, received such a marvellous interpretation at the hands of this celebrated orchestra, that the picture I had had of it in my mind in the enthusiastic days of my youth now stood before me almost tangibly in brilliant colours, undimmed, as though it had never been effaced by the Leipzig orchestra who had slaughtered it under Pohlenz's baton. Where formerly I had

only seen mystic constellations and weird shapes without meaning, I now found, flowing from innumerable sources, a stream
of the most touching and heavenly melodies which delighted
my heart.

The whole of that period of the deterioration of my musical
tastes which dated, practically speaking, from those selfsame
confusing ideas about Beethoven, and which had grown so
much worse through my acquaintance with that dreadful
theatre — all these wrong views now sank down as if into an
abyss of shame and remorse.

This inner change had been gradually prepared by many
painful experiences during the last few years. I owed the
recovery of my old vigour and spirits to the deep impression
the rendering of the Ninth Symphony had made on me when
performed in a way I had never dreamed of. This important
event in my life can only be compared to the upheaval caused
within me when, as a youth of sixteen, I saw Schröder-Devrient
act in *Fidelio*.

The direct result of this was my intense longing to compose
something that would give me a similar feeling of satisfaction,
and this desire grew in proportion to my anxiety about my
unfortunate position in Paris, which made me almost despair
of success.

In this mood I sketched an overture to *Faust* which,
according to my original scheme, was only to form the first
part of a whole *Faust* Symphony, as I had already got
the 'Gretchen' idea in my head for the second movement.
This is the same composition that I rewrote in several parts
fifteen years later; I had forgotten all about it, and I owed
its reconstruction to the advice of Liszt, who gave me many
valuable hints. This composition has been performed many
times under the title of *eine Faust-ouvertüre,* and has met
with great appreciation. At the time of which I am speaking, I hoped that the Conservatoire orchestra would have
been willing to give the work a hearing, but I was told they
thought they had done enough for me, and hoped to be rid of
me for some time.

Having failed everywhere, I now turned to Meyerbeer for
more introductions, especially to singers. I was very much

surprised when, in consequence of my request, Meyerbeer introduced me to a certain M. Gouin, a post-office official, and
Meyerbeer's sole agent in Paris, whom he instructed to do his
utmost for me. Meyerbeer specially wished me to know M.
Anténor Joly, director of the Théâtre de la Renaissance, the
musical theatre already mentioned. M. Gouin, with almost
suspicious levity, promised me to produce my opera *Liebesverbot,* which now only required translation. There was a
question of having a few numbers of my opera sung to the
committee of the theatre at a special audience. When I
suggested that some of the singers of this very theatre should
undertake to sing three of the numbers which had been already
translated by Dumersan, I was refused on the plea that all
these artists were far too busy. But Gouin saw a way out
of the difficulty; on the authority of *Maître* Meyerbeer, he
won over to our cause several singers who were under an
obligation to Meyerbeer: Mme. Dorus-Gras, a real prima-
donna of the Grand Opera, Mme. Widmann and M. Dupont
(the two last-named had previously refused to help me) now
promised to sing for me at this audience.

This much, then, did I achieve in six months. It was now
nearly Easter of the year 1840. Encouraged by Gouin's
negotiations, which seemed to spell hope, I made up my mind
to move from the obscure Quartier des Innocents to a part
of Paris nearer to the musical centre; and in this I was
encouraged by Lehrs' foolhardy advice.

What this change meant to me, my readers will learn when
they hear under what circumstances we had dragged on our
existence during our stay in Paris.

Although we were living in the cheapest possible way,
dining at a very small restaurant for a franc a head, it was
impossible to prevent the rest of our money from melting
away. Our friend Möller had given us to understand that we
could ask him if we were in need, as he would put aside for us
the first money that came in from any successful business
transaction. There was no alternative but to apply to him for
money; in the meantime we pawned all the trinkets we
possessed that were of any value. As I was too shy to make
inquiries about a pawnshop, I looked up the French equivalent

in the dictionary in order to be able to recognise such a place when I saw it. In my little pocket dictionary I could not find any other word than 'Lombard.' On looking at a map of Paris I found, situated in the middle of an inextricable maze of streets, a very small lane called Rue des Lombards. Thither I wended my way, but my expedition was fruitless. Often, on reading by the light of the transparent lanterns the inscription 'Mont de Piété,' I became very curious to know its meaning, and on consulting my advisory board at home about this 'Mount of Piety,' [1] I was told, to my great delight, that it was precisely there that I should find salvation. To this 'Mont de Piété' we now carried all we possessed in the way of silver, namely, our wedding presents. After that followed my wife's trinkets and the rest of her former theatrical wardrobe, amongst which was a beautiful silver-embroidered blue dress with a court train, once the property of the Duchess of Dessau. Still we heard nothing from our friend Möller, and we were obliged to wait on from day to day for the sorely needed help from Königsberg, and at last, one dark day, we pledged our wedding rings. When all hope of assistance seemed vain, I heard that the pawn-tickets themselves were of some value, as they could be sold to buyers, who thereby acquired the right to redeem the pawned articles. I had to resort even to this, and thus the blue court-dress, for instance, was lost for ever. Möller never wrote again. When later on he called on me at the time of my conductorship in Dresden, he admitted that he had been embittered against me owing to humiliating and derogatory remarks we were said to have made about him after we parted, and had resolved not to have anything further to do with us. We were certain of our innocence in the matter, and very grieved at having, through pure slander, lost the chance of such assistance in our great need.

At the beginning of our pecuniary difficulties we sustained a loss which we looked upon as providential, in spite of the grief it caused us. This was our beautiful dog, which we had managed to bring across to Paris with endless difficulty. As he was a very valuable animal, and attracted much attention,

[1] This is the correct translation of the words *Berg der Frömmigkeit* used in the original. — EDITOR.

he had probably been stolen. In spite of the terrible state of the traffic in Paris, he had always found his way home in the same clever manner in which he had mastered the difficulties of the London streets. Quite at the beginning of our stay in Paris he had often gone off by himself to the gardens of the Palais Royal, where he used to meet many of his friends, and had returned safe and sound after a brilliant exhibition of swimming and retrieving before an audience of gutter children. At the Quai du Pont-neuf he generally begged us to let him bathe; there he used to draw a large crowd of spectators round him, who were so loud in their enthusiasm about the way in which he dived for and brought to land various objects of clothing, tools, etc., that the police begged us to put an end to the obstruction. One morning I let him out for a little run as usual; he never returned, and in spite of our most strenuous efforts to recover him, no trace of him was to be found. This loss seemed to many of our friends a piece of luck, for they could not understand how it was possible for us to feed such a huge animal when we ourselves had not enough to eat. About this time, the second month of our stay in Paris, my sister Louisa came over from Leipzig to join her husband, Friedrich Brockhaus, in Paris, where he had been waiting for her for some time. They intended to go to Italy together, and Louisa made use of this opportunity to buy all kinds of expensive things in Paris. I did not expect them to feel any pity for us on account of our foolish removal to Paris, and its attendant miseries, or that they should consider themselves bound to help us in any way; but although we did not try to conceal our position, we derived no benefit from the visit of our rich relations. Minna was even kind enough to help my sister with her luxurious shopping, and we were very anxious not to make them think we wanted to rouse their pity. In return my sister introduced me to an extraordinary friend of hers, who was destined to take a great interest in me. This was the young painter, Ernst Kietz, from Dresden; he was an exceptionally kind-hearted and unaffected young man, whose talent for portrait painting (in a sort of coloured pastel style) had made him such a favourite in his own town, that he had been induced by his financial successes to come to Paris for a time

to finish his art studies. He had now been working in Delaroche's studio for about a year. He had a curious and
almost childlike disposition, and his lack of all serious education, combined with a certain weakness of character, had made
him choose a career in which he was destined, in spite of all
his talent, to fail hopelessly. I had every opportunity of recognising this, as I saw a great deal of him. At the time,
however, the simple-hearted devotion and kindness of this
young man were very welcome both to myself and my wife,
who often felt lonely, and his friendship was a real source of
help in our darkest hours of adversity. He became almost a
member of the family, and joined our home circle every night,
providing a strange contrast to nervous old Anders and the
grave-faced Lehrs. His good-nature and his quaint remarks
soon made him indispensable to us; he amused us tremendously
with his French, into which he would launch with the greatest
confidence, although he could not put together two consecutive
sentences properly, in spite of having lived in Paris for twenty
years. With Delaroche he studied oil-painting, and had obviously considerable talent in this direction, although it was
the very rock on which he stranded. The mixing of the colours
on his palette, and especially the cleaning of his brushes, took
up so much of his time that he rarely came to the actual painting. As the days were very short in midwinter, he never had
time to do any work after he had finished washing his palette
and brushes, and, as far as I can remember, he never completed
a single portrait. Strangers to whom he had been introduced,
and who had given him orders to paint their portraits, were
obliged to leave Paris without seeing them even half done,
and at last he even complained because some of his sitters
died before their portraits were completed. His landlord, to
whom he was always in debt for rent, was the only creature
who succeeded in getting a portrait of his ugly person from
the painter, and, as far as I know, this is the only finished
portrait in existence by Kietz. On the other hand, he was
very clever at making little sketches of any subject suggested
by our conversation during the evening, and in these he displayed both originality and delicacy of execution. During
the winter of that year he completed a good pencil portrait

of me, which he touched up two years afterwards when he knew me more intimately, finishing it off as it now stands. It pleased him to sketch me in the attitude I often assumed during our evening chats when I was in a cheerful mood. No evening ever passed during which I did not succeed in shaking off the depression caused by my vain endeavours, and by the many worries I had gone through during the day, and in regaining my natural cheerfulness, and Kietz was anxious to represent me to the world as a man who, in spite of the hard times he had to face, had confidence in his success, and rose smiling above the troubles of life. Before the end of the year 1839, my youngest sister Cecilia also arrived in Paris with her husband, Edward Avenarius. It was only natural that she should feel embarrassed at the idea of meeting us in Paris in our extremely straitened circumstances, especially as her husband was not very well off. Consequently, instead of calling on them frequently, we preferred waiting until they came to see us, which, by the way, took them a long time. On the other hand, the renewal of our acquaintance with Heinrich Laube, who came over to Paris at the beginning of 1840 with his young wife, Iduna (née Budäus), was very cheering. She was the widow of a wealthy Leipzig doctor, and Laube had married her under very extraordinary circumstances, since we last saw him in Berlin; they intended to enjoy themselves for a few months in Paris. During the long period of his detention, while awaiting his trial, this young lady had been so touched by his misfortunes that without knowing much of him, she had shown great sympathy and interest in his case. Laube's sentence was pronounced soon after I left Berlin; it was unexpectedly light, consisting of only one year's imprisonment in the town gaol. He was allowed to undergo this term in the prison at Muskau in Silesia, where he had the advantage of being near his friend, Prince Pückler, who in his official capacity, and on account of his influence with the governor of the prison, was permitted to afford the prisoner even the consolation of personal intercourse.

The young widow resolved to marry him at the beginning of his term of imprisonment, so that she might be near him at Muskau with her loving assistance. To see my old friend under such favourable conditions was in itself a pleasure to me; I also experienced the liveliest satisfaction at finding there was no change in his former sympathetic attitude. We met frequently; our wives also became friends, and Laube was the first to approve in his kindly humorous way of our folly in moving to Paris.

In his house I made the acquaintance of Heinrich Heine, and both of them joked good-humouredly over my extraordinary position, making even me laugh. Laube felt himself compelled to talk seriously to me about my expectations of succeeding in Paris, as he saw that I treated my situation, based on such trivial hopes, with a humour that charmed him even against his better judgment. He tried to think how he could help me without prejudicing my future. With this object he wanted me to make a more or less plausible sketch of my future plans, so that on his approaching visit to our native land he might procure some help for me. I happened just at that time to have come to an exceedingly promising understanding with the management of the Théâtre de la Renaissance. I thus seemed to have obtained a footing, and I thought it safe to assert, that if I were guaranteed the means of livelihood for six months, I could not fail within that period to accomplish something. Laube promised to make this provision, and kept his word. He induced one of his wealthy friends in Leipzig, and, following this example, my well-to-do relations, to provide me for six months with the necessary resources, to be paid in monthly instalments through Avenarius.

We therefore decided, as I have said, to leave our furnished apartments and take a flat for ourselves in the Rue du Helder. My prudent, careful wife had suffered greatly on account of the careless and uncertain manner in which I had hitherto controlled our meagre resources, and in now undertaking the responsibility, she explained that she understood how to keep house more cheaply than we could do by living in furnished rooms and restaurants. Success justified the step; the serious part of the question lay in the fact that we had to start housekeeping without any furniture of our own, and everything necessary for domestic purposes had to be procured, though we had not the wherewithal to get it. In this matter Lehrs, who was well versed in the peculiarities of Parisian life, was able to advise us. In his opinion the only compensation for the experiences we had undergone hitherto would be a success equivalent to my daring. As I did not possess the resources to allow of long years of patient waiting for success in Paris, I must either count on extraordinary luck or renounce all my hopes forthwith. The longed-for success must come within a year, or I should be ruined. Therefore I must dare all, as befitted my name, for in my case he was not inclined to derive ' Wagner ' [1] from *Fuhrwerk*. I was to pay my rent, twelve hundred francs, in quarterly instalments; for the furniture and fittings, he recommended me, through his landlady, to a carpenter who provided everything that was necessary for what seemed to be a reasonable sum, also to be paid by instalments, all of which appeared very simple. Lehrs maintained that I should do no good in Paris unless I showed the world that I had confidence in myself. My trial audience was impending; I felt sure of the Théâtre de la Renaissance, and Dumersan was keenly anxious to make a complete translation of my *Liebesverbot* into French. So we decided to run the risk. On 15th April, to the astonishment of the concierge of the house in the Rue du Helder, we moved with an exceedingly small amount of luggage into our comfortable new apartments.

The very first visit I received in the rooms I had taken with such high hopes was from Anders, who came with the tidings that the Théâtre de la Renaissance had just gone bankrupt, and was closed. This news, which came on me like a thunderclap, seemed to portend more than an ordinary stroke of bad luck; it revealed to me like a flash of lightning the absolute emptiness of my prospects. My friends openly expressed the opinion that Meyerbeer, in sending me from the Grand Opera to this theatre, probably knew the whole of the circumstances. I did not pursue the line of thought to which this supposition might lead, as I felt cause enough for bitterness when I wondered what I should do with the rooms in which I was so nicely installed.

As my singers had now practised the portions of *Liebes-*

---

[1] ' Wagner ' in German means one who dares, also a Wagoner; and ' Fuhrwerk ' means a carriage. — EDITOR.

verbot intended for the trial audience, I was anxious at least
to have them performed before some persons of influence.
M. Edouard Monnaie, who had been appointed temporary director of the Grand Opera after Duponchel's retirement, was
the less disposed to refuse as the singers who were to take part
belonged to the institution over which he presided; moreover,
there was no obligation attached to his presence at the audience.
I also took the trouble to call on Scribe to invite him to attend,
and he accepted with the kindest alacrity. At last my three
pieces were performed before these two gentlemen in the green
room of the Grand Opera, and I played the piano accompaniment. They pronounced the music charming, and Scribe expressed his willingness to arrange the libretto for me as soon
as the managers of the opera had decided on accepting the
piece; all that M. Monnaie had to reply to this offer was that
it was impossible for them to do so at present. I did not fail
to realise that these were only polite expressions; but at all
events I thought it very nice of them, and particularly condescending of Scribe to have got so far as to think me deserving
of a little politeness.

But in my heart of hearts I felt really ashamed of having
gone back again seriously to that superficial early work from
which I had taken these three pieces. Of course I had only
done this because I thought I should win success more rapidly
in Paris by adapting myself to its frivolous taste. My aversion
from this kind of taste, which had been long growing, coincided
with my abandonment of all hopes of success in Paris. I was
placed in an exceedingly melancholy situation by the fact
that my circumstances had so shaped themselves that I dared
not express this important change in my feelings to any one,
especially to my poor wife. But if I continued to make the best
of a bad bargain, I had no longer any illusions as to the possibility of success in Paris. Face to face with unheard-of misery,
I shuddered at the smiling aspect which Paris presented in the
bright sunshine of May. It was the beginning of the slack
season for any sort of artistic enterprise in Paris, and from
every door at which I knocked with feigned hope I was turned
away with the wretchedly monotonous phrase, *Monsieur est à
la campagne.*

On our long walks, when we felt ourselves absolute strangers in the midst of the gay throng, I used to romance to my wife about the South American Free States, far away from all this sinister life, where opera and music were unknown, and the foundations of a sensible livelihood could easily be secured by industry. I told Minna, who was quite in the dark as to my meaning, of a book I had just read, Zschokke's *Die Gründung von Maryland,* in which I found a very seductive account of the sensation of relief experienced by the European settlers after their former sufferings and persecutions. She, being of a more practical turn of mind, used to point out to me the necessity of procuring means for our continued existence in Paris, for which she had thought out all sorts of economies.

I, for my part, was sketching out the plan of the poem of my *Fliegender Holländer,* which I kept steadily before me as a possible means of making a début in Paris. I put together the material for a single act, influenced by the consideration that I could in this way confine it to the simple dramatic developments between the principal characters, without troubling about the tiresome operatic accessories. From a practical point of view, I thought I could rely on a better prospect for the acceptance of my proposed work if it were cast in the form of a one-act opera, such as was frequently given as a curtain raiser before a ballet at the Grand Opera. I wrote about it to Meyerbeer in Berlin, asking for his help. I also resumed the composition of *Rienzi,* to the completion of which I was now giving my constant attention.

In the meantime our position became more and more gloomy; I was soon compelled to draw in advance on the subsidies obtained by Laube, but in so doing I gradually alienated the sympathy of my brother-in-law Avenarius, to whom our stay in Paris was incomprehensible.

One morning, when we had been anxiously consulting as to the possibility of raising our first quarter's rent, a carrier appeared with a parcel addressed to me from London; I thought it was an intervention of Providence, and broke open the seal. At the same moment a receipt-book was thrust into my face for signature, in which I at once saw that I had to pay seven francs for carriage. I recognised, moreover, that the parcel

contained my overture *Rule Britannia,* returned to me from
the London Philharmonic Society. In my fury I told the
bearer that I would not take in the parcel, whereupon he
remonstrated in the liveliest fashion, as I had already opened it.
It was no use; I did not possess seven francs, and I told him
he should have presented the bill for the carriage before I had
opened the parcel. So I made him return the only copy of
my overture to Messrs. Laffitte and Gaillard's firm, to do what
they liked with it, and I never cared to inquire what became
of that manuscript.

Suddenly Kietz devised a way out of these troubles. He
had been commissioned by an old lady of Leipzig, called Fräulein Leplay, a rich and very miserly old maid, to find a cheap
lodging in Paris for her and for his stepmother, with whom she
intended to travel. As our apartment, though not spacious,
was larger than we actually needed, and had very quickly
become a troublesome burden to us, we did not hesitate for a
moment to let the larger portion of it to her for the time of her
stay in Paris, which was to last about two months. In addition,
my wife provided the guests with breakfast, as though they
were in furnished apartments, and took a great pride in looking
at the few pence she earned in this way. Although we found
this amazing example of old-maidishness trying enough, the
arrangement we had made helped us in some degree to tide
over the anxious time, and I was able, in spite of this dis-
organisation of our household arrangements, to continue working in comparative peace at my *Rienzi.*

This became more difficult after Fräulein Leplay's departure,
when we let one of our rooms to a German commercial traveller,
who in his leisure hours zealously played the flute. His name
was Brix; he was a modest, decent fellow, and had been recommended to us by Pecht the painter, whose acquaintance we
had recently made. He had been introduced to us by Kietz,
who studied with him in Delaroche's studio. He was the very
antithesis of Kietz in every way, and obviously endowed with
less talent, yet he grappled with the task of acquiring the art
of oil-painting in the shortest possible time under difficult
circumstances with an industry and earnestness quite out of
the common. He was, moreover, well educated, and eagerly

assimilated information, and was very straightforward, earnest, and trustworthy. Without attaining to the same degree of intimacy with us as our three older friends, he was, nevertheless, one of the few who continued to stand by us in our troubles, and habitually spent nearly every evening in our company.

One day I received a fresh surprising proof of Laube's continued solicitude on our behalf. The secretary of a certain Count Kuscelew called on us, and after some inquiry into our affairs, the state of which he had heard from Laube at Karlsbad, informed us in a brief and friendly way that his patron wished to be of use to us, and with that object in view desired to make my acquaintance. In fact, he proposed to engage a small light opera company in Paris, which was to follow him to his Russian estates. He was therefore looking for a musical director of sufficient experience to assist in recruiting the members in Paris. I gladly went to the hotel where the count was staying, and there found an elderly gentleman of frank and agreeable bearing, who willingly listened to my little French compositions. Being a shewd reader of human nature, he saw at a glance that I was not the man for him, and though he showed me the most polite attention, he went no further into the opera scheme. But that very day he sent me, accompanied by a friendly note, ten golden napoleons, in payment for my services. What these services were I did not know. I thereupon wrote to him, and asked for more precise details of his wishes, and begged him to commission a composition, the fee for which I presumed he had sent in advance. As I received no reply, I made more than one effort to approach him again, but in vain. From other sources I afterwards learned that the only kind of opera Count Kuscelew recognised was Adam's. As for the operatic company to be engaged to suit his taste, what he really wanted was more a small harem than a company of artists.

So far I had not been able to arrange anything with the music publisher Schlesinger. It was impossible to persuade him to publish my little French songs. In order to do something, however, towards making myself known in this direction, I decided to have my *Two Grenadiers* engraved by him at my own expense. Kietz was to lithograph a magnificent title-page for it. Schlesinger ended by charging me fifty francs for the cost of production. The story of this publication is curious from beginning to end; the work bore Schlesinger's name, and as I had defrayed all expenses, the proceeds were, of course, to be placed to my account. I had afterwards to take the publisher's word for it that not a single copy had been sold. Subsequently, when I had made a quick reputation for myself in Dresden through my *Rienzi,* Schott the publisher in Mainz, who dealt almost exclusively in works translated from the French, thought it advisable to bring out a German edition of the *Two Grenadiers.* Below the text of the French translation he had the German original by Heine printed; but as the French poem was a very free paraphrase, in quite a different metre to the original, Heine's words fitted my composition so badly that I was furious at the insult to my work, and thought it necessary to protest against Schott's publication as an entirely unauthorised reprint. Schott then threatened me with an action for libel, as he said that, according to his agreement, his edition was not a reprint (*Nachdruck*), but a reimpression (*Abdruck*). In order to be spared further annoyance, I was induced to send him an apology in deference to the distinction he had drawn, which I did not understand.

In 1848, when I made inquiries of Schlesinger's successor in Paris (M. Brandus) as to the fate of my little work, I learned from him that a new edition had been published, but he declined to entertain any question of rights on my part. Since I did not care to buy a copy with my own money, I have to this day had to do without my own property. To what extent, in later years, others profited by similar transactions relating to the publication of my works, will appear in due course.

For the moment the point was to compensate Schlesinger for the fifty francs agreed upon, and he proposed that I should do this by writing articles for his *Gazette Musicale.*

As I was not expert enough in the French language for literary purposes, my article had to be translated and half the fee had to go to the translator. However, I consoled myself by thinking I should still receive sixty francs per sheet for the work. I was soon to learn, when I presented myself

to the angry publisher for payment, what was meant by a
sheet. It was measured by an abominable iron instrument,
on which the lines of the columns were marked off with figures;
this was applied to the article, and after careful subtraction
of the spaces left for the title and signature, the lines were added
up. After this process had been gone through, it appeared
that what I had taken for a sheet was only half a sheet.

So far so good. I began to write articles for Schlesinger's
wonderful paper. The first was a long essay, *De la musique
allemande,* in which I expressed with the enthusiastic exaggeration characteristic of me at that time my appreciation of the
sincerity and earnestness of German music. This article led
my friend Anders to remark that the state of affairs in Germany
must, indeed, be splendid if the conditions were really as I
described. I enjoyed what was to me the surprising satisfaction of seeing this article subsequently reproduced in Italian,
in a Milan musical journal, where, to my amusement, I saw
myself described as *Dottissimo Musico Tedesco,* a mistake
which nowadays would be impossible. My essay attracted
favourable comment, and Schlesinger asked me to write an
article in praise of the arrangement made by the Russian
General Lwoff of Pergolesi's *Stabat Mater,* which I did as
superficially as possible. On my own impulse I then wrote
an essay in a still more amiable vein called *Du métier du
virtuose et de l'indépendance de la composition.*

In the meantime I was surprised in the middle of the summer
by the arrival of Meyerbeer, who happened to come to Paris
for a fortnight. He was very sympathetic and obliging. When
I told him my idea of writing a one-act opera as a curtain
raiser, and asked him to give me an introduction to M. Léon
Pillet, the recently appointed manager of the Grand Opera,
he at once took me to see him, and presented me to him. But
alas, I had the unpleasant surprise of learning from the serious
conversation which took place between those two gentlemen
as to my future, that Meyerbeer thought I had better decide
to compose an act for the ballet in collaboration with another
musician. Of course I could not entertain such an idea for a
moment. I succeeded, however, in handing over to M. Pillet
my brief sketch of the subject of the *Flying Dutchman.*

Things had reached this point when Meyerbeer again left Paris, this time for a longer period of absence.

As I did not hear from M. Pillet for quite a long time, I now began to work diligently at my composition of *Rienzi*, though, to my great distress, I had often to interrupt this task in order to undertake certain pot-boiling hack-work for Schlesinger.

As my contributions to the *Gazette Musicale* proved so unremunerative, Schlesinger one day ordered me to work out a method for the *Cornet à pistons*. When I told him about my embarrassment, in not knowing how to deal with the subject, he replied by sending me five different published 'Methods' for the *Cornet à pistons,* at that time the favourite amateur instrument among the younger male population of Paris. I had merely to devise a new sixth method out of these five, as all Schlesinger wanted was to publish an edition of his own. I was racking my brains how to start, when Schlesinger, who had just obtained a new complete method, released me from the onerous task. I was, however, told to write fourteen 'Suites' for the *Cornet à pistons* — that is to say, airs out of operas arranged for this instrument. To furnish me with material for this work, Schlesinger sent me no less than sixty complete operas arranged for the piano. I looked them through for suitable airs for my 'Suites,' marked the pages in the volumes with paper strips, and arranged them into a curious-looking structure round my work-table, so that I might have the greatest possible variety of the melodious material within my reach. When I was in the midst of this work, however, to my great relief and to my poor wife's consternation, Schlesinger told me that M. Schlitz, the first cornet player in Paris, who had looked my 'Études' through, preparatory to their being engraved, had declared that I knew absolutely nothing about the instrument, and had generally adopted keys that were too high, which Parisians would never be able to use. The part of the work I had already done was, however, accepted, Schlitz having agreed to correct it, but on condition that I should share my fee with him. The remainder of the work was then taken off my hands, and the sixty pianoforte arrangements went back to the curious shop in the Rue Richelieu.

So my exchequer was again in a sorry plight. The distressing poverty of my home grew more apparent every day, and yet I was now free to give a last touch to *Rienzi*, and by the 19th of November I had completed this most voluminous of all my operas. I had decided, some time previously, to offer the first production of this work to the Court Theatre at Dresden, so that, in the event of its being a success, I might thus resume my connection with Germany. I had decided upon Dresden as I knew that there I should have in Tichatschek the most suitable tenor for the leading part. I also reckoned on my acquaintance with Schröder-Devrient, who had always been nice to me and who, though her efforts were ineffectual, had been at great pains, out of regard for my family, to get my *Feen* introduced at the Court Theatre, Dresden. In the secretary of the theatre, Hofrat Winkler (known as Theodor Hell), I also had an old friend of my family, besides which I had been introduced to the conductor, Reissiger, with whom I and my friend Apel had spent a pleasant evening on the occasion of our excursion to Bohemia in earlier days. To all these people I now addressed most respectful and eloquent appeals, wrote out an official note to the director, Herr von Lüttichau, as well as a formal petition to the King of Saxony, and had everything ready to send off.

Meantime, I had not omitted to indicate the exact *tempi* in my opera by means of a metronome. As I did not possess such a thing, I had to borrow one, and one morning I went out to restore the instrument to its owner, carrying it under my thin overcoat. The day when this occurred was one of the strangest in my life, as it showed in a really horrible way the whole misery of my position at that time. In addition to the fact that I did not know where to look for the few francs wherewith Minna was to provide for our scanty household requirements, some of the bills which, in accordance with the custom in Paris in those days, I had signed for the purpose of fitting up our apartments, had fallen due. Hoping to get help from one source or another, I first tried to get those bills prolonged by the holders. As such documents pass through many hands, I had to call on all the holders across the length and breadth of the city. That day I was to propitiate a cheese-monger who occupied a fifth-floor apartment in the Cité. I also intended to ask for help from Heinrich, the brother of my brother-in-law, Brockhaus, as he was then in Paris; and I was going to call at Schlesinger's to raise the money to pay for the despatch of my score that day by the usual mail service.

As I had also to deliver the metronome, I left Minna early in the morning after a sad good-bye. She knew from experience that as I was on a money-raising expedition, she would not see me back till late at night. The streets were enveloped in a dense fog, and the first thing I recognised on leaving the house was my dog Robber, who had been stolen from us a year before. At first I thought it was a ghost, but I called out to him sharply in a shrill voice. The animal seemed to recognise me, and approached me cautiously, but my sudden movement towards him with outstretched arms seemed only to revive memories of the few chastisements I had foolishly inflicted on him during the latter part of our association, and this memory prevailed over all others. He drew timidly away from me and, as I followed him with some eagerness, he ran, only to accelerate his speed when he found he was being pursued. I became more and more convinced that he had recognised me, because he always looked back anxiously when he reached a corner; but seeing that I was hunting him like a maniac, he started off again each time with renewed energy. Thus I followed him through a labyrinth of streets, hardly distinguishable in the thick mist, until I eventually lost sight of him altogether, never to see him again. It was near the church of St. Roch, and I, wet with perspiration and quite breathless, was still bearing the metronome. For a while I stood motionless, glaring into the mist, and wondered what the ghostly reappearance of the companion of my travelling adventures on this day might portend! The fact that he had fled from his old master with the terror of a wild beast filled my heart with a strange bitterness and seemed to me a horrible omen. Sadly shaken, I set out again, with trembling limbs, upon my weary errand.

Heinrich Brockhaus told me he could not help me, and I left him. I was sorely ashamed, but made a strong effort to conceal the painfulness of my situation. My other undertakings turned out equally hopeless, and after having been kept waiting for hours at Schlesinger's, listening to my employer's very trivial conversations with his callers — conversations which he seemed purposely to protract — I reappeared under the windows of my home long after dark, utterly unsuccessful. I saw Minna looking anxiously from one of the windows. Half expecting my misfortune she had, in the meantime, succeeded in borrowing a small sum of our lodger and boarder, Brix, the flute-player, whom we tolerated patiently, though at some inconvenience to ourselves, as he was a good-natured fellow. So she was able to offer me at least a comfortable meal. Further help was to come to me subsequently, though at the cost of great sacrifices on my part, owing to the success of one of Donizetti's operas, *La Favorita,* a very poor work of the Italian maestro's, but welcomed with great enthusiasm by the Parisian public, already so much degenerated. This opera, the success of which was due mainly to two lively little songs, had been acquired by Schlesinger, who had lost heavily over Halévy's last operas.

Taking advantage of my helpless situation, of which he was well aware, he rushed into our rooms one morning, beaming all over with amusing good-humour, called for pen and ink, and began to work out a calculation of the enormous fees which he had arranged for me! He put down: ' *La Favorita,* complete arrangement for pianoforte, arrangement without words, for solo; ditto, for duet; complete arrangement for quartette; the same for two violins; ditto for a *Cornet à piston.* Total fee, frcs. 1100. Immediate advance in cash, frcs. 500.' I could see at a glance what an enormous amount of trouble this work would involve, but I did not hesitate a moment to undertake it.

Curiously enough, when I brought home these five hundred francs in hard shining five-franc pieces, and piled them up on the table for our edification, my sister Cecilia Avenarius happened to drop in to see us. The sight of this abundance of wealth seemed to produce a good effect on her, as she had hitherto been rather chary of coming to see us; and after that we used to see rather more of her, and were often invited to dine with them on Sundays. But I no longer cared for any amusements. I was so deeply impressed by my past experiences that I made up my mind to work through this humiliating, albeit profitable task, with untiring energy, as though it were a penance imposed on me for the expiation of my bygone sins. To save fuel, we limited ourselves to the use of the bedroom, making it serve as a drawing-room, dining-room, and study, as well as dormitory. It was only a step from my bed to my work-table; to be seated at the dining-table, all I had to do was to turn my chair round, and I left my seat altogether only late at night when I wanted to go to bed again. Every fourth day I allowed myself a short constitutional. This penitential process lasted almost all through the winter, and sowed the seeds of those gastric disorders which were to be more or less of a trouble to me for the rest of my life.

In return for the minute and almost interminable work of correcting the score of Donizetti's opera, I managed to get three hundred francs from Schlesinger, as he could not get any one else to do it. Besides this, I had to find the time to copy out the orchestra parts of my overture to *Faust,* which I was still hoping to hear at the Conservatoire; and by the way of counteracting the depression produced by this humiliating occupation, I wrote a short story, *Eine Pilgerfahrt zu Beethoven* (A Pilgrimage to Beethoven), which appeared in the *Gazette Musicale,* under the title *Une Visite à Beethoven.* Schlesinger told me candidly that this little work had created quite a sensation, and had been received with very marked approval; and, indeed, it was actually reproduced, either complete or in parts, in a good many fireside journals.

He persuaded me to write some more of the same kind; and in a sequel entitled *Das Ende eines Musikers in Paris (Un Musicien étranger à Paris)* I avenged myself for all the misfortunes I had had to endure. Schlesinger was not quite so pleased with this as with my first effort, but it received touching signs of approval from his poor assistant; while Heinrich Heine praised it by saying that 'Hoffmann would have been incapable of writing such a thing.' Even Berlioz was touched by it, and spoke of the story very favourably in one of his articles in the *Journal des Débats.* He also gave me signs of his sympathy, though only during a conversation, after the appearance of another of my musical articles entitled *Ueber die Ouvertüre* (Concerning Overtures), mainly because I had illustrated my principle by pointing to Gluck's overture to *Iphigenia in Aulis* as a model for compositions of this class.

Encouraged by these signs of sympathy, I felt anxious to become more intimately acquainted with Berlioz. I had been introduced to him some time previously at Schlesinger's office, where we used to meet occasionally. I had presented him with a copy of my *Two Grenadiers*, but could, however, never learn any more from him concerning what he really thought of it than the fact that as he could only strum a little on the guitar, he was unable to play the music of my composition to himself on the piano. During the previous winter I had often heard his grand instrumental pieces played under his own direction, and had been most favourably impressed by them. During that winter (1839-40) he conducted three performances of his new symphony, *Romeo and Juliet,* at one of which I was present.

All this, to be sure, was quite a new world to me, and I was desirous of gaining some unprejudiced knowledge of it. At first the grandeur and masterly execution of the orchestral part almost overwhelmed me. It was beyond anything I could have conceived. The fantastic daring, the sharp precision with which the boldest combinations — almost tangible in their clearness — impressed me, drove back my own ideas of the poetry of music with brutal violence into the very depths of my soul. I was simply all ears for things of which till then I had never dreamt, and which I felt I must try to realise. True, I found a great deal that was empty and shallow in his *Romeo and Juliet,* a work that lost much by its length and form of combination; and this was the more painful to me seeing that, on the other hand, I felt overpowered by many really bewitching passages which quite overcame any objections on my part.

During the same winter Berlioz produced his *Sinfonie Fantastique* and his *Harald* ('Harold en Italie'). I was also much impressed by these works; the musical genre-pictures woven into the first-named symphony were particularly pleasing, while *Harald* delighted me in almost every respect.

It was, however, the latest work of this wonderful master, his *Trauer-Symphonie für die Opfer der Juli-Revolution* (*Grande Symphonie Funèbre et Triomphale*), most skilfully composed for massed military bands during the summer of 1840 for the anniversary of the obsequies of the July heroes, and conducted by him under the column of the Place de la Bastille, which had at last thoroughly convinced me of the greatness and enterprise of this incomparable artist. But while admiring this genius, absolutely unique in his methods, I could never quite shake off a certain peculiar feeling of anxiety. His works left me with a sensation as of something strange, something with which I felt I should never be able to be familiar, and I was often puzzled at the strange fact that, though ravished by his compositions, I was at the same time repelled and even wearied by them. It was only much later that I succeeded in clearly grasping and solving this problem, which for years exercised such a painful spell over me.

It is a fact that at that time I felt almost like a little school-boy by the side of Berlioz. Consequently I was really embarrassed when Schlesinger, determined to make good use of the success of my short story, told me he was anxious to produce some of my orchestral compositions at a concert arranged by the editor of the *Gazette Musicale*. I realised that none of my available works would in any way be suitable for such an occasion. I was not quite confident as to my *Faust* Overture because of its zephyr-like ending, which I presumed could only be appreciated by an audience already familiar with my methods. When, moreover, I learned that I should have only a second-rate orchestra — the Valentino from the Casino, Rue St. Honoré — and, moreover, that there could be only one rehearsal, my only alternative lay between declining altogether, or making another trial with my *Columbus* Overture, the work composed in my early days at Magdeburg. I adopted the latter course.

When I went to fetch the score of this composition from Habeneck, who had it stored among the archives of the Conservatoire, he warned me somewhat dryly, though not without kindness, of the danger of presenting this work to the Parisian public, as, to use his own words, it was too ' vague.' One great objection was the difficulty of finding capable musicians for the six cornets required, as the music for this instrument, so skilfully played in Germany, could hardly, if ever, be satis-factorily executed in Paris. Herr Schlitz, the corrector of my 'Suites' for *Cornet à piston,* offered his assistance. I was compelled to reduce my six cornets to four, and he told me that only two of these could be relied on.

As a matter of fact, the attempts made at the rehearsal to produce those very passages on which the effect of my work chiefly depended were very discouraging. Not once were the soft high notes played but they were flat or altogether wrong. In addition to this, as I was not going to be allowed to conduct the work myself, I had to rely upon a conductor who, as I was well aware, had fully convinced himself that my composition was the most utter rubbish — an opinion that seemed to be shared by the whole orchestra. Berlioz, who was present at the rehearsal, remained silent throughout. He gave me no encouragement, though he did not dissuade me. He merely said afterwards, with a weary smile, ' that it was very difficult to get on in Paris.'

On the night of the performance (4th February 1841) the audience, which was largely composed of subscribers to the *Gazette Musicale,* and to whom, therefore, my literary successes were not unknown, seemed rather favourably disposed towards me. I was told later on that my overture, however wearisome it had been, would certainly have been applauded if those unfortunate cornet players, by continually failing to produce the effective passages, had not excited the public almost to the point of hostility; for Parisians, for the most part, care only for the skilful parts of performances, as, for instance, for the faultless production of difficult tones. I was clearly con-scious of my complete failure. After this misfortune Paris no longer existed for me, and all I had to do was to go back to my miserable bedroom and resume my work of arranging Donizetti's operas.

So great was my renunciation of the world that, like a penitent, I no longer shaved, and to my wife's annoyance, for the first and only time in my life allowed my beard to grow quite long. I tried to bear everything patiently, and the only

thing that threatened really to drive me to despair was a
pianist in the room adjoining ours who during the livelong day
practised Liszt's fantasy on *Lucia di Lammermoor*. I had
to put a stop to this torture, so, to give him an idea of what he
made us endure, one day I moved our own piano, which was
terribly out of tune, close up to the party wall. Then Brix
with his piccolo-flute played the piano-and-violin (or flute)
arrangement of the *Favorita* Overture I had just completed,
while I accompanied him on the piano. The effect on our
neighbour, a young piano-teacher, must have been appalling.
The concierge told me the next day that the poor fellow was
leaving, and, after all, I felt rather sorry.

The wife of our concierge had entered into a sort of arrangement with us. At first we had occasionally availed ourselves
of her services, especially in the kitchen, also for brushing
clothes, cleaning boots, and so on; but even the slight outlay
that this involved was eventually too heavy for us, and after
having dispensed with her services, Minna had to suffer the
humiliation of doing the whole work of the household, even the
most menial part of it, herself. As we did not like to mention
this to Brix, Minna was obliged, not only to do all the cooking
and washing up, but even to clean our lodger's boots as well.
What we felt most, however, was the thought of what the
concierge and his wife would think of us; but we were mistaken,
for they only respected us the more, though of course we could
not avoid a little familiarity at times. Now and then, therefore, the man would have a chat with me on politics. When
the Quadruple Alliance against France had been concluded,
and the situation under Thiers' ministry was regarded as very
critical, my concierge tried to reassure me one day by saying:
' *Monsieur, il y a quatre hommes en Europe qui s'appellent: le roi
Louis Philippe, l'empereur d'Autriche, l'empereur de Russie,
le roi de Prusse; eh bien, ces quatre sont des c . . .; et nous
n'aurons pas la guerre.'*

Of an evening I very seldom lacked entertainment; but the
few faithful friends who came to see me had to put up with my
going on scribbling music till late in the night. Once they
prepared a touching surprise for me in the form of a little
party which they arranged for New Year's Eve (1840). Lehrs

arrived at dusk, rang the bell, and brought a leg of veal; Kietz
brought some rum, sugar, and a lemon; Pecht supplied a goose;
and Anders two bottles of the champagne with which he had
been presented by a musical instrument-maker in return for a
flattering article he had written about his pianos. Bottles
from that stock were produced only on very great occasions.
I soon threw the confounded *Favorita* aside, therefore, and
entered enthusiastically into the fun.

We all had to assist in the preparations, to light the fire in
the salon, give a hand to my wife in the kitchen, and get what
was wanted from the grocer. The supper developed into a
dithyrambic orgy. When the champagne was drunk, and the
punch began to produce its effects, I delivered a fiery speech
which so provoked the hilarity of the company that it seemed
as though it would never end. I became so excited that I first
mounted a chair, and then, by way of heightening the effect,
at last stood on the table, thence to preach the maddest gospel
of the contempt of life together with a eulogy on the South
American Free States. My charmed listeners eventually broke
into such fits of sobs and laughter, and were so overcome, that
we had to give them all shelter for the night — their condition
making it impossible for them to reach their own homes in
safety. On New Year's Day (1841) I was again busy with my
Favorita.

I remember another similar though far less boisterous feast,
on the occasion of a visit paid us by the famous violinist Vieuxtemps, an old schoolfellow of Kietz's. We had the great
pleasure of hearing the young virtuoso, who was then greatly
fêted in Paris, play to us charmingly for a whole evening — a
performance which lent my little salon an unusual touch of
'fashion.' Kietz rewarded him for his kindness by carrying
him on his shoulders to his hotel close by.

We were hard hit in the early part of this year by a mistake
I made owing to my ignorance of Paris customs. It seemed
to us quite a matter of course that we should wait until the
proper quarter-day to give notice to our landlady. So I called
on the proprietress of the house, a rich young widow living in
one of her own houses in the Marias quarter. She received me,
but seemed much embarrassed, and said she would speak to

her agent about the matter, and eventually referred me to him. The next day I was informed by letter that my notice would have been valid had it been given two days earlier. By this omission I had rendered myself liable, according to the agreement, for another year's rent. Horrified by this news, I went to see the agent himself, and after having been kept waiting for a long time — as a matter of fact they would not let me in at all — I found an elderly gentleman, apparently crippled by some very painful malady, lying motionless before me. I frankly told him my position, and begged him most earnestly to release me from my agreement, but I was merely told that the fault was mine, and not his, that I had given notice a day too late, and consequently that I must find the rent for the next year. My concierge, to whom, with some emotion, I related the story of this occurrence, tried to soothe me by saying: ' J'aurais pu vous dire cela, car voyez, monsieur, cet homme ne vaut pas l'eau qu'il boit.'

This entirely unforeseen misfortune destroyed our last hopes of getting out of our disastrous position. We consoled ourselves for awhile with the hope of finding another lodger, but the fates were once more against us. Easter came, the new term began, and our prospects were as hopeless as ever. At last our concierge recommended us to a family who were willing to take the whole of our apartment, furniture included, off our hands for a few months. We gladly accepted this offer; for, at any rate, it ensured the payment of the rent for the ensuing quarter. We thought if only we could get away from this unfortunate place we should find some way of getting rid of it altogether. We therefore decided to find a cheap summer residence for ourselves in the outskirts of Paris.

Meudon had been mentioned to us as an inexpensive summer resort, and we selected an apartment in the avenue which joins Meudon to the neighbouring village of Bellevue. We left full authority with our concierge as to our rooms in Rue du Helder, and settled down in our new temporary abode as well as we could. Old Brix, the good-natured flutist, had to stay with us again, for, owing to the fact that his usual receipts had been delayed, he would have been in great straits had we refused to give him shelter. The removal of our scanty possessions took place on the 29th of April, and was, after all, no more than a flight from the impossible into the unknown, for how we were going to live during the following summer we had not the faintest idea. Schlesinger had no work for me, and no other sources were available.

The only help we could hope for seemed to lie in journalistic work which, though rather unremunerative, had indeed given me the opportunity of making a little success. During the previous winter I had written a long article on Weber's *Freischütz* for the *Gazette Musicale.* This was intended to prepare the way for the forthcoming first performance of this opera, after recitatives from the pen of Berlioz had been added to it. The latter was apparently far from pleased at my article. In the article I could not help referring to Berlioz's absurd idea of polishing up this old-fashioned musical work by adding ingredients that spoiled its original characteristics, merely in order to give it an appearance suited to the luxurious repertoire of Opera House. The fact that the result fully justified my forecasts did not in the least tend to diminish the ill-feeling I had roused among all those concerned in the production; but I had the satisfaction of hearing that the famous George Sand had noticed my article. She commenced the introduction to a legendary story of French provincial life by repudiating certain doubts as to the ability of the French people to understand the mystic, fabulous element which, as I had shown, was displayed in such a masterly manner in *Freischütz,* and she pointed to my article as clearly explaining the characteristics of that opera.

Another journalistic opportunity arose out of my endeavours to secure the acceptance of my *Rienzi* by the Court Theatre at Dresden. Herr Winkler, the secretary of that theatre, whom I have already mentioned, regularly reported progress; but as editor of the *Abendzeitung,* a paper then rather on the wane, he seized the opportunity presented by our negotiations in order to ask me to send him frequent and gratuitous contributions. The consequence was, that whenever I wanted to know anything concerning the fate of my opera, I had to oblige him by enclosing an article for his paper. Now, as these negotiations with the Court Theatre lasted a very long time, and involved a large number of contributions from me, I often got into the most extraordinary fixes simply owing to the fact that I was now once more a prisoner in my room, and had been so for some time, and therefore knew nothing of what was going on in Paris.

I had serious reasons for thus withdrawing from the artistic and social life of Paris. My own painful experiences and my disgust at all the mockery of that kind of life, once so attractive to me and yet so alien to my education, had quickly driven me away from everything connected with it. It is true that the production of the *Huguenots,* for instance, which I then heard for the first time, dazzled me very much indeed. Its beautiful orchestral execution, and the extremely careful and effective *mise en scène,* gave me a grand idea of the great possibilities of such perfect and definite artistic means. But, strange to say, I never felt inclined to hear the same opera again. I soon became tired of the extravagant execution of the vocalists, and I often amused my friends exceedingly by imitating the latest Parisian methods and the vulgar exaggerations with which the performances teemed. Those composers, moreover, who aimed at achieving success by adopting the style which was then in vogue, could not help, either, incurring my sarcastic criticism. The last shred of esteem which I still tried to retain for the ' first lyrical theatre in the world ' was at last rudely destroyed when I saw how such an empty, altogether un-French work as Donizetti's *Favorita* could secure so long and important a run at this theatre.

During the whole time of my stay in Paris I do not think I went to the opera more than four times. The cold productions at the Opéra Comique, and the degenerate quality of the music produced there, had repelled me from the start; and the same lack of enthusiasm displayed by the singers also drove me from Italian opera. The names, often very famous ones, of these artists who sang the same four operas for years could not compensate me for the complete absence of sentiment which characterised their performance, so unlike that of Schröder-Devrient, which I so thoroughly enjoyed. I clearly saw that everything was on the down grade, and yet I cherished no hope or desire to see this state of decline superseded by a period of newer and fresher life. I preferred the small theatres, where French talent was shown in its true light; and yet, as the result of my own longings, I was too intent upon finding points of relationship in them which would excite my sympathy, for it to be possible for me to realise those peculiar excellences in them which did not happen to interest me at all. Besides, from the very beginning my own troubles had proved so trying, and the consciousness of the failure of my Paris schemes had become so cruelly apparent, that, either out of indifference or annoyance, I declined all invitations to the theatres. Again and again, much to Minna's regret, I returned tickets for performances in which *Rachel* was to appear at the Théâtre Français, and, in fact, saw that famous theatre only once, when, some time later, I had to go there on business for my Dresden patron, who wanted some more articles.

I adopted the most shameful means for filling the columns of the *Abendzeitung;* I just strung together whatever I happened to hear in the evening from Anders and Lehrs. But as they had no very exciting adventures either, they simply told me all they had picked up from papers and table-talk, and this I tried to render with as much piquancy as possible in accordance with the journalistic style created by Heine, which was all the rage at the time. My one fear was lest old Hofrath Winkler should some day discover the secret of my wide knowledge of Paris. Among other things which I sent to his declining paper was a long account of the production of *Freischütz.* He was particularly interested in it, as he was the guardian of Weber's children; and when in one of his letters he assured me that he would not rest until he had got the definite assurance that *Rienzi* had been accepted, I sent him, with my most profuse thanks, the German manuscript of my ' Beethoven ' story for his paper. The 1841 edition of this gazette, then published by Arnold, but now no longer in existence, contains the only print of this manuscript.

My occasional journalistic work was increased by a request from Lewald, the editor of *Europa,* a literary monthly, asking me to write something for him. This man was the first who, from time to time, had mentioned my name to the public. As he used to publish musical supplements to his elegant and rather widely read magazine, I sent him two of my compositions from Königsberg for publication. One of these was the music I had set to a melancholy poem by Scheuerlin, entitled *Der Knabe und der Tannenbaum* (a work of which even to-day I am still proud), and my beautiful *Carnevals Lied* out of *Liebesverbot.*

When I wanted to publish my little French compositions — *Dors, mon enfant,* and the music to Hugo's *Attente* and Ronsard's *Mignonne* — Lewald not only sent me a small fee — the first I had ever received for a composition — but commissioned some long articles on my Paris impressions, which he begged me to write as entertainingly as possible. For his paper I wrote *Pariser Amusements* and *Pariser Fatalitäten,* in which I gave vent in a humorous style, à la Heine, to all my disappointing experiences in Paris, and to all my contempt for the life led by its inhabitants. In the second I described the existence of a certain Hermann Pfau, a strange good-for-nothing with whom, during my early Leipzig days, I had become more intimately acquainted than was desirable. This man had been wandering about Paris like a vagrant ever since the beginning of the previous winter, and the meagre income I derived from arrangements of *La Favorita* was often partly consumed in helping this completely broken-down fellow. So it was only fair that I should get back a few francs of the money spent on him in Paris by turning his adventures to some account in Lewald's newspapers.

When I came into contact with Léon Pillet, the manager of the Opera, my literary work took yet another direction. After numerous inquiries I eventually discovered that he had taken a fancy to my draft of the *Fliegender Holländer.* He informed me of this, and asked me to sell him the plot, as he was under contract to supply various composers with subjects for operettas. I tried to explain to Pillet, both verbally and in writing, that he could hardly expect that the plot would be properly treated except by myself, as this draft was in fact my own idea, and that it had only come to his knowledge by my having submitted it to him. But it was all to no purpose. He was obliged to admit quite frankly that the expectations I had cherished as to the result of Meyerbeer's recommendation to him would not come to anything. He said there was no likelihood of my getting a commission for a composition, even of a light opera, for the next seven years, as his already existing contracts extended over that period. He asked me to be sensible, and to sell him the draft for a small amount, so that he might have the music written by an author to be selected by him; and he added that if I still wished to try my luck at the Opera House, I had better see the ' ballet-master,' as he might want some music for a certain dance. Seeing that I contemptuously refused this proposal, he left me to my own devices.

After endless and unsuccessful attempts at getting the matter settled, I at last begged Edouard Monnaie, the Commissaire for the Royal Theatres, who was not only a friend of mine, but also editor of the *Gazette Musicale*, to act as mediator. He candidly confessed that he could not understand Pillet's liking for my plot, which he also was acquainted with; but as Pillet seemed to like it — though he would probably lose it — he advised me to accept anything for it, as Monsieur Paul Faucher, a brother-in-law of Victor Hugo's, had had an offer to work out the scheme for a similar libretto. This gentleman had, moreover, declared that there was nothing new in my plot, as the story of the *Vaisseau Fantôme* was well known in France. I now saw how I stood, and, in a conversation with Pillet, at which M. Faucher was present, I said I would come to an arrangement. My plot was generously estimated by Pillet at five hundred francs, and I received that amount from the cash office at the theatre, to be subsequently deducted from the author's rights of the future poet.

Our summer residence in the Avenue de Meudon now assumed quite a definite character. These five hundred francs had to help me to work out the words and music of my *Fliegender Holländer* for Germany, while I abandoned the French *Vaisseau Fantôme* to its fate.

The state of my affairs, which was getting ever worse and worse, was slightly improved by the settlement of this matter. May and June had gone by, and during these months our troubles had grown steadily more serious. The lovely season of the year, the stimulating country air, and the sensation of freedom following upon my deliverance from the wretchedly paid musical hack-work I had had to do all the winter, wrought their beneficial effects on me, and I was inspired to write a small story entitled *Ein glücklicher Abend*. This was translated and published in French in the *Gazette Musicale*. Soon, however, our lack of funds began to make itself felt with a severity that was very discouraging. We felt this all the more keenly when my sister Cecilia and her husband, following our example, moved to a place quite close to us. Though not wealthy, they were fairly well-to-do. They came to see us every day, but we never thought it desirable to let them know how terribly hard-up we were. One day it came to a climax. Being absolutely without money, I started out, early one morning, to walk to Paris — for I had not even enough to pay the railway fare thither — and I resolved to wander about the whole day, trudging from street to street, even until late in the afternoon, in the hope of raising a five-franc piece; but my errand proved absolutely vain, and I had to walk all the way back to Meudon again, utterly penniless.

When I told Minna, who came to meet me, of my failure, she informed me in despair that Hermann Pfau, whom I have mentioned before, had also come to us in the most pitiful plight, and actually in want of food, and that she had had to give him the last of the bread delivered by the baker that morning. The only hope that now remained was that, at any rate, my lodger Brix, who by a singular fate was now our companion in misfortune, would return with some success from the expedition to Paris which he also had made that morning. At last he, too, returned bathed in perspiration and exhausted, driven home by the craving for a meal, which he had been unable to procure in the town, as he could not find any of the acquaintances he went to see. He begged most piteously for a piece of bread. This climax to the situation at last inspired my wife with heroic resolution; for she felt it her duty to exert herself to appease at least the hunger of her menfolk. For the first time during her stay on French soil, she persuaded the baker, the butcher, and wine-merchant, by plausible arguments, to supply her with the necessaries of life without immediate cash payment, and Minna's eyes beamed when, an hour later. she was able to put before us an excellent meal, during which, as it happened, we were surprised by the Avenarius family, who were evidently relieved at finding us so well provided for.

This extreme distress was relieved for a time, at the beginning of July, by the sale of my *Vaisseau Fantôme,* which meant my final renunciation of my success in Paris. As long as the five hundred francs lasted, I had an interval of respite for carrying on my work. The first object on which I spent my money was on the hire of a piano, a thing of which I had been entirely deprived for months. My chief intention in so doing was to revive my faith in myself as a musician, as, ever since the autumn of the previous year, I had exercised my talents as a journalist and adapter of operas only. The libretto of the *Fliegender Holländer,* which I had hurriedly written during the recent period of distress, aroused considerable interest in Lehrs; he actually declared I would never write anything better, and that the *Fliegender Holländer* would be my *Don Juan;* the only thing now was to find the music for it. As towards the end of the previous winter I still entertained the hopes of being permitted to treat this subject for the French Opera, I had already finished some of the words and music of the lyric parts, and had had the libretto translated by Émile Deschamps, intending it for a trial performance, which, alas, never took place. These parts were the ballad of Senta, the song of the Norwegian sailors, and the ' Spectre Song ' of the crew of the *Fliegender Holländer.* Since that time I had been so violently torn away from the music that, when the piano arrived at my rustic retreat, I did not dare to touch it for a whole day. I was terribly afraid lest I should discover that my inspiration had left me — when suddenly I was seized with the idea that I had forgotten to write out the song of the helmsman in the first act, although, as a matter of fact, I could not remember having composed it at all, as I had in reality only just written the lyrics. I succeeded, and was pleased with the result. The same thing occurred with the ' Spinner's Song,' and when I had written out these two pieces, and, on further reflection, could not help admitting that they had really only taken shape in my mind at that moment, I was quite delirious with joy at the discovery. In seven weeks the whole of the music of the *Fliegender Holländer*, except the orchestration, was finished.

Thereupon followed a general revival in our circle; my exuberant good spirits astonished every one, and my Avenarius relations in particular thought I must really be prospering, as I was such good company. I resumed my long walks in the woods of Meudon, frequently even consenting to help Minna gather mushrooms, which, unfortunately, were for her the chief charm of our woodland retreat, though it filled our landlord with terror when he saw us returning with our spoils, as he felt sure we should be poisoned if we ate them.

My destiny, which almost invariably led me into strange adventures, here once more introduced me to the most eccentric character to be found not only in the neighbourhood of Meudon, but even in Paris. This was M. Jadin, who, though he was old enough to be able to say that he remembered seeing Madame de Pompadour at Versailles, was still vigorous beyond belief. It appeared to be his aim to keep the world in a constant state of conjecture as to his real age; he made everything for himself with his own hands, including even a quantity of wigs of every shade, ranging in the most comic variety from youthful flaxen to the most venerable white, with intermediate shades of grey; these he wore alternately, as the fancy pleased him. He dabbled in everything, and I was pleased to find he had a particular fancy for painting. The fact that all the walls of his rooms were hung with the most childish caricatures of animal life, and that he had even embellished the outside of his blinds with the most ridiculous paintings, did not disconcert me in the least; on the contrary, it confirmed my belief that he did not dabble in music, until, to my horror, I discovered that the strangely discordant sounds of a harp which kept reaching my ears from some unknown region were actually proceeding from his basement, where he had two harpsichords of his own invention. He informed me that he had unfortunately neglected playing them for a long time, but that he now meant to begin practising again assiduously in order to give me pleasure. I succeeded in dissuading him from this, by assuring him that the doctor had forbidden me to listen to the harp, as it was bad for my nerves. His figure as I saw him for the last time remains impressed on my memory, like an apparition from the world of Hoffmann's fairy-tales. In the late autumn, when we were going back to Paris, he asked us to take with us on our furniture van an enormous stove-pipe, of which he promised to relieve us shortly. One very cold day Jadin actually presented himself at our new abode in Paris, in a most preposterous costume of his own manufacture, consisting of very thin light-yellow trousers, a very short pale-green dress-coat with conspicuously long tails, projecting lace shirt frills and cuffs, a very fair wig, and a hat so small that it was constantly dropping off; he wore in addition a quantity of imitation jewellery — and all this on the undisguised assumption that he could not go about in fashionable Paris dressed as simply as in the country. He had come for the stove-pipe; we asked him where the men to carry it were; in reply he simply smiled, and expressed his surprise at our helplessness; and thereupon took the enormous stove-pipe under his arm and absolutely refused to accept our help when we offered to assist him in carrying it down the stairs, though this operation, notwithstanding his vaunted skill, occupied him quite half an hour. Every one in the house assembled to witness this removal, but he was by no means disconcerted, and managed to get the pipe through the street door, and then tripped gracefully along the pavement with it, and disappeared from our sight.

For this short though eventful period, during which I was quite free to give full scope to my inmost thoughts, I indulged in the consolation of purely artistic creations. I can only say that, when it came to an end, I had made such progress that I could look forward with cheerful composure to the much longer period of trouble and distress I felt was in store for me. This, in fact, duly set in, for I had only just completed the last scene when I found that my five hundred francs were coming to an end, and what was left was not sufficient to secure me the necessary peace and freedom from worry for composing the overture; I had to postpone this until my luck should take another favourable turn, and meanwhile I was forced to engage in the struggle for a bare subsistence, making efforts of all kinds that left me neither leisure nor peace of mind. The concierge from the Rue du Helder brought us the news that the mysterious family to whom we had let our rooms had left, and that we were now once more responsible for the rent. I had to tell him that I would not under any circumstances trouble about the rooms any more, and that the landlord might recoup himself by the sale of the furniture we had left there. This was done at a very heavy loss, and the furniture, the greater part of which was still unpaid for, was sacrificed to pay the rent of a dwelling which we no longer occupied.

Under the stress of the most terrible privations I still endeavoured to secure sufficient leisure for working out the orchestration of the score of the *Fliegender Holländer*. The rough autumn weather set in at an exceptionally early date; people were all leaving their country houses for Paris, and, among them, the Avenarius family. We, however, could not dream of doing so, for we could not even raise the funds for the journey. When M. Jadin expressed his surprise at this, I pretended to be so pressed with work that I could not interrupt it, although I felt the cold that penetrated through the thin walls of the house very severely.

So I waited for help from Ernst Castel, one of my old Königsberg friends, a well-to-do young merchant, who a short time before had called on us in Meudon and treated us to a luxurious repast in Paris, promising at the same time to relieve our necessities as soon as possible by an advance, which we knew was an easy matter to him.

By way of cheering us up, Kietz came over to us one day, with a large portfolio and a pillow under his arm; he intended to amuse us by working at a large caricature representing myself and my unfortunate adventures in Paris, and the pillow was to enable him, after his labours, to get some rest on our hard couch, which he had noticed had no pillows at the head. Knowing that we had a difficulty in procuring fuel, he brought with him some bottles of rum, to 'warm' us with punch during the cold evenings; under these circumstances I read Hoffmann's *Tales* to him and my wife.

At last I had news from Königsberg, but it only opened my eyes to the fact that the gay young dog had not meant his promise seriously. We now looked forward almost with despair to the chilly mists of approaching winter, but Kietz, declaring that it was his place to find help, packed up his portfolio, placed it under his arm with the pillow, and went off to Paris. On the next day he returned with two hundred francs, that he had managed to procure by means of generous self-sacrifice. We at once set off for Paris, and took a small apartment near our friends, in the back part of No. 14 Rue Jacob. I afterwards heard that shortly after we left it was occupied by Proudhon.

We got back to town on 30th October. Our home was exceedingly small and cold, and its chilliness in particular made it very bad for our health. We furnished it scantily with the little we had saved from the wreck of the Rue du Helder, and awaited the results of my efforts towards getting my works accepted and produced in Germany. The first necessity was at all costs to secure peace and quietness for myself for the short time which I should have to devote to the overture of the *Fliegender Holländer;* I told Kietz that he would have to procure the money necessary for my household expenses until this work was finished and the full score of the opera sent off. With the aid of a pedantic uncle, who had lived in Paris a long time and who was also a painter, he succeeded in providing me with the necessary assistance, in instalments of five or ten francs at a time. During this period I often pointed with cheerful pride to my boots, which became mere travesties of footgear, as the soles eventually disappeared altogether.

As long as I was engaged on the *Dutchman,* and Kietz was looking after me, this made no difference, for I never went out: but when I had despatched my completed score to the management of the Berlin Court Theatre at the beginning of December, the bitterness of the position could no longer be disguised. It was necessary for me to buckle to and look for help myself.

What this meant in Paris I learned just about this time from the hapless fate of the worthy Lehrs. Driven by need such as I myself had had to surmount a year before at about the same time, he had been compelled on a broiling hot day in the previous summer to scour the various quarters of the city breathlessly, to get grace for bills he had accepted, and which had fallen due. He foolishly took an iced drink, which he hoped would refresh him in his distressing condition, but it immediately

made him lose his voice, and from that day he was the victim
of a hoarseness which with terrific rapidity ripened the seeds
of consumption, doubtless latent in him, and developed that
incurable disease. For months he had been growing weaker
and weaker, filling us at last with the gloomiest anxiety: he
alone believed the supposed chill would be cured, if he could
heat his room better for a time. One day I sought him out in
his lodging, where I found him in the icy-cold room, huddled
up at his writing-table, and complaining of the difficulty of his
work for Didot, which was all the more distressing as his
employer was pressing him for advances he had made.

He declared that if he had not had the consolation in those
doleful hours of knowing that I had, at any rate, got my
Dutchman finished, and that a prospect of success was thus
opened to the little circle of friends, his misery would have
been hard indeed to bear. Despite my own great trouble, I
begged him to share our fire and work in my room. He smiled
at my courage in trying to help others, especially as my quarters offered barely space enough for myself and my wife. However, one evening he came to us and silently showed me a letter
he had received from Villemain, the Minister of Education at
that time, in which the latter expressed in the warmest terms
his great regret at having only just learned that so distinguished
a scholar, whose able and extensive collaboration in Didot's
issue of the Greek classics had made him participator in a work
that was the glory of the nation, should be in such bad health
and straitened circumstances. Unfortunately, the amount of
public money which he had at his disposal at that moment for
subsidising literature only allowed of his offering him the sum
of five hundred francs, which he enclosed with apologies, asking
him to accept it as a recognition of his merits on the part of
the French Government, and adding that it was his intention
to give earnest consideration as to how he might materially
improve his position.

This filled us with the utmost thankfulness on poor Lehrs'
account, and we looked on the incident almost as a miracle.
We could not help assuming, however, that M. Villemain had
been influenced by Didot, who had been prompted by his own
guilty conscience for his despicable exploitation of Lehrs, and

by the prospect of thus relieving himself of the responsibility
of helping him. At the same time, from similar cases within
our knowledge, which were fully confirmed by my own subsequent experience, we were driven to the conclusion that such
prompt and considerate sympathy on the part of a minister
would have been impossible in Germany. Lehrs would now
have a fire to work by, but alas! our fears as to his declining
health could not be allayed. When we left Paris in the following spring, it was the certainty that we should never see our
dear friend again that made our parting so painful.

In my own great distress I was again exposed to the annoyance of having to write numerous unpaid articles for the
Abendzeitung, as my patron, Hofrath Winkler, was still unable
to give me any satisfactory account of the fate of my *Rienzi* in
Dresden. In these circumstances I was obliged to consider it
a good thing that Halévy's latest opera was at last a success.
Schlesinger came to us radiant with joy at the success of *La
Reine de Chypre,* and promised me eternal bliss for the piano
score and various other arrangements I had made of this
newest rage in the sphere of opera. So I was again forced to
pay the penalty for composing my own *Fliegender Holländer* by
having to sit down and write out arrangements of Halévy's
opera. Yet this task no longer weighed on me so heavily.
Apart from the wellfounded hope of being at last recalled
from my exile in Paris, and thus being able, as I thought, to
regard this last struggle with poverty as the decisive one, the
arrangement of Halévy's score was far and away a more interesting piece of hack-work than the shameful labour I had spent
on Donizetti's *Favorita.*

I paid another visit, the last for a long time to come, to the
Grand Opera to hear this *Reine de Chypre.* There was, indeed, much for me to smile at. My eyes were no longer shut to
the extreme weakness of this class of work, and the caricature
of it that was often produced by the method of rendering it. I
was sincerely rejoiced to see the better side of Halévy again.
I had taken a great fancy to him from the time of his *La Juive,*
and had a very high opinion of his masterly talent.

At the request of Schlesinger I also willingly consented to
write for his paper a long article on Halévy's latest work. In

it I laid particular stress on my hope that the French school
might not again allow the benefits obtained by studying the
German style to be lost by relapsing into the shallowest Italian
methods. On that occasion I ventured, by way of encouraging
the French school, to point to the peculiar significance of Auber,
and particularly to his *Stumme von Portici,* drawing attention,
on the other hand, to the overloaded melodies of Rossini, which
often resembled sol-fa exercises. In reading over the proof
of my article I saw that this passage about Rossini had been
left out, and M. Edouard Monnaie admitted to me that, in
his capacity as editor of a musical paper, he had felt himself
bound to suppress it. He considered that if I had any adverse
criticism to pass on the composer, I could easily get it published in any other kind of paper, but not in one devoted to
the interests of music, simply because such a passage could not
be printed there without seeming absurd. It also annoyed him
that I had spoken in such high terms of Auber, but he let it
stand. I had to listen to much from that quarter which enlightened me for ever with regard to the decay of operatic
music in particular, and artistic taste in general, among Frenchmen of the present day.

I also wrote a longer article on the same opera for my
precious friend Winkler at Dresden, who was still hesitating
about accepting my *Rienzi.* In doing so I intentionally made
merry over a mishap that had befallen Lachner the conductor.
Küstner, who was theatrical director at Munich at the time,
with a view to giving his friend another chance, ordered a
libretto to be written for him by St. Georges in Paris, so that,
through his paternal care, the highest bliss which a German
composer could dream of might be assured to his protégé.
Well, it turned out that when Halévy's *Reine de Chypre* appeared, it treated the same subject as Lachner's presumably
original work, which had been composed in the meantime. It
mattered very little that the libretto was a really good one, the
value of the bargain lay in the fact that it was to be glorified
by Lachner's music. It appeared, however, that St. Georges
had, as a matter of fact, to some extent altered the book sent
to Munich, but only by the omission of several interesting
features. The fury of the Munich manager was great, where-

upon St. Georges declared his astonishment that the latter could have imagined he would supply a libretto intended solely for the German stage at the paltry price offered by his German customer. As I had formed my own private opinion as to procuring French librettos for operas, and as nothing in the world would have induced me to set to music even the most effective piece of writing by Scribe or St. Georges, this occurrence delighted me immensely, and in the best of spirits I let myself go on the point for the benefit of the readers of the *Abendzeitung,* who, it is to be hoped, did not include my future ' friend ' Lachner.

In addition, my work on Halévy's opera (*Reine de Chypre*) brought me into closer contact with that composer, and was the means of procuring me many an enlivening talk with that peculiarly good-hearted and really unassuming man, whose talent, alas, declined all too soon. Schlesinger, in fact, was exasperated at his incorrigible laziness. Halévy, who had looked through my piano score, contemplated several changes with a view to making it easier, but he did not proceed with them: Schlesinger could not get the proof-sheets back; the publication was consequently delayed, and he feared that the popularity of the opera would be over before the work was ready for the public. He urged me to get firm hold of Halévy very early in the morning in his rooms, and compel him to set to work at the alterations in my company.

The first time I reached his house at about ten in the morning, I found him just out of bed, and he informed me that he really must have breakfast first. I accepted his invitation, and sat down with him to a somewhat luxurious meal; my conversation seemed to appeal to him, but friends came in, and at last Schlesinger among the number, who burst into a fury at not finding him at work on the proofs he regarded as so important. Halévy, however, remained quite unmoved. In the best of good tempers he merely complained of his latest success, because he had never had more peace than of late, when his operas, almost without exception, had been failures, and he had not had anything to do with them after the first production. Moreover, he feigned not to understand why this *Reine de Chypre* in particular should have been a success; he declared that Schlesinger had engineered it on purpose to worry him. When he spoke a few words to me in German, one of the visitors was astonished, whereupon Schlesinger said that all Jews could speak German. Thereupon Schlesinger was asked if he also was a Jew. He answered that he had been, but had become a Christian for his wife's sake. This freedom of speech was a pleasant surprise to me, because in Germany in such cases we always studiously avoided the point, as discourteous to the person referred to. But as we never got to the proof correcting, Schlesinger made me promise to give Halévy no peace until we had done them.

The secret of his indifference to success became clear to me in the course of further conversation, as I learned that he was on the point of making a wealthy marriage. At first I was inclined to think that Halévy was simply a man whose youthful talent was only stimulated to achieve one great success with the object of becoming rich; in his case, however, this was not the only reason, as he was very modest in regard to his own capacity, and had no great opinion of the works of those more fortunate composers who were writing for the French stage at that time. In him I thus, for the first time, met with the frankly expressed admission of disbelief in the value of all our modern creations in this dubious field of art. I have since come to the conclusion that this incredulity, often expressed with much less modesty, justifies the participation of all Jews in our artistic concerns. Only once did Halévy speak to me with real candour, when, on my tardy departure for Germany, he wished me the success he thought my works deserved.

In the year 1860 I saw him again. I had learned that, while the Parisian critics were giving vent to the bitterest condemnation of the concerts I was giving at that time, he had expressed his approval, and this determined me to visit him at the Palais de l'Institut, of which he had for some time been permanent secretary. He seemed particularly eager to learn from my own lips what my new theory about music really was, of which he had heard such wild rumours. For his own part, he said, he had never found anything but music in my music, but with this difference, that mine had generally

seemed very good. This gave rise to a lively discussion on my
part, to which he good-humouredly agreed, once more wishing
me success in Paris. This time, however, he did so with less
conviction than when he bade me good-bye for Germany, which
I thought was because he doubted whether I could succeed
in Paris. From this final visit I carried away a depressing
sense of the enervation, both moral and æsthetic, which had
overcome one of the last great French musicians, while, on
the other hand, I could not help feeling that a tendency to a
hypocritical or frankly impudent exploitation of the universal
degeneracy marked all who could be designated as Halévy's
successors.

Throughout this period of constant hack-work my thoughts
were entirely bent on my return to Germany, which now presented itself to my mind in a wholly new and ideal light. I
endeavoured in various ways to secure all that seemed most
attractive about the project, or which filled my soul with longing. My intercourse with Lehrs had, on the whole, given a
decided spur to my former tendency to grapple seriously with
my subjects, a tendency which had been counteracted by closer
contact with the theatre. This desire now furnished a basis
for closer study of philosophical questions. I had been astonished at times to hear even the grave and virtuous Lehrs,
openly and quite as a matter of course, give expression to
grave doubts concerning our individual survival after death.
He declared that in many great men this doubt, even though
only tacitly held, had been the real incitement to noble deeds.
The natural result of such a belief speedily dawned on me
without, however, causing me any serious alarm. On the contrary, I found a fascinating stimulus in the fact that boundless regions of meditation and knowledge were thereby opened
up which hitherto I had merely skimmed in light-hearted
levity.

In my renewed attempts to study the Greek classics in the
original, I received no encouragement from Lehrs. He dissuaded me from doing so with the well-meant consolation, that
as I could only be born once, and that with music in me, I
should learn to understand this branch of knowledge without
the help of grammar or lexicon; whereas if Greek were to be

studied with real enjoyment, it was no joke, and would not suffer being relegated to a secondary place.

On the other hand, I felt strongly drawn to gain a closer acquaintance of German history than I had secured at school. I had Raumer's *History of the Hohenstaufen* within easy reach to start upon. All the great figures in this book lived vividly before my eyes. I was particularly captivated by the personality of that gifted Emperor Frederick II., whose fortunes aroused my sympathy so keenly that I vainly sought for a fitting artistic setting for them. The fate of his son Manfred, on the other hand, provoked in me an equally well-grounded, but more easily combated, feeling of opposition.

I accordingly made a plan of a great five-act dramatic poem, which should also be perfectly adapted to a musical setting. My impulse to embellish the story with the central figure of romantic significance was prompted by the fact of Manfred's enthusiastic reception in Luceria by the Saracens, who supported him and carried him on from victory to victory till he reached his final triumph, and this, too, in spite of the fact that he had come to them betrayed on every hand, banned by the Church, and deserted by all his followers during his flight through Apulia and the Abruzzi.

Even at this time it delighted me to find in the German mind the capacity of appreciating beyond the narrow bounds of nationality all purely human qualities, in however strange a garb they might be presented. For in this I recognised how nearly akin it is to the mind of Greece. In Frederick II. I saw this quality in full flower. A fair-haired German of ancient Swabian stock, heir to the Norman realm of Sicily and Naples, who gave the Italian language its first development, and laid a basis for the evolution of knowledge and art where hitherto ecclesiastical fanaticism and feudal brutality had alone contended for power, a monarch who gathered at his court the poets and sages of eastern lands, and surrounded himself with the living products of Arabian and Persian grace and spirit — this man I beheld betrayed by the Roman clergy to the infidel foe, yet ending his crusade, to their bitter disappointment, by a pact of peace with the Sultan, from whom he obtained a

grant of privileges to Christians in Palestine such as the
bloodiest victory could scarcely have secured.

In this wonderful Emperor, who finally, under the ban of
that same Church, struggled hopelessly and in vain against the
savage bigotry of his age, I beheld the German ideal in its
highest embodiment. My poem was concerned with the fate
of his favourite son Manfred. On the death of an elder brother,
Frederick's empire had entirely fallen to pieces, and the young
Manfred was left, under papal suzerainty, in nominal possession
of the throne of Apulia. We find him at Capua, in surroundings, and attended by a court, in which the spirit of his great
father survives, in a state of almost effeminate degeneration.
In despair of ever restoring the imperial power of the Hohenstaufen, he seeks to forget his sadness in romance and song.
There now appears upon the scene a young Saracen lady, just
arrived from the East, who, by appealing to the alliance between
East and West concluded by Manfred's noble father, conjures
the desponding son to maintain his imperial heritage. She
acts the part of an inspired prophetess, and though the prince
is quickly filled with love for her, she succeeds in keeping
him at a respectful distance. By a skilfully contrived flight
she snatches him, not only from the pursuit of rebellious Apulian
nobles, but also from the papal ban which is threatening to
depose him from his throne. Accompanied only by a few
faithful followers, she guides him through mountain fastnesses,
where one night the wearied son beholds the spirit of Frederick
II. passing with feudal array through the Abruzzi, and beckon-
ing him on to Luceria.

To this district, situated in the Papal States, Frederick had,
by a peaceful compact, transplanted the remnant of his Saracen
retainers, who had previously been wreaking terrible havoc in
the mountains of Sicily. To the great annoyance of the Pope,
he had handed the town over to them in fee-simple, thus securing
for himself a band of faithful allies in the heart of an ever-
treacherous and hostile country.

Fatima, as my heroine is called, has prepared, through the
instrumentality of trusty friends, a reception for Manfred in
this place. When the papal governor has been expelled by a
revolution, he slips through the gateway into the town, is

recognised by the whole population as the son of their beloved
Emperor, and, amid wildest enthusiasm, is placed at their head,
to lead them against the enemies of their departed benefactor.
In the meantime, while Manfred is marching on from victory
to victory in his reconquest of the whole kingdom of Apulia,
the tragic centre of my action still continues to be the unvoiced
longing of the lovelorn victor for the marvellous heroine.

She is the child of the great Emperor's love for a noble
Saracen maiden. Her mother, on her deathbed, had sent her
to Manfred, foretelling that she would work wonders for his
glory provided she never yielded to his passion. Whether
Fatima was to know that she was his sister I left undecided in
framing my plot. Meanwhile she is careful to show herself
to him only at critical moments, and then always in such a way
as to remain unapproachable. When at last she witnesses the
completion of her task in his coronation at Naples, she deter-
mines, in obedience to her vow, to slip away secretly from the
newly anointed king, that she may meditate in the solitude
of her distant home upon the success of her enterprise.

The Saracen Nurreddin, who had been a companion of her
youth, and to whose help she had chiefly owed her success in
rescuing Manfred, is to be the sole partner of her flight. To
this man, who loves her with passionate ardour, she had been
promised in her childhood. Before her secret departure she
pays a last visit to the slumbering king. This rouses her lover's
furious jealousy, as he construes her act into a proof of unfaithfulness on the part of his betrothed. The last look of
farewell which Fatima casts from a distance at the young
monarch, on his return from his coronation, inflames the jealous
lover to wreak instant vengeance for the supposed outrage upon
his honour. He strikes the prophetess to the earth, whereupon
she thanks him with a smile for having delivered her from
an unbearable existence. At the sight of her body Manfred
realises that henceforth happiness has deserted him for ever.

This theme I had adorned with many gorgeous scenes and
complicated situations, so that when I had worked it out I
could regard it as a fairly suitable, interesting, and effective
whole, especially when compared with other well-known subjects of a similar nature. Yet I could never rouse myself to

sufficient enthusiasm over it to give my serious attention to
its elaboration, especially as another theme now laid its grip
upon me. This was suggested to me by a pamphlet on the
'Venusberg,' which accidentally fell into my hands.

If all that I regarded as essentially German had hitherto
drawn me with ever-increasing force, and compelled me to its
eager pursuit, I here found it suddenly presented to me in the
simple outlines of a legend, based upon the old and well-known
ballad of 'Tannhäuser.' True, its elements were already familiar
to me from Tieck's version in his *Phantasus*. But his conception of the subject had flung me back into the fantastic regions
created in my mind at an earlier period by Hoffmann, and
I should certainly never have been tempted to extract the
framework of a dramatic work from his elaborate story. The
point in this popular pamphlet which had so much weight with
me was that it brought 'Tannhäuser,' if only by a passing
hint, into touch with 'The Minstrel's War on the Wartburg.'
I had some knowledge of this also from Hoffmann's account
in his *Serapionsbrüdern*. But I felt that the writer had only
grasped the old legend in a distorted form, and therefore endeavoured to gain a closer acquaintance with the true aspect
of this attractive story. At this juncture Lehrs brought me
the annual report of the proceedings of the Königsberg German
Society, in which the 'Wartburg contest' was criticised with
a fair amount of detail by Lukas. Here I also found the
original text. Although I could utilise but little of the real
setting for my own purpose, yet the picture it gave me of Germany in the Middle Ages was so suggestive that I found I had
not previously had the smallest conception of what it was like.

As a sequel to the Wartburg poem, I also found in the same
copy a critical study, 'Lohengrin,' which gave in full detail
the main contents of that widespread epic.

Thus a whole new world was opened to me, and though as
yet I had not found the form in which I might cope with
Lohengrin, yet this image also lived imperishably within me.
When, therefore, I afterwards made a close acquaintance with
the intricacies of this legend, I could visualise the figure of the
hero with a distinctness equal to that of my conception of
Tannhäuser at this time.

Under these influences my longing for a speedy return to Germany grew ever more intense, for there I hoped to earn a new home for myself where I could enjoy leisure for creative work. But it was not yet possible even to think of occupying myself with such grateful tasks. The sordid necessities of life still bound me to Paris. While thus employed, I found an opportunity of exerting myself in a way more congenial to my desires. When I was a young man at Prague, I had made the acquaintance of a Jewish musician and composer called Dessauer — a man who was not devoid of talent, who in fact achieved a certain reputation, but was chiefly known among his intimates on account of his hypochondria. This man, who was now in flourishing circumstances, was so far patronised by Schlesinger that the latter seriously proposed to help him to a commission for Grand Opera. Dessauer had come across my poem of the *Fliegender Holländer*, and now insisted that I should draft a similar plot for him, as M. Léon Pillet's *Vaisseau Fantôme* had already been given to M. Dietsch, the latter's musical conductor, to set to music. From this same conductor Dessauer obtained the promise of a like commission, and he now offered me two hundred francs to provide him with a similar plot, and one congenial to his hypochondriacal temperament.

To meet this wish I ransacked my brain for recollections of Hoffmann, and quickly decided to work up his *Bergwerke von Falun*. The moulding of this fascinating and marvellous material succeeded as admirably as I could wish. Dessauer also felt convinced that the topic was worth his while to set to music. His dismay was accordingly all the greater when Pillet rejected our plot on the ground that the staging would be too difficult, and that the second act especially would entail insurmountable obstacles for the ballet, which had to be given each time. In place of this Dessauer wished me to compose him an oratorio on 'Mary Magdalene.' As on the day that he expressed this wish he appeared to be suffering from acute melancholia, so much so that he declared he had that morning seen his own head lying beside his bed, I thought well not to refuse his request. I asked him, therefore, to give me time, and I regret to say that ever since that day I have continued to take it.

It was amid such distractions as these that this winter at
length drew to an end, while my prospects of getting to Germany
gradually grew more hopeful, though with a slowness that
sorely tried my patience. I had kept up a continuous correspondence with Dresden respecting *Rienzi*, and in the worthy
chorus-master Fischer I at last found an honest man who was
favourably disposed to me. He sent me reliable and reassuring
reports as to the state of my affairs.

After receiving news, early in January, 1842, of renewed delay, I at last heard that by the end of February the work would
be ready for performance. I was seriously uneasy at this, as I
was afraid of not being able to accomplish the journey by that
date. But this news also was soon contradicted, and the honest
Fischer informed me that my opera had had to be postponed till
the autumn of that year. I realised fully that it would never
be performed if I could not be present in person at Dresden.
When eventually in March Count Redern, the director of the
Theatre Royal in Berlin, told me that my *Fliegender Holländer*
had been accepted for the opera there, I thought I had sufficient
reason to return to Germany at all costs as soon as possible.

I had already had various experiences as to the views of
German managers on this work. Relying on the plot, which
had pleased the manager of the Paris Opera so much, I had
sent the libretto in the first instance to my old acquaintance
Ringelhardt, the director of the Leipzig theatre. But the man
had cherished an undisguised aversion for me since my *Liebesverbot*. As he could not this time possibly object to any
levity in my subject, he now found fault with its gloomy solemnity and refused to accept it. As I had met Councillor
Küstner, at that time manager of the Munich Court Theatre,
when he was making arrangements about *La Reine de Chypre*
in Paris, I now sent him the text of the *Dutchman* with a
similar request. He, too, returned it, with the assurance that
it was not suited to German stage conditions, or to the taste
of the German public. As he had ordered a French libretto
for Munich, I knew what he meant. When the score was
finished, I sent it to Meyerbeer in Berlin, with a letter for
Count Redern, and begged him, as he had been unable to help
me to anything in Paris, in spite of his desire to do so, to be

kind enough to use his influence in Berlin in favour of my composition. I was genuinely astonished at the truly prompt acceptance of my work two months later, which was accompanied by very gratifying assurances from the Count, and I was delighted to see in it a proof of Meyerbeer's sincere and energetic intervention in my favour. Strange to say, on my return to Germany soon afterwards, I was destined to learn that Count Redern had long since retired from the management of the Berlin Opera House, and that Küstner of Munich had already been appointed his successor: the upshot of this was that Count Redern's consent, though very courteous, could not by any means be taken seriously, as the realisation of it depended not on him but on his successor. What the result was remains to be seen.

A circumstance that eventually facilitated my long-desired return to Germany, which was now justified by my good prospects, was the tardily awakened interest taken in my position by the wealthy members of my family. If Didot had had reasons of his own for applying to the Minister Villemain for support for Lehrs, so also Avenarius, my brother-in-law in Paris, when he heard how I was struggling against poverty, one day took it into his head to surprise me with some quite unexpected help secured by his appeal to my sister Louisa. On 26th December of the fast-waning year 1841 I went home to Minna carrying a goose under my arm, and in the beak of the bird we found a five-hundred-franc note. This note had been given me by Avenarius as the result of a request on my behalf made by my sister Louisa to a friend of hers, a wealthy merchant named Schletter. This welcome addition to our extremely straitened resources might not in itself have been sufficient to put me in an exceedingly good-humour, had I not clearly seen in it the prospect of escaping altogether from my position in Paris. As the leading German managers had now consented to the performance of two of my compositions, I thought I might seriously approach my brother-in-law, Friedrich Brockhaus, who had repulsed me the year before when I applied to him in great distress, on the ground that he ' disapproved of my profession.' This time I might be more successful in securing the wherewithal for my return. I was not mistaken, and when the time came I was supplied from this source with the necessary travelling expenses.

With these prospects, and my position thus improved, I found myself spending the second half of the winter 1841–42 in high spirits, and affording constant entertainment to the small circle of friends which my relationship to Avenarius had created around me. Minna and I frequently spent our evenings with this family and others, amongst whom I have pleasant recollections of a certain Herr Kühne, the head of a private school, and his wife. I contributed so greatly to the success of their little soirées, and was always so willing to improvise dances on the piano for them to dance to, that I soon ran the risk of enjoying an almost burdensome popularity.

At length the hour struck for my deliverance; the day came on which, as I devoutly hoped, I might turn my back on Paris for ever. It was the 7th of April, and Paris was already gay with the first luxuriant buddings of spring. In front of our windows, which all the winter had looked upon a bleak and desolate garden, the trees were burgeoning, and the birds sang. Our emotion at parting from our dear friends Anders, Lehrs, and Kietz, however, was great, almost overwhelming. The first seemed already doomed to an early death, for his health was exceedingly bad, and he was advanced in years. About Lehrs' condition, as I have already said, there could no longer be any doubt, and it was dreadful, after so short an experience as the two and a half years which I had spent in Paris, to see the ravages that want had wrought among good, noble, and sometimes even distinguished men. Kietz, for whose future I was concerned, less on grounds of health than of morals, touched our hearts once more by his boundless and almost childlike good-nature. Fancying, for instance, that I might not have enough money for the journey, he forced me, in spite of all resistance, to accept another five-franc piece, which was about all that remained of his own fortune at the moment: he also stuffed a packet of good French snuff for me into the pocket of the coach, in which we at last rumbled through the boulevards to the barriers, which we passed but were unable to see this time, because our eyes were blinded with tears.

PART II

1842–1850

THE journey from Paris to Dresden at that time took five days and nights. On the German frontier, near Forbach, we met with stormy weather and snow, a greeting which seemed inhospitable after the spring we had already enjoyed in Paris. And, indeed, as we continued our journey through our native land once more, we found much to dishearten us, and I could not help thinking that the Frenchmen who on leaving Germany breathed more freely on reaching French soil, and unbuttoned their coats, as though passing from winter into summer, were not so very foolish after all, seeing that we, for our part, were now compelled to seek protection against this conspicuous change of temperature by being very careful to put on sufficient clothing. The unkindness of the elements became perfect torture when, later on, between Frankfort and Leipzig, we were swept into the stream of visitors to the Great Easter Fair.

The pressure on the mail-coaches was so great, that for two days and a night, amid ceaseless storm, snow and rain, we were continually changing from one wretched 'substitute' to another, thus turning our journey into an adventure of almost the same type as our former voyage at sea.

One solitary flash of brightness was afforded by our view of the Wartburg, which we passed during the only sunlit hour of this journey. The sight of this mountain fastness, which, from the Fulda side, is clearly visible for a long time, affected me deeply. A neighbouring ridge further on I at once christened the Hörselberg, and as we drove through the valley, pictured to myself the scenery for the third act of my *Tannhäuser*. This scene remained so vividly in my mind, that long afterwards I was able to give Despléchin, the Parisian scene-painter, exact details when he was working out the scenery under my

direction. If I had already been impressed by the significance of the fact that my first journey through the German
Rhine district, so famous in legend, should have been made
on my way home from Paris, it seemed an even more omi-
nous coincidence that my first sight of Wartburg, which was
so rich in historical and mythical associations, should come
just at this moment. The view so warmed my heart against
wind and weather, Jews and the Leipzig Fair, that in the
end I arrived, on 12th April, 1842, safe and sound, with my
poor, battered, half-frozen wife, in that selfsame city of Dresden which I had last seen on the occasion of my sad separation from my Minna, and my departure for my northern place
of exile.

We put up at the ' Stadt Gotha ' inn. The city, in which
such momentous years of my childhood and boyhood had been
spent, seemed cold and dead beneath the influences of the wild,
gloomy weather. Indeed, everything there that could remind
me of my youth seemed dead. No hospitable house received
us. We found my wife's parents living in cramped and dingy
lodgings in very straitened circumstances, and were obliged
at once to look about for a small abode for ourselves. This we
found in the Töpfergasse for twenty-one marks a month. After
paying the necessary business visits in connection with *Rienzi*,
and making arrangements for Minna during my brief absence,
I set out on 15th April direct for Leipzig, where I saw my
mother and family for the first time in six years.

During this period, which had been so eventful for my own
life, my mother had undergone a great change in her domestic
position through the death of Rosalie. She was living in a
pleasant roomy flat near the Brockhaus family, where she was
free from all those household cares to which, owing to her
large family, she had devoted so many years of anxious thought.
Her bustling energy, which had almost amounted to hardness,
had entirely given place to a natural cheerfulness and interest
in the family prosperity of her married daughters. For the
blissful calm of this happy old age she was mainly indebted to
the affectionate care of her son-in-law, Friedrich Brockhaus,
to whom I expressed my heartfelt thanks for his goodness.
She was exceedingly astonished and pleased to see me unex-

pectedly enter her room. Any bitterness that ever existed between us had utterly vanished, and her only complaint was that she could not put me up in her house, instead of my brother Julius, the unfortunate goldsmith, who had none of the qualities that could make him a suitable companion for her. She was full of hope for the success of my undertaking, and felt this confidence strengthened by the favourable prophecy which our dear Rosalie had made about me shortly before her sad death.

For the present, however, I only stayed a few days in Leipzig, as I had first to visit Berlin in order to make definite arrangements with Count Redern for the performance of the *Fliegender Holländer*. As I have already observed, I was here at once destined to learn that the Count was on the point of retiring from the directorship, and he accordingly referred me for all further decisions to the new director, Küstner, who had not yet arrived in Berlin. I now suddenly realised what this strange circumstance meant, and knew that, so far as the Berlin negotiations went, I might as well have remained in Paris. This impression was in the main confirmed by a visit to Meyerbeer, who, I found, regarded my coming to Berlin as over hasty. Nevertheless, he behaved in a kind and friendly manner, only regretting that he was just on the point of 'going away,' a state in which I always found him whenever I visited him again in Berlin.

Mendelssohn was also in the capital about this time, having been appointed one of the General Musical Directors to the King of Prussia. I also sought him out, having been previously introduced to him in Leipzig. He informed me that he did not believe his work would prosper in Berlin, and that he would rather go back to Leipzig. I made no inquiry about the fate of the score of my great symphony performed at Leipzig in earlier days, which I had more or less forced upon him so many years ago. On the other hand, he did not betray to me any signs of remembering that strange offering. In the midst of the lavish comforts of his home he struck me as cold, yet it was not so much that he repelled me as that I recoiled from him. I also paid a visit to Rellstab, to whom I had a letter of introduction from his trusty publisher, my brother-in-law Brockhaus. Here it was not so much smug ease that I encountered; I doubtless felt repulsed more by the fact that he showed no inclination whatever to interest himself in my affairs.

I grew very low spirited in Berlin. I could almost have wished Commissioner Cerf back again. Miserable as had been the time I had spent here years before, I had then, at any rate, met one man, who, for all the bluntness of his exterior, had treated me with true friendliness and consideration. In vain did I try to call to mind the Berlin through whose streets I had walked, with all the ardour of youth, by the side of Laube. After my acquaintance with London, and still more with Paris, this city, with its sordid spaces and pretensions to greatness, depressed me deeply, and I breathed a hope that, should no luck crown my life, it might at least be spent in Paris rather than in Berlin.

On my return from this wholly fruitless expedition, I first went to Leipzig for a few days, where, on this occasion, I stayed with my brother-in-law, Hermann Brockhaus, who was now Professor of Oriental Languages at the University. His family had been increased by the birth of two daughters, and the atmosphere of unruffled content, illuminated by mental activity and a quiet but vivid interest in all things relating to the higher aspects of life, greatly moved my homeless and vagabond soul. One evening, after my sister had seen to her children, whom she had brought up very well, and had sent them with gentle words to bed, we gathered in the large richly stocked library for our evening meal and a long confidential chat. Here I broke out into a violent fit of weeping, and it seemed as though the tender sister, who five years before had known me during the bitterest straits of my early married life in Dresden, now really understood me. At the express suggestion of my brother-in-law Hermann, my family tendered me a loan, to help me to tide over the time of waiting for the performance of my *Rienzi* in Dresden. This, they said, they regarded merely as a duty, and assured me that I need have no hesitation whatever in accepting it. It consisted of a sum of six hundred marks, which was to be paid me in monthly instalments for six months. As I had no prospect of being able to rely on any other source of income, there was every chance of Minna's talent for management being put severely to the test, if this were to carry us through; it could be done, however, and I was able to return to Dresden with a great sense of relief.

While I was staying with my relatives I played and sang them the *Fliegender Holländer* for the first time connectedly, and seemed to arouse considerable interest by my performance, for when, later on, my sister Louisa heard the opera in Dresden, she complained that much of the effect previously produced by my rendering did not come back to her. I also sought out my old friend Apel again. The poor man had gone stone blind, but he astonished me by his cheeriness and contentment, and thereby once and for all deprived me of any reason for pitying him. As he declared that he knew the blue coat I was wearing very well, though it was really a brown one, I thought it best not to argue the point, and I left Leipzig in a state of wonder at finding every one there so happy and contented.

When I reached Dresden, on 26th April, I found occasion to grapple more vigorously with my lot. Here I was enlivened by closer intercourse with the people on whom I had to rely for a successful production of *Rienzi*. It is true that the results of my interviews with Lüttichau, the general manager, and Reissiger, the musical conductor, left me cold and incredulous. Both were sincerely astonished at my arrival in Dresden; and the same might even be said of my frequent correspondent and patron, Hofrath Winkler, who also would have preferred my remaining in Paris. But, as has been my constant experience both before and since, help and encouragement have always come to me from humbler and never from the more exalted ranks of life.

So in this case, too, I met my first agreeable sensation in the overwhelmingly cordial reception I received from the old chorus-master, Wilhelm Fischer. I had had no previous acquaintance with him, yet he was the only person who had taken the trouble to read my score carefully, and had not only conceived serious hopes for the success of my opera, but had worked energetically to secure its being accepted and practised. The moment I entered his room and told him my name, he rushed to embrace me with a loud cry, and in a second I was translated to an atmosphere of hope. Besides this man, I met in the actor Ferdinand Heine and his family another sure foundation for hearty and, indeed, deep-rooted friendship. It is true that I had known him from childhood, for at that time he was one of the few young people whom my stepfather Geyer liked to see about him. In addition to a fairly decided talent for drawing, it was chiefly his pleasant social gifts that had won him an entrance into our more intimate family circle. As he was very small and slight, my stepfather nicknamed him Davidchen, and under this appellation he used to take part with great affability and good-humour in our little festivities, and above all in our friendly excursions into the neighbouring country, in which, as I mentioned in its place, even Carl Maria von Weber used to join. Belonging to the good old school, he had become a useful, if not prominent, member of the Dresden stage. He possessed all the knowledge and qualities for a good stage manager, but never succeeded in inducing the committee to give him that appointment. It was only as a designer of costumes that he found further scope for his talents, and in this capacity he was included in the consultations over the staging of *Rienzi*.

Thus it came about that he had the opportunity of busying himself with the work of a member, now grown to man's estate, of the very family with whom he had spent such pleasant days in his youth. He greeted me at once as a child of the house, and we two homeless creatures found in our memories of this long-lost home the first common basis to our friendship. We generally spent our evenings with old Fischer at Heine's, where, amid hopeful conversation, we regaled ourselves on potatoes and herrings, of which the meal chiefly consisted. Schröder-Devrient was away on a holiday; Tichatschek, who was also on the point of going away, I had just time to see, and with him I went quickly through a part of his rôle in *Rienzi*. His brisk and lively nature, his glorious voice and great musical talent, gave special weight to his encouraging assurance that he delighted in the rôle of Rienzi. Heine also told me that the mere prospect of having many new costumes, and especially new silver armour, had inspired Tichatschek with the liveliest desire to play this part, so that I might rely on him under any circumstances. Thus I could at once give closer attention to the preparations for practice, which was fixed to begin in the late summer, after the principal singers had returned from their holiday.

I had to make special efforts to pacify my friend Fischer by my readiness to abbreviate the score, which was excessively lengthy. His intentions in the matter were so honest that I gladly sat down with him to the wearisome task. I played and sang my score to the astonished man on an old grand piano in the rehearsing-room of the Court Theatre, with such frantic vigour that, although he did not mind if the instrument came to grief, he grew concerned about my chest. Finally, amid hearty laughter, he ceased to argue about cutting down passages, as precisely where he thought something might be omitted I proved to him with headlong eloquence that it was precisely here that the main point lay. He plunged with me head over heels into the vast chaos of sound, against which he could raise no objection, beyond the testimony of his watch, whose correctness I also ended by disputing. As sops I light-heartedly flung him the big pantomime and most of the ballet in the second act, whereby I reckoned we might save a whole half-hour. Thus, thank goodness, the whole monster was at last handed over to the clerks to make a fair copy of, and the rest was left for time to accomplish.

We next discussed what we should do in ₄he summer, and I decided upon a stay of several months at Töplitz, the scene of my first youthful flights, whose fine air and baths, I hoped, would also benefit Minna's health. But before we could carry out this intention I had to pay several more visits to Leipzig to settle the fate of my *Dutchman*. On 5th May I proceeded thither to have an interview with Küstner, the new director of the Berlin Opera, who I had been told had just arrived there. He was now placed in the awkward position of being about to produce in Berlin the very opera which he had before declined in Munich, as it had been accepted by his predecessor in office. He promised me to consider what steps he would take in this predicament. In order to learn the result of

Küstner's deliberations, I determined, on 2nd June, to seek him out, and this time in Berlin itself. But at Leipzig I found a letter in which he begged me to wait patiently a little longer for his final verdict. I took advantage of being in the neighbourhood of Halle to pay a visit to my eldest brother Albert. I was very much grieved and depressed to find the poor fellow, whom I must give the credit of having the greatest perseverance and a quite remarkable talent for dramatic song, living in the unworthy and mean circumstances which the Halle Theatre offered to him and his family. The realisation of conditions into which I myself had once nearly sunk now filled me with indescribable abhorrence. Still more harrowing was it to hear my brother speak of this state in tones which showed, alas, only too plainly, the hopeless submission with which he had already resigned himself to its horrors. The only consolation I could find was the personality and childlike nature of his stepdaughter Johanna, who was then fifteen, and who sang me Spohr's *Rose, wie bist du so schön* with great expression and in a voice of an extraordinarily beautiful quality.

Then I returned to Dresden, and at last, in wonderful weather, undertook the pleasant journey to Töplitz with Minna and one of her sisters, reaching that place on 9th June, where we took up our quarters at a second-class inn, the Eiche, at Schönau. Here we were soon joined by my mother, who paid her usual yearly visit to the warm baths all the more gladly this time because she knew she would find me there. If she had before had any prejudice against Minna because of my premature marriage to her, a closer acquaintance with her domestic gifts soon changed it into respect, and she quickly learned to love the partner of my doleful days in Paris. Although my mother's vagaries demanded no small consideration, yet what particularly delighted me about her was the astonishing vivacity of her almost childlike imagination, a faculty she retained to such a degree that one morning she complained that my relation of the *Tannhäuser* legend on the previous evening had given her a whole night of pleasant but most tiring sleeplessness.

By dint of appealing letters to Schletter, a wealthy patron of art in Leipzig, I managed to do something for Kietz, who, had remained behind in misery in Paris, and also to provide Minna with medical treatment. I also succeeded to a certain extent in ameliorating my own woeful financial position. Scarcely were these tasks accomplished, when I started off in my old boyish way on a ramble of several days on foot through the Bohemian mountains, in order that I might mentally work out my plan of the 'Venusberg' amid the pleasant associations of such a trip. Here I took the fancy of engaging quarters in Aussig on the romantic Schreckenstein, where for several days I occupied the little public room, in which straw was laid down for me to sleep on at night. I found recreation in daily ascents of the Wostrai, the highest peak in the neighbourhood, and so keenly did the fantastic solitude quicken my youthful spirit, that I clambered about the ruins of the Schreckenstein the whole of one moonlit night, wrapped only in a blanket, in order myself to provide the ghost that was lacking, and delighted myself with the hope of scaring some passing wayfarer.

Here I drew up in my pocket-book the detailed plan of a three-act opera on the 'Venusberg,' and subsequently carried out the composition of this work in strict accordance with the sketch I then made.

One day, when climbing the Wostrai, I was astonished, on turning the corner of a valley, to hear a merry dance tune whistled by a goatherd perched up on a crag. I seemed immediately to stand among the chorus of pilgrims filing past the goatherd in the valley; but I could not afterwards recall the goatherd's tune, so I was obliged to help myself out of the matter in the usual way.

Enriched by these spoils, I returned to Töplitz in a wonderfully cheerful frame of mind and robust health, but on receiving the interesting news that Tichatschek and Schröder-Devrient were on the point of returning, I was impelled to set off once more for Dresden. I took this step, not so much to avoid missing any of the early rehearsals of *Rienzi*, as because I wanted to prevent the management replacing it by something else. I left Minna for a time with my mother, and reached Dresden on 18th July.

I hired a small lodging in a queer house, since pulled down, facing the Maximilian Avenue, and entered into a fairly lively intercourse with our operatic stars who had just returned. My old enthusiasm for Schröder-Devrient revived when I saw her again more frequently in opera. Strange was the effect produced upon me when I heard her for the first time in Grétry's *Blaubart,* for I could not help remembering that this was the first opera I had ever seen. I had been taken to it as a boy of five (also in Dresden), and I still retained my wondrous first impressions of it. All my earliest childish memories were revived, and I recollected how frequently and with what emphasis I had myself sung Bluebeard's song: *Ha, die Falsche! Die Thüre offen!* to the amusement of the whole house, with a paper helmet of my own making on my head. My friend Heine still remembered it well.

In other respects the operatic performances were not such as to impress me very favourably: I particularly missed the rolling sound of the fully equipped Parisian orchestra of string instruments. I also noticed that, when opening the fine new theatre, they had quite forgotten to increase the number of these instruments in proportion to the enlarged space. In this, as well as in the general equipment of the stage, which was materially deficient in many respects, I was impressed by the sense of a certain meanness about theatrical enterprise in Germany, which became most noticeable when reproductions were given, often with wretched translations of the text, of the Paris opera repertoire. If even in Paris my dissatisfaction with this treatment of opera had been great, the feeling which once drove me thither from the German theatres now returned with redoubled energy. I actually felt degraded again, and nourished within my breast a contempt so deep that for a time I could hardly endure the thought of signing a lasting contract, even with one of the most up-to-date of German opera houses, but sadly wondered what steps I could take to hold my ground between disgust and desire in this strange world.

Nothing but the sympathy inspired by communion with persons endowed with exceptional gifts enabled me to triumph over my scruples. This statement applies above all to my great ideal, Schröder-Devrient, in whose artistic triumphs it had once been my most burning desire to be associated. It is true that many years had elapsed since my first youthful impressions of her were formed. As regards her looks, the verdict which, in the following winter, was sent to Paris by Berlioz during his stay in Dresden, was so far correct that her somewhat 'maternal' stoutness was unsuited to youthful parts, especially in male attire, which, as in *Rienzi*, made too great a demand upon the imagination. Her voice, which in point of quality had never been an exceptionally good medium for song, often landed her in difficulties, and in particular she was forced, when singing, to drag the time a little all through. But her achievements were less hampered now by these material hindrances than by the fact that her repertoire consisted of a limited number of leading parts, which she had sung so frequently that a certain monotony in the conscious calculation of effect often developed into a mannerism which, from her tendency to exaggeration, was at times almost painful.

Although these defects could not escape me, yet I, more than any one, was especially qualified to overlook such minor weaknesses, and realise with enthusiasm the incomparable greatness of her performances. Indeed, it only needed the stimulus of excitement, which this actress's exceptionally eventful life still procured, fully to restore the creative power of her prime, a fact of which I was subsequently to receive striking demonstrations. But I was seriously troubled and depressed at seeing how strong was the disintegrating effect of theatrical life upon the character of this singer, who had originally been endowed with such great and noble qualities. From the very mouth through which the great actress's inspired musical utterances reached me, I was compelled to hear at other times very similar language to that in which, with but few exceptions, nearly all heroines of the stage indulge. The possession of a naturally fine voice, or even mere physical advantages, which might place her rivals on the same footing as herself in public favour, was more than she could endure; and so far was she from acquiring the dignified resignation worthy of a great artist, that her jealousy increased to a painful extent as years went on. I noticed this all the more because I had reason to suffer from it. A fact which caused me even greater trouble, however, was that she did not grasp music easily, and the study of a new part involved difficulties which meant many a painful hour for the composer who had to make her master his work. Her difficulty in learning new parts, and particularly that of Adriano in *Rienzi*, entailed disappointments for her which caused me a good deal of trouble.

If, in her case, I had to handle a great and sensitive nature very tenderly, I had, on the other hand, a very easy task with Tichatschek, with his childish limitations and superficial, but exceptionally brilliant, talents. He did not trouble to learn his parts by heart, as he was so musical that he could sing the most difficult music at sight, and thought all further study needless, whereas with most other singers the work consisted in mastering the score. Hence, if he sang through a part at rehearsals often enough to impress it on his memory, the rest, that is to say, everything pertaining to vocal art and dramatic delivery, would follow naturally. In this way he picked up any clerical errors there might be in the libretto, and that with such incorrigible pertinacity, that he uttered the wrong words with just the same expression as if they were correct. He waved aside good-humouredly any expostulations or hints as to the sense with the remark, ' Ah! that will be all right soon.' And, in fact, I very soon resigned myself and quite gave up trying to get the singer to use his intelligence in the interpretation of the part of the hero, for which I was very agreeably compensated by the light-hearted enthusiasm with which he flung himself into his congenial rôle, and the irresistible effect of his brilliant voice.

With the exception of these two actors who played the leading parts, I had only very moderate material at my disposal. But there was plenty of goodwill, and I had recourse to an ingenious device to induce Reissiger the conductor to hold frequent piano rehearsals. He had complained to me of the difficulty he had always found in securing a well-written libretto, and thought it was very sensible of me to have acquired the habit of writing my own. In his youth he had unfortunately neglected to do this for himself, and yet this was all he lacked to make a successful dramatic composer. I feel bound to confess that he possessed ' a good deal of melody '; but this, he added, did not seem sufficient to inspire the singers with the requisite enthusiasm. His experience was that Schröder-Devrient, in his *Adèle de Foix,* would render very indifferently the same final passage with which, in Bellini's *Romeo and Juliet,* she would put the audience into an ecstasy. The reason for this, he presumed, must lie in the subject-matter. I at once promised him that I would supply him with a libretto in which he would be able to introduce these and similar melodies to the greatest advantage. To this he gladly agreed, and I therefore set aside for versification, as a suitable text for Reissiger, my *Hohe Braut,* founded on König's romance, which I had once before submitted to Scribe. I promised to bring Reissiger a page of verse for every piano rehearsal, and this I faithfully did until the whole book was done. I was much surprised to learn some time later that Reissiger had had a new libretto written for him by an actor named Kriethe. This was called the *Wreck of the Medusa.* I then learned that the wife of the conductor, who was a suspicious woman, had been filled with the greatest concern at my readiness to give up a libretto to her husband. They both thought the book was good and full of striking effects, but they suspected some sort of trap in the background, to escape from which they must certainly exercise the greatest caution. The result was that I regained possession of my libretto and was able, later on, to help my old friend Kittl with it in Prague; he set it to music of his own, and entitled it *Die Franzosen vor Nizza.* I heard that it was frequently performed in Prague with great success, though I never saw it myself; and I was also told at the same time by a local critic that this text was a proof of my real aptitude as a librettist, and that it was a mistake for me to devote myself to composition. As regards my *Tannhäuser,* on the other hand, Laube used to declare it was a misfortune that I had not got an experienced dramatist to supply me with a decent text for my music.

For the time being, however, this work of versification had the desired result, and Reissiger kept steadily to the study of *Rienzi.* But what encouraged him even more than my verses was the growing interest of the singers, and above all the genuine enthusiasm of Tichatschek. This man, who had been

so ready to leave the delights of the theatre piano for a shooting
party, now looked upon the rehearsals of Rienzi as a genuine
treat. He always attended them with radiant eyes and boisterous good-humour. I soon felt myself in a state of constant ex-
hilaration: favourite passages were greeted with acclamation by
the singers at every rehearsal, and a concerted number of the
third finale, which unfortunately had afterwards to be omitted
owing to its length, actually became on that occasion a source
of profit to me. For Tichatschek maintained that this B minor
was so lovely that something ought to be paid for it every
time, and he put down a silver penny, inviting the others to
do the same, to which they all responded merrily. From that
day forward, whenever we came to this passage at rehearsals,
the cry was raised, ' Here comes the silver penny part,' and
Schröder-Devrient, as she took out her purse, remarked that
these rehearsals would ruin her. This gratuity was conscientiously handed to me each time, and no one suspected that
these contributions, which were given as a joke, were often a
very welcome help towards defraying the cost of our daily food.
For Minna had returned from Töplitz, at the beginning of
August, accompanied by my mother.

We lived very frugally in chilly lodgings, hopefully awaiting
the tardy day of our deliverance. The months of August
and September passed, in preparation for my work, amid
frequent disturbances caused by the fluctuating and scanty
repertoire of a German opera house, and not until October
did the combined rehearsals assume such a character as to
promise the certainty of a speedy production. From the
very beginning of the general rehearsals with the orchestra
we all shared the conviction that the opera would, without
doubt, be a great success. Finally, the full dress rehearsals
produced a perfectly intoxicating effect. When we tried the
first scene of the second act with the scenery complete, and
the messengers of peace entered, there was a general outburst
of emotion, and even Schröder-Devrient, who was bitterly
prejudiced against her part, as it was not the rôle of the
heroine, could only answer my questions in a voice stifled
with tears. I believe the whole theatrical body, down to its
humblest officials, loved me as though I were a real prodigy,

and I am probably not far wrong in saying that much of this arose from sympathy and lively fellow-feeling for a young man, whose exceptional difficulties were not unknown to them, and who now suddenly stepped out of perfect obscurity into splendour. During the interval at the full dress rehearsal, while other members had dispersed to revive their jaded nerves with lunch, I remained seated on a pile of boards on the stage, in order that no one might realise that I was in the quandary of being unable to obtain similar refreshment. An invalid Italian singer, who was taking a small part in the opera, seemed to notice this, and kindly brought me a glass of wine and a piece of bread. I was sorry that I was obliged to deprive him of even his small part in the course of the year, for its loss provoked such ill-treatment from his wife, that by conjugal tyranny he was driven into the ranks of my enemies. When, after my flight from Dresden in 1849, I learned that I had been denounced to the police by this same singer for supposed complicity in the rising which took place in that town, I bethought me of this breakfast during the *Rienzi* rehearsal, and felt I was being punished for my ingratitude, for I knew I was guilty of having brought him into trouble with his wife.

The frame of mind in which I looked forward to the first performance of my work was a unique experience which I have never felt either before or since. My kind sister Clara fully shared my feelings. She had been living a wretched middle-class life at Chemnitz, which, just about this time, she had left to come and share my fate in Dresden. The poor woman, whose undoubted artistic gifts had faded so early, was laboriously dragging out a commonplace bourgeois existence as a wife and mother; but now, under the influence of my growing success, she began joyously to breathe a new life. She and I and the worthy chorus-master Fischer used to spend our evenings with the Heine family, still over potatoes and herrings, and often in a wonderfully elated frame of mind. The evening before our first performance I was able to crown our happiness by myself ladling out a bowl of punch. With mingled tears and laughter we skipped about like happy children, and then in sleep prepared ourselves for the triumphant day to which we looked forward with such confidence.

Although on the morning of 20th October, 1842 I had resolved not to disturb any of my singers by a visit, yet I happened to come across one of them, a stiff Philistine called
Risse, who was playing a minor bass part in a dull but respectable way. The day was rather cool, but wonderfully bright
and sunshiny, after the gloomy weather we had just been
having. Without a word this curious creature saluted me and
then remained standing, as though bewitched. He simply
gazed into my face with wonder and rapture, in order to find
out, so he at last managed to tell me in strange confusion, how
a man looked who that very day was to face such an exceptional
fate. I smiled and reflected that it was indeed a day of crisis,
and promised him that I would soon drink a glass with him, at
the Stadt Hamburg inn, of the excellent wine he had recommended to me with so much agitation.

No subsequent experience of mine can be compared with
the sensations which marked the day of the first production of
Rienzi. At all the first performances of my works in later days,
I have been so absorbed by an only too well-founded anxiety
as to their success, that I could neither enjoy the opera nor
form any real estimate of its reception by the public. As for
my subsequent experiences at the general rehearsal of *Tristan
und Isolde,* this took place under such exceptional circumstances, and its effect upon me differed so fundamentally from
that produced by the first performance of *Rienzi,* that no comparison can possibly be drawn between the two.

The immediate success of *Rienzi* was no doubt assured beforehand. But the emphatic way in which the audience declared
their appreciation was thus far exceptional, that in cities like
Dresden the spectators are never in a position to decide con-
clusively upon a work of importance on the first night, and
consequently assume an attitude of chilling restraint towards
the works of unknown authors. But this was, in the nature
of things, an exceptional case, for the numerous staff of the
theatre and the body of musicians had inundated the city beforehand with such glowing reports of my opera, that the
whole population awaited the promised miracle in feverish expectation. I sat with Minna, my sister Clara, and the Heine
family in a pit-box, and when I try to recall my condition

during that evening, I can only picture it with all the para-
phernalia of a dream. Of real pleasure or agitation I felt none
at all: I seemed to stand quite aloof from my work; whereas
the sight of the thickly crowded auditorium agitated me so
much, that I was unable even to glance at the body of the
audience, whose presence merely affected me like some natural
phenomenon — something like a continuous downpour of rain —
from which I sought shelter in the farthest corner of my box
as under a protecting roof. I was quite unconscious of applause,
and when at the end of the acts I was tempestuously called for,
I had every time to be forcibly reminded by Heine and driven
on to the stage. On the other hand, one great anxiety filled
me with growing alarm: I noticed that the first two acts had
taken as long as the whole of *Freischütz*, for instance. On
account of its warlike calls to arms the third act begins with an
exceptional uproar, and when at its close the clock pointed to
ten, which meant that the performance had already lasted full
four hours, I became perfectly desperate. The fact that after
this act, also, I was again loudly called, I regarded merely
as a final courtesy on the part of the audience, who wished to
signify that they had had quite enough for one evening, and
would now leave the house in a body. As we had still two acts
before us, I thought it settled that we should not be able to
finish the piece, and apologised for my lack of wisdom in not
having previously effected the necessary curtailments. Now,
thanks to my folly, I found myself in the unheard-of predicament of being unable to finish an opera, otherwise extremely
well received, simply because it was absurdly long. I could
only explain the undiminished zeal of the singers, and particularly of Tichatschek, who seemed to grow lustier and cheerier
the longer it lasted, as an amiable trick to conceal from me
the inevitable catastrophe. But my astonishment at finding
the audience still there in full muster, even in the last act —
towards midnight — filled me with unbounded perplexity. I
could no longer trust my eyes or ears, and regarded the whole
events of the evening as a nightmare. It was past midnight
when, for the last time, I had to obey the thunderous calls of
the audience, side by side with my trusty singers.

My feeling of desperation at the unparalleled length of my

opera was augmented by the temper of my relatives, whom I saw for a short time after the performance. Friedrich Brockhaus and his family had come over with some friends from Leipzig, and had invited us to the inn, hoping to celebrate an agreeable success over a pleasant supper, and possibly to drink my health. But on arriving, kitchen and cellar were closed, and every one was so worn out that nothing was to be heard but outcries at the unparalleled case of an opera lasting from six o'clock till past twelve. No further remarks were exchanged, and we stole away feeling quite stupefied.

About eight the next morning I put in an appearance at the clerks' office, in order that in case there should be a second performance I might arrange the necessary curtailment of the parts. If, during the previous summer, I had contested every beat with the faithful chorus-master Fischer, and proved them all to be indispensable, I was now possessed by a blind rage for striking out. There was not a single part of my score which seemed any longer necessary — what the audience had been made to swallow the previous evening now appeared but a chaos of sheer impossibilities, each and all of which might be omitted without the slightest damage or risk of being unintelligible. My one thought now was how to reduce my convolution of monstrosities to decent limits. By dint of unsparing and ruthless abbreviations handed over to the copyist, I hoped to avert a catastrophe, for I expected nothing less than that the general manager, together with the city and the theatre, would that very day give me to understand that such a thing as the performance of my *Last of the Tribunes* might perhaps be permitted once as a curiosity, but not oftener. All day long, therefore, I carefully avoided going near the theatre, so as to give time for my heroic abbreviations to do their salutary work, and for news of them to spread through the city. But at midday I looked in again upon the copyists, to assure myself that all had been duly performed as I had ordered. I then learned that Tichatschek had also been there, and, after inspecting the omissions that I had arranged, had forbidden their being carried out. Fischer, the chorus-master, also wished to speak to me about them: work was suspended, and I foresaw great confusion. I could not understand what it all meant, and feared mischief if the arduous task were delayed. At length, towards evening, I sought out Tichatschek at the theatre. Without giving him a chance to speak, I brusquely asked him why he had interrupted the copyists' work. In a half-choked voice he curtly and defiantly rejoined, ' I will have none of my part cut out — it is too heavenly.' I stared at him blankly, and then felt as though I had been suddenly bewitched: such an unheard-of testimony to my success could not but shake me out of my strange anxiety. Others joined him, Fischer radiant with delight and bubbling with laughter. Every one spoke of the enthusiastic emotion which thrilled the whole city. Next came a letter of thanks from the Commissioner acknowledging my splendid work. Nothing now remained for me but to embrace Tichatschek and Fischer, and go on my way to inform Minna and Clara how matters stood.

After a few days' rest for the actors, the second performance took place on 26th October, but with various curtailments, for which I had great difficulty in obtaining Tichatschek's consent. Although it was still of much more than average length, I heard no particular complaints, and at last adopted Tichatschek's view that, if he could stand it, so could the audience. For six performances therefore, all of which continued to receive a similar avalanche of applause, I let the matter run its course.

My opera, however, had also excited interest among the elder princesses of the royal family. They thought its exhausting length a drawback, but were nevertheless unwilling to miss any of it. Lüttichau consequently proposed that I should give the piece at full length, but half of it at a time on two successive evenings. This suited me very well, and after an interval of a few weeks we announced *Rienzi's Greatness* for the first day, and *His Fall* for the second. The first evening we gave two acts, and on the second three, and for the latter I composed a special introductory prelude. This met with the entire approval of our august patrons, and especially of the two eldest, Princesses Amalie and Augusta. The public, on the contrary, simply regarded this in the light of now being asked to pay two entrance fees for one opera, and pronounced the new arrangement a decided fraud. Its annoyance at the change was so great that it actually threatened to be fatal to the attendance, and after three performances of the divided *Rienzi* the management was obliged to go back to the old arrangement, which I willingly made possible by introducing my cuttings again.

From this time forward the piece used to fill the house to overflowing as often as it could be presented, and the permanence of its success became still more obvious when I began to realise the envy it drew upon me from many different quarters. My first experience of this was truly painful, and came from the hands of the poet, Julius Mosen, on the very day after the first performance. When I first reached Dresden in the summer I had sought him out, and, having a really high opinion of his talent, our intercourse soon became more intimate, and was the means of giving me much pleasure and instruction. He had shown me a volume of his plays, which on the whole appealed to me exceptionally. Among these was a tragedy, *Cola Rienzi*, dealing with the same subject as my opera, and in a manner partly new to me, and which I thought effective. With reference to this poem, I had begged him to take no notice of my libretto, as in the quality of its poetry it could not possibly bear comparison with his own; and it cost him little sacrifice to grant the request. It happened that just before the first performance of my *Rienzi*, he had produced in Dresden *Bernhard von Weimar*, one of his least happy pieces, the result of which had brought him little pleasure. Dramatically it was a thing with no life in it, aiming only at political harangue, and had shared the inevitable fate of all such aberrations. He had therefore awaited the appearance of my *Rienzi* with some vexation, and confessed to me his bitter chagrin at not being able to procure the acceptance of his tragedy of the same name in Dresden. This, he presumed, arose from its somewhat pronounced political tendency, which, certainly in a spoken play on a similar subject, would be more noticeable than in an opera, where from the very start no one pays any heed to the words. I had genially confirmed him in this depreciation of the subject matter in opera; and was therefore the more startled when, on finding him at my sister Louisa's the day after the first performance, he straightway overwhelmed me with a scornful outburst of irritation at my success. But he found in me a strange sense of the essential unreality in opera of such a subject as that which I had just illustrated with so much success in *Rienzi,* so that, oppressed by a secret sense of shame, I had no serious rejoinder to offer to his candidly poisonous abuse. My line of defence was not yet sufficiently clear in my own mind to be available offhand, nor was it yet backed by so obvious a product of my own peculiar genius that I could venture to quote it. Moreover, my first impulse was only one of pity for the unlucky playwright, which I felt all the more constrained to express, because his burst of fury gave me the inward satisfaction of knowing that he recognised my great success, of which I was not yet quite clear myself.

But this first performance of *Rienzi* did far more than this. It gave occasion for controversy, and made an ever-widening breach between myself and the newspaper critics. Herr Karl Bank, who for some time had been the chief musical critic in Dresden, had been known to me before at Magdeburg, where he once visited me and listened with delight to my playing of several fairly long passages from my *Liebesverbot.* When we met again in Dresden, this man could not forgive me for having been unable to procure him tickets for the first performance of *Rienzi.* The same thing happened with a certain Herr Julius Schladebach, who likewise settled in Dresden about that time as a critic. Though I was always anxious to be gracious to everybody, yet I felt just then an invincible repugnance for showing special deference to any man because he was a critic. As time went on, I carried this rule to the point of almost systematic rudeness, and was consequently all my life through the victim of unprecedented persecution from the press. As yet, however, this ill-will had not become pronounced, for at that time journalism had not begun to give itself airs in Dresden. There were so few contributions sent from there to the outside press that our artistic doings excited very little notice elsewhere, a fact which was certainly not without its disadvantages for me. Thus for the present the unpleasant side of my success scarcely affected me at all, and for a brief space I felt myself, for the first and only time in my life, so pleasantly borne along on the breath of general good-will, that all my former troubles seemed amply requited.

For further and quite unexpected fruits of my success now appeared with astonishing rapidity, though not so much in the form of material profit, which for the present resolved itself into nine hundred marks, paid me by the General Board as an exceptional fee instead of the usual twenty golden louis. Nor did I dare to cherish the hope of selling my work advantageously to a publisher, until it had been performed in some other important towns. But fate willed it, that by the sudden death of Rastrelli, royal director of music, which occurred shortly after the first production of *Rienzi*, an office should unexpectedly become vacant, for the filling of which all eyes at once turned to me.

While the negotiations over this matter were slowly proceeding, the General Board gave proof in another direction of an almost passionate interest in my talents. They insisted that the first performance of the *Fliegender Holländer* should on no account be conceded to the Berlin opera, but reserved as an honour for Dresden. As the Berlin authorities raised no obstacle, I very gladly handed over my latest work also to the Dresden theatre. If in this I had to dispense with Tichatschek's assistance, as there was no leading tenor part in the play, I could count all the more surely on the helpful co-operation of Schröder-Devrient, to whom a worthier task was assigned in the leading female part than that which she had had in *Rienzi*. I was glad to be able thus to rely entirely upon her, as she had grown strangely out of humour with me, owing to her scanty share in the success of *Rienzi*. The completeness of my faith in her I proved with an exaggeration by no means advantageous to my own work, by simply forcing the leading male part on Wächter, a once capable, but now somewhat delicate baritone. He was in every respect wholly unsuited to the task, and only accepted it with unfeigned hesitation. On submitting my play to my adored prima donna, I was much relieved to find that its poetry made a special appeal to her. Thanks to the genuine personal interest awakened in me under very peculiar circumstances by the character and fate of this exceptional woman, our study of the part of Senta, which often brought us into close contact, became one of the most thrilling and momentously instructive periods of my life.

It is true that the great actress, especially when under the influence of her famous mother, Sophie Schröder, who was just then with her on a visit, showed undisguised vexation at my having composed so brilliant a work as *Rienzi* for Dresden without having specifically reserved the principal part for her. Yet the magnanimity of her disposition triumphed even over this selfish impulse: she loudly proclaimed me ' a genius,' and honoured me with that special confidence which, she said, none but a genius should enjoy. But when she invited me to become both the accomplice and adviser in her really dreadful love affairs, this confidence certainly began to have its risky side; nevertheless there were at first occasions on which she openly proclaimed herself before all the world as my friend, making most flattering distinctions in my favour.

First of all I had to accompany her on a trip to Leipzig, where she was giving a concert for her mother's benefit, which she thought to make particularly attractive by including in its programme two selections from *Rienzi* — the aria of Adriano and the hero's prayer (the latter sung by Tichatschek), and both under my personal conductorship. Mendelssohn, who was also on very friendly terms with her, had been enticed to this concert too, and produced his overture to *Ruy Blas,* then quite new. It was during the two busy days spent on this occasion in Leipzig that I first came into close contact with him, all my previous knowledge of him having been limited to a few rare and altogether profitless visits. At the house of my brother-in-law, Fritz Brockhaus, he and Devrient gave us a good deal of music, he playing her accompaniment to a number of Schubert's songs. I here became conscious of the peculiar unrest and excitement with which this master of music, who, though still young, had already reached the zenith of his fame and life's work, observed or rather watched me. I could see clearly that he thought but little of a success in opera, and that merely in Dresden. Doubtless I seemed in his eyes one of a class of musicians to whom he attached no value, and with whom he proposed to have no intercourse. Nevertheless my success had certain characteristic features, which gave it a more or less alarming aspect. Mendelssohn's most ardent desire for a long time past had been to write a successful opera, and it was possible he now felt annoyed that, before he had succeeded in doing so, a triumph of this nature should suddenly be thrust into his face with blunt brutality, and based upon a style of music which he might feel justified in regarding as poor. He probably found it no less exasperating that Devrient, whose gifts he acknowledged, and who was his own devoted admirer, should now so openly and loudly sound my praises. These thoughts were dimly shaping themselves in my mind, when Mendelssohn, by a very remarkable statement, drove me, almost with violence, to adopt this interpretation. On our way home together, after the joint concert rehearsal, I was talking very warmly on the subject of music. Although by no means a talkative man, he suddenly interrupted me with curiously hasty excitement by the assertion that music had but one great fault, namely, that more than any other art it stimulated not only our good, but also our evil qualities, such, for instance, as jealousy. I blushed with shame to have to apply this speech to his own feelings towards me; for I was profoundly conscious of my innocence of ever having dreamed, even in the remotest degree, of placing my own talents or performances as a musician in comparison with his. Yet, strange to say, at this very concert he showed himself in a light by no means calculated to place him beyond all possibility of comparison with myself. A rendering of his *Hebrides* Overture would have placed him so immeasurably above my two operatic airs, that all shyness at having to stand beside him would have been spared me, as the gulf between our two productions was impassable. But in his choice of the *Ruy Blas* Overture he appears to have been prompted by a desire to place himself on this occasion so close to the operatic style that its effectiveness might be reflected upon his own work. The overture was evidently calculated for a Parisian audience, and the astonishment Mendelssohn caused by appearing in such a connection was shown by Robert Schumann in his own ungainly fashion at its close. Approaching the musician in the orchestra, he blandly, and with a genial smile, expressed his admiration of the 'brilliant orchestral piece' just played.

But in the interests of veracity let me not forget that neither he nor I scored the real success of that evening. We were both wholly eclipsed by the tremendous effect produced by the grey-haired Sophie Schröder in a recitation of Bürger's *Lenore*. While the daughter had been taunted in the newspapers with unfairly employing all sorts of musical attractions to cozen a benefit concert out of the music lovers of Leipzig for a mother who never had anything to do with that art, we, who were there as her musical aiders and abettors, had to stand like so many idle conjurers, while this aged and almost toothless dame declaimed Bürger's poem with truly terrifying beauty and grandeur. This episode, like so much else that I saw during these few days, gave me abundant food for thought and meditation.

A second excursion, also undertaken with Devrient, took me in the December of that year to Berlin, where the singer had been invited to appear at a grand state concert. I for my part wanted an interview with Director Küstner about the *Fliegender Holländer*. Although I arrived at no definite result regarding my own personal business, this short visit to Berlin was memorable for my meeting with Franz Liszt, which afterwards proved of great importance. It took place under singular circumstances, which placed both him and me in a situation of peculiar embarrassment, brought about in the most wanton fashion by Devrient's exasperating caprice.

I had already told my patroness the story of my earlier meeting with Liszt. During that fateful second winter of my stay in Paris, when I had at last been driven to be grateful for Schlesinger's hack-work, I one day received word from Laube, who always bore me in mind, that F. Liszt was coming to Paris. He had mentioned and recommended me to him when he was in Germany, and advised me to lose no time in looking him up, as he was 'generous,' and would certainly find means of helping me. As soon as I heard that he had really arrived, I presented myself at the hotel to see him. It was early in the morning. On my entrance I found several strange gentlemen waiting in the drawing-room, where, after some time, we were joined by Liszt himself, pleasant and affable, and wearing his indoor coat. The conversation was carried on in French, and turned upon his experiences during his last professional journey in Hungary. As I was unable to take part, on account of the language, I listened for some time, feeling heartily bored, until at last he asked me pleasantly what he could do for me. He seemed unable to recall Laube's recommendation, and all the answer I could give was that I desired to make his acquaintance. To this he had evidently no objection, and informed me he would take care to have a ticket sent me for his great matinée, which was to take place shortly. My sole attempt to introduce an artistic theme of conversation was a question as to whether he knew Löwe's *Erlkönig* as well as Schubert's. His reply in the negative frustrated this somewhat awkward attempt, and I ended my visit by giving him my address. Thither his secretary, Belloni, presently sent me, with a few polite words, a card of admission to a concert to be given entirely by the master himself in the Salle Erard. I duly wended my way to the overcrowded hall, and beheld the platform on which the grand piano stood, closely beleaguered by the cream of Parisian female society, and witnessed their enthusiastic ovations of this virtuoso, who was at that time the wonder of the world. Moreover, I heard several of his most brilliant pieces, such as ' Variations on *Robert le Diable,*' but carried away with me no real impression beyond that of being stunned. This took place just at the time when I abandoned a path which had been contrary to my truer nature, and had led me astray, and on which I now emphatically turned my back in silent bitterness. I was therefore in no fitting mood for a just appreciation of this prodigy, who at that time was shining in the blazing light of day, but from whom I had turned my face to the night. I went to see Liszt no more.

As already mentioned, I had given Devrient a bare outline of this story, but she had noted it with particular attention, for I happened to have touched her weak point of professional jealousy. As Liszt had also been commanded by the King of Prussia to appear at the grand state concert at Berlin, it so happened that the first time they met Liszt questioned her with great interest about the success of *Rienzi*. She thereupon observed that the composer of that opera was an altogether unknown man, and proceeded with curious malice to taunt him with his apparent lack of penetration, as proved by the fact that the said composer, who now so keenly excited his interest, was the very same poor musician whom he had lately ' turned away so contemptuously ' in Paris. All this she told me with an air of triumph, which distressed me very much, and I at once set to work to correct the false impression conveyed by my former account. As we were still debating this point in her room, we were startled by hearing from the next the famous bass part in the ' Revenge ' air from *Donna Anna,* rapidly executed in octaves on the piano. ' That 's Liszt himself,' she cried. Liszt then entered the room to fetch her for the rehearsal. To my great embarrassment she introduced me to him with malicious delight as the composer of *Rienzi,* the man whose acquaintance he now wished to make after having previously shown him the door in his glorious Paris. My solemn asseverations that my patroness — no doubt only in fun — was deliberately distorting my account of my former visit to him, apparently pacified him so far as I was concerned, and, on the other hand, he had no doubt already formed his own opinion of the impulsive singer. He certainly regretted that he could not remember my visit in Paris, but it nevertheless shocked and alarmed him to learn that any one should have had reason to complain of such treatment at his hands. The hearty sincerity of Listz's simple words to me about this misunderstanding, as contrasted with the strangely passionate raillery of the incorrigible lady, made a most pleasing and captivating impression upon me. The whole bearing of the man, and the way in which he tried to ward off the pitiless scorn of her attacks, was something new to me, and gave me a deep insight into his character, so firm in its amiability and boundless good-nature. Finally, she teased him about the Doctor's degree which had just been conferred on him by the University of Königsberg, and pretended to mistake him for a chemist. At last he stretched himself out flat on the floor, and implored her mercy, declaring himself quite defenceless against the storm of her invective. Then turning to me with a hearty assurance that he would make it his business to hear *Rienzi,* and would in any case endeavour to give me a better opinion of himself than his evil star had hitherto permitted, we parted for that occasion.

The almost naïve simplicity and naturalness of his every phrase and word, and particularly his emphatic manner, left a most profound impression upon me. No one could fail to be equally affected by these qualities, and I now realised for the first time the almost magic power exerted by Liszt over all who came in close contact with him, and saw how erroneous had been my former opinion as to its cause.

These two excursions to Leipzig and Berlin found but brief interruptions of the period devoted at home to our study of the *Fliegender Holländer*. It was therefore, of paramount importance to me to maintain Schröder-Devrient's keen interest in her part, since, in view of the weakness of the rest of the cast, I was convinced that it was from her alone I could expect any adequate interpretation of the spirit of my work.

The part of Senta was essentially suited to her, and there were just at that moment peculiar circumstances in her life which brought her naturally emotional temperament to a high pitch of tension. I was amazed when she confided to me that she was on the point of breaking off a regular *liaison* of many years' standing, to form, in passionate haste, another much less desirable one. The forsaken lover, who was tenderly devoted to her, was a young lieutenant in the Royal Guards, and the son of Müller, the ex-Minister of Education; her new choice, whose acquaintance she had formed on a recent visit to Berlin, was Herr von Münchhausen. He was a tall, slim young man, and her predilection for him was easily explained when I became more closely acquainted with her love affairs. It seemed to me that the bestowal of her confidence on me in this matter arose from her guilty conscience; she was aware that Müller, whom I liked on account of his excellent disposition, had loved her with the earnestness of a first love, and also that she was now betraying him in the most faithless way on a trivial pretext. She must have known that her new lover was entirely unworthy of her, and that his intentions were frivolous and selfish. She knew, too, that no one, and certainly none of her older friends who knew her best, would approve of her behaviour. She told me candidly that she had felt impelled to confide in me because I was a genius, and would understand the demands of her temperament. I hardly knew what to think. I was repelled alike by her passion and the circumstances attending it; but to my astonishment I had to confess that the infatuation, so repulsive to me, held this strange woman in so powerful a grasp that I could not refuse her a certain amount of pity, nay, even real sympathy.

She was pale and distraught, ate hardly anything, and her faculties were subjected to a strain so extraordinary that I thought she would not escape a serious, perhaps a fatal illness. Sleep had long since deserted her, and whenever I brought her my unlucky *Fliegender Holländer,* her looks so alarmed me that the proposed rehearsal was the last thing I thought of. But in this matter she insisted; she made me sit down at the piano, and then plunged into the study of her rôle as if it were a matter of life and death. She found the actual learning of the part very difficult, and it was only by repeated and persevering rehearsal that she mastered her task. She would sing for hours at a time with such passion that I often sprang up in terror and begged her to spare herself; then she would point smiling to her chest, and expand the muscles of her still magnificent person, to assure me that she was doing herself no harm. Her voice really acquired at that time a youthful freshness and power of endurance. I had to confess that which often astonished me: this infatuation for an insipid nobody was very much to the advantage of my Senta. Her courage under this intense strain was so great that, as time pressed, she consented to have the general rehearsal on the very day of the first performance, and a delay which would have been greatly to my disadvantage was thus avoided.

The performance took place on 2nd January, in the year 1843. Its result was extremely instructive to me, and led to the turning-point of my career. The ill-success of the performance taught me how much care and forethought were essential to secure the adequate dramatic interpretation of my latest works. I realised that I had more or less believed that my score would explain itself, and that my singers would arrive at the right interpretation of their own accord. My good old friend Wächter, who at the time of Henriette Sontag's first success was a favourite ' Barber of Seville,' had from the first discreetly thought otherwise. Unfortunately, even Schröder-Devrient only saw when the rehearsals were too far advanced how utterly incapable Wächter was of realising the horror and supreme suffering of my Mariner. His distressing corpulence, his broad fat face, the extraordinary movements of his arms and legs, which he managed to make look like mere stumps, drove my passionate Senta to despair. At one rehearsal, when in the great scene in Act ii. she comes to him in the guise of a guardian angel to bring the message of salvation, she broke off to whisper despairingly in my ear, ' How can I say it when I look into those beady eyes? Good God, Wagner, what a muddle you have made! ' I consoled her as well as I could, and secretly placed my dependence on Herr von Münchhausen, who promised faithfully to sit that evening in the front row of the stalls, so that Devrient's eyes must fall on him. And the magnificent performance of my great artiste, although she stood horribly alone on the stage, did succeed in rousing enthusiasm in the second act. The first act offered the audience nothing but a dull conversation between Herr Wächter and that Herr Risse who had invited me to an excellent glass of wine on the first night of *Rienzi,* and in the third the loudest raging of the orchestra did not rouse the sea from its dead calm nor the phantom ship in its cautious rocking. The audience fell to wondering how I could have produced this crude, meagre, and gloomy work after *Rienzi,* in every act of which incident abounded, and Tichatschek shone in an endless variety of costumes.

As Schröder-Devrient soon left Dresden for a considerable time, the *Fliegender Holländer* saw only four performances, at which the diminishing audiences made it plain that I had not pleased Dresden taste with it. The management was compelled to revive *Rienzi* in order to maintain my prestige; and the triumph of this opera compared with the failure of the *Dutchman* gave me food for reflection. I had to admit, with some misgivings, that the success of my *Rienzi* was not entirely due to the cast and staging, although I was fully alive to the defects from which the *Fliegender Holländer* suffered in this

respect. Although Wächter was far from realising my conception of the *Fliegender Holländer* I could not conceal from
myself the fact that Tichatschek was quite as far removed
from the ideal *Rienzi*. His abominable errors and deficiencies
in his presentation of the part had never escaped me; he had
never been able to lay aside his brilliant and heroic leading-
tenor manners in order to render that gloomy demonic
strain in Rienzi's temperament on which I had laid unmistakable stress at the critical points of the drama. In the
fourth act, after the pronouncement of the curse, he fell on his
knees in the most melancholy fashion and abandoned himself
to bewailing his fate in piteous tones. When I suggested to
him that *Rienzi*, though inwardly despairing, must take up
an attitude of statuesque firmness before the world, he pointed
out to me the great popularity which the end of this very
act had won as interpreted by himself, with an intimation that
he intended making no change in it.

And when I considered the real causes of the success of
Rienzi, I found that it rested on the brilliant and extraordinarily fresh voice of the soaring, happy singer, in the refreshing
effect of the chorus and the gay movement and colouring on
the stage. I received a still more convincing proof of this
when we divided the opera into two, and found that the second
part, which was the more important from both the dramatic
and the musical point of view, was noticeably less well attended
than the first, for the very obvious reason, as I thought, that
the ballet occurred in the first part. My brother Julius, who
had come over from Leipzig for one of the performances of
Rienzi, gave me a still more naïve testimony as to the real
point of interest in the opera. I was sitting with him in an
open box, in full sight of the audience, and had therefore
begged him to desist from giving any applause, even if directed
only to the efforts of the singers; he restrained himself all
through the evening, but his enthusiasm at a certain figure
of the ballet was too much for him, and he clapped loudly,
to the great amusement of the audience, telling me that he
could not hold himself in any longer. Curiously enough, this
same ballet secured for *Rienzi*, which was otherwise received
with indifference, the enduring preference of the present King

of Prussia,[1] who many years afterwards ordered the revival of this opera, although it had utterly failed in arousing public interest by its merits as a drama.

I found, when I had to be present later on at a representation of the same opera at Darmstadt, that while wholesale cuts had to be made in its best parts, it had been found necessary to expand the ballets by additions and repetitions. This ballet music, which I had put together with contemptuous haste at Riga in a few days without any inspiration, seemed to me, moreover, so strikingly weak that I was thoroughly ashamed of it even in those days at Dresden, when I had found myself compelled to suppress its best feature, the tragic pantomime. Further, the resources of the ballet in Dresden did not even admit of the execution of my stage directions for the combat in the arena, nor for the very significant round dances, both admirably carried out at a later date in Berlin. I had to be content with the humiliating substitution of a long, foolish step-dance by two insignificant dancers, which was ended by a company of soldiers marching on, bearing their shields on high so as to form a roof and remind the audience of the Roman *testudo;* then the ballet-master with his assistant, in flesh-coloured tights, leaped on to the shields and turned somersaults, a proceeding which they thought was reminiscent of the gladiatorial games. It was at this point that the house was always moved to resounding applause, and I had to own that this moment marked the climax of my success.

I thus had my doubts as to the intrinsic divergence between my inner aims and my outward success; at the same time a decisive and fatal change in my fortunes was brought about by my acceptance of the conductorship at Dresden, under circumstances as perplexing in their way as those preceding my marriage. I had met the negotiations which led up to this appointment with a hesitation and a coolness by no means affected. I felt nothing but scorn for theatrical life; a scorn that was by no means lessened by a closer acquaintance with the apparently distinguished ruling body of a court theatre, the splendours of which only conceal, with arrogant ignorance, the humiliating conditions appertaining to it and to the modern

[1] William the First.

theatre in general. I saw every noble impulse stifled in those occupied with theatrical matters, and a combination of the vainest and most frivolous interests maintained by a ridiculously rigid and bureaucratic system; I was now fully convinced that the necessity of handling the business of the theatre would be the most distasteful thing I could imagine. Now that, through Rastrelli's death, the temptation to be false to my inner conviction came to me in Dresden, I explained to my old and trusted friends that I did not think I should accept the vacant post.

But everything calculated to shake human resolution combined against this decision. The prospect of securing the means of livelihood through a permanent position with a fixed salary was an irresistible attraction. I combated the temptation by reminding myself of my success as an operatic composer, which might reasonably be expected to bring in enough to supply my moderate requirements in a lodging of two rooms, where I could proceed undisturbed with fresh compositions. I was told in answer to this that my work itself would be better served by a fixed position without arduous duties, as for a whole year since the completion of the *Fliegender Holländer* I had not, under existing circumstances, found any leisure at all for composition. I still remained convinced that Rastrelli's post of musical director, in subordination to the conductor, was unworthy of me, and I declined to entertain the proposal, thus leaving the management to look elsewhere for some one to fill the vacancy.

There was therefore no further question of this particular post, but I was then informed that the death of Morlacchi had left vacant a court conductorship, and it was thought that the King would be willing to offer me the post. My wife was very much excited at this prospect, for in Germany the greatest value is laid on these court appointments, which are tenable for life, and the dazzling respectability pertaining to them is held out to German musicians as the acme of earthly happiness. The offer opened up for us in many directions the prospect of friendly relations in a society which had hitherto been outside our experience. Domestic comfort and social prestige were very alluring to the homeless wanderers who, in bygone days of misery, had often longed for the comfort and security of an assured and permanent position such as was now open to them under the august protection of the court. The influence of Caroline von Weber did much in the long-run to weaken my opposition. I was often at her house, and took great pleasure in her society, which brought back to my mind very vividly the personality of my still dearly beloved master. She begged me with really touching tenderness not to withstand this obvious command of fate, and asserted her right to ask me to settle in Dresden, to fill the place left sadly empty by her husband's death. 'Just think,' she said, 'how can I look Weber in the face again when I join him if I have to tell him that the work for which he made such devoted sacrifices in Dresden is neglected; just imagine my feelings when I see that indolent Reissiger stand in my noble Weber's place, and when I hear his operas produced more mechanically every year. If you loved Weber, you owe it to his memory to step into his place and to continue his work.' As an experienced woman of the world she also pointed out energetically and prudently the practical side of the matter, impressing on me the duty of thinking of my wife, who would, in case of my death, be sufficiently provided for if I accepted the post.

The promptings of affection, prudence and good sense, however, had less weight with me than the enthusiastic conviction, never at any period of my life entirely destroyed, that wherever fate led me, whether to Dresden or elsewhere, I should find the opportunity which would convert my dreams into reality through currents set in motion by some change in the everyday order of events. All that was needed for this was the advent of an ardent and aspiring soul who, with good luck to back him, might make up for lost time, and by his ennobling influence achieve the deliverance of art from her shameful bonds. The wonderful and rapid change which had taken place in my fortunes could not fail to encourage such a hope, and I was seduced on perceiving the marked alteration that had taken place in the whole attitude of Lüttichau, the general director, towards me. This strange individual showed me a kindliness of which no one would hitherto have thought him capable, and that he was prompted by a genuine feeling of personal benevolence towards me I could not help being absolutely convinced, even at the time of my subsequent ceaseless differences with him.

Nevertheless, the decision came as a kind of surprise. On 2nd February 1843 I was very politely invited to the director's office, and there met the general staff of the royal orchestra, in whose presence Lüttichau, through the medium of my never-to-be-forgotten friend Winkler, solemnly read out to me a royal rescript appointing me forthwith conductor to his Majesty, with a life salary of four thousand five hundred marks a year. Lüttichau followed the reading of this document by a more or less ceremonious speech, in which he assumed that I should gratefully accept the King's favour. At this polite ceremony it did not escape my notice that all possibility of future negotiations over the figure of the salary was cut off; on the other hand, a substantial exemption in my favour, the omission of the condition, enforced even on Weber in his time, of serving a year's probation under the title of mere musical director, was calculated to secure my unconditional acceptance. My new colleagues congratulated me, and Lüttichau accompanied me with the politest phrases to my own door, where I fell into the arms of my poor wife, who was giddy with delight. Therefore I fully realised that I must put the best face I could on the matter, and unless I wished to give unheard-of offence, I must even congratulate myself on my appointment as royal conductor.

A few days after taking the oath as a servant of the King in solemn session, and undergoing the ceremony of presentation to the assembled orchestra by means of an enthusiastic speech from the general director, I was summoned to an audience with his Majesty. When I saw the features of the kind, courteous, and homely monarch, I involuntarily thought of my youthful attempt at a political overture on the theme of *Friedrich und Freiheit.* Our somewhat embarrassed conversation brightened with the King's expression of his satisfaction with those two of my operas which had been performed in Dresden. He expressed with polite hesitation his feeling that if my operas left anything to be desired, it was a clearer definition of the various characters in my musical dramas. He thought the interest in the persons was overpowered by the elemental forces figuring beside them — in *Rienzi* the mob, in the *Fliegender Holländer* the sea. I thought I understood his meaning perfectly, and this proof of his sincere sympathy and original judgment pleased me very much. He also made his excuses in advance for a possible rare attendance at my operas on his part, his sole reason for this being that he had a peculiar aversion from theatre-going, as the result of one of the rules of his early training, under which he and his brother John, who had acquired a similar aversion, were for a long time compelled regularly to attend the theatre, when he, to tell the truth, would often have preferred to be left alone to follow his own pursuits independent of etiquette.

As a characteristic instance of the courtier spirit, I after-wards learned that Lüttichau, who had had to wait for me in the anteroom during this audience, had been very much put out by its long duration. In the whole course of my life I was only admitted twice more to personal intercourse and speech with the good King. The first occasion was when I presented him with the dedication copy of the pianoforte score of my *Rienzi;* and the second was after my very successful arrange-ment and performance of the *Iphigenia in Aulis,* by Gluck, of whose operas he was particularly fond, when he stopped me in the public promenade and congratulated me on my work.

That first audience with the King marked the zenith of my hastily adopted career at Dresden; thenceforward anxiety reasserted itself in manifold ways. I very quickly realised the difficulties of my material situation, since it soon became evident that the advantage won by new exertions and my present appointment bore no proportion to the heavy sacrifices and obligations which I incurred as soon as I entered on an independent career. The young musical director of Riga, long since forgotten, suddenly reappeared in an astonishing reincarnation as royal conductor to the King of Saxony. The first-fruits of the universal estimate of my good fortune took the shape of pressing creditors and threats of prosecution; next followed demands from the Königsberg tradesmen, from whom I had escaped from Riga by means of that horribly wretched and miserable flight. I also heard from people in

the most distant parts, who thought they had some claim on
me, dating even from my student, nay, my school days, until at
last I cried out in my astonishment that I expected to receive
a bill next from the nurse who had suckled me. All this
did not amount to any very large sum, and I merely mention
it because of the ill-natured rumours which, I learned years
later, had been spread abroad about the extent of my debts
at that time.   Out of three thousand marks, borrowed at
interest from Schröder-Devrient, I not only paid these debts,
but also fully compensated the sacrifices which Kietz had
made on my behalf, without ever expecting any return, in the
days of my poverty in Paris. I was, moreover, able to be of
practical use to him. But where was I to find even this sum,
as my distress had hitherto been so great that I was obliged
to urge Schröder-Devrient to hurry on the rehearsals of the
Fliegender Holländer by pointing out to her the enormous
importance to me of the fee for the performance? I had no
allowance for the expenses of my establishment in Dresden,
though it had to be suitable for my position as royal conductor,
nor even for the purchase of a ridiculous and expensive court
uniform, so that there would have been no possibility of my
making a start at all, as I had no private means, unless I
borrowed money at interest.

But no one who knew of the extraordinary success of *Rienzi*
at Dresden could help believing in an immediate and remunerative rage for my operas on the German stage. My own relatives,
even the prudent Ottilie, were so convinced of it that they
thought I might safely count on at least doubling my salary
by the receipts from my operas. At the very beginning the
prospects did indeed seem bright; the score of my *Fliegender
Holländer* was ordered by the Royal Theatre at Cassel and by
the Riga theatre, which I had known so well in the old days,
because they were anxious to perform something of mine at an
early date, and had heard that this opera was on a smaller
scale, and made smaller demands on the stage management,
than *Rienzi*. In May, 1843 I heard good reports of the success
of the performances from both those places. But this was all
for the time being, and a whole year went by without the
smallest inquiry for any of my scores. An attempt was made

to secure me some benefit by the publication of the pianoforte score of the *Fliegender Holländer,* as I wanted to reserve *Rienzi,* after the successes it had gained, as useful capital for a more favourable opportunity; but the plan was spoilt by the opposition of Messrs. Härtel of Leipzig, who, although ready enough to publish my opera, would only do so on the condition that I abstained from asking any payment for it.

So I had, for the present, to content myself with the moral satisfaction of my successes, of which my unmistakable popularity with the Dresden public, and the respect and attention paid to me, formed part. But even in this respect my Utopian dreams were destined to be disturbed. I think that my appearance at Dresden marked the beginning of a new era in journalism and criticism, which found food for its hitherto but slightly developed vitality in its vexation at my success. The two gentlemen I have already mentioned, C. Bank and J. Schladebach, had, as I now know, first taken up their regular abode in Dresden at that time; I know that when difficulties were raised about the permanence of Bank's appointment, they were waived, owing to the testimonials and recommendation of my present colleague Reissiger. The success of my *Rienzi* had been the source of great annoyance to these gentlemen, who were now established as musical critics to the Dresden press, because I made no effort to win their favour; they were not ill-pleased, therefore, to find an opportunity of pouring out the vitriol of their hatred over the universally popular young musician who had won the sympathy of the kindly public, partly on account of the poverty and ill-luck which had hitherto been his lot. The need for any kind of human consideration had suddenly vanished with my 'unheard-of' appointment to the royal conductorship. Now 'all was well with me,' 'too well,' in fact; and envy found its congenial food; this provided a perfectly clear and comprehensible point of attack; and soon there spread through the German press, in the columns given to Dresden news, an estimate of me which has never fundamentally changed, except in one point, to this day. This single modification, which was purely temporary and confined to papers of one political colour, occurred on my first settlement as a political refugee in Switzerland, but lasted only until, through Liszt's exertions, my operas began to be produced all over Germany, in spite of my exile. The orders from two theatres, immediately after the Dresden performance, for one of my scores, were merely due to the fact that up to that time the activity of my journalistic critics was still limited. I put down the cessation of all inquiries, certainly not without due justification, mainly to the effect of the false and calumnious reports in the papers.

My old friend Laube tried, indeed, to undertake my defence in the press. On New Year's Day, 1843 he resumed the editorship of the *Zeitung für die Elegante Welt,* and asked me to provide him with a biographical notice of myself for the first number. It evidently gave him great pleasure to present me thus in triumph to the literary world, and in order to give the subject more prominence he added a supplement to that number in the shape of a lithograph reproduction of my portrait by Kietz. But after a time even he became anxious and confused in his judgment of my works, when he saw the systematic and increasingly virulent detraction, depreciation, and scorn to which they were subjected. He confessed to me later that he had never imagined such a desperate position as mine against the united forces of journalism could possibly exist, and when he heard my view of the question, he smiled and gave me his blessing, as though I were a lost soul.

Moreover, a change was observable in the attitude of those immediately connected with me in my work, and this provided very acceptable material for the journalistic campaign. I had been led, though by no ambitious impulse, to ask to be allowed to conduct the performances of my own works. I found that at every performance of *Rienzi* Reissiger became more negligent in his conducting, and that the whole production was slipping back into the old familiar, expressionless, and humdrum performance; and as my appointment was already mooted, I had asked permission to conduct the sixth performance of my work in person. I conducted without having held a single rehearsal, and without any previous experience, at the head of the Dresden orchestra. The performance went splendidly; singers and orchestra were inspired with new life, and everybody was obliged to admit that this was the finest performance

of *Rienzi* that had yet been given. The rehearsing and conducting of the *Fliegender Holländer* were willingly handed over
to me, because Reissiger was overwhelmed with work, in consequence of the death of the musical director, Rastrelli. In
addition to this I was asked to conduct Weber's *Euryanthe*,
by way of providing a direct proof of my capacity to interpret scores other than my own. Apparently everybody was
pleased, and it was the tone of this performance that made
Weber's widow so anxious that I should accept the Dresden
conductorship; she declared that for the first time since her
husband's death she had heard his work correctly interpreted,
both in expression and time.

Thereupon, Reissiger, who would have preferred to have a
musical director under him, but had received instead a colleague
on an equal footing, felt himself aggrieved by my appointment.
Though his own indolence would have inclined him to the side
of peace and a good understanding with me, his ambitious wife
took care to stir up his fear of me. This never led to an openly
hostile attitude on his part, but I noticed certain indiscretions
in the press from that time onwards, which showed me that
the friendliness of my colleague, who never talked to me
without first embracing me, was not of the most honourable
type.

I also received a quite unexpected proof that I had attracted
the bitter envy of another man whose sentiments I had no
reason to suspect. This was Karl Lipinsky, a celebrated
violinist in his day, who had for many years led the Dresden
orchestra. He was a man of ardent temperament and original
talent, but of incredible vanity, which his emotional, suspicious
Polish temperament rendered dangerous. I always found him
annoying, because however inspiring and instructive his playing
was as to the technical execution of the violinists, he was certainly ill-fitted to be the leader of a first-class orchestra. This
extraordinary person tried to justify Director Lüttichau's praise
of his playing, which could always be heard above the rest of
the orchestra; he came in a little before the other violins; he
was a leader in a double sense, as he was always a little ahead.
He acted in much the same way with regard to expression,
marking his slight variations in the piano passages with fanatical

precision. It was useless to talk to him about it, as nothing but the most skilful flattery had any effect on him. So I had to endure it as best I could, and to think out ways and means of diminishing its ill effects on the orchestral performances as a whole by having recourse to the most polite circumlocutions. Even so he could not endure the higher estimation in which the performances of the orchestra under my conductorship were held, because he thought that the playing of an orchestra in which he was the leader must invariably be excellent, whoever stood at the conductor's desk. Now it happened, as is always the case when a new man with fresh ideas is installed in office, that the members of the orchestra came to me with the most varied suggestions for improvements which had hitherto been neglected; and Lipinsky, who was already annoyed about this, turned a certain case of this kind to a peculiarly treacherous use. One of the oldest contrabassists had died. Lipinsky urged me to arrange that the post should not be filled in the usual way by promotion from the ranks of our own orchestra, but should be given, on his recommendation, to a distinguished and skilful contrabassist from Darmstadt named Müller. When the musician whose rights of seniority were thus threatened, appealed to me, I kept my promise to Lipinsky, explained my views about the abuses of promotion by seniority, and declared that, in accordance with my sworn oath to the King, I held it my paramount duty to consider the maintenance of the artistic interests of the institution before everything else. I then found to my great astonishment, though it was foolish of me to be surprised, that the whole of the orchestra turned upon me as one man, and when the occasion arose for a discussion between Lipinsky and myself as to his own numerous grievances, he actually accused me of having threatened, by my remarks in the contrabassist case, to undermine the well-established rights of the members of the orchestra, whose welfare it was my duty to protect. Lüttichau, who was on the point of absenting himself from Dresden for some time, was extremely uneasy, as Reissiger was away on his holiday, at leaving musical affairs in such a dangerous state of unrest. The deceit and impudence of which I had been the victim was a revelation to me, and I gathered from this experience the calm sense necessary to set the harassed director at ease by the most conclusive assurances that I understood the people with whom I had to deal, and would act accordingly. I faithfully kept my word, and never again came into collision either with Lipinsky or any other member of the orchestra. On the contrary, all the musicians were soon so firmly attached to me that I could always pride myself on their devotion.

From that day forward, however, one thing at least was certain, namely, that I should not die as conductor at Dresden. My post and my work at Dresden thenceforward became a burden, of which the occasionally excellent results of my efforts made me all the more sensible.

My position at Dresden, however, brought me one friend whose intimate relations with me long survived our artistic collaboration in Dresden. A musical director was assigned to each conductor; he had to be a musician of repute, a hard worker, adaptable, and, above all, a Catholic, for the two conductors were Protestants, a cause of much annoyance to the clergy of the Catholic cathedral, numerous positions in which had to be filled from the orchestra. August Röckel, a nephew of Hummel, who sent in his application for this position from Weimar, furnished evidence of his suitability under all these heads. He belonged to an old Bavarian family; his father was a singer, and had sung the part of Florestan at the time of the first production of Beethoven's *Fidelio,* and had himself remained on terms of close intimacy with the Master, many details about whose life have been preserved through his care. His subsequent position as a teacher of singing led him to take up theatrical management, and he introduced German opera to the Parisians with so much success, that the credit for the popularity of *Fidelio* and *Der Freischütz* with French audiences, to whom these works were quite unknown, must be awarded to his admirable enterprise, which was also responsible for Schröder-Devrient's début in Paris. August Röckel, his son, who was still a young man, by helping his father in these and similar undertakings, had gained practical experience as a musician. As his father's business had for some time even extended to England, August had won practical knowledge of all sorts by contact with many men and things, and in addition had learned

French and English. But music had remained his chosen vocation, and his great natural talent justified the highest hopes of success. He was an excellent pianist, read scores with the utmost ease, possessed an exceptionally fine ear, and had indeed every qualification for a practical musician. As a composer he was actuated, not so much by a strong impulse to create, as the desire to show what he was capable of; the success at which he aimed was to gain the reputation of a clever operatic composer rather than recognition as a distinguished musician, and he hoped to obtain his end by the production of popular works. Actuated by this modest ambition he had completed an opera, *Farinelli*, for which he had also written the libretto, with no other aspiration than that of attaining the same reputation as his brother-in-law Lortzing.

He brought this score to me, and begged me — it was his first visit before he had heard one of my operas in Dresden — to play him something from *Rienzi* and the *Fliegender Holländer*. His frank, agreeable personality induced me to try and meet his wishes as far as I could, and I am convinced that I soon made such a great and unexpectedly powerful impression on him that from that moment he determined not to bother me further with the score of his opera. It was not until we had become more intimate and had discovered mutual personal interests, that the desire of turning his work to account induced him to ask me to show my practical friendship by turning my attention to his score. I made various suggestions as to how it might be improved, but he was soon so hopelessly disgusted with his own work that he put it absolutely aside, and never again felt seriously moved to undertake a similar task. On making a closer acquaintance with my completed operas and plans for new works, he declared to me that he felt it his vocation to play the part of spectator, to be my faithful helper and the interpreter of my new ideas, and, as far as in him lay, to remove entirely, and at all events to relieve me as far as possible from, all the unpleasantnesses of my official position and of my dealings with the outside world. He wished, he said, to avoid placing himself in the ridiculous position of composing operas of his own while living on terms of close friendship with me.

Nevertheless, I tried to urge him to turn his own talent to

account, and to this end called his attention to several plots
which I wished him to work out. Among these was the idea
contained in a small French drama entitled *Cromwell's Daugh-*
ter, which was subsequently used as the subject for a sentimental
pastoral romance, and for the elaboration of which I presented
him with an exhaustive plan.

But in the end all my efforts remained fruitless, and it became
evident that his productive talent was feeble. This perhaps
arose partly from his extremely needy and trying domestic
circumstances, which were such that the poor fellow wore himself out to support his wife and numerous growing children.
Indeed, he claimed my help and sympathy in quite another
fashion than by arousing my interest in his artistic development. He was unusually clear-headed, and possessed a rare
capacity for teaching and educating himself in every branch
of knowledge and experience; he was, moreover, so genuinely
true and good-hearted that he soon became my intimate friend
and comrade. He was, and continued to be, the only person
who really appreciated the singular nature of my position
towards the surrounding world, and with whom I could fully
and sincerely discuss the cares and sorrows arising therefrom.
What dreadful trials and experiences, what painful anxieties our common fate was to bring upon us, will soon be
seen.

The earlier period of my establishment in Dresden brought
me also another devoted and lifelong friend, though his
qualities were such that he exerted a less decisive influence
upon my career. This was a young physician, named Anton
Pusinelli, who lived near me. He seized the occasion of a
serenade sung in honour of my thirtieth birthday by the
Dresden Glee Club to express to me personally his hearty and
sincere attachment. We soon entered upon a quiet friendship
from which we derived a mutual benefit. He became my
attentive family doctor, and during my residence in Dresden,
marked as it was by accumulating difficulties, he had abundant opportunities of helping me. His financial position was
very good, and his ready self-sacrifice enabled him to give me
substantial succour and bound me to him by many heartfelt
obligations.

A further development of my association with Dresden society was provided by the kindly advances of Chamberlain von Könneritz's family. His wife, Marie von Könneritz (*née* Fink), was a friend of Countess Ida Hahn-Hahn, and expressed her appreciation of my success as a composer with great warmth, I might almost say, with enthusiasm. I was often invited to their house, and seemed likely, through this family, to be brought into touch with the higher aristocracy of Dresden. I merely succeeded in touching the fringe, however, as we really had nothing in common. True, I here made the acquaintance of Countess Rossi, the famous Sontag, by whom, to my genuine astonishment, I was most heartily greeted, and I thereby obtained the right of afterwards approaching her in Berlin with a certain degree of familiarity. The curious way in which I was disillusioned about this lady on that occasion will be related in due course. I would only mention here that, through my earlier experiences of the world, I had become fairly impervious to deception, and my desire for closer acquaintance with these circles speedily gave way to a complete hopelessness and an entire lack of ease in their sphere of life.

Although the Könneritz couple remained friendly during the whole of my prolonged sojourn in Dresden, yet the connection had not the least influence either upon my development or my position. Only once, on the occasion of a quarrel between Lüttichau and myself, the former observed that Frau von Könneritz, by her unmeasured praises, had turned my head and made me forget my position towards him. But in making this taunt he forgot that, if any woman in the higher ranks of Dresden society had exerted a real and invigorating influence upon my inward pride, that woman was his own wife, Ida von Lüttichau (*née* von Knobelsdorf).

The power which this cultured, gentle, and distinguished lady exercised over my life was of a kind I now experienced for the first time, and might have become of great importance had I been favoured with more frequent and intimate intercourse. But it was less her position as wife of the general director than her constant ill-health and my own peculiar unwillingness to appear obtrusive, that hindered our meeting, except at rare intervals. My recollections of her merge somewhat, in my memory, with those of my own sister Rosalie. I remember the tender ambition which inspired me to win the encouraging sympathy of this sensitive woman, who was painfully wasting away amid the coarsest surroundings. My earliest hope for the fulfilment of this ambition arose from her appreciation of my *Fliegender Holländer,* in spite of the fact that, following close upon *Rienzi,* it had so puzzled the Dresden public. In this way she was the first, so to speak, who swam against the tide and met me upon my new path. So deeply was I touched by this conquest that, when I afterwards published the opera, I dedicated it to her. In the account of my later years in Dresden I shall have more to record of the warm sympathy for my new development and dearest artistic aims for which I was indebted to her. But of real intercourse we had none, and the character of my Dresden life was not affected by this acquaintance, otherwise so important in itself.

On the other hand, my theatrical acquaintances thrust themselves with irresistible importunancy into the wide foreground of my life, and in fact, after my brilliant successes, I was still restricted to the same limited and familiar sphere in which I had prepared myself for these triumphs. Indeed, the only one who joined my old friends Heine and Gaffer Fischer was Tichatschek, with his strange domestic circle. Any one who lived in Dresden at that time and chanced to know the court lithographer, Fürstenau, will be astonished to hear that, without really being aware of it myself, I entered into a familiarity that was to prove a lasting one with this man who was an intimate friend of Tichatschek's. The importance of this singular connection may be judged from the fact that my complete withdrawal from him coincided exactly with the collapse of my civic position in Dresden.

My good-humoured acceptance of election to the musical committee of the Dresden Glee Club also brought me further chance acquaintances. This club consisted of a limited number of young merchants and officials, who had more taste for any kind of convivial entertainment than for music. But it was seduously kept together by a remarkable and ambitious man, Professor Löwe, who nursed it with special objects in view, for the attainment of which he felt the need of an authority such as I possessed at that time in Dresden.

Among other aims he was particularly and chiefly concerned in arranging for the transfer of Weber's remains from London to Dresden. As this project was one which interested me also, I lent him my support, though he was in reality merely following the voice of personal ambition. He furthermore desired, as head of the Glee Club — which, by the way, from the point of view of music was quite worthless — to invite all the male choral unions of Saxony to a great gala performance in Dresden. A committee was appointed for the execution of this plan, and as things soon became pretty warm, Löwe turned it into a regular revolutionary tribunal, over which, as the great day of triumph approached, he presided day and night without resting, and by his furious zeal earned from me the nickname of ' Robespierre.'

In spite of the fact that I had been placed at the head of this enterprise, I luckily managed to evade his terrorism, as I was fully occupied with a great composition promised for the festival. The task had been assigned to me of writing an important piece for male voices only, which, if possible, should occupy half an hour. I reflected that the tiresome monotony of male singing, which even the orchestra could only enliven to a slight extent, can only be endured by the introduction of dramatic themes. I therefore designed a great choral scene, selecting the apostolic Pentecost with the outpouring of the Holy Ghost as its subject. I completely avoided any real solos, but worked out the whole in such a way that it should be executed by detached choral masses according to requirement. Out of this composition arose my *Liebesmahl der Apostel* ('Love-feast of the Apostles '), which has recently been performed in various places.

As I was obliged at all costs to finish it within a limited time, I do not mind including this in the list of my uninspired compositions. But I was not displeased with it when it was done, more especially when it was played at the rehearsals given by the Dresden choral societies under my personal supervision. When, therefore, twelve hundred singers from all parts of Saxony gathered around me in the Frauenkirche, where the

performance took place, I was astonished at the comparatively
feeble effect produced upon my ear by this colossal human
tangle of sounds. The conclusion at which I arrived was, that
these enormous choral undertakings are folly, and I never again
felt inclined to repeat the experiment.

It was with much difficulty that I shook myself free of the
Dresden Glee Club, and I only succeeded in doing so by introducing to Professor Löwe another ambitious man in the person
of Herr Ferdinand Hiller. My most glorious exploit in connection with this association was the transfer of Weber's ashes,
of which I will speak later on, though it occurred at an earlier
date. I will only refer now to another commissioned composition which, as royal bandmaster, I was officially commanded to produce. On the 7th of June of this year (1843)
the statue of King Frederick Augustus by Rietschl was
unveiled in the Dresden Zwinger [1] with all due pomp and
ceremony. In honour of this event I, in collaboration with
Mendelssohn, was commanded to compose a festal song, and to
conduct the gala performance. I had written a simple song
for male voices of modest design, whereas to Mendelssohn had
been assigned the more complicated task of interweaving the
National Anthem (the English 'God Save the King,' which
in Saxony is called *Heil Dir im Rautenkranz*) into the male
chorus he had to compose. This he had effected by an artistic
work in counterpoint, so arranged that from the first eight
beats of his original melody the brass instruments simultaneously played the Anglo-Saxon popular air. My simpler song
seems to have sounded very well from a distance, whereas I
understood that Mendelssohn's daring combination quite
missed its effect, because no one could understand why the
vocalists did not sing the same air as the wind instruments
were playing. Nevertheless Mendelssohn, who was present, left
me a written expression of thanks for the pains I had taken
in the production of his composition. I also received a gold
snuff-box from the grand gala committee, presumably meant
as a reward for my male chorus, but the hunting scene which
was engraved on the top was so badly done that I found, to

[1] This is the name by which the famous Dresden Art Galleries are known. —
EDITOR.

my surprise, that in several places the metal was cut through.

Amid all the distractions of this new and very different mode of life, I diligently strove to concentrate and steel my soul against these influences, bearing in mind my experiences of success in the past. By May of my thirtieth year I had finished my poem *Der Venusberg* (' The Mount of Venus '), as I called *Tannhäuser* at that time. I had not yet by any means gained any real knowledge of mediæval poetry. The classical side of the poetry of the Middle Ages had so far only faintly dawned upon me, partly from my youthful recollections, and partly from the brief acquaintance I had made with it through Lehrs' instruction in Paris.

Now that I was secure in the possession of a royal appointment that would last my lifetime, the establishment of a permanent domestic hearth began to assume great importance; for I hoped it would enable me to take up my serious studies once more, and in such a way as to make them productive — an aim which my theatrical life and the miseries of my years in Paris had rendered impossible. My hope of being able to do this was strengthened by the character of my official employment, which was never very arduous, and in which I met with exceptional consideration from the general management. Though I had only held my appointment for a few months, yet I was given a holiday this first summer, which I spent in a second visit to Töplitz, a place which I had grown to like, and whither I had sent on my wife in advance.

Keenly indeed did I appreciate the change in my position since the preceding year. I could now engage four spacious and well-appointed rooms in the same house — the *Eiche* at Schönau — where I had before lived in such straitened and frugal circumstances. I invited my sister Clara to pay us a visit, and also my good mother, whose gout necessitated her taking the Töplitz baths every year. I also seized the opportunity of drinking the mineral waters, which I hoped might have a beneficial effect on the gastric troubles from which I had suffered ever since my vicissitudes in Paris. Unfortunately the attempted cure had a contrary effect, and when I complained of the painful irritation produced, I learned that my constitution was not adapted for water cures. In fact, on my morning promenade, and while drinking my water, I had been observed to race through the shady alleys of the adjacent Thurn Gardens, and it was pointed out to me that such a cure could only be properly wrought by leisurely calm and easy sauntering. It was also remarked that I usually carried about a fairly stout volume, and that, armed with this and my bottle of mineral water, I used to take rest in lonely places.

This book was J. Grimm's *German Mythology*. All who know the work can understand how the unusual wealth of its contents, gathered from every side, and meant almost exclusively for the student, would react upon me, whose mind was everywhere seeking for something definite and distinct. Formed from the scanty fragments of a perished world, of which scarcely any monuments remained recognisable and intact, I here found a heterogeneous building, which at first glance seemed but a rugged rock clothed in straggling brambles. Nothing was finished, only here and there could the slightest resemblance to an architectonic line be traced, so that I often felt tempted to relinquish the thankless task of trying to build from such materials. And yet I was enchained by a wondrous magic. The baldest legend spoke to me of its ancient home, and soon my whole imagination thrilled with images; long-lost forms for which I had sought so eagerly shaped themselves ever more and more clearly into realities that lived again. There rose up soon before my mind a whole world of figures, which revealed themselves as so strangely plastic and primitive, that, when I saw them clearly before me and heard their voices in my heart, I could not account for the almost tangible familiarity and assurance of their demeanour. The effect they produced upon the inner state of my soul I can only describe as an entire rebirth. Just as we feel a tender joy over a child's first bright smile of recognition, so now my own eyes flashed with rapture as I saw a world, revealed, as it were, by miracle, in which I had hitherto moved blindly as the babe in its mother's womb.

But the result of this reading did not at first do much to help me in my purpose of composing part of the *Tannhäuser* music. I had had a piano put in my room at the *Eiche*, and though

I smashed all its strings, nothing satisfactory would emerge. With much pain and toil I sketched the first outlines of my music for the *Venusberg,* as fortunately I already had its theme in my mind. Meanwhile I was very much troubled by excitability and rushes of blood to the brain. I imagined I was ill, and lay for whole days in bed, where I read Grimm's German legends, or tried to master the disagreeable mythology. It was quite a relief when I hit upon the happy thought of freeing myself from the torments of my condition by an excursion to Prague. Meanwhile I had already ascended Mount Millischau once with my wife, and in her company I now made the journey to Prague in an open carriage. There I stayed once more at my favourite inn, the Black Horse, met my friend Kittl, who had now grown fat and rotund, made various excursions, revelled in the curious antiquities of the old city, and learned to my joy that the two lovely friends of my youth, Jenny and Auguste Pachta, had been happily married to members of the highest aristocracy. Thereupon, having reassured myself that everything was in the best possible order, I returned to Dresden and resumed my functions as musical conductor to the King of Saxony.

We now set to work on the preparations and furnishing of a roomy and well-situated house in the Ostra Allee, with an outlook upon the Zwinger. Everything was good and substantial, as is only right for a man of thirty who is settling down at last for the whole of his life. As I had not received any subsidy towards this outlay, I had naturally to raise the money by loan. But I could look forward to a certain harvest from my operatic successes in Dresden, and what was more natural than for me to expect soon to earn more than enough? The three most valued treasures which adorned my house were a concert grand piano by Breitkopf and Härtel, which I had bought with much pride; a stately writing-desk, now in possession of Otto Kummer, the chamber-music artist; and the title-page by Cornelius for the *Nibelungen,* in a handsome Gothic frame — the only object which has remained faithful to me to the present day. But the thing which above all else made my house seem homelike and attractive was the presence of a library, which I procured in accordance with a systematic

plan laid down by my proposed line of study. On the failure
of my Dresden career this library passed in a curious way into
the possession of Herr Heinrich Brockhaus, to whom at that
time I owed fifteen hundred marks, and who took it as security
for the amount. My wife knew nothing at the time of this
obligation, and I never afterwards succeeded in recovering this
characteristic collection from his hands. Upon its shelves
old German literature was especially well represented, and also
the closely related work of the German Middle Ages, including
many a costly volume, as, for instance, the rare old work,
Romans des douze Paris. Beside these stood many excellent
historical works on the Middle Ages, as well as on the German
people in general. At the same time I made provision for the
poetical and classical literature of all times and languages.
Among these were the Italian poets, Shakespeare and the French
writers, of whose language I had a passable knowledge. All
these I acquired in the original, hoping some day to find time
to master their neglected tongues. As for the Greek and Roman
classics, I had to content myself with standard German translations. Indeed, on looking once more into my Homer — whom
I secured in the original Greek — I soon recognised that I should
be presuming on more leisure than my conductorship was likely
to leave me, if I hoped to find time for regaining my lost knowledge of that language. Moreover, I provided most thoroughly
for a study of universal history, and to this end did not fail to
equip myself with the most voluminous works. Thus armed,
I thought I could bid defiance to all the trials which I clearly
foresaw would inevitably accompany my calling and position.
In hopes, therefore, of long and peaceable enjoyment of this
hard-earned home, I entered into possession with the best of
spirits in October of this year (1843), and though my conductor's quarters were by no means magnificent, they were
stately and substantial.

The first leisure in my new home which I could snatch from
the claims of my profession and my favourite studies was
devoted to the composition of *Tannhäuser,* the first act of which
was completed in January of the new year, 1844. I have
no recollections of any importance regarding my activities in
Dresden during this winter. The only memorable events were

two enterprises which took me away from home, the first to Berlin early in the year, for the production of my *Fliegender Holländer,* and the other in March to Hamburg for *Rienzi.*

Of these the former made the greater impression upon my mind. The manager of the Berlin theatre, Küstner, quite took me by surprise when he announced the first performance of the *Fliegender Holländer* for an early date.

As the opera house had been burnt down only about a year before, and could not possibly have been rebuilt, it had not occurred to me to remind them about the production of my opera. It had been performed in Dresden with very poor scenic accessories, and knowing how important a careful and artistic execution of the difficult scenery was for my dramatic sea-scapes, I had relied implicitly on the admirable management and staging capacities of the Berlin opera house. Consequently I was very much annoyed that the Berlin manager should select my opera as a stopgap to be produced at the Comedy Theatre, which was being used as a temporary opera house. All remonstrances proved useless, for I learned that they were not merely thinking about rehearsing the work, but that it was already actually being rehearsed, and would be produced in a few days. It was obvious that this arrangement meant that my opera was to be condemned to quite a short run in their repertoire, as it was not to be expected that they would remount it when the new opera house was opened. On the other hand, they tried to appease me by saying that this first production of the *Fliegender Holländer* was to be associated with a special engagement of Schröder-Devrient, which was to begin in Berlin immediately. They naturally thought I should be delighted to see the great actress in my own work. But this only confirmed me in the suspicion that this opera was simply wanted as a makeshift for the duration of Schröder-Devrient's visit. They were evidently in a dilemma with regard to her repertoire, which consisted mainly of so-called grand operas — such as Meyerbeer's — destined exclusively for the opera house, and which were being specially reserved for the brilliant future of the new building. I therefore realised beforehand that my *Fliegender Holländer* was to be relegated to the category of conductor's operas, and would meet with the usual predestined

fate of such productions. The whole treatment meted out to
me and my works all pointed in the same direction; but in
consideration of the expected co-operation of Schröder-Devrient
I fought against these vexatious premonitions, and set out for
Berlin to do all I could for the success of my opera. I saw at
once that my presence was very necessary. I found the conductor's desk occupied by a man calling himself Conductor
Henning (or Henniger), an official who had won promotion from
the ranks of ordinary musicians by an upright observance of
the laws of seniority, but who knew precious little about conducting an orchestra at all, and about my opera had not the
faintest glimmer of an idea. I took my seat at the desk, and
conducted one full rehearsal and two performances, in neither
of which, however, did Schröder-Devrient take part. Although
I found much to complain of in the weakness of the string
instruments and the consequent mean sound of the orchestra,
yet I was well satisfied with the actors both as regards their
capacity and their zeal. The careful staging, moreover,
which under the supervision of the really gifted stage manager,
Blum, and with the co-operation of his skilful and ingenious
mechanics, was truly excellent, gave me a most pleasant
surprise.

I was now very curious to learn what effect these pleasing
and encouraging preparations would have upon the Berlin
public when the full performance took place. My experiences
on this point were very curious. Apparently the only thing
that interested the large audience was to discover my weak
points. During the first act the prevalent opinion seemed to
be that I belonged to the category of bores. Not a single hand
was moved, and I was afterwards informed that this was fortunate, as the slightest attempt at applause would have been
ascribed to a paid claque, and would have been energetically
opposed. Küstner alone assured me that the composure with
which, on the close of this act, I quitted my desk and appeared
before the curtain, had filled him with wonder, considering this
entire absence — lucky as it appears to have been — of all applause. But so long as I myself felt content with the execution,
I was not disposed to let the public apathy discourage me,
knowing, as I did, that the crucial test was in the second act.

It lay, therefore, much nearer my heart to do all I could for the success of this than to inquire into the reasons for this attitude on the part of the Berlin public. And here the ice was really broken at last. The audience seemed to abandon all idea of finding a proper niche for me, and allowed itself to be carried away into giving vent to applause, which at last grew into the most boisterous enthusiasm. At the close of the act, amid a storm of shouts, I led forward my singers on to the stage for the customary bows of thanks. As the third act was too short to be tedious, and as the scenic effects were both new and impressive, we could not help hoping that we had won a veritable triumph, especially as renewed outbursts of applause marked the end of the performance. Mendelssohn, who happened at that time to be in Berlin, with Meyerbeer, on business relating to the general musical conductorship, was present in a stage box during this performance. He followed its progress with a pale face, and afterwards came and murmured to me in a weary tone of voice, ' Well, I should think you are satisfied now! ' I met him several times during my brief stay in Berlin, and also spent an evening with him listening to various pieces of chamber-music. But never did another word concerning the *Fliegender Holländer* pass his lips, beyond inquiries as to the second performance, and as to whether Devrient or some one else would appear in it. I heard, moreover, that he had responded with equal indifference to the earnest warmth of my allusions to his own music for the *Midsummer Night's Dream*, which was being frequently played at that time, and which I had heard for the first time. The only thing he discussed with any detail was the actor Gern, who was playing in *Zettel*, and who he considered was overacting his part.

A few days later came a second performance with the same cast. My experiences on this evening were even more startling than on the former. Evidently the first night had won me a few friends, who were again present, for they began to applaud after the overture. But others responded with hisses, and for the rest of the evening no one again ventured to applaud. My old friend Heine had arrived in the meantime from Dresden, sent by our own board of directors to study the scenic arrange-

ments of the *Midsummer Night's Dream* for our theatre. He
was present at this second performance, and had persuaded
me to accept the invitation from one of his Berlin relatives to
have supper after the performance in a wine-bar *unter den
Linden*. Very weary, I followed him to a nasty and badly
lighted house, where I gulped down the wine with hasty ill-
humour to warm myself, and listened to the embarrassed conversation of my good-natured friend and his companion, whilst
I turned over the day's papers. I now had ample leisure to
read the criticisms they contained on the first performance of
my *Fliegender Holländer*. A terrible spasm cut my heart as
I realised the contemptible tone and unparalleled shamelessness
of their raging ignorance regarding my own name and work.
Our Berlin friend and host, a thorough Philistine, said that he
had known how things would go in the theatre that night, after
having read these criticisms in the morning. The people of
Berlin, he added, wait to hear what Rellstab and his mates
have to say, and then they know how to behave. The good
fellow was anxious to cheer me up, and ordered one wine after
another. Heine hunted up his reminiscences of our merry
Rienzi times in Dresden, until at last the pair conducted me,
staggering along in an addled condition, to my hotel.

It was already midnight. As I was being lighted by the
waiter through its gloomy corridors to my room, a gentleman
in black, with a pale refined face, came forward and said he
would like to speak to me. He informed me that he had
waited there since the close of the play, and as he was determined to see me, had stopped till now. I excused myself on
the ground of being quite unfit for business, and added that,
although not exactly inclined to merriment, I had, as he might
perceive, somewhat foolishly drunk a little too much wine.
This I said in a stammering voice; but my strange visitor
seemed only the more unwilling to be repulsed. He accompanied me to my room, declaring that it was all the more imperative for him to speak with me. We seated ourselves in
the cold room, by the meagre light of a single candle, and then
he began to talk. In flowing and impressive language he related that he had been present at the performance that night
of my *Fliegender Holländer*, and could well conceive the humour

in which the evening's experiences had left me. For this very reason he felt that nothing should hinder him from speaking to me that night, and telling me that in the *Fliegender Holländer* I had produced an unrivalled masterpiece. Moreover, the acquaintance he had made with this work had awakened in him a new and unforeseen hope for the future of German art; and that it would be a great pity if I yielded to any sense of discouragement as the result of the unworthy reception accorded to it by the Berlin public. My hair began to stand on end. One of Hoffmann's fantastic creations had entered bodily into my life. I could find nothing to say, except to inquire the name of my visitor, at which he seemed surprised, as I had talked with him the day before at Mendelssohn's house. He said that my conversation and manner had created such an impression upon him there, and had filled him with such sudden regret at not having sufficiently overcome his dislike for opera in general, to be present at the first performance, that he had at once resolved not to miss the second. His name, he added, was Professor Werder. That was no use to me, I said, he must write his name down. Getting paper and ink, he did as I desired, and we parted. I flung myself unconsciously on the bed for a deep and invigorating sleep. Next morning I was fresh and well. I paid a farewell call on Schröder-Devrient, who promised me to do all she could for the *Fliegender Holländer* as soon as possible, drew my fee of a hundred ducats, and set off for home. On my way through Leipzig I utilised my ducats for the repayment of sundry advances made me by my relatives during the earlier and poverty-stricken period of my sojourn in Dresden, and then continued my journey, to recuperate among my books and meditate upon the deep impression made on me by Werder's midnight visit.

Before the end of this winter I received a genuine invitation to Hamburg for the performance of *Rienzi*. The enterprising director, Herr Cornet, through whom it came, confessed that he had many difficulties to contend against in the management of his theatre, and was in need of a great success. This, after the reception with which it had met in Dresden, he thought he could secure by the production of *Rienzi*. I accordingly betook myself thither in the month of March. The journey at that time was not an easy one, as after Hanover one had to proceed by mail-coach, and the crossing of the Elbe, which was full of floating ice, was a risky business. Owing to a great fire that had recently broken out, the town of Hamburg was in process of being rebuilt, and there were still many wide spaces encumbered with ruins. Cold weather and an ever-gloomy sky make my recollections of my somewhat prolonged sojourn in this town anything but agreeable. I was tormented to such an extent by having to rehearse with bad material, fit only for the poorest theatrical trumpery, that, worn out and exposed to constant colds, I spent most of my leisure time in the solitude of my inn chamber. My earlier experiences of ill-arranged and badly managed theatres came back to me afresh. I was particularly depressed when I realised that I had made myself an unconscious accomplice of Director Cornet's basest interests. His one aim was to create a sensation, which he thought should be of great service to me also; and not only did he put me off with a smaller fee, but even suggested that it should be paid by gradual instalments. The dignity of scenic decoration, of which he had not the smallest idea, was completely sacrificed to the most ridiculous and tawdry showiness. He imagined that pageantry was all that was really needed to secure my success. So he hunted out all the old fairy-ballet costumes from his stock, and fancied that if they only looked gay enough, and if plenty of people were bustling about on the stage, I ought to be satisfied. But the most sorry item of all was the singer he provided for the title-rôle. He was a man of the name of Wurda, an elderly, flabby and voiceless tenor, who sang Rienzi with the expression of a lover — like Elvino, for instance, in the *Somnambula*. He was so dreadful that I conceived the idea of making the Capitol tumble down in the second act, so as to bury him sooner in its ruins, a plan which would have cut out several of the processions, which were so dear to the heart of the director. I found my one ray of light in a lady singer, who delighted me with the fire with which she played the part of Adriano. This was a Mme. Fehringer, who was afterwards engaged by Liszt for the rôle of Ortrud in the production of *Lohengrin* at Weimar, but by that time her powers had greatly deteriorated. Nothing could be more

depressing than my connection with this opera under such
dismal circumstances. And yet there were no outward signs
of failure. The manager hoped in any case to keep *Rienzi* in
his repertoire until Tichatschek was able to come to Hamburg
and give the people of that town a true idea of the play. This
actually took place in the following summer.

My discouragement and ill-humour did not escape the notice
of Herr Cornet, and discovering that I wished to present my
wife with a parrot, he managed to procure a very fine bird,
which he gave me as a parting gift. I carried it with me in
its narrow cage on my melancholy journey home, and was
touched to find that it quickly repaid my care and became
very much attached to me. Minna greeted me with great
joy when she saw this beautiful grey parrot, for she regarded
it as a self-evident proof that I should do something in life.
We already had a pretty little dog, born on the day of the first
Rienzi rehearsal in Dresden, which, owing to its passionate
devotion to myself, was much petted by all who knew me and
visited my house during those years. This sociable bird,
which had no vices and was an apt scholar, now formed an
addition to our household; and the pair did much to brighten
our dwelling in the absence of children. My wife soon taught
the bird snatches of songs from *Rienzi,* with which it would
good-naturedly greet me from a distance when it heard me
coming up the stairs.

And thus at last my domestic hearth seemed to be established with every possible prospect of a comfortable competency.

No further excursions for the performance of any of my
operas took place, for the simple reason that no such performances were given. As I saw it was quite clear that the diffusion of my works through the theatrical world would be a very
slow business, I concluded that this was probably due to the
fact that no adaptations of them for the piano existed. I
therefore thought that I should do well to press forward such
an issue at all costs, and in order to secure the expected profits,
I hit upon the idea of publishing at my own expense. I
accordingly made arrangements with F. Meser, the court
music-dealer, who had hitherto not got beyond the publication
of a valse, and signed an agreement with him for his firm to

appear as the nominal publishers on the understanding that they should receive a commission of ten per cent., whilst I provided the necessary capital.

As there were two operas to be issued, including *Rienzi*, a work of exceptional bulk, it was not likely that these publications would prove very profitable unless, in addition to the usual piano selections, I also published adaptations, such as the music without words, for duet or solo. For this a fairly large capital was necessary. I also needed funds for the repayment of the loans already mentioned, and for the settlement of old debts, as well as to pay off the remaining expenses of my house-furnishing. I was therefore obliged to try and procure much larger sums. I laid my project and its motive before Schröder-Devrient, who had just returned to Dresden, at Easter, 1844, to fulfil a fresh engagement. She believed in the future of my works, recognised the peculiarity of my position, as well as the correctness of my calculations, and declared her willingness to provide the necessary capital for the publication of my operas, refusing to consider the act as one involving any sacrifice on her part. This money she proposed to get by selling out her investments in Polish state-bonds, and I was to pay the customary rate of interest. The thing was so easily done, and seemed so much a matter of course, that I at once made all needful arrangements with my Leipzig printer, and set to work on the publication of my operas.

When the amount of work delivered brought with it a demand for considerable payments on account, I approached my friend for a first advance. And here I became confronted with a new phase of that famous lady's life, which placed me in a position which proved as disastrous as it was unexpected. After having broken away from the unlucky Herr von Münchhausen some time previously, and returned, as it appeared, with penitential ardour to her former connection with my friend, Hermann Müller, it now turned out that she had found no real satisfaction in this fresh relationship. On the contrary, the star of her being, whom she had so long and ardently desired, had now at last arisen in the person of another lieutenant of the Guards. With a vehemence which made light of her treachery to her old friend, she elected this slim young man, whose moral and intellectual weaknesses were patent to every eye, as the chosen keystone of her life's love. He took the good luck that befell him so seriously, that he would brook no jesting, and at once laid hands on the fortune of his future wife, as he considered that it was disadvantageously and insecurely invested, and thought that he knew of much more profitable ways of employing it. My friend therefore explained, with much pain and evident embarrassment, that she had renounced all control over her capital, and was unable to keep her promise to me.

Owing to this I entered upon a series of entanglements and troubles which henceforth dominated my life, and plunged me into sorrows that left their dismal mark on all my subsequent enterprises. It was clear that I could not now abandon the proposed plan of publication. The only satisfactory solution of my perplexities was to be found in the execution of my project and the success which I hoped would attend it. I was compelled, therefore, to turn all my energies to the raising of the money wherewith to publish my two operas, to which in all probability *Tannhäuser* would shortly have to be added. I first applied to my friends, and in some cases had to pay exorbitant rates of interest, even for short terms. For the present these details are sufficient to prepare the reader for the catastrophe towards which I was now inevitably drifting.

The hopelessness of my position did not at first reveal itself. There seemed no reason to despair of the eventual spread of my operatic works among the theatres in Germany, though my experience of them indicated that the process would be slow. In spite of the depressing experiences in Berlin and Hamburg, there were many encouraging signs to be seen. Above all, *Rienzi* maintained its position in favour of the people of Dresden, a place which undoubtedly occupied a position of great importance, especially during the summer months, when so many strangers from all parts of the world pass through it. My opera, which was not to be heard anywhere else, was in great request, both among the Germans and other visitors, and was always received with marked approbation, which surprised me very much. Thus a performance of *Rienzi,* especially in summer, became quite a Dionysian revelry, whose effect upon me could not fail to be encouraging.

On one occasion Liszt was among the number of these visitors. As *Rienzi* did not happen to be in the repertoire when he arrived, he induced the management at his earnest request to arrange a special performance. I met him between the acts in Tichatschek's dressing-room, and was heartily encouraged and touched by his almost enthusiastic appreciation, expressed in his most emphatic manner. The kind of life to which Liszt was at that time condemned, and which bound him to a perpetual environment of distracting and exciting elements, debarred us from all more intimate and fruitful intercourse. Yet from this time onward I continued to receive constant testimonies of the profound and lasting impression I had made upon him, as well as of his sympathetic remembrance of me. From various parts of the world, wherever his triumphal progress led him, people, chiefly of the upper classes, came to Dresden for the purpose of hearing *Rienzi*. They had been so interested by Liszt's reports of my work, and by his playing of various selections from it, that they all came expecting something of unparalleled importance.

Besides these indications of Liszt's enthusiastic and friendly sympathy, other deeply touching testimonies appeared from different quarters. The startling beginning made by Werder, on the occasion of his midnight visit after the second performance of the *Fliegender Holländer* in Berlin, was shortly afterwards followed by a similarly unsolicited approach in the form of an effusive letter from an equally unknown personage, Alwine Frommann, who afterwards became my faithful friend. After my departure from Berlin she heard Schröder-Devrient twice in the *Fliegender Holländer,* and the letter in which she described the effect produced upon her by my work conveyed to me for the first time the vigorous and profound sentiments of a deep and confident recognition such as seldom falls to the lot of even the greatest master, and cannot fail to exercise a weighty influence on his mind and spirit, which long for self-confidence.

I have no very vivid recollections of my own doings during

this first year of my position as conductor in a sphere of action which gradually grew more and more familiar. For the anniversary of my appointment, and to some extent as a personal recognition, I was commissioned to procure Gluck's *Armida.* This we performed in March, 1843, with the co-operation of Schröder-Devrient, just before her temporary departure from Dresden. Great importance was attached to this production, because, at the same moment, Meyerbeer was inaugurating his general-directorship in Berlin by a performance of the same work. Indeed, it was in Berlin that the extraordinary respect entertained for such a commemoration of Gluck had its origin. I was told that Meyerbeer went to Rellstab with the score of *Armida* in order to obtain hints as to its correct interpretation.

As not long afterwards I also heard a strange story of two silver candlesticks, wherewith the famous composer was said to have enlightened the no less famous critic when showing him the score of his *Feldlager in Schlesien,* I decided to attach no great importance to the instructions he might have received, but rather to help myself by a careful handling of this difficult score, and by introducing some softness into it through modulating the variations in tone as much as possible. I had the gratification later of receiving an exceedingly warm appreciation of my rendering from Herr Eduard Devrient, a great Gluck connoisseur. After hearing this opera as presented by us, and comparing it with the Berlin performance, he heartily praised the tenderly modulated character of our rendering of certain parts, which, he said, had been given in Berlin with the coarsest bluntness. He mentioned, as a striking instance of this, a brief chorus in C major of male and female nymphs in the third act. By the introduction of a more moderate *tempo* and very soft *piano* I had tried to free this from the original coarseness with which Devrient had heard it rendered in Berlin — presumably with traditional fidelity. My most innocent device, and one which I frequently adopted, for disguising the irritating stiffness or the orchestral movement in the original, was a careful modification of the *Basso-continuo,* which was taken uninterruptedly in common time. This I felt obliged to remedy, partly by *legato* playing, and partly by *pizzicato.*

Our management were lavish in their expenditure on externals, especially decoration, and as a spectacular opera the piece drew fairly large houses, thus earning me the reputation of being a very suitable conductor for Gluck, and one who was in close sympathy with him. This result was the more conspicuous from the fact that *Iphigenia in Tauris* which is a far superior work, and in which Devrient's interpretation of the title-rôle was admirable had been performed to empty houses.

I had to live upon this reputation for a long time, as it often happened that I was compelled to give inferior performances of repertoire pieces, including Mozart's operas. The mediocrity of these was particularly disappointing to those who, after my success in *Armida*, had expected a great deal from my rendering of these pieces, and were much disappointed in consequence. Even sympathetic hearers sought to explain their disappointment on the ground that I did not appreciate Mozart and could not understand him. But they failed to realise how impossible it was for me, as a mere conductor, to exercise any real influence on such desultory performances, which were merely given as stopgaps, and often without rehearsal. Indeed, in this matter I often found myself in a false position, which, as I was powerless to remedy it, contributed not a little to render unbearable both my new office and my dependence upon the meanest motives of a paltry theatrical routine, already overweighted with the cares of business. This, in fact, became worse than I had expected, in spite of my previous knowledge of the precariousness of such a life. My colleague Reissiger, to whom from time to time I poured out my woes regarding the scant attention given by the general management to our demands for the maintenance of correct representations in the realm of opera, comforted me by saying that I, like himself, would sooner or later relinquish all these fads and submit to the inevitable fate of a conductor. Thereupon he proudly smote his stomach, and hoped that I might soon be able to boast of one as round as his own.

I received further provocation for my growing dislike of these jog-trot methods from a closer acquaintance with the spirit in which even eminent conductors undertook the reproduction of our masterpieces. During this first year Mendelssohn was invited to conduct his *St. Paul* for one of the Palm Sunday concerts in the Dresden chapel, which was famous at that time. The knowledge I thus acquired of this work, under such favourable circumstances, pleased me so much, that I made a fresh attempt to approach the composer with sincere and friendly motives; but a remarkable conversation which I had with him on the evening of this performance quickly and strangely repelled my impulse. After the oratorio Reissiger was to produce Beethoven's Eighth Symphony. I had noticed in the preceding rehearsal that Reissiger had fallen into the error of all the ordinary conductors of this work by taking the *tempo di minuetto* of the third movement at a meaningless waltz time, whereby not only does the whole piece lose its imposing character, but the trio is rendered absolutely ridiculous by the impossibility of the violoncello part being interpreted at such a speed. I had called Reissiger's attention to this defect, and he acquiesced in my opinion, promising to take the part in question at true *minuetto tempo*. I related this to Mendelssohn, when he was resting after his own performance in the box beside me, listening to the symphony. He, too, acknowledged that I was right, and thought that it ought to be played as I said. And now the third movement began. Reissiger, who, it is true, did not possess the needful power suddenly to impress so momentous a change of time upon his orchestra with success, followed the usual custom and took the *tempo di minuetto* in the same old waltz time. Just as I was about to express my anger, Mendelssohn gave me a friendly nod, as though he thought that this was what I wanted, and that I had understood the music in this way. I was so amazed by this complete absence of feeling on the part of the famous musician, that I was struck dumb, and thenceforth my own particular opinion of Mendelssohn gradually matured, an opinion which was afterwards confirmed by R. Schumann. The latter, in expressing the sincere pleasure he had felt on listening to the time at which I had taken the first movement of Beethoven's Ninth Symphony, told me that he had been compelled to hear it year after year taken by Mendelssohn at a perfectly distracting speed.

Amid my yearning anxiety to exert some influence upon the

spirit in which our noblest masterpieces were executed, I had
to struggle against the profound dissatisfaction I felt with my
employment on the ordinary theatre repertoire. It was not
until Palm Sunday of the year 1844, just after my dispiriting
expedition to Hamburg, that my desire to conduct the Pastoral
Symphony was satisfied. But many faults still remained un-
remedied, and for the removal of these I had to adopt indirect
methods which gave me much trouble. For instance, at these
famous concerts the arrangement of the orchestra, the members of which were seated in a long, thin, semicircular row
round the chorus of singers, was so inconceivably stupid that
it required the explanation given by Reissiger to make me
understand such folly. He told me that all these arrangements dated from the time of the late conductor Morlacchi,
who, as an Italian composer of operas, had no true realisation of the importance of the orchestra nor of its necessities.
When, therefore, I asked why they had permitted him to
meddle with things he did not understand, I learned that the
preference shown to this Italian, both by the court and the
general management, even in opposition to Carl Maria von
Weber, had always been absolute and brooked no contradiction. I was warned that, even now, we should experience
great difficulty in ridding ourselves of these inherited vices,
because the opinion still prevailed in the highest circles that
he must have understood best what he was about.

Once more my childish memories of the eunuch Sassaroli
flashed through my mind, and I remembered the warning of
Weber's widow as to the significance of my succession to her
husband's post of conductor in Dresden. But, in spite of all
this, our performance of the Pastoral Symphony succeeded
beyond expectation, and the incomparable and wonderfully
stimulating enjoyment, which I was in future to derive from
my intercourse with Beethoven's works, now first enabled me
to realise his prolific strength. Röckel shared in this enjoyment with heartfelt sympathy; he supported me with eye
and ear at every rehearsal, always stood by my side, and was
at one with me both in his appreciation and his aims.

After this encouraging success I was to receive the gratification of another triumph in the summer, which, although it

was of no particular moment from the musical point of view, was of great social importance. The King of Saxony, towards whom, as I have already said, I had felt warmly drawn when he was Prince Friedrich, was expected home from a long visit to England. The reports received of his stay there had greatly rejoiced my patriotic soul. While this homely monarch, who shrank from all pomp and noisy demonstration, was in England, it happened that the Tsar Nicholas arrived quite unexpectedly on a visit to the Queen. In his honour great festivities and military reviews were held, in which our King, much against his will, was obliged to participate, and he was consequently compelled to receive the enthusiastic acclamations of the English crowd, who were most demonstrative in showing their preference for him, as compared with the unpopular Tsar. This preference was also reflected in the newspapers, so that a flattering incense floated over from England to our little Saxony which filled us all with a peculiar pride in our King. While I was in this mood, which absorbed me completely, I learned that preparations were being made in Leipzig for a special welcome to the King on his return, which was to be further dignified by a musical festival in the directing of which Mendelssohn was to take part. I made inquiries as to what was going to be done in Dresden, and learned that the King did not propose to call there at all, but was going direct to his summer residence at Pillnitz.

A moment's reflection showed me that this would only further my desire of preparing a pleasant and hearty reception for his Majesty. As I was a servant of the Crown, any attempt on my part to render an act of homage in Dresden might have had the appearance of an official parade which would not be admissible. I seized the idea, therefore, of hurriedly collecting together all who could either play or sing, so that we might perform a Reception song hastily composed in honour of the event. The obstacle to my plan was that my Director Lüttichau was away at one of his country seats. To come to an understanding with my colleague Reissiger would, moreover, have involved delay, and given the enterprise the very aspect of an official ovation which I wished to avoid. As no time was to be lost, if anything worthy of the occasion was to be done —

as the King was due to arrive in a few days — I availed myself
of my position as conductor of the Glee Club, and summoned all
its singers and instrumentalists to my aid. In addition to these,
I invited the members of our theatrical company, and also
those of the orchestra, to join us. This done, I drove quickly
to Pillnitz to arrange matters with the Lord Chamberlain,
whom I found favourably disposed towards my project. The
only leisure I could snatch for composing the verses of my song
and setting them to music was during the rapid drive there
and back, for by the time I reached home I had to have every
thing ready for the copyist and lithographer. The agreeable
sensation of rushing through the warm summer air and lovely
country, coupled with the sincere affection with which I was
inspired for our German Prince, and which had prompted my
effort, elated me and worked me up to a high pitch of tension,
in which I now formed a clear conception of the lyrical outlines
of the ' Tannhäuser March,' which first saw the light of day
on the occasion of this royal welcome. I soon afterwards developed this theme, and thus produced the march which became
the most popular of the melodies I had hitherto composed.

On the next day it had to be tried over with a hundred and
twenty instrumentalists and three hundred singers. I had
taken the liberty of inviting them to meet me on the stage of
the Court Theatre, where everything went off capitally. Every
one was delighted, and I not the least so, when a messenger
arrived from the director, who had just returned to town,
requesting an immediate interview. Lüttichau was enraged
beyond measure at my high-handed proceedings in this matter,
of which he had been informed by our good friend Reissiger.
If his baronial coronet had been on his head during this interview, it would assuredly have tumbled off. The fact that I
should have conducted my negotiations in person with the
court officials, and could report that my endeavours had met
with extraordinarily prompt success, aroused his deepest fury,
for the chief importance of his own position consisted in always
representing everything which had to be obtained by these
means as surrounded by the greatest obstacles, and hedged
in by the strictest etiquette. I offered to cancel everything,
but that only embarrassed him the more. I thereupon asked

him what he wanted me to do, if the plan was still to be carried out. On this point he seemed uncertain, but thought I had shown a great lack of fellow-feeling in having not only ignored him, but Reissiger as well. I answered that I was perfectly ready to hand over my composition and the conducting of the piece to Reissiger. But he could not swallow this, as he really had an exceedingly poor opinion of Reissiger, of which I was very well aware. His real grievance was that I had arranged the whole business with the Lord Chamberlain, Herr von Reizenstein, who was his personal enemy, and he added that I could form no conception of the rudeness he had been obliged to endure from the hands of this official. This outburst of confidence made it easier for me to exhibit an almost sincere emotion, to which he responded by a shrug of the shoulders, meaning that he must resign himself to a disagreeable necessity.

But my project was even more seriously threatened by the wretched weather than by this storm with the director; for it rained all day in torrents. If it lasted, which it seemed only too likely to do, I could hardly start on the special boat at five o'clock in the morning, as proposed, with my hundreds of helpers, to give an early morning concert at Pillnitz, two hours away. I anticipated such a disaster with genuine dismay. But Röckel consoled me by saying that I could rely upon it that we should have glorious weather the next day; for I was lucky! This belief in my luck has followed me ever since, even down to my latest days; and amid the great misfortunes which have so often hampered my enterprises, I have felt as if this statement were a wicked insult to fate. But this time, at least, my friend was right; the 12th of August, 1844 was from sunrise till late at night the most perfect summer day that I can remember in my whole life. The sensation of blissful content with which I saw my light-hearted legion of gaily dressed bandsmen and singers gathering through the auspicious morning mists on board our steamer, swelled my breast with a fervent faith in my lucky star.

By my friendly impetuosity I had succeeded in overcoming Reissiger's smouldering resentment, and had persuaded him to share the honour of our undertaking by conducting the performance of my composition himself. When we arrived at the spot, everything went off splendidly. The King and royal family were visibly touched, and in the evil times that followed the Queen of Saxony spoke of this occasion, I am told, with peculiar emotion, as the fairest day of her life. After Reissiger had wielded his baton with great dignity, and I had sung with the tenors in the choir, we two conductors were summoned to the presence of the royal family. The King warmly expressed his thanks, while the Queen paid us the high compliment of saying that I composed very well and that Reissiger conducted very well. His Majesty asked us to repeat the last three stanzas only, as, owing to a painful ulcerated tooth, he could not remain much longer out of doors. I rapidly devised a combined evolution, the remarkably successful execution of which I am very proud, even to this day. I had the entire song repeated, but, in accordance with the King's wish, only one verse was sung in our original crescent formation. At the beginning of the second verse I made my four hundred un-disciplined bandsmen and singers file off in a march through the garden, which, as they gradually receded, was so arranged that the final notes could only reach the royal ear as an echoing dream-song. Thanks to my unexampled activity and ever-present help, this retreat was so steadily carried out that not the slightest faltering was perceptible either in time or delivery, and the whole might have been taken for a carefully rehearsed theatrical manœuvre. On reaching the castle court we found that, by the Queen's kindly forethought, an ample breakfast had been provided for our party on the lawn, where the tables were already spread. We often saw our royal hostess herself busily supervising the attendants, or moving with excited de-light about the windows and corridors of the castle. Every eye beamed rapture to my soul, as the successful author of the general happiness, and I almost felt amid the glories of that day as though the millennium had been proclaimed. After roaming in a body through the lovely grounds of the castle, and not omitting to pay a visit to the Keppgrund which had been so dear to me in my youth, we returned late at night, and in the highest spirits, to Dresden.

Next morning I was again summoned to the presence of the director. But a change had come over him during the night.

As I began to offer my apologies for the anxiety I had caused
him, the tall thin man, with the hard dry face, seized me by
the hand and addressed me with a rapturous expression, which
I am sure no one else ever saw on his face. He told me to say
no more about these anxieties. I was a great man, and soon
no one would know anything about him, whereas I should
be universally admired and loved. I was deeply moved, and
wished only to express my embarrassment at so unexpected an
outburst, when he kindly interrupted me and sought an escape
from his own emotion in good-humoured confidences. He referred, with a smile, to the self-denial which had yielded the
place of honour on so extraordinary an occasion to an undeserving man like Reissiger. When I assured him that this act
had afforded me the liveliest satisfaction, and that I had myself persuaded my colleague to take the baton, he confessed
that at last he began to understand me, but failed altogether
to comprehend how the other could accept a position to which
he had no right.

Lüttichau's altered attitude towards me was such that for
some time our intercourse on matters of business assumed an
almost confidential tone. But, unfortunately, in course of time
things changed for the worse, so that our relationship became one of open enmity; nevertheless, a certain peculiar
tenderness towards me on the part of this singular man was
always clearly perceptible. Indeed, I might almost say that
much of his subsequent abuse of me sounded more like the
strangely perverted plaints of a love that met with no response.

For my holiday this year I went, early in September, to
Fischer's vineyard, near Loschwitz, not far from the famous
Findlater vineyard, where, somewhat late in the year, I rented
a summer residence. Here, under the kindly and strengthening stimulus of six week of open-air life, I composed my music
for the second act of *Tannhäuser*, which I completed by the
15th of October. During this period a performance of *Rienzi*
was given before an audience of no ordinary importance. For
this event I went up to town. Spontini, Meyerbeer, and
General Lwoff, the composer of the Russian National Anthem,
were seated together in a stage box. I sought no opportunity
of learning the impression made by my opera upon these learned

judges and magnates of the musical world. It was enough for me to have the complacent satisfaction of knowing that they had heard my oft-repeated work performed before a crowded house and amid overwhelming applause. I was delighted at the close of the opera to have my little dog Peps, which had run after me all the way from the country, brought to me; and without waiting to greet the European celebrities, I drove off with it at once to our quiet vineyard, where Minna was greatly relieved to recover her little pet, which for hours she had believed to be lost.

Here I also received a visit from Werder, the man whose friendship I had made in Berlin under such dramatic circumstances. But this time he appeared in ordinary human guise, beneath the kindly light of heaven, by which we disputed in a friendly way concerning the true worth of the *Fliegender Holländer,* my mind having somewhat turned against this work since *Tannhäuser* had got into my head. It certainly seemed odd to find myself contradicted on this point by my friend, and to receive instruction from him on the significance of my own work.

When we returned to our winter quarters I tried to avoid allowing so lengthy an interval to elapse between the composition of the second and third acts as had separated that of the first and second. In spite of many absorbing engagements I succeeded in my aim. By carefully cultivating a habit of taking solitary walks, and thanks to their soothing influence over me, I managed to finish the music of Act iii. by the 29th of December, that is to say, before the end of the year.

During this period my time was otherwise very seriously occupied by a visit paid us by Spontini with reference to a proposed presentation of his *Vestalin,* the preparation for which had just begun. The singular episodes and characteristic features of the intercourse which I thus gained with this eminent and hoary-headed master are still so vividly imprinted on my memory that they seem worthy of a place in this record.

Since, with the co-operation of Schröder-Devrient, we could, on the whole, rely upon an admirable presentation of the opera, I had inspired Lüttichau with the idea of inviting Spontini to undertake the personal superintendence of his justly famous work. He had just left Berlin for ever, after enduring great humiliation there, and such an invitation at this moment would be a well-timed proof of respect. This was accordingly sent, and as I had myself been entrusted with the conductorship of the opera, I was given the singular task of deciding this point with the master. My letter, it appears, although written in French, inspired him with a high opinion of my zeal for the enterprise, and in a gracious reply he informed me what his special wishes were regarding the arrangements to be made for his collaboration. As far as the vocalists were concerned, and seeing that a Schröder-Devrient was among the number, he frankly expressed his satisfaction. As for chorus and ballet, he took it for granted that nothing would be lacking to the dignity of the performance; and finally, as regarded the orchestra, he expected that this also would be sure to please him, as he presumed it contained the necessary complement of excellent instruments which, to use his own words, ' he hoped would furnish the performance with twelve good contrabassi' (*le tout garni de douze bonnes contre-basses*). This phrase bowled me over, for the proportion thus bluntly stated in figures gave me so logical a conception of his exalted expectations, that I hurried away at once to the director to warn him that the enterprise on which we had embarked would not, after all, prove as easy as we thought. His alarm was great, and he said that some plan must at once be devised for breaking off the engagement.

When Schröder-Devrient heard of our dilemma, knowing Spontini well, she laughed as though she would never stop at the ingenuous impudence with which we had issued our invitation. A trifling indisposition from which she then suffered provided a reasonable excuse for a delay, more or less prolonged, and this she generously placed at our disposal. Spontini had, in fact, urged us to use all possible despatch in the execution of our project, for, as he was impatiently awaited in Paris, he could spare us but little time. It fell to my lot to weave the tissue of innocent deceptions by which we hoped to divert the master from a definite acceptance of our invitation. Now we could breathe again, and duly began rehearsing. But

on the very day before we proposed to hold our full-dress
rehearsal at our leisure, lo and behold! about noon a carriage
drove up to my door, in which, clad in a long blue coat of pilot-
cloth, sat no other than the haughty master himself, whose manners resembled those of a Spanish grandee. All unattended and
greatly excited, he entered my room, showed me my letters,
and proved from our correspondence that the invitation had
not been declined, but that he had in all points accurately
complied with our wishes. Forgetting for the moment all the
possible embarrassments which might arise, in my genuine delight at beholding the wonderful man before me, and hearing
his work conducted by himself, I at once undertook to do everything I possibly could to meet his desires. This declaration I
made with the utmost sincerity of zeal. He smiled with almost
childlike kindliness on hearing me, and I at once begged him
to conduct the rehearsal arranged for the morrow. He thereupon
grew suddenly thoughtful, and began to weigh the numerous
disadvantages of such an action on his part. So acute did his
agitation become that he had the greatest difficulty in expressing
himself clearly on any point, and I found it no easy matter
to inquire what arrangements on our part would persuade him
to undertake the morrow's rehearsal. After a moment's reflection he asked what sort of baton I was accustomed to
use when conducting. With my hands I indicated the approxi-
mate length and thickness of a medium-sized wooden rod, such
as our choir-attendant was in the habit of supplying, freshly
covered with white paper. He sighed, and asked if I thought
it possible to procure him by to-morrow a baton of black ebony,
whose very respectable length and thickness he indicated by a
gesture, and on each end of which a fairly large knob of ivory
was to be affixed. I promised to have one prepared for the next
rehearsal, which should at least be similar in appearance to
what he desired, and another of the specified materials in time
for the actual performance. Visibly relieved, he then passed
his hand over his brow, and granted me permission to announce
his consent to conduct on the following day. After once more
strongly enforcing his instructions as to the baton, he went back
to his hotel.

I seemed to be moving in a dream, and hastened in a whirlwind of excitement to publish the news of what had happened and was to be expected. We were fairly trapped. Schröder-Devrient offered to become our scapegoat, while I entered into precise details with the theatre carpenter concerning the baton. This turned out so far correct that it possessed the requisite length and breadth, was black in its colour, and had two large white knobs. Then came the fateful rehearsal. Spontini was evidently ill at ease on his seat in the orchestra. First of all he wished to have the oboists placed behind him. As this partial change of position just at that moment would have caused much confusion in the disposition of the orchestra, I promised to effect the alteration after the rehearsal. He said no more, and took up his baton. In a moment I understood why he attached such importance to its form and size. He held it, not as other conductors do, by the end, but gripped it about the middle with his clenched fist, waving it so as to make it evident that he wielded his baton like a field-marshal's staff, not for beating time, but for command.

Confusion arose in the very first scene, which was increased by the fact that the master's instructions, both to orchestra and singers, were rendered almost unintelligible by his confused use of the German language. This much at least we were soon able to grasp, that he was particularly anxious to dis-abuse us of the idea that this was a full-dress rehearsal, and to show us that he was set upon a thorough re-study of the opera from the very beginning. Great, indeed, was the despair of my good old chorus-master and stage manager, Fischer — who before had enthusiastically advocated the invitation of Spontini — when he recognised that the dislocation of our repertoire was now inevitable. This feeling swelled by degrees to open anger, in the blindness of which every fresh suggestion of Spontini's appeared but frivolous fault-finding, to which he bluntly responded in the coarsest German. After one of the choruses Spontini beckoned me to his side and whispered: ' Mais savez-vous, vos chœurs ne chantent pas mal'; whereupon Fischer, regarding this with suspicion, shouted out to me in a rage: ' What does the old hog want now?' and I had some trouble to pacify the speedily converted enthusiast.

But our most serious delay arose, during the first act,

through the evolutions of a triumphal march. With the most
vociferous emphasis the master expressed intense dissatisfaction with the apathetic demeanour of our populace during the
procession of vestal virgins. He was quite unaware of the fact
that, in obedience to our stage manager's instructions, they
had fallen on their knees upon the appearance of the priest-
esses; for he was so excited, and withal so terribly short-
sighted, that nothing which appealed to the eye alone was perceptible to his senses. What he demanded was that the Roman
army should manifest its devout respect in more drastic
fashion by flinging themselves as one man to the ground, and
marking this by delivering a crashing blow of their spears on
their shields. Endless attempts were made, but some one always clattered either too soon or too late. Then he repeated
the action himself several times with his baton on the desk, but
all to no purpose; the crash was not sufficiently sharp and
emphatic. This reminded me of the impression made upon
me some years before in Berlin by the wonderful precision and
almost alarming effect with which I had seen similar evolutions
carried out in the play of *Ferdinand Cortez*, and I realized that
it would require an immediate and tedious accentuation of our
customary softness of action in such manœuvres before we
could meet the fastidious master's requirements. At the end
of the first act Spontini went on the stage himself, in order to
give a detailed explanation of his reasons for wishing to defer
his opera for a considerable time, so as to prepare by multi-
tudinous rehearsals for its production in accordance with his
taste. He expected to find the actors of the Dresden Court
Theatre gathered there to hear him; but the company had
already dispersed. Singers and stage manager had hastily
scattered in every direction to give vent, each in his own
fashion, to the misery of the situation. None but the workmen, lamp-cleaners, and a few of the chorus gathered in a
semicircle around Spontini, in order to have a look at that
remarkable man, as he held forth with wonderful effect on the
requirements of true theatrical art. Turning towards the dismal scene, I gently and respectfully pointed out to Spontini
the uselessness of his declamation, and promised that everything should eventually be done precisely as he desired.

Finally, I succeeded in extricating him from the undignified position in which, to my horror, he had been placed, by telling him that Herr Eduard Devrient, who had seen the *Vestalin* in Berlin, and carried every detail of the performance in his mind, should personally drill our chorus and supers into a becoming solemnity during the reception of the vestals. This pacified him, and we proceeded to settle on a plan for a series of rehearsals according to his wishes. But, in spite of all this, I was the only person to whom this strange turn of affairs was not unwelcome; for through the burlesque extravagances of Spontini, and notwithstanding his extraordinary eccentricities, which, however, I learned in time to understand, I could perceive the miraculous energy with which he pursued and attained an ideal of theatrical art such as in our days had become almost unknown.

We began, therefore, with a pianoforte rehearsal, at which the master made a point of telling the singers what he wanted. He did not tell us anything new, however, for he said little about the details of the rendering; on the other hand, he expatiated upon the general interpretation, and I noticed that in doing this, he had accustomed himself to make the most decided allowances for the great singers, especially Schröder-Devrient and Tichatschek. The only thing he did was to forbid the latter to use the word *Braut* (bride) with which Licinius had to address Julia in the German translation; this word sounded horrible in his ears, and he could not understand how anybody could set such a vulgar sound as that to music. He gave a long lecture, however, to the somewhat coarse and less talented singer who took the part of the high-priest, and explained to him how to understand and interpret this character from the dialogue (in recitative) between him and Haruspex. He told him that he must understand that the whole thing was based upon priestcraft and superstition. Pontifex must make it clear that he does not fear his antagonist at the head of the Roman army, because, should the worst come to the worst, he has his machines ready, which, if necessary, will miraculously rekindle the dead fire of Vesta. In this way, even though Julia should escape the sacrifice, the power of the priesthood would still be unassailable.

During one of the rehearsals I asked Spontini why he, who, as a rule, made such very effective use of the trombone, should have left it entirely out in the magnificent triumphal march of the first act. Very much astonished he asked: ' *Est-ce que je n'ai pas de trombones?* ' I showed him the printed score, and he then asked me to add the trombones to the march, so that, if possible, they might be used at the next rehearsal. He also said: ' *J'ai entendu dans votre* Rienzi *un instrument, que vous appelez Basse-tuba; je ne veux pas bannir cet instrument de l'orchestre: faites m'en une partie pour la* Vestale.' It gave me great pleasure to perform this task for him with all the care and good judgment I could dispose of. When at the rehearsal he heard the effect for the first time, he threw me a really grateful glance, and so much appreciated the really simple additions I had made to his score, that a little later on he wrote me a very friendly letter from Paris in which he asked me kindly to send him the extra instrumental parts I had prepared for him. His pride would not allow him, however, to ask outright for something for which I alone had been responsible, so he wrote: ' *Envoyez-moi une partition des trombones pour la marche triomphale et de la Basse-tuba telle qu'elle a été exécutée sous ma direction à Dresde.*' Apart from this, I also showed how greatly I respected him, in the eagerness with which, at his special request, I regrouped all the instruments in the orchestra. He was forced to this request more by habit than by principle, and how very important it seemed to him not to make the slightest change in his customary arrangements, was proved to me when he explained his method of conducting. He conducted the orchestra, so he said, only with his eyes: ' My left eye is the first violin, my right eye the second, and if the eye is to have power, one must not wear glasses (as so many bad conductors do), even if one is short-sighted. I,' he admitted confidentially, ' cannot see twelve inches in front of me, but all the same I can make them play as I want, merely by fixing them with my eye.' In some respects the arbitrary way in which he used to arrange his orchestra was really very irrational. From his old days in Paris he had retained the habit of placing the two oboists immediately behind him, and although this was a fad which owed its origin to a mere accident.

it was one to which he always adhered. The consequence was
that these players had to avert the mouthpiece of their instruments from the audience, and our excellent oboist was so angry
about this arrangement, that it was only by dint of great diplo-
macy that I succeeded in pacifying him.

Apart from this, Spontini's method was based upon the absolutely correct system (which even at the present time is misunderstood by some German orchestras) of spreading the string
quartette over the whole orchestra. This system further consisted in preventing the brass and percussion instruments from
culminating in one point (and drowning each other) by dividing them on both sides, and by placing the more delicate wind
instruments at a judicious distance from each other, thus forming a chain between the violins. Even some great and celebrated orchestras of the present day still retain the custom of
dividing the mass of instruments into two halves, the string
and the wind instruments, an arrangement that denotes rough-
ness and a lack of understanding of the sound of the
orchestra, which ought to blend harmoniously and be well
balanced.

I was very glad to have the chance of introducing this excellent improvement in Dresden, for now that Spontini himself
had initiated it, it was an easy matter to get the King's command
to let the alteration stand. Nothing remained after Spontini's
departure but to modify and correct certain eccentricities and
arbitrary features in his arrangements; and from that moment
I attained a high level of success with my orchestra.

With all the peculiarities he showed at rehearsals, this exceptional man fascinated both musicians and singers to such an
extent that the production attracted quite an unusual amount
of attention. Very characteristic was the energy with which
he insisted on exceptionally sharp rhythmic accents; through
his association with the Berlin orchestra he had acquired the
habit of marking the note that he wished to be brought out
with the word *diese* (this), which at first was quite incomprehensible to me. The great singer Tichatschek, who had a positive genius for rhythm, was highly pleased by this; for he
also had acquired the habit of compelling the chorus to great
precision in very important entries, and maintained that if one

only accentuated the first note properly, the rest followed as a
matter of course. On the whole, therefore, a spirit of devotion
to the master gradually pervaded the orchestra; the violas
alone bore him a grudge for a while, and for this reason. In
the accompaniment of the lugubrious cantilena of Julia at the
end of the second act, he would not put up with the way in
which the violas played the horribly sentimental accompaniment. Suddenly turning towards them he called in a sepulchral
tone, 'Are the violas dying?' The two pale and incurably
melancholy old men who held on tenaciously to their posts in
the orchestra, notwithstanding their right to a pension, stared
at Spontini with real fright, reading a threat in his words, and
I had to explain Spontini's wish in sober language in order to
call them back to life.

On the stage Herr Eduard Devrient helped very materially
in bringing about wonderfully distinct *ensembles;* he also knew
how to gratify a certain wish of Spontini's, which threw us
all into tremendous confusion. In accordance with the cuts
adopted by all the German theatres, we too ended the opera
with the fiery duet, supported by the chorus, between Licinius
and Julia after their rescue. The master, however, insisted on
adding a lively chorus and ballet to the finale, according to the
antiquated method of ending common to French *opera seria.*
He was absolutely against finishing his work with a dismal
churchyard episode; consequently the whole scene had to be
altered. Venus was to shine resplendent in a rose bower, and
the long-suffering lovers were to be wedded at her altar, amid
lively dancing and singing, by rose-bedecked priests and priest-
esses. We performed it like this, but unluckily not with the
success we had all hoped for.

In the course of the production, which was proceeding with
wonderful accuracy and verve, we came across a difficulty with
regard to the principal part for which none of us had been
prepared. Our great Schröder-Devrient was obviously no longer
of an age to give the desired effect as the youngest of the vestal
virgins; she had acquired matronly contours, and her age
was moreover accentuated by the extremely girlish-looking high-
priestess with whom she had to act, and whose youth it
was difficult to dissimulate. This was my niece, Johanna

Wagner, who, because of her marvellous voice and great talent as an actress, made every one in the audience long to see the parts of the two women reversed. Schröder-Devrient, who was well aware of this fact, tried by every effective means in her power to overcome her most difficult position; this effort, however, resulted not infrequently in great exaggeration and straining of the voice, and in one very important place her part was sadly overacted. When, after the great trio in the second act, she had to gasp the words, ' *er ist frei* ' (' he is free '), and to move away from her rescued lover towards the front of the stage, she made the mistake of speaking the words instead of singing them.

She had often proved the effect of a decisive word uttered with an exaggerated and yet careful imitation of the ordinary accents of the spoken language, by exciting the audience's wildest enthusiasm when she almost whispered the words, ' *Noch einen Schritt und du bist todt!* ' (' Just one more step and thou art dead! ') in *Fidelio*. This terrific effect, which I too had felt, was produced by the shock — like unto the blow of an executioner's axe — which I received on suddenly coming down from the ideal sphere to which music itself can exalt the most awful situations, to the naked surface of dreadful reality. This sensation was due simply to the knowledge of the utmost height of the sublime, and the memory of the impression I received led me to call that particular moment the moment of lightning; for it was as if two different worlds that meet, and yet are divided, were suddenly illumined and revealed as by a flash. Thoroughly to understand such a moment, and not to treat it wrongly, was the whole secret, and this I fully realised on that day from the absolute failure on the great singer's part to produce the right effect. The toneless, hoarse way in which she uttered the words was like throwing cold water over the audience and myself, and not one of those present could see any more in the incident than a botched theatrical effect. It is possible that the public had expected too much, for they were curious to see Spontini conduct, and the prices had been raised accordingly; it may also have been that the whole style of the work, with its antiquated French plot, seemed rather obsolete in spite of the majestic beauty of the music; or, perhaps, the very tame end left the same cold impression as Devrient's dramatic failure. In any case there was no real enthusiasm, and the only sign of approval was a rather lukewarm call for the celebrated master, who, covered with numerous decorations, made a sad impression on me as he bowed his thanks to the audience for their very moderate applause.

Nobody was less blind to the somewhat disappointing result than Spontini himself. He decided, however, to defy fate, and to this end had recourse to means which he had often employed in Berlin, in order to get packed houses for his operatic productions. Thus, he always gave Sunday performances, for experience had taught him that he could always have a full house on that day. As the next Sunday on which his *Vestalin* was to be produced was still some time ahead, his prolonged stay gave us several more chances of enjoying his interesting company. I have such a vivid recollection of the hours spent with him either at Madame Devrient's or at my house, that I shall be pleased to quote a few reminiscences.

I shall never forget a dinner at Schröder-Devrient's house at which we had a charming conversation with Spontini and his wife (a sister of the celebrated pianoforte maker, Erard). Spontini generally listened deferentially to what the others had to say, his attitude being that of a man who expected to be asked for his opinion. When he did speak in the end it was with a sort of rhetorical solemnity, in sharp and precise sentences, categorical and well accentuated, which forbade contradiction from the outset. Herr Ferdinand Hiller was among the invited guests, and he began to speak about Liszt. After some time Spontini gave his opinion in his characteristic fashion, but in a spirit which showed only too clearly, that from the heights of his Berlin throne he had not judged the affairs of the world either with impartiality or goodwill. While he was laying down the law in this style he could not brook any interruption. When, therefore, during the dessert, the general conversation became livelier, and Madame Devrient happened to laugh with her neighbour at the table in the middle of a long harangue of Spontini's, he shot an extremely angry glance at his wife. Madame Devrient apologised for her at once by saying that it was she (Madame Devrient) who had been laughing about some lines on a *bonbonnière,* whereupon Spontini retorted: '*Pourtant je suis sûr que c'est ma femme qui a suscité ce rire; je ne veux pas que l'on rie devant moi, je ne rie jamais moi, j'aime le sérieux.*' In spite of that he sometimes succeeded in being jovial. For instance, it amused him to set us all wondering at the way in which he crunched enormous lumps of sugar with his marvellous teeth. After dinner, when we drew our chairs closer together, he usually became very excited.

As far as he was capable of affection he seemed really to like me; he declared openly that he loved me, and said that he would prove this best by trying to keep me from the misfortune of proceeding in my career as a dramatic composer. He said he knew it would be difficult to convince me of the value of this friendly service, but as he felt it his sacred duty to look after my happiness in this particular line, he was prepared to stay in Dresden for another half-year, during which period he suggested that we should produce his other operas, and especially *Agnes von Hohenstaufen,* under his direction. To explain his views about the fatal mistake of trying to succeed as a dramatic composer 'after Spontini,' he began by praising me in these terms: '*Quand j'ai entendu votre* Rienzi, *j'ai dit, c'est un homme de génie, mais déjà il a plus fait qu'il ne peut faire.*' In order to show me what he meant by this paradox, he proceeded as follows: '*Après* Gluck *c'est moi qui ai fait la grande révolution avec la* Vestale; *j'ai introduit le* Vorhalt *de la sexte*' (the suspension of the sixth) '*dans l'harmonie et la grosse caisse dans l'orchestre; avec* Cortez *j'ai fait un pas de plus en avant; puis j'ai fait trois pas avec* Olympie. Nurmahal, Alcidor *et tout ce que j'ai fait dans les premiers temps à Berlin, je vous les livre, c'étaient des œuvres occasionnelles; mais depuis j'ai fait cent pas en avant avec* Agnès de Hohenstaufen, *où j'ai imaginé un emploi de l'orchestre remplaçant parfaitement l'orgue.*'

Since then he had tried his hand at a new work, *Les Athéniennes;* the Crown Prince (now King of Prussia [1]) had urged him to finish this work, and to testify to the truth of his words, he took several letters which he had received from this monarch

[1] William the First.

out of his pocket-book, and handed them to us for inspection.
Not until he had insisted upon our reading them carefully
through did he continue by saying that, in spite of this flattering invitation, he had given up the idea of setting this excellent
subject to music, because he felt sure he could never surpass
his *Agnes von Hohenstaufen*, nor invent anything new. In
conclusion he said: '*Or, comment voulez-vous que quiconque
puisse inventer quelque chose de nouveau, moi Spontini déclarant
ne pouvoir en aucune façon surpasser mes œuvres précédentes,
d'autre part etant avise que depuis la* Vestale *il n'a point été
écrit une note qui ne fut volée de mes partitions.*'
     To prove that this assertion was not merely talk, but that it
was based on scientific investigations, he quoted his wife, who
was supposed to have read with him an elaborate discussion on
the subject by a celebrated member of the French academy,
and he added that the essay in question had, for some mysterious
reason, never been printed. In this very important and scientific treatise it was proved that without Spontini's invention of the suspension of the sixth in his *Vestalin,* the whole of
modern melody would not have existed, and that any and
every form of melody that had been used since had been borrowed from his compositions. I was thunderstruck, but hoped
all the same to bring the inexorable master to a better frame
of mind, especially in regard to certain reservations he had
made. I acknowledged that the academician in question was
right in many ways, but I asked him if he did not believe that
if somebody brought him a dramatic poem full of an absolutely new and hitherto unknown spirit, it would not inspire
him to invent new musical combinations? With a ring of compassion in his voice, he replied that my question was wholly
mistaken; in what would the novelty consist? '*Dans la* Vestale *j'ai composé un sujet romain, dans* Ferdinand Cortez
un sujet espagnol-mexicain, dans Olympie *un sujet gréco-
macédonien, enfin dans* Agnès de Hohenstaufen *un sujet alle-
mand: tout le reste ne vaut rien!*' He hoped that I was not
thinking of the so-called romantic style *à la Freischütz?* With
such childish stuff no serious man could have anything to do;
for art was a serious thing, and *he* had exhausted serious art!
And, after all, what nation could produce the composer who

could surpass *him?* Surely not the Italians, whom he characterised simply as *cochons;* certainly not the French, who had only imitated the Italians; nor the Germans, who would never get beyond their childhood in music, and who, if they had ever possessed any talent, had had it all spoilt for them by the Jews? ' *Oh, croyez-moi, il y avait de l'espoir pour l'Allemagne lorsque j'étais empereur de la musique à Berlin; mais depuis que le roi de Prusse a livré sa musique au désordre occasionné par les deux juifs errants qu'il a attirés, tout espoir est perdu.*'

Our charming hostess now thought it time to change the subject, and to divert the master's thoughts. The theatre was situated quite near to her house; she invited him to go across with our friend Heine, who was amongst the guests, and to have a look at *Antigone,* which was then being given, and which was sure to interest him on account of the antique equipment of the stage, which had been carried out according to Semper's excellent plans. At first he wanted to refuse, on the plea that he had seen all this so much better when his *Olympia* had been performed. After a while he consented; but in a very short time he returned to his original opinion, and, smiling scornfully, assured us that he had seen and heard enough to strengthen him in his verdict. Heine told us that shortly after he and Spontini had taken their seats in the almost empty amphitheatre, and as soon as the Bacchus chorus had started, Spontini had said to him: ' *C'est de la Berliner Sing-Academie, allons-nous-en.*' Through an open door a streak of light had fallen on a lonely figure behind one of the columns; Heine had recognised Mendelssohn, and concluded that he had overheard Spontini's remark.

From the master's very excited conversations we soon realised very distinctly that he intended to stay longer in Dresden, so as to get all his operas performed. It was Schröder-Devrient's idea to save Spontini, in his own interest, from the mortifying disappointment of finding all his enthusiastic hopes in regard to a second performance of *Vestalin* unfounded, and, if possible, to prevent this second performance during his stay in Dresden. She pretended to be ill, and the director requested me to inform Spontini of the fact that his production would have to be indefinitely postponed. This visit was so distasteful to

me, that I was glad to make it in Röckel's company. He was
also a friend of Spontini's, and his French was moreover much
better than mine. As we were quite prepared for a bad reception, we were really frightened to enter. Imagine, therefore,
our astonishment when we found the master, who had already
been informed of the news in a letter from Devrient, in the
very brightest spirits.

He told us that he had to leave immediately for Paris, and
that from there he was to travel to Rome, the Holy Father
having commanded him to come in order to receive the title
of 'Count of San Andrea.' Then he showed us a second document, in which the King of Denmark was supposed to have
raised him to the Danish nobility. This meant, however, only
that the title of 'Ritter' of the 'Elephanten-Order' had been
conferred upon him; and although this was indeed a high
honour, in speaking about it he only mentioned the word
'Ritter' without referring to the particular order, because this
seemed to him too ordinary for a person of his dignity. He
was, however, childishly pleased over the affair, and felt that
he had been miraculously rescued from the narrow sphere of
his Dresden *Vestalin* production to find himself suddenly transported into regions of glory, from which he looked down upon
the distressing 'opera' world with sublime self-content.

Meanwhile Röckel and I silently thanked the Holy Father
and the King of Denmark from the bottom of our hearts. We
bade an affectionate farewell to the strange master, and to
cheer him I promised him seriously to think over his friendly
advice with regard to my career as a composer of opera.

Later on I heard what Spontini had said about me, on hearing that I had fled from Dresden for political reasons, and had
sought refuge in Switzerland. He thought that this was in
consequence of my share in a plot of high treason against the
King of Saxony, whom he looked upon as my benefactor, because I had been nominated conductor of the royal orchestra,
and he expressed his opinion about me by ejaculating in tones
of the deepest anguish: '*Quelle ingratitude!*'

From Berlioz, who was at Spontini's deathbed until the end,
I heard that the master had struggled most determinedly
against death, and had cried repeatedly, '*Je ne veux pas*

mourir, je ne veux pas mourir!' When Berlioz tried to comfort him by saying, *' Comment pouvez-vous penser mourir vous, mon maître, qui êtes immortel!'* Spontini retorted angrily, *' Ne faites pas de mauvaises plaisanteries!'* In spite of all the extraordinary experiences I had had with him, the news of his death, which I received in Zürich, touched me very deeply. Later on I expressed my feelings towards him, and my opinion of him as an artist, in a somewhat condensed form in the *Eidgenossischen Zeitung,* and in this article the quality I extolled more particularly in him was that, unlike Meyerbeer, who was then the rage, and the very aged Rossini, he believed absolutely in himself and his art. All the same, and somewhat to my disgust, I could not but see that this belief in himself had deteriorated into a veritable superstition.

I do not remember in those days having gone deeply into my feelings about Spontini's exceedingly strange individuality, nor do I recollect having troubled to discover how far they were consistent with the high opinion I formed of him after I had got to know him more intimately. Obviously I had only seen the caricature of the man, although the tendency towards such plainly overweening self-confidence may, at all events, have manifested itself earlier in life. At the same time, one could trace in all this the influence of the decay of the musical and dramatic life of the period, which Spontini, situated as he was in Berlin, was well able to witness. The surprising fact that he saw his chief merit in unessential details showed plainly that his judgment had become childish; in my opinion this did not detract from the great value of his works, however much he might exaggerate their value. In a sense I could justify his boundless self-confidence, which was principally the outcome of the comparison between himself and the great composers who were now replacing him; for in my heart of hearts I shared the contempt which he felt for these artists, although I did not dare to say so openly. And thus it came about that, in spite of his many somewhat absurd idiosyncrasies, I learned during this meeting at Dresden to feel a deep sympathy for this man, the like of whom I was never again to meet.

My next experiences of important musical celebrities of this age were of quite a different character. Amongst the more distinguished of these was Heinrich Marschner, who, as a very young man, had been nominated musical director of the Dresden orchestra by Weber. After Weber's death he seemed to have hoped that he would take his place entirely, and it was due less to the fact that his talent was still unknown, than to his repellent manner, that he was disappointed in his expectations. His wife, however, suddenly came into some money, and this windfall enabled him to devote all his energies to his work as composer of operas, without being obliged to fill any fixed post.

During the wild days of my youth Marschner lived in Leipzig, where his operas *Der Vampir* and *Templer und Jüdin* saw their first appearance. My sister Rosalie had once taken me to him in order to hear his opinion about me. He did not treat me uncivilly, but my visit led to nothing. I was also present at the first night of his opera *Des Falkner's Braut,* which however was not a success. Then he went to Hanover. His opera *Hans Heiling,* which was originally produced in Berlin, I heard for the first time in Würzburg; it showed vacillation in its tendency, and a decrease in constructive power. After that he produced several other operas, such as *Das Schloss am Aetna* and *Der Bäbu,* which never became popular. He was always neglected by the management at Dresden, as though they bore him some grudge, and only his *Templer* was played at all often. My colleague, Reissiger, had to conduct this opera, and as in his absence I always had to take his place, it also fell to my lot on one occasion to direct a performance of this work.

This was during the time that I worked at my *Tannhäuser.* I remember that, although I had often conducted this opera before in Magdeburg, on this occasion the wild nature of the instrumentation and its lack of mastership affected me to such an extent that it literally made me ill, and as soon as he returned, therefore, I implored Reissiger at any cost to resume the leadership. On the other hand, immediately after my nomination I had started on the production of *Hans Heiling,* but merely for the sake of the artistic honour. The insufficient distribution of the parts, however, a difficulty which in those days could not be overcome, made a complete success impossible. In any case, though, the whole spirit of the work seemed to be terribly old-fashioned.

I now heard that Marschner had finished another opera called *Adolph von Nassau*, and in a criticism of this work, of the genuineness of which I was unable to judge, particular stress was laid upon the 'patriotic and noble German atmosphere' of this new creation. I did my best to make the Dresden theatre take the initiative, and to urge Lüttichau to secure this opera before it was produced elsewhere. Marschner, who did not seem to have been treated with particular consideration by the Hanoverian opera authorities, accepted the invitation with great joy, sent his score, and declared himself willing to come to Dresden for the first performance. Lüttichau, however, was not anxious to see him take his place at the head of the orchestra; while I, also, was of the opinion that the too frequent appearance of outside conductors, even if it were for the purpose of conducting their own works, would not only lead to confusion, but might also fail to be as amusing and instructive as Spontini's visit had proved to be. It was therefore decided that I should conduct the new opera myself. And how I lived to regret it!

The score arrived: to a weak plot by Karl Golmick the composer of the *Templer* had written such superficial music, that the principal effect lay in a drinking song for a quartette, in which the German Rhine and German wine played the usual stereotyped part peculiar to such male quartettes. I lost all courage; but we had to go on with it now, and all I could do was to try, by maintaining a grave bearing, to make the singers take an interest in their task; this, however, was not easy. To Tichatschek and Mitterwurzer were assigned the two principal male parts; being both eminently musical, they sang everything at first sight, and after each number looked up at me as if to say, 'What do you think of it all?' I maintained that it was good German music; they must not allow themselves to get confused. But all they did was to stare at each other in amazement, not knowing what to make of me. Nevertheless, in the end they could not stand it any longer, and when they saw that I still retained my gravity, they burst into loud laughter, in which I could not help joining.

I now had to take them into my confidence, and make them promise to follow my lead and pretend to be serious, for it was impossible to give up the opera at this stage. A Viennese 'colorature' singer of the latest style — Madame Spatser Gentiluomo — who came to us from Hanover, and on whose services Marschner greatly relied, was rather taken with her part chiefly because it gave her the chance of showing 'brilliancy.' And, indeed, there was a finale in which my 'German master' had actually tried to steal a march on Donizetti. The Princess had been poisoned by a golden rose, a present from the wicked Bishop of Mainz, and had become delirious. Adolph von Nassau, with the knights of the German empire, swears vengeance, and, accompanied by the chorus, pours out his feelings in a *stretta* of such incredible vulgarity and amateurishness that Donizetti would have thrown it at the head of any of his pupils who had dared to compose such a thing. Marschner now arrived for the dress rehearsal; he was very pleased, and, without compelling me to falsehood, he gave me sufficient opportunities for exercising my powers in the art of concealing my real thoughts. At all events I must have succeeded fairly well, for he had every reason to think himself considerately and kindly treated by me.

During the performance the public behaved very much as the singers had done at the rehearsals. We had brought a still-born child into the world. But Marschner was comforted by the fact that his drinking quartette was encored. This was reminiscent of one of Becker's songs: *Sie sollen ihn nicht haben, den freien deutschen Rhein* ('They shall not have it, our free German Rhine'). After the performance the composer was my guest at a supper party at which, I am sorry to say, the singers, who had had enough of it, would not attend. Herr Ferdinand Hiller had the presence of mind to insist, in his toast to Marschner, that 'whatever one might say, all stress must be laid on the *German* master and *German* art.' Strangely enough, Marschner himself contradicted him by saying that there was something wrong with German operatic compositions, and that one ought to consider the singers and how to write more brilliantly for their voices than he had succeeded in doing up to the present.

Highly gifted as Marschner was, there can be no doubt
that the decline of his genius was due partly to a tendency
which even in the ageing master himself, as he frankly admitted,
was effecting an important and most salutary change. In
later years I met him once more in Paris at the time of my
memorable production of *Tannhäuser*. I did not feel inclined
to renew the old relations, for, to tell the truth, I wanted to
spare myself the unpleasantness of witnessing the consequences
of his change of views, of which we had seen the beginning in
Dresden. I learned that he was in a state of almost helpless
childishness, and that he was in the hands of a young and
ambitious woman, who was trying to make a last attempt
at conquering Paris for him. Among other puff paragraphs
calculated to spread Marschner's glory, I read one which said
that the Parisians must not believe that I (Wagner) was
representative of German art; no — if only Marschner were
given a hearing, it would be discovered that he was beyond
a doubt better suited to the French taste than I could ever be.
Marschner died before his wife had succeeded in establishing
this point.

Ferdinand Hiller, on the other hand, who was in Dresden,
behaved in a very charming and friendly manner, particularly
at this time. Meyerbeer also stayed in the same town from
time to time; precisely why, nobody knew. Once he had
rented a little house for the summer near the Pirnaischer
Schlag, and under a pretty tree in the garden of this place
he had had a small piano installed, whereon, in this idyllic
retreat, he worked at his *Feldlager in Schlesien*. He lived in
great retirement, and I saw very little of him. Ferdinand
Hiller, on the contrary, took a commanding position in the
Dresden musical world in so far as this was not already
monopolised by the royal orchestra and its masters, and for
many years he worked hard for its success. Having a little
private capital, he established himself comfortably amongst us,
and was soon known as a delightful host, who kept a pleasant
house, which, thanks to his wife's influence, was frequented
by a numerous Polish colony. Frau Hiller was indeed an
exceptional Jewish woman of Polish origin, and she was
perhaps all the more exceptional seeing that she, in company

with her husband, had been baptized a Protestant in Italy. Hiller began his career in Dresden with the production of his opera, *Der Traum in der Christnacht*. Since the unheard-of fact that *Rienzi* had been able to rouse the Dresden public to lasting enthusiasm, many an opera composer had felt himself drawn towards our ' Florence on the Elbe,' of which Laube once said that as soon as one entered it one felt bound to apologise because one found so many good things there which one promptly forgot the moment one departed.

The composer of *Der Traum in der Christnacht* looked upon this work as a peculiarly ' German composition.' Hiller had set to music a gruesome play by Raupach, *Der Müller und sein Kind* (' The Miller and his Child '), in which father and daughter, within but a short space of time, both die of consumption. He declared that he had conceived the dialogue and the music of this opera in what he called the ' popular style,' but this work met with the same fate as that which, according to Liszt, befell all his compositions. In spite of his undoubted musical merits, which even Rossini acknowledged, and whether he gave them in French in Paris or in Italian in Italy, it was his sad experience always to see his operas fail. In Germany he had tried the Mendelssohnian style, and had succeeded in composing an oratorio called *Die Zerstörung Jerusalems,* which luckily was not taken notice of by the moody theatre-going public, and which consequently received the unassailable reputation of being ' a solid German work.' He also took Mendelssohn's place as director of the Leipzig Gewandhaus concerts when the latter was called to Berlin in the capacity of general director. Hiller's evil fortune still pursued him, however, and he was unable to retain his position, everybody being given to understand that it was because his wife was not sufficiently acknowledged as concert prima-donna. Mendelssohn returned and made Hiller leave, and Hiller boasted of having quarrelled with him.

Dresden and the success of my *Rienzi* now weighed so much upon his mind that he naturally made another attempt to succeed as an opera composer. Owing to his great energy, and to his position as son of a rich banker (a special attraction even to the director of a court theatre), it happened that he induced them to put aside my poor friend Röckel's *Farinelli* (the production of which had been promised him) in favour of his (Hiller's) own work, *Der Traum in der Christnacht.* He was of the opinion that next to Reissiger and myself, a man of greater musical reputation than Röckel was needed. Lütti-chau, however, was quite content to have Reissiger and myself as celebrities, particularly as we got on so well together, and he remained deaf to Hiller's wishes. To me *Der Traum in der Christnacht* was a great nuisance. I had to conduct it a second time, and before an empty house. Hiller now saw that he had been wrong in not taking my advice before, and in not shorten-ing the opera by one act and altering the end, and he now fancied that he was doing me a great favour by at last declaring himself ready to act on my suggestion in the event of another performance of his opera being possible. I really managed to have it played once more. This was, however, to be the last time, and Hiller, who had read my book of *Tannhäuser,* thought that I had a great advantage over him in writing my own words. He therefore made me promise to help him with the choice and writing of a subject for his next opera.

Shortly afterwards Hiller was present at a performance of *Rienzi,* which was again given before a crowded and enthusi-astic house. When, at the end of the second act, and after frantic recalls from the audience, I left the orchestra in a great state of excitement, Hiller, who was waiting for me in the passage, took the opportunity of adding to his very hasty congratulations, ' Do give my *Traum* once more ! ' I promised him laughingly to do this if I had the chance, but I can-not remember whether it came off or not. While he was waiting for the creation of an entirely new plot for his next opera, Hiller devoted himself to the study of chamber music, to which his large and well-furnished room lent itself most admirably.

A beautiful and solemn event added to the seriousness of the mood in which I finished the music to *Tannhäuser* towards the end of the year, and neutralised the more superficial impres-sions made upon me by the stirring events above described. This was the removal of the remains of Carl Maria von Weber from London to Dresden in December, 1844. As I have already said, a committee had for years been agitating for this removal. From information given by a certain traveller, it had become known that the insignificant coffin which contained Weber's ashes had been disposed of in such a careless way in a remote corner of St. Paul's, that it was feared it might soon become impossible to identify it.

My energetic friend, Professor Löwe, whom I have already mentioned, had availed himself of this information in order to urge the Dresden Glee Club, which constituted his hobby, to take the matter in hand. The concert of male singers arranged to this end had been a fair success financially, and they now wanted to induce the theatre management to make similar efforts, when suddenly they met with serious opposition from this very quarter. The management of the Dresden theatre told the committee that the King had religious scruples with regard to disturbing the peace of the dead. However much we felt inclined to doubt the genuineness of these reasons, nothing could be done, and I was next approached on the subject, in the hope that my influential position might lend weight to my appeal. I entered into the spirit of the enterprise with great fervour. I consented to be made president; Herr Hofrat Schulz, director of the ' Antiken-Cabinet,' who was a well-known authority on artistic matters, and another gentleman, a Christian banker, were also elected members of the committee, and the movement thus received fresh life. Prospectuses were sent round, exhaustive plans were made, and numerous meetings held. Here, again, I met with opposition on the part of my chief, Lüttichau; if he could have done so, he would have forbidden me to move in the matter by making the most of the King's scruples referred to above. But he had had a warning not to pick a quarrel with me after his experience in the summer, when, contrary to his expectations, the music written by me to celebrate the King's arrival had found favour with the monarch. As his antipathy to the proceedings was not so very serious, Lüttichau must have seen that even the direct opposition of his Majesty could not have prevented the enterprise from being carried out privately, and that, on the contrary, the court would cut a sorry figure if the Royal Court Theatre (to which Weber once belonged) should assume a hostile attitude. He therefore tried in a would-be friendly way to make me desist from furthering the cause, well knowing that, without me, the plan would fail. He tried to convince me that it would be wrong to pay this exaggerated honour to Weber's memory, whereas nobody thought of removing the ashes of Morlacchi from Italy, although the latter had given his services to the royal orchestra for a much longer period than Weber had done. What would be the consequence? By way of argument he said, ' Suppose Reissiger died on his journey to some watering-place — his wife would then be as much justified as was Frau von Weber (who had annoyed him quite enough already) in expecting her husband's dead body to be brought home with music and pomp.' I tried to calm him, and if I did not succeed in making him see the difference between Reissiger and Weber, I managed to make him understand that the affair must take its course, as the Berlin Court Theatre had already announced a benefit performance to support our undertaking.

Meyerbeer, to whom my committee had applied, was instrumental in bringing this about, and a performance of *Euryanthe* was actually given which yielded the handsome balance of six thousand marks. A few theatres of lesser importance now followed our lead. The Dresden Court Theatre, therefore, could not hold back any longer, and as we now had a fairly large sum at the bank, we were able to cover the expenses of the removal, as well as the cost of an appropriate vault and monument; we even had a nucleus fund for a statue of Weber, which we were to fight for later on. The elder of the two sons of the immortal master travelled to London to fetch the remains of his father. He brought them by boat down the Elbe, and finally arrived at the Dresden landing-stage, from whence they were to be conducted to German soil. This last journey of the remains was to take place at night. A solemn torchlight procession was to be formed, and I had undertaken to see to the funeral music.

I arranged this from two motives out of *Euryanthe,* using that part of the music in the overture which relates to the vision of spirits. I introduced the Cavatina from *Euryanthe* — *Hier dicht am Quell* ('Here near the source '), which I left unaltered, except that I transposed it into B flat major, and I finished the whole, as Weber finished his opera, by a return to the first sublime motive. I had orchestrated this symphonic piece, which was well suited to the purpose, for eight chosen wind instruments, and notwithstanding the volume of sound, I had not forgotten softness and delicacy of instrumentation. I substituted the gruesome *tremolo* of the violas, which appears in that part of the overture adapted by me, by twenty muffled drums, and as a whole attained to such an exceedingly impressive effect, especially to us who were full of thoughts of Weber, that, even in the theatre where we rehearsed, Schröder-Devrient, who was present, and who had been an intimate friend of Weber's, was deeply moved. I had never carried out anything more in keeping with the character of the subject; and the procession through the town was equally impressive.

As the very slow tempo, devoid of any strongly marked accents, offered numerous difficulties, I had had the stage cleared for the rehearsal, in order to command a sufficient space for the musicians, once they had thoroughly practised the piece, to walk round me in a circle playing all the while. Several of those who witnessed the procession from their windows assured me that the effect of the procession was indescribably and sublimely solemn. After we had placed the coffin in the little mortuary chapel of the Catholic cemetery in Friedrichstadt, where Madame Devrient met it with a wreath of flowers, we performed, on the following morning, the solemn ceremony of lowering it into the vault. Herr Hofrat Schulz and myself, as presidents of the committee, were allowed the honour of speaking by the graveside, and what afforded me an appropriate subject for the few, somewhat affecting, words which I had to pronounce, was the fact that, shortly before the removal of Weber's remains, the second son of the master, Alexander von Weber, had died. The poor mother had been so terribly affected by the sudden death of this youth, so full of life and health, that had we not been in the very midst of our arrangements, we should have been compelled to abandon them; for in this new loss the widow saw a judgment of God who, in her opinion, looked upon the removal of the remains as an act of sacrilege prompted by vanity. As the public seemed particularly disposed to hold the same view, it fell to my lot to set the nature of our undertaking in the proper light before the eyes of the world. And this I so far succeeded in doing that, to my satisfaction, I learned from all sides that my justification of our action had received the most general acceptance.

On this occasion I had a strange experience with regard to myself, when for the first time in my life I had to deliver a solemn public speech. Since then I have always spoken extemporarily; this time, however, as it was my first appearance as an orator, I had written out my speech, and carefully learned it by heart. As I was thoroughly under the influence of my subject, I felt so sure of my memory that I never thought of making any notes. Thanks to this omission, however, I made my brother Albert very unhappy. He was standing near me at the ceremony, and he told me afterwards that, in spite of being deeply moved, he felt at one moment as if he could have sworn at me for not having asked him to prompt me. It happened in this way: I began my speech in a clear and full voice, but suddenly the sound of my own words, and their particular intonation, affected me to such an extent that, carried away as I was by my own thoughts, I imagined I *saw* as well as *heard* myself before the breathless multitude. While I thus appeared objectively to myself I remained in a sort of trance, during which I seemed to be waiting for something to happen, and felt quite a different person from the man who was supposed to be standing and speaking there. It was neither nervousness nor absent-mindedness on my part; only at the end of a certain sentence there was such a long pause that those who saw me standing there must have wondered what on earth to think of me. At last my own silence and the stillness round me reminded me that I was not there to listen, but to speak. I at once resumed my discourse, and I spoke with such fluency to the very end that the celebrated actor, Emil Devrient, assured me that, apart from the solemn service, he had been deeply impressed simply from the standpoint of a dramatic orator.

The ceremony concluded with a poem written and set to music by myself, and, though it presented many difficulties

for men's voices, it was splendidly rendered by some of the best
opera singers. Lüttichau, who was present, was now not only
convinced of the justice of the enterprise, but also strongly
in favour of it. I was deeply thankful that everything had
succeeded so well, and when Weber's widow, upon whom I
called after the ceremony, told me how profoundly she, too,
had been moved, the only cloud that still darkened my horizon
was dispelled. In my youth I had learned to love music through
my admiration for Weber's genius, and the news of his death
was a terrible blow to me. To have, as it were, come into
contact with him again and after so many years by this second
funeral, was an event that stirred the very depths of my
being.

From all the particulars I have given concerning my intimacy
with the great masters who were my contemporaries, it is
easy to see at what sources I had been able to quench my
thirst for intellectual intercourse. It was not a very satisfactory outlook to turn from Weber's grave to his living successors; but I had still to find out how absolutely hopeless
this was.

I spent the winter of 1844-5 partly in yielding to attractions from outside, and partly in indulging in the deepest
meditation. By dint of great energy, and by getting up very
early, even in winter, I succeeded in completing my score to
Tannhäuser early in April, having, as already stated, finished
the composition of it at the end of the preceding year. In
writing down the orchestration I made things particularly
difficult for myself by using the specially prepared paper which
the printing process renders necessary, and which involved me
in all kinds of trying formalities. I had each page transferred
to the stone immediately, and a hundred copies printed from
each, hoping to make use of these proofs for the rapid circulation of my work. Whether my hopes were to be fulfilled or
not, I was at all events fifteen hundred marks out of pocket
when all the expenses of the publication were paid.

In regard to this work which called for so many sacrifices,
and which was so slow and difficult, more details will appear
in my autobiography. At all events, when May came round I
was in possession of a hundred neatly bound copies of my first

new work since the production of the *Fliegender Holländer,* and Hiller, to whom I showed some parts of it, formed a tolerably good impression of its value.

These plans for rapidly spreading the fame of my *Tannhäuser* were made with the hope of a success which, in view of my needy circumstances, seemed ever more and more desirable. In the course of one year since I had begun my own publication of my operas, much had been done to this end. In September of the year 1844 I had presented the King of Saxony with a special richly bound copy of the complete pianoforte arrangement of *Rienzi,* dedicated to his Majesty. The *Fliegender Holländer* had also been finished, and the pianoforte arrangement of *Rienzi* for duet, as well as some songs selected from both operas, had either been published or were about to be published. Apart from this I had had twenty-five copies made of the scores of both these operas by means of the so-called autographic transfer process, although only from the writing of the copyists. All these heavy expenses made it absolutely imperative that I should try to send my scores to the different theatres, and induce them to produce my operas, as the outlay on the piano scores had been heavy, and these could only have a sale if my works got to be known sufficiently well through the theatre.

I now sent the score of my *Rienzi* to the more important theatres, but they all returned my work to me, the Munich Court Theatre even sending it back unopened! I therefore knew what to expect, and spared myself the trouble of sending my *Dutchman.* From a speculative business point of view the situation was this: the hoped-for success of *Tannhäuser* would bring in its wake a demand for my earlier works. The worthy Meser, my agent, who was the music publisher appointed to the court, had also begun to feel a little doubtful, and saw that this was the only thing to do. I started at once on the publication of a pianoforte arrangement of *Tannhäuser,* preparing it myself while Röckel undertook the *Fliegender Holländer,* and a certain Klink did *Rienzi.*

The only thing that Meser was absolutely opposed to was the title of my new opera, which I had just named *Der Venusberg;* he maintained that, as I did not mix with the public, I had no idea what horrible jokes were made about this title. He said the students and professors of the medical school in Dresden would be the first to make fun of it, as they had a predilection for that kind of obscene joke. I was sufficiently disgusted by these details to consent to the change. To the name of my hero, Tannhäuser, I added the name of the subject of the legend which, although originally not belonging to the *Tannhäuser* myth, was thus associated with it by me, a fact which later on Simrock, the great investigator and innovator in the world of legend, whom I esteemed so highly, took very much amiss.

Tannhäuser un der Sängerkrieg auf Wartburg should henceforth be its title, and to give the work a mediæval appearance I had the words specially printed in Gothic characters upon the piano arrangement, and in this way introduced the work to the public.

The extra expenses this involved were very heavy; but I went to great pains to impress Meser with my belief in the success of my work. So deeply were we involved in this scheme, and so great were the sacrifices it had compelled us to make, that there was nothing else for it but to trust to a special turn of Fortune's wheel. As it happened, the management of the theatre shared my confidence in the success of *Tannhäuser*. I had induced Lüttichau to have the scenery for *Tannhäuser* painted by the best painters of the great opera house in Paris. I had seen their work on the Dresden stage: it belonged to the style of German scenic art which was then fashionable, and really gave the effect of first-class work.

The order for this, as well as the necessary negotiations with the Parisian painter, Despléchin, had already been settled in the preceding autumn. The management agreed to all my wishes, even to the ordering of beautiful costumes of mediæval character designed by my friend Heine. The only thing Lüttichau constantly postponed was the order for the Hall of Song on the Wartburg; he maintained that the Hall for Kaiser Karl the Great in Oberon, which had only recently been delivered by some French painters, would answer the purpose just as well. With superhuman efforts I had to convince my chief that we did not want a brilliant throne-room, but a scenic picture of a certain character such as I saw before my mind's eye, and that it could be painted only according to my directions. As in the end I became very irritable and cross, he soothed me by saying that he had no objection to having this scene painted, and that he would order it to be commenced at once, adding that he had not agreed immediately, only with the view of making my joy the greater, because, what one obtained without difficulty, one rarely appreciated. This Hall of Song was fated to cause me great trouble later on.

Thus everything was in full swing; circumstances were favourable, and seemed to cast a hopeful light upon the production of my new work at the beginning of the autumn season. Even the public was looking forward to it, and for the first time I saw my name mentioned in a friendly manner in a communication to the *Allgemeine Zeitung*. They actually spoke of the great expectations they had of my new work, the poem of which had been written ' with undoubted poetic feeling.'

Full of hope, I started in July on my holiday, which consisted of a journey to Marienbad in Bohemia, where my wife and I intended to take the cure. Again I found myself on the 'volcanic' soil of this extraordinary country, Bohemia, which always had such an inspiring effect on me. It was a marvellous summer, almost too hot, and I was therefore in high spirits. I had intended to follow the easy-going mode of life which is a necessary part of this somewhat trying treatment, and had selected my books with care, taking with me the poems of Wolfram von Eschenbach, edited by Simrock and San Marte, as well as the anonymous epic *Lohengrin*, with its lengthy introduction by Görres. With my book under my arm I hid myself in the neighbouring woods, and pitching my tent by the brook in company with *Titurel* and *Parcival*, I lost myself in Wolfram's strange, yet irresistibly charming, poem. Soon, however, a longing seized me to give expression to the inspiration generated by this poem, so that I had the greatest difficulty in overcoming my desire to give up the rest I had been prescribed while partaking of the water of Marienbad.

The result was an ever-increasing state of excitement. *Lohengrin*, the first conception of which dates from the end of my time in Paris, stood suddenly revealed before me, complete in every detail of its dramatic construction. The legend

of the swan which forms such an important feature of all the
many versions of this series of myths that my studies had
brought to my notice, exercised a singular fascination over my
imagination.

Remembering the doctor's advice, I struggled bravely against
the temptation of writing down my ideas, and resorted to the
most strange and energetic methods. Owing to some comments I had read in Gervinus's *History of German Literature,*
both the *Meistersinger von Nürnberg* and *Hans Sachs* had
acquired quite a vital charm for me. The Marker alone,
and the part he takes in the Master-singing, were particularly
pleasing to me, and on one of my lonely walks, without knowing
anything particular about Hans Sachs and his poetic contemporaries, I thought out a humorous scene, in which the cobbler
— as a popular artisan-poet — with the hammer on his last,
gives the Marker a practical lesson by making him sing, thereby
taking revenge on him for his conventional misdeeds. To me
the force of the whole scene was concentrated in the two following points: on the one hand the Marker, with his slate
covered with chalk-marks, and on the other Hans Sachs holding
up the shoes covered with his chalk-marks, each intimating to
the other that the singing had been a failure. To this picture,
by way of concluding the second act, I added a scene consisting of a narrow, crooked little street in Nuremberg, with
the people all running about in great excitement, and ultimately
engaging in a street brawl. Thus, suddenly, the whole of my
Meistersinger comedy took shape so vividly before me, that,
inasmuch as it was a particularly cheerful subject, and not in
the least likely to over-excite my nerves, I felt I must write it
out in spite of the doctor's orders. I therefore proceeded to
do this, and hoped it might free me from the thrall of the idea
of *Lohengrin;* but I was mistaken; for no sooner had I got
into my bath at noon, than I felt an overpowering desire to
write out *Lohengrin,* and this longing so overcame me that I
could not wait the prescribed hour for the bath, but when a
few minutes elapsed, jumped out and, barely giving myself time
to dress, ran home to write out what I had in my mind. I
repeated this for several days until the complete sketch of
Lohengrin was on paper.

The doctor then told me I had better give up taking the waters and baths, saying emphatically that I was quite unfit for such cures. My excitement had grown to such an extent that even my efforts to sleep as a rule ended only in nocturnal adventures. Among some interesting excursions that we made at this time, one to Eger fascinated me particularly, on account of its association with Wallenstein and of the peculiar costumes of the inhabitants.

In mid-August we travelled back to Dresden, where my friends were glad to see me in such good spirits; as for myself, I felt as if I had wings. In September, when all our singers had returned from their summer holidays, I resumed the rehearsals of *Tannhäuser* with great earnestness. We had now got so far, at least with the musical part of the performance, that the possible date of the production seemed quite close at hand. Schröder-Devrient was one of the first to realise the extraordinary difficulties which the production of *Tannhäuser* would entail. And, indeed, she saw these difficulties so clearly that, to my great discomfiture, she was able to lay them all before me. Once, when I called upon her, she read the principal passages aloud with great feeling and force, and then she asked me how I could have been so simple-minded as to have thought that so childish a creature as Tichatschek would be able to find the proper tones for Tannhäuser. I tried to bring her attention and my own to bear upon the nature of the music, which was written so clearly in order to bring out the necessary accent, that, in my opinion, the music actually spoke for him who interpreted the passage, even if he were only a musical singer and nothing more. She shook her head, saying that this would be all right in the case of an oratorio.

She now sang Elizabeth's prayer from the piano score, and asked me if I really thought that this music would answer my intentions if sung by a young and pretty voice without any soul or without that experience of life which alone could give the real expression to the interpretation. I sighed and said that, in that case, the youthfulness of the voice and of its owner must make up for what was lacking: at the same time, I asked her as a favour to see what she could do towards making my niece, Johanna, understand her part. All this, however, did not solve the Tannhäuser problem, for any effort at teaching Tichatschek would only have resulted in confusion. I was therefore obliged to rely entirely upon the energy of his voice, and on the singer's peculiarly sharp ' speaking ' tone.

Devrient's anxiety about the principal parts arose partly out of concern about her own. She did not know what to do with the part of Venus; she had undertaken it for the sake of the success of the performance, for although a small part, so much depended upon its being ideally interpreted! Later on, when the work was given in Paris, I became convinced that this part had been written in too sketchy a style, and this induced me to reconstruct it by making extensive additions, and by supplying all that which I felt it lacked. For the moment, however, it looked as if no art on the part of the singer could give to this sketch anything of what it ought to represent. The only thing that might have helped towards a satisfactory impersonation of Venus would have been the artist's confidence in her own great physical attraction, and in the effect it would help to produce by appealing to the purely material sympathies of the public. The certainty that these means were no longer at her disposal paralysed this great singer, who could hide her age and matronly appearance no longer. She therefore became self-conscious, and unable to use even the usual means for gaining an effect. On one occasion, with a little smile of despair, she expressed herself incapable of playing Venus, for the very simple reason that she could not appear dressed like the goddess. ' What on earth am I to wear as Venus ? ' she exclaimed. ' After all, I cannot be clad in a belt alone. A nice figure of fun I should look, and you would laugh on the wrong side of your face ! '

On the whole, I still built my hopes upon the general effect of the music alone, the great promise of which at the rehearsals greatly encouraged me. Hiller, who had looked through the score and had already praised it, assured me that the instrumentation could not have been carried out with greater sobriety. The characteristic and delicate sonority of the orchestra delighted me, and strengthened me in my resolve to be extremely sparing in the use of my orchestral material, in order to attain that abundance of combinations which I needed for my later works.

At the rehearsal my wife alone missed the trumpets and trombones that gave such brightness and freshness to *Rienzi*. Although I laughed at this, I could not help feeling anxious when she confided to me how great had been her disappointment when, at the theatre rehearsal, she noticed the really feeble impression made by the music of the *Sängerkrieg*. Speaking from the point of view of the public, who always want to be amused or stirred in some way or other, she had thus very rightly called attention to an exceedingly questionable side of the performance. But I saw at once that the fault lay less with the conception than with the fact that I had not controlled the production with sufficient care.

In regard to the conception of this scene I was literally on the horns of a dilemma, for I had to decide once for all whether this *Sängerkrieg* was to be a concert of arias or a competition in dramatic poetry. There are many people even nowadays, who, in spite of having witnessed a perfectly successful production of this scene, have not received the right impression of its purport. Their idea is that it belongs to the traditional operatic 'genre,' which demands that a number of vocal evolutions shall be juxtaposed or contrasted, and that these different songs are intended to amuse and interest the audience by means of their purely musical changes in rhythm and time on the principle of a concert programme, *i.e.* by various items of different styles. This was not at all my idea: my real intention was, if possible, to force the listener, for the first time in the history of opera, to take an interest in a poetical idea, by making him follow all its necessary developments. For it was only by virtue of this interest that he could be made to understand the catastrophe, which in this instance was not to be brought about by any outside influence, but must be the outcome simply of the natural spiritual processes at work. Hence the need of great moderation and breadth in the conception of the music; first, in order that according to my principle it might prove helpful rather than the reverse to the understanding of the poetical lines, and secondly, in order that the increasing rhythmic character of the melody which marks the ardent growth of passion may not be interrupted too arbitrarily by unnecessary changes in modulation and rhythm. Hence, too, the need of a very sparing use of orchestral instruments for the accompaniment, and an intentional suppression of all those purely musical effects which must be utilised, and that gradually, only when the situation becomes so intense that one almost ceases to think, and can only feel the tragic nature of the crisis. No one could deny that I had contrived to produce the proper effect of this principle the moment I played the *Sängerkrieg* on the piano. With the view of ensuring all my future successes, I was now confronted with the exceptional difficulty of making the opera singers understand how to interpret their parts precisely in the way I desired. I remembered how, through lack of experience, I had neglected properly to superintend the production of the *Fliegender Holländer,* and as I now fully realised all the disastrous consequences of this neglect, I began to think of means by which I could teach the singers my own interpretation. I have already stated that it was impossible to influence Tichatschek, for if he were made to do things he could not understand, he only became nervous and confused. He was conscious of his advantages. He knew that with his metallic voice he could sing with great musical rhythm and accuracy, while his delivery was simply perfect. But, to my great astonishment, I was soon to learn that all this did not by any means suffice; for, to my horror, at the first performance, that which had strangely escaped my notice in the rehearsals became suddenly apparent to me. At the close of the *Sängerkrieg,* when Tannhäuser (in frantic excitement, and forgetful of everybody present) has to sing his praise to Venus, and I saw Tichatschek moving towards Elizabeth and addressing his passionate outburst to her, I thought of Schröder-Devrient's warning in very much the same way as Crœsus must have thought when he cried, 'O Solon! Solon!' at the funeral pyre. In spite of the musical excellence of Tichatschek, the enormous life and melodic charm of the *Sängerkrieg* failed entirely.

On the other hand, I succeeded in calling into life an entirely new element such as probably had never been seen in opera! I had watched the young baritone Mitterwurzer with great interest in some of his parts — he was a strangely reticent man, and not at all sociably inclined, and I had noticed that his delightfully mellow voice possessed the rare quality of bringing out the inner note of the soul. To him I entrusted Wolfram, and I had every reason to be satisfied with his zeal and with the success of his studies. Therefore, if I wished my intention and method to become known, especially in regard to this difficult *Sängerkrieg*, I had to rely on him for the proper execution of my plans and everything they involved. I began by going through the opening song of this scene with him; but, after I had done my utmost to make him understand how I wanted it done, I was surprised to find how very difficult this particular rendering of the music appeared to him. He was absolutely incapable of repeating it after me, and with each renewed effort his singing became so commonplace and so mechanical that I realised clearly that he had not understood this piece to be anything more than a phrase in recitative form, which he might render with any inflections of the voice that happened to be prescribed, or which might be sung either this way or that, according to fancy, as was usual in operatic pieces. He, too, was astonished at his own want of capacity, but was so struck by the novelty and the justice of my views, that he begged me not to try any more for the present, but to leave him to find out for himself how best to become familiar with this newly revealed world. During several rehearsals he only sang in a whisper in order to get over the difficulty, but at the last rehearsal he acquitted himself so admirably of his task, and threw himself into it so heartily, that his work has remained to this day as my most conclusive reason for believing that, in spite of the unsatisfactory state of the world of opera to-day, it is possible not only to find, but also properly to train, the singer whom I should regard as indispensable for a correct interpretation of my works. It was through the impression made by Mitterwurzer that I ultimately succeeded in making the public understand the whole of my work. This man, who had utterly changed himself in bearing, look, and appearance in order to fit himself to the rôle of Wolfram, had, in thus solving the problem, not only become a thorough artist, but by his interpretation of his part had also proved himself my saviour at the very moment when my work was threatening to fail through the unsatisfactory result of the first performance.

By his side the part of Elizabeth made a sweet impression. The youthful appearance of my niece, her tall and slender form, the decidedly German cast of her features, as well as the incomparable beauty of her voice, with its expression of almost childlike innocence, helped her to gain the hearts of the audience, even though her talent was more theatrical than dramatic. She soon rose to fame by her impersonation of this part, and often in later years, when speaking about *Tannhäuser* performances in which she had appeared, people used to tell me that its success had been entirely due to her. Strange to say, in such reports people referred principally to the charm of her acting at the moment when she received the guests in the Wartburg Hall; and I used to account for this by remembering the untiring efforts with which my talented brother and I had trained her to perform this very part. And yet it was never possible to make her understand the proper interpretation of the prayer in the third act, and I felt inclined to say, ' O Solon! Solon!' as I had done in the case of Tichatschek, when after the first performance I was obliged to make a considerable cut in this solo, a proceeding which greatly reduced its importance for ever afterwards. I heard later that Johanna, who for a short period actually had the reputation of being a great singer, had never succeeded in singing the prayer as it ought to be sung, whereas a French singer, Mademoiselle Marie Sax, achieved this in Paris to my entire satisfaction.

In the beginning of October we had so far progressed with our rehearsals that nothing stood in the way of an immediate production of *Tannhäuser* save the scenery, which was not yet complete. A few only of the scenes ordered from Paris had arrived, and even these had come very late. The Wartburg Valley was beautifully effective and perfect in every detail. The inner part of the Venusberg, however, gave me much anxiety: the painter had not understood me; he had

painted clusters of trees and statues, which reminded one of
Versailles, and had placed them in a wild cave; he had evidently not known how to combine the weird with the alluring.
I had to insist on extensive alterations, and chiefly on the painting out of the shrubs and statues, all of which required time.
The grotto had to lie half hidden in a rosy cloud, through which
the Wartburg Valley had to loom in the distance; this was to
be done in strict obedience to my own ideas.

The greatest misfortune, however, was to befall me in the
shape of the tardy delivery of the scenery for the Hall of Song.
This was due to great negligence on the part of the Paris
artists; and we waited and waited until every detail of the
opera had been studied and studied again *ad nauseam*. Daily
I went to the railway station and examined all the packages
and boxes that had arrived, but there was no Hall of Song.
At last I allowed myself to be persuaded not to postpone the
first performance any longer, and I decided to use the Hall of
Karl the Great out of *Oberon,* originally suggested to me by
Lüttichau, instead of the real thing. Considering the importance I attached to practical effect, this entailed a great sacrifice
of my personal feelings. And true enough, when the curtain
rose for the second act, the reappearance of this throne-room,
which the public had seen so often, added considerably to the
general disappointment of the audience, who had anticipated
astonishing surprises in this opera.

On the 19th of October the first performance took place.
In the morning of that day a very beautiful young lady was
introduced to me by the leader Lipinsky. Her name was Mme.
Kalergis, and she was a niece of the Russian Chancellor, Count
von Nesselrode. Liszt had spoken to her about me with such
enthusiasm that she had travelled all the way to Dresden especially to hear the first production of my new work. I thought
I was right in regarding this flattering visit as a good omen.
But although on this occasion she turned away from me, somewhat perplexed and disappointed by the very unintelligible
performance and the somewhat doubtful reception with which
it met, I had sufficient cause in after-years to know how deeply
this remarkable and energetic woman had nevertheless been
impressed.

A great contrast to this visit was one I received from a peculiar man called C. Gaillard. He was the editor of a Berlin musical paper, which had only just started, and in which I had read with great astonishment an entirely favourable and important criticism of my *Fliegender Holländer*. Although necessity had compelled me to remain indifferent to the attitude of the critics, yet this particular notice gave me much pleasure, and I had invited my unknown critic to come and hear the first production of *Tannhäuser* in Dresden.

This he did, and I was deeply touched to find that I had to deal with a young man who, in spite of being threatened by consumption, and being also exceedingly badly off, had come at my invitation, simply from a sense of duty and honour, and not with any mercenary motive. I saw from his knowledge and capacities that he would never be able to attain a position of great influence, but his kindness of heart and his extraordinarily receptive mind filled me with a feeling of profound respect for him. A few years later I was very sorry to hear that he had at last succumbed to the terrible disease from which I knew him to be suffering; for to the very end he remained faithful and devoted to me, in spite of the most trying circumstances.

Meanwhile I had renewed my acquaintance with the friend I had won through the production of the *Fliegender Holländer* in Berlin, and who for a long time I had never had an opportunity of knowing more thoroughly. The second time I met her was at Schröder-Devrient's, with whom she was already on friendly terms, and of whom she used to speak as ' one of my greatest conquests.'

She was already past her first youth, and had no beauty of feature except remarkably penetrating and expressive eyes that showed the greatness of soul with which she was gifted. She was the sister of Frommann, the bookseller of Jena, and could relate many intimate facts about Goethe, who had stayed at her brother's house when he was in that town. She had held the position of reader and companion to the Princess Augusta of Prussia, and had thus become intimately acquainted with her, and was regarded by her own association as almost a bosom friend and confidante of that great lady. Nevertheless, she lived in extreme poverty, and seemed proud of being able, by means of her talent as a painter of arabesques, to secure for herself some sort of independence. She always remained faithfully devoted to me, as she was one of the few who were uninfluenced by the unfavourable impression produced by the first performance of *Tannhäuser,* and promptly expressed her appreciation of my latest work with the greatest enthusiasm.

With regard to the production itself the conclusions I drew from it were as follows: the real faults in the work, which I have already mentioned incidentally, lay in the sketchy and clumsy portrayal of the part of Venus, and consequently of the whole of the introductory scene of the first act. In consequence of this defect the drama never even rose to the level of genuine warmth, still less did it attain to the heights of passion which, according to the poetic conception of the part, should so strongly work upon the feelings of the audience as to prepare them for the inevitable catastrophe in which the scene culminates, and thus lead up to the tragic *dénouement.* This great scene was a complete failure, in spite of the fact that it was entrusted to so great an actress as Schröder-Devrient, and a singer so unusually gifted as Tichatschek. The genius of Devrient might yet have struck the right note of passion in the scene had she not chanced to be acting with a singer incapable of all dramatic seriousness, and whose natural gifts only fitted him for joyous or declamatory accents, and who was totally incapable of expressing pain and suffering. It was not until Wolfram's touching song and the closing scene of this act were reached that the audience showed any signs of emotion. Tichatschek wrought such a tremendous effect in the concluding phrase by the jubilant music of his voice that, as I was afterwards informed, the end of this first act left the audience in a great state of enthusiasm. This was maintained, and even exceeded in the second act, during which Elizabeth and Wolfram made a very sympathetic impression. It was only the hero of *Tannhäuser* who continued to lose ground, and at last so completely failed to hold the audience that in the final scene he almost broke down himself in dejection, as though the failure of *Tannhäuser* were his own. The fatal defect of his performance lay in his inability to find the right expression for the theme of the great Adagio passage of the finale beginning with the words: ' To lead the sinner to salvation, the Heaven-sent messenger drew near.' The importance of this passage I have explained at length in my subsequent instructions for the production of *Tannhäuser*. Indeed, owing to Tichatschek's absolutely expressionless rendering, which made it seem terribly long and tedious, I had to omit it entirely from the second performance. As I did not wish to offend so devoted and, in his way, so deserving a man as Tichatschek, I let it be understood I had come to the conclusion that this theme was a failure. Moreover, as Tichatschek was thought to be an actor chosen by myself to take the parts of the heroes in my works, this passage, which was so immeasurably vital to the opera, continued to be omitted in all the subsequent productions of *Tannhäuser,* as though this proceeding had been approved and demanded by me. I therefore cherished no illusions about the value of the subsequent universal success of this opera on the German stage. My hero, who, in rapture as in woe, should always have asserted his feelings with boundless energy, slunk away at the end of the second act with the humble bearing of a penitent sinner, only to reappear in the third with a demeanour designed to awaken the charitable sympathy of the audience. His pronunciation of the Pope's excommunication, however, was rendered with his usual full rhetorical power, and it was refreshing to hear his voice dominating the accompanying trombones. Granted that this radical defect in the hero's acting had left the public in a doubtful and unsatisfied state of suspense regarding the meaning of the whole, yet the mistake in the execution of the final scene, arising from my own inexperience in this new field of dramatic creation, undoubtedly contributed to produce a chilling uncertainty as to the true significance of the scenic action. In my first complete version I had made Venus, on the occasion of her second attempt to recall her faithless lover, appear in a vision to Tannhäuser when he is in a frenzy of madness, and the awfulness of the situation is merely suggested by a faint roseate glow upon the distant Hörselberg. Even the definite announcement of Elizabeth's death was a sudden inspiration on the part of Wolfram. This idea I intended to convey to the listening audience solely by the sound of bells tolling in the distance, and by a faint gleam of torches to attract their eyes to the remote Wartburg. Moreover, there was a lack of precision and clearness in the appearance of the chorus of young pilgrims, whose duty it was to announce the miracle by their song alone. At that time I had given them no budding staves to carry, and had unfortunately spoiled their refrain by a tedious and unbroken monotony of accompaniment.

When at last the curtain fell, I was under the impression, not so much from the behaviour of the audience, which was friendly, as from my own inward conviction, that the failure of this work was to be attributed to the immature and unsuitable material used in its production. My depression was extreme, and a few friends who were present after the piece, among them my dear sister Clara and her husband, were equally affected. That very evening I decided to remedy the defects of the first night before the second performance. I was conscious of where the principal fault lay, but hardly dared give expression to my conviction. At the slightest attempt on my part to explain anything to Tichatschek I had to abandon it, as I realised the impossibility of success. I should only have made him so embarrassed and annoyed, that on one pretext or another he would never have sung *Tannhäuser* again. In order to ensure the repetition of my opera, therefore, I took the only course open to me by arrogating to myself all blame for the failure. I could thus make considerable curtailments, whereby, of course, the dramatic significance of the leading rôle was considerably lessened; this, however, did not interfere with the other parts of the opera, which had been favourably received. Consequently, although inwardly very humiliated, I hoped to gain some advantage for my work at the second performance, and was particularly desirous that this should take place with as little delay as possible. But Tichatschek was hoarse, and I had to possess my soul in patience for fully a week.

I can hardly describe what I suffered during that time; it seemed as if this delay would completely ruin my work. Every day that elapsed between the first and second performance left the result of the former more and more problematic, until at last it appeared to be a generally acknowledged failure. While the public as a whole expressed angry astonishment that, after the approval they had shown of my *Rienzi*, I had paid no attention to their taste in writing my new work, there were may kind and judicious friends who were utterly perplexed at its inefficiency, the principal parts of which they had been unable to understand, or thought were imperfectly sketched and finished. The critics, with unconcealed joy, attacked it as ravens attack carrion thrown out to them. Even the passions and prejudices of the day were drawn into the controversy in order, if possible, to confuse men's minds, and prejudice them against me. It was just at the time when the German-Catholic agitation, set in motion by Czersky and Ronge as a highly meritorious and liberal movement, was causing a great commotion. It was now made' out that by *Tannhäuser* I had provoked a reactionary tendency, and that precisely as Meyerbeer with his *Huguenots* had glorified Protestantism, so I with my latest opera would glorify Catholicism.

The rumour that in writing *Tannhäuser* I had been bribed by the Catholic party was believed for a long time. While the effort was being made to ruin my popularity by this means, I had the questionable honour of being approached, first by letter, afterwards in person, by a certain M. Rousseau, at that time editor of the Prussian *Staatszeitung*, who wished for my friendship and help. I knew of him only in connection with a scathing criticism of my *Fliegender Holländer*. He informed me that he had been sent from Austria to further the Catholic cause in Berlin, but that he had had so many sad experiences of the fruitlessness of his efforts, that he was now returning to Vienna to continue his work in this direction undisturbed, with which work I had, by my *Tannhäuser*, proclaimed myself fully in accord.

That remarkable paper, the *Dresdener Anzeiger*, which was a local organ for the redress of slander and scandal, daily published some fresh bit of news to my prejudice. At last I noticed that these attacks were met by witty and forcible little snubs, and also that encouraging comments appeared in my favour, which for some time surprised me very much, as

I knew that only enemies and never friends interested themselves in such cases. But I learned, to my amusement, from Röckel, that he and my friend Heine had carried out this inspiriting campaign on my behalf.

The ill-feeling against me in this quarter was only troublesome because at that unfortunate period I was hindered from expressing myself through my work. Tichatschek continued hoarse, and it was said he would never sing in my opera again. I heard from Lüttichau that, scared by the failure of *Tannhäuser*, he was holding himself in readiness to countermand the order for the promised scenery for the Hall of Song, or to cancel it altogether. I was so terrified at the cowardice which was thus revealed, that I myself began to look upon *Tannhäuser* as doomed. My prospects and my whole position, when viewed in this mood, may be readily gathered from my communications, especially those referring to my negotiations for the publication of my works.

This terrible week dragged out like an endless eternity. I was afraid to look anybody in the face, but was one day obliged to go to Meser's music shop, where I met Gottfried Semper just buying a text-book of *Tannhäuser*. Only a short time before I had been very much put out in discussing this subject with him; he would listen to nothing I had to say about the Minnesängers and Pilgrims of the Middle Ages in connection with art, but gave me to understand that he despised me for my choice of such material.

While Meser assured me that no inquiry whatever had been received for the numbers of *Tannhäuser* already published, it was strange that my most energetic antagonist should be the only person who had actually bought and paid for a copy. In a peculiarly earnest and impressive manner he remarked to me that it was necessary to be thoroughly acquainted with the subject if a just opinion was to be passed on it, and that for this purpose, unfortunately, nothing but the text was available. This very meeting with Semper, strange as it may appear, was the first really encouraging sign that I can remember.

But I found my greatest consolation in those days of trouble and anxiety in Röckel, who from that time forward entered into a lifelong intimacy with me. He had, without my being aware of it, disputed, explained, quarrelled, and petitioned on my behalf, and thereby roused himself to a veritable enthusiasm for *Tannhäuser*. The evening before the second performance, which was at last to take place, we met over a glass of beer, and his bright demeanour had such a cheering effect upon me that we became very lively. After contemplating my head for some time, he swore that it was impossible to destroy me, that there was a something in me, something, probably, in my blood, as similar characteristics also appeared in my brother Albert, who was otherwise so unlike me. To speak more plainly, he called it the peculiar *heat* of my temperament; this heat, he thought, might consume others, whereas I appeared to feel at my best when it glowed most fiercely, for he had several times seen me positively ablaze. I laughed, and did not know what to make of his nonsense. Well, he said, I should soon see what he meant in *Tannhäuser*, for it was simply absurd to think the work would not live; and he was absolutely certain of its success. I thought over the matter on my way home, and came to the conclusion that if *Tannhäuser* did indeed win its way, and become really popular, incalculable possibilities might be attained.

At last the time arrived for our second performance. For this I thought I had made due preparation by lessening the importance of the principal part, and lowering my original ideals about some of the more important portions, and I hoped by accentuating certain undoubtedly attractive passages to secure a genuine appreciation of the whole. I was greatly delighted with the scenery which had at last arrived for the Hall of Song in the second act, the beautiful and imposing effect of which cheered us all, for we looked upon it as a good omen. Unfortunately I had to bear the humiliation of seeing the theatre nearly empty. This, more than anything else, sufficed to convince me what the opinion of the public really was in regard to my work. But, if the audience was scanty, the majority, at any rate, consisted of the first friends of my art, and the reception of the piece was very cordial. Mitterwurzer especially aroused the greatest enthusiasm. As for Tichatschek, my anxious friends, Röckel and Heine, thought it necessary to endeavour by every artifice to keep him in a good humour for his part. In order to give practical assistance in making the undoubted obscurity of the last scene clear, my friends had asked several young people, more especially artists, to give vent to torrents of applause at those parts which are not generally regarded by the opera-going public as provoking any demonstration. Strange to say, the outburst of applause thus provoked after the words, ' An angel flies to God's throne for thee, and will make his voice heard; Heinrich, thou art saved,' made the entire situation suddenly clear to the public. At all subsequent productions this continued to be the principal moment for the expression of sympathy on the part of the audience, although it had passed quite unnoticed on the first night. A few days later a third performance took place, but this time before a full house. Schröder-Devrient, depressed at the small share she was able to take in the success of my work, watched the progress of the opera from the small stage box; she informed me that Lüttichau had come to her with a beaming face, saying he thought we had now carried *Tannhäuser* happily through.

And this certainly proved to be the case; we often repeated it in the course of the winter, but noticed that when two performances followed close upon one another, there was not such a rush for the second, from which we concluded that I had not yet gained the approval of the great opera-going public, but only of the more cultured section of the community. Among these real friends of *Tannhäuser* there were many, as I gradually discovered, who as a rule never visited the theatre at all, and least of all the opera. This interest on the part of a totally new public continued to grow in intensity, and expressed itself in a delightful and hitherto unknown manner by a strong sympathy for the author. It was particularly painful to me, on Tichatschek's account, to respond alone to the calls of the audience after almost every act; however, I had at last to submit, as my refusal would only have exposed the vocalist to fresh humiliations, for when he appeared on the stage with his colleagues without me, the loud shouts for me were almost insulting to him. With what genuine eagerness did I wish that the contrary were the case, and that the

excellence of the execution might overshadow the author. The
conviction that I should never attain this with my *Tannhäuser*
in Dresden guided me in all my future undertakings. But, at
all events, in producing *Tannhäuser* in this city I had succeeded
in making at least the cultured public acquainted with my
peculiar tendencies, by stimulating their mental faculties and
stripping the performance of all realistic accessories. I did
not, however, succeed in making these tendencies sufficiently
clear in a dramatic performance, and in such an irresistible
and convincing manner as also to familiarise the uncultivated
taste of the ordinary public with them when they saw them
embodied on the stage.

By enlarging the circle of my acquaintances, and making
interesting friends, I had a good opportunity during the
winter of obtaining further information on this point in a way
that was both instructive and encouraging. My acquaintance
and close intimacy at this time with Dr. Hermann Franck
of Breslau, who had for some time been living quietly in
Dresden, was also very inspiring. He was very comfortably
off, and was one of those men who, by a wide knowledge and
good judgment, combined with considerable gifts as an author,
won an excellent reputation for himself in a large and select
circle of private friends, without, however, making any great
name for himself with the public. He endeavoured to use his
knowledge and abilities for the general good, and was induced
by Brockhaus to edit the *Deutsche Allgemeine Zeitung* when it
first started. This paper had been founded by Brockhaus
some years earlier. However, after editing it for a year,
Franck resigned this post, and from that time forward it was
only on the very rarest occasions that he could be persuaded
to touch anything connected with journalism. His curt and
spirited remarks about his experiences in connection with the
Deutsche Allgemeine Zeitung justified his disinclination to
engage in any work connected with the public press. My appreciation was all the greater, therefore, when, without any
persuasion on my part, he wrote a full report on *Tannhäuser*
for the *Augsburger Allgemeine Zeitung*. This appeared in
October or November, 1845, in a supplement to that paper,
and although it contained the first account of a work which

has since been so widely discussed, I regard it, after mature consideration, as the most far-reaching and exhaustive that has ever been written. By this means my name figured for the first time in the great European political paper, whose columns, in consequence of a remarkable change of front which was to the interests of the proprietors, have since been open to any one who wished to make merry at the expense of me or my work.

The point which particularly attracted me in Dr. Franck was the delicate and tactful art he displayed in his criticism and his methods of discussion. There was something distinguished about them that was not so much the outcome of rank and social position as of genuine world-wide culture.

The delicate coldness and reserve of his manner charmed rather than repelled me, as it was a characteristic I had not met with hitherto. When I found him expressing himself with some reserve in regard to persons who enjoyed a reputation to which I did not think they were always entitled, I was very pleased to see during my intercourse with him that in many ways I exercised a decisive influence over his opinion. Even at that time I did not care to let it pass unchallenged when people evaded the close analysis of the work of this or that celebrity, by referring in terms of eulogy to his ' good-nature.' I even cornered my worldly wise friend on this point, when a few years later I had the satisfaction of getting from him a very concise explanation of Meyerbeer's ' good-nature,' of which he had once spoken, and he recalled with a smile the extraordinary questions I had put to him at the time. He was, however, quite alarmed when I gave him a very lucid explanation of the disinterestedness and conspicuous altruism of Mendelssohn in the service of art, of which he had spoken enthusiastically. In a conversation about Mendelssohn he had remarked how delightful it was to find a man able to make real sacrifices in order to free himself from a false position that was of no service to art. It was assuredly a grand thing, he said, to have renounced a good salary of nine thousand marks as general musical conductor in Berlin, and to have retired to Leipzig as a simple conductor at the Gewandhaus concerts, and Mendelssohn was much to be admired on that

account. Just at that time I happened to be in a position to
give some correct details regarding this apparent sacrifice on
the part of Mendelssohn, because when I had made a serious
proposal to our general management about increasing the
salaries of several of the poorer members of the orchestra,
Lüttichau was requested to inform me that, according to the
King's latest commands, the expenditure on the state bands
was to be so restricted that for the present the poorer chamber
musicians could not claim any consideration, for Herr von
Falkenstein, the governor of the Leipzig district, who was a
passionate admirer of Mendelssohn's, had gone so far as to
influence the King to appoint the latter secret conductor,
with a secret salary of six thousand marks. This sum,
together with the salary of three thousand marks openly granted
him by the management of the Leipzig Gewandhaus, would
amply compensate him for the position he had renounced in
Berlin, and he had consequently consented to migrate to Leipzig.
This large grant had, for decency's sake, to be kept secret by
the board administering the band funds, not only because it
was detrimental to the interests of the institution, but also
because it might give offence to those who were acting as
conductors at a lower salary, if they knew another man had
been appointed to a sinecure. From these circumstances Mendelssohn derived not only the advantage of having the grant
kept a secret, but also the satisfaction of allowing his friends
to applaud him as a model of self-sacrificing zeal for going
to Leipzig; which they could easily do, although they knew
him to be in a good financial position. When I explained this
to Franck, he was astonished, and admitted it was one of the
strangest cases he had ever come across in connection with
undeserved fame.

We soon arrived at a mutual understanding in our views
about many other artistic celebrities with whom we came in
contact at that time in Dresden. This was a simple matter
in the case of Ferdinand Hiller, who was regarded as the chief
of the 'good-natured' ones. Regarding the more famous
painters of the so-called Düsseldorf School, whom I met frequently through the medium of *Tannhäuser,* it was not quite
so easy to come to a conclusion, as I was to a great extent

influenced by the fame attached to their well-known names;
but here again Franck startled me with opportune and conclusive reasons for disappointment. When it was a question
between Bendemann and Hübner, it seemed to me that Hübner
might very well be sacrificed to Bendemann. The latter, who
had only just completed the frescoes for one of the reception-
rooms at the royal palace, and had been rewarded by his
friends with a banquet, appeared to me to have the right to be
honoured as a great master. I was very much astonished,
therefore, when Franck calmly pitied the King of Saxony
for having had his room 'bedaubed' by Bendemann! Nevertheless, there was no denying that these people were 'good-
natured.' My intercourse with them became more frequent,
and at all events offered me opportunities of mixing with the
more cultured artistic society, in distinction to the theatrical
circles with which I had usually associated; yet I never derived from it the least enthusiasm or inspiration. The latter,
however, appears to have been Hiller's main object, and that
winter he organised a sort of social circle which held weekly
meetings at the home of one or the other of its members in
turn. Reinecke, who was both painter and poet, joined this
society, together with Hübner and Bendemann, and had the
bad fortune to write the new text for an opera for Hiller,
the fate of which I will describe later on. Robert Schumann,
the musician, who was also in Dresden at this time, and was
busy working out on opera, which eventually developed into
Genovefa, made advances to Hiller and myself. I had already
known Schumann in Leipzig, and we had both entered upon
our musical careers at about the same time. I had also occasionally sent small contributions to the *Neue Zeitschrift für Musik*,
of which he had formerly been editor, and more recently a longer
one from Paris on Rossini's *Stabat Mater*. He had been asked
to conduct his *Paradies und Peri* at a concert to be given at
the theatre; but his peculiar awkwardness in conducting on
that occasion aroused my sympathy for the conscientious and
energetic musician whose work made so strong an appeal
to me, and a kindly and friendly confidence soon grew up
between us. After a performance of *Tannhäuser*, at which
he was present, he called on me one morning and declared

himself fully and decidedly in favour of my work. The only objection he had to make was that the *stretta* of the second finale was too abrupt, a criticism which proved his keenness of perception; and I was able to show him, by the score, how I had been compelled, much against my inclination, to curtail the opera, and thereby create the position to which he had taken exception. We often met when out walking and, as far as it was possible with a person so sparing of words, we exchanged views on matters of musical interest. He was looking forward to the production, under my baton, of Beethoven's Ninth Symphony, as he had attended the performances at Leipzig, and had been very much disappointed by Mendelssohn's conducting, which had quite misunderstood the time of the first movement. Otherwise his society did not inspire me particularly, and the fact that he was too conservative to benefit by my views was soon shown, more especially in his conception of the poem of *Genovefa*. It was clear that my example had only made a very transient impression on him, only just enough, in fact, to make him think it advisable to write the text of an opera himself. He afterwards invited me to hear him read his libretto, which was a combination of the styles of Hebbel and Tieck. When, however, out of a genuine desire for the success of his work, about which I had serious misgivings, I called his attention to some grave defects in it, and suggested the necessary alterations, I realised how matters stood with this extraordinary person: he simply wanted me to be swayed by himself, but deeply resented any interference with the product of his own ideals, so that thenceforward I let matters alone.

In the following winter, our circle, thanks to the assiduity of Hiller, was considerably widened, and it now became a sort of club whose object was to meet freely every week in a room at Engel's restaurant at the Postplatz. Just about this time the famous J. Schnorr of Munich was appointed director of the museums in Dresden, and we entertained him at a banquet. I had already seen some of his large and well-executed cartoons, which made a deep impression on me, not only on account of their dimensions, but also by reason of the events they depicted from old German history, in which

I was at that time particularly interested. It was through Schnorr that I now became acquainted with the 'Munich School' of which he was the master. My heart overflowed when I thought what it meant for Dresden, if such giants of German art were to shake hands there. I was much struck by Schnorr's appearance and conversation, and I could not reconcile his whining pedagogic manner with his mighty cartoons; however, I thought it a great stroke of luck when he also took to frequenting Engel's restaurant on Saturdays. He was well versed in the old German legends, and I was delighted when they formed the topic of conversation. The famous sculptor, Hänel, used also to attend these meetings, and his marvellous talent inspired me with the greatest respect, although I was not an authority on his work, and could only judge of it by my own feelings. I soon saw that his bearing and manner were affected; he was very fond of expressing his opinion and judgment on questions of art, and I was not in a position to decide whether they were reliable or otherwise. In fact, it often occurred to me that I was listening to a Philistine swaggerer. It was only when my old friend Pecht, who had also settled in Dresden for a time, clearly and emphatically explained to me Hänel's standing as an artist, that I conquered all my secret doubts, and tried to find some pleasure in his works. Rietschel, who was also a member of our society, was the very antithesis of Hänel. I often found it difficult to believe that the pale delicate man, with the whining nervous way of expressing himself, was really a sculptor; but as similar peculiarities in Schnorr did not prevent me from recognising him as a marvellous painter, this helped me to make friends with Rietschel, as he was quite free from affectation, and had a warm sympathetic soul that drew me ever closer to him. I also remember hearing from him a very enthusiastic appreciation of my personality as a conductor. In spite, however, of being fellow-members of our versatile art club, we never attained a footing of real comradeship, for, after all, no one thought much of anybody else's talents. For instance, Hiller had arranged some orchestral concerts, and to commemorate them he was entertained at the usual banquet by his friends, when his services were gratefully acknowledged with due rhetorical pathos. Yet I never found, in my private intercourse with Hiller's friends, the least enthusiasm in regard to his work; on the contrary, I only noticed expressions of doubt and apprehensive shrugs.

These fêted concerts soon came to an end. At our social evenings we never discussed the works of the masters who were present; they were not even mentioned, and it was soon evident that none of the members knew what to talk about. Semper was the only man who, in his extraordinary fashion, often so enlivened our entertainments that Rietschel, inwardly sympathetic, though painfully startled, would heartily complain against the unrestrained outbursts that led not infrequently to hot discussions between Semper and myself. Strange to say, we two always seemed to start from the hypothesis that we were antagonists, for he insisted upon regarding me as the representative of mediæval Catholicism, which he often attacked with real fury. I eventually succeeded in persuading him that my studies and inclinations had always led me to German antiquity, and to the discovery of ideals in the early Teutonic myths. When we came to paganism, and I expressed my enthusiasm for the genuine heathen legends, he became quite a different being, and a deep and growing interest now began to unite us in such a way that it quite isolated us from the rest of the company. It was, however, impossible ever to settle anything without a heated argument, not only because Semper had a peculiar habit of contradicting everything flatly, but also because he knew his views were opposed to those of the entire company. His paradoxical assertions, which were apparently only intended to stir up strife, soon made me realise, beyond any doubt, that he was the only one present who was passionately in earnest about everything he said, whereas all the others were quite content to let the matter drop when convenient. A man of the latter type was Gutzkow, who was often with us; he had been summoned to Dresden by the general management of our court theatre, to act in the capacity of dramatist and adapter of plays. Several of his pieces had recently met with great success: *Zopf und Schwert, Das Urbild des Tartüffe,* and *Uriel Acosta,* shed an unexpected lustre on the latest dramatic

repertoire, and it seemed as though the advent of Gutzkow
would inaugurate a new era of glory for the Dresden theatre,
where my operas had also been first produced. The good
intentions of the management were certainly undeniable. My
only regret on that occasion was that the hopes my old friend
Laube entertained of being summoned to Dresden to fill that
post were unrealised. He also had thrown himself enthusiastically into the work of dramatic literature. Even in Paris
I had noticed the eagerness with which he used to study the
technique of dramatic composition, especially that of Scribe,
in the hope of acquiring the skill of that writer, without which,
as he soon discovered, no poetical drama in German could be
successful. He maintained that he had thoroughly mastered
this style in his comedy, *Rococo*, and he cherished the conviction that he could work up any imaginable material into an
effective stage play.

At the same time, he was very careful to show equal skill
in the selection of his material. In my opinion this theory of
his was a complete failure, as his only successful pieces were
those in which popular interest was excited by catch-phrases.
This interest was always more or less associated with the
politics of the day, and generally involved some obvious dia-
tribes about ' German unity' and ' German Liberalism.' As
this important stimulus was first applied by way of experiment to the subscribers to our Residenz Theater, and afterwards
to the German public generally, it had, as I have already said,
to be worked out with the consummate skill which, presumably,
could only be learned from modern French writers of comic
opera.

I was very glad to see the result of this study in Laube's
plays, more especially as when he visited us in Dresden, which
he often did on the occasion of a new production, he admitted his
indebtedness with modest candour, and was far from pretending to be a real poet. Moreover, he displayed great skill and
an almost fiery zeal, not only in the preparation of his pieces,
but also in their production, so that the offer of a post at
Dresden, the hope of which had been held out to him, would
at least, from a practical point of view, have been a benefit
to the theatre. Finally, however, the choice fell on his rival

Gutzkow, in spite of his obvious unsuitability for the practical
work of dramatist. It was evident that even as regards his
successful plays his triumph was mainly due to his literary
skill, because these effective plays were immediately followed
by wearisome productions which made us realise, to our astonishment, that he himself could not have been aware of the skill
he had previously displayed. It was, however, precisely these
abstract qualities of the genuine man of letters which, in the
eyes of many, cast over him the halo of literary greatness; and
when Lüttichau, thinking more of a showy reputation than of
permanent benefit to his theatre, decided to give the preference to Gutzkow, he thought his choice would give a special
impetus to the cause of higher culture. To me the appointment of Gutzkow as the director of dramatic art at the theatre
was peculiarly objectionable, as it was not long before I was
convinced of his utter incompetence for the task, and it was
probably owing to the frankness with which I expressed my
opinion to Lüttichau that our subsequent estrangement was
originally due. I had to complain bitterly of the want of judgment and the levity of those who so recklessly selected men to
fill the posts of managers and conductors in such precious
institutions of art as the German royal theatres. To obviate
the failure I felt convinced must follow on this important
appointment, I made a special request that Gutzkow should
not be allowed to interfere in the management of the opera;
he readily yielded, and thus spared himself great humiliation.
This action, however, created a feeling of mistrust between us,
though I was quite ready to remove this as far as possible
by coming into personal contact with him whenever opportunity offered on those evenings when the artists used to
gather at the club, as already described. I would gladly have
made this strange man, whose head was anxiously bowed down
on his breast, relax and unburden himself in his conversations
with me, but I was unsuccessful, on account of his constant
reserve and suspicion, and his studied aloofness. An opportunity arose for a discussion between us when he wanted the
orchestra to take a melodramatic part (which they afterwards
did) in a certain scene of his *Uriel Acosta*, where the hero had
to recant his alleged heresy. The orchestra had to execute

the soft tremolo for a given time on certain chords, but when I heard the performance it appeared to me absurd, and equally derogatory both for the music and the drama.

On one of these evenings I tried to come to an understanding with Gutzkow concerning this, and the employment of music generally as a melodramatic auxiliary to the drama, and I discussed my views on the subject in accordance with the highest principles I had conceived. He met all the chief points of my discussion with a nervous distrustful silence, but finally explained that I really went too far in the significance which I claimed for music, and that he failed to understand how music would be degraded if it were applied more sparingly to the drama, seeing that the claims of verse were often treated with much less respect when it was used as a mere accessory to operatic music. To put it practically, in fact, it would be advisable for the librettist not to be too dainty in this matter; it was n't possible always to give the actor a brilliant exit; at the same time, however, nothing could be more painful than when the chief performer made his exit without any applause. In such cases a little distracting noise in the orchestra really supplied a happy diversion. This I actually heard Gutzkow say; moreover, I saw that he really meant it! After this I felt I had done with him.

It was not long before I had equally little to do with all the painters, musicians, and other zealots in art belonging to our society. At the same time, however, I came into closer contact with Berthold Auerbach. With great enthusiasm, Alwine Frommann had already drawn my attention to Auerbach's *Pastoral Stories*. The account she gave of these modest works (for that is how she characterised them) sounded quite attractive. She said that they had had the same refreshing effect on her circle of friends in Berlin as that produced by opening the window of a scented boudoir (to which she compared the literature they had hitherto been used to), and letting in the fresh air of the woods. After that I read the *Pastoral Stories of the Black Forest,* which had so quickly become famous, and I, too, was strongly attracted by the contents and tone of these realistic anecdotes about the life of the people in a locality which it was easy enough to identify

from the vivid descriptions. As at this time Dresden seemed
to be becoming ever more and more the rendezvous for the
lights of our literary and artistic world, Auerbach also reconciled himself to taking up his quarters in this city; and for
quite a long time lived with his friend Hiller, who thus again
had a celebrity at his side of equal standing with himself. The
short, sturdy Jewish peasant boy, as he was placed to represent himself to be, made a very agreeable impression. It was
only later that I understood the significance of his green
jacket, and above all of his green hunting-cap, which made
him look exactly what the author of *Swabian Pastoral Stories*
ought to look like, and this significance was anything but a
naïve one. The Swiss poet, Gottfried Keller, once told me
that, when Auerbach was in Zürich, and he had decided on
taking him up, he (Auerbach) had drawn his attention to the
best way in which to introduce one's literary effusions to the
public, and to make money, and he advised him, above all
things, to get a coat and cap like his own, for being, as he said,
like himself, neither handsome nor well grown, it would be
far better deliberately to make himself look rough and queer;
so saying, he placed his cap on his head in such a way as to
look a little rakish. For the time being, I perceived no real
affectation in Auerbach; he had assimilated so much of the
tone and ways of the people, and had done this so happily,
that, in any case, one could not help asking oneself why, with
these delightful qualities, he should move with such tremendous ease in spheres that seemed absolutely antagonistic. At
all events, he always seemed in his true element even in those
circles which really seemed most opposed to his assumed
character; there he stood in his green coat, keen, sensitive,
and natural, surrounded by the distinguished society that
flattered him; and he loved to show letters he had received
from the Grand Duke of Weimar and his answers to them, all
the time looking at things from the standpoint of the Swabian
peasant nature which suited him so admirably.

What especially attracted me to him was the fact that he
was the first Jew I ever met with whom one could discuss
Judaism with absolute freedom. He even seemed particularly
desirous of removing, in his agreeable manner, all prejudice

on this score; and it was really touching to hear him speak
of his boyhood, and declare that he was perhaps the only
German who had read Klopstock's *Messiah* all through. Having one day become absorbed in this work, which he read
secretly in his cottage home, he had played the truant from
school, and when he finally arrived too late at the school-house,
his teacher angrily exclaimed: 'You confounded Jew-boy,
where have you been? Lending money again?' Such experiences had only made him feel pensive and melancholy, but not
bitter, and he had even been inspired with real compassion
for the coarseness of his tormentors. These were traits in his
character which drew me very strongly to him. As time
went on, however, it seemed to me a serious matter that he
could not get away from the atmosphere of these ideas, for I
began to feel that the universe contained no other problem
for him than the elucidation of the Jewish question. One day,
therefore, I protested as good-naturedly and confidentially as
I could, and advised him to let the whole problem of Judaism
drop, as there were, after all, many other standpoints from
which the world might be criticised. Strange to say, he
thereupon not only lost his ingeniousness, but also fell to
whining in an ecstatic fashion, which did not seem to me very
genuine, and assured me that that would be an impossibility
for him, as there was still so much in Judaism which needed
his whole sympathy. I could not help recalling the surprising
anguish which he had manifested on this occasion, when I
learned, in the course of time, that he had repeatedly arranged
Jewish marriages, concerning the happy result of which I heard
nothing, save that he had, by this means, made quite a fortune.
When, several years afterwards, I again saw him in Zürich, I
observed that his appearance had unfortunately changed in a
manner quite disconcerting: he looked really extraordinarily
common and dirty; his former refreshing liveliness had turned
into the usual Jewish restlessness, and it was easy to see that
all he said was uttered as if he regretted that his words could
not be turned to better account in a newspaper article.

During his time in Dresden, however, Auerbach's warm
agreement with my artistic projects really did me good, even
though it may have been only from his Semitic and Swabian

standpoint; so did the novelty of the experience I was at that time undergoing as an artist, in meeting with ever-increasing regard and recognition among people of note, of acknowledged importance and of exceptional culture. If, after the success obtained by *Rienzi,* I still remained with the circle of the real theatrical world, the greater success following on *Tannhäuser* certainly brought me into contact with such people as I have mentioned above, who, though to be sure they considerably enlarged my ideas, at the same time impressed me very unfavourably with what was apparently the pinnacle of the artistic life of the period. At any rate, I felt neither rewarded nor, fortunately, even diverted by the acquaintances I won by the first performance of my *Tannhäuser* that winter. On the contrary, I felt an irresistible desire to withdraw into my shell and leave these gay surroundings into which, strangely enough, I had been introduced at the instigation of Hiller, whom I soon recognised as being a nonentity. I felt I must quickly compose something, as this was the only means of ridding myself of all the disturbing and painful excitement *Tannhäuser* had produced in me.

Only a few weeks after the first performances I had worked out the whole of the *Lohengrin* text. In November I had already read this poem to my intimate friends, and soon afterwards to the Hiller set. It was praised, and pronounced 'effective.' Schumann also thoroughly approved of it, although he did not understand the musical form in which I wished to carry it out, as he saw no resemblance in it to the old methods of writing individual solos for the various artists. I then had some fun in reading different parts of my work to him in the form of arias and cavatinas, after which he laughingly declared himself satisfied.

Serious reflection, however, aroused my gravest doubts as to the tragic character of the material itself, and to these doubts I had been led, in a manner both sensible and tactful, by Franck. He thought it offensive to effect Elsa's punishment through Lohengrin's departure; for although he understood that the characteristics of the legend were expressed precisely by this highly poetical feature, he was doubtful as to whether it did full justice to the demands of tragic feeling in its relation to dramatic realism. He would have preferred to see Lohengrin die before our eyes owing to Elsa's loving treachery. As, however, this did not seem feasible, he would have liked to see Lohengrin spell-bound by some powerful motive, and prevented from getting away. Although, of course, I would not agree to any of these suggestions, I went so far as to consider whether I could not do away with the cruel separation, and still retain the incident of Lohengrin's departure, which was essential. I then sought for a means of letting Elsa go away with Lohengrin, as a form of penance which would withdraw her also from the world. This seemed more promising to my talented friend. While I was still very doubtful about all this, I gave my poem to Frau von Lüttichau, so that she might peruse it, and criticise the point raised by Franck. In a little letter, in which she expressed her pleasure at my poem, she wrote briefly, but very decidedly, on the knotty question, and declared that Franck must be devoid of all poetry if he did not understand that it was exactly in the way I had chosen, and in no other, that Lohengrin must depart. I felt as if a load had fallen from my heart. In triumph I showed the letter to Franck, who, much abashed, and by way of excusing himself, opened a correspondence with Frau von Lüttichau, which certainly cannot have been lacking in interest, though I was never able to see any of it. In any case, the upshot of it was that *Lohengrin* remained as I had originally conceived it. Curiously enough, some time later, I had a similar experience with regard to the same subject, which again put me in a temporary state of uncertainty. When Adolf Stahr gravely raised the same objection to the solution of the *Lohengrin* question, I was really taken aback by the uniformity of opinion; and as, owing to some excitement, I was just then no longer in the same mood as when I composed *Lohengrin,* I was foolish enough to write a hurried letter to Stahr in which, with but a few slight reservations, I declared him to be right. I did not know that, by this, I was causing real grief to Liszt, who was now in the same position with regard to Stahr as Frau von Lüttichau had been with regard to Franck. Fortunately, however, the displeasure of my great friend at my supposed treachery to myself did not last long; for, without

having got wind of the trouble I had caused him, and thanks to
the torture I myself was going through, I came to the proper
decision in a few days, and, as clear as daylight, I saw what
madness it had been. I was therefore able to rejoice Liszt
with the following laconical protest which I sent him from my
Swiss resort: ' Stahr is wrong, and Lohengrin is right.'

For the present I remained occupied with the revision of
my poem, for there could be no question of planning the music
to it just now. That peaceful and harmonious state of mind
which is so favourable to creative work, and always so necessary to me for composing, I now had to secure with the greatest
difficulty, for it was one of the things I always had the
hardest struggle to obtain. All the experiences connected with
the performance of *Tannhäuser* having filled me with true
despair as to the whole future of my artistic operations, I saw
it was hopeless to think of its production being extended to
other German theatres — for I had not been able to achieve
this end even with the successful *Rienzi*. It was perfectly
obvious, therefore, that my work would, at the utmost, be
conceded a permanent place in the Dresden repertoire. As
the result of all this, my pecuniary affairs, which have already
been described, had got into such a serious state that a catastrophe seemed inevitable. While I was preparing to meet
this in the best way I could, I tried to stupefy myself, on the
one hand, by plunging into the study of history, mythology,
and literature, which were becoming ever dearer and dearer
to me, and on the other by working incessantly at my artistic
enterprises. As regards the former, I was chiefly interested
in the German Middle Ages, and tried to make myself familiar
with every point relative to this period. Although I could not
set about this task with philological precision, I proceeded
with such earnestness that I studied the German records,
published by Grimm, for instance, with the greatest interest.
As I could not put the results of such studies immediately into
my scenes, there were many who could not understand why,
as an operatic composer, I should waste my time on such
barren work. Different people remarked later on, that the
personality of Lohengrin had a charm quite its own; but this
was ascribed to the happy selection of the subject, and I was

specially praised for choosing it. Material from the German Middle Ages, and later on, subjects from Scandinavian antiquity, were therefore looked forward to by many, and, in the end, they were astonished that I gave them no adequate result of all my labours. Perhaps it will be of help to them if I now tell them to take the old records and such works to their aid. I forgot at that time to call Hiller's attention to my documents, and with great pride he seized upon a subject out of the history of the Hohenstaufen. As, however, he had no success with his work, he may perhaps think I was a little artful for not having spoken to him of the old records.

Concerning my other duties, my chief undertaking for this winter consisted in an exceptionally carefully prepared performance of Beethoven's Ninth Symphony, which took place in the spring on Palm Sunday. This performance involved many a struggle, besides a host of experiences which were destined to exercise a strong influence over my further development. Roughly they were as follows: the royal orchestra had only one opportunity a year of showing their powers independently in a musical performance outside the Opera or the church. For the benefit of the Pension Fund for their widows and orphans, the old so-called Opera House was given up to a big performance originally only intended for oratorios. Ultimately, in order to make it more attractive, a symphony was always added to the oratorio; and, as already mentioned, I had performed on such occasions, once the Pastoral Symphony, and later Haydn's *Creation*. The latter was a great joy to me, and it was on this occasion that I first made its acquaintance. As we two conductors had stipulated for alternate performances, the Symphony on Palm Sunday of the year 1846 fell to my lot. I had a great longing for the Ninth Symphony, and I was led to the choice of this work by the fact that it was almost unknown in Dresden. When the directors of the orchestra, who were the trustees of the Pension Fund, and who had to promote its increase, got to know of this, such a fright seized them that they interviewed the general director, Lüttichau, and begged him, by virtue of his high authority, to dissuade me from carrying out my intention. They gave as a reason for this request, that the Pension Fund would surely

suffer through the choice of this symphony, as the work was in
ill-repute in the place, and would certainly keep people from
going to the concert. The symphony had been performed
many years before by Reissiger at a charity concert, and, as
the conductor himself honestly admitted, had been an absolute
failure. Now it needed my whole ardour, and all the eloquence
I could command, to prevail over the doubts of our principal.
With the orchestral directors, however, there was nothing for
me to do but quarrel, as I heard that they were complaining all
over the town about my indiscretion. In order to add shame
to their trouble, I made up my mind to prepare the public in
such a way for the performance, upon which I had resolved,
and for the work itself, that at least the sensation caused would
lead to a full hall and thus, in a very favourable manner,
guarantee satisfactory returns, and contradict their belief
that the fund was menaced. Thus the Ninth Symphony had,
in every conceivable way, become for me a point of honour,
for the success of which I had to exercise all my powers to the
utmost. The committee had misgivings regarding the outlay
needed for procuring the orchestral parts, so I borrowed them
from the Leipzig Concert Society.

Imagine my feelings, however, on now seeing for the first
time since my earliest boyhood the mysterious pages of this
score, which I studied conscientiously! In those days the
sight of these same pages had filled me with the most mystic
reveries, and I had stayed up for nights together to copy them
out. Just as at the time of my uncertainty in Paris, on hearing
the rehearsal of the first three movements performed by the
incomparable orchestra of the Conservatoire, I had been
carried back through years of error and doubt to be placed in
marvellous touch with my earliest days, while all my inmost
aspirations had been fruitfully stimulated in a new direction,
so now in the same way the memory of that music was secretly
awakened in me as I again saw before my own eyes that which
in those early days had likewise been only a mysterious vision.
I had by this time experienced much which, in the depths
of my soul, drove me almost unconsciously to a process of
summing-up, to an almost despairing inquiry concerning my
fate. What I dared not acknowledge to myself was the fact

of the absolute insecurity of my existence both from the artistic and financial point of view; for I saw that I was a stranger to my own mode of life as well as to my profession, and I had no prospects whatsoever. This despair, which I tried to conceal from my friends, was now converted into genuine exaltation, thanks entirely to the Ninth Symphony. It is not likely that the heart of a disciple has ever been filled with such keen rapture over the work of a master, as mine was at the first movement of this symphony. If any one had come upon me unexpectedly while I had the open score before me, and had seen me convulsed with sobs and tears as I went through the work in order to consider the best manner of rendering it, he would certainly have asked with astonishment if this were really fitting behaviour for the Conductor Royal of Saxony! Fortunately, on such occasions I was spared the visits of our orchestra directors, and their worthy conductor Reissiger, and even those of F. Hiller, who was so versed in classical music.

In the first place I drew up a programme, for which the book of words for the chorus — always ordered according to custom — furnished me with a good pretext. I did this in order to provide a guide to the simple understanding of the work, and thereby hoped to appeal not to the critical judgment, but solely to the feelings, of the audience. This programme, in the framing of which some of the chief passages in Goethe's *Faust* were exceedingly helpful to me, was very well received, not only on that occasion in Dresden, but later on in other places. Besides this, I made use of the Dresden *Anzeiger,* by writing all kinds of short and enthusiastic anonymous paragraphs, in order to whet the public taste for a work which hitherto had been in ill-repute in Dresden.

Not only did these purely extraneous exertions succeed in making the receipts of that year by far exceed any that had been taken theretofore, but the orchestra directors themselves, during the remaining years of my stay in Dresden, made a point of ensuring similarly large profits by repeated performances of the celebrated symphony. Concerning the artistic side of the performance, I aimed at making the orchestra give as expressive a rendering as possible, and to this end made all kinds of notes, myself, in the various parts, so as to make quite sure that their interpretation would be as clear and as coloured as could be desired. It was principally the custom which existed then of doubling the wind instruments, that led me to a most careful consideration of the advantages this system presented, for, in performances on a large scale, the following somewhat crude rule prevailed: all those passages marked *piano* were executed by a single set of instruments, while those marked *forte* were carried out by a duplicated set. As an instance of the way in which I took care to ensure an intelligible rendering by this means, I might point to a certain passage in the second movement of the symphony, where the whole of the string instruments play the principal and rhythmical figure in C major for the first time; it is written in triple octaves, which play uninterruptedly in unison and, to a certain degree, serve as an accompaniment to the second theme, which is only performed by feeble wood instruments. As *fortissimo* is indicated alike for the whole orchestra, the result in every imaginable rendering must be that the melody for the wood instruments not only completely disappears, but cannot even be heard through the strings, which, after all, are only accompanying. Now, as I never carried my piety to the extent of taking directions absolutely literally, rather than sacrifice the effect really intended by the master to the erroneous indications given, I made the strings play only moderately loudly instead of real *fortissimo,* up to the point where they alternate with the wind instruments in taking up the continuation of the new theme: thus the motive, rendered as it was as loudly as possible by a double set of wind instruments, was, I believe for the first time since the existence of the symphony, heard with real distinctness. I proceeded in this manner throughout, in order to guarantee the greatest exactitude in the dynamical effects of the orchestra. There was nothing, however difficult, which was allowed to be performed in such a way as not to arouse the feelings of the audience in a particular manner. For example, many brains had been puzzled by the *Fugato* in $\frac{6}{8}$ time which comes after the chorus, *Froh wie seine Sonnen fliegen,* in the movement of the finale marked *alla marcia.* In view of the preceding inspiriting verses, which seemed to be preparing for combat and victory, I conceived this *Fugato* really as a glad but earnest war-song, and I took it at a continuously fiery tempo, and with the utmost vigour. The day following the first performance I had the satisfaction of receiving a visit from the musical director Anacker of Freiburg, who came to tell me somewhat penitently, that though until then he had been one of my antagonists, since the performance of the symphony he certainly reckoned himself among my friends. What had absolutely overwhelmed him, he said, was precisely my conception and interpretation of the *Fugato.* Furthermore, I devoted special attention to that extraordinary passage, resembling a recitative for the 'cellos and basses, which comes at the beginning of the last movement, and which had once caused my old friend Pohlenz such great humiliation in Leipzig. Thanks to the exceptional excellence of our bass players, I felt certain of attaining to absolute perfection in this passage. After twelve special rehearsals of the instruments alone concerned, I succeeded in getting them to perform in a way which sounded not only perfectly free, but which also expressed the most exquisite tenderness and the greatest energy in a thoroughly impressive manner.

From the very beginning of my undertaking I had at once recognised, that the only method of achieving overwhelming popular success with this symphony was to overcome, by some ideal means, the extraordinary difficulties presented by the choral parts. I realised that the demands made by these parts could be met only by a large and enthusiastic body of singers. It was above all necessary, then, to secure a very gcod and large choir; so, besides adding the somewhat feeble Dreissig ' Academy of Singing' to our usual number of members in the theatre chorus, in spite of great difficulties I also enlisted the help of the choir from the Kreuzschule, with its fine boys' voices, and the choir of the Dresden seminary, which had had much practice in church singing. In a way quite my own I now tried to get these three hundred singers, who were frequently united for rehearsals, into a state of genuine ecstasy; for instance, I succeeded in demonstrating to the basses that the celebrated passage *Seid umschlungen, Millionen,* and especially *Brüder, über'm Sternenzelt muss ein guter Vater wohnen,* could not be

sung in an ordinary manner, but must, as it were, be proclaimed
with the greatest rapture. In this I took the lead in a manner
so elated that I really think I literally transported them to a
world of emotion uttery strange to them for a while; and I
did not desist till my voice, which had been heard clearly above
all the others, began to be no longer distinguishable even to
myself, but was drowned, so to speak, in the warm sea of
sound.

It gave me particular pleasure, with Mitterwurzer's co-
operation, to give a most overwhelmingly expressive rendering
of the recitative for baritone: *Freunde, nicht diese Töne.* In
view of its exceptional difficulties this passage might almost be
considered impossible to perform, and yet he executed it in a
way which showed what fruit our mutual interchange of ideas
had borne. I also took care that, by means of the complete
reconstruction of the hall, I should obtain good acoustic conditions for the orchestra, which I had arranged according to
quite a new system of my own. As may be imagined, it was
only with the greatest difficulty that the money for this could
be found; however, I did not give up, and owing to a totally
new construction of the platform, I was able to concentrate the
whole of the orchestra towards the centre, and surround it,
in amphitheatre fashion, by the throng of singers who were
accommodated on seats very considerably raised. This was
not only of great advantage to the powerful effect of the choir,
but it also gave great precision and energy to the finely organised
orchestra in the purely symphonic movements.

Even at the general rehearsal the hall was overcrowded.
Reissiger was guilty of the incredible stupidity of working up
the public mind against the symphony and drawing attention
to Beethoven's very regrettable error. Gade, on the other
hand, who came to visit us from Leipzig, where he was then
conducting the Gewandhaus Concerts, assured me after the
general rehearsal, that he would willingly have paid double
the price of his ticket in order to hear the recitative by the
basses once more; whilst Hiller considered that I had gone
too far in my modification of the tempo. What he meant by this
I learned subsequently when I heard him conducting intricate
orchestral works; but of this I shall have more to say later on.

There was no denying that the performance was, on the whole, a success; in fact, it exceeded all our expectations, and was particularly well received by the non-musical public. Among these I remember the philologist Dr. Köchly, who came to me at the end of the evening and confessed that it was the first time he had been able to follow a symphonic work from beginning to end with intelligent interest. This experience left me with a pleasant feeling of ability and power, and strongly confirmed me in the belief, that if I only desired anything with sufficient earnestness, I was able to achieve it with irresistible and overwhelming success. I now had to consider, however, what the difficulties were, which hitherto had prevented a similarly happy production of my own new conceptions. Beethoven's Ninth Symphony, which was still such a problem to so many, and had, at all events, never attained to popularity, I had been able to make a complete success; yet, as often as it was put on the stage, my *Tannhäuser* taught me that the possibilities of its success had yet to be discovered. How was this to be done? This was and remained the secret question which influenced all my subsequent development.

I dared not, however, indulge at that time in any meditation on this point with the view of arriving at any particular results, for the real significance of my failure, of which I was inwardly convinced, stood absolutely bare before me with all its terrifying lessons. Albeit, I could no longer delay taking even the most disagreeable steps with the view of warding off the catastrophe which menaced my financial position.

I was led to this, thanks to the influence of a ridiculous omen. My agent, the purely nominal publisher of my three operas — *Rienzi,* the *Fliegender Holländer,* and *Tannhäuser* — the eccentric court music publisher, C. F. Meser, invited me one day to the café known as the ' Verderber ' to discuss our money affairs. With great qualms we talked over the possible results of the Annual Easter Fair, and wondered whether they would be tolerably good or altogether bad. I gave him courage, and ordered a bottle of the best Haut-Sauterne. A venerable flask made its appearance; I filled the glasses, and we drank to the good success of the Fair; when suddenly we both yelled as though we had gone mad, while, with horror, we tried to rid our mouths of the strong Tarragon vinegar with which we had been served by mistake. 'Heavens!' cried Meser, 'nothing could be worse!' 'True enough,' I answered, 'no doubt there is much that will turn to vinegar for us.' My good-humour revealed to me in a flash that I must try some other way of saving myself than by means of the Easter Fair.

Not only was it necessary to refund the capital which had been got together by dint of ever-increasing sacrifices, in order to defray the expenses of the publication of my operas; but, owing to the fact that I had been obliged ultimately to seek aid from the usurers, the rumour of my debts had spread so far abroad, that even those friends who had helped me at the time of my arrival in Dresden were seized with anxiety on my account. At this time I met with a really sad experience at the hands of Madame Schröder-Devrient, who, as the result of her incomprehensible lack of discretion, did much to bring about my final undoing. When I first settled in Dresden, as I have already pointed out, she lent me three thousand marks, not only to help me to discharge my debts, but also to allow me to contribute to the maintenance of my old friend Kietz in Paris. Jealousy of my niece Johanna, and suspicion that I had made her (my niece) come to Dresden in order to make it easier for the general management to dispense with the services of the great artist, had awakened in this otherwise so noble-minded woman the usual feelings of animosity towards me, which are so often met with in the theatrical profession. She had now given up her engagement; she even declared openly that I had been partly instrumental in obtaining her dismissal; and abandoning all friendly regard for me, whereby she deeply wronged me in every respect, she placed the I.O.U. I had given her in the hands of an energetic lawyer, and without further ado this man sued me for the payment of the money. Thus I was forced to make a clean breast of everything to Lüttichau, and to beseech him to intervene for me, and if possible to obtain a royal advance that would enable me to clear my position, which was so seriously compromised.

My principal declared himself willing to support any request I might wish to address to the King on this matter. To this end I had to note down the amount of my debts; but as I

soon discovered that the necessary sum could only be assigned
to me as a loan from the Theatre Pension Fund, at an interest
of five per cent., and that I should moreover have to secure
the capital of the Pension Fund by a life insurance policy,
which would cost me annually three per cent. of the capital
borrowed, I was, for obvious reasons, tempted to leave out of
my petition all those of my debts which were not of a pressing
nature, and for the payment of which I thought I could count
on the receipts which I might finally expect from my publishing enterprises. Nevertheless, the sacrifices I had to make
in order to repay the help offered me increased to such an
extent, that my salary of conductor, in itself very slender,
promised to be materially diminished for some time to come.
I was forced to make the most irksome efforts to gather
together the necessary sum for the life insurance policy, and
was therefore obliged frequently to appeal to Leipzig. In
addition to this, I had to overcome the most appalling doubts
in regard both to my health and to the probable length of my
life, concerning which I fancied I had heard all sorts of
malicious apprehensions expressed by those who had observed
me but casually in the miserable condition which I was in at
that time. My friend Pusinelli, as a doctor who was very
intimate with me, eventually managed to give such satisfactory
information concerning the state of my health, that I succeeded
in insuring my life at the rate of three per cent.

The last of these painful journeys to Leipzig was, at all
events, made under pleasant circumstances owing to a kind
invitation from the old Maestro Louis Spohr. I was particularly pleased over this, because to me it meant nothing less than
an act of reconciliation. As a matter of fact, Sophr had written
to me on one occasion, and had declared that, stimulated by
the success of my *Fliegender Holländer* and his own enjoyment
of it, he had once more decided to take up the career of a
dramatic composer, which of recent years had brought him
such scant success. His last work was an opera — *Die Kreuz-
fahrer* — which he had sent to the Dresden theatre in the course
of the preceding year in the hope, as he himself assured me,
that I would urge on its production. After asking this favour,
he drew my attention to the fact that in this work he had made

an absolutely new departure from his earlier operas, and had kept to the most precise rhythmically dramatic declamation, which had certainly been made all the more easy for him by the ' excellent subject.' Without being actually surprised, my horror was indeed great when, after studying not only the text, but also the score, I discovered that the old maestro had been absolutely mistaken in regard to the account he had given me of his work. The custom in force at that time that the decision concerning the production of works should not, as a rule, rest with one of the conductors alone, did not tend to make me any less fearful of declaring myself emphatically in favour of this work. In addition to this, it was Reissiger, who, as he had often boasted, was an old friend of Spohr's, whose turn it was to select and produce a new work. Unfortunately, as I learned later, the general management had returned Spohr's opera to its author in such a curt manner as to offend him, and he complained bitterly of this to me. Genuinely concerned at this, I had evidently managed to calm and appease him, for the invitation mentioned above was clearly a friendly acknowledgment of my efforts. He wrote that it was very painful for him to have to touch at Dresden on his way to one of the watering-places; as, however, he had a real longing to make my acquaintance, he begged me to meet him in Leipzig, where he was going to stay for a few days.

This meeting with him did not leave me unimpressed. He was a tall, stately man, distinguished in appearance, and of a serious and calm temperament. He gave me to understand, in a touching, almost apologetic manner, that the essence of his education and of his aversion from the new tendencies in music, had its origin in the first impressions he had received on hearing, as a very young boy, Mozart's *Magic Flute,* a work which was quite new at that time, and which had a great influence on his whole life. Regarding my libretto to *Lohengrin,* which I had left behind for him to read, and the general impression which my personal acquaintance had made on him, he expressed himself with almost surprising warmth to my brother-in-law, Hermann Brockhaus, at whose house we had been invited to dine, and where, during the meal, the conversation was most animated. Besides this, we had met at real musical evenings at the conductor Hauptmann's as well as at Mendelssohn's, on which occasion I heard the master take the violin in one of his own quartettes. It was precisely in these circles that I was impressed by the touching and venerable dignity of his absolutely calm demeanour. Later on, I learned from witnesses — for whose testimony, be it said, I cannot vouch — that *Tannhäuser,* when it was performed at Cassel, had caused him so much confusion and pain that he declared he could no longer follow me, and feared that I must be on the wrong road.

In order to recover from all the hardships and cares I had gone through, I now managed to obtain a special favour from the management, in the form of a three months' leave, in which to improve my health in rustic retirement, and to get pure air to breathe while composing some new work. To this end I had chosen a peasant's house in the village of Gross-Graupen, which is half-way between Pillnitz and the border of what is known as ' Saxon Switzerland.' Frequent excursions to the Porsberg, to the adjacent Liebethaler, and to the far distant bastion helped to strengthen my unstrung nerves. While I was first planning the music to *Lohengrin,* I was disturbed incessantly by the echoes of some of the airs in Rossini's *William Tell,* which was the last opera I had had to conduct. At last I happened to hit on an effective means of stopping this annoying obtrusion: during my lonely walks I sang with great emphasis the first theme from the Ninth Symphony, which had also quite lately been revived in my memory. This succeeded! At Pirna, where one can bathe in the river, I was surprised, on one of my almost regular evening constitutionals, to hear the air from the Pilgrim's Chorus out of *Tannhäuser* whistled by some bather, who was invisible to me. This first sign of the possibility of popularising the work, which I had with such difficulty succeeded in getting performed in Dresden, made an impression on me which no similar experience later on has ever been able to surpass. Sometimes I received visits from friends in Dresden, and among them Hans von Bülow, who was then sixteen years old, came accompanied by Lipinsky. This gave me great pleasure, because I had already noticed the interest which he took in me. Generally, however, I had to rely only on my wife's company, and during my long walks I had to be satisfied with my little dog Peps. During this summer holiday, of which a great part of the time had at the beginning to be devoted to the unpleasant task of arranging my business affairs, and also to the improvement of my health, I nevertheless succeded in making a sketch of the music to the whole of the three acts of *Lohengrin,* although this cannot be said to have consisted of anything more than a very hasty outline.

With this much gained, I returned in August to Dresden, and resumed my duties as conductor, which every year seemed to become more and more burdensome to me. Moreover, I immediately plunged once more into the midst of troubles which had only just been temporarily allayed. The business of publishing my operas, on the success of which I still counted as the only means of liberating me from my difficult position, demanded ever-fresh sacrifices if the enterprise were to be made worth while. But as my income was now very much reduced, even the smallest outlays necessarily led me into ever-new and more painful complications; and I once more lost all courage.

On the other hand, I tried to strengthen myself by again working energetically at *Lohengrin.* While doing this, I proceeded in a manner that I have not since repeated. I first of all completed the third act, and in view of the criticism already mentioned of the characters and conclusion of this act, I determined to try to make it the very pivot of the whole opera. I wished to do this, if only for the sake of the musical motive appearing in the story of the Holy Grail; but in other respects the plan struck me as perfectly satisfactory.

Owing to previous suggestions on my part, Gluck's *Iphigenia in Aulis* was to be produced this winter. I felt it my duty to give more care and attention to this work, which interested me particularly on account of its subject, than I had given to the study of the *Armida.* In the first place, I was upset by the translation in which the opera with the Berlin score was presented to us. In order not to be led into false interpretations through the instrumental additions which I considered very badly applied in this score, I wrote for the original edition from Paris. When I had made a thorough revision of the translation, with a view merely to the correctness of declamation, I was spurred on by my increasing interest to revise the score itself. I tried to bring the poem as far as possible into agreement with Euripides' play of the same name, by the elimination of everything which, in deference to French taste, made the relationship between Achilles and Iphigenia one of tender love. The chief alteration of all was to cut out the inevitable marriage at the end. For the sake of the vitality of the drama I tried to join the arias and choruses, which generally followed immediately upon each other without rhyme or reason, by connecting links, prologues and epilogues. In this I did my best, by the use of Gluck's themes, to make the interpolations of a strange composer as unnoticeable as possible. In the third act alone was I obliged to give Iphigenia, as well as Artemis, whom I had myself introduced, recitatives of my own composition. Throughout the rest of the work I revised the whole instrumentation more or less thoroughly, but only with the object of making the existing version produce the effect I desired. It was not till the end of the year that I was able to finish this tremendous task, and I had to postpone the completion of the third act of *Lohengrin*, which I had already begun, until the New Year.

The first thing to claim my attention at the beginning of the year (1847) was the production of *Iphigenia*. I had to act as stage manager in this case, and was even obliged to help the scene-painters and the mechanicians over the smallest details. Owing to the fact that the scenes in this opera were generally strung together somewhat clumsily and without any apparent connection, it was necessary to recast them completely, in order so to animate the representation as to give to the dramatic action the life it lacked. A good deal of this faultiness of construction seemed to me due to the many conventional practices which were prevalent at the Paris Opera in Gluck's time. Mitterwurzer was the only actor in the whole cast who gave me any pleasure. In the rôle of Agamemnon he showed a thorough grasp of that character, and carried out my instructions and suggestions to the letter, so that he succeeded in giving a really splendid and intelligent rendering of the part. The success of the whole performance was far beyond my expectations, and even the directors were so surprised at the exceptional enthusiasm aroused by one of Gluck's operas, that for the second performance they, on their own initiative, had my name put on the programme as ' Reviser.' This at once drew the attention of the critics to this work, and for once they almost did me justice; my treatment of the overture, the only part of the opera which these gentlemen heard rendered in the usual trivial way, was the only thing that they could find fault with. I have discussed and given an accurate account of all that relates to this in a special article on ' Gluck's Overture to *Iphigenia in Aulis,*' and I only wish to add here that the musician who made such strange comments on this occasion was Ferdinand Hiller.

As in former years, the winter meetings of the various artistic elements in Dresden which Hiller had inaugurated, continued to take place; but they now assumed more the character of ' salons ' in Hiller's own house, and it seemed to me intended solely for the purpose of laying the foundations for a general recognition of Hiller's artistic greatness. He had already founded, among the more wealthy patrons of art, the chief of whom was the banker Kaskel, a society for running subscription concerts. As it was impossible for the royal orchestra to be placed at his disposal for this purpose, he had to content himself with members of the town and military bands for his orchestra, and it cannot be denied that, thanks to his perseverance, he attained a praiseworthy result. As he produced many compositions which were still unknown in Dresden, especially from the domain of more modern music, I was often tempted to go to his concerts. His chief bait to the general public, however, seemed to lie in the fact that he presented unknown singers (among whom, unfortunately, Jenny Lind was not to be found) and virtuosos, one of which, Joachim, who was then very young, I became acquainted with.

Hiller's treatment of those works with which I was already well acquainted, showed what his musical power was really worth. The careless and indifferent manner in which he interpreted a Triple Concerto by Sebastian Bach positively astounded me. In the *tempo di minuetto* of the Eighth Symphony of Beethoven, I found that Hiller's rendering was even more astonishing than Reissiger's and Mendelssohn's. I promised to be present at the performance of this symphony if I could rely on his giving a correct rendering of the tempo of the third phrase, which was generally so painfully distorted. He assured me that he thoroughly agreed with me about it, and my disappointment at the performance was all the greater when I found the well-known waltz measure adopted again. When I called him to account about it he excused himself with a smile, saying that he had been seized with a fit of temporary abstraction just at the beginning of the phrase in question, which had made him forget his promise. For inaugurating these concerts, which, as a matter of fact, only lasted for two seasons, Hiller was given a banquet, which I also had much pleasure in attending.

People in these circles were surprised at that time to hear me speak, often with great animation, about Greek literature and history, but never about music. In the course of my reading, which I zealously pursued, and which drew me away from my professional activities to retirement and solitude, I was at that time impelled by my spiritual needs to turn my attention once more to a systematic study of this all-important source of culture, with the object of filling the perceptible gap between my boyhood's knowledge of the eternal elements of human culture and the neglect of this field of learning due to the life I had been obliged to lead. In order to approach the real goal of my desires — the study of Old and Middle High German — in the right frame of mind, I began again from the beginning with Greek antiquity, and was now filled with such overwhelming enthusiasm for this subject that, whenever I entered into conversation, and by hook or by crook had managed to get it round to this theme, I could only speak in terms of the strongest emotion. I occasionally met some one who seemed to listen to what I had to say; on the whole, however, people preferred to talk to me only about the theatre because, since my production of Gluck's *Iphigenia,* they thought themselves justified in thinking I was an authority on this subject. I received special recognition from a man to whom I quite rightly gave the credit of being at least as well versed as myself in the matter. This was Eduard Devrient, who had been forced at that time to resign his position as stage manager-in-chief owing to a plot against him on the part of the actors, headed by his own brother Emil. We were brought into closer sympathy by our conversations in connection with this, which led him into dissertations on the triviality and thorough hopelessness of our whole theatrical life, especially under the ruining influence of ignorant court managers, which could never be overcome.

We were also drawn together by his intelligent understanding of the part I had played in the production of *Iphigenia*, which he compared with the Berlin production of the same piece, that had been utterly condemned by him. He was for a long time the only man with whom I could discuss, seriously and in detail, the real needs of the theatre and the means by which its defects might be remedied. Owing to his longer and more specialised experience, there was much he could tell me and make clear to me; in particular he helped me successfully to overcome the idea that mere literary excellence is enough for the theatre, and confirmed my conviction that the path to true prosperity lay only with the stage itself and with the actors of the drama.

From this time forward, till I left Dresden, my intercourse with Eduard Devrient grew more and more friendly, though his dry nature and obvious limitations as an actor had attracted me but little before. His highly meritorious work, *Die Geschichte der deutschen Schauspielkunst* (' History of German Dramatic Art '), which he finished and published about that time, threw a fresh and instructive light on many problems which exercised my mind, and helped me to master them for the first time.

At last I managed once more to resume my task of composing the third act of *Lohengrin*, which had been interrupted in the middle of the Bridal Scene, and I finished it by the end of the winter. After the repetition, by special request, of the Ninth Symphony at the concert on Palm Sunday had revived me, I tried to find comfort and refreshment for the further progress of my new work by changing my abode, this time without asking permission. The old Marcolini palace, with a very large garden laid out partly in the French style, was situated in an outlying and thinly populated suburb of Dresden.

It had been sold to the town council, and a part of it was to be let. The sculptor, Hänel, whom I had known for a long time, and who had given me as a mark of friendship an ornament in the shape of a perfect plaster cast of one of the basreliefs from Beethoven's monument representing the Ninth Symphony, had taken the large rooms on the ground floor of a side-wing of this palace for his dwelling and studio. At Easter I moved into the spacious apartments above him, the rent of which was extremely low, and found that the large garden planted with glorious trees, which was placed at my disposal, and the pleasant stillness of the whole place, not only provided mental food for the weary artist, but at the same time, by lessening my expenses, improved my straitened finances. We soon settled down quite comfortably in the long row of pleasant rooms without having incurred any unnecessary expense, as Minna was very practical in her arrangements. The only real inconvenience which in the course of time I found our new home possessed, was its inordinate distance from the theatre. This was a great trial to me after fatiguing rehearsals and tiring performances, as the expense of a cab was a serious consideration. But we were favoured by an exceptionally fine summer, which put me in a happy frame of mind, and soon helped to overcome every inconvenience.

At this time I insisted with the utmost firmness on refraining from taking any further share in the management of the theatre, and I had most cogent reasons to bring forth in defence of my conduct. All my endeavours to set in order the wilful chaos which prevailed in the use of the costly artistic materials at the disposal of this royal institution were repeatedly thwarted, merely because I wished to introduce some method into the arrangements. In a carefully written pamphlet which, in addition to my other work, I had compiled during the past winter, I had drawn up a plan for the reorganisation of the orchestra, and had shown how we might increase the productive power of our artistic capital by making a more methodical use of the royal funds intended for its maintenance, and showing greater discretion regarding salaries. This increase in the productive power would raise the artistic spirit as well as improve the economic position of the members of the

orchestra, for I should have liked them at the same time to
form an independent concert society. In such a capacity it
would have been their task to present to the people of Dresden,
in the best possible way, a kind of music which they had
hitherto hardly had the opportunity of enjoying at all. It
would have been possible for such a union, which, as I pointed
out, had so many external circumstances in its favour, to
provide Dresden with a suitable concert-hall. I hear, however,
that such a place is wanting to this day.

With this object in view I entered into close communication
with architects and builders, and the plans were completed,
according to which the scandalous buildings facing a wing of the
renowned prison opposite the Ostra Allee, and consisting of
a shed for the members of the theatre and a public wash-house,
were to be pulled down and replaced by a beautiful building,
which, besides containing a large concert-hall adapted to our
requirements, would also have had other large rooms which
could have been, let out on hire at a profit. The practicality
of these plans was disputed by no one, as even the administrators
of the orchestra's widows' fund saw in them an opportunity for
the safe and advantageous laying out of capital; yet they were
returned to me, after long consideration on the part of the
general management, with thanks and an acknowledgment
of my careful work, and the curt reply that it was thought
better for things to remain as they were.

All my proposals for meeting the useless waste and drain
upon our artistic capital by a more methodical arrangement,
met with the same success in every detail that I suggested.
I had also found out by long experience that every proposal
which had to be discussed and decided upon in the most tiring
committee meetings, as for instance the starting of a repertoire, might at any moment be overthrown and altered for the
worse by the temper of a singer or the plan of a junior business
inspector. I was therefore driven to renounce my wasted
efforts and, after many a stormy discussion and outspoken
expression of my sentiments, I withdrew from taking any
part whatever in any branch of the management, and limited
myself entirely to holding rehearsals and conducting performances of the operas provided for me.

Although my relations with Lüttichau grew more and more strained on this account, for the time being it mattered little whether my conduct pleased him or not, as otherwise my position was one which commanded respect, on account of the ever-increasing popularity of *Tannhäuser* and *Rienzi*, which were presented during the summer to houses packed with distinguished visitors, and were invariably chosen for the gala performances.

By thus going my own way and refusing to be interfered with, I succeeded this summer, amid the delightful and perfect seclusion of my new home, in preserving myself in a frame of mind exceedingly favourable to the completion of my *Lohengrin*. My studies, which, as I have already mentioned, I pursued eagerly at the same time as I was working on my opera, made me feel more light-hearted than I had ever done before. For the first time I now mastered Æschylus with real feeling and understanding. Droysen's eloquent commentaries in particular helped to bring before my imagination the intoxicating effect of the production of an Athenian tragedy, so that I could see the *Oresteia* with my mind's eye, as though it were actually being performed, and its effect upon me was indescribable. Nothing, however, could equal the sublime emotion with which the *Agamemnon* trilogy inspired me, and to the last word of the *Eumenides* I lived in an atmosphere so far removed from the present day that I have never since been really able to reconcile myself with modern literature. My ideas about the whole significance of the drama and of the theatre were, without a doubt, moulded by these impressions. I worked my way through the other tragedians, and finally reached Aristophanes. When I had spent the morning industriously upon the completion of the music for *Lohengrin,* I used to creep into the depths of a thick shrubbery in my part of the garden to get shelter from the summer heat, which was becoming more intense every day. My delight in the comedies of Aristophanes was boundless, when once his *Birds* had plunged me into the full torrent of the genius of this wanton favourite of the Graces, as he used to call himself with conscious daring. Side by side with this poet I read the principal dialogues of Plato, and from the *Symposium* I gained such a deep

insight into the wonderful beauty of Greek life that I felt
myself more truly at home in ancient Athens than in any
conditions which the modern world has to offer.

As I was following out a settled course of self-education,
I did not wish to pursue my way further in the leading-strings
of any literary history, and I consequently turned my attention
from the historical studies, which seemed to be my own peculiar
province, and in which department Droysen's history of
Alexander and the Hellenistic period, as well as Niebuhr and
Gibbon, were of great help to me, and fell back once more
upon my old and trusty guide, Jakob Grimm, for the study
of German aniquity.   In my efforts to master the myths of
Germany more thoroughly than had been possible in my former
perusal of the *Nibelung* and the *Heldenbuch,* Mone's particularly suggestive commentary on this *Heldensage* filled me with
delight, although stricter scholars regarded this work with suspicion on account of the boldness of some of its statements.
By this means I was drawn irresistibly to the northern sagas;
and I now tried, as far as was possible without a fluent knowledge of the Scandinavian languages, to acquaint myself with
the *Edda,* as well as with the prose version which existed of a
considerable portion of the *Heldensage.*

Read by the light of Mone's Commentaries, the *Wolsungasaga*
had a decided influence upon my method of handling this material.   My conceptions as to the inner significance of these
old-world legends, which had been growing for a long time,
gradually gained strength and moulded themselves with the
plastic forms which inspired my later works.

All this was sinking into my mind and slowly maturing,
whilst with unfeigned delight I was finishing the music of the
first two acts of *Lohengrin,* which were now at last completed.
I now succeeded in shutting out the past and building up for
myself a new world of the future, which presented itself with
ever-growing clearness to my mind as the refuge whither I
might retreat from all the miseries of modern opera and theatre
life.   At the same time, my health and temper were settling
down into a mood of almost unclouded serenity, which made
me oblivious for a long time of all the worries of my position.
I used to walk every day up into the neighbouring hills, which

rose from the banks of the Elbe to the Plauenscher Grund. I generally went alone, except for the company of our little dog Peps, and my excursions always resulted in producing a satisfactory number of ideas. At the same time, I found I had developed a capacity, which I had never possessed before, for good-tempered intercourse with the friends and acquaintances who liked to come from time to time to the Marcolini garden to share my simple supper. My visitors used often to find me perched on a high branch of a tree, or on the neck of the Neptune which was the central figure of a large group of statuary in the middle of an old fountain, unfortunately always dry, belonging to the palmy days of the Marcolini estate. I used to enjoy walking with my friends up and down the broad footpath of the drive leading to the real palace, which had been laid especially for Napoleon in the fatal year 1813, when he had fixed his headquarters there.

By August, the last month of summer, I had completely finished the composition of *Lohengrin,* and felt that it was high time for me to have done so, as the needs of my position demanded imperatively that I should give my most serious attention to improving it, and it became a matter of supreme importance for me once more to take steps for having my operas produced in the German theatres.

Even the success of *Tannhäuser* in Dresden, which became more obvious every day, did not attract the smallest notice anywhere else. Berlin was the only place which had any influence in the theatrical world of Germany, and I ought long before to have given my undivided attention to that city. From all I had heard of the special tastes of Friedrich Wilhelm IV., I felt perfectly justified in assuming that he would feel sympathetically inclined towards my later works and conceptions if I could only manage to bring them to his notice in the right light. On this hypothesis I had already thought of dedicating *Tannhäuser* to him, and to gain permission to do so I had to apply to Count Redern, the court musical director. From him I heard that the King could only accept the dedication of works which had actually been performed in his presence, and of which he thus had a personal knowledge. As my *Tannhäuser* had been refused by the managers of the court theatre because it was considered too epic in form, the Count added that if I wished to remain firm in my resolve, there was only one way out of the difficulty, and that was to adapt my opera as far as possible to a military band, and try to bring it to the King's notice on parade. This drove me to determine upon another plan of attack on Berlin.

After this experience I saw that I must open my campaign there with the opera that had won the most decided triumph in Dresden. I therefore obtained an audience of the Queen of Saxony, the sister of the King of Prussia, and begged her to use her influence with her brother to obtain a performance in Berlin by royal command of my *Rienzi*, which was also a favourite with the court of Saxony. This manœuvre was successful, and I soon received a communication from my old friend Küstner to say that the production of *Rienzi* was fixed for a very early date at the Berlin Court Theatre, and at the same time expressing the hope that I would conduct my work in person. As a very handsome author's royalty had been paid by this theatre, at the instigation of Küstner, on the occasion of the production of his old Munich friend Lachner's opera, *Katharina von Cornaro,* I hoped to realise a very substantial improvement in my finances if only the success of *Rienzi* in this city in any degree rivalled that in Dresden. But my chief desire was to make the acquaintance of the King of Prussia, so that I might read him the text of my *Lohengrin,* and arouse his interest in my work. This from various signs I flattered myself was perfectly possible, in which case I intended to beg him to command the first performance of *Lohengrin* to be given at his court theatre.

After my strange experiences as to the way in which my success in Dresden had been kept secret from the rest of Germany, it seemed to me a matter of vital importance to make the future centre of my artistic enterprises the only place which exercised any influence on the outside world, and as such I was forced to regard Berlin. Inspired by the success of my recommendation to the Queen of Prussia, I hoped to gain access to the King himself, which I regarded as a most important step. Full of confidence, and in excellent spirits, I set out for Berlin in September, trusting to a favourable turn of

Fortune's wheel, in the first place for the rehearsals of *Rienzi,* though my interests were no longer centred in this work.

Berlin made the same impression on me as on the occasion of my former visit, when I saw it again after my long absence in Paris. Professor Werder, my friend of the *Fliegender Holländer,* had taken lodgings for me in advance in the renowned Gensdarmeplatz, but when I looked at the view from my windows every day I could not believe that I was in a city which was the very centre of Germany. Soon, however, I was completely absorbed by the cares of the task I had in hand.

I had nothing to complain of with regard to the official preparations for *Rienzi,* but I soon noticed that it was looked upon merely as a conductor's opera, that is to say, all the materials to hand were duly placed at my disposal, but the management had not the slightest intention of doing anything more for me. All the arrangements for my rehearsals were entirely upset as soon as a visit from Jenny Lind was announced, and she occupied the Royal Opera exclusively for some time.

During the delay thus caused I did all I could to attain my main object — an introduction to the King — and for this purpose made use of my former acquaintance with the court musical director, Count Redern. This gentleman received me at once with the greatest affability, invited me to dinner and a soirée, and entered into a hearty discussion with me about the steps necessary for attaining my purpose, in which he promised to do his utmost to help me. I also paid frequent visits to Sans-Souci, in order to pay my respects to the Queen and express my thanks to her. But I never got further than an interview with the ladies-in-waiting, and I was advised to put myself into communication with M. Illaire, the head of the Royal Privy Council. This gentleman seemed to be impressed by the seriousness of my request, and promised to do what he could to further my wish for a personal introduction to the King. He asked what my real object was, and I told him it was to get permission from the King to read my libretto *Lohengrin* to him. On the occasion of one of my oft-repeated visits from Berlin, he asked me whether I did not think it would be advisable to bring a recommendation of my work from Tieck. I was able to tell him that I had already had the pleasure of bringing my case to the notice of the old poet, who lived near Potsdam as a royal pensioner.

I remembered very well that Frau von Lüttichau had sent the themes *Lohengrin* and *Tannhäuser* to her old friend some years ago, when these matters were first mentioned between us. When I called upon Tieck, I was welcomed by him almost as a friend, and I found my long talks with him exceedingly valuable. Although Tieck had perhaps gained a somewhat doubtful reputation for the leniency with which he would give his recommendation for the dramatic works of those who applied to him, yet I was pleased by the genuine disgust with which he spoke of our latest dramatic literature, which was modelling itself on the style of modern French stagecraft, and his complaint at the utter lack of any true poetic feeling in it was heartfelt. He declared himself delighted with my poem of *Lohengrin,* but could not understand how all this was to be set to music without a complete change in the conventional structure of an opera, and on this score he objected to such scenes as that between Ortrud and Frederick at the beginning of the second act. I thought I had roused him to a real enthusiasm when I explained how I proposed to solve these apparent difficulties, and also described my own ideals about musical drama. But the higher I soared the sadder he grew when I had once made known to him my hope of securing the patronage of the King of Prussia for these conceptions, and the working out of my scheme for an ideal drama. He had no doubt that the King would listen to me with the greatest interest, and even seize upon my ideas with warmth, only I must not entertain the smallest hope of any practical result, unless I wished to expose myself to the bitterest disappointment. 'What can you expect from a man who to-day is enthusiastic about Gluck's *Iphigenia in Tauris,* and to-morrow mad about Donizetti's *Lucrezia Borgia?'* he said. Tieck's conversation about these and similar topics was much too entertaining and charming for me to give any serious weight to the bitterness of his views. He gladly promised to recommend my poem, more particularly to Privy Councillor Illaire, and dismissed me with hearty goodwill and his sincere though anxious blessing.

The only result of all my labours was that the desired invitation from the King still hung fire. As the rehearsals for *Rienzi*, which had been postponed on account of Jenny Lind's visit, were being carried on seriously again, I made up my mind to take no further trouble before the performance of my opera, as I thought myself, at any rate, justified in counting on the presence of the monarch on the first night, as the piece was being played at his express command, and at the same time I hoped this would conduce to the fulfilment of my main object. However, the nearer we came to the event the lower did the hopes I had built upon it sink. To play the part of the hero I had to be satisfied with a tenor who was absolutely devoid of talent, and far below the average. He was a conscientious, painstaking man, and had moreover been strongly recommended to me by my kind host, the renowned Meinhard. After I had taken infinite pains with him, and had in consequence, as so often happens, conjured up in my mind certain illusions as to what I might expect from his acting, I was obliged, when it came to the final test of the dress rehearsal, to confess my true opinion. I realised that the scenery, chorus, ballet, and minor parts were on the whole excellent, but that the chief character, around whom in this particular opera everything centred, faded into an insignificant phantom. The reception which this opera met with at the hands of the public when it was produced in October was also due to him; but in consequence of the fairly good rendering of a few brilliant passages, and more especially on account of the enthusiastic recognition of Frau Köster in the part of Adriano, it might have been concluded from all the external signs that the opera had been fairly successful. Nevertheless, I knew very well that this seeming triumph could have no real substance, as only the immaterial parts of my work could reach the eyes and ears of the audience; its essential spirit had not entered their hearts. Moreover, the Berlin reviewers in their usual way began their attacks immediately, with the view of demolishing any success my opera might have won, so that after the second performance, which I also conducted myself, I began to wonder whether my desperate labours were really worth while.

When I asked the few intimate friends I had their opinion on

this point, I elicited much valuable information. Among these
friends I must mention, in the first place, Hermann Franck,
whom I found again. He had lately settled in Berlin, and did
much to encourage me. I spent the most enjoyable part of
those sad two months in his company, of which, however, I
had but too little. Our conversation generally turned upon
reminiscences of the old days, and on to topics which had no
connection with the theatre, so that I was almost ashamed to
trouble him with my complaints on this subject, especially as
they concerned my worries about a work which I could not
pretend was of any practical importance to the stage. He for
his part soon arrived at the conclusion that it had been foolish
of me to choose my *Rienzi* for this occasion, as it was an opera
which appealed merely to the general public, in preference to
my *Tannhäuser*, which might have educated a party in Berlin
useful to my higher aims. He maintained that the very nature
of this work would have aroused a fresh interest in the drama
in the minds of people who, like himself, were no longer to
be counted among regular theatre-goers, precisely because they
had given up all hope of ever finding any nobler ideals of the
stage.

The curious information as to the character of Berlin art
in other respects, which Werder gave me from time to time,
was most discouraging. With regard to the public, he told
me once that at a performance of an unknown work, it was
quite useless for me to expect a single member of the audience
from the stalls to the gallery to take his seat with any better
object in view than to pick as many holes as possible in the
production. Although Werder did not wish to discourage me
in any of my endeavours, he felt himself obliged to warn me
continually not to expect anything above the average from
the cultured society of Berlin. He liked to see proper respect
paid to the really considerable gifts of the King; and when
I asked him how he thought the latter would receive my ideas
about the ennobling of opera, he answered, after having listened
attentively to a long and fiery tirade on my part: ' The King
would say to you, " Go and consult Stawinsky! " ' This was
the opera manager, a fat, smug creature who had grown rusty
in following out the most jog-trot routine. In short, every-

thing I learned was calculated to discourage me. I called on Bernhard Marx, who some years ago had shown a kindly interest in my *Fliegender Holländer,* and was courteously received by him. This man, who in his earlier writings and musical criticisms had seemed to me filled with a fire of energy, now struck me as extraordinarily limp and listless when I saw him by the side of his young wife, who was radiantly and bewitchingly beautiful. From his conversation I soon learned that he also had abandoned even the remotest hope of success for any efforts directed towards the object so dear to both our hearts, on account of the inconceivable shallowness of all the officials connected with the head authority. He told me of the extraordinary fate which had befallen a scheme he had brought to the notice of the King for founding a school of music. In a special audience the King had gone into the matter with the greatest interest, and noticed the minutest detail, so that Marx felt justified in entertaining the strongest possible hopes of success. However, all his labours and negotiations about the business, in the course of which he was driven from pillar to post, proved utterly futile, until at last he was told to have an interview with a certain general. This personage, like the King, had Marx's proposals explained to him in the minutest detail, and expressed his warmest sympathy with the undertaking. ' And there,' said Marx, at the end of this long rigmarole, ' the matter ended, and I never heard another word about it.'

One day I learned that Countess Rossi, the renowned Henriette Sontag, who was living in quiet seclusion in Berlin, had pleasant recollections of me in Dresden, and wished me to visit her. She had at this time already fallen into the unfortunate position which was so detrimental to her artistic career. She too complained bitterly of the general apathy of the influential classes in Berlin, which effectually prevented any artistic aims from being realised. It was her opinion that the King found a sort of satisfaction in knowing that the theatre was badly managed, for though he never opposed any criticisms which he received on the subject, he likewise never supported any proposal for its improvement. She expressed a wish to know something of my latest work, and I gave her my poem of

Lohengrin for perusal. On the occasion of my next morning call she told me she would send me an invitation to a musical evening which she was going to have at her house in honour of the Grand Duke of Mecklenburg-Strelitz, her elderly patron, and she also gave me back the manuscript of *Lohengrin,* with the assurance that it had appealed to her very much, and that while she was reading it she had often seen the little fairies and elves dancing about in front of her. As in the old days I had been heartily encouraged by the warm and friendly sympathy of this naturally cultured woman, I now felt as if cold water had been suddenly poured down my back. I soon took my leave, and never saw her again. Indeed, I had no particular object in doing so, as the promised invitation never came. Herr E. Kossak also sought me out, and although our acquaintance did not lead to much, I was sufficiently kindly received by him to give him my poem of *Lohengrin* to read. I went one day by appointment to see him, and found that his room had just been scrubbed with boiling water. The steam from this operation was so unbearable that it had already given him a headache, and was not less disagreeable to me. He looked into my face with an almost tender expression when he gave me back the manuscript of my poem, and assured me, in accents which admitted of no doubt of his sincerity, that he thought it ' very pretty.'

I found my casual intercourse with H. Truhn rather more entertaining. I used to treat him to a good glass of wine at Lutter and Wegener's, where I went occasionally on account of its association with Hoffmann, and he would then listen with apparently growing interest to my ideas as to the possible development of opera and the goal at which we should aim. His comments were generally witty and very much to the point, and his lively and animated ways pleased me very much. After the production of *Rienzi,* however, he too, as a critic, joined the majority of scoffers and detractors. The only person who supported me stoutly but uselessly, through thick and thin, was my old friend Gaillard. His little music-shop was not a success, his musical journal had already failed, so that he was only able to help me in small ways. Unfortunately I discovered not only that he was the author of many exceedingly dubious dramatic works, for which he wished to gain my support, but also that he was apparently in the last stages of the disease from which he was suffering, so that the little intercourse I had with him, in spite of all his fidelity and devotion, only exercised a melancholy and depressing influence upon me.

But as I had embarked upon this Berlin enterprise in contradiction to all my inmost wishes, and prompted solely by the desire of winning the success so vital to my position, I made up my mind to make a personal appeal to Rellstab.

As in the case of the *Fliegender Holländer* he had taken exception more particularly to its 'nebulousness' and 'lack of form,' I thought I might with advantage point out to him the brighter and clearer outline of *Rienzi*. He seemed to be pleased at my thinking I could get anything out of him, but told me at once of his firm conviction that any new art form was utterly impossible after Gluck, and that the only thing that the best of good luck and hard work was capable of producing was meaningless bombast. I then realised that in Berlin all hope had been abandoned. I was told that Meyerbeer was the only man who had been able in any way to master the situation.

This former patron of mine I met once more in Berlin, and he declared that he still took an interest in me. As soon as I arrived I called on him, but in the hall I found his servant busy packing up trunks, and learned that Meyerbeer was just going away. His master confirmed this assertion, and regretted that he would not be able to do anything for me, so I had to say good-bye and how-do-you-do at the same time. For some time I thought he really was away, but after a few weeks I learned to my surprise that he was still staying in Berlin without letting himself be seen by any one, and at last he made his appearance again at one of the rehearsals of *Rienzi*. What this meant I only discovered later from a rumour which was circulated among the initiated, and imparted to me by Eduard von Bülow, my young friend's father. Without having the slightest idea how it originated, I learned, about the middle of my stay in Berlin, from the conductor Taubert, that he had heard on very good authority that I was trying for a director's post at the court theatre, and had good expectations of securing the appointment in addition to special privileges. In

order to remain on good terms with Taubert, as it was very
necessary for me to do, I had to give him the most solemn
assurances that such an idea had never even entered my head,
and that I would not accept such a position if it were offered
to me. On the other hand, all my endeavours to get access to
the King continued to be fruitless. My chief mediator, to
whom I always turned, was still Count Redern, and although
my attention had been called to his staunch adherence to
Meyerbeer, his extraordinary open and friendly manner always
strengthened my belief in his honesty. At last the only
medium that remained open to me was the fact that the King
could not possibly stay away from the performance of *Rienzi,*
given at his express command, and on this conviction I based
all further hope of approaching him. Whereupon Count
Redern informed me, with an expression of deep despair, that
on the very day of the first performance the monarch would
be away on a hunting party. Once more I begged him to
make very effort in his power to secure the King's presence,
at least at the second performance, and at length my inexhaustible patron told me that he could not make head or tail
of it, but his Majesty seemed to have conceived an utter disinclination to accede to my wish; he himself had heard these
hard words fall from the royal lips: ' Oh bother! have you
come to me again with your *Rienzi?* '

At this second performance I had a pleasant experience.
After the impressive second act the public showed signs of
wishing to call me, and as I went from the orchestra to the
vestibule, in order to be ready if necessary, my foot slipped
on the smooth parquet, and I might have had perhaps a serious
fall had I not felt my arm prasped by a strong hand. I turned,
and recognised the Crown Prince of Prussia,[1] who had come out
of his box, and who at once seized the opportunity of inviting
me to follow him to his wife, who wished to make my acquaintance. She had only just arrived in Berlin, and told me that
she had heard my opera for the first time that evening, and

---

[1] This Prince subsequently became the Emperor William the First. He was
given the title of Crown Prince in 1840 on the death of his father, Frederick
William III., as he was then heir-presumptive to his brother, Frederick William
IV., whose marriage was without issue. — EDITOR.

expressed her appreciation of it. She had, however, long ago received very favourable reports of me and my artistic aims from a common friend, Alwine Frommann. The whole tenor of this interview, at which the Prince was present, was unusually friendly and pleasant.

It was indeed my old friend Alwine who in Berlin had not only followed all my fortunes with the greatest sympathy, but had also done all in her power to give me consolation and courage to endure. Almost every evening, when the day's business made it possible, I used to visit her for an hour of recreation, and gain strength from her ennobling conversation for the struggle against the reverses of the following day. I was particularly pleased by the warm and intelligent sympathy which she and our mutual friend Werder devoted to *Lohengrin,* the object of all my labours at that time. On the arrival of her friend and patroness, the Crown Princess, which had been delayed till now, she hoped to hear something more definite as to how my affairs stood with the King, although she intimated to me that even this great lady was in deep disfavour, and could only bring her influence to bear upon the King by observing the strictest etiquette. But from this source also no news reached me till it was time for me to leave Berlin and I could postpone my departure no longer.

As I had to conduct a third performance of *Rienzi,* and there still remained a remote possibility of receiving a sudden command to Sans-Souci, I accordingly fixed on a date which would be the very latest I could wait to ascertain the fate of the projects I had nearest to heart. This period passed by, and I was forced to realise that my hopes of Berlin were wholly shattered.

I was in a very depressed state when I made up my mind to this conclusion. I can seldom remember having been so dreadfully affected by the influence of cold and wet weather and an eternally grey sky as during those last wretched weeks in Berlin, when everything that I heard, in addition to my own private anxieties, weighed upon me with a leaden weight of discouragement.

My conversations with Hermann Franck about the social and political situation had assumed a peculiarly gloomy tone,

as the King of Prussia's efforts to summon a united conference
had failed. I was among those who had at first been inclined
to see a hopeful significance in this undertaking, but it was a
shock to have all the intimate details relating to the project
clearly set before me by so well informed a man as Franck.
His dispassionate views on this subject, as well as on the
Prussian State in particular, which was supposed to be representative of German intelligence, and was universally considered
to be a model of order and good government, so completely disillusioned me and destroyed all the favourable and hopeful
opinions I had formed of it, that I felt as if I had plunged
into chaos, and realised the utter futility of expecting a prosperous settlement of the German question from this quarter.
If in the midst of my misery in Dresden I had founded great
hopes from gaining the King of Prussia's sympathy for my
ideas, I could no longer close my eyes to the fearful hollowness
which the state of affairs disclosed to me on every side.

In this despairing mood I felt but little emotion when, on
going to say good-bye to Count Redern, he told me with a
very sad face the news, which had just arrived, of Mendelssohn's
death. I certainly did not realise this stroke of fate, which
Redern's obvious grief first brought to my notice. At all
events, he was spared more detailed and heartfelt explanation
of my own affairs, which he had so much at heart.

The only thing that remained for me to do in Berlin was to
try and make my material success balance my material loss.
For a stay of two months, during which my wife and my sister
Clara had been with me, lured on by the hope that the production of *Rienzi* in Berlin would be a brilliant success, I found
my old friend, Director Küstner, by no means inclined to compensate me. From his correspondence with me he could prove
up to the hilt that legally he had only expressed the desire for
my co-operation in studying *Rienzi,* but had given me no positive invitation. As I was prevented by Count Redern's grief
over Mendelssohn's death from going to him for help in these
trivial private concerns, there was no alternative but for me to
accept with a good grace Küstner's beneficence in paying me
on the spot the royalties on the three performances which had
already taken place. The Dresden authorities were surprised

when I found myself obliged to beg an advance of income from them in order to conclude this brilliant undertaking in Berlin.

As I was travelling with my wife in the most horrible weather through the deserted country on my way home, I fell into a mood of the blackest despair, which I thought I might perhaps survive once in a lifetime but never again. Nevertheless, it amused me, as I sat silently looking out of the carriage into the grey mist, to hear my wife enter into a lively discussion with a commercial traveller who, in the course of friendly conversation, had spoken in a disparaging way about the ' new opera *Rienzi.*' My wife, with great heat and even passion, corrected various mistakes made by this hostile critic, and to her great satisfaction made him confess that he had not heard the opera himself, but had only based his opinion upon hearsay and the reviews. Whereupon my wife pointed out to him most earnestly that ' he could not possibly know whose future he might not injure by such irresponsible comment.'

These were the only cheering and consoling impressions which I carried back with me to Dresden, where I soon felt the direct results of the reverses I had suffered in Berlin in the condolences of my acquaintances. The papers had spread abroad the news that my opera had been a dismal failure. The most painful part of the whole proceeding was that I had to meet these expressions of pity with a cheerful countenance and the assurance that things were by no means so bad as had been made out, but that, on the contrary, I had had many pleasant experiences.

This unaccustomed effort placed me in a position strangely similar to that in which I found Hiller on my return to Dresden. He had given a performance of his new opera, *Conradin von Hohenstaufen,* here just about this time. He had kept the composition of this work a secret from me, and had hoped to make a decided hit with it after the three performances which took place in my absence. Both the poet and the composer thought that in this work they had combined the tendencies and effects of my *Rienzi* with those of my *Tannhäuser* in a manner peculiarly suited to the Dresden public. As he was just setting out for Düsseldorf, where he had been appointed concert-director, he commended his work with great confidence

to my tender mercies, and regretted not having the power of
appointing me the conductor of it. He acknowledged that he
owed his great success partly to the wonderfully happy rendering of the male part of *Conradin* by my niece Johanna. She,
in her turn, told me with equal confidence that without her
Hiller's opera would not have had such an extraordinary
triumph. I was now really anxious to see this fortunate work
and its wonderful staging for myself; and this I was able
to do, as a fourth performance was announced after Hiller and
his family had left Dresden for good. When I entered the
theatre at the beginning of the overture to take my place in
the stalls, I was astonished to find all the seats, with a few
scarcely noticeable exceptions, absolutely empty. At the other
end of my row I saw the poet who had written the libretto,
the gentle painter Reinike. We moved, naturally, towards the
middle of the space and discussed the strange position in which
we found ourselves. He poured out melancholy complaints
to me about Hiller's musical setting to his poetry; the secret
of the mistake which Hiller had made about the success of
his work he did not explain, and was evidently very much
upset at the conspicuous failure of the opera. It was from
another quarter that I learned how it had been possible for
Hiller to deceive himself in such an extraordinary way. Frau
Hiller, who was of Polish origin, had managed at the frequent
Polish gatherings which took place in Dresden to persuade a
large contingent of her countrymen, who were keen theatre-
goers, to attend her husband's opera. On the first night these
friends, with their usual enthusiasm, incited the public to
applaud, but had themselves found so little pleasure in the
work that they had stayed away from the second performance,
which was otherwise badly attended, so that the opera could
only be considered a failure. By commandeering all the help
that could possibly be got from the Poles by way of applause,
every effort was made to secure a third performance on a Sunday, when the theatre generally filled of its own accord. This
object was achieved, and the Polish theatre aristocracy, with
the charity that was habitual to them, fulfilled their duty
towards the needy couple in whose drawing-room they had
often spent such pleasant evenings.

Once more the composer was called before the curtain, and everything went off well. Hiller thereupon placed his confidence in the verdict on the third performance, according to which his opera was an undoubted success, just as had been the case with my *Tannhäuser*. The artificiality of this proceeding was, however, exposed by this fourth performance, at which I was present, and at which no one was under an obligation to the departed composer to attend. Even my niece was disgusted with it, and thought that the best singer in the world could not make a success of such a tedious opera. Whilst we were watching this miserable performance I managed to point out to the poet some weaknesses and faults that were to be found in the subject-matter. The latter reported my criticisms to Hiller, whereupon I received a warm and friendly letter from Düsseldorf, in which Hiller acknowledged the mistake he had made in rejecting my advice on this point. He gave me plainly to understand that it was not too late to alter the opera according to my suggestions; I should thus have had the inestimable benefit of having such an obviously well-intentioned, and, in its way, so significant, a work in the repertoire, but I never got so far as that.

On the other hand, I experienced the small satisfaction of hearing the news that two performances of my *Rienzi* had taken place in Berlin, for the success of which Conductor Taubert, as he informed me himself, thought he had won some credit on account of the extremely effective combinations he had arranged. In spite of this, I was absolutely convinced that I must abandon all hope of any lasting and profitable success from Berlin, and I could no longer hide from Lüttichau that, if I were to continue in the discharge of my duties with the necessary good spirits, I must insist on a rise of salary, as, beyond my regular income, I could not rely on any substantial success wherewith to meet my unlucky publishing transactions. My income was so small that I could not even live on it, but I asked nothing more than to be placed on an equal footing with my colleague Reissiger, a prospect which had been held out to me from the beginning.

At this juncture Lüttichau saw a favourable opportunity for making me feel my dependence on his goodwill, which

could only be secured by my showing due deference to his
wishes. After I had laid my case before the King, at a personal interview, and asked for the favour of the moderate increase in income which was my object, Lüttichau promised to
make the report he was obliged to give of me as favourable as
possible. How great was my consternation and humiliation
when one day he opened our interview by telling me that his
report had come back from the King. In it was set forth
that I had unfortunately overestimated my talent on account
of the foolish praise of various friends in a high position
(among whom he counted Frau v. Könneritz), and had thus
been led to consider that I had quite as good a right to success
as Meyerbeer. I had thereby caused such serious offence that it
might, perhaps, be considered advisable to dismiss me altogether.
On the other hand, my industry and my praiseworthy performance with regard to the revision of Gluck's *Iphigenia,* which
had been brought to the notice of the management, might
justify my being given another chance, in which case my
material condition must be given due consideration. At this
point I could read no further, and stupefied by surprise I gave
my patron back the paper. He tried at once to remove the
obviously bad impression it had made upon me by telling me
that my wish had been granted, and I could draw the nine
hundred marks belonging to me at once from the bank. I
took my leave in silence, and pondered over what course of
action I must pursue in face of this disgrace, as it was quite
out of the question for me to accept the nine hundred marks.

But in the midst of these adversities a visit of the King of
Prussia to Dresden was one day announced, and at the same
time by his special request a performance of *Tannhäuser* was
arranged. He really did make his appearance in the theatre
at this performance in the company of the royal family of
Saxony, and stayed with apparent interest from beginning to
end. On this occasion the King gave a curious explanation
for having stayed away from the performances of *Rienzi* in
Berlin, which was afterwards reported to me. He said he had
denied himself the pleasure of hearing one of my operas in
Berlin, because it was important to get a good impression of
them, and he knew that in his own theatre they would only

be badly produced. This strange event had, at any rate, the
result of giving me back sufficient self-confidence to accept the
nine hundred marks of which I was in such desperate need.

Lüttichau also seemed to make a point of winning back my
trust to some extent, and I gathered from his calm friendliness
that I must suppose this wholly uncultured man had no consciousness of the outrage he had done me. He returned to the
idea of having orchestral concerts, in accordance with the suggestions I had made in my rejected report on the orchestra,
and in order to induce me to arrange such musical performances
in the theatre, said the initiative had come from the management and not from the orchestra itself. As soon as I discovered
that the profits were to go to the orchestra I willingly entered
into the plan. By a special device of my own the stage
of the theatre was made into a concert-hall (afterwards considered first-class) by means of a sounding board enclosing the
whole orchestra, which proved a great success. In future six
performances were to take place during the winter months.
This time, however, as it was the end of the year, and we only
had the second half of the winter before us, subscription tickets
were issued for only three concerts, and the whole available
space in the theatre was filled by the public. I found the
preparations for this fairly diverting, and entered upon the
fateful year 1848 in a rather more reconciled and amiable
frame of mind.

Early in the New Year the first of these orchestral concerts
took place, and brought me much popularity on account of its
unusual programme. I had discovered that if any real significance were to be given to these concerts, in distinction to
those consisting of heterogeneous scraps of music of every
different species under the sun, and which are so opposed
to all serious artistic taste, we could only afford to give two
kinds of genuine music alternately if a good effect was to
be produced. Accordingly between two symphonies I placed
one or two longer vocal pieces, which were not to be heard
elsewhere, and these were the only items in the whole concert.
After the Mozart Symphony in D major, I made all the
musicians move from their places to make room for an imposing choir, which had to sing Palestrina's *Stabat Mater,* from

an adaptation of the original recitative, which I had carefully
revised, and Bach's Motet for eight voices: *Singet dem Herrn
ein neues Lied* ('Sing unto the Lord a new song'); thereupon
I let the orchestra again take its place to play Beethoven's
Sinfonia Eroica, and with that to end the concert.

This success was very encouraging, and disclosed to me a
somewhat consoling prospect of increasing my influence as
musical conductor at a time when my disgust was daily growing stronger at the constant meddling with our opera repertoire,
which made me lose more and more influence as compared with
the wishes of my would-be prima donna niece, whom even
Tichatschek supported. Immediately on my return from Berlin
I had begun the orchestration of *Lohengrin,* and in all other
respects had given myself up to greater resignation, which
made me feel I could face my fate calmly, when I suddenly
received a very disturbing piece of news.

In the beginning of February my mother's death was announced to me. I at once hastened to her funeral at Leipzig,
and was filled with deep emotion and joy at the wonderfully
calm and sweet expression of her face. She had passed the
latter years of her life, which had before been so active and
restless, in cheerful ease, and at the end in peaceful and almost
childlike happiness. On her deathbed she exclaimed in humble
modesty, and with a bright smile on her face: 'Oh! how
beautiful! how lovely! how divine! Why do I deserve such
favour?' It was a bitterly cold morning when we lowered the
coffin into the grave in the churchyard, and the hard, frozen
lumps of earth which we scattered on the lid, instead of the
customary handful of dust, frightened me by the loud noise
they made. On the way home to the house of my brother-
in-law, Hermann Brockhaus, where the whole family were to
gather together for an hour, Laube, of whom my mother had
been very fond, was my only companion. He expressed his
anxiety at my unusually exhausted appearance, and when he
afterwards accompanied me to the station, we discussed the
unbearable burden which seemed to us to lie like a dead weight
on every noble effort made to resist the tendency of the time
to sink into utter worthlessness. On my return to Dresden
the realisation of my complete loneliness came over me for the

first time with full consciousness, as I could not help knowing that with the loss of my mother every natural bond of union was loosened with my brothers and sisters, each of whom was taken up with his or her own family affairs. So I plunged dully and coldly into the only thing which could cheer and warm me, the working out of my *Lohengrin* and my studies of German antiquity.

Thus dawned the last days of February, which were to plunge Europe once more into revolution. I was among those who least expected a probable or even possible overthrow of the political world. My first knowledge of such things had been gained in my youth at the time of the July Revolution, and the long and peaceful reaction that followed it. Since then I had become acquainted with Paris, and from all the signs of public life which I saw there, I thought all that had occurred had been merely the preliminaries of a great revolutionary movement. I had been present at the erection of the *forts détachés* around Paris, which Louis Philippe had carried out, and been instructed about the strategic value of the various fixed sentries scattered about Paris, and I agreed with those who considered that everything was ready to make even an attempt at a rising on the part of the populace of Paris quite impossible. When, therefore, the Swiss War of Separation at the end of the previous year, and the successful Sicilian Revolution at the beginning of the New Year, turned all men's eyes in great excitement to watch the effect of these risings on Paris, I did not take the slightest interest in the hopes and fears which were aroused. News of the growing restlessness in the French capital did indeed reach us, but I disputed Röckel's belief that any significance could be attached to it. I was sitting in the conductor's desk at a rehearsal of *Martha* when, during an interval, Röckel, with the peculiar joy of being in the right, brought me the news of Louis Philippe's flight, and the proclamation of the Republic in Paris. This made a strange and almost astonishing impression on me, although at the same time the doubt as to the true significance of these events made it possible for me to smile to myself. I too caught the fever of excitement which had spread everywhere. The German March days were coming, and from all directions ever

more alarming news kept coming in. Even within the narrow
confines of my native Saxony serious petitions were framed,
which the King withstood for a long time; even he was deceived, in a way which he was soon to acknowledge, as to
the meaning of this commotion and the temper that prevailed
in the country.

On the evening of one of these really anxious days, when
the very air was heavy and full of thunder, we gave our third
great orchestral concert, at which the King and his court were
present, as on the two previous occasions. For the opening of
this one I had chosen Mendelssohn's Symphony in A minor,
which I had played on the occasion of his funeral. The mood
of this piece, which even in the would-be joyful phrases is
always tenderly melancholy, corresponded strangely with the
anxiety and depression of the whole audience, which was more
particularly accentuated in the demeanour of the royal family.
I did not conceal from Lipinsky, the leader of the orchestra,
my regret at the mistake I had made in the arrangement of
that day's programme, as Beethoven's Fifth Symphony, also
in a minor key, was to follow this minor symphony. With
a merry twinkle in his eyes the eccentric Pole comforted me
by exclaiming: ' Oh, let us play only the first two movements
of the Symphony in C minor, then no one will know whether
we have played Mendelssohn in the major or the minor key.'
Fortunately before these two movements began, to our great
surprise, a loud shout was raised by some patriotic spirit in the
middle of the audience, who called out ' Long live the King! '
and the cry was promptly repeated with unusual enthusiasm
and energy on all sides. Lipinsky was perfectly right: the
symphony, with the passionate and stormy excitement of the
first theme, swelled out like a hurricane of rejoicing, and had
seldom produced such an effect on the audience as on that
night. This was the last of the newly inaugurated concerts
that I ever conducted in Dresden.

Shortly after this the inevitable political changes took place.
The King dismissed his ministry and elected a new one, consisting partly of Liberals and partly even of really enthusiastic
Democrats, who at once proclaimed the well-known regulations,
which are the same all over the world, for founding a thoroughly

democratic constitution. I was really touched by this result,
and by the heartfelt joy which was evident among the whole
population, and I would have given much to have been able
to gain access to the King, and convince myself of his hearty
confidence in the people's love for him, which seemed to me
so desirable a consummation. In the evening the town was
gaily illuminated, and the King drove through the streets in
an open carriage. In the greatest excitement I went out
among the dense crowds and followed his movements, often
running where I thought it likely that a particularly hearty
shout might rejoice and reconcile the monarch's heart. My
wife was quite frightened when she saw me come back late at
night, tired out and very hoarse from shouting.

The events which took place in Vienna and Berlin, with their
apparently momentous results, only moved me as interesting
newspaper reports, and the meeting of a Frankfort parliament
in the place of the dissolved *Bundestag* sounded strangely
pleasant in my ears. Yet all these significant occurrences
could not tear me for a single day from my regular hours of
work. With immense, almost overweening satisfaction, I
finished, in the last days of this eventful and historic month
of March, the score of *Lohengrin* with the orchestration of
the music up to the vanishing of the Knight of the Holy Grail
into the remote and mystic distance.

About this time a young Englishwomen, Madame Jessie
Laussot, who had married a Frenchman in Bordeaux, one day
presented herself at my house in the company of Karl Ritter,
who was barely eighteen years of age. This young man, who
was born in Russia of German parents, was a member of one
of those northern families who had settled down permanently
in Dresden, on account of the pleasant artistic atmosphere of
that place. I remembered that I had seen him once before
not long after the first performance of *Tannhäuser,* when he
asked me for my autograph for a copy of the score of that opera,
which was on sale at the music-shop. I now learned that this
copy really belonged to Frau Laussot, who had been present
at those performances, and who was now introduced to me.
Overcome with shyness, the young lady expressed her admiration in a way I had never experienced before, and at the same

time told me how great was her regret at being called away
by family affairs from her favourite home in Dresden with the
Ritter family, who, she gave me to understand, were deeply
devoted to me. It was with a strange, and in its way quite
a new, sensation that I bade farewell to this young lady. This
was the first time since my meeting with Alwine Frommann
and Werder, when the *Fliegender Holländer* was produced, that
I came across this sympathetic tone, which seemed to come
like an echo from some old familiar past, but which I never
heard close at hand. I invited young Ritter to come and see
me whenever he liked, and to accompany me sometimes on
my walks. His extraordinary shyness, however, seemed to
prevent him from doing this, and I only remember seeing him
very occasionally at my house. He used to turn up more often
with Hans von Bülow, whom he seemed to know pretty well,
and who had already entered the Leipzig University as a
student of law. This well-informed and talkative young man
showed his warm and hearty devotion to me more openly,
and I felt bound to reciprocate his affection. He was the first
person who made me realise the genuine character of the new
political enthusiasm. On his hat, as well as on his father's, the
black, red, and gold cockade was paraded before my eyes.

Now that I had finished my *Lohengrin,* and had leisure to
study the course of events, I could no longer help myself sympathising with the ferment aroused by the birth of German
ideals and the hopes attached to their realisation. My old
friend Franck had already imbued me with a fairly sound
political judgment, and, like many others, I had grave doubts
as to whether the German parliament now assembling would
serve any useful purpose. Nevertheless, the temper of the
populace, of which there could be no question, although it
might not have been given very obvious expression, and the
belief, everywhere prevalent, that it was impossible to return
to the old conditions, could not fail to exercise its influence
upon me. But I wanted actions instead of words, and actions
which would force our princes to break for ever with their old
traditions, which were so detrimental to the cause of the German
commonwealth. With this object I felt inspired to write a
popular appeal in verse, calling upon the German princes and

peoples to inaugurate a great crusade against Russia, as the
country which had been the prime instigator of that policy in
Germany which had so fatally separated the monarchs from their
subjects. One of the verses ran as follows : —

> The old fight against the East
> Returns again to-day.
> The people's sword must not rust
> Who freedom wish for aye.

As I had no connection with political journals, and had
learned by chance that Berthold Auerbach was on the staff
of a paper in Mannheim, where the waves of revolution ran
high, I sent him my poem with the request to do whatever he
thought best with it, and from that day to this I have never
heard or seen anything of it.

Whilst the Frankfort Parliament continued to sit on from
day to day, and it seemed idle to conjecture whither this big
talk by small men would lead, I was much impressed by the
news which reached us from Vienna. In the May of this year
an attempt at a reaction, such as had succeeded in Naples
and remained indecisive in Paris, had been triumphantly nipped
in the bud by the enthusiasm and energy of the Viennese people
under the leadership of the students' band, who had acted with
such unexpected firmness. I had arrived at the conclusion
that, in matters directly concerning the people, no reliance
could be placed on reason or wisdom, but only on sheer force
supported by fanaticism or absolute necessity; but the course
of events in Vienna, where I saw the youth of the educated
classes working side by side with the labouring man, filled
me with peculiar enthusiasm, to which I gave expression in
another popular appeal in verse. This I sent to the *Oester-
reichischen Zeitung,* where it was printed in their columns with
my full signature.

In Dresden two political unions had been formed, as a result
of the great changes that had taken place. The first was
called the *Deutscher Verein* (German Union), whose programme
aimed at ' a constitutional monarchy on the broadest democratic foundation.' The names of its principal leaders, among
which, in spite of its broad democratic foundation, my friends

Eduard Devrient and Professor Rietschel had the courage
openly to appear, guaranteed the safety of its objects. This
union, which tried to include every element that regarded a
real revolution with abhorrence, conjured into existence an
opposition club which called itself the *Vaterlands-Verein*
(Patriotic Union). In this the 'democratic foundation'
seemed to be the chief basis, and the 'constitutional monarchy'
only provided the necessary cloak.

Röckel canvassed passionately for the latter, as he seemed
to have lost all confidence in the monarchy. The poor fellow
was, indeed, in a very bad way. He had long ago given up
all hope of rising to any position in the musical world; his
directorship had become pure drudgery, and was, unfortunately,
so badly paid that he could not possibly keep himself and his
yearly increasing family on the income he derived from his
post. He always had an unconquerable aversion from teaching,
which was a fairly profitable employment in Dresden among
the many wealthy visitors. So he went on from bad to worse,
running miserably into debt, and for a long time saw no hope
for his position as the father of a family except in emigration
to America, where he thought he could secure a livelihood for
himself and his dependants by manual labour, and for his practical mind by working as a farmer, from which class he had originally sprung. This, though tedious, would at least be certain.
On our walks he had of late been entertaining me almost
exclusively with ideas he had gleaned from reading books on
farming, doctrines which he applied with zeal to the improvement of his encumbered position. This was the mood in which
the Revolution of 1848 found him, and he immediately went
over to the extreme socialist side, which, owing to the example
set by Paris, threatened to become serious. Every one who
knew him was utterly taken aback at the apparently vital
change which had so suddenly taken place in him, when he
declared that he had at last found his real vocation — that of an
agitator.

His persuasive faculties, on which, however, he could not rely
sufficiently for platform purposes, developed in private intercourse into stupefying energy. It was impossible to stop his
flow of language with any objection, and those he could not

draw over to his cause he cast aside for ever. In his enthusiasm about the problems which occupied his mind day and night, he sharpened his intellect into a weapon capable of demolishing every foolish objection, and suddenly stood in our midst like a preacher in the wilderness. He was at home in every department of knowledge. The *Vaterlands-Verein* had elected a committee for carrying into execution a plan for arming the populace; this included Röckel and other thoroughgoing democrats, and, in addition, certain military experts, among whom was my old friend Hermann Müller, the lieutenant of the Guards who had once been engaged to Schröder-Devrient. He and another officer named Zichlinsky were the only members of the Saxon army who joined the political movement. The part I played in the meetings of this committee, as in everything else, was dictated by artistic motives. As far as I can remember, the details of this plan, which at last became a nuisance, afforded very sound foundation for a genuine arming of the people, though it was impossible to carry it out during the political crisis.

My interest and enthusiasm about the social and political problems which were occupying the whole world increased every day, until public meetings and private intercourse, and the shallow platitudes which formed the staple eloquence of the orators of the day, proved to me the terrible shallowness of the whole movement.

If only I could rest assured that, while such senseless confusion was the order of the day, people well versed in these matters would withhold from any demonstration (which to my great regret I observed in Hermann Franck, and told him of, openly), then, on the contrary, I should feel myself compelled, as soon as the opportunity arose, to discuss the purport of such questions and problems according to my judgment. Needless to say, the newspapers played an exciting and prominent part on this occasion. Once, when I went incidentally (as I might go to see a play) to a meeting of the *Vaterlands-Verein,* when they were assembled in a public garden, they chose for the subject of their discussion, ' Republic or Monarchy ? ' I was astonished to hear and to read with what incredible triviality it was carried on, and how the sum-total of their explanation was, that, to be sure, a republic is best, but, at the worst, one could put up with a monarchy if it were well conducted. As the result of many heated discussions on this point, I was incited to lay bare my views on the subject in an article which I published in the *Dresdener Anzeiger*, but which I did not sign. My special aim was to turn the attention of the few who really took the matter seriously, from the external form of the government to its intrinsic value. When I had pursued and consistently discussed the utmost idealistic conclusions of all that which, to my mind, was necessary and inseparable from the perfect state and from social order, I inquired whether it would not be possible to realise all this with a king at the head, and entered so deeply into the matter as to portray the king in such a fashion, that he seemed even more anxious than any one else that his state should be organised on genuinely republican lines, in order that he might attain to the fulfilment of his own highest aims. I must own, however, that I felt bound to urge this king to assume a much more familiar attitude towards his people than the court atmosphere and the almost exclusive society of his nobles would seem to render possible. Finally, I pointed to the King of Saxony as being specially chosen by Fate to lead the way in the direction I had indicated, and to give the example to all the other German princes. Röckel considered this article a true inspiration from the Angel of Propitiation, but as he feared that it would not meet with proper recognition and appreciation in the paper, he urged me to lecture on it publicly at the next meeting of the *Vaterlands-Verein,* for he attached great importance to my discoursing on the subject personally. Quite uncertain as to whether I could really persuade myself to do this, I attended the meeting, and there, owing to the intolerable balderdash uttered by a certain barrister named Blöde and a master-furrier Klette, whom at that time Dresden venerated as a Demosthenes and a Cleon, I passionately decided to appear at this extraordinary tribunal with my paper, and to give a very spirited reading of it to about three thousand persons.

The success I had was simply appalling. The astounded audience seemed to remember nothing of the speech of the

Orchestral Conductor Royal save the incidental attack I had made upon the court sycophants. The news of this incredible event spread like wildfire. The next day I rehearsed *Rienzi,* which was to be performed the following evening. I was congratulated on all sides upon my self-sacrificing audacity. On the day of the performance, however, I was informed by Eisolt, the attendant of the orchestra, that the plans had been changed, and he gave me to understand that thereby there hung a tale. True enough, the terrible sensation I had made became so great, that the directors feared the most unheard-of demonstrations at any performance of *Rienzi.* Then a perfect storm of derision and vituperation broke loose in the press, and I was besieged on all sides to such an extent that it was useless to think of self-defence. I had even offended the Communal Guard of Saxony, and was challenged by the commander to make a full apology. But the most inexorable enemies I made were the court officials, especially those holding a minor office, and to this day I still continue to be persecuted by them. I learned that, as far as it lay in their power, they incessantly besought the King, and finally the director, to deprive me at once of my office. On account of this I thought it necessary to write to the monarch personally, in order to explain to him that my action was to be regarded more in the light of a thoughtless indiscretion than as a culpable offence. I sent this letter to Herr von Lüttichau, begging him to deliver it to the King, and to arrange at the same time a short leave for me, so that the provoking disturbance should have a chance of dying down during my absence from Dresden. The striking kindness and goodwill which Herr von Lüttichau showed me on this occasion made no little impression upon me, and this I took no pains to conceal from him. As in the course of time, however, his ill-controlled rage at various things, and especially at a good deal that he had misunderstood in my pamphlet, broke loose, I learned that it was not from any humane motives that he had spoken in such a propitiatory manner to me, but rather by desire of the King himself. On this point I received most accurate information, and heard that when everybody, and even von Lüttichau himself, were besieging the King to visit me with punishment, the King had forbidden any further talk on the subject. After this very encouraging experience, I flattered myself that the King had understood not only my letter, but also my pamphlet, better than many others.

In order to change my mind a little, I determined for the present (it was the beginning of July) to take advantage of the short period of leave granted to me, by going to Vienna. I travelled by way of Breslau, where I looked up an old friend of my family, the musical director Mosewius, at whose house I spent an evening. We had a most lively conversation, but, unfortunately, were unable to steer clear of the stirring political questions of the day. What interested me most was his exceptionally large, or even, if I remember rightly, complete collection of Sebastian Bach's cantatas in most excellent copies. Besides this, he related, with a humour quite his own, several amusing musical anecdotes which were a pleasant memory for many a year. When Mosewius returned my visit in the course of the summer at Dresden, I played a part of the first act of *Lohengrin* on the piano for him, and the expression of his genuine astonishment at this conception was very gratifying to me. In later years, however, I found that he had spoken somewhat scoffingly about me; but I did not stop to reflect as to the truth of this information, or as to the real character of the man, for little by little I had had to accustom myself to the most inconceivable things. At Vienna the first thing I did was to call on Professor Fischhof, as I knew that he had in his keeping important manuscripts, chiefly by Beethoven, among which the original of the C minor Sonata, opus 111, I was particularly curious to see. Through this new friend, whom I found somewhat dry, I made the acquaintance of Herr Vesque von Püttlingen, who, as the composer of a most insignificant opera (*Joan of Arc*), which had been performed in Dresden, had with cautious good taste adopted only the last two syllables of Beethoven's name — *Hoven.* One day we were at his house to dinner, and I then recognised in him a former confidential official of Prince Metternich, who now, with his ribbon of black, red, and gold, followed the current of the age, apparently quite convinced. I made another interesting acquaintance in the person of Herr von Fonton, the Russian state councillor, and attaché at the Russian Embassy in

Vienna. I frequently met this man, both at Fischhof's house
and on excursions into the surrounding country; and it was
interesting to me for the first time to run up against a man
who could so strongly profess his faith in the pessimistic standpoint that a consistent despotism guarantees the only order
of things which can be tolerated. Not without interest, and
certainly not without intelligence — for he boasted of having
been educated at the most enlightened schools in Switzerland
— he listened to my enthusiastic narration of the art ideal
which I had in my mind, and which was destined to exercise
a great and decided influence upon the human race. As he
had to allow that the realisation of this ideal could not be
effected through the strength of despotism, and as he was unable
to foresee any rewards for my exertions, by the time we came
to the champagne he thawed to such a degree of affable good-
nature as to wish me every success. I learned later on that this
man, of whose talent and energetic character I had at the time
no small opinion, was last heard of as being in great distress.

Now, as I never undertook anything whatever without some
serious object in view, I had made up my mind to avail myself
of this visit to Vienna, in order to try in some practical manner
to promote my ideas for the reform of the theatre. Vienna
seemed to me specially suitable for this purpose, as at that time
it had five theatres, all totally different in character, which
were dragging on a miserable existence. I quickly worked out
a plan, according to which these various theatres might be
formed into a sort of co-operative organisation, and placed
under one administration composed not only of active members,
but also of all those having any literary connection with the
theatre. With a view to submitting my plan to them, I then
made inquiries about persons with such capacities as seemed
most likely to answer my requirements. Besides Herr Friedrich Uhl, whom I had got to know at the very beginning through
Fischer, and who did me very good service, I was told of a
Herr Franck (the same, I presume, who later on published a
big epic work called *Tannhäuser*), and a Dr. Pacher, an agent
of Meyerbeer's, and a pettifogger of whose acquaintance later
on I was to have no reason to be proud. The most sympathetic,
and certainly the most important, of those chosen by me for

the conference meeting at Fischhof's house, was undoubtedly
Dr. Becher, a passionate and exceedingly cultivated man.
He was the only one present who seriously followed the reading of my plan, although, of course, he by no means agreed
with everything. I observed in him a certain wildness and
vehemence, the impression of which returned to me very
vividly some months later, when I heard of his being shot
as a rebel who had participated in the October Insurrection at
Vienna. For the present, then, I had to satisfy myself with
having read the plan of my theatre reform to a few attentive
listeners. All seemed to be convinced that the time was not
opportune for putting forward such peaceable schemes of
reform. On the other hand, Uhl thought it right to give me
an idea of what was at present all the rage in Vienna, by taking
me one evening to a political club of the most advanced tendencies. There I heard a speech by Herr Sigismund Engländer,
who shortly afterwards attracted much attention in the political
monthly papers; the unblushing audacity with which he and
others expressed themselves that evening with regard to the
most dreaded persons in public power astounded me almost
as much as the poverty of the political views expressed on that
occasion. By way of contrast I received a very nice impression
of Herr Grillparzer, the poet, whose name was like a fable to
me, associated as it was, from my earliest days, with his *Ahnfrau.*
I approached him also with respect to the matter of my theatre
reform. He seemed quite disposed to listen in a friendly
manner to what I had to say to him; he did not, however,
attempt to conceal his surprise at my direct appeals and the
personal demands I made of him. He was the first playwright
I had ever seen in an official uniform.

After I had paid an unsuccessful visit to Herr Bauernfeld, relative to the same business, I concluded that Vienna was of no
more use for the present, and gave myself up to the exceptionally stimulating impressions produced by the public life of
the motley crowd, which of late had undergone such marked
changes. If the student band, which was always represented
in great numbers in the streets, had already amused me with
the extraordinary constancy with which its members sported
the German colours, I was very highly diverted by the effect

produced when at the theatres I saw even the ices served by attendants in the black, red, and gold of Austria. At the Karl Theatre, in the Leopold quarter of the town, I saw a new farce, by Nestroy, which actually introduced the character of Prince Metternich, and in which this statesman, on being asked whether he had poisoned the Duke of Reichstadt, had to make his escape behind the wings as an unmasked sinner. On the whole, the appearance of this imperial city — usually so fond of pleasure — impressed one with a feeling of youthful and powerful confidence. And this impression was revived in me when I heard of the energetic participation of the youthful members of the population, during those fateful October days, in the defence of Vienna against the troops of Prince Windisch-grätz.

On the homeward journey I touched at Prague, where I found my old friend Kittl (who had grown very much more corpulent) still in the most terrible fright about the riotous events which had taken place there. He seemed to be of opinion that the revolt of the Tschech party against the Austrian Government was directed at him personally, and he thought fit to reproach himself with the terrible agitation of the time, which he believed he had specially inflamed by his composition of my operatic text of *Die Franzosen vor Nizza,* out of which a kind of revolutionary air seemed to have become very popular. To my great pleasure, on my homeward journey I had the company of Hänel the sculptor, whom I met on the steamer. There travelled with us also a Count Albert Nostitz, with whom he had just settled up his business concerning the statue of the Emperor Charles IV., and he was in the gayest mood, as the extremely insecure state of Austrian paper money had led to his being paid at a great profit to himself, in silver coin in accordance with his agreement. I was very pleased to find that, thanks to this circumstance, he was in such a confident mood, and so free from prejudice, that on arriving at Dresden he accompanied me the whole way — a very long distance — from the landing-stage at which we had left the steamer to my house, in an open carriage; and this despite the fact that he very well knew that, only a few weeks before, I had caused a really terrible stir in this very city.

As far as the public were concerned, the storm seemed quite to have died down, and I was able to resume my usual occupations and mode of life without any further trouble. I am sorry to say, however, that my old worries and anxieties started afresh; I stood in great need of money, and had not the vaguest notion whither to go in search of it. I then examined very thoroughly the answer I had received during the preceding winter to my petition for a higher salary. I had left it unread, as the modifications made in it had already disgusted me. If I had till now believed that it was Herr von Lüttichau who had brought about the increase of salary I had demanded, in the shape of a supplement which I was to receive annually — in itself a humiliating thing — I now saw to my horror that all the time there had been no mention save of one single supplement, and that there was nothing to show that this should be repeated annually. On learning this, I saw that I should now be at the hopeless disadvantage of coming too late with a remonstrance if I should attempt to make one; so there was nothing left for me but to submit to an insult which, under the circumstances, was quite unprecedented. My feelings towards Herr von Lüttichau, which shortly before had been rather warm owing to his supposed kind attitude towards me during the last disturbance, now underwent a serious change, and I soon had a new reason (actually connected with the above-mentioned affair) for altering my favourable opinion of him, and for turning finally against him for good and all. He had informed me that the members of the Imperial Orchestra had sent him a deputation demanding my instant dismissal, as they thought that it affected their honour to be any longer under a conductor who had compromised himself politically to the extent which I had. He also informed me that he had not only reprimanded them very severely, but that he had also been at great pains to pacify them concerning me. All this, which Lüttichau had put in a highly favourable light, had latterly made me feel very friendly towards him. Then, however, as the result of inquiries into the matter, I heard accidentally through members of the orchestra that the facts of the case were almost exactly the reverse. What had happened was this, that the members of the Imperial Orchestra had been

approached on all sides by the officials of the court, and had
been not only earnestly requested to do what Lüttichau had
declared they had done of their own accord, but also threatened
with the displeasure of the King, and of incurring the strongest
suspicion if they refused to comply. In order to protect themselves against this intrigue, and to avoid all evil consequences
should they *not* take the required step, the musicians had turned
to their principal, and had sent him a deputation, through
which they declared that, as a corporation of artists, they did
not in the least feel called upon to mix themselves up in a
matter that did not concern them. Thus the halo with which
my former attachment to Herr von Lüttichau had surrounded
him at last disappeared for good and all, and it was chiefly
my shame at having been so very much upset by his false conduct that now inspired me for ever with such bitter feelings
for this man. What determined this feeling even more than
the insults I had suffered, was the recognition of the fact that
I was now utterly incapable of ever being able to enlist his
influence in the cause of theatrical reform, which was
so dear to me. It was natural that I should learn to attach
ever less and less importance to the mere retention of the post
of orchestral conductor on so extraordinarily inadequate and
reduced a salary; and in keeping to this office, I merely bowed
to what was an inevitable though purely accidental circumstance of a wretched fate. I did nothing to make the post
more intolerable, but, at the same time, I moved not a finger
to ensure its permanence.

The very next thing I must do was to attempt to establish
my hopes of a larger income, so sadly doomed hitherto, upon a
very much sounder basis. In this respect it occurred to me
that I might consult my friend Liszt, and beg him to suggest a
remedy for my grievous position. And lo and behold, shortly
after those fateful March days, and not long before the completion of my *Lohengrin* score, to my very great delight and
astonishment, the very man I wanted walked into my room.
He had come from Vienna, where he had lived through the
' Barricade Days,' and he was going on to Weimar, where he
intended to settle permanently. We spent an evening together
at Schumann's, had a little music, and finally began a discussion

on Mendelssohn and Meyerbeer, in which Liszt and Schumann differed so fundamentally that the latter, completely losing his temper, retired in a fury to his bedroom for quite a long time. This incident did indeed place us in a somewhat awkward position towards our host, but it furnished us with a most amusing topic of conversation on the way home. I have seldom seen Liszt so extravagantly cheerful as on that night, when, in spite of the cold and the fact that he was clad only in ordinary evening-dress, he accompanied first the music director Schubert, and then myself, to our respective homes. Subsequently I took advantage of a few days' holiday in August to make an excursion to Weimar, where I found Liszt permanently installed and, as is well known, enjoying a life of most intimate intercourse with the Grand Duke. Even though he was unable to help me in my affairs, except by giving me a recommendation which finally proved useless, his reception of me on this short visit was so hearty and so exceedingly stimulating, that it left me profoundly cheered and encouraged. On returning to Dresden I tried as far as possible to curtail my expenses and to live within my means; and, as every means of assistance failed me, I resorted to the expedient of sending out a circular letter addressed jointly to my remaining creditors, all of whom were really friends; and in this I told them frankly of my situation, and enjoined them to relinquish their demands for an indefinite time, till my affairs took a turn for the better, as without this I should certainly never be in a position to satisfy them. By this means they would, at all events, be in a position to oppose my general manager, whom I had every reason to suspect of evil designs, and who would have been only too glad to seize any signs of hostility towards me, on the part of my creditors, as a pretext for taking the worst steps against me. The assurance I required was given me unhesitatingly; my friend Pusinelli, and Frau Klepperbein (an old friend of my mother's), even going so far as to declare that they were prepared to give up all claim to the money they had lent me. Thus, in some measure reassured, and with my position relative to Lüttichau so far improved that I could consult my own wishes as to whether and when I should give up my post entirely, I now continued to fulfil my duties as a conductor as patiently and conscientiously as I was able, while with great zeal I also resumed my studies, which were carrying me ever further and further afield.

Thus settled, I now began to watch the wonderful developments in the fate of my friend Röckel. As every day brought fresh rumours of threatened reactionary *coups d'état* and similar violent outbreaks, which Röckel thought it right to prevent, he drew up an appeal to the soldiers of the army of Saxony, in which he explained every detail of the cause for which he stood, and which he then had printed and distributed broadcast. This was too flagrant a misdeed for the public prosecutors: he was therefore immediately placed under arrest, and had to remain three days in gaol while an action for high treason was lodged against him. He was only released when the solicitor Minkwitz stood bail for the requisite three thousand marks (equal to £150). This return home to his anxious wife and children was celebrated by a little public festival, which the committee of the *Vaterlands-Verein* had arranged in his honour, and the liberated man was greeted as the champion of the people's cause. On the other hand, however, the general management of the court theatre, who had before suspended him temporarily, now gave him his final dismissal. Röckel let a full beard grow, and began the publication of a popular journal called the *Volksblatt,* of which he was sole editor. He must have counted on its success to compensate him for the loss of his salary as musical director, for he at once hired an office in the Brüdergasse for his undertaking. This paper succeeded in attracting the attention of a great many people to its editor, and showed up his talents in quite a new light. He never got involved in his style or indulged in any elaboration of words, but confined himself to matters of immediate importance and general interest; it was only after having discussed them in a calm and sober fashion, that he led up from them to further deductions of still greater interest connected with them. The individual articles were short, and never contained anything superfluous, in addition to which they were so clearly written, that they made an instructive and convincing appeal to the most uneducated mind. By always going to the root of things, instead of indulging in circum-

locutions which, in politics, have caused such great confusion
in the minds of the uneducated masses, he soon had a large
circle of readers, both among cultivated and uncultivated
people. The only drawback was that the price of the little
weekly paper was too small to yield him a corresponding profit.
Moreover, it was necessary to warn him that if the reactionary
party should ever come into power again, it could never
possibly forgive him for this newspaper. His younger brother,
Edward, who was paying a visit at the time in Dresden, declared
himself willing to accept a post as piano-teacher in England,
which, though most uncongenial to him, would be lucrative
and place him in a position to help Röckel's family, if, as
seemed probable, he met his reward in prison or on the gallows.
Owing to his connection with various societies, his time was so
much taken up that my intercourse with him was limited to
walks, which became more and more rare. On these occasions
I often got lost in the most wildly speculative and profound
discussions, while this wonderfully exciteable man always remained calmly reflective and clear-headed. First and foremost, he had planned a drastic social reform of the middle
classes — as at present constituted — by aiming at a complete
alteration of the basis of their condition. He constructed a
totally new moral order of things, founded on the teaching of
Proudhon and other socialists regarding the annihilation of
the power of capital, by immediately productive labour, dis-
pensing with the middleman. Little by little he converted
me, by most seductive arguments, to his own views, to such an
extent that I began to rebuild my hopes for the realisation
of my ideal in art upon them. Thus there were two questions
which concerned me very nearly: he wished to abolish matrimony, in the usual acceptation of the word, altogether. I thereupon asked him what he thought the result would be of
promiscuous intercourse with women of a doubtful character.
With amiable indignation he gave me to understand that we
could have no idea about the purity of morals in general, and of
the relations of the sexes in particular, so long as we were unable
to free people completely from the yoke of the trades, guilds,
and similar coercive institutions. He asked me to consider
what the only motive would be which would induce a woman

to surrender herself to a man, when not only the considerations of money, fortune, position, and family prejudices, but also the various influences necessarily arising from these, had disappeared. When I, in my turn, asked him whence he would obtain persons of great intellect and of artistic ability, if everybody were to be merged in the working classes, he met my objection by replying, that owing to the very fact that everybody would participate in the necessary labour according to his strength and capacity, work would cease to be a burden, and would become simply an occupation which would finally assume an entirely artistic character. He demonstrated this on the principle that, as had already been proved, a field, worked laboriously by a single peasant, was infinitely less productive than when cultivated by several persons in a scientific way. These and similar suggestions, which Röckel communicated to me with a really delightful enthusiasm, led me to further reflections, and gave birth to new plans upon which, to my mind, a possible organisation of the human race, which would correspond to my highest ideals in art, could alone be based. In reference to this, I immediately turned my thoughts to what was close at hand, and directed my attention to the theatre. The motive for this came not only from my own feelings, but also from external circumstances. In accordance with the latest democratic suffrage laws, a general election seemed imminent in Saxony; the election of extreme radicals, which had now taken place nearly everywhere else, showed us that if the movement lasted, there would be the most extraordinary changes even in the administration of the revenue. Apparently a general resolution had been passed to subject the Civil List to a strict revision; all that was deemed superfluous in the royal household was to be done away with; the theatre, as an unnecessary place of entertainment for a depraved portion of the public, was threatened with the withdrawal of the subsidy granted it from the Civil List. I now resolved, in view of the importance which I attached to the theatre, to suggest to the ministers that they should inform the members of parliament, that if the theatre in its present condition were not worth any sacrifice from the state, it would sink to still more doubtful tendencies — and might even become dangerous

to public morals — if deprived of that state control which had
for its aim the ideal, and, at the same time, felt itself called
upon to place culture and education under its beneficial protection. It was of the highest importance to me to secure an
organisation of the theatre, which would make the carrying
out its loftiest ideals not only a possibility but also a certainty.
Accordingly I drew up a project by which the same sum as
that which was allotted from the Civil List for the support of
a court theatre should be employed for the foundation and
upkeep of a national theatre for the kingdom of Saxony. In
showing the practical nature of the well-planned particulars
of my scheme, I defined them with such great precision, that
I felt assured my work would serve as a useful guide to the
ministers as to how they should put this matter before parliament. The point now was to have a personal interview with
one of the ministers, and it occurred to me that the best man
to apply to in the matter would be Herr von der Pfordten,
the Minister of Education. Although he already enjoyed the
reputation of being a turncoat in politics, and was said to be
struggling to efface the origin of his political promotion, which
had taken place at a time of great agitation, the mere fact of
his having formerly been a professor was sufficient to make
me suppose that he was a man with whom I could discuss the
question that I had so much at heart. I learned, however, that
the real art institutions of the kingdom, such, for instance, as
the Academy of Fine Arts, to whose number I so ardently
desired to see the theatre added, belonged to the department
of the Minister of the Interior. To this man — the worthy
though not highly cultivated or artistic Herr Oberländer — I
submitted my plans, not, however, without having first made
myself known to Herr von der Pfordten, in order, for the reasons
above stated, to command my project to him. This man, who
apparently was very busy, received me in a polite and reassuring
manner; but his whole bearing, indeed the very expression
of his face, seemed to destroy all hopes I might ever have
cherished of finding in him that understanding which I had
expected. The minister Oberländer, on the other hand, earned
my confidence by the straightforward earnestness with which
he promised a thorough inquiry into the matter. Unfortu-

nately, however, at the same time, he informed me with the most simple frankness, that he could entertain but very little hope of getting the King's authorisation for any unusual treatment of a question hitherto given over to routine. It must be understood that the relations of the King to his ministers were both strained and unconfidential, and that this was more especially so in the case of Oberländer, who never approached the monarch on any other business than that which the strictest discharge of his current duties rendered indispensable. He therefore thought it would be better if my plan could be brought forward, in the first place, by the Chamber of Deputies. As, in the event of the new Civil List being discussed, I was particularly anxious to avoid the question of the continuation of the court theatre being treated in the ignorant and short-sighted radical fashion, which was to be feared above all, I did not despair of making the acquaintance of some of the most influential among the new members of parliament. In this wise I found myself suddenly plunged into quite a new and strange world, and became acquainted with persons and opinions, the very existence of which until then I had not even suspected. I found it somewhat trying always to be obliged to meet these gentlemen at their beer and shrouded in the dense clouds of their tobacco smoke, and to have to discuss with them matters which, though very dear to me, must have seemed a little fantastic to their mind. After a certain Herr von Trütschler, a very handsome, energetic man, whose seriousness was almost gloomy, had listened to me calmly for some time, and had told me that he no longer knew anything about the state, but only about society, and that the latter would know, without either his or my aid, how it should act in regard to art and to the theatre, I was filled with such extraordinary feelings, half mingled with shame, that there and then I gave up, not only all my exertions, but all my hopes as well. The only reminder I ever had of the whole affair came some while after when, on meeting Herr von Lüttichau, I quickly gathered from his attitude to me that he had got wind of the episode, and that it only inspired him with fresh hostility towards me.

During my walks, which I now took absolutely alone, I thought ever more deeply — and much to the relief of my mind

— over my ideas concerning that state of human society for which the boldest hopes and efforts of the socialists and communists, then busily engaged in constructing their system, offered me but the roughest foundation. These efforts could begin to have some meaning and value for me only when they had attained to that political revolution and reconstruction which they aimed at; for it was only then that I, in my turn, could start my reforms in art.

At the same time my thoughts were busy with a drama, in which the Emperor Frederick I. (surnamed ' Barbarossa ') was to be the hero. In it the model ruler was portrayed in a manner which lent him the greatest and most powerful significance. His dignified resignation at the impossibility of making his ideals prevail was intended not only to present a true transcript of the arbitrary multifariousness of the things of this world, but also to arouse sympathy for the hero. I wished to carry out this drama in popular rhyme, and in the style of the German used by our epic poets of the Middle Ages, and in this respect the poem *Alexander,* by the priest Lambert, struck me as a good example; but I never got further with this play than to sketch its outline in the broadest manner possible. The five acts were planned in the following manner: Act i. Imperial Diet in the Roncaglian fields, a demonstration of the significance of imperial power which should extend even to the investiture of water and air; Act ii. the siege and capture of Milan; Act iii. revolt of Henry the Lion and his overthrow at Ligano; Act iv. Imperial Diet in Augsburg, the humiliation and punishment of Henry the Lion; Act v. Imperial Diet and grand court assembly at Mainz; peace with the Lombards, reconciliation with the Pope, acceptance of the Cross, and the departure for the East. I lost all interest, however, in the carrying out of this dramatic scheme directly I discovered its resemblance to the subject-matter of the Nibelungen and Siegfried myths, which possessed a more powerful attraction for me. The points of similarity which I recognised between the history and the legend in question then induced me to write a treatise on the subject; and in this I was assisted by some stimulating monographs (found in the royal library), written by authors whose names have now escaped my memory, but which taught

me in a very attractive manner a considerable amount about the
old original kingdom of Germany. Later on I published this
fairly extensive essay with the title of *Die Nibelungen,* but in
working it out I finally lost all inclination to elaborate the
historical material for a real drama.

In direct connection with this I began to sketch a clear
summary of the form which the old original Nibelungen myth
had assumed in my mind in its immediate association with the
mythological legend of the gods — a form which, though full
of detail, was yet much condensed in its leading features.
Thanks to this work, I was able to convert the chief part of the
material itself into a musical drama. It was only by degrees,
however, and after long hesitation that I dared to enter more
deeply into my plans for this work; for the thought of the
practical realisation of such a work on our stage literally
appalled me. I must confess that it required all the despair
which I then felt of ever having the chance of doing anything
more for our theatre, to give me the necessary courage to
begin upon this new work. Until that time I simply allowed
myself to drift, while I meditated listlessly upon the possibility
of things pursuing their course further under the existing circumstances. In regard to *Lohengrin,* I had got to that point
when I hoped for nothing more than the best possible production
of it at the Dresden theatre, and felt that I should have to be
satisfied in all respects, and for all time, if I were able to achieve
even that. I had duly announced the completion of the score to
Herr von Lüttichau; but, in consideration of the unfavourable
nature of my circumstances at the time, I had left it entirely
to him to decide when my work should be produced.

Meanwhile the time arrived when the keeper of the Archives
of the Royal Orchestra called to mind that it was just three
hundred years since this royal institution had been founded,
and that a jubilee would therefore have to be celebrated. To
this end a great concert festival was planned, the programme
of which was to be made up of the compositions of all the Saxon
orchestral conductors that had lived since the institution had
been founded. The whole body of musicians, with both their
conductors at their head, were first to present their grateful
homage to the King in Pillnitz; and on this occasion a musician

was, for the first time, to be elevated to the rank of Knight of the Civil Order of Merit of Saxony. This musician was my colleague Reissiger. Until then he had been treated by the court, and by the manager himself, in the most scornful manner possible, but had, owing to his conspicuous loyalty at this critical time, especially to me, found exceptional favour in the eyes of our committees. When he appeared before the public decorated with the wonderful order, he was greeted with great jubilation by the loyal audience that filled the theatre on the evening of the festival concert. His overture to *Yelva* was also received with a perfect uproar of enthusiastic applause, such as had never fallen to his lot; whereas the finale of the first act from *Lohengrin,* which was produced as the work of the youngest conductor, was accorded only an indifferent reception. This was all the more strange as I was quite un-accustomed to such coolness in regard to my work on the part of the Dresden public. Following upon the concert, there was a festive supper, and when this was over, as all kinds of speeches were being made, I freely proclaimed to the orchestra, in a loud and decided tone, my views as to what was desirable for their perfection in the future. Hereupon Marschner, who, as a former musical conductor in Dresden, had been invited to the jubilee celebrations, expressed the opinion that I should do myself a great deal of harm by holding too good an opinion of the musicians. He said I ought just to consider how uncultivated these people were with whom I had to deal; he pointed out that they were trained simply for the one instrument they played; and asked me whether I did not think that by discoursing to them on the aspirations of art I would produce not only con-fusion, but even perhaps bad blood? Far more pleasant to me than these festivities is the remembrance of the quiet memorial ceremony which united us on the morning of the Jubilee Day, with the object of placing wreaths on Weber's grave. As nobody could find a word to utter, and even Marschner was able to give expression only to the very driest and most trivial of speeches about the departed master, I felt it incumbent upon me to say a few heartfelt words concerning the memorial ceremony for which we were gathered together.

This brief spell of artistic activity was speedily broken by

fresh excitements, which kept pouring in upon us from the
political world. The events of October in Vienna awakened
our liveliest sympathy, and our walls daily blazed with red
and black placards, with summonses to march on Vienna, with
the curse of ' Red Monarchy,' as opposed to the hated ' Red
Republic,' and with other equally startling matter. Except
for those who were best informed as to the course of events —
and who certainly did not swarm in our streets — these occurrences aroused great uneasiness everywhere. With the entry
of Windischgrätz into Vienna, the acquittal of Fröbel and the
execution of Blum, it seemed as though even Dresden were
on the eve of an explosion. A vast demonstration of mourning
was organised for Blum, with an endless procession through
the streets. At the head marched the ministry, among whom
the people were particularly glad to see Herr von der Pfordten
taking a sympathetic share in the ceremony, as he had already
become an object of suspicion to them. From that day
gloomy forebodings of disaster grew ever more prevalent on
every side. People even went so far as to say, with little
attempt at circumlocution, that the execution of Blum had
been an act of friendship on the part of the Archduchess Sophia
to her sister, the Queen of Saxony, for during his agitation in
Leipzig the man had made himself both hated and feared.
Troops of Viennese fugitives, disguised as members of the student bands, began to arrive in Dresden, and made a formidable
addition to its population, which from this time forth paraded
the streets with ever-increasing confidence. One day, as I
was on my way to the theatre to conduct a performance of
Rienzi, the choir-master informed me that several foreign
gentlemen had been asking for me. Thereupon half a dozen
persons presented themselves, greeted me as a brother democrat,
and begged me to procure them free entrance tickets. Among
them I recognised a former dabbler in literature, a man named
Häfner, a little hunchback, in a Calabrian hat cocked at a
terrific angle, to whom I had been introduced by Uhl on the
occasion of my visit to the Vienna political club. Great as
was my embarrassment at this visit, which evidently astonished
our musicians, I felt in no wise compelled to make any compromising admission, but quietly went to the booking-office,

took six tickets and handed them to my strange visitors, who parted from me before all the world with much hearty shaking of hands. Whether this evening call improved my position as musical conductor in Dresden in the minds of the theatrical officials and others, may well be doubted; but, at all events, on no occasion was I so frantically called for after every act as at this particular performance of *Rienzi*.

Indeed, at this time I seemed to have won over to my side a party of almost passionate adherents among the theatre-going public, in opposition to the clique which had shown such marked coldness on the occasion of the gala concert already mentioned. It mattered not whether *Tannhäuser* or *Rienzi* were being played, I was always greeted with special applause; and although the political tendencies of this party may have given our management some cause for alarm, yet it forced them to regard me with a certain amount of awe. One day Lüttichau proposed to have my *Lohengrin* performed at an early date. I explained my reasons for not having offered it to him before, but declared myself ready to further his wishes, as I considered the opera company was now sufficiently powerful. The son of my old friend, F. Heine, had just returned from Paris, where he had been sent by the Dresden management to study scene-painting under the artists Despléchin and Dieterle. By way of testing his powers, with a view to an engagement at the Dresden Royal Theatre, the task of preparing suitable scenery for this opera was entrusted to him. He had already asked permission to do this for *Lohengrin* at the instigation of Lüttichau, who wished to call attention to my latest work. Consequently, when I gave my consent, young Heine's wish was granted.

I regarded this turn of events with no little satisfaction, believing that in the study of this particular work I should find a wholesome and effective diversion from all the excitement and confusion of recent events. My horror, therefore, was all the greater, when young Wilhelm Heine one day came to my room with the news that the scenery for *Lohengrin* had been suddenly countermanded, and instructions given him to prepare for another opera. I did not make any remark, nor ask the reason for this singular behaviour. The assurances which Lüttichau afterwards made to my wife — if they were really true — made me regret having laid the chief blame for this mortification at his door, and having thereby irrevocably alienated my sympathy from him. When she asked him about this many years later, he assured her that he had found the court vehemently hostile to me, and that his well-meant attempts to produce my work had met with insuperable obstacles.

However that may have been, the bitterness I now experienced wrought a decisive effect upon my feelings. Not only did I relinquish all hope of a reconciliation with the theatre authorities by a splendid production of my *Lohengrin,* but I determined to turn my back for ever on the theatre, and to make no further attempt to meddle with its concerns. By this act I expressed not merely my utter indifference as to whether I kept my position as musical conductor or no, but my artistic ambitions also entirely cut me off from all possibility of ever cultivating modern theatrical conditions again.

I at once proceeded to execute my long-cherished plans for *Siegfried's Tod,* which I had been half afraid of before. In this work I no longer gave a thought to the Dresden or any other court theatre in the world; my sole preoccupation was to produce something that should free me, once and for all, from this irrational subservience. As I could get nothing more from Röckel in this connection, I now corresponded exclusively with Eduard Devrient on matters connected with the theatre and dramatic art. When, on the completion of my poem, I read it to him, he listened with amazement, and at once realised the fact that such a production would be an absolute drug in the modern theatrical market, and he naturally could not agree to let it remain so. On the other hand, he tried so far to reconcile himself to my work as to try and make it less startling and more adapted for actual production. He proved the sincerity of his intentions by pointing out my error in asking too much of the public, and requiring it to supply from its own knowledge many things necessary for a right understanding of my subject-matter, at which I had only hinted in brief and scattered suggestions. He showed me, for instance, that before Siegfried and Brunhilda are displayed in a position of bitter hostility towards each other, they ought first to have been presented in their true and calmer relationship. I had, in fact, opened the poem of *Siegfried's Tod* with those scenes which now form the first act of the *Götterdämmerung*. The details of Siegfried's relation to Brunhilda had been merely outlined to the listeners in a lyrico-episodical dialogue between the hero's wife, whom he had left behind in solitude, and a crowd of Valkyries passing before her rock. To my great joy, Devrient's hint on this point directed my thoughts to those scenes which I afterwards worked out in the prologue of this drama.

This and other matters of a similar nature brought me into intimate contact with Eduard Devrient, and made our intercourse much more lively and pleasant. He often invited a select circle of friends to attend dramatic readings at his house in which I gladly took part, for I found, to my surprise, that his gift for declamation, which quite forsook him on the stage, here stood out in strong relief. It was, moreover, a consolation to pour into a sympathetic ear my worries about my growing unpopularity with the director. Devrient seemed particularly anxious to prevent a definite breach; but of this there was little hope. With the approach of winter the court had returned to town, and once more frequented the theatre, and various signs of dissatisfaction in high quarters with my behaviour as conductor began to be manifested. On one occasion the Queen thought that I had conducted *Norma* badly, and on another that I 'had taken the time wrongly' in *Robert the Devil*. As Lüttichau had to communicate these reprimands to me, it was natural that our intercourse at such times should hardly be of a nature to restore our mutual satisfaction with each other.

Notwithstanding all this, it still seemed possible to prevent matters from coming to a crisis, though everything continued in a state of agitating uncertainty and fermentation. At all events the forces of reaction, which were holding themselves in readiness on every side, were not yet sufficiently certain that the hour of their triumph had come as not to consider it advisable for the present, at least, to avoid all provocation. Consequently our management did not meddle with the musicians of the royal orchestra, who, in obedience to the spirit of the times, had formed a union for debate and the protection of their artistic and civic interests. In this matter one of our youngest musicians, Theodor Uhlig, had been particularly active. He was a young man, still in his early twenties, and was a violinist in the orchestra. His face was strikingly mild, intelligent and noble, and he was conspicuous among his fellows on account of his great seriousness and his quiet but unusually firm character. He had particularly attracted my notice on several occasions by his quick insight and extensive knowledge of music. As I recognised in him a spirit keenly alert in every direction, and unusually eager for culture, it was not long before I chose him as my companion in my regular walks — a habit I still continued to cultivate — and on which Röckel had hitherto accompanied me. He induced me to come to a meeting of this union of the orchestral company, in order that I might form an opinion about it, and encourage and support so praiseworthy a movement. On this occasion I communicated to its members the contents of my memorandum to the director, which had been rejected a year before, and in which I had made suggestions for reforms in the band, and I also explained further intentions and plans arising therefrom. At the same time I was obliged to confess that I had lost all hope of carrying out any projects of the kind through the general management, and must therefore recommend them to take the initiative vigorously into their own hands. They acclaimed the idea with enthusiastic approval. Although, as I have said before, Lüttichau left these musicians unmolested in their more or less democratic union, yet he took care to be informed through spies of what took place at their highly treasonable gatherings. His chief instrument was a bugler named Lewy, who, much to the disgust of all his comrades in the orchestra, was in particularly high favour with the director. He consequently received precise, or rather exaggerated, accounts of my appearance there, and thought it was now high time to let me once more feel the weight of his authority. I was officially summoned to his presence, and had to listen to a long and wrathful tirade which he had been bottling up for some time about several matters. I also learned that he knew all about the plan of theatre reform which I had laid before the ministry. This knowledge he betrayed in a popular Dresden phrase, which until then I had never heard; he knew very well, he said, that in a memorandum respecting the theatre I had ' made him look ridiculous ' (*ihm an den Laden gelegt*). In answer to this I did not refrain from telling him how I intended to act in retaliation, and when he threatened to report me to the King and demand my dismissal, I calmly replied that he might do as he pleased, as I was well assured that I could rely on his Majesty's justice to hear, not only his charges, but also my defence. Moreover, I added, this was the only befitting manner for me to discuss with the King the many points on which I had to complain, not only in my own interests, but also in those of the theatre and of art. This was not pleasant hearing for Lüttichau, and he asked how it was possible for him to try and co-operate with me, when I for my part had openly declared (to use his own expression) that all labour was wasted upon him (*Hopfen und Malz verloren seien*). We had at last to part with mutual shruggings of the shoulder. My conduct seemed to trouble my former patron, and he therefore enlisted the tact and moderation of Eduard Devrient in his service, and asked him to use his influence with me to facilitate some further arrangement between us. But, in spite of all his zeal, Devrient had to admit with a smile, after we had discussed his message, that nothing much could be done; and as I persisted in my refusal to meet the director again in consultation respecting the service of the theatre, he had at last to recognise that his own wisdom would have to help him out of the difficulty.

Throughout the whole period during which I was fated to fill the post of conductor at Dresden, the effects of this dislike on the part of the court and the director continued to make themselves felt in everything. The orchestral concerts, which had been organised by me in the previous winter, were this year placed under Reissiger's control, and at once sank to the usual level of ordinary concerts. Public interest quickly waned, and the undertaking could only with difficulty be kept alive. In opera I was unable to carry out the proposed revival of the *Fliegender Holländer,* for which I had found in Mitterwurzer's maturer talent an admirable and promising exponent. My niece Johanna, whom I had destined for the part of Senta, did not like the rôle, because it offered little opportunity for splendid costumes. She preferred *Zampa* and *Favorita*, partly to please her new protector, my erstwhile *Rienzi* enthusiast, Tichatschek, partly for the sake of *three brilliant costumes* which the management had to furnish for each of these parts. In fact, these two ringleaders of the Dresden opera of that day had formed an alliance of rebellion against my vigorous rule in the matter of operatic repertoire. Their opposition, to my great discomfiture, was crowned by success when they secured the production of this *Favorita* of Donizetti's, the arrangement of which I had once been obliged to undertake for Schlesinger in Paris. I had at first emphatically refused to have anything to do with this opera, although its principal part suited my niece's voice admirably, even in her father's judgment. But now that they knew of my feud with the director, and of my voluntary loss of influence, and finally of my evident disgrace, they thought the opportunity ripe for compelling me to conduct this tiresome work myself, as it happened to be my turn.

Besides this, my chief occupation at the royal theatre during this period consisted in conducting Flotow's opera *Martha*, which, although it failed to attract the public, was nevertheless produced with excessive frequency, owing to its convenient cast. On reviewing the results of my labours in Dresden — where I had now been nearly seven years — I could not help feeling humiliated when I considered the powerful and energetic impetus I knew I had given in many directions to the court theatre, and I found myself obliged to confess that, were I now to leave Dresden, not the smallest trace of my influence would remain behind. From various signs I also gathered that, if ever it should come to a trial before the King between the director and myself, even if his Majesty were in my favour, yet out of consideration for the courtier the verdict would go against me.

Nevertheless, on Palm Sunday of the new year, 1849, I received ample amends. In order to ensure liberal receipts, our orchestra had again decided to produce Beethoven's Ninth

Symphony. Every one did his utmost to make this one of
our finest performances, and the public took up the matter
with real enthusiasm. Michael Bakunin, unknown to the police,
had been present at the public rehearsal. At its close he walked
unhesitatingly up to me in the orchestra, and said in a loud
voice, that if all the music that had ever been written were
lost in the expected world-wide conflagration, we must pledge
ourselves to rescue this symphony, even at the peril of our lives.
Not many weeks after this performance it really seemed as
though this world-wide conflagration would actually be kindled
in the streets of Dresden, and that Bakunin, with whom I had
meanwhile become more closely associated through strange
and unusual circumstances, would undertake the office of chief
stoker.

It was long before this date that I first made the acquaintance
of this most remarkable man. For years I had come across
his name in the newspapers, and always under extraordinary
circumstances. He turned up in Paris at a Polish gathering, but although he was a Russian, he declared that it mattered
little whether a man were a Russian or a Pole, so long as he
wanted to be a free man, and that this was all that mattered.
I heard afterwards, through George Herwegh, that he had
renounced all his sources of income as a member of an influential
Russian family, and that one day, when his entire fortune
consisted of two francs, he had given them away to a beggar
on the boulevard, because it was irksome to him to be bound
by this possession to take any thought for the morrow. I was
informed of his presence in Dresden one day by Röckel, after
the latter had become a rampant republican. He had taken
the Russian into his house, and invited me to come and make
his acquaintance. Bakunin was at that time being persecuted
by the Austrian government for his share in the events which
took place in Prague in the summer of 1848, and because he was
a member of the Slav Congress which had preceded them.
He had consequently sought refuge in our city, as he did not
wish to settle too far from the Bohemian frontier. The extraordinary sensation he had created in Prague arose from the fact
that, when the Czechs sought the protection of Russia against
the dreaded Germanising policy of Austria, he conjured them

to defend themselves with fire and sword against those very
Russians, and indeed against any other people who lived under
the rule of a despotism like that of the Tsars. This superficial
acquaintance with Bakunin's aims had sufficed to change the
purely national prejudices of the Germans against him into
sympathy. When I met him, therefore, under the humble
shelter of Röckel's roof, I was immediately struck by his singular
and altogether imposing personality. He was in the full bloom
of manhood, anywhere between thirty and forty years of age.
Everything about him was colossal, and he was full of a primitive exuberance and strength. I never gathered that he set
much store by my acquaintance. Indeed, he did not seem
to care for merely intellectual men; what he demanded was
men of reckless energy. As I afterwards perceived, theory
in this case had more weight with him than purely personal
sentiment; and he talked much and expatiated freely on the
matter. His general mode of discussion was the Socratic
method, and he seemed quite at his ease when, stretched on
his host's hard sofa, he could argue discursively with a crowd
of all sorts of men on the problems of revolution. On these
occasions he invariably got the best of the argument. It was
impossible to triumph against his opinions, stated as they were
with the utmost conviction, and overstepping in every direction
even the extremest bounds of radicalism. So communicative
was he, that on the very first evening of our meeting he gave
me full details about the various stages of his development.
He was a Russian officer of high birth, but smarting under the
yoke of the narrowest martial tyranny, he had been led by a
study of Rousseau's writings to escape to Germany under pretence of taking furlough. In Berlin he had flung himself into
the study of philosophy with all the zest of a barbarian newly
awakened to civilisation. Hegel's philosophy was the one which
was the rage at that moment, and he soon became such an
expert in it, that he had been able to hurl that master's most
famous disciples from the saddle of their own philosophy, in a
thesis couched in terms of the strictest Hegelian dialectic.
After he had got philosophy off his chest, as he expressed it,
he proceeded to Switzerland, where he preached communism,
and thence wandered over France and Germany back to the

borderland of the Slav world, from which quarter he looked
for the regeneration of humanity, because the Slavs had been
less enervated by civilisation. His hopes in this respect were
centred in the more strongly pronounced Slav type characteristic of the Russian peasant class. In the natural detestation
of the Russian serf for his cruel oppressor the nobleman, he
believed he could trace a substratum of simple-minded brotherly
love, and that instinct which leads animals to hate the men
who hunt them. In support of this idea he cited the childish,
almost demoniac delight of the Russian people in fire, a quality
on which Rostopschin calculated in his strategic burning of
Moscow. He argued that all that was necessary to set in
motion a world-wide movement was to convince the Russian
peasant, in whom the natural goodness of oppressed human
nature had preserved its most childlike characteristics, that
it was perfectly right and well pleasing to God for them to burn
their lords' castles, with everything in and about them The
least that could result from such a movement would be the
destruction of all those things which, rightly considered, must
appear, even to Europe's most philosophical thinkers, the real
source of all the misery of the modern world. To set these
destructive forces in action appeared to him the only object
worthy of a sensible man's activity. (Even while he was
preaching these horrible doctrines, Bakunin, noticing that my
eyes troubled me, shielded them with his outstretched hand
from the naked light for a full hour, in spite of my protestations.) This annihilation of all civilisation was the goal upon
which his heart was set. Meanwhile it amused him to utilise
every lever of political agitation he could lay hands on for the
advancement of this aim, and in so doing he often found cause
for ironical merriment. In his retreat he received people belonging to every shade of revolutionary thought. Nearest to
him stood those of Slav nationality, because these, he thought,
would be the most convenient and effective weapons he could
use in the uprooting of Russian despotism. In spite of their
republic and their socialism à la Proudhon, he thought nothing
of the French, and as for the Germans, he never mentioned
them to me. Democracy, republicanism, and anything else
of the kind he regarded as unworthy of serious consideration.

Every objection raised by those who had the slightest wish to reconstruct what had been demolished, he met with overwhelming criticism. I well remember on one occasion that a Pole, startled by his theories, maintained that there must be an organised state to guarantee the individual in the possession of the fields he had cultivated. ' What ! ' he answered; ' would you carefully fence in your field to provide a livelihood for the police again ! ' This shut the mouth of the terrified Pole. He comforted himself by saying that the creators of the new order of things would arise of themselves, but that our sole business in the meantime was to find the power to destroy. Was any one of us so mad as to fancy that he would survive the desired destruction ? We ought to imagine the whole of Europe with St. Petersburg, Paris, and London transformed into a vast rubbish-heap. How could we expect the kindlers of such a fire to retain any consciousness after so vast a devastation? He used to puzzle any who professed their readiness for self-sacrifice by telling them it was not the so-called tyrants who were so obnoxious, but the smug Philistines. As a type of these he pointed to a Protestant parson, and declared that he would not believe he had really reached the full stature of a man until he saw him commit his own parsonage, with his wife and child, to the flames.

I was all the more perplexed for a while, in the face of such dreadful ideas, by the fact that Bakunin in other respects proved a really amiable and tender-hearted man. He was fully alive to my own anxiety and despair with regard to the risk I ran of forever destroying my ideals and hopes for the future of art. It is true, he declined to receive any further instruction concerning these artistic schemes, and would not even look at my work on the Nibelungen saga. I had just then been inspired by a study of the Gospels to conceive the plan of a tragedy for the ideal stage of the future, entitled *Jesus of Nazareth*. Bakunin begged me to spare him any details; and when I sought to win him over to my project by a few verbal hints, he wished me luck, but insisted that I must at all costs make Jesus appear as a weak character. As for the music of the piece, he advised me, amid all the variations, to use only one set of phrases, namely: for the tenor, ' Off with His head ! ';

for the soprano, 'Hang Him!'; and for the basso continuo,
'Fire! fire!' And yet I felt more sympathetically drawn
towards this prodigy of a man when I one day induced him to
hear me play and sing the first scenes of my *Fliegender
Holländer*. After listening with more attention than most
people gave, he exclaimed, during a momentary pause, ' That is
stupendously fine!' and wanted to hear more.

As his life of permanent concealment was very dull, I occasionally invited him to spend an evening with me. For supper
my wife set before him finely cut slices of sausage and meat,
which he at once devoured wholesale, instead of spreading
them frugally on his bread in Saxon fashion. Noticing Minna's
alarm at this, I was guilty of the weakness of telling him how
we were accustomed to consume such viands, whereupon he
reassured me with a laugh, saying that it was quite enough,
only he would like to eat what was set before him in his own
way. I was similarly astonished at the manner in which he
drank wine from our ordinary-sized small glasses. As a matter
of fact he detested wine, which only satisfied his craving for
alcoholic stimulants in such paltry, prolonged, and subdivided
doses; whereas a stiff glass of brandy, swallowed at a gulp,
at once produced the same result, which, after all, was only
temporarily attained. Above all, he scorned the sentiment
which seeks to prolong enjoyment by moderation, arguing that
a true man should only strive to still the cravings of nature, and
that the only real pleasure in life worthy of a man was love.

These and other similar little characteristics showed clearly
that in this remarkable man the purest impulses of an ideal
humanity conflicted strangely with a savagery entirely inimical
to all civilisation, so that my feelings during my intercourse
with him fluctuated between involuntary horror and irresistible
attraction. I frequently called for him to share my lonely
wanderings. This he gladly did, not only for the sake of
necessary bodily exercise, but also because he could do so in this
part of the world without fear of meeting his pursuers. My
attempts during our conversations to instruct him more fully
regarding my artistic aims remained quite unavailing as long
as we were unable to quit the field of mere discussion. All
these things seemed to him premature. He refused to admit

that out of the very needs of the evil present all laws for the future would have to be evolved, and that these, moreover, must be moulded upon quite different ideas of social culture. Seeing that he continued to urge destruction, and again destruction, I had at last to inquire how my wonderful friend proposed to set this work of destruction in operation. It then soon became clear, as I had suspected it would, and as the event soon proved, that with this man of boundless activity everything rested upon the most impossible hypotheses. Doubtless I, with my hopes of a future artistic remodelling of human society, appeared to him to be floating in the barren air; yet it soon became obvious to me that his assumptions as to the unavoidable demolition of all the institutions of culture were at least equally visionary. My first idea was that Bakunin was the centre of an international conspiracy; but his practical plans seem originally to have been restricted to a project for revolutionising Prague, where he relied merely on a union formed among a handful of students. Believing that the time had now come to strike a blow, he prepared himself one evening to go there. This proceeding was not free from danger, and he set off under the protection of a passport made out for an English merchant. First of all, however, with the view of adapting himself to the most Philistine culture, he had to submit his huge beard and bushy hair to the tender mercies of the razor and shears. As no barber was available, Röckel had to undertake the task. A small group of friends watched the operation, which had to be executed with a dull razor, causing no little pain, under which none but the victim himself remained passive. We bade farewell to Bakunin with the firm conviction that we should never see him again alive. But in a week he was back once more, as he had realised immediately what a distorted account he had received as to the state of things in Prague, where all he found ready for him was a mere handful of childish students. These admissions made him the butt of Röckel's good-humoured chaff, and after this he won the reputation among us of being a mere revolutionary, who was content with theoretical conspiracy. Very similar to his expectations from the Prague students were his presumptions with regard to the Russian people. These also afterwards proved to be entirely groundless, and based merely on gratuitous assumptions drawn from the supposed nature of things. I consequently found myself driven to explain the universal belief in the terrible dangerousness of this man by his theoretical views, as expressed here and elsewhere, and not as arising from any actual experience of his practical activity. But I was soon to become almost an eye-witness of the fact that his personal conduct was never for a moment swayed by prudence, such as one is accustomed to meet in those whose theories are not seriously meant. This was shortly to be proved in the momentous insurrection of May, 1849.

The winter of this year, up to the spring of 1849, passed in a many-sided development of my position and temper, as I have described them, that is to say, in a sort of dull agitation. My latest artistic occupation had been the five-act drama, *Jesus of Nazareth,* just mentioned. Henceforth I lingered on in a state of brooding instability, full of expectation, yet without any definite wish. I felt fully convinced that my activity in Dresden, as an artist, had come to an end, and I was only waiting for the pressure of circumstances to shake myself free. On the other hand, the whole political situation, both in Saxony and the rest of Germany, tended inevitably towards a catastrophe. Day by day this drew nearer, and I flattered myself into regarding my own personal fate as interwoven with this universal unrest. Now that the powers of reaction were everywhere more and more openly bracing themselves for conflict, the final decisive struggle seemed indeed close at hand. My feelings of partisanship were not sufficiently passionate to make me desire to take any active share in these conflicts. I was merely conscious of an impulse to give myself up recklessly to the stream of events, no matter whither it might lead.

Just at this moment, however, an entirely new influence forced itself in a most strange fashion into my fortunes, and was at first greeted by me with a smile of scepticism. Liszt wrote announcing an early production in Weimar of my *Tannhäuser* under his own conductorship — the first that had taken place outside Dresden — and he added with great modesty that this was merely a fulfilment of his own personal desire. In order to ensure success he had sent a special invitation to

Tichatschek to be his guest for the two first performances. When the latter returned he said that the production had, on the whole, been a success, which surprised me very much. I received a gold snuff-box from the Grand Duke as a keepsake, which I continued to use until the year 1864. All this was new and strange to me, and I was still inclined to regard this other-wise agreeable occurrence as a fleeting episode, due to the friendly feeling of a great artist. ' What does this mean for me ? ' I asked myself. ' Has it come too early or too late ? ' But a very cordial letter from Liszt induced me to visit Weimar for a few days later on, for a third performance of *Tannhäuser,* which was to be carried out entirely by native talent, with a view to the permanent addition of this opera to the repertoire. For this purpose I obtained leave of absence from my manage-ment for the second week in May.

Only a few days elapsed before the execution of this little plan; but they were destined to be momentous ones. On the 1st of May the Chambers were dissolved by the new Beust ministry, which the King had charged with carrying out his proposed reactionary policy. This event imposed upon me the friendly task of caring for Röckel and his family. Hitherto his position as a deputy had shielded him from the danger of criminal prosecution; but as soon as the Chambers were dissolved this protection was withdrawn, and he had to escape by flight from being arrested again. As I could do little to help him in this matter, I promised at least to provide for the con-tinued publication of his popular *Volksblatt,* mainly because the proceeds from this would support his family. Scarcely was Röckel safely across the Bohemian frontier, while I was still toiling at great inconvenience to myself in the printer's office, in order to provide material for an issue of his paper, when the long-expected storm burst over Dresden. Emergency deputations, nightly mob demonstrations, stormy meetings of the various unions, and all the other signs that precede a swift decision in the streets, manifested themselves. On the 3rd May the demeanour of the crowds moving in our thoroughfares plainly showed that this consummation would soon be reached, as was undoubtedly desired. Each local deputation which petitioned for the recognition of the German constitution, which was the universal cry, was refused an audience by the government, and this with a peremptoriness which at last became startling. I was present one afternoon at a committee meeting of the *Vaterlands-Verein,* although merely as a representative of Röckel's *Volksblatt,* for whose continuance, both from economic as well as humane motives, I felt pledged. Here I was at once absorbed in watching the conduct and demeanour of the men whom popular favour had raised to the leadership of such unions. It was quite evident that events had passed beyond the control of these persons; more particularly were they utterly at a loss as to how to deal with that peculiar terrorism exerted by the lower classes which is always so ready to react upon the representatives of democratic theories. On every side I heard a medley of wild proposals and hesitating responses. One of the chief subjects under debate was the necessity of preparing for defence. Arms, and how to procure them, were eagerly discussed, but all in the midst of great disorder; and when at last they discovered that it was time to break up, the only impression I received was one of the wildest confusion. I left the hall with a young painter named Kaufmann, from whose hand I had previously seen a series of cartoons in the Dresden Art Exhibition, illustrating ' The History of the Mind.' One day I had seen the King of Saxony standing before one of these, representing the torture of a heretic under the Spanish Inquisition, and observed him turn away with a disapproving shake of the head from so abstruse a subject. I was on my way home, deep in conversation with this man, whose pale face and troubled look betrayed that he foresaw the disaster that was imminent, when, just as we reached the Postplatz, near the fountain erected from Semper's design, the clang of bells from the neighbouring tower of St. Ann's Church suddenly sounded the tocsin of revolt. With a terrified cry, ' Good God, it has begun! ' my companion vanished from my side. He wrote to me afterwards to say that he was living as a fugitive in Berne, but I never saw his face again.

The clang of this bell, so close at hand, made a profound impression upon me also. It was a very sunny afternoon, and I at once noticed the same phenomenon which Goethe describes in his attempt to depict his own sensations during the bom-

bardment of Valmy. The whole square looked as though it
were illuminated by a dark yellow, almost brown, light, such
as I had once before seen in Magdeburg during an eclipse of
the sun. My most pronounced sensation beyond this was one
of great, almost extravagant, satisfaction. I felt a sudden
strange longing to play with something hitherto regarded as
dangerous and important. My first idea, suggested probably
by the vicinity of the square, was to inquire at Tichatschek's
house for the gun which, as an enthusiastic Sunday sportsman,
he was accustomed to use. I only found his wife at home, as
he was away on a holiday tour. Her evident terror as to what
was going to happen provoked me to uncontrollable laughter.
I advised her to lodge her husband's gun in a place of safety,
by handing it to the committee of the *Vaterlands-Verein* in
return for a receipt, as it might otherwise soon be requisitioned
by the mob. I have since learned that my eccentric behaviour
on this occasion was afterwards reckoned against me as a
serious crime. I then returned to the streets, to see whether
anything beyond a ringing of bells and a yellowish eclipse of
the sun might be going on in the town. I first made my way
to the Old Market-place, where I noticed a group of men
gathered round a vociferous orator. It was also an agreeable surprise to me to see Schröder-Devrient descending at the door of
a hotel. She had just arrived from Berlin, and was keenly
excited by the news which had reached her, that the populace
had already been fired upon. As she had only recently seen
an abortive insurrection crushed by arms in Berlin, she was
indignant to find the same things happening in her ' peaceful
Dresden,' as she termed it.

When she turned to me from the stolid crowd, which had
complacently been listening to her passionate outpourings, she
seemed relieved at finding some one to whom she could appeal
to oppose these horrible proceedings with all his might. I
met her on another occasion at the house of my old friend
Heine, where she had taken refuge. When she noticed my
indifference she again adjured me to use every possible effort
to prevent the senseless, suicidal conflict. I heard afterwards
that a charge of high treason on account of sedition had been
brought against Schröder-Devrient by reason of her conduct

in regard to this matter. She had to prove her innocence in a court of law, so as to establish beyond dispute her claim to the pension which she had been promised by contract for her many years' service in Dresden as an opera-singer.

On the 3rd of May I betook myself direct to that quarter of the town where I heard unpleasant rumours of a sanguinary conflict having taken place. I afterwards learned that the actual cause of the dispute between the civil and military power had arisen when the watch had been changed in front of the Arsenal. At that moment the mob, under a bold leader, had seized the opportunity to take forcible possession of the armoury. A display of military force was made, and the crowd was fired upon by a few cannon loaded with grape-shot. As I approached the scene of operations through the Rampische Gasse, I met a company of the Dresden Communal Guards, who, although they were quite innocent, had apparently been exposed to this fire. I noticed that one of the citizen guards, leaning heavily on the arm of a comrade, was trying to hurry along, in spite of the fact that his right leg seemed to be dragging helplessly behind him. Some of the crowd, seeing the blood on the pavement behind him, shouted 'He is bleeding.' In the midst of this excitement I suddenly became conscious of the cry raised on all sides: 'To the barricades! to the barricades!' Driven by a mechanical impulse I followed the stream of people, which moved once more in the direction of the Town Hall in the Old Market-place. Amid the terrific tumult I particularly noticed a significant group stretching right across the street, and striding along the Rosmaringasse. It reminded me, though the simile was rather exaggerated, of the crowd that had once stood at the doors of the theatre and demanded free entrance to *Rienzi;* among them was a hunchback, who at once suggested Goethe's Vansen in *Egmont,* and as the revolutionary cry rose about his ears, I saw him rub his hands together in great glee over the long-desired ecstasy of revolt which he had realised at last.

I recollect quite clearly that from that moment I was attracted by surprise and interest in the drama, without feeling any desire to join the ranks of the combatants. However, the agitation caused by my sympathy as a mere spectator increased with every step I felt impelled to take. I was able to press right into the rooms of the town council, escaping notice in the tumultuous crowd, and it seemed to me as if the officials were guilty of collusion with the mob. I made my way unobserved into the council-chamber; what I saw there was utter disorder and confusion. When night fell I wandered slowly through the hastily made barricades, consisting chiefly of market stalls, back to my house in the distant Friedrichstrasse, and next morning I again watched these amazing proceedings with sympathetic interest.

On Thursday, 4th May, I could see that the Town Hall was gradually becoming the undoubted centre of the revolution. That section of the people who had hoped for a peaceful understanding with the monarch was thrown into the utmost consternation by the news that the King and his whole court, acting on the advice of his minister Beust, had left the palace, and had gone by ship down the Elbe to the fortress of Königstein. In these circumstances the town council saw they were no longer able to face the situation, and thereupon took part in summoning those members of the Saxon Chamber who were still in Dresden. These latter now assembled in the Town Hall to decide what steps should be taken for the protection of the state. A deputation was sent to the ministry, but returned with the report that they were nowhere to be found. At the same moment news arrived from all sides that, in accordance with a previous compact, the King of Prussia's troops would advance to occupy Dresden. A general outcry immediately arose for measures to be adopted to prevent this incursion of foreign troops.

Simultaneously with this, came the intelligence of the national uprising in Würtemberg, where the troops themselves had frustrated the intentions of the government by their declaration of fidelity to the parliament, and the ministry had been compelled against their will to acknowledge the Pan-German Constitution. The opinion of our politicians, who were assembled in consultation, was that the matter might still be settled by peaceful means, if it were possible to induce the Saxon troops to take up a similar attitude, as by this means the King would at least be placed under the wholesome necessity of offering patriotic resistance to the Prussian occupation of his country.

Everything seemed to depend on making the Saxon battalions
in Dresden understand the paramount importance of their
action. As this seemed to me the only hope of an honourable
peace in this senseless chaos, I confess that, on this one occasion,
I did allow myself to be led astray so far as to organise a
demonstration which, however, proved futile.

I induced the printer of Röckel's *Volksblatt,* which was for
the moment at a standstill, to employ all the type he would
have used for his next number, in printing in huge characters
on strips of paper the words: *Seid Ihr mit uns gegen fremde
Truppen?* (' Are you on our side against the foreign troops ? ').
Placards bearing these words were fixed on those barricades
which it was thought would be the first to be assaulted, and
were intended to bring the Saxon troops to a halt if they were
commanded to attack the revolutionaries. Of course no one
took any notice of these placards except intending informers.
On that day nothing but confused negotiations and wild excitement took place which threw no light on the situation. The
Old Town of Dresden, with its barricades, was an interesting
enough sight for the spectators. I looked on with amazement
and disgust, but my attention was suddenly distracted by
seeing Bakunin emerge from his hiding-place and wander
among the barricades in a black frockcoat. But I was very
much mistaken in thinking he would be pleased with what he
saw; he recognised the childish inefficiency of all the measures
that had been taken for defence, and declared that the only
satisfaction he could feel in the state of affairs was that he need
not trouble about the police, but could calmly consider the
question of going elsewhere, as he found no inducement to take
part in an insurrection conducted in such a slovenly fashion.
While he walked about smoking his cigar, and making fun of
the *naïveté* of the Dresden revolution, I watched the Communal
Guards assembling under arms in front of the Town Hall at the
summons of their commandant. From the ranks of its most
popular corps, the Schützen-Compagnie, I was accosted by
Rietschel, who was most anxious about the nature of the rising,
and also by Semper. Rietschel, who seemed to think I was
better informed of the facts than he was, assured me that he
felt his position was a very difficult one. He said the select

company to which he belonged was very democratic, and as his professorship at the Fine Arts Academy placed him in a peculiar position, he did not know how to reconcile the sentiments he shared with his company with his duty as a citizen. The word ' citizen ' amused me; I glanced sharply at Semper and repeated the word ' citizen.' Semper responded with a peculiar smile, and turned away without further comment.

The next day (Friday the 5th of May), when I again took my place as a passionately interested spectator of the proceedings at the Town Hall, events took a decisive turn. The remnant of the leaders of the Saxon people there assembled thought it advisable to constitute themselves into a provisional government, as there was no Saxon government in existence with which negotiations could be conducted. Professor Köchly, who was an eloquent speaker, was chosen to proclaim the new administration. He performed this solemn ceremony from the balcony of the Town Hall, facing the faithful remnant of the Communal Guards and the not very numerous crowd. At the same time the legal existence of the Pan-German Constitution was proclaimed, and allegiance to it was sworn by the armed forces of the nation. I recollect that these proceedings did not seem to me imposing, and Bakunin's reiterated opinion about their triviality gradually became more comprehensible. Even from a technical point of view these reflections were justified when, to my great amusement and surprise, Semper, in the full uniform of a citizen guard, with a hat bedecked with the national colours, asked for me at the Town Hall, and informed me of the extremely faulty construction of the barricades in the Wild Strufergasse and the neighbouring Brüdergasse. To pacify his artistic conscience as an engineer I directed him to the office of the ' Military Commission for the Defence.' He followed my advice with conscientious satisfaction; possibly he obtained the necessary authorisation to give instructions for the building of suitable works of defence at that neglected point. After that I never saw him again in Dresden; but I presume that he carried out the strategic works entrusted to him by that committee with all the conscientiousness of a Michael Angelo or a Leonardo da Vinci.

The rest of the day passed in continuous negotiations over

the truce which, by arrangement with the Saxon troops, was
to last until noon of the next day. In this business I noticed
the very pronounced activity of a former college friend, Marschall von Bieberstein, a lawyer who, in his capacity as senior
officer of the Dresden Communal Guard, distinguished himself by his boundless zeal amid the shouts of a mighty band of
fellow-orators. On that day a certain Heinz, formerly a Greek
colonel, was placed in command of the armed forces. These proceedings did not seem at all satisfactory to Bakunin, who put in
an occasional appearance. While the provisional government
placed all its hopes on finding a peaceful settlement of the
conflict by moral persuasion, he, on the contrary, with his
clear vision foresaw a well-planned military attack by the
Prussians, and thought it could only be met by good strategic
measures. He therefore urgently pressed for the acquisition
of some experienced Polish officers who happened to be in
Dresden, as the Saxon revolutionaries appeared to be absolutely lacking in military tactics. Everybody was afraid to
take this course; on the other hand, great expectations were
entertained from negotiations with the Frankfort States Assembly, which was on its last legs. Everything was to be
done as far as possible in legal form. The time passed pleasantly enough. Elegant ladies with their cavaliers promenaded
the barricaded streets during those beautiful spring evenings.
It seemed to be little more than an entertaining drama. The
unaccustomed aspect of things even afforded me genuine pleasure, combined with a feeling that the whole thing was not
quite serious, and that a friendly proclamation from the government would put an end to it. So I strolled comfortably
home through the numerous barricades at a late hour, thinking
as I went of the material for a drama, *Achilleus*, with which
I had been occupied for some time.

At home I found my two nieces, Clara and Ottilie Brockhaus,
the daughters of my sister Louisa. They had been living for
a year with a governess in Dresden, and their weekly visits
and contagious good spirits delighted me. Every one was in
a high state of glee about the revolution; they all heartily
approved of the barricades, and felt no scruples about desiring
victory for their defenders. Protected by the truce, this state

of mind remained undisturbed the whole of Friday (5th May).
From all parts came news which led us to believe in a universal
uprising throughout Germany. Baden and the Palatinate were
in the throes of a revolt on behalf of the whole of Germany.
Similar rumours came in from free towns like Breslau. In
Leipzig, volunteer student corps had mustered contingents for
Dresden, which arrived amid the exultation of the populace.
A fully equipped defence department was organised at the
Town Hall, and young Heine, disappointed like myself in his
hopes of the performance of *Lohengrin,* had also joined this
body. Vigorous promises of support came from the Saxon
Erzgebirge, as well as announcements that armed contingents
were forthcoming. Every one thought, therefore, that if only
the Old Town were kept well barricaded, it could safely defy
the threat of foreign occupation. Early on Saturday, 6th May,
it was obvious that the situation was becoming more serious.
Prussian troops had marched into the New Town, and the
Saxon troops, which it had not been considered advisable to
use for an attack, were kept loyal to the flag. The truce expired
at noon, and the troops, supported by several guns, at once
opened the attack on one of the principal positions held by the
people on the Neumarkt.

So far I had entertained no other conviction than that the
matter would be decided in the most summary fashion as soon
as it came to an actual conflict, for there was no evidence in
the state of my own feelings (or, indeed, in what I was able to
gather independently of them) of that passionate seriousness
of purpose, without which tests as severe as this have never
been successfully withstood. It was irritating to me, while I
heard the sharp rattle of fire, to be unable to gather anything
of what was going on, and I thought by climbing the Kreuz
tower I might get a good view. Even from this elevation I
could not see anything clearly, but I gathered enough to satisfy
myself that after an hour of heavy firing the advance artillery
of the Prussian troops had retired, and had at last been completely silenced, their withdrawal being signalled by a loud
shout of jubilation from the populace. Apparently the first
attack had exhausted itself; and now my interest in what was
going on began to assume a more and more vivid hue. To

obtain information in greater detail I hurried back to the Town
Hall. I could extract nothing, however, from the boundless
confusion which I met, until at last I came upon Bakunin 'in
the midst of the main group of speakers. He was able to give
me an extraordinarily accurate account of what had happened. Information had reached headquarters from a barricade
in the Neumarkt where the attack was most serious, that
everything had been in a state of confusion there before the on-
slaught of the troops; thereupon my friend Marschall von
Bieberstein, together with Leo von Zichlinsky, who were officers
in the citizen corps, had called up some volunteers and conducted them to the place of danger. Kreis-Amtmann Heubner
of Freiberg, without a weapon to defend himself, and with
bared head, jumped immediately on to the top of the barricade,
which had just been abandoned by all its defenders. He was
the sole member of the provisional government to remain on the
spot, the leaders, Todt and Tschirner, having disappeared at
the first sign of a panic. Heubner turned round to exhort the
volunteers to advance, addressing them in stirring words. His
success was complete, the barricade was taken again, and a
fire, as unexpected as it was fierce, was directed upon the
troops, which, as I myself saw, were forced to retire. Bakunin
had been in close touch with this action, he had followed
the volunteers, and he now explained to me that however narrow might be the political views of Heubner (he belonged to the
moderate Left of the Saxon Chamber), he was a man of noble
character, at whose service he had immediately placed his own
life.

Bakunin had only needed this example to determine his own
line of conduct; he had decided to risk his neck in the attempt
and to ask no further questions. Heubner too was now bound
to recognise the necessity for extreme measures, and no longer
recoiled from any proposal on the part of Bakunin which was
directed to this end. The military advice of experienced
Polish officers was brought to bear on the commandant, whose
incapacity had not been slow to reveal itself; Bakunin, who
openly confessed that he understood nothing of pure strategy,
never moved from the Town Hall, but remained at Heubner's
side, giving advice and information in every direction with

wonderful sangfroid. For the rest of the day the battle confined itself to skirmishes by sharpshooters from the various
positions. I was itching to climb the Kreuz tower again, so
as to get the widest possible survey over the whole field of
action. In order to reach this tower from the Town Hall, one
had to pass through a space which was under a cross-fire of
rifle-shots from the troops posted in the royal palace. At a
moment when this square was quite deserted, I yielded to my
daring impulse, and crossed it on my way to the Kreuz tower
at a slow pace, remembering that in such circumstances the
young soldier is advised never to hurry, because by so doing
he may draw the shot upon himself. On reaching this post of
vantage I found several people who had gathered there, some
of them driven by a curiosity like my own, others in obedience
to an order from the headquarters of the revolutionaries to
reconnoitre the enemy's movements. Amongst them I made
the acquaintance of a schoolmaster called Berthold, a man of
quiet and gentle disposition, but full of conviction and determination. I lost myself in an earnest philosophical discussion
with him which extended to the widest spheres of religion. At
the same time he showed a homely anxiety to protect us from
the cone-shaped bullets of the Prussian sharpshooters by placing us ingeniously behind a barricade consisting of one of the
straw mattresses which he had cajoled out of the warder. The
Prussian sharpshooters were posted on the distant tower of
the Frauenkirche, and had chosen the height occupied by us
as their target. At nightfall I found it impossible to make up
my mind to go home and leave my interesting place of refuge,
so I persuaded the warder to send a subordinate to Friedrichstadt with a few lines to my wife, and with instructions to ask
her to let me have some necessary provisions. Thus I spent
one of the most extraordinary nights of my life, taking turns
with Berthold to keep watch and sleep, close beneath the great
bell with its terrible groaning clang, and with the accompaniment of the continuous rattle of the Prussian shot as it beat
against the tower walls.

Sunday (the 7th of May) was one of the most beautiful days
in the year. I was awakened by the song of a nightingale, which
rose to our ears from the Schütze garden close by. A sacred

calm and peacefulness lay over the town and the wide suburbs of Dresden, which were visible from my point of vantage. Towards sunrise a mist settled upon the outskirts, and suddenly through its folds we could hear the music of the *Marseillaise* making its way clearly and distinctly from the district of the Tharanderstrasse. As the sound drew nearer and nearer, the mist dispersed, and the glow of the rising sun spread a glittering light upon the weapons of a long column which was winding its way towards the town. It was impossible not to feel deeply impressed at the sight of this continuous procession. Suddenly a perception of that element which I had so long missed in the German people was borne in upon me in all its essential freshness and vital colour. The fact that until this moment I had been obliged to resign myself to its absence, had contributed not a little to the feelings by which I had been swayed. Here I beheld some thousand men from the Erzgebirge, mostly miners, well armed and organised, who had rallied to the defence of Dresden. Soon we saw them march up the Altmarkt opposite the Town Hall, and after receiving a joyful welcome, bivouac there to recover from their journey. Reinforcements continued to pour in the whole day long, and the heroic achievement of the previous day now received its reward in the shape of a universal elevation of spirits. A change seemed to have been made in the plan of attack by the Prussian troops. This could be gathered from the fact that numerous simultaneous attacks, but of a less concentrated type, were made upon various positions. The troops which had come to reinforce us brought with them four small cannon, the property of a certain Herr Thade von Burgk, whose acquaintance I had made before on the occasion of the anniversary of the founding of the Dresden Choral Society, when he had made a speech which was well intentioned but wearisome to the point of being ludicrous. The recollection of this speech returned to me with peculiar irony, now that his cannon were being fired from the barricade upon the enemy. I felt a still deeper impression, however, when, towards eleven o'clock, I saw the old Opera House, in which a few weeks ago I had conducted the last performance of the Ninth Symphony, burst into flames. As I have had occasion to mention before, the danger from fire to which this building was exposed, full as it was with wood and all kind of textile fabric, and originally built only for a temporary purpose, had always been a subject of terror and apprehension to those who visited it.

I was told that the Opera House had been set alight on strategical grounds, in order to face a dangerous attack on this exposed side, and also to protect the famous ' Semper ' barricade from an overpowering surprise.   From this I concluded that reasons of this kind act as far more powerful motives in the world than æsthetic considerations.   For a long time men of taste had vainly cried aloud for abolition of this ugly building which was such an eyesore by the side of the elegant proportions of the Zwinger Gallery in its neighbourhood.   In a few moments the Opera House (which as regards size was, it is true, an imposing edifice), together with its highly inflammable contents, was a vast sea of flames.   When this reached the metal roofs of the neighbouring wings of the Zwinger, and enveloped them in wonderful bluish waves of fire, the first expression of regret made itself audible amongst the spectators. What a disaster!   Some thought that the Natural History collection was in danger;   others maintained that it was the Armoury, upon which a citizen soldier retorted that if such were the case, it would be a very good job if the ' stuffed noblemen ' were burnt to cinders.   But it appeared that a keen sense of the value of art knew how to curb the fire's lust for further dominion, and, as a matter of fact, it did but little damage in that quarter.   Finally our post of observation, which until now had remained comparatively quiet, was filled itself with swarms and swarms of armed men, who had been ordered thither to defend the approach from the church to the Altmarkt, upon which an attack was feared from the side of the ill-secured Kreuzgasse.   Unarmed men were now in the way; moreover, I had received a message from my wife summoning me home after the long and terrible anxiety she had suffered.

At last, after meeting with innumerable obstacles and overcoming a host of difficulties, I succeeded, by means of all sorts of circuitous routes, in reaching my remote suburb, from which I was cut off by the fortified portions of the town, and especially by a cannonade directed from the Zwinger.   My lodgings were

full to overflowing with excited women who had collected round
Minna; among them the panic-stricken wife of Röckel, who suspected her husband of being in the very thick of the fight, as she
thought that on the receipt of the news that Dresden had risen he
would probably have returned. As a matter of fact, I had
heard a rumour that Röckel had arrived on this very day, but as
yet I had not obtained a glimpse of him. My young nieces
helped once more to raise my spirits. The firing had put them
into a high state of glee, which to some extent infected my wife,
as soon as she was reassured as to my personal safety. All of
them were furious with the sculptor Hänel, who had never
ceased insisting upon the expedience of bolting the house to prevent an entry of the revolutionaries. All the women without
exception were joking about his abject terror at the sight of
some men armed with scythes who had appeared in the street. In
this way Sunday passed like a sort of family jollification.

On the following morning (Monday, 8th May) I tried again
to get information as to the state of affairs by forcing my way
to the Town Hall from my house, which was cut off from the
place of action. As in the course of my journey I was making
my way over a barricade near St. Ann's Church, one of the
Communal Guard shouted out to me, 'Hullo, conductor,
your *der Freude schöner Götterfunken* [1] has indeed set fire to
things. The rotten building is rased to the ground.' Obviously the man was an enthusiastic member of the audience
at my last performance of the Ninth Symphony. Coming upon
me so unexpectedly, this pathetic greeting filled me with a
curious sense of strength and freedom. A little further on,
in a lonely alley in the suburb of Plauen, I fell in with the
musician Hiebendahl, the first oboist in the royal orchestra,
and a man who still enjoyed a very high reputation; he was in
the uniform of the Communal Guards, but carried no gun, and
was chatting with a citizen in a similar costume. As soon as he
saw me, he felt he must immediately make an appeal to me to
use my influence against Röckel, who, accompanied by ordnance
officers of the revolutionary party, was instituting a search for
guns in this quarter. As soon as he realised that I was making

---

[1] These words refer to the opening of the Ninth Symphony chorus:
'Freude, Freude, Freude, schöner götterfunken Tochter aus Elysium' —
(Praise her, praise oh praise Joy, the god-descended daughter of Elysium.)
English version by Natalia Macfarren. — EDITOR.

sympathetic inquiries about Röckel, he drew back frightened, and said to me in tones of the deepest anxiety: ' But, conductor, have you no thought for your position, and what you may lose by exposing yourself in this fashion ? ' This remark had the most drastic effect upon me; I burst into a loud laugh, and told him that my position was not worth a thought one way or the other. This indeed was the expression of my real feelings, which had long been suppressed, and now broke out into almost jubilant utterance. At that moment I caught sight of Röckel, with two men of the citizen army who were carrying some guns, making his way towards me. He gave me a most friendly greeting, but turned at once to Hiebendahl and his companion and asked him why he was idling about here in uniform instead of being at his post. When Hiebendahl made the excuse that his gun had been requisitioned, Röckel cried out to him, ' You 're a fine lot of fellows! ' and went away laughing. He gave me a brief account as we proceeded of what had happened to him since I had lost sight of him, and thus spared me the obligation of giving him a report of his *Volksblatt*. We were interrupted by an imposing troop of well-armed young students of the gymnasium who had just entered the city and wished to have a safe conduct to their place of muster. The sight of these serried ranks of youthful figures, numbering several hundreds, who were stepping bravely to their duty, did not fail to make the most elevating impression upon me. Röckel undertook to accompany them over the barricade in safety to the mustering place in front of the Town Hall. He took the opportunity of lamenting the utter absence of true spirit which he had hitherto encountered in those in command. He had proposed, in case of extremity, to defend the most seriously threatened barricades by firing them with pitch brands; at the mere word the provisional government had fallen into a veritable state of panic. I let him go his way in order that I might enjoy the privilege of a solitary person and reach the Town Hall by a short cut, and it was not until thirteen years later that I again set eyes upon him.

In the Town Hall I learned from Bakunin that the provisional government had passed a resolution, on his advice, to abandon the position in Dresden, which had been entirely neglected

from the beginning, and was consequently quite untenable for
any length of time. This resolution proposd an armed retreat
to the Erzgebirge, where it would be possible to concentrate
the reinforcements pouring in from all sides, especially from
Thuringia, in such strength, that the advantageous position
could be used to inaugurate a German civil war that would
sound no hesitating note at its outset. To persist in defending
isolated barricaded streets in Dresden could, on the other hand,
lend little but the character of an urban riot to the contest,
although it was pursued with the highest courage. I must
confess that this idea seemed to me magnificent and full of
meaning. Up to this moment I had been moved only by a
feeling of sympathy for a method of procedure entered upon at
first with almost ironical incredulity, and then pursued with
the vigour of surprise. Now, however, all that had before
seemed incomprehensible, unfolded itself before my vision in
the form of a great and hopeful solution. Without either feeling that I was in any way being compelled, or that it was my
vocation to get some part or function allotted to me in these
events, I now definitely abandoned all consideration for my
personal situation, and determined to surrender myself to the
stream of developments which flowed in the direction towards
which my feelings had driven me with a delight that was full
of despair. Still, I did not wish to leave my wife helpless in
Dresden, and I rapidly devised a means of drawing her into
the path which I had chosen, without immediately informing
her of what my resolve meant. During my hasty return to
Friedrichstadt I recognised that this portion of the town had
been almost entirely cut off from the inner city by the occupation of the Prussian troops; I saw in my mind's eye our
own suburb occupied, and the consequences of a state of military
siege in their most repulsive light. It was an easy job to persuade Minna to accompany me on a visit, by way of the Tharanderstrasse, which was still free, to Chemnitz, where my married sister Clara lived. It was only a matter of a moment for
her to arrange her household orders, and she promised to follow
me to the next village in an hour with the parrot. I went on
in advance with my little dog Peps, in order to hire a carriage
in which to proceed on our journey to Chemnitz. It was a

smiling spring morning when I traversed for the last time the paths I had so often trod on my lonely walks, with the knowledge that I should never wander along them again. While the larks were soaring to dizzy heights above my head, and singing in the furrows of the fields, the light and heavy artillery did not cease to thunder down the streets of Dresden. The noise of this shooting, which had continued uninterruptedly for several days, had hammered itself so indelibly upon my nerves, that it continued to re-echo for a long time in my brain; just as the motion of the ship which took me to London had made me stagger for some time afterwards. Accompanied by this terrible music, I threw my parting greeting to the towers of the city that lay behind me, and said to myself with a smile, that if, seven years ago, my entry had taken place under thoroughly obscure auspices, at all events my exit was conducted with some show of pomp and ceremony.

When at last I found myself with Minna in a one-horse carriage on the way to the Erzgebirge, we frequently met armed reinforcements on their way to Dresden. The sight of them always kindled an involuntary joy in us; even my wife could not refrain from addressing words of encouragement to the men; at present it seemed not a single barricade had been lost. On the other hand, a gloomy impression was made upon us by a company of regulars which was making its way towards Dresden in silence. We asked some of them whither they were bound; and their answer, 'To do their duty,' had been obviously impressed upon them by command. At last we reached my relations in Chemnitz. I terrified all those near and dear to me when I declared my intention to return to Dresden on the following day at the earliest possible hour, in order to ascertain how things were going there. In spite of all attempts to dissuade me, I carried out my decision, pursued by a suspicion that I should meet the armed forces of the Dresden people on the country highroad in the act of retreat. The nearer I approached the capital, the stronger became the confirmation of the rumours that, as yet, there was no thought in Dresden of surrender or withdrawal, but that, on the contrary, the contest was proving very favourable for the national party. All this appeared to me like one miracle after another. On

this day, Tuesday, 9th of May, I once more forced my way in
a high state of excitement over ground which had become more
and more inaccessible. All the highways had to be avoided,
and it was only possible to make progress through such houses
as had been broken through. At last I reached the Town Hall
in the Altstadt, just as night was falling. A truly terrible
spectacle met my eyes, for I crossed those parts of the town in
which preparations had been made for a house-to-house fight.
The incessant groaning of big and small guns reduced to an
uncanny murmur all the other sounds that came from armed
men ceaselessly crying out to one another from barricade to
barricade, and from one house to another, which they had
broken through. Pitch brands burnt here and there, pale-
faced figures lay prostrate around the watch-posts, half dead
with fatigue, and any unarmed wayfarer forcing a path for
himself was sharply challenged. Nothing, however, that I
have lived through can be compared with the impression that
I received on my entry into the chambers of the Town Hall.
Here was a gloomy, and yet fairly compact and serious mass
of people; a look of unspeakable fatigue was upon all faces;
not a single voice had retained its natural tone. There was a
hoarse jumble of conversation inspired by a state of the highest
tension. The only familiar sight that survived was to be found
in the old servants of the Town Hall in their curious antiquated
uniform and three-cornered hats. These tall men, at other
times an object of considerable fear, I found engaged partly
in buttering pieces of bread, and cutting slices of ham and
sausage, and partly in piling into baskets immense stores of
provisions for the messengers sent by the defenders of the
barricades for supplies. These men had turned into veritable
nursing mothers of the revolution.

As I proceeded further, I came at last upon the members of
the provisional government, among whom Todt and Tschirner,
after their first panic-stricken flight, were once more to be
found gliding to and fro, gloomy as spectres, now that they
were chained to the performance of their heavy duties.
Heubner alone had preserved his full energy; but he was a
really piteous sight: a ghostly fire burned in his eyes which had
not had a wink of sleep for seven nights. He was delighted

to see me again, as he regarded my arrival as a good omen for
the cause which he was defending; while on the other hand,
in the rapid succession of events, he had come into contact
with elements about which no conclusion could shape itself
to his complete satisfaction. I found Bakunin's outlook undisturbed, and his attitude firm and quiet. He did not show
the smallest change in his appearance, in spite of having had
no sleep during the whole time, which I afterwards heard was a
fact. With a cigar in his mouth he received me, seated on one
of the mattresses which lay distributed over the floor of the
Town Hall. At his side was a very young Pole (a Galician)
named Haimberger, a violinist whom he had once asked me
to recommend to Lipinsky, in order that he might give him
lessons, as he did not want this raw and inexperienced boy,
who had become passionately attached to him, to get drawn
into the vortex of the present upheavals. Now that Haimberger had shouldered a gun, and presented himself for service
at the barricades, however, Bakunin had greeted him none the
less joyfully. He had drawn him down to sit by his side on
the couch, and every time the youth shuddered with fear at
the violent sound of the cannon-shot, he slapped him vigorously on the back and cried out: ' You are not in the company of your fiddle here, my friend. What a pity you did n't
stay where you were! ' Bakunin then gave me a short and
precise account of what had happened since I had left him
on the previous morning. The retreat which had then been
decided upon soon proved unadvisable, as it would have discouraged the numerous reinforcements which had already arrived on that day. Moreover, the desire for fighting had been
so great, and the force of the defenders so considerable, that
it had been possible to oppose the enemy's troops successfully
so far. But as the latter had also got large reinforcements,
they again had been able to make an effective combined attack
on the strong Wildstruf barricade. The Prussian troops had
avoided fighting in the streets, choosing instead the method of
fighting from house to house by breaking through the walls.
This had made it clear that all defence by barricades had
become useless, and that the enemy would succeed slowly
but surely in drawing near the Town Hall, the seat of the

provisional government. Bakunin had now proposed that all
the powder stores should be brought together in the lower rooms
of the Town Hall, and that on the approach of the enemy it
should be blown up. The town council, who were still in consultation in a back room, had remonstrated with the greatest
vehemence. Bakunin, however, had insisted with great firmness on the execution of the measure, but in the end had
been completely outwitted by the removal of all the powder
stores. Moreover, Heubner, to whom Bakunin could refuse
nothing, had been won over to the other side. It was now
decided that as everything was ready, the retreat to the Erzgebirge, which had originally been intended for the previous
day, should be fixed for the early morrow. Young Zichlinsky
had already received orders to cover the road to Plauen so as
to make it strategically safe. When I inquired after Röckel,
Bakunin replied swiftly that he had not been seen since the
previous evening, and that he had most likely allowed himself
to be caught: he was in such a nervous state. I now gave
an account of what I had observed on my way to and from
Chemnitz, describing the great masses of reinforcements,
amongst which was the communal guard of that place, several
thousands strong. In Freiberg I had met four hundred reserv-
ists, who had come in excellent form to back the citizen
army, but could not proceed further, as they were tired out by
their forced march. It seemed obvious that this was a case
in which the necessary energy to requisition wagons had been
lacking, and that if the bounds of loyalty were transgressed
in this matter, the advent of fresh forces would be considerably promoted. I was begged to make my way back at once,
and convey the opinion of the provisional government to the
people whose acquaintance I had made. My old friend Marschall von Bieberstein immediately proposed to accompany me.
I welcomed his offer, as he was an officer of the provisional
government, and was consequently more fitted than I was to
communicate orders. This man, who had been almost extravagant in his enthusiasm before, was now utterly exhausted
by sleeplessness, and unable to emit another word from his
hoarse throat. He now made his way with me from the Town
Hall to his house in the suburb of Plauen by the devious ways

that had been indicated to us, in order to requisition a carriage for our purpose from a coachman he knew, and to bid farewell to his family, from whom he assumed he would in all probability have to separate himself for some time.

While we were waiting for the coachman we had tea and supper, talking the while, in a fairly calm and composed manner, with the ladies of the house. We arrived at Freiberg early the following morning, after various adventures, and I set out forthwith to find the leaders of the reservist contingent with whom I was already acquainted. Marschall advised them to requisition horses and carts in the villages wherever they could do so. When they had all set off in marching order for Dresden, and while I was feeling impelled by my passionate interest in the fate of that city to return to it once more, Marschall conceived the desire to carry his commission further afield, and for this purpose asked to be allowed to leave me. Whereupon I again turned my back on the heights of the Erzgebirge, and was travelling by special coach in the direction of Tharand, when I too was overcome with sleep, and was only awakened by violent shouts and the sound of some one holding a parley with the postillion. On opening my eyes I found, to my astonishment, that the road was filled with armed revolutionaries marching, not towards, but away from Dresden, and some of them were trying to commandeer the coach to relieve their weariness on the way back.

'What is the matter?' I cried. 'Where are you going?'

'Home,' was the reply. 'It is all over in Dresden. The provincial government is close behind us in that carriage down there.'

I shot out of the coach like a dart, leaving it at the disposal of the tired men, and hurried on, down the steeply sloping road, to meet the ill-fated party. And there I actually found them — Heubner, Bakunin, and Martin, the energetic post-office clerk, the two latter armed with muskets — in a smart hired carriage from Dresden which was coming slowly up the hill. On the box were, as I supposed, the secretaries, while as many as possible of the weary National Guard struggled for seats behind. I hastened to swing myself into the coach, and so came in for a conversation which thereupon took place between the driver, who was also the owner of the coach, and the provisional government. The man was imploring them to spare his carriage, which, he said, was very lightly sprung and quite unequal to carrying such a load; he begged that the people should be told not to seat themselves behind and in front. But Bakunin remained quite unconcerned, and elected to give me a short account of the retreat from Dresden, which had been successfully achieved without loss. He had had the trees in the newly planted Maximilian Avenue felled early in the morning to form a barricade against a possible flank attack of cavalry, and had been immensely entertained by the lamentations of the inhabitants, who during the process did nothing but bewail their *Scheene Beeme*.[1] All this time our driver's lamentations over his coach were growing more importunate. Finally he broke into loud sobs and tears, upon which Bakunin, regarding him with positive pleasure, called out: ' The tears of a Philistine are nectar for the gods.' He would not vouchsafe him a word, but Heubner and I found the scene tiresome, whereupon he asked me whether we two at least should not get out, as he could not ask it of the others. As a matter of fact, it was high time to leave the coach, as some new contingents of revolutionaries had formed up in rank and file all along the highway to salute the provisional government and receive orders. Heubner strode down the line with great dignity, acquainted the leaders with the state of affairs, and exhorted them to keep their trust in the righteousness of the cause for which so many had shed their blood. All were now to retire to Freiberg, there to await further orders.

A youngish man of serious mien. now stepped forward from the ranks of the rebels to place himself under the special protection of the provisional government. He was a certain Menzdorff, a German Catholic priest whom I had had the advantage of meeting in Dresden. (It was he who, in the course of a significant conversation, had first induced me to read Feuerbach.) He had been dragged along as a prisoner and abominably treated by the Chemnitz municipal guard on this particular march, having originally been the instigator of a demonstration to force that body to take up arms and march

[1] Saxon corruption of *schöne Baume,* beautiful trees. — EDITOR.

to Dresden. He owed his freedom only to the chance meeting with other better disposed volunteer corps. We saw this Chemnitz town guard ourselves, stationed far away on a hill. They sent representatives to beseech Heubner to tell them how things stood. When they had received the information rquired, and had been told that the fight would be continued in a determined manner, they invited the provisional government to quarter at Chemnitz. As soon as they rejoined their main body we saw them wheel round and turn back.

With many similar interruptions the somewhat disorganised procession reached Freiberg. Here some friends of Heubner's came to meet him in the streets with the urgent request not to plunge their native place into the misery of desperate street-fighting by establishing the provisional government there. Heubner made no reply to this, but requested Bakunin and myself to accompany him into his house for a consultation. First we had to witness the painful meeting between Heubner and his wife; in a few words he pointed out the gravity and importance of the task assigned to him, reminding her that it was for Germany and the high destiny of his country that he was staking his life.

Breakfast was then prepared, and after the meal, during which a fairly cheerful mood prevailed, Heubner made a short speech to Bakunin, speaking quietly but firmly. ' My dear Bukanin,' he said (his previous acquaintance with Bakunin was so slight that he did not even know how to pronounce his name), ' before we decide anything further, I must ask you to state clearly whether your political aim is really the Red Republic, of which they tell me you are a partisan. Tell me frankly, so that I may know if I can rely on your friendship in the future ? '

Bakunin explained briefly that he had no scheme for any political form of government, and would not risk his life for any of them. As for his own far-reaching desires and hopes, they had nothing whatever to do with the street-fighting in Dresden and all that this implied for Germany. He had looked upon the rising in Dresden as a foolish, ludicrous movement until he realised the effect of Heubner's noble and courageous example. From that moment every political consideration and aim had been put in the background by his sympathy with

this heroic attitude, and he had immediately resolved to assist
this excellent man with all the devotion and energy of a friend.
He knew, of course, that he belonged to the so-called moderate
party, of whose political future he was not able to form an
opinion, as he had not profited much by his opportunities of
studying the position of the various parties in Germany.

Heubner declared himself satisfied by this reply, and proceeded to ask Bakunin's opinion of the present state of things —
whether it would not be conscientious and reasonable to dismiss
the men and give up a struggle which might be considered
hopeless. In reply Bakunin insisted, with his usual calm assurance, that whoever else threw up the sponge, Heubner must
certainly not do so. He had been the first member of the
provisional government, and it was he who had given the call
to arms. The call had been obeyed, and hundreds of lives
had been sacrificed; to scatter the people again would look
as if these sacrifices had been made to idle folly. Even if
they were the only two left, they still ought not to forsake
their posts. If they went under their lives might be forfeit,
but their honour must remain unsullied, so that a similar appeal in the future might not drive every one to despair.

This was quite enough for Heubner. He at once made out
a summons for the election of a representative assembly for
Saxony, to be held at Chemnitz. He thought that, with the
assistance of the populace and of the numerous insurgent bands
who were arriving from all quarters, he would be able to hold
the town as the headquarters of a provisional government until
the general situation in Germany had become more settled.
In the midst of these discussions, Stephan Born walked into the
room to report that he had brought the armed bands right into
Freiberg, in good order and without any losses. This young
man was a compositor who had contributed greatly to Heubner's
peace of mind during the last three days in Dresden by taking
over the chief command. His simplicity of manner made a very
encouraging impression on us, particularly when we heard his
report. When, however, Heubner asked whether he would
undertake to defend Freiberg against the troops which might be
expected to attack at any moment, he declared that this was
an experienced officer's job, and that he himself was no soldier

and knew nothing of strategy.   Under these circumstances it
seemed better, if only to gain time, to fall back on the more
thickly populated town of Chemnitz.   The first thing to be
done, however, was to see that the revolutionaries, who were
assembled in large numbers at Freiberg, were properly cared
for, and Born went off immediately to make preliminary arrangements.   Heubner also took leave of us, and went to refresh
his tired brain by an hour's sleep.   I was left alone on the sofa
with Bakunin, who soon fell towards me, overcome by irresistible drowsiness, and dropped the terrific weight of his head
on to my shoulder.   As I saw that he would not wake if I
shook off this burden, I pushed him aside with some difficulty,
and took leave both of the sleeper and of Heubner's house;
for I wished to see for myself, as I had done for many days past,
what course these extraordinary events were taking.   I therefore went to the Town Hall, where I found the townspeople
entertaining to the best of their ability a blustering horde
of excited revolutionaries both within and without the walls.
To my surprise, I found Heubner there in the full swing of
work.   I thought he was asleep at home, but the idea of
leaving the people even for an hour without a counsellor had
driven away all thought of rest.   He had lost no time in
superintending the organisation of a sort of commandant's
office, and was again occupied with drafting and signing
documents in the midst of the uproar that raged on all sides.
It was not long before Bakunin too put in an appearance,
principally in search of a good officer — who was not, however,
forthcoming.   The commandant of a large contingent from
the Vogtland, an oldish man, raised Bakunin's hopes by the
impassioned energy of his speeches, and he would have had
him appointed commandant-general on the spot.   But it seemed
as if any real decision were impossible in that frenzy and
confusion, and as the only hope of mastering it seemed to be
in reaching Chemnitz, Heubner gave the order to march on
towards that town as soon as every one had had food.   Once
this was settled, I told my friends I should go on in advance of
their column to Chemnitz, where I should find them again next
day; for I longed to be quit of this chaos.   I actually caught
the coach, the departure of which was fixed for that time, and

obtained a seat in it. But the revolutionaries were just marching off on the same road, and we were told that we must wait
until they had passed to avoid being caught in the whirlpool.
This meant considerable delay, and for a long while I watched
the peculiar bearing of the patriots as they marched out. I
noticed in particular a Vogtland regiment, whose marching step
was fairly orthodox, following the beat of a drummer who
tried to vary the monotony of his instrument in an artistic
manner by hitting the wooden frame alternately with the
drumhead. The unpleasant rattling tone thus produced reminded me in ghostly fashion of the rattling of the skeletons'
bones in the dance round the gallows by night which Berlioz
had brought home to my imagination with such terrible
realism in his performance of the last movement of his *Sinfonie
Fantastique* in Paris.

Suddenly the desire seized me to look up the friends I had
left behind, and travel to Chemnitz in their company if possible.
I found they had quitted the Town Hall, and on reaching
Heubner's house I was told that he was asleep. I therefore
went back to the coach, which, however, was still putting off
its departure, as the road was blocked with troops. I walked
nervously up and down for some time, then, losing faith in
the journey by coach, I went back again to Heubner's house to
offer myself definitely as a travelling companion. But Heubner
and Bakunin had already left home, and I could find no traces
of them. In desperation I returned once more to the coach,
and found it by this time really ready to start. After various
delays and adventures it brought me late at night to Chemnitz, where I got out and betook myself to the nearest inn.
At five o'clock the next morning I got up (after a few hours'
sleep) and set out to find my brother-in-law Wolfram's house,
which was about a quarter of an hour's walk from the town.
On the way I asked a sentinel of the town guard whether
he knew anything about the arrival of the provisional
government.

'Provisional government?' was the reply. 'Why, it's all
up with that.' I did not understand him, nor was I able to
learn anything about the state of things when I first reached
the house of my relatives, for my brother-in-law had been sent

into the town as special constable. It was only on his return home, late in the afternoon, that I heard what had taken place in one hotel at Chemnitz while I had been resting in another inn. Heubner, Bakunin, and the man called Martin, whom I have mentioned already, had, it seemed, arrived before me in a hackney-coach at the gates of Chemnitz. On being asked for their names Heubner had announced himself in a tone of authority, and had bidden the town councillors come to him at a certain hotel. They had no sooner reached the hotel than they all three collapsed from excessive fatigue. Suddenly the police broke into the room and arrested them in the name of the local government, upon which they only begged to have a few hours' quiet sleep, pointing out that flight was out of the question in their present condition. I heard further that they had been removed to Altenburg under a strong military escort. My brother-in-law was obliged to confess that the Chemnitz municipal guard, which had been forced to start for Dresden much against its will, and had resolved at the very outset to place itself at the disposal of the royal forces on arriving there, had deceived Heubner by inviting him to Chemnitz, and had lured him into the trap. They had reached Chemnitz long before Heubner, and had taken over the guard at the gates with the object of seeing him arrive and of preparing for his arrest at once. My brother-in-law had been very anxious about me too, as he had been told in furious tones by the leaders of the town guard that I had been seen in close association with the revolutionaries. He thought it a wonderful intervention of Providence that I had not arrived at Chemnitz with them and gone to the same inn, in which case their fate would certainly have been mine. The recollection of my escape from almost certain death in duels with the most experienced swordsmen in my student days flashed across me like a flash of lightning. This last terrible experience made such an impression on me that I was incapable of breathing a word in connection with what had happened. My brother-in-law, in response to urgent appeals — from my wife in particular, who was much concerned for my personal safety — undertook to convey me to Altenburg in his carriage by night. From there I continued my journey by coach to Weimar, where I had originally planned to spend my holidays, little thinking that I should arrive by such devious ways.

The dreamy unreality of my state of mind at this time is best explained by the apparent seriousness with which, on meeting Liszt again, I at once began to discuss what seemed to be the sole topic of any real interest to him in connection with me — the forthcoming revival of *Tannhäuser* at Weimar. I found it very difficult to confess to this friend that I had not left Dresden in the regulation way for a conductor of the royal opera. To tell the truth, I had a very hazy conception of the relation in which I stood to the law of my country (in the narrow sense). Had I done anything criminal in the eye of the law or not? I found it impossible to come to any conclusion about it. Meanwhile, alarming news of the terrible conditions in Dresden continued to pour into Weimar. Genast, the stage manager, in particular, aroused great excitement by spreading the report that Röckel, who was well known at Weimar, had been guilty of arson. Liszt must soon have gathered from my conversation, in which I did not take the trouble to dissimulate, that I too was suspiciously connected with these terrible events, though my attitude with regard to them misled him for some time. For I was not by any means prepared to proclaim myself a combatant in the recent fights, and that for reasons quite other than would have seemed valid in the eyes of the law. My friend was therefore encouraged in his delusion by the unpremeditated effect of my attitude. When we met at the house of Princess Caroline of Wittgenstein, to whom I had been introduced the year before when she paid her flying visit to Dresden, we were able to hold stimulating conversations on all sorts of artistic topics. One afternoon, for instance, a lively discussion sprang up from a description I had given of a tragedy to be entitled *Jesus of Nazareth*. Liszt maintained a discreet silence after I had finished, whereas the Princess protested vigorously against my proposal to bring such a subject on to the stage. From the lukewarm attempt I made to support the paradoxical theories I had put forward, I realised the state of my mind at that time. Although it was not very evident to onlookers, I had been, and still was, shaken to the very depths of my being by my recent experiences.

In due course an orchestral rehearsal of *Tannhäuser* took place, which in various ways stimulated the artist in me afresh. Liszt's conducting, though mainly concerned with the musical rather than the dramatic side, filled me for the first time with the flattering warmth of emotion roused by the consciousness of being understood by another mind in full sympathy with my own. At the same time I was able, in spite of my dreamy condition, to observe critically the standard of capacity exhibited by the singers and their chorus-master. After the rehearsal I, together with the musical director, Stöhr, and Götze the singer, accepted Liszt's invitation to a simple dinner, at a different inn from the one where he lived. I thus had occasion to take alarm at a trait in his character which was entirely new to me. After being stirred up to a certain pitch of excitement his mood became positively alarming, and he almost gnashed his teeth in a passion of fury directed against a certain section of society which had also aroused my deepest indignation. I was strongly affected by this strange experience with this wonderful man, but I was unable to see the association of ideas which had led to his terrible outburst. I was therefore left in a state of amazement, while Liszt had to recover during the night from a violent attack of nerves which his excitement had produced. Another surprise was in store for me the next morning, when I found my friend fully equipped for a journey to Karlsruhe—the circumstances which made it necessary being absolutely incomprehensible to me. Liszt invited Director Stöhr and myself to accompany him as far as Eisenach. On our way there we were stopped by Beaulieu, the Lord Chamberlain, who wished to know whether I was prepared to be received by the Grand Duchess of Weimar, a sister of the Emperor Nicolas, at Eisenach castle. As my excuse on the score of unsuitable travelling costume was not admitted, Liszt accepted in my name, and I really met with a surprisingly kind reception that evening from the Grand Duchess, who chatted with me in the friendliest way, and introduced me to her chamberlain with all due ceremony. Liszt maintained afterwards that his noble patroness had been informed that I should be wanted by the authorities in Dresden within the next few days, and had therefore hastened to make my personal acquaintance

at once, knowing that it would compromise her too heavily
later on.

Liszt continued his journey from Eisenach, leaving me to
be entertained and looked after by Stöhr and the musical
director Kühmstedt, a diligent and skilful master of counterpoint with whom I paid my first visit to the Wartburg, which
had not then been restored. I was filled with strange musings
as to my fate when I visited this castle. Here I was actually
on the point of entering, for the first time, the building which
was so full of meaning for me; here, too, I had to tell myself
that the days of my further sojourn in Germany were numbered.
And in fact the news from Dresden, when we returned to Weimar the next day, was serious indeed. Liszt, on his return on
the third day, found a letter from my wife, who had not dared to
write direct to me. She reported that the police had searched
my house in Dresden, to which she had returned, and that she
had, moreover, been warned on no account to allow me to return
to that city, as a warrant had been taken out against me, and I
was shortly to be served with a writ and arrested. Liszt, who
was now solely concerned for my personal safety, called in a
friend who had some experience of law, to consider what should
be done to rescue me from the danger that threatened me.
Von Watzdorf, the minister whom I had already visited, had
been of opinion that I should, if required, submit quietly to
being taken to Dresden, and that the journey would be made
in a respectable private carriage. On the other hand, reports
which had reached us of the brutal way in which the Prussian
troops in Dresden had gone to work in applying the state of
siege were of so alarming a nature that Liszt and his friends in
council urged my speedy departure from Weimar, where it
would be impossible to protect me. But I insisted on taking
leave of my wife, whose anxiety was great, before leaving
Germany, and begged to be allowed to stay a little longer at
least in the neighbourhood of Weimar. This was taken into
consideration, and Professor Siebert suggested my taking
temporary shelter with a friendly steward at the village of
Magdala, which was three hours distant. I drove there the
following morning to introduce myself to this kind steward and
protector as Professor Werder from Berlin, who, with a letter

of recommendation from Professor Siebert, had come to turn his financial studies to practical account in helping to administer these estates. Here in rural seclusion I spent three days, entertainment of a peculiar nature being provided by the meeting of a popular assembly, which consisted of the remainder of the contingent of revolutionaries which had marched off towards Dresden and had now returned in disorder. I listened with curious feelings, amounting almost to contempt, to the speeches on this occasion, which were of every kind and description. On the second day of my stay my host's wife came back from Weimar (where it was market-day) full of a curious tale: the composer of an opera which was being performed there on that very day had been obliged to leave Weimar suddenly because the warrant for his arrest had arrived from Dresden. My host, who had been let into my secret by Professor Seibert, asked playfully what his name was. As his wife did not seem to know, he came to her assistance with the suggestion that perhaps it was Röckel whose name was familiar at Weimar.

'Yes,' she said, 'Röckel, that was his name, quite right.'

My host laughed loudly, and said that he would not be so stupid as to let them catch him, in spite of his opera.

At last, on 22nd May, my birthday, Minna actually arrived at Magdala. She had hastened to Weimar on receiving my letter, and had proceeded from there according to instructions, bent on persuading me at all costs to flee the country immediately and for good. No attempt to raise her to the level of my own mood was successful; she persisted in regarding me as an ill-advised, inconsiderate person who had plunged both himself and her into the most terrible situation. It had been arranged that I should meet her the next evening in the house of Professor Wolff at Jena to take a last farewell. She was to go by way of Weimar, while I took the footpath from Magdala. I started accordingly on my walk of about six hours, and came over the plateau into the little university town (which now received me hospitably for the first time) at sunset. I found my wife again at the house of Professor Wolff, who, thanks to Liszt, was already my friend, and with the addition of a certain

Professor Widmann another conference was held on the subject of my further escape. A writ was actually out against me for being strongly suspected of participation in the Dresden rising, and I could not under any circumstances depend on a safe refuge in any of the German federal states. Liszt insisted on my going to Paris, where I could find a new field for my work, while Widmann advised me not to go by the direct route through Frankfort and Baden, as the rising was still in full swing there, and the police would certainly exercise praiseworthy vigilance over incoming travellers with suspicious-looking passports. The way through Bavaria would be the safest, as all was quiet there again; I could then make for Switzerland, and the journey to Paris from there could be engineered without any danger. As I needed a passport for the journey, Professor Widmann offered me his own, which had been issued at Tübingen and had not been brought up to date. My wife was quite in despair, and the parting from her caused me real pain. I set off in the mail-coach and travelled, without further hindrance, through many towns (amongst them Rudolstadt, a place full of memories for me) to the Bavarian frontier. From there I continued my journey by mail-coach straight to Lindau. At the gates I, together with the other passengers, was asked for my passport. I passed the night in a state of strange, feverish excitement, which lasted until the departure of the steamer on Lake Constance early in the morning. My mind was full of the Swabian dialect, as spoken by Professor Widmann, with whose passport I was travelling. I pictured to myself my dealings with the Bavarian police should I have to converse with them in accordance with the above-mentioned irregularities in that document. A prey to feverish unrest, I spent the whole night trying to perfect myself in the Swabian dialect, but, as I was amused to find, without the smallest success. I had braced myself to meet the crucial moment early the next morning, when the policeman came into my room and, not knowing to whom the passports belonged, gave me three at random to choose from. With joy in my heart I seized my own, and dismissed the dreaded messenger in the most friendly way. Once on board the steamer I realised with true satisfaction that I had now stepped on to Swiss territory. It was a lovely spring

morning; across the broad lake I could gaze at the Alpine
landscape as it spread itself before my eyes. When I stepped
on to Republican soil at Rorschach, I employed the first
moments in writing a few lines home to tell of my safe arrival
in Switzerland and my deliverance from all danger. The
coach drive through the pleasant country of St. Gall to Zürich
cheered me up wonderfully, and when I drove down from
Oberstrass into Zürich that evening, the last day in May, at six
o'clock, and saw for the first time the Glarner Alps that encircle
the lake gleaming in the sunset, I at once resolved, though
without being fully conscious of it, to avoid everything that
could prevent my settling here.

I had been the more willing to accept my friends' suggestion
to take the Swiss route to Paris, as I knew I should find an old
acquaintance, Alexander Müller, at Zürich. I hoped with his
help to obtain a passport to France, as I was anxious not to
arrive there as a political refugee. I had been on very friendly
terms with Müller once upon a time at Würzburg. He had
been settled at Zürich for a long time as a teacher of music;
this I learned from a pupil of his, Wilhelm Baumgartner, who
had called on me in Dresden some years back to bring me a
greeting from this old friend. On that occasion I entrusted the
pupil with a copy of the score of *Tannhäuser* for his master,
by way of remembrance, and this kind attention had not fallen
on barren soil: Müller and Baumgartner, whom I visited
forthwith, introduced me at once to Jacob Sulzer and Franz
Hagenbuch, two cantonal secretaries who were the most likely,
among all their good friends, to compass the immediate fulfilment of my desire. These two people, who had been joined by
a few intimates, received me with such respectful curiosity and
sympathy that I felt at home with them at once. The great
assurance and moderation with which they commented on the
persecutions which had overtaken me, as seen from their usual
simple republican standpoint, opened to me a conception of
civil life which seemed to lift me to an entirely new sphere.
I felt so safe and protected here, whereas in my own country
I had, without quite realising it, come to be considered a
criminal owing to the peculiar connection between my disgust
at the public attitude towards art and the general political

disturbances. To prepossess the two secretaries entirely in my favour (one of them, Sulzer, had enjoyed an excellent classical education), my friends arranged a meeting one evening at which I was to read my poem on the *Death of Siegfried*. I am prepared to swear that I never had more attentive listeners, among men, than on that evening. The immediate effect of my success was the drawing up of a fully valid federal passport for the poor German under warrant of arrest, armed with which I started gaily on my journey to Paris after quite a short stay at Zürich. From Strassburg, where I was enthralled by the fascination of the world-famous minster, I travelled towards Paris by what was then the best means of locomotion, the so-called *malle-poste*. I remember a remarkable phenomenon in connection with this conveyance. Till then the noise of the cannonade and musketry in the fighting at Dresden had been persistently re-echoing in my ears, especially in a half-waking condition; now the humming of the wheels, as we rolled rapidly along the highroad, cast such a spell upon me that for the whole of the journey I seemed to hear the melody of *Freude, schöner Götterfunken* [1] from the Ninth Symphony being played, as it were, on deep bass instruments.

From the time of my entering Switzerland till my arrival in Paris my spirits, which had sunk into a dreamlike apathy, rose gradually to a level of freedom and comfort that I had never enjoyed before. I felt like a bird in the air whose destiny is not to founder in a morass; but soon after my arrival in Paris, in the first week of June, a very palpable reaction set in. I had had an introduction from Liszt to his former secretary Belloni, who felt it his duty, in loyalty to the instructions received, to put me into communication with a literary man, a certain Gustave Vaisse, with the object of being commissioned to write an opera libretto for production in Paris. I did not, however, make the personal acquaintance of Vaisse. The idea did not please me, and I found sufficient excuse for warding off the negotiations by saying I was afraid of the epidemic of cholera which was said to be raging in the city. I was staying in the Rue Notre Dame de Lorette for the sake of being near Belloni. Through this street funeral processions, announced by the muffled drum

<hr />

[1] See note on page 486.

beats of the National Guard, passed practically every hour. Though the heat was stifling, I was strictly forbidden to touch water, and was advised to exercise the greatest precaution with regard to diet in every respect. Besides this weight of uneasiness on my spirits, the whole outward aspect of Paris, as it then appeared, had the most depressing effect on me. The motto, *liberté, égalité, fraternité,* was still to be seen on all the public buildings and other establishments, but, on the other hand, I was alarmed at seeing the first *garçons caissiers* making their way from the bank with their long money-sacks over their shoulders and their large portfolios in their hands. I had never met them so frequently as now, just when the old capitalist régime, after its triumphant struggle against the once dreaded socialist propaganda, was exerting itself vigorously to regain the public confidence by its almost insulting pomp. I had gone, as it were, mechanically into Schlesinger's music-shop, where a successor was now installed — a much more pronounced type of Jew named Brandus, of a very dirty appearance. The only person there to give me a friendly welcome was the old clerk, Monsieur Henri. After I had talked to him in loud tones for some time, as the shop was apparently empty, he at length asked me with some embarrassment whether I had not seen my master (*votre maître*) Meyerbeer.

'Is Monsieur Meyerbeer here?' I asked.

'Certainly,' was the even more embarrassed reply; 'quite near, over there behind the desk.'

And, sure enough, as I walked across to the desk Meyerbeer came out, covered with confusion. He smiled and made some excuse about pressing proof-sheets. He had been hiding there quietly for over ten minutes since first hearing my voice. I had had enough after my strange encounter with this apparition. It recalled so many things affecting myself which reflected suspicion on the man, in particular the significance of his behaviour towards me in Berlin on the last occasion. However, as I had now nothing more to do with him, I greeted him with a certain easy gaiety induced by the regret I felt at seeing his manifest confusion on becoming cognisant of my arrival in Paris. He took it for granted that I should again seek my fortune there, and seemed much surprised when I assured him, on the contrary, that the idea of having any work there was odious to me.

' But Liszt published such a brilliant article about you in the *Journal des Débats*,' he said.

' Ah,' I replied, ' it really had not occurred to me that the enthusiastic devotion of a friend should be regarded as a mutual speculation.'

' But the article made a sensation. It is incredible that you should not seek to make any profit out of it.'

This offensive meddlesomeness roused me to protest to Meyerbeer with some violence that I was concerned with anything rather than with the production of artistic work, particularly just at that time when the course of events seemed to indicate that the whole world was undergoing a reaction.

' But what do you expect to get out of the revolution ? ' he replied. ' Are you going to write scores for the barricades ? '

Whereupon I assured him that I was not thinking of writing any scores at all. We parted, obviously without having arrived at a mutual understanding.

In the street I was also stopped by Moritz Schlesinger, who, being equally under the influence of Liszt's brilliant article, evidently considered me a perfect prodigy. He too thought I must be counting on making a hit in Paris, and was sure that I had a very good chance of doing so.

' Will you undertake my business ? ' I asked him. ' I have no money. Do you really think the performance of an opera by an unknown composer can be anything but a matter of money ? '

' You are quite right,' said Moritz, and left me on the spot.

I turned from these disagreeable encounters in the plague-stricken capital of the world to inquire the fate of my Dresden companions, for some of those with whom I was intimate had also reached Paris, when I called on Despléchins, who had painted the scenery for *Tannhäuser*. I found Semper there, who had, like myself, been deposited in this city. We met again with no little pleasure, although we could not help smiling at our grotesque situation. Semper had retired from the battle when the famous barricade, which he in his capacity of architect kept under close observation, had been surrounded. (He thought it

impossible for it to be captured.)   All the same, he considered
that he had exposed himself quite sufficiently to make it
unsafe for him to stay after the Prussians had announced a
state of siege and were occupying Dresden.   He considered
himself lucky as a native of Holstein to be dependent, not on
the German, but on the Danish government for a passport,
as this had helped him to reach Paris without difficulty.   When
I expressed my real and heartfelt regret at the turn of affairs
which had torn him from a professional undertaking on which
he had just started — the completion of the Dresden Museum
— he refused to take it too seriously, saying it had given him
a great deal of worry.   In spite of our trying situation, it
was with Semper that I spent the only bright hours of my stay
in Paris.   We were soon joined by another refugee, young
Heine, who had once wished to paint my *Lohengrin* scenery.
He had no qualms about his future, for his master Despléchins
was willing to give him employment.   I alone felt I had been
pitched quite aimlessly into Paris.   I had a passionate desire
to leave this cholera-laden atmosphere, and Belloni offered me
an opportunity which I promptly and joyfully seized.   He
invited me to follow himself and his family to a country place
near La Ferté-sous-Jouarre, where I could be refreshed by pure
air and absolute quiet, and wait for a change for the better in
my position.   I made the short journey to Rueil after another
week in Paris, and took for the time being a poor lodging (one
room, built with recesses) in the house of Monsieur Raphaël,
a wine merchant, close by the village *mairie* where the Belloni
family were staying.   Here I waited further developments.
During the period when all news from Germany ceased I tried
to occupy myself as far as possible with reading.   After going
through Proudhon's writings, and in particular his *De la
propriété,* in such a manner as to glean comfort for my situation
in curiously divers ways, I entertained myself for a considerable time with Lamartine's *Histoire des Girondins,* a most
alluring and attractive work.   One day Belloni brought me news
of the unfortunate rising in Paris, which had been attempted
on the 13th June by the Republicans under Ledru-Rollin against
the provisional government, which was then in the full tide of
reaction.   Great as was the indignation with which the news

was received by my host and the mayor of the place (a relative
of his, at whose table we ate our modest daily meal), it made, on
the whole, little impression on me, as my attention was still
fixed in great agitation on the events which were taking place
on the Rhine, and particularly on the grand-duchy of Baden,
which had been made forfeit to a provisional government.
When, however, the news reached me from this quarter also
that the Prussians had succeeded in subduing a movement which
had not at first seemed hopeless, I felt extraordinarily
downcast.

I was compelled to consider my position carefully, and the
necessity of conquering my difficulties helped to allay the
excitement to which I was a prey. The letters from my
Weimar friends, as well as those from my wife, now brought me
completely to my senses. The former expressed themselves
very curtly about my behaviour with regard to recent events.
The opinion was, that for the moment there would be nothing
for me to do, and especially not in Dresden, or at the grand-
ducal court, ' as one could not very well knock at battered
doors '; ' on ne frappe pas à des portes enfoncées ' (Princess
von Wittgenstein to Belloni).

I did not know what to reply, for I had never dreamt of
expecting anything to come from their intervening on my
behalf in that quarter; consequently I was quite satisfied that
they sent me temporarily financial assistance. With this money
I made up my mind to leave for Zürich and ask Alex Müller to
give me shelter for a while, as his house was sufficiently large
to accommodate a guest. My saddest moment came when, after
a long silence, I at last received a letter from my wife. She
wrote that she could not dream of living with me again; that
after I had so unscrupulously thrown away a connection and
position, the like of which would never again present itself to
me, no woman could reasonably be expected to take any further
interest in my future enterprises.

I fully appreciated my wife's unfortunate position; I could
in no way assist her, except by advising her to sell our Dresden
furniture, and by making an appeal on her behalf to my relatives
in Leipzig.

Until then I had been able to think more lightly of the

misery of her position, simply because I had imagined her to be more deeply in sympathy with what agitated me. Often during the recent extraordinary events I had even believed that she understood my feelings. Now, however, she had disillusioned me on this point: she could see in me no more than what the public saw, and the one redeeming point of her severe judgment was that she excused my behaviour on the score that I was reckless. After I had begged Liszt to do what he could for my wife, I soon began to regard her unexpected behaviour with more equanimity. In reply to her announcement that she would not write to me again for the present, I said that I had also resolved to spare her all further anxiety about my very doubtful fate, by ceasing from communicating with her. I surveyed the panorama of our long years of association critically in my mind's eye, beginning with that first stormy year of our married life, that had been so full of sorrow. Our youthful days of worry and care in Paris had undoubtedly been of benefit to us both. The courage and patience with which she had faced our difficulties, while I on my part had tried to end them by dint of hard work, had linked us together with bonds of iron. Minna was rewarded for all these privations by Dresden successes, and more especially by the highly enviable position I had held there. Her position as wife of the conductor (Frau Kapellmeisterin) had brought her the fulfilment of her dearest wishes, and all those things which conspired to make my work in this official post so intolerable to me, were to her no more than so many threats directed against her smug content. The course I had adopted with regard to *Tannhäuser* had already made her doubtful of my success at the theatres, and had robbed her of all courage and confidence in our future. The more I deviated from the path which she regarded as the only profitable one, due partly to the change of my views (which I grew ever less willing to communicate to her), and partly to the modification in my attitude towards the stage, the more she retreated from that position of close fellowship with me which she had enjoyed in former years, and which she thought herself justified in connecting in some way with my successes.

She looked upon my conduct with regard to the Dresden catastrophe as the outcome of this deviation from the right path, and attributed it to the influence of unscrupulous persons (particularly the unfortunate Röckel), who were supposed to have dragged me with them to ruin, by appealing to my vanity. Deeper than all these disagreements, however, which, after all, were concerned only with external circumstances, was the consciousness of our fundamental incompatibility, which to me had become ever more and more apparent since the day of our reconciliation. From the very beginning we had had scenes of the most violent description; never once after these frequent quarrels had she admitted herself in the wrong or tried to be friends again.

The necessity of speedily restoring our domestic peace, as well as my conviction (confirmed by every one of her extravagant outbursts) that, in view of the great disparity of our characters and especially of our educations, it devolved upon me to prevent such scenes by observing great caution in my behaviour, always led me to take the entire blame for what had happend upon myself, and to mollify Minna by showing her that I was sorry. Unfortunately, and to my intense grief, I was forced to recognise that by acting in this way I lost all my power over her affections, and especially over her character. Now we stood in a position in which I could not possibly resort to the same means of reconciliation, for it would have meant my being inconsistent in all my views and actions. And then I found myself confronted by such hardness in the woman whom I had spoilt by my leniency, that it was out of the question to expect her to acknowledge the injustice done to myself. Suffice it to say that the wreck of my married life had contributed not inconsiderably to the ruin of my position in Dresden, and to the careless manner in which I treated it, for instead of finding help, strength, and consolation at home, I found my wife unwittingly conspiring against me, in league with all the other hostile circumstances which then beset me. After I had got over the first shock of her heartless behaviour, I was absolutely clear about this. I remember that I did not suffer any great sorrow, but that on the contrary, with the conviction of being now quite helpless, an almost exalted calm came over me when I realised that up to the present my life had been built on a foundation of sand and nothing more. At all events, the fact that I stood absolutely alone did much towards restoring my peace of mind, and in my distress I now found strength and comfort even in the fact of my dire poverty. At last assistance arrived from Weimar. I accepted it eagerly, and it was the means of extricating me from my present useless life and stranded hopes.

My next move was to find a place of refuge — one, however, which had but little attraction for me, seeing that in it there was not the slightest hope of my being able to make any further headway in the paths along which I had hitherto progressed. This refuge was Zürich, a town devoid of all art in the public sense, and where for the first time I met simple-hearted people who knew nothing about me as a musician, but who, as it appeared, felt drawn towards me by the power of my personality alone. I arrived at Müller's house and asked him to let me have a room, at the same time giving him what remained of my capital, namely twenty francs. I quickly discovered that my old friend was embarrassed by my perfectly open confidence in him, and that he was at his wit's end to know what to do with me. I soon gave up the large room containing a grand piano, which he had allotted to me on the impulse of the moment, and retired to a modest little bedroom. The meals were my great trial, not because I was fastidious, but because I could not digest them. Outside my friend's house, on the contrary, I enjoyed what, considering the habits of the locality, was the most luxurious reception. The same young men who had been so kind to me on my first journey through Zürich again showed themselves anxious to be continually in my company, and this was especially the case with one young fellow called Jakob Sulzer. He had to be thirty years of age before he was entitled to become a member of the Zürich government, and he therefore still had several years to wait. In spite of his youth, however, the impression he made on all those with whom he came in contact was that of a man of riper years, whose character was formed. When I was asked long afterwards whether I had ever met a man who, morally speaking, was the beau-ideal of real character and uprightness, I could, on reflection, think of none other than this newly gained friend, Jakob Sulzer.

He owed his early appointment as permanent Cantonal Secretary (*Staatsschreiber*), one of the most excellent government posts in the canton of Zürich, to the recently returned liberal party, led by Alfred Escher. As this party could not employ the more experienced members of the older conservative side in the public offices, their policy was to choose exceptionally gifted young men for these positions. Sulzer showed extraordinary promise, and their choice accordingly soon lighted on him. He had only just returned from the Berlin and Bonn universities with the intention of establishing himself as professor of philology at the university in his native town, when he was made a member of the new government. To fit himself for his post he had to stay in Geneva for six months to perfect himself in the French language, which he had neglected during his philological studies. He was quick-witted and industrious, as well as independent and firm, and he never allowed himself to be swayed by any party tactics. Consequently he rose very rapidly to high positions in the government, to which he rendered valuable and important services, first as Minister of Finance, a post he held for many years, and later with particular distinction as member of the School Federation. His unexpected acquaintance with me seemed to place him in a sort of dilemma; from the philological and classical studies which he had entered upon of his own choice, he suddenly found himself torn away in the most bewildering manner by this unexpected summons from the government. It almost seemed as if his meeting with me had made him regret having accepted the appointment. As he was a person of great culture, my poem, *Siegfried's Death,* naturally revealed to him my knowledge of German antiquity. He had also studied this subject, but with greater philological accuracy than I could possibly have aspired to. When, later on, he became acquainted with my manner of writing music, this peculiarly serious and reserved man became so thoroughly interested in my sphere of art, so far removed from his own field of labour, that, as he himself confessed, he felt it his duty to fight against these disturbing influences by being intentionally brusque and curt with me. In the beginning of my stay in Zürich, however, he delighted in being led some distance astray in the realms of art. The old-fashioned official residence of the first Cantonal Secretary was often the scene of unique gatherings, composed of people such as I would be sure to attract. It might even be said that these social functions occurred rather more frequently than was advisable for the reputation of a civil servant of this little philistine state. What attracted the musician Baumgartner more particularly to these meetings was the product of Sulzer's vineyards in Winterthur, to which our hosts treated his guests with the greatest liberality. When in my moods of mad exuberance I gave vent in dithyrambic effusions to my most extreme views on art and life, my listeners often responded in a manner which, more often than not, I was perfectly right in ascribing to the effects of the wine rather than to the power of my enthusiasm. Once when Professor Ettmüller, the Germanist and Edda scholar, had been invited to listen to a reading of my *Siegfried* and had been led home in a state of melancholy enthusiasm, there was a regular outburst of wanton spirits among those who had remained behind. I conceived the absurd idea of lifting all the doors of the state official's house off their hinges.

Herr Hagenbuch, another servant of the state, seeing what exertion this cost me, offered me the help of his gigantic physique, and with comparative ease we succeeded in removing every single door, and laying it aside, a proceeding at which Sulzer merely smiled good-naturedly. The next day, however, when we made inquiries, he told us that the replacing of those doors (which must have been a terrible strain on his delicate constitution) had taken him the whole night, as he had made up his mind to keep the knowledge of our orgies from the sergeant, who always arrived at a very early hour in the morning.

The extraordinary birdlike freedom of my existence had the effect of exciting me more and more. I was often frightened at the excessive outbursts of exaltation to which I was prone — no matter whom I was with — and which led me to indulge in the most extraordinary paradoxes in my conversation. Soon after I had settled in Zürich I began to write down my various ideas about things at which I had arrived through my private and artistic experiences, as well as through the influence of the political unrest of the day. As I had no choice but to try, to the best of my ability, to earn something by my pen, I thought of sending a series of articles to a great French journal such as the *National,* which in those days was still extant. In these articles I meant to propound my ideas (in my revolutionary way) on the subject of modern art in its relation to society. I sent six of them to an elderly friend of mine, Albert Franck, requesting him to have them translated into French and to get them published. This Franck was the brother of the better-known Hermann Franck, now the head of the Franco-German bookselling firm, which had originally belonged to my brother-in-law, Avenarius. He sent me back my work with the very natural remark that it was out of the question to expect the Parisian public to understand or appreciate my articles, especially at such a critical moment.

I headed the manuscript *Kunst und Revolution* ('Art and Revolution') and sent it to Otto Wigand in Leipzig, who actually undertook to publish it in the form of a pamphlet, and sent me five louis d'or for it. This unexpected success induced me to continue to exploit my literary gifts. I looked among my papers for the essay I had written the year before as the outcome of my historical studies of the 'Nibelungen' legend; I gave it the title of *Die Nibelungen Weltgeschichte aus der Sage,* and again tried my luck by sending it to Wigand.

The sensational title of *Kunst und Revolution,* as well as the notoriety the 'royal conductor' had gained as a political refugee, had made the radical publisher hope that the scandal that would arise on the publication of my articles would redound to his benefit! I soon discovered that he was on the point of issuing a second edition of *Kunst und Revolution,* without, however, informing me of the fact. He also took over my new pamphlet for another five louis d'or. This was the first time I had earned money by means of published work, and I now began to believe that I had reached that point when I should be able to get the better of my misfortunes. I thought it over, and decided to give public lectures in Zürich on subjects related to my writings during the coming winter, hoping in that free and haphazard fashion to keep body and soul together for a little while, although I had no fixed appointment and did not intend to work at music.

It seemed necessary for me to resort to these means, as I did not know how otherwise to keep myself alive. Shortly after my arrival in Zürich I had witnessed the coming of the fragments of the Baden army, dispersed over Swiss territory, and accompanied by fugitive volunteers, and this had made a painful and uncanny impression upon me. The news of the surrender near Villagos by Görgey paralysed the last hopes as to the issue of the great European struggle for liberty, which so far had been left quite undecided. With some misgiving and anxiety I now turned my eyes from all these occurrences in the outside world inwards to my own soul.

I was accustomed to patronise the *café littéraire,* where I took my coffee after my heavy mid-day meal, in a smoky atmosphere surrounded by a merry and joking throng of men playing dominoes and ' fast.' One day I stared at its common wall-paper representing antique subjects, which in some inexplicable way recalled a certain water-colour by Genelli to my mind, portraying ' The education of Dionysos by the Muses.' I had seen it at the house of my brother-in-law Brockhaus in my young days, and it had made a deep impression on me at the time. At this same place I conceived the first ideas of my *Kunstwerk der Zukunft* (' The Art-Work of the Future '), and it seemed a significant omen to me to be roused one day out of one of my post-prandial dreams by the news that Schröder-Devrient was staying in Zürich. I immediately got up with the intention of calling on her at the neighbouring hotel, ' Zum Schwerte,' but to my great dismay heard that she had just left by steamer. I never saw her again, and long afterwards only heard of her painful death from my wife, who in later years became fairly intimate with her in Dresden.

After I had spent two remarkable summer months in this wild and extraordinary fashion, I at last received reassuring news of Minna, who had remained in Dresden. Although her manner of taking leave of me had been both harsh and wounding, I could not bring myself to believe I had completely parted from her. In a letter I wrote to one of her relations, and which I presumed they would forward, I made sympathetic inquiries about her, while I had already done all that lay in my power.

through repeated appeals to Liszt, to ensure her being well cared for. I now received a direct reply, which, in addition to the fact that it testified to the vigour and activity with which she had fought her difficulties, at the same time showed me that she earnestly desired to be reunited with me. It was almost in terms of contempt that she expressed her grave doubts as to the possibility of my being able to make a living in Zürich, but she added that, inasmuch as she was my wife, she wished to give me another chance. She also seemed to take it for granted that I intended making Zürich only our temporary home, and that I would do my utmost to promote my career as a composer of opera in Paris. Whereupon she announced her intention of arriving at Rorschach in Switzerland on a certain date in September of that year, in the company of the little dog Peps, the parrot Papo, and her so-called sister Nathalie. After having engaged two rooms for our new home, I now prepared to set out on foot for St. Gall and Rorschach through the lovely and celebrated Toggenburg and Appenzell, and felt very touched after all when the peculiar family, which consisted half of pet animals, landed at the harbour of Rorschach. I must honestly confess that the little dog and the bird made me very happy. My wife at once threw cold water on my emotions, however, by declaring that in the event of my behaving badly again she was ready to return to Dresden any moment, and that she had numerous friends there, who would be glad to protect and succour her if she were forced to carry out her threat. Be this as it may, one look at her convinced me how greatly she had aged in this short time, and how much I ought to pity her, and this feeling succeeded in banishing all bitterness from my heart.

I did my utmost to give her confidence and to make her believe that our present misfortunes were but momentary. This was no easy task, as she would constantly compare the diminutive aspect of the town of Zürich with the more noble majesty of Dresden, and seemed to feel bitterly humiliated. The friends whom I introduced to her found no favour in her eyes. She looked upon the Cantonal Secretary, Sulzer, as a ' mere town clerk who would not be of any importance in Germany '; and the wife of my host Müller absolutely disgusted her when, in answer to Minna's complaints about my terrible position, she replied that my greatness lay in the very fact of my having faced it. Then again Minna appeased me by telling me of the expected arrival of some of my Dresden belongings, which she thought would be indispensable to our new home.

The property of which she spoke consisted of a Breitkopf and Härtel grand-piano that looked better than it sounded, and of the ' title-page ' of the *Nibelungen* by Cornelius in a Gothic frame that used to hang over my desk in Dresden.

With this nucleus of household effects we now decided to take small lodgings in the so-called ' hinteren Escherhäusern ' in the Zeltweg. With great cleverness Minna had succeeded in selling the Dresden furniture to advantage, and out of the proceeds of this sale she had brought three hundred marks with her to Zürich to help towards setting up our new home. She told me that she had saved my small but very select library for me by giving it into the safe custody of the publisher, Heinrich Brockhaus (brother of my sister's husband and member of the Saxon Diet), who had insisted upon looking after it. Great, therefore, was her dismay when, upon asking this kind friend to send her the books, he replied that he was holding them as security for a debt of fifteen hundred marks which I had contracted with him during my days of trouble in Dresden, and that he intended to keep them until that sum was returned. As even after the lapse of many years I found it impossible to refund this money, these books, collected for my own special wants, were lost to me for ever.

Thanks more particularly to my friend Sulzer, the Cantonal Secretary, whom my wife at first despised so much on account of his title which she misunderstood, and who, although he was far from well-off himself, thought it only natural that he should help me, however moderately, out of my difficulties, we soon succeeded in making our little place look so cosy that my simple Zürich friends felt quite at home in it. My wife, with all her undeniable talents, here found ample scope in which to distinguish herself, and I remember how ingeniously she made a little what-not out of the box in which she had kindly brought my music and manuscript to Zürich.

But it was soon time to think of how to earn enough money to provide for us all. My idea of giving public lectures was treated with contempt by my wife, who looked upon it as an insult to her pride. She could acquiesce only in one plan, that suggested by Liszt, namely, that I should write an opera for Paris. To satisfy her, and in view of the fact that I could see no chance of a remunerative occupation close at hand, I actually reopened a correspondence on this matter with my great friend and his secretary Belloni in Paris. In the meantime I could not be idle, so I accepted an invitation from the Zürich musical society to conduct a classical composition at one of their concerts, and to this end I worked with their very poor orchestra at Beethoven's Symphony in A major. Although the result was successful, and I received five napoleons for my trouble, it made my wife very unhappy, for she could not forget the excellent orchestra, and the much more appreciative public, which a short time before in Dresden would have seconded and rewarded similar efforts on my part. Her one and only ideal for me was that, by hook or by crook, and with a total disregard of all artistic scruples, I should make a brilliant reputation for myself in Paris. While we were both absolutely at a loss to discover whence we should obtain the necessary funds for our journey to Paris and our sojourn there, I again plunged into my philosophical study of art, as being the only sphere still left open to me.

Harrassed by the cares of a terrible struggle for existence, I wrote the whole of *Das Kunstwerk der Zukunft* in the chilly atmosphere of a sunless little room on the ground floor during the months of November and December of that year. Minna had no objection to this occupation when I told her of the success of my first pamphlet, and the hope I had of receiving even better pay for this more extensive work.

Thus for a while I enjoyed comparative peace, although in my heart a spirit of unrest had begun to reign, thanks to my growing acquaintance with Feuerbach's works. I had always had an inclination to fathom the depths of philosophy, just as I had been led by the mystic influence of Beethoven's Ninth Symphony to search the deepest recesses of music. My first efforts at satisfying this longing had failed. None of the Leipzig professors had succeeded in fascinating me with their lectures on fundamental philosophy and logic. I had procured Schelling's work, *Transcendental Idealism,* recommended to me by Gustav Schlesinger, a friend of Laube's, but it was in vain that I racked my brains to try and make something out of the first pages, and I always returned to my Ninth Symphony.

During the latter part of my stay in Dresden I had returned to these old studies, the longing for which suddenly revived within me, and to these I added the deeper historical studies which had always fascinated me. As an introduction to philosophy I now chose Hegel's *Philosophy of History.* A good deal of this impressed me deeply, and it now seemed as if I should ultimately penetrate into the Holy of Holies along this path. The more incomprehensible many of his speculative conclusions appeared, the more I felt myself desirous of probing the question of the ' Absolute ' and everything connected therewith to the core. For I so admired Hegel's powerful mind that it seemed to me he was the very keystone of all philosophical thought.

The revolution intervened; the practical tendencies of a social reconstruction distracted my attention, and as I have already stated, it was a German Catholic priest and political agitator (formerly a divinity student named Menzdorff, who used to wear a Calabrian hat) [1] who drew my attention to ' the only real philosopher of modern times,' Ludwig Feuerbach. My new Zürich friend, the piano teacher, Wilhelm Baumgartner, made me a present of Feuerbach's book on *Tod und Unsterblichkeit* (' Death and Immortality '). The well-known and stirring lyrical style of the author greatly fascinated me as a layman. The intricate questions which he propounds in this book as if they were being discussed for the first time by him, and which he treats in a charmingly exhaustive manner, had often occupied my mind since the very first days of my acquaintance with Lehrs in Paris, just as they occupy the mind of every imaginative and serious man. With me, however, this was not lasting, and I had contented myself with the poetic suggestions on these important subjects which appear here and there in the works of our great poets.

---

[1] A broad-rimmed, tall, white felt hat, tapering to a point, originally worn by the inhabitants of Calabria, and in 1848 a sign of Republicanism. — EDITOR.

The frankness with which Feuerbach explains his views on
these interesting questions, in the more mature parts of his
book, pleased me as much by their tragic as by their social-
radical tendencies.   It seemed right that the only true immortality should be that of sublime deeds and great works of
art.   It was more difficult to sustain any interest in *Das Wesen
des Christenthums* (' The Essence of Christianity ') by the same
author, for it was impossible whilst reading this work not to
become conscious, however involuntarily, of the prolix and
unskilful manner in which he dilates on the simple and fundamental idea, namely, religion explained from a purely subjective
and psychological point of view.   Nevertheless, from that day
onward I always regarded Feuerbach as the ideal exponent
of the radical release of the individual from the thraldom of
accepted notions, founded on the belief in authority.   The
initiated will therefore not wonder that I dedicated my *Kunstwerk der Zukunft* to Feuerbach and addressed its preface to him.

My friend Sulzer, a thorough disciple of Hegel, was very sorry
to see me so interested in Feuerbach, whom he did not even
recognise as a philosopher at all.   He said that the best thing
that Feuerbach had done for me was that he had been the means
of awakening my ideas, although he himself had none.   But
what had really induced me to attach so much importance to
Feuerbach was the conclusion by means of which he had seceded
from his master Hegel, to wit, that the best philosophy was to
have no philosophy — a theory which greatly simplified what I
had formerly considered a very terrifying study — and secondly,
that only that was real which could be ascertained by the
senses.

The fact that he proclaimed what we call ' spirit ' to be an
æsthetic perception of our senses, together with his statement
concerning the futility of philosophy—these were the two things
in him which rendered me such useful assistance in my conceptions of an all-embracing work of art, of a perfect drama
which should appeal to the simplest and most purely human
emotions at the very moment when it approached its fulfilment
as *Kunstwerk der Zukunft*.   It must have been this which
Sulzer had in his mind when he spoke deprecatingly of Feuerbach's influence over me.   At all events, after a while I certainly

could not return to his works, and I remember that his newly published book, *Uber das Wesen der Religion* ('Lectures on the Essence of Religion'), scared me to such an extent by the dullness of its title alone, that when Herwegh opened it for my benefit, I closed it with a bang under his very nose.

At that time I was working with great enthusiasm upon the draft of a connected essay, and was delighted one day to receive a visit from the novelist and Tieckian scholar, Eduard von Bülow (the father of my young friend Bülow), who was passing through Zürich. In my tiny little room I read him my chapter on poetry, and could not help noticing that he was greatly startled at my ideas on literary drama and on the advent of the new Shakespeare. I thought this all the more reason why Wigand the publisher should accept my new revolutionary book, and expected him to pay me a fee which would be in proportion to the greater size of the work. I asked for twenty lous d'or, and this sum he agreed to pay me.

The prospect of receiving this amount induced me to carry out the plan, which need had forced upon me, of travelling to Paris and of trying my luck there as a composer of opera. This plan had very serious drawbacks; not only did I hate the idea, but I knew that I was doing an injustice to myself by believing in the success of my enterprise, for I felt that I could never seriously throw myself into it heart and soul. Everything, however, combined to make me try the experiment, and it was Liszt in particular who, confident of this being my only way to fame, insisted upon my reopening the negotiations into which Belloni and I had entered during the previous summer. To show with what earnestness I tried to consider the chances of carrying out my plan, I drafted out the plot of the opera, which the French poet would only have to put into verse, because I never for a moment fancied that it would be possible for him to think out and write a libretto for which I would only need to compose the music. I chose for my subject the legend of *Wieland der Schmied,* upon which I commented with some stress at the end of my recently finished *Kunstwerk der Zukunft,* and the version of which by Simrock, taken from the Wilkyna legend, had greatly attracted me.

I sketched out the complete scenario with precise indication

of the dialogue for three acts, and with a heavy heart decided to
hand it over to my Parisian author to be worked out. Liszt
thought he saw a means of making my music known through
his relations with Seghers, the musical director of a society then
known as the ' Concerts de St. Cécile.' In January of the following year the *Tannhäuser* Overture was to be given under his
baton, and it therefore seemed advisable that I should reach
Paris some time before this event. This undertaking, which
appeared to be so difficult owing to my complete lack of funds,
was at last facilitated in a manner quite unexpected.

I had written home for help, and had appealed to all the old
friends I could think of, but in vain. By the family of my
brother Albert in particular, whose daughter had recently entered
upon a brilliant theatrical career, I was treated in much the
same way as one treats an invalid by whom one dreads to become
infected. In contrast to their harshness I was deeply touched
by the devotion of the Ritter family, who had remained in
Dresden; for, apart from my acquaintance with young Karl,
I scarcely knew these people at all. Through the kindness of
my old friend Heine, who had been informed of my position,
Frau Julie Ritter, the venerable mother of the family, had
thought it her duty to place, through a business friend, the
sum of fifteen hundred marks at my disposal. At about the
same time I received a letter from Mme. Laussot, who had
called upon me in Dresden the year before, and who now in
the most affecting terms assured me of her continued sympathy.

These were the first signs of that new phase in my life upon
which I entered from this day forth, and in which I accustomed
myself to look upon the outward circumstances of my existence
as being merely subservient to my will. And by this means
I was able to escape from the hampering narrowness of my
home life.

For the moment the proffered financial assistance was very
distasteful to me, for it seemed to forbid my raising any further
objections to the realisation of the detested Paris schemes.
When, however, on the strength of this favourable change in
my affairs, I suggested to my wife that we might, after all,
content ourselves with remaining in Zürich, she flew into the
most violent passion over my weakness and lack of spirit, and

declared that if I did not make up my mind to achieve something in Paris, she would lose all faith in me. She said, moreover, that she absolutely refused to be a witness of my misery
and grief as a wretched literary man and insignificant conductor of local concerts in Zürich.

We had entered upon the year 1850; I had decided to go to
Paris, if only for the sake of peace, but had to postpone my
journey on account of ill-health. The reaction following upon
the terrible excitement of recent times had not failed to have
its effect on my overwrought nerves, and a state of complete
exhaustion had followed. The continual colds, in spite of which
I had been obliged to work in my very unhealthy room, had
at last given rise to alarming symptoms. A certain weakness
of the chest became apparent, and this the doctor (a political
refugee) undertook to cure by the application of pitch plasters.
As the result of this treatment and the irritating effect it had
upon my nerves, I lost my voice completely for a while; whereupon I was told that I must go away for a change. On going
out to buy my ticket for the journey, I felt so weak and broke
out into such terrible perspiration that I hastened to return
to my wife in order to consult her as to the advisability, in
the circumstances, of abandoning the idea of the expedition
altogether. She, however, maintained (and perhaps rightly)
not only that my condition was not dangerous, but that it was
to a large extent due to imagination, and that, once in the right
place, I would soon recover.

An inexpressible feeling of bitterness stimulated my nerves
as in anger and despair I quickly left the house to buy the
confounded ticket for the journey, and in the beginning of
February I actually started on the road to Paris. I was filled
with the most extraordinary feelings, but the spark of hope
which was then kindled in my breast certainly had nothing whatever to do with the belief that had been imposed upon me from
without, that I was to make a success in Paris as a composer
of operas.

I was particularly anxious to find quiet rooms, for peace had
now become my first necessity, no matter where I happened to
be staying. The cabman who drove me from street to street
through the most isolated quarters, and whom I at last accused

of keeping always to the most animated parts of the city, finally protested in despair that one did not come to Paris to live in a convent. At last it occurred to me to look for what I wanted in one of the *cités* through which no vehicle seemed to drive, and I decided to engage rooms in the Cité de Provence.

True to the plans which had been forced upon me, I at once called on Herr Seghers about the performance of the *Tannhäuser* Overture.

It turned out that in spite of my late arrival I had missed nothing, for they were still racking their brains as to how to procure the necessary orchestral parts.

I therefore had to write to Liszt, asking him to order the copies, and had to wait for their arrival. Belloni was not in town, things were therefore at a standstill, and I had plenty of time to think over the object of my visit to Paris, while an unceasing accompaniment was poured out to my meditations by the barrel-organs which infest the *cités* of Paris.

I had much difficulty in convincing an agent of the government, from whom I received a visit soon after my arrival, that my presence in Paris was due to artistic reasons, and not to my doubtful position as a political refugee.

Fortunately he was impressed by the score, which I showed him, as well as by Liszt's article on the *Tannhäuser* Overture, written the year before in the *Journal des Débats,* and he left me, politely inviting me to continue my avocations peacefully and industriously, as the police had no intention of disturbing me.

I also looked up my older Parisian acquaintances. At the hospitable house of Despléchins I met Semper, who was trying to make his position as tolerable as possible by writing some inferior artistic work. He had left his family in Dresden, from which town we soon received the most alarming news. The prisons were gradually filling there with the unfortunate victims of the recent Saxon movement. Of Röckel, Bakunin, and Heubner, all we could hear was that they had been charged with high treason, and that they were awaiting the death sentence.

In view of the tidings which continually arrived concerning the cruelty and brutality with which the soldiers treated the prisoners, we could not help considering our own lot a very happy one.

My intercourse with Semper, whom I saw frequently, was generally enlivened by a gaiety which was occasionally of rather a risky nature; he was determined to rejoin his family in London, where the prospect of various appointments was open to him. My latest attempts at writing, and the thoughts expressed in my work, interested him greatly, and gave rise to animated conversations in which we were joined by Kietz, who was at first amusing, but evidently boring Semper considerably. I found the former in the identical position in which I had left him many years ago: he had made no headway with his painting, and would have been glad if the revolution had taken a more decided turn, so that, under cover of the general confusion, he might have escaped from his embarrassing position with his landlord. He made at this time quite a good pastel portrait of me in his very best and earliest style. While I was sitting I unfortunately spoke to him about my *Das Kunstwerk der Zukunft,* and thereby laid the foundation for him of troubles that lasted many years, as he tried to instil my new ideas into the Parisian bourgeoisie at whose tables he had hitherto been a welcome guest. Notwithstanding, he remained as of old a good, obliging, true-hearted fellow, and even Semper could not help putting up with him cheerfully. I also looked up my friend Anders. It was a difficult matter to find him at any hour of the day, since out of sleeping hours he was closeted in the library, where he could receive no one, and afterwards retired to the reading-room to spend his hours of rest, and generally went to dine with certain bourgeois families where he gave music lessons. He had aged considerably, but I was glad to find him, comparatively speaking, in better health than the state in which I had last seen him had allowed me to hope, as when I left Paris before he had seemed to be in a decline. Curiously enough, a broken leg had been the means of improving his health, the treatment necessary for it having taken him to a hydro, where his condition had much improved. His one idea was to see me achieve a great success in Paris, and he wished to secure a seat in advance for the first performance of my opera, which he took for granted was to appear, and kept repeating that it would be so very trying for him to occupy a place in any part of the theatre where there would be likely to be a crush. He could not see the use of my present literary work; in spite of this I was again engaged on it exclusively, as I soon ascertained there was no likelihood of my overture to *Tannhäuser* being produced. Liszt had shown the greatest zeal in obtaining and forwarding the orchestral parts; but Herr Seghers informed me that as far as his own orchestra was concerned, he found himself in a republican democracy where each instrument had an equal right to voice its opinion, and it had been unanimously decided that for the remainder of the winter season, which was now drawing to a close, my overture could be dispensed with. I gathered enough from this turn of affairs to realise how precarious my position was.

It is true, the result of my writings was hardly less discouraging. A copy of the Wigand edition of my *Kunstwerk der Zukunft* was forwarded to me full of horrible misprints, and instead of the expected remuneration of twenty louis d'or, my publisher explained that for the present he could only pay me half this sum, as, owing to the fact that at first the sale of the *Kunst und Revolution* had been very rapid, he had been led to attach too high a commercial value to my writings, a mistake he had speedily discovered when he found there was no demand for *Die Nibelungen*.

On the other hand, I received an offer of remunerative work from Adolph Kolatschek, who was also a fugitive, and was just going to bring out a German monthly journal as the organ of the progressive party. In response to this invitation I wrote a long essay on *Kunst und Klima* ('Art and Climate'), in which I supplemented the ideas I had already touched upon in my *Kunstwerk der Zukunft*. Besides this I had, since my arrival in Paris, worked out a more complete sketch of *Wieland der Schmied*. It is true that this work had no longer any value, and I wondered with apprehension what I could write home to my wife, now that the last precious remittance had been so aimlessly sacrificed. The thought of returning to Zürich was as distasteful to me as the prospect of remaining any longer in Paris. My feelings with regard to the latter alternative were intensified by the impression made upon me by Meyerbeer's opera *The Prophet,* which had just been produced and which I had not heard before. Rearing itself on the ruins of the hopes for new and more noble endeavour which had animated the better works of the past year — the only result of the negotiations of the provisional French republic for the encouragement of art — I saw this work of Meyerbeer's break upon the world like the dawn heralding this day of disgraceful desolation. I was so sickened by this performance, that though I was unfortunately placed in the centre of the stalls and would willingly have avoided the disturbance necessarily occasioned by one of the audience moving during the middle of an act, even this consideration did not deter me from getting up and leaving the house. When the famous mother of the prophet finally gives vent to her grief in the well-known series of ridiculous roulades, I was filled with rage and despair at the thought that I should be called upon to listen to such a thing, and never again did I pay the slightest heed to this opera.

But what was I to do next? Just as the South American republics had attracted me during my first miserable sojourn in Paris, so now my longing was directed towards the East, where I could live my life in a manner worthy of a human being far away from this modern world. While I was in this frame of mind I was called upon to answer another inquiry as to my state of health from Mme. Laussot in Bordeaux. It turned out that my answer prompted her to send me a kind and pressing invitation to go and stay at her house, at least for a short time, to rest and forget my troubles. In any circumstances an excursion to more southerly regions, which I had not yet seen, and a visit to people who, though utter strangers, showed such friendly interest in me, could not fail to prove attractive and flattering. I accepted, settled my affairs in Paris, and went by coach via Orléans, Tours, and Angoulême, down the Gironde to the unknown town, where I was received with great courtesy and cordiality by the young wine merchant Eugène Laussot, and presented to my sympathetic young friend, his wife. A closer acquaintance with the family, in which Mrs. Taylor, Mme. Laussot's mother, was now also included, led to a clearer understanding of the character of the sympathy bestowed upon me in such a cordial and unexpected manner by people hitherto unknown to me.   Jessie, as the young wife was called at home, had, during a somewhat lengthy stay in Dresden, become very intimate with the Ritter family, and I had no reason to doubt the assurance given me, that the Laussots' interest in me and my work was principally owing to this intimacy.   After my flight from Dresden, as soon as the news of my difficulties had reached the Ritters, a correspondence had been carried on between Dresden and Bordeaux with a view to ascertaining how best to assist me.   Jessie attributed the whole idea to Frau Julie Ritter who, while not being well enough off herself to make me a sufficient allowance, was endeavouring to come to an understanding with Jessie's mother, the well-to-do widow of an English lawyer, whose income entirely supported the young couple in Bordeaux. This plan had so far succeeded, that shortly after my arrival in Bordeaux Mrs. Taylor informed me that the two families had combined, and that it had been decided to ask me to accept the help of three thousand francs a year until the return of better days.   My one object now was to enlighten my benefactors as to the exact conditions under which I should be accepting such assistance.   I could no longer reckon upon achieving any success as a composer of opera either in Paris or elsewhere; what line I should take up instead I did not know; but, at all events, I was determined to keep myself free from the disgrace which would reflect upon my whole life if I used such means as this offer presented to secure success.   I feel sure I am not wrong in believing that Jessie was the only one who understood me, and though I only experienced kindness from the rest of the family, I soon discovered the gulf by which she, as well as myself, was separated from her mother and husband.   While the husband, who was a handsome young man, was away the greater part of the day attending to his business, and the mother's deafness excluded her to a great extent from our conversations, we soon discovered by a rapid exchange of ideas that we shared the same opinions on many important matters, and this led to a great feeling of friendship between us.   Jessie, who was at that time about twenty-two, bore little resemblance to her mother, and no doubt took after her father, of whom I heard most flattering accounts.   A large and varied collection of books left by this man to his daughter showed his tastes, for besides carrying on his lucrative profession as a lawyer, he had devoted himself to the study of literature and science. From him Jessie had also learned German as a child, and she spoke that language with great fluency. She had been brought up on Grimm's fairy-tales, and was, moreover, thoroughly acquainted with German poetry, as well as with that of England and France, and her knowledge of them was as thorough as the most advanced education could demand. French literature did not appeal to her much. Her quick powers of comprehension were astonishing. Everything which I touched upon she immediately grasped and assimilated. It was the same with music: she read at sight with the greatest facility, and was an accomplished player. During her stay in Dresden she had been told that I was still in search of the pianist who could play Beethoven's great Sonata in B flat major, and she now astonished me by her finished rendering of this most difficult piece. The emotion aroused in me by finding such an exceptionally developed talent suddenly changed to anxiety when I heard her sing. Her sharp, shrill voice, in which there was strength but no real depth of feeling, so shocked me that I could not refrain from begging her to desist from singing in future. With regard to the execution of the sonata, she listened eagerly to my instructions as to how it should be interpreted, though I could not feel that she would succeed in rendering it according to my ideas. I read her my latest essays, and she seemed to understand even the most extraordinary descriptions perfectly. My poem on *Siegfried's Tod* moved her deeply, but she preferred my sketch of *Wieland der Schmied*. She admitted afterwards that she would prefer to imagine herself filling the rôle of Wieland's worthy bride than to find herself in the position and forced to endure the fate of Gutrune in *Siegfried*. It followed inevitably that the presence of the other members of the family proved embarrassing when we wanted to talk over and discuss these various subjects. If we felt somewhat troubled at having to confess to ourselves that Mrs. Taylor would certainly never be able to understand why I was being offered assistance, I was still more disconcerted at realising after a time the complete want of harmony between the young couple, particularly from

an intellectual point of view. The fact that Laussot had
for some time been well aware of his wife's dislike for him
was plainly shown when he one day so far forgot himself
as to complain loudly and bitterly that she would not even
love a child of his if she had one, and that he therefore thought
it fortunate that she was not a mother. Astonished and saddened, I suddenly gazed into an abyss which was hidden here,
as is often the case, under the appearance of a tolerably happy
married life. About this time, and just as my visit, which
had already lasted three weeks, was drawing to a close, I received a letter from my wife that could not have had a more
unfortunate effect on my state of mind. She was, on the
whole, pleased at my having found new friends, but at the
same time explained that if I did not immediately return to
Paris, and there endeavour to secure the production of my
overture with the results anticipated, she would not know
what to think of me, and would certainly fail to understand me
if I returned to Zürich without having effected my purpose.
At the same time my depression was intensified in a terrible
way by a notice in the papers announcing that Röckel, Bakunin,
and Heubner had been sentenced to death, and that the date
of their execution was fixed. I wrote a short but stirring letter
of farewell to the two first, and as I saw no possibility of having
it conveyed to the prisoners, who were confined in the fortress
of Königstein, I decided to send it to Frau von Lüttichau, to
be forwarded to them by her, because I thought she was the
only person in whose power it might lie to do this for me,
while at the same time she had sufficient generosity and independence of mind to enable her to respect and carry out my
wishes, in spite of any possible difference of opinion she might
entertain. I was told some time afterwards that Lüttichau
had got hold of the letter and thrown it into the fire. For the
time being this painful impression helped me to the determination to break with every one and everything, to lose all desire
to learn more of life or of art, and, even at the risk of having
to endure the greatest privations, to trust to chance and put
myself beyond the reach of everybody. The small income
settled upon me by my friends I wished to divide between
myself and my wife, and with my half go to Greece or Asia

Minor, and there, Heaven alone knew how, seek to forget and be forgotten. I communicated this plan to the only confidante I had left to me, chiefly in order that she might be able to enlighten my benefactors as to how I intended disposing of the income they had offered me. She seemed pleased with the idea, and the resolve to abandon herself to the same fate seemed to her also, in her resentment against her position, to be quite an easy matter. She expressed as much by hints and a word dropped here and there. Without clearly realising what it would lead to, and without coming to any understanding with her, I left Bordeaux towards the end of April, more excited than soothed in spirit, and filled with regret and anxiety. I returned to Paris, for the time being, stunned and full of uncertainty as to what to do next. Feeling very unwell, exhausted, and at the same time excited from want of sleep, I reached my destination and put up at the Hôtel Valois, where I remained a week, struggling to gain my self-control and to face my strange position. Even if I had wished to resume the plans which had been instrumental in bringing me to Paris, I soon convinced myself that little or nothing could be done. I was filled with distress and anger at being called upon to waste my energies in a direction contrary to my tastes, merely to satisfy the unreasonable demands made upon me. I was at length obliged to answer my wife's last pressing communication, and wrote her a long and detailed letter in which I kindly, but at the same time frankly, retraced the whole of our life together, and explained that I was fully determined to set her free from any immediate participation in my fate, as I felt quite incapable of so arranging it so as to meet with her approval. I promised her the half of whatever means I should have at my disposal now or in the future, and told her she must accept this arrangement with a good grace, because the occasion had now arisen to take that step of parting from me which, on our first meeting again in Switzerland, she had declared herself ready to do. I ended my letter without bidding her a final farewell. I thereupon wrote to Bordeaux immediately to inform Jessie of the step I had taken, though my means did not as yet allow of my forming any definite plan which I could communicate to her for my complete flight from the world. In return she announced that she was determined to do likewise, and asked for my protection, under which she intended to place herself when once she had set herself free. Much alarmed, I did all in my power to make her realise that it was one thing for a man, placed in such a desperate situation as myself, to cut himself adrift in the face of insurmountable difficulties, but quite another matter for a young woman, at least to all outward appearances, happily settled, to decide to break up her home, for reasons which probably no one except myself would be in a position to understand. Regarding the unconventionality of her resolve in the eyes of the world, she assured me that it would be carried out as quietly as possible, and that for the present she merely thought of arranging to visit her friends the Ritters in Dresden. I felt so upset by all this that I yielded to my craving for retirement, and sought it at no great distance from Paris. Towards the middle of April I went to Montmorency, of which I had heard many agreeable accounts, and there sought a modest hiding-place. With great difficulty I dragged myself to the outskirts of the little town, where the country still bore a wintry aspect, and turned into the little strip of garden belonging to a wine merchant, which was filled with visitors only on Sundays, and there refreshed myself with some bread and cheese and a bottle of wine. A crowd of hens surrounded me, and I kept throwing them pieces of bread, and was touched by the self-sacrificing abstemiousness with which the cock gave all to his wives though I aimed particularly at him. They became bolder and bolder, and finally flew on to the table and attacked my provisions; the cock flew after them, and noticing that everything was topsy-turvy, pounced upon the cheese with the eagerness of a craving long unsatisfied. When I found myself being driven from the table by this chaos of fluttering wings, I was filled with a gaiety to which I had long been a stranger. I laughed heartily, and looked round for the signboard of the inn. I thereby discovered that my host rejoiced in the name of Homo. This seemed a hint from Fate, and I felt I must seek shelter here at all costs. An extraordinarily small and narrow bedroom was shown me, which I immediately engaged. Besides the bed it held a rough table and two cane-bottomed chairs. I arranged one of these as a washhand-stand, and on the table I placed some books, writing materials, and the score of *Lohengrin,* and almost heaved a sigh of content in spite of my extremely cramped accommodation.   Though the weather remained uncertain and the woods with their leafless trees did not seem to offer the prospect of very enticing walks, I still felt that here there was a possibility of my being forgotten, and being also in my turn allowed to forget the events that had lately filled me with such desperate anxiety.   My old artistic instinct awoke again.   I looked over my *Lohengrin* score, and quickly decided to send it to Liszt and leave it to him to bring it out as best he could.   Now that I had got rid of this score also, I felt as free as a bird and as careless as Diogenes about what might befall me.   I even invited Kietz to come and stay with me and share the pleasures of my retreat. He did actually come, as he had done during my stay in Meudon; but he found me even more modestly installed than I had been there.   He was quite prepared to take pot-luck, however, and cheerfully slept on an improvised bed, promising to keep the world in touch with me upon his return to Paris.   I was suddenly startled from my state of complacency by the news that my wife had come to Paris to look me up.   I had an hour's painful struggle with myself to settle the course I should pursue, and decided not to allow the step I had taken in regard to her to be looked upon as an ill-considered and excusable vagary. I left Montmorency and betook myself to Paris, summoned Kietz to my hotel, and instructed him to tell my wife, who had already been trying to gain admittance to him, that he knew nothing more of me except that I had left Paris.   The poor fellow, who felt as much pity for Minna as for me, was so utterly bewildered on this occasion, that he declared that he felt as though he were the axis upon which all the misery in the world turned.   But he apparently realised the significance and importance of my decision, as it was necessary he should, and acquitted himself in this delicate matter with intelligence and good feeling.   That night I left Paris by train for Clermont-Tonnerre, from whence I travelled on to Geneva, there to await news from Frau Ritter in Dresden.   My exhaustion was such that, even had I possessed the necessary means, I could not as yet have contemplated undergoing the fatigue of a long journey. By way of gaining time for further developments I retired to Villeneuve, at the other end of the Lake of Geneva, where I put up at the Hôtel Byron, which was quite empty at the time. Here I learned that Karl Ritter had arrived in Zürich, as he said he would, with the intention of paying me a visit. Impressing upon him the necessity for the strictest secrecy, I invited him to join me at the Lake of Geneva, and in the second week in May we met at the Hôtel Byron. The characteristic which pleased me in him was his absolute devotion, his quick comprehension of my position and the necessity of my resolutions, as well as his readiness to submit without question to all my arrangements, even where he himself was concerned. He was full of my latest literary efforts, told me what an impression they had made on his acquaintances, and thereby induced me to spend the few days of rest I was enjoying in preparing my poem of *Siegfried's Tod* for publication.

I wrote a short preface dedicating this poem to my friends as a relic of the time when I had hoped to devote myself entirely to art, and especially to the composition of music. I sent this manuscript to Herr Wigand in Leipzig, who returned it to me after some time with the remark, that if I insisted on its being printed in Latin characters he would not be able to sell a single copy of it. Later on I discovered that he deliberately refused to pay me the ten louis d'or due to me for *Das Kunstwerk der Zukunft,* which I had directed him to send to my wife. Disappointing as all this was, I was nevertheless unable to engage in any further work, as only a few days after Karl's arrival the realities of life made themselves felt in an unexpected manner, most upsetting to my tranquillity of mind. I received a wildly excited letter from Mme. Laussot to tell me that she had not been able to resist telling her mother of her intentions, that in so doing she had immediately aroused the suspicion that I was to blame, and in consequence of this her disclosure had been communicated to M. Laussot, who vowed he would search everywhere for me in order to put a bullet through my body. The situation was clear enough, and I decided to go to Bordeaux immediately in order to come to an understanding with my opponent. I at once wrote fully to M. Eugène,

endeavouring to make him see matters in their true light, but
at the same time declared myself incapable of understanding
how a man could bring himself to keep a woman with him by
force, when she no longer wished to remain. I ended by informing him that I should reach Bordeaux at the same time as my
letter, and immediately upon my arrival there would let him
know at what hotel to find me; also that I would not tell his
wife of the step I was taking, and that he could consequently
act without restraint. I did not conceal from him, what indeed
was the fact, that I was undertaking this journey under great
difficulties, as under the circumstances I considered it impossible
to wait to have my passport endorsed by the French envoy.
At the same time I wrote a few lines to Mme. Laussot, exhorting
her to be calm and self-possessed, but, true to my purpose,
refrained from even hinting at any movement on my part.
(When, years afterwards, I told Liszt this story, he declared
I had acted very stupidly in not telling Mme. Laussot of my
intentions.) I took leave of Karl the same day, in order to set
out next morning from Geneva on my tedious journey across
France. But I was so exhausted by all this that I could not
help thinking I was going to die. That same night I wrote to
Frau Ritter in Dresden, to this effect, giving her a short account
of the incredible difficulties I had been drawn into. As a
matter of fact, I suffered great inconvenience at the French
frontier on account of my passport; I was made to give my
exact place of destination, and it was only upon my assuring
them that pressing family affairs required my immediate
presence, that the authorities showed exceptional leniency and
allowed me to proceed.

I travelled by Lyons through Auvergne by stage-coach for
three days and two nights, till at length I reached Bordeaux.
It was the middle of May, and as I surveyed the town from a
height at early dawn I saw it lit up by a fire that had broken
out. I alighted at the Hôtel Quatre Sœurs, and at once sent
a note to M. Laussot, informing him that I held myself at
his disposal and would remain in all day to receive him. It
was nine o'clock in the morning when I sent him this message.
I waited in vain for an answer, till at last, late in the afternoon, I received a summons from the police-station to present

myself immediately. There I was first of all asked whether my passport was in order. I acknowledged the difficulty I found myself in with regard to it, and explained that family matters had necessitated my placing myself in this position.

I was thereupon informed that precisely this family matter, which had no doubt brought me there, was the cause of their having to deny me the permission to remain in Bordeaux any longer. In answer to my question, they did not conceal the fact that these proceedings against me were being carried out at the express wish of the family concerned. This extraordinary revelation immediately restored my good-humour. I asked the police inspector whether, after such a trying journey, I might not be allowed a couple of days' rest before returning; this request he readily granted, and told me that in any case there could be no chance of my meeting the family in question, as they had left Bordeaux at mid-day. I used these two days to recover from my fatigue, and also wrote a letter to Jessie, in which I told her exactly what had taken place, without concealing my contempt at the behaviour of her husband, who could expose his wife's honour by a denunciation to the police. I also added that our friendship could certainly not continue until she had released herself from so humiliating a position. The next thing was to get this letter safely delivered. The information furnished me by the police officials was not sufficient to enlighten me as to what had exactly taken place in the Laussot family, whether they had left home for some length of time or merely for a day, so I simply made up my mind to go to their house. I rang the bell and the door sprang open; without meeting any one I walked up to the first-floor flat, the door of which stood open, and went from room to room till I reached Jessie's boudoir, where I placed my letter in her work-basket and returned the way I had come. I received no reply, and set out upon my return journey as soon as the term of rest granted me had expired. The fine May weather had a cheering effect upon me, and the clear water, as well as the agreeable name of the Dordogne, along whose banks the post-chaise travelled for some distance, gave me great pleasure.

I was also entertained by the conversation of two fellow-travellers, a priest and an officer, about the necessity of putting an end to the French Republic. The priest showed himself much more humane and broad-minded than his military interlocutor, who could only repeat the one refrain, ' *Il faut en finir.*' I now had a look at Lyons, and in a walk round the town tried to recall the scenes in Lamartine's *Histoire des Girondins*, where he so vividly describes the siege and surrender of the town during the period of the Convention Nationale. At last I arrived at Geneva, and returned to the Byron hotel, where Karl Ritter was awaiting me. During my absence he had heard from his family, who wrote very kindly concerning me. His mother had at once reassured him as to my condition, and pointed out that with people suffering from nervous disorders the idea of approaching death was a frequent symptom, and that there was consequently no occasion to feel anxious about me. She also announced her intention of coming to visit us in Villeneuve with her daughter Emilie in a few days' time. This news made me take heart again; this devoted family, so solicitous for my welfare, seemed sent by Providence to lead me, as I so longed to be led, to a new life. Both ladies arrived in time to celebrate my thirty-seventh birthday on the twenty-second of May. The mother, Frau Julie, particularly made a deep impression upon me. I had only met her once before in Dresden, when Karl had invited me to be present at the performance of a quartette of his own composition, given at his mother's house. On this occasion the respect and devotion shown me by each member of the family had delighted me. The mother had hardly spoken to me, but when I was leaving she was moved to tears as she thanked me for my visit. I was unable to understand her emotion at the time, but now when I reminded her of it she was surprised, and explained that she had felt so touched at my unexpected kindness to her son.

She and her daughter remained with us about a week. We sought diversion in excursions to the beautiful Valais, but did not succeed in dispelling Frau Ritter's sadness of heart, caused by the knowledge of recent events of which she had now been informed, as well as by her anxiety at the course my life was taking. As I afterwards learned, it had cost the nervous, delicate woman a great effort to undertake this journey, and when I urged her to leave her house to come and settle in

Switzerland with her family, so that we might all be united,
she at last pointed out to me that in proposing what seemed
to her such an eccentric undertaking, I was counting upon a
strength and energy she no longer possessed. For the present
she commended her son, whom she wished to leave with me,
to my care, and gave me the necessary means to keep us both
for the time being. Regarding the state of her fortune, she
told me that her income was limited, and now that it was
impossible to accept any help from the Laussots, she did not
know how she would be able to come to my assistance sufficiently
to assure my independence. Deeply moved, we took leave of
this venerable woman at the end of a week, and she returned to
Dresden with her daughter, and I never saw her again.

Still bent upon discovering a means of disappearing from the
world, I thought of choosing a wild mountain spot where I could
retire with Karl. For this purpose we sought the lonely Visper
Thal in the canton Valais, and not without difficulty made our
way along the impracticable roads to Zermatt. There, at the
foot of the colossal and beautiful Matterhorn, we could indeed
consider ourselves cut off from the outer world. I tried to
make things as comfortable as I could in this primitive wilderness, but discovered only too soon that Karl could not reconcile himself to his surroundings. Even on the second day he
owned that he thought it horrid, and suggested that it would
be more pleasant in the neighbourhood of one of the lakes.
We studied the map of Switzerland, and chose Thun for our
next destination. Unfortunately I again found myself reduced to a state of extreme nervous fatigue, in which the slightest effort produced a profuse and weakening perspiration. Only
by the greatest strength of will was I able to make my way
out of the valley; but at last we reached Thun, and with renewed courage engaged a couple of modest but cheerful rooms
looking out on to the road, and proposed to wait and see how
we should like it. In spite of the reserve which still betrayed
his shyness of character, I found conversation with my young
friend always pleasant and enlivening. I now realised the
pitch of fluent and overflowing vivacity to which the young
man could attain, particularly at night before retiring to
rest, when he would squat down beside my bed, and in the

agreeable, pure dialect of the German Baltic provinces, give free expression to whatever had excited his interest. I was exceedingly cheered during these days by the perusal of the *Odyssey,* which I had not read for so long and which had fallen into my hands by chance. Homer's long-suffering hero, always homesick yet condemned to perpetual wandering, and always valiantly overcoming all difficulties, was strangely sympathetic to me. Suddenly the peaceful state I had scarcely yet entered upon was disturbed by a letter which Karl received from Mme. Laussot. He did not know whether he ought to show it to me, as he thought Jessie had gone mad. I tore it out of his hand, and found she had written to say that she felt obliged to let my friend know that she had been sufficiently enlightened about me to make her drop my acquaintance entirely. I afterwards discovered, chiefly through the help of Frau Ritter, that in consequence of my letter and my arrival in Bordeaux, M. Laussot, together with Mrs. Taylor, had immediately taken Jessie to the country, intending to remain there until the news was received of my departure, to accelerate which he had applied to the police authorities. While they were away, and without telling her of my letter and my journey, they had obtained a promise from the young woman to remain quiet for a year, give up her visit to Dresden, and, above all, to drop all correspondence with me; since, under these conditions, she was promised her entire freedom at the end of that time, she had thought it better to give her word. Not content with this, however, the two conspirators had immediately set about calumniating me on all sides, and finally to Mme. Laussot herself, saying that I was the initiator of this plan of elopement. Mrs. Taylor had written to my wife complaining of my intention to commit adultery, at the same time expressing her pity for her and offering her support; the unfortunate Minna, who now thought she had found a hitherto unsuspected reason for my resolve to remain separated from her, wrote back complaining of me to Mrs. Taylor. The meaning of an innocent remark I had once made had been strangely misinterpreted, and matters were now aggravated by making it appear as though I had intentionally lied. In the course of playful conversation Jessie had once told me that she belonged

to no recognised form of religion, her father having been a
member of a certain sect which did not baptise either according
to the Protestant or the Roman Catholic ritual; whereupon
I had comforted her by assuring her that I had come in contact
with much more questionable sects, as shortly after my marriage
in Königsberg I had learned that it had been solemnised by
a hypocrite. God alone knows in what form this had been
repeated to the worthy British matron, but, at all events, she
told my wife that I had said I was ' not legally married to
her.' In any case, my wife's answer to this had no doubt
furnished further material with which to poison Jessie's mind
against me, and this letter to my young friend was the result.
I must admit that, seen by this light, the circumstance at
which I felt most indignant was the way my wife had been
treated, and while I was perfectly indifferent as to what the
rest of the party thought of me, I immediately accepted Karl's
offer to go to Zürich and see her, so as to give her the explanation
necessary to her peace of mind. While awaiting his return,
I received a letter from Liszt, telling me of the deep impression
made upon him by my *Lohengrin* score, which had caused him
to make up his mind as to the future in store for me. He at
the same time announced that, as I had given him the permission
to do so, he intended doing all in his power to bring about the
production of my opera at the forthcoming Herder festival in
Weimar. About this time I also heard from Frau Ritter, who,
in consequence of events of which she was well aware, thought
herself called upon to beg me not to take the matter too much
to heart. At this moment Karl also returned from Zürich, and
spoke with great warmth of my wife's attitude. Not having
found me in Paris, she had pulled herself together with remarkable energy, and in pursuance of an earlier wish of mine,
had rented a house on the lake of Zürich, installed herself
comfortably, and remained there in the hope of at last hearing
from me again. Besides this, he had much to tell me of Sulzer's
good sense and friendliness, the latter having stood by, my wife
and shown her great sympathy. In the midst of his narrative
Karl suddenly exclaimed, ' Ah! these could be called sensible
people; but with such a mad Englishwoman nothing could be
done.' To all this I said not a word, but finally with a smile

asked him whether he would like to go over to Zürich? He sprang up exclaiming, 'Yes, and as soon as possible.' 'You shall have your way,' said I; 'let us pack. I can see no sense in anything either here or there.' Without breathing another syllable about all that had happened, we left the next day for Zürich.

PART III

1850–1861

MINNA had been lucky enough to find quarters near Zürich which corresponded very closely with the wishes I had so emphatically expressed before leaving. The house was situated in the parish of Enge, a good fifteen minutes' walk from the town, on a site overlooking the lake, and was an old-fashioned hostelry called 'Zum Abendstern,' belonging to a certain Frau Hirel, who was a pleasant old lady. The second floor, which was quite self-contained and very quiet, offered us humble but adequate accommodations for a modest rent.

I arrived early in the morning and found Minna still in bed. She was anxious to know whether I had returned simply out of pity; but I quickly succeeded in obtaining her promise that she would never again refer to what had taken place. She was soon quite herself again when she began to show me the progress she had made in arranging the rooms.

Our position had for some years been growing more comfortable, in spite of the fact that at this time various difficulties again arose, and our domestic happiness seemed tolerably secure. Yet I could never quite master a restless inclination to deviate from anything that was regarded as conventional.

Our two pets, Peps and Papo, largely helped to make our lodgings homelike; both were very fond of me, and were sometimes even too obtrusive in showing their affection. Peps would always lie behind me in the armchair while I was working, and Papo, after repeatedly calling out 'Richard' in vain, would often come fluttering into my study if I stayed away from the sitting-room too long. He would then settle down on my desk and vigorously shuffle about the papers and pens. He was so well trained that he never uttered the ordinary cry of a bird, but expressed his sentiments only by talking or singing. As soon as he heard my step on the staircase he would begin whistling a tune, as, for instance, the great march in the finale of the Symphony in C minor, the beginning of the Eighth Symphony in F major, or even a bright bit out of the *Rienzi* Overture. Peps, our little dog, on the other hand, was a highly sensitive and nervous creature. My friends used to call him 'Peps the petulant,' and there were times when we could not speak to him even in the friendliest way without bringing on paroxysms of howls and sobs. These two pets of course helped very much to increase the mutual understanding between myself and my wife.

Unfortunately, there was one perpetual source of quarrel, arising from my wife's behaviour towards poor Nathalie. Until her death she shamefully withheld from the girl the fact that she was her mother. Nathalie, therefore, always believed that she was Minna's sister, and consequently could not understand why she should not have the same rights as my wife, who always treated her in an authoritative way, as a strict mother would do, and seemed to think herself justified in complaining of Nathalie's behaviour. Apparently the latter had been much neglected and spoiled just at the critical age, and deprived of any proper training. She was short in stature and inclined to become stout, her manners were awkward and her opinions narrow. Minna's hasty temper and continual jeering made the girl, who was naturally very good-natured, stubborn and spiteful, so that the behaviour of the 'sisters' often caused the most hateful scenes in our quiet home. I never lost my patience at these incidents, however, but remained completely indifferent to everything going on around me.

The arrival of my young friend Karl was a pleasant diversion in our small household. He occupied a tiny attic above our rooms and shared our meals. Sometimes he would accompany me on my walks, and for a time seemed quite satisfied.

But I soon noticed in him a growing restlessness. He had not been slow to recognise, by the unpleasant scenes that again became daily occurrences in our married life, at what point the shoe pinched that I had good-naturedly put on again at his request. However, when one day I reminded him that in coming back to Zürich I had other objects in view besides the longing for a quiet domestic life, he remained silent. But I saw that there was another peculiar reason for his uneasiness; he took to coming in late for meals, and even then he had no appetite. At first I was anxious at this, fearing he might have taken a dislike to our simple fare, but I soon discovered that my young friend was so passionately addicted to sweets that I feared he might eventually ruin his health by trying to live on large quantities of confectionery. My remarks seemed to annoy him, as his absences from the house became more frequent, I thought that probably his small room did not afford him the comfort he required, and I therefore made no objection when he left us and took a room in town.

As his state of uneasiness still seemed to increase and he did not appear at all happy in Zürich, I was glad to be able to suggest a little change for him, and persuade him to go for a holiday to Weimar, where the first performance of *Lohengrin* was to take place about the end of August.

About the same time I induced Minna to go with me for our first ascent of the Righi, a feat we both accomplished very energetically on foot. I was very much grieved on this occasion to discover that my wife had symptoms of heart disease, which continued to develop subsequently. We spent the evening of the 28th of August, while the first performance of *Lohengrin* was taking place at Weimar, in Lucerne, at the Schwan inn, watching the clock as the hands went round, and marking the various times at which the performance presumably began, developed, and came to a close.

I always felt somewhat distressed, uncomfortable, and ill at ease whenever I tried to pass a few pleasant hours in the society of my wife.

The reports received of that first performance gave me no clear or reassuring impression of it. Karl Ritter soon came back to Zürich, and told me of deficiencies in staging and of the unfortunate choice of a singer for the leading part, but remarked that on the whole it had gone fairly well. The reports sent me by Liszt were the most encouraging. He did not seem to think it worth while to allude to the inadequacy of the means at his command for such a bold undertaking, but preferred to dwell on the sympathetic spirit that prevailed in the company and the effect it produced on the influential personages he had invited to be present.

Although everything in connection with this important enterprise eventually assumed a bright aspect, the direct result on my position at the time was very slight. I was more interested in the future of the young friend who had been entrusted to my care than in anything else. At the time of his visit to Weimar he had been to stay with his family in Dresden, and after his return expressed an anxious wish to become a musician, and possibly to secure a position as a musical director at a theatre. I had never had an opportunity of judging of his gifts in this line. He had always refused to play the piano in my presence, but I had seen his setting of an alliterative poem of his own, *Die Walküre,* which, though rather awkwardly put together, struck me by its precise and skilful compliance with the rules of composition.

He proved himself to be the worthy pupil of his master, Robert Schumann, who, long before, had told me that Karl possessed great musical gifts, and that he could not remember ever having had any other pupil endowed with such a keen ear and such a ready facility for assimilation. Consequently I had no reason to discourage the young man's confidence in his capacity for the career of a musical director. As the winter season was approaching, I asked the manager of the theatre for the address of Herr Kramer, who was coming for the season, and learned that he was still engaged at Winterthur.

Sulzer, who was always ready when help or advice was needed, arranged for a meeting with Herr Kramer at a dinner at the 'Wilden Mann' in Winterthur. At this meeting it was decided, on my recommendation, that Karl Ritter should be appointed musical director at the theatre for the ensuing winter, starting from October, and the remuneration he was to receive was really a very fair one. As my protégé was admittedly a beginner, I had to guarantee his capacity by undertaking to perform his duties in the event of any trouble arising at the theatre on the ground of his inefficiency. Karl seemed delighted. As October drew near and the opening of the theatre was announced to take place 'under exceptional artistic auspices,' I thought it advisable to see what Karl's views were.

By way of a début I had selected *Der Freischütz,* so that he might open his career with a well-known opera. Karl did not entertain the slightest doubt of being able to master such a simple score, but when he had to overcome his reserve in playing the piano before me, as I wanted to go through the whole opera with him, I was amazed at seeing that he had no idea of accompaniment. He played the arrangement for the pianoforte with the characteristic carelessness of an amateur who attaches no importance to lengthening a bar by incorrect fingering. He knew nothing whatever about rhythmic precision or tempo, the very essentials of a conductor's career. I felt completely nonplussed and was absolutely at a loss what to say. However, I still hoped the young man's talent might suddenly break out, and I looked forward to an orchestral rehearsal, for which I provided him with a pair of large spectacles. I had never noticed before that he was so shortsighted, but when reading he had to keep his face so close to the music that it would have been impossible for him to control both orchestra and singers. When I saw him, hitherto so confident, standing at the conductor's desk staring hard at the score, in spite of his spectacles, and making meaningless signs in the air like one in a trance, I at once realised that the time for carrying out my guarantee had arrived.

It was, nevertheless, a somewhat difficult and trying task to make young Ritter understand that I should be compelled to take his place; but there was no help for it, and it was I who had to inaugurate Kramer's winter season under such 'exceptional artistic auspices.' The success of *Der Freischütz* placed me in a peculiar position as regards both the company and the public, but it was quite out of the question to suppose that Karl could continue to act as musical director at the theatre by himself.

Strange to say, this trying experience coincided with an important change in the life of another young friend of mine, Hans von Bülow, whom I had known in Dresden. I had met his father at Zürich in the previous year just after his second marriage. He afterwards settled down at Lake Constance, and it was from this place that Hans wrote to me expressing his regret that he was unable to pay his long-desired visit to Zürich, as he had previously promised to do.

As far as I could make out, his mother, who had been divorced from his father, did all in her power to restrain him from embracing the career of an artist, and tried to persuade him to enter the civil or the diplomatic service, as he had studied law. But his inclinations and talents impelled him to a musical career. It seemed that his mother, when giving him permission to go to visit his father, had particularly urged him to avoid any meeting with me. When I afterwards heard that he had been advised by his father also not to come to Zürich, I felt sure that the latter, although he had been on friendly terms with me, was anxious to act in accordance with his first wife's wishes in this serious matter of his son's future, so as to avoid any further disputes after the friction of the divorce had barely been allayed. Later on I learned that these statements, which roused a strong feeling of resentment in me against Eduard von Bülow, were unfounded; but the despairing tone of Hans's letter, clearly showing that any other career would be repugnant to him and would be a constant source of misery, seemed to be ample reason for my interference. This was one of the occasions when my easily excited indignation roused me to activity. I replied very fully, and eloquently pointed out to him the vital importance of this moment in his life. The desperate tone of his letter justified me in telling him very plainly that this was not a case in which he could deal hastily with his views as to the future, but that it was a matter profoundly affecting his whole heart and soul. I told him what I myself would do in his case, that is to say, if he really felt an overwhelming and irresistible impulse to become an artist, and would prefer to endure the greatest hardships and trials rather than be forced into a course he felt was a wrong one, he ought, in defiance of everything, to make up his mind to accept the helping hand I was holding out to him at once. If, in spite of his father's prohibition, he still wished to come to me, he ought not to hesitate, but should carry out his wishes immediately on the receipt of my letter.

Karl Ritter was pleased when I entrusted him with the duty of delivering the letter personally at Bülow's country villa.

When he arrived he asked to see his friend at the door, and went for a stroll with him, during which he gave him my letter. Thereupon Hans, who like Karl had no money, at once decided, in spite of storm and rain, to accompany Karl back to Zürich on foot. So one day they turned up absolutely tired out, and came into my room looking like a couple of tramps, with visible signs about them of their mad expedition. Karl beamed with joy over this feat, while young Bülow was quite overcome with emotion.

I at once realised that I had taken a very serious responsibility on my shoulders, yet I sympathised deeply with the overwrought youth, and my conduct towards him was guided by all that had occurred for a long time afterwards.

At first we had to console him, and stimulate his confidence by our cheerfulness. His appointment was soon arranged. He was to share Karl's contract at the theatre, and enjoy the same rights; both were to receive a small salary, and I was to continue to act as surety for their capabilities.

At this time they happened to be rehearsing a musical comedy, and Hans, without any knowledge of the subject, took up his position at the conductor's desk and handled the baton with great vigour and remarkable skill. I felt safe as far as he was concerned, and all doubt as to his ability as musical director vanished on the spot. But it was a somewhat difficult task to overcome Karl's misgivings about himself, owing to the idea ingrained in his mind that he never could become a practical musician. A growing shyness and secret antipathy towards me soon manifested itself and became more noticeable in this young man, in spite of the fact that he was certainly gifted. It was impossible to keep him any longer in his position or to ask him to conduct again.

Bülow also soon encountered unexpected difficulties. The manager and his staff, who had been spoiled by my having conducted on the occasion already mentioned, were always on the look-out for some fresh excuse for requisitioning my services.

I did, in fact, conduct again a few times, partly to give the public a favourable impression of the operatic company, which was really quite a good one, and partly to show my young friends, especially Bülow, who was so eminently adapted for a conductor, the most essential points which the leader of an orchestra ought to know.

Hans was always equal to the occasion, and I could with a clear conscience say there was no need for me to take his place whenever he was called upon to conduct. However, one of the artistes, a very conceited singer, who had been somewhat spoiled by my praise, annoyed him so much by her ways that she succeeded in forcing me to take up the baton again. When a couple of months later we realised the impossibility of carrying on this state of things indefinitely, and were tired of the whole affair, the management consented to free us from our irksome duties. About this time Hans was offered the post of musical director at St. Gall without any special conditions being attached to his engagement, so I sent the two boys off to try their luck in the neighbouring town, and thus gained time for further developments.

Herr Eduard von Bülow had, after all, come to the conclusion that it would be wiser to abide by his son's decision, though he did not do so without evincing a good deal of ill-humour towards me. He had not replied to a letter I had written him to explain my conduct in the matter, but I afterwards learned that he had visited his son in Zürich by way of patching up a reconciliation.

I went several times to St. Gall to see the young men, as they remained there during the winter months. I found Karl lost in gloomy thought: he had again met with an unfavourable reception when conducting Gluck's Overture to *Iphigenia*, and was keeping aloof from everybody. Hans was busily rehearsing with a very poor company and a horrible orchestra, in a hideous theatre. Seeing all this misery, I told Hans that for the time being he had picked up enough to pass for a practical musician or even for an experienced conductor.

The question now was to find him a sphere which would give him a suitable scope for his talents. He told me that his father was going to send him to Freiherr von Poissl, the manager of the Munich Court Theatre, with a letter of introduction. But his mother soon intervened, and wanted him to go to Weimar to continue his musical training under Liszt. This was all I could desire; I felt greatly relieved and heartily recommended the young man, of whom I was very fond, to my distinguished friend.

He left St. Gall at Easter, 1851, and during the long period of his stay in Weimar I was released from the responsibility of looking after him.

Meanwhile Ritter remained in melancholy retirement, and not being able to make up his mind whether or not he should return to Zürich, where he would be disagreeably reminded of his unlucky début, he preferred for the present to stay in seclusion at St. Gall.

The sojourn of my young friends at St. Gall had been pleasantly varied during the previous winter by a visit to Zürich, when Hans made his appearance as pianist at one of the concerts of the musical society there. I also took an active part in it by conducting one of Beethoven's symphonies, and it was a great pleasure to us both to give each other mutual encouragement.

I had been asked to appear again at this society's concerts during the winter. However, I only did so occasionally, to conduct a Beethoven symphony, making it a conditon that the orchestra, and more especially the string instruments, should be reinforced by capable musicians from other towns.

As I always required three rehearsals for each symphony, and many of the musicians had to come from a great distance, our work acquired quite an imposing and solemn character. I was able to devote the time usually taken up by a rehearsal to the study of one symphony, and accordingly had leisure to work out the minutest details of the execution, particularly as the technical difficulties were not of an insuperable character. My facility in interpreting music at that time attained a degree of perfection I had not hitherto reached, and I recognised this by the unexpected effect my conducting produced.

The orchestra contained some really talented and clever musicians, among whom I may mention Fries, an oboist, who, starting from a subordinate place, had been appointed a leading player. He had to practice with me, just as a singer would do, the more important parts allotted to his instrument in Beethoven's symphonies. When we first produced the Symphony in C minor, this extraordinary man played the small passage

marked *adagio* at the *fermata* of the first movement in a manner
I have never heard equalled. After my retirement from the
directorship of these concerts he left the orchestra and went
into business as a music-seller.

The orchestra could further boast of a Herr Ott-Imhoff, a
highly cultured and well-to-do man who belonged to a noble
family, and had joined the orchestra as a patron and as an
amateur musician. He played the clarionet with a soft and
charming tone which was somewhat lacking in spirit. I must
also mention the worthy Herr Bär, a cornet-player, whom I
appointed leader of the brass instruments, as he exercised a
great influence on that part of the orchestra. I cannot remember ever having heard the long, powerful chords of the last
movement of the C minor Symphony executed with such intense
power as by this player in Zürich, and can only compare the
recollection of it with the impressions I had when, in my early
Parisian days, the Conservatoire orchestra performed Beethoven's Ninth Symphony.

Our production of the Symphony in C minor made a great
impression on the audience, especially on my intimate friend
Sulzer, who had previously kept aloof from any kind of music.
He became so incensed when an attack was made on me by a
newspaper that he answered the gratuitous critic in a satirical
poem composed with the skill of a Platen.

As I have already said, Bülow was invited in the course of
the winter to give a pianoforte recital at a concert at which I
promised to produce the *Sinfonia Eroica*.

With his usual audacity he chose Liszt's piano arrangement
of the *Tannhäuser* Overture, a work as brilliant as it is difficult,
and therefore a somewhat hazardous undertaking. However,
he caused quite a sensation, and I myself was astounded at his
execution. Up to this time I had not paid it the attention it
deserved, and it inspired me with the greatest confidence in his
future. I frequently had occasion to admire his masterly
skill both as conductor and accompanist.

During that winter, apart from the occasions in my young
friend's life already briefly alluded to, there were frequent
opportunities of displaying his capabilities. My acquaintances used to foregather in my house, and formed quite a

little club for the purposes of mutual enjoyment, which, however, would hardly have been successful without Bülow's assistance.

I sang suitable passages from my opera, which Hans accompanied with an expressiveness which delighted me very much. On an occasion like this I also read aloud extracts from my manuscripts. For instance, during a series of successive evenings I read the whole of my longer work, *Oper und Drama*, written in the course of this winter, and was favoured by a steadily growing and remarkably attentive audience.

Now that after my return I had secured a certain degree of peace and tranquillity of mind, I began to think of resuming my more serious studies. But somehow the composition of *Siegfried's Death* did not seem to appeal to me. The idea of sitting down deliberately to write a score which should never go further than the paper on which it was written, again discouraged me; whereas I felt more and more strongly impelled to lay a foundation on which it might some day be possible to present such a work, even though the end had to be gained by roundabout means. To secure this object it seemed above all necessary to approach those friends, both at home and abroad, who interested themselves in my art, in order to expound to them more clearly the problems that demanded solution, which, although definite enough to my own mind, had scarcely as yet even entered into their heads. A singularly favourable opportunity for so doing offered itself one day when Sulzer showed me an article on 'Opera' in Brockhaus's *Modern Encyclopædia*. The good man was fully convinced that in the opinions expressed in this article I should find a preliminary basis for my own theories. But a hasty glance sufficed to show me at once how entirely erroneous they were, and I tried hard to point out to Sulzer the fundamental difference between the accepted views, even of very sensible people, and my own conceptions of the heart of the matter. Finding it naturally impossible, even with all the eloquence at my command, to elucidate my ideas all at once, I set about preparing a methodical plan for detailed treatment of the subject as soon as I got home. In this way I was lead to write this book which was published under the title of *Oper und Drama*, a task which kept me fully occupied for several months, in fact until February, 1851.

But I had to pay heavily for the exhausting toil expended on the conclusion of this work. According to my calculations, only a few days of persevering industry were needed for the completion of my manuscript, when my parrot, which usually watched me on my writing-table, was taken seriously ill. As it had already completely recovered from several similar attacks, I did not feel very anxious. Although my wife begged me to fetch a veterinary surgeon who lived in a village which was rather far off, I preferred to stick to my desk, and I put off going from one day to the next. At last one evening the all-important manuscript was finished, and the next morning our poor Papo lay dead on the floor. My inconsolable grief over this melancholy loss was fully shared by Minna, and by our mutual affection for this treasured pet we were once more tenderly united in a way likely to conduce to our domestic happiness.

In addition to our pets, our older Zürich friends had also remained faithful to us, in spite of the catastrophe which had befallen my family life. Sulzer was without a doubt the worthiest and most important of these friends. The profound difference between us both in intellect and temperament seemed only to favour this relationship, for each was constantly providing surprises for the other; and as the divergencies between us were radical, they aften gave rise to most exhilarating and instructive experiences. Sulzer was extraordinarily excitable and very delicate in health. It was quite against his own original desire that he had entered the service of the state, and in doing so he had sacrificed his own wishes to a conscientious performance of duty in the extremest sense of the word, and now, through his acquaintance with me, he was drawn more deeply into the sphere of æsthetic enjoyment than he regarded as justifiable. Probably he would have indulged less freely in these excesses, had I taken my art a little less seriously. But as I insisted upon attaching an importance to the artistic destiny of mankind which far transcended the mere aims of citizenship, I sometimes completely upset him. Yet, on the other hand, it was just this intense earnestness which so strongly attracted him to me and my speculations. This

not only gave rise to pleasant conversation and calm discussion
between us, but also, owing to a fiery temper on both sides,
sometimes provoked violent explosions, so that, with trembling
lips, he would seize hat and stick and hurry away without a
word of farewell.   Such, however, was the intrinsic worth of
the man, that he was sure to turn up again the next evening
at the accustomed hour, when we both felt as though nothing
whatever had passed between us.   But when certain bodily
ailments compelled him to remain indoors for many days, it
was difficult to gain access to him, for he was apt to become
furious when any one inquired about his health.   On these
occasions there was only one way of putting him in a good
temper, and that was to say that one had called to ask a favour
of him.   Thereupon he was pleasantly surprised, and would
not only declare himself ready to oblige in any way that was
in his power, but would assume a really cheerful and benevolent
demeanour.

A remarkable contrast to him was presented by the musician
Wilhelm Baumgartner, a merry, jovial fellow, without any
aptitude for concentration, who had learned just enough about
the piano to be able, as teacher at so much an hour, to earn
what he required for a living.   He had a taste for what was
beautiful, provided it did not soar too high, and possessed a
true and loyal heart, full of a great respect for Sulzer, which
unfortunately could not cure him of a craving for the public-
house.

Besides this man, there were two others who had also from
the very first formed part of our circle.   Both of them were
friends of the pair I have already mentioned; their names were
Hagenbuch, a worthy and respectable deputy cantonal secretary; and Bernhard Spyri, a lawyer, and at that time editor
of the *Eidgenössische Zeitung*.   The latter was a singularly good-
tempered man, but not overburdened with intellect, for which
reason Sulzer always treated him with special consideration.

Alexander Müller soon disappeared from our midst, as he
became more and more engrossed by domestic calamities, bodily
infirmities, and the mechanical drudgery of giving lessons by
the hour.   As for the musician Abt, I had never felt particularly drawn towards him, in spite of his *Schwalben,* and he

too speedily left us to carve a brilliant career for himself in Brunswick.

In the meantime, however, our Zürich circle was enriched by all kinds of additions from without, mainly due to the political shipwrecks. On my return, in January, 1850, I had already found Adolph Kolatschek, a plain, though not unprepossessing-looking man, though he was a bit of a bore. He imagined himself born to be an editor, and had founded a German monthly magazine, which was to open a field for those who had been outwardly conquered in the recent movements to continue their fight in the inner realm of the spirit. I felt almost flattered at being picked out by him as an author, and being informed that ' a power like mine ' ought not to be absent from a union of spiritual forces such as was to be established by his enterprise. I had previously sent him from Paris my treatise on *Kunst und Klima;* and he now gladly accepted some fairly long extracts from my still unpublished *Oper und Drama,* for which he moreover paid me a handsome fee. This man made an indelible impression on my mind as the only instance I have met of a really tactful editor. He once handed me the manuscript of a review on my *Kunstwerk der Zukunft,* written by a certain Herr Palleske, to read, saying that he would not print it without my express consent, though he did not press me to give it. It was a superficial article, without any true comprehension of the subject, and couched in most arrogant terms. I felt that if it appeared in this particular journal it would certainly demand inconvenient and wearisome rejoinders from me, in which I should have to restate my original thesis. As I was by no means inclined to enter upon such a controversy, I agreed to Kolatschek's proposal, and suggested that he had better return the manuscript to its author for publication elsewhere.

Through Kolatschek I also learned to know Reinhold Solger, a really excellent and interesting man. But it did not suit his restless and adventurous spirit to remain cooped up in the small and narrow Swiss world of Zürich, so that he soon left us and went to North America, where I heard that he went about giving lectures and denouncing the political situation in Europe. It was a pity that this talented man never succeeded

in making a name for himself by more important work. His
contributions to our monthly journal, during the brief term of
his stay in Zürich, were certainly among the best ever written
on these topics by a German.

In the new year, 1851, Georg Herwegh also joined us, and
I was delighted to meet him one day at Kolatschek's lodgings.
The vicissitudes which had brought him to Zürich came to my
knowledge afterwards in a somewhat offensive and aggressive
manner. For the present, Herwegh put on an aristocratic swag-
ger and gave himself the airs of a delicately nurtured and
luxurious son of his times, to which a fairly liberal interpolation
of French expletives at least added a certain distinction. Nevertheless, there was something about his person, with his quick,
flashing eye and kindliness of manner, which was well calculated to exert an attractive influence. I felt almost flattered
by his ready acceptance of my invitation to my informal
evening parties, which may, perhaps, have been fairly agreeable gatherings, as Bülow entertained us with music, though
to me personally they afforded no mental sustenance whatever.
My wife used to declare that, when I proceeded to read from
my manuscript, Kolatschek promptly fell asleep, while Herwegh gave all his attention to her punch. When, later on,
as I have already mentioned, I read my *Oper und Drama* for
twelve consecutive evenings to our Zürich friends, Herwegh
stayed away, because he did not wish to mix with those for
whom such things had not been written. Yet my intercourse
with him became gradually more cordial. Not only did I respect his poetical talent, which had recently gained recognition, but I also learned to realise the delicate and refined qualities of his richly cultivated intellect, and in course of time
learned that Herwegh, on his side, was beginning to covet my
society. My steady pursuit of those deeper and more serious
interests which so passionately engrossed me seemed to arouse
him to an ennobling sympathy, even for those topics which,
since his sudden leap into poetic fame, had been, greatly to his
prejudice, smothered under mere showy and trivial mannerisms,
altogether alien to his original nature. Possibly this process
was accelerated by the growing difficulties of his position, which
he had hitherto regarded as demanding a certain amount of

outward show. In short, he was the first man in whom I met with a sensitive and sympathetic comprehension of my most daring schemes and opinions, and I soon felt compelled to believe his assertion that he occupied himself solely with my ideas, into which, certainly, no other man entered so profoundly as he did.

This familiarity with Herwegh, in which an element of affection was certainly mingled, was further stimulated by news which reached me respecting a new dramatic poem which I had sketched out for the coming spring. Liszt's preparations in the late summer of the previous year for the production in Weimar of my *Lohengrin* had met with more success than, with such limited resources, had hitherto seemed possible. This result could naturally only have been obtained by the zeal of a friend endowed with such rich and varied gifts as Liszt. Though it was beyond his power to attract quickly to the Weimar stage such singers as *Lohengrin* demanded, and he had been compelled on many points to content himself with merely suggesting what was intended to be represented, yet he was now endeavouring by sundry ingenious methods to make these suggestions clearly comprehensible. First of all, he prepared a detailed account of the production of *Lohengrin*. Seldom has a written description of a work of art won for it such attentive friends, and commanded their enthusiastic appreciation from the outset, as did this treatise of Liszt's, which extended even to the most insignificant details. Karl Ritter distinguished himself by providing an excellent German translation of the French original, which was first published in the *Illustrirte Zeitung*. Shortly after this Liszt also issued *Tannhäuser* in French, accompanied by a similar preface on its origin, and these pamphlets were the chief means of awakening, now and for long after, especially in foreign countries, not only a surprisingly sympathetic interest in these works, but also an intimate understanding of them such as could not possibly have been attained by the mere study of my pianoforte arrangements. But, far from being satisfied with this, Liszt contrived to attract the attention of intellects outside Weimar to the performances of my operas, in order, with kindly compulsion, to force them upon the notice of all who had ears to hear and eyes to see. Although his good intentions did not altogether succeed with Franz Dingelstedt, who would only commit himself to a confused report on *Lohengrin* in the *Allgemeine Zeitung*, yet his enthusiastic eloquence completely and decisively captured Adolf Stahr for my work. His detailed view of *Lohengrin* in the Berlin *National-Zeitung*, in which he claimed a high importance for my opera, did not remain without permanent influence upon the German public. Even in the narrow circle of professional musicians its effects seem not to have been unimportant; for Robert Franz, whom Liszt dragged almost by force to a performance of *Lohengrin*, spoke of it with unmistakable enthusiasm. This example gave the lead to many other journals, and for some time it seemed as though the otherwise dull-witted musical press would energetically champion my cause.

I shall shortly have occasion to describe what it was that eventually gave quite a different direction to this movement. Meanwhile Liszt felt emboldened by these kindly signs to encourage me to renew my creative activity, which had now for some time been interrupted. His success with *Lohengrin* gave him confidence in his ability to execute a yet more hazardous undertaking, and he invited me to set my poem of *Siegfried's Death* to music for production at Weimar. On his recommendation, the manager of the Weimar theatre, Herr von Ziegesar, offered to make a definite contract with me in the name of the Grand Duke. I was to finish the work within a year, and during that period was to receive a payment of fifteen hundred marks (£75).

It was a curious coincidence that about this time, and also through Liszt, the Duke of Coburg invited me to arrange the instrumentation for an opera of his own composition, for which he offered me the sum of two thousand seven hundred marks (£135). In spite of my position as an outlaw, my noble patron and would-be employer offered to receive me in his castle at Coburg, where, in quiet seclusion with himself and Frau Birchpfeiffer, the writer of the libretto, I might execute the work. Liszt naturally expected nothing more from me than a decent excuse for declining this offer, and suggested my pleading ' bodily and mental depression.' My friend told me afterwards that the Duke had desired my co-operation with him in his score on

account of my skilful use of trombones. When he inquired,
through Liszt, what my rules for their manipulation were,
I replied that before I could write anything for trombones I
required first to have some ideas in my head.

On the other hand, however, I felt very much tempted to
entertain the Weimar proposal. Still weary from my exhausting labour on *Oper und Drama*, and worried by many things
which had a depressing effect on my spirits, I seated myself
for the first time for many months at my Härtel grand-piano,
which had been rescued from the Dresden catastrophe, to see
whether I could settle down to composing the music for my
ponderous heroic drama. In rapid outline I sketched the music
for the Song of the Norns, or Daughters of the Rhine, which
in this first draft was only roughly suggested. But when I
attempted to turn Brunhilda's first address to Siegfried into
song my courage failed me completely, for I could not help
asking myself whether the singer had yet been born who was
capable of vitalising this heroic female figure. The idea of my
niece Johanna occurred to me, whom, as a matter of fact,
I had already destined for this rôle when I was still in Dresden
on account of her various personal charms. She had now
entered upon the career of prima donna at Hamburg, but,
judging from all the reports I had received, and especially from
the attitude towards me that she openly adopted in her letters
to her family, I could only conclude that my modest hopes of
enlisting her talents on my behalf were doomed to disappointment. I was, moreover, confused by the fact that a second
Dresden prima donna, Mme. Gentiluomo Spatzer, who had once
enraptured Marschner with Donizetti's dithyrambics, kept
hovering perpetually before my mind as a possible substitute
for Johanna. At last, in a rage, I sprang up from the piano,
and swore that I would write nothing more for these silly
fastidious schoolgirls. Whenever I saw any likelihood of being
again brought into closer contact with the theatre I was filled
with an indescribable disgust which, for the time being, I was
unable to overcome. It was some little consolation to discover
that bodily ill-health might possibly be at the bottom of this
mental disorder. During the spring of this year I had been
suffering from a curious rash, which spread over my whole body.

For this my doctor prescribed a course of sulphur-baths, to be taken regularly every morning. Although the remedy excited my nerves so much that later on I was obliged to adopt radical measures for the restoration of my health, yet in the meantime the regular morning walk to the town and back, surrounded by the fresh green and early spring flowers of May, acted as a cheerful stimulant on my mental condition. I now conceived the idea of the poem of *Junger Siegfried*, which I proposed to issue as a heroic comedy by way of prelude and complement to the tragedy of *Siegfrieds Tod*. Carried away by my conception, I tried to persuade myself that this piece would be easier to produce than the other more serious and terrible drama. With this idea in my mind I informed Liszt of my purpose, and offered the Weimar management to compose a score for *Junger Siegfried*, which as yet was unwritten, in return for which I would definitely accept their proposal to grant me a year's salary of fifteen hundred marks. This they agreed to without delay, and I took up my quarters in the attic-room evacuated the previous year by Karl Ritter, where, with the aid of sulphur and May-blossom, and in the highest spirits, I proposed to complete the poem of *Junger Siegfried*, as already outlined in my original design.

I must now give some account of the cordial relations which, ever since my departure from Dresden, I had maintained with Theodor Uhlig, the young musician of the Dresden orchestra, which I have already described, and which by this time had developed into a genuinely productive association. His independent and indeed somewhat uncultivated disposition had been moulded into a warm, almost boundless devotion to myself, inspired both by sympathy for my fate and a thorough understanding of my works. He also had been among the number of those who had visited Weimar to hear my *Lohengrin*, and had sent me a very detailed account of the performance. As Härtel, the music-dealer in Leipzig, had willingly agreed to my request to publish *Lohengrin* on condition that I should not demand any share in the profits, I entrusted Uhlig with the preparation of the pianoforte arrangement. But it was more the theoretical questions discussed in my works that formed the chief link that bound us together by a serious correspond-

ence. The characteristic which especially touched me about
this man, whom from his training I could regard merely
as an instrumentalist, was that he had grasped with clear understanding and perfect agreement those very tendencies of
mine which many musicians of apparently wider culture than
his own regarded with almost despairing horror, as being
dangerous to the orthodox practice of their art. He forthwith
acquired the literary facility necessary for the expression of his
agreement with my views, and gave tangible proof of this in
a lengthy treatise on ' Instrumental Music,' which appeared in
Kolatschek's German monthly journal. He also sent to me
another strictly theoretical work on the ' Structure of Musical
Theme and Phrase.' In this he showed the originality of his
ideas about Mozart's and Beethoven's methods, to an extent
which was only equalled by the thoroughness with which he
had mastered the question, especially where he discussed their
highly characteristic differences. This clear and exhaustive
treatise appeared to me admirably adapted to form the basis
for a new theory of the higher art of musical phrasing, whereby
Beethoven's most obscure construction might be explained, and
elaborated into a comprehensible system that would allow of
further application. These treatises attracted the attention of
Franz Brendel, the astute publisher of the *Neue Zeitschrift
für Musik,* to their brilliant young author. He was invited
by Brendel to join the staff of his paper, and soon succeeded
in changing his chief's previous attitude of indecision. As
Brendel's aims were on the whole perfectly honourable and
serious, he was quickly and definitely led to adopt those views
which from this time began to make a stir in the musical world
under the title of the ' New Tendency.' I thereupon felt
impelled to contribute an epoch-making article to his paper
on these lines. I had noticed for some time that such ill-
sounding catch-phrases as ' Jewish ornamental flourishes '
(Melismas), 'Synagogue Music,' and the like were being bandied
about without any rhyme or reason beyond that of giving
expression to meaningless irritation. The question thus raised
regarding the significance of the modern Jew in music stimulated me to make a closer examination of Jewish influence
and the characteristics peculiar to it. This I did in a lengthy

treatise on 'Judaism in Music.' Although I did not wish to hide my identity, as its author, from all inquiries, yet I considered it advisable to adopt a pseudonym, lest my very seriously intended effort should be degraded to a purely personal matter, and its real importance be thereby vitiated. The stir, nay, the genuine consternation, created by this article defies comparison with any other similar publication. The unparalleled animosity with which, even up to the present day, I have been pursued by the entire press of Europe can only be understood by those who have taken an account of this article and of the dreadful commotion which it caused at the time of its publication. It must also be remembered that almost all the newspapers of Europe are in the hands of Jews. Apart from these facts, it would be impossible to understand the unqualified bitterness of this lasting persecution, which cannot be adequately explained on the mere ground of a theoretical or practical dislike for my opinions or artistic works. The first outcome of the article was a storm which broke over poor Brendel, who was entirely innocent, and, indeed, hardly conscious of his offence. This erelong developed into a savage persecution which aimed at nothing less than his ruin. Another immediate result was that the few friends whom Liszt had induced to declare themselves in my favour forthwith took refuge in a discreet silence. As it soon seemed advisable, in the interests of their own productions, to give direct evidence of their estrangement from me, most of them passed over to the ranks of my enemies. But Uhlig clung to me all the more closely on this account. He strengthened Brendel's weaker will to endurance, and kept helping him with contributions for his paper, some of them profound and others witty and very much to the point. He fixed his eye more particularly on one of my chief antagonists, a man named Bischoff, whom Hiller had discovered in Cologne, and who first invented for me and my friends the title of *Zukunftsmusiker* ('Musicians of the Future'). With him he entered into a prolonged and somewhat diverting controversy. The foundation had now been laid for the problem of the so-called *Zukunftsmusik* ('Music of the Future'), which was to become a European scandal, in spite of the fact that Liszt quickly adopted the title himself with good-humoured pride. It is true that I had to some extent suggested this name in the title of my book, *Kunstwerk der Zukunft;* but it only developed into a battle-cry when ' Judaism in Music ' unbarred the sluices of wrath upon me and my friends.

My book, *Oper und Drama,* was published in the second half of this year, and, so far as it was noticed at all by the leading musicians of the day, naturally only helped to add fuel to the wrath which blazed against me. This fury, however, assumed more the character of slander and malice, for our movement had meantime been reduced by a great connoisseur in such things, Meyerbeer, to a clearly defined system, which he maintained and practised with a sure hand until his lamented death.

Uhlig had come across my book, *Oper und Drama,* during the early stages of the furious uproar against me. I had presented him with the original manuscript, and as it was nicely bound in red, I hit upon the idea of writing in it, by way of dedication, the words, ' *Red,* my friend, is *my* theory,' in contradistinction to the Gothic saying, ' Grey, my friend, is all theory.' This gift elicited an exhilarating and most delightful correspondence with my lively and keen-sighted young friend, who, after two long years of separation, I felt sincerely desirous of seeing again. It was not an easy matter for the poor fiddler, whose pay was barely that of a chamber musician, to comply with my invitation. But he gladly tried to overcome all difficulties, and said he would come early in July. I decided to go as far as Rorschach, on the Lake of Constance, to meet him, so that we might make an excursion through the Alps as far as Zürich. I went by a pleasant detour through the Toggenburg, travelling on foot as usual. In this way, cheerful and refreshed, I reached St. Gall, where I sought out Karl Ritter, who, since Bülow's departure, had remained there alone in curious seclusion. I could guess the reason of his retirement, although he said that he had enjoyed very agreeable intercourse with a St. Gall musician named Greitel, of whom I never heard anything further. Though very tired after my long walking tour, I could not refrain from submitting the manuscript of my *Junger Siegfried,* which I had just finished, to the quick and critical judgment of this intelligent young man, who was thus the first person to hear it. I was more than gratified by its effect upon him, and, in high spirits, persuaded him to forsake his strange retreat and go with me to meet Uhlig, so that we might all three proceed over the Säntis for a long and pleasant stay in Zürich.

My first glance at my guest, as he landed at the familiar harbour of Rorschach, filled me at once with anxiety for his health, for it revealed but too plainly his tendency to consumption. In order to spare him, I wished to give up the proposed mountain climb, but he eagerly protested that exercise of this kind in the fresh air could only do him good after the drudgery of his wretched fiddling. After crossing the little canton of Appenzell, we had to face the by no means easy crossing of the Säntis. It was my first experience also of travelling over an extensive snow-field in summer. After reaching our guide's hut, which was perched on a rugged slope, where we regaled ourselves with exceedingly frugal fare, we had to climb the towering and precipitous pinnacle of rock which forms the summit of the mountain, a few hundred feet above us. Here Karl suddenly refused to allow us, and to shake him out of his effeminacy I had to send back the guide for him, who, at our request, succeeded in bringing him along, half by force. But now that we had to clamber from stone to stone along the precipitous cliff, I soon began to realise how foolish I had been in compelling Karl to share our perilous adventure. His dizziness evidently stupefied him, for he stared in front of him as though he could not see, and we had to hold him fast between our alpenstocks, every moment expecting to see him collapse, and tumble into the abyss. When we at last attained the summit, he sank senseless on the ground, and I now fully understood what a terrible responsibility I had undertaken, as the yet more dangerous descent had still to be made. In an agony of fear, which, while it made me forget my own danger altogether, filled me with a vision of my young friend lying shattered on the rocks below, we at last reached the guide's cottage in safety. As Uhlig and myself were still determined to descend the precipitous further side of the mountain, a feat which the guide informed us was not without danger, I resolved to leave young Ritter behind in the hut, as the indescribable

anguish I had just endured on his behalf had been a warning
to me. Here he was to await the return of our guide, and in
his company take the not very dangerous path by which we
had come. We accordingly parted, as he was to return in the
direction of Gall, while we two roamed through the lovely
Toggenburg valley, and the next day by Rappersweil to the
Lake of Zürich, and so home. Not until many days later did
Karl relieve our anxiety concerning him by arriving at Zürich.
He remained with us a short time, and then departed, probably
wishing to escape being tempted into more mountain climbing,
which we had certainly planned. I heard from him afterwards
when he had settled for some time in Stuttgart, where he
seemed to be doing well. He soon made great friends with
a young actor, and lived on terms of great intimacy with him.

I was sincerely delighted by the close intercourse I now had
with the gentle young Dresden chamber musician, whose manly
strength of character and extraordinary mental endowments
greatly endeared him to me. My wife said that his curly golden
hair and bright blue eyes made her think an angel had come
to stay with us. For me his features had a peculiar and,
considering his fate, pathetic interest, on account of his striking
resemblance to King Friedrich August of Saxony, my former
patron, who was still alive at that time, and seemed to confirm
a rumour which had reached me that Uhlig was his natural
son. It was entertaining to hear his news of Dresden, and all
about the theatre, and the condition of musical affairs in that
city. My operas, which had once been its glory, had now quite
vanished from the repertoire. He gave me a choice example
of my late colleagues' opinion of me by relating the following
incident. When *Kunst und Revolution* and *Kunstwerk der
Zukunft* appeared, and were being discussed among them, one
of them remarked: 'Ha! he may worry a long time before
he will be able to write conductor before his name again.' By
way of illustrating the advance made in music. he related the
manner in which Reissiger, having on one occasion to conduct
Beethoven's Symphony in A major, which had been previously
executed by me, had helped himself out of a sudden dilemma.
Beethoven, as is well known, marks the great finale of the last
movement with a prolonged *forte,* which he merely heightens

by a *sempre più forte*. At this point Reissiger, who had conducted the Symphony before me, thinking the opportunity a
favourable one, had introduced a *piano*, in order at least to
secure an effective *crescendo*. This I had naturally ignored,
and had instructed the orchestra to play with their full strength
throughout. Now, therefore, that the conducting of this work
had once more fallen into my predecessor's hands, he found it
difficult to restore his unlucky *piano;* but, feeling that he must
save his authority, which had been compromised, he made a
rule that *mezzo forte* should be played instead of *forte*.

But the most painful news he gave me was about the state
of utter neglect into which my unhappy operatic publications
had fallen in the hands of the court music-dealer Meser, who,
seeing that money had to be continually paid out, while nothing
came in, regarded himself as a sacrificial lamb whom I had
lured to the slaughter. Yet he steadily refused all inspection
of his books, maintaining that he thereby protected my property,
as all I possessed having been confiscated, it would otherwise
be seized at once. A pleasanter topic than this was *Lohengrin*.
My friend had completed the pianoforte arrangement, and was
already busy correcting the engraver's proofs.

By his enthusiastic advocacy of the water cure, Uhlig gained
an influence over me in another direction, and one which was
of long duration. He brought me a book on the subject by
a certain Rausse, which pleased me greatly, especially by its
radical principles, which had something of Feuerbach about
them. Its bold repudiation of the entire science of medicine,
with all its quackeries, combined with its advocacy of the
simplest natural processes by means of a methodical use of
strengthening and refreshing water, quickly won my fervent
adherence. He maintained, for instance, that every genuine
medicine can only act upon our organism in so far as it is a
poison, and is therefore not assimilated by our system; and
proved, moreover, that men who had become weak owing to a
continuous absorption of medicine, had been cured by the
famous Priesnitz, who had effectually driven out the poison
contained in their bodies by expelling it through the skin. I
naturally thought of the disagreeable sulphur baths I had
taken during the spring, and to which I attributed my chronic

and severe state of irritability. In so doing I was probably
not far wrong. For a long while after this I did my best to
expel this and all other poisons which I might have absorbed
in the course of time, and by an exclusive water regimen restore
my original healthy condition. Uhlig asserted that by persevering conscientiously in a water cure, he was perfectly confident of being able to renew his own bodily health entirely,
and my own faith in it also grew daily.

At the end of July we started on an excursion through the
centre of Switzerland. From Brunnen, on the Lake of Lucerne,
we proceeded via Beckenried to Engelberg, from which place
we crossed the wild Surenen-Eck, and on this occasion learned
how to glide over the snow fairly easily. But in crossing a
swollen mountain torrent Uhlig had the misfortune to fall into
the water. By way of quieting my uneasiness about him, he
at once exclaimed that this was a very good way of carrying
out the water cure. He made no fuss about the drying of his
clothes, but simply spread them out in the sun, and in the
meanwhile calmly promenaded about in a state of nature in
the open air, protesting that this novel form of exercise would
do him good. We occupied the interval in discussing the important problem of Beethoven's theme construction, until, by
way of a joke, I told him that I could see Councillor Carns of
Dresden coming up behind him with a party, which for a moment
quite frightened him. Thus with light hearts we reached the
Reuss valley near Attinghausen, and in the evening wandered
on as far as Amsteg, and the next morning, in spite of our
great fatigue, at once visited the Madran valley. There we
climbed the Hüfi glacier, whence we enjoyd a splendid view
over an impressive panorama of mountains, bounded at this
point by the Tödy range. We returned the same day to Amsteg, and as we were both thoroughly tired out, I dissuaded my
companion from attempting the ascent of the Klausen Pass
to the Schächen valley, which we had planned for the following
day, and induced him to take the easier way home via Flüelen.
When, early in August, my young friend, who was always calm
and very deliberate in his manner, set out on his return journey
to Dresden, I could detect no signs of exhaustion about him.
He was hoping on his arrival to lighten the heavy burden of

life a little by undertaking the conductorship of the *entr'acte* music at the theatre, which he proposed to organise artistically, and thus set himself free from the oppressive and demoralising service of the opera.   It was with sincere grief that I accompanied him to the mail-coach, and he too seemed to be seized with sudden foreboding.   As a matter of fact, this was the last time we ever met.

But for the present we carried on an active correspondence, and as his communications were always pleasant and entertaining, and for a long time constituted almost my sole link with the outside world, I begged him to write me long letters as often as possible.   As postage was expensive at that time, and voluminous letters touched our pockets severely, Uhlig conceived the ingenious idea of using the parcel post for our correspondence.   As only packets of a certain weight might be sent in this way, a German translation of Beaumarchais' *Figaro*, of which Uhlig possessed an ancient copy, enjoyed the singular destiny of acting as ballast for our letters to and fro. Every time, therefore, that our epistles had swelled, to the requisite length, we announced them with the words: ' Figaro brings tidings to-day.'

Uhlig meanwhile found much pleasure in the *Mittheilung an meine Freunde* (' A Communication to my Friends'), which, immediately after our separation, I wrote as a preface to an edition of my three operas, the *Fliegender Holländer, Tannhäuser,* and *Lohengrin.*   He was also amused to hear that Härtel, who had accepted the book for publication on payment of ten louis d'or, protested so vigorously against certain passages in this preface, which wounded his orthodoxy and political feelings, that I thought seriously of giving the book to another firm.   However, he finally persuaded me to give way, and I pacified his tender conscience by a few trifling alterations.

With this comprehensive preface, which had occupied me during the whole of the month of August, I hoped that my excursion into the realms of literature would be ended once and for all.   However, as soon as I began to think seriously about taking up the composition of *Junger Siegfried,* which I had promised for Weimar, I was seized with depressing doubts which almost amounted to a positive reluctance to attempt this work. As I could not clearly discern the reason of this dejection, I concluded that its source lay in the state of my health, so I determined one day to carry out my theories about the advantages of a water cure, which I had always propounded with great enthusiasm. I made due inquiries about a neighbouring hydropathic establishment, and informed my wife that I was going off to Albisbrunnen, which was situated about three miles from our abode. It was then about the middle of September, and I had made up my mind not to come back until I was completely restored to health.

Minna was quite frightened when I announced my intention, and looked upon it as another attempt on my part to abandon my home. I begged of her, however, to devote herself during my absence to the task of furnishing and arranging our new flat as comfortably as possible. This, although small, was conveniently situated on the ground floor of the Vordern Escher Häuser im Zeltweg. We had determined to move back to the town, on account of the great inconvenience of the situation of our present quarters, especially during winter time. Everybody, of course, was astonished at the idea of my undertaking a water cure so late in the season. Nevertheless, I soon succeeded in securing a fellow-patient. I was not fortunate enough to get Herwegh, but Fate was kind in sending me Hermann Müller, an ex-lieutenant in the Saxon Guards, and a former lover of Schröder-Devrient, who proved a most cheerful and pleasant companion. It had become impossible for him to maintain his position in the Saxon army, and although he was not exactly a political refugee, every career was closed to him in Germany, and yet he met with all the consideration of an exiled patriot when he came to Switzerland to try and make a fresh start in life. We had seen a good deal of each other in my early Dresden days, and he soon felt at home in my house, where my wife always gave him a warm welcome. I easily persuaded him to follow me shortly to Albisbrunnen to undergo a thorough treatment for an infirmity from which he was suffering. I established myself there as comfortably as I could, and I looked forward to excellent results. The cure itself was superintended in the usual superficial way by a Dr. Brunner, whom my wife, on one of her visits to this place, promptly christened the

'Water Jew,' and whom she heartily detested. Early at five o'clock in the morning I was wrapped up and kept in a state of perspiration for several hours; after that I was plunged into an icy cold bath at a temperature of only four degrees; then I was made to take a brisk walk to restore my circulation in the chilly air of late autumn. In addition I was kept on a water diet; no wine, coffee, or tea was allowed; and this régime, in the dismal company of nothing but incurables, with dull evenings only enlivened by desperate attempts at games of whist, and the prohibition of all intellectual occupation, resulted in irritability and overwrought nerves. I led this life for nine weeks, but I was determined not to give in until I felt that every kind of drug or poison I had ever absorbed into my system had been brought to the surface. As I considered that wine was most dangerous, I presumed that my system still contained many unassimilated substances which I had absorbed at various dinner-parties at Sulzer's, and which must evaporate in profuse perspiration. This life, so full of privations, which I led in rooms miserably furnished with common deal and the usual rustic appointments of a Swiss *pension,* awoke in me by way of contrast an insuperable longing for a cosy and comfortable home; indeed, as the year went on, this longing became a passionate desire. My imagination was for ever picturing to itself the manner and style in which a house or a dwelling ought to be appointed and arranged, in order to keep my mind pleasantly free for artistic creation.

At this time symptoms of a possible improvement in my position appeared. Karl Ritter, unfortunately for himself, wrote to me from Stuttgart while I was at the hydro, describing his own private attempts to secure the benefits of a water cure — not by means of baths, but by drinking quantities of water. I had found out that it was most dangerous to drink large quantities of water without undergoing the rest of the treatment, so I implored Karl to submit to the regular course, and not to have an effeminate fear of privations, and to come at once to Albisbrunnen. He took me at my word, and to my great delight arrived in a few days' time at Albisbrunnen. Theoretically he was filled with enthusiasm for hydropathy, but he soon objected to it in practice; and he denounced the

use of cold milk as indigestible and against the dictates of
Nature, as mother's milk was always warm. He found the
cold packs and the cold baths too exciting, and preferred
treating himself in a comfortable and pleasant way behind the
doctor's back. He soon discovered a wretched confectioner's
shop in the neighbouring village, and when he was caught buying cheap pastry on the sly, he was very angry. He soon grew
perfectly miserable, and would fain have escaped, had not a
certain feeling of honour prevented him from doing so. The
news reached him here of the sudden death of a rich uncle, who
had left a considerable fortune to every member of Karl's
family. His mother, in telling him and me of the improvement
in her position, declared that she was now able to assure me
the income which the two families of Laussot and Ritter had
offered me some time ago. Thus I stepped into an annual
income of two thousand four hundred marks for as long as I
required it, and into partnership with the Ritter family.

This happy and encouraging turn of events made me decide
to complete my original sketch of the *Nibelungen,* and to bring
it out in our theatres without paying any regard to the practica-
bility of its various parts. In order to do this I felt that I
must free myself from all obligations to the management of
the Weimar theatre. I had already drawn six hundred marks
salary from this source, but Karl was enchanted to place this
sum at my disposal in order that I might return it. I sent the
money back to Weimar with a letter expressing my most grateful acknowledgments to the management for their conduct
towards me, and at the same time I wrote to Liszt, giving him
the fullest particulars of my great plan, and explaining how I
felt absolutely compelled to carry it out.

Liszt, in his reply, told me how delighted he was to know
that I was now in a position to undertake such a remarkable
work, which he considered in every respect worthy of me if
only on account of its surprising originality. I began to
breathe freely at last, because I had always felt that it was
merely self-deception on my part to maintain that it would be
possible to produce *Junger Siegfried* with the limited means at
the disposal of even the best German theatre.

My water cure and the hydropathic establishment became

more and more distasteful to me; I longed for my work, and
the desire to get back to it made me quite ill. I tried obstinately to conceal from myself that the object of my cure had
entirely failed; indeed, it had really done me more harm than
good, for although the evil secretions had not returned, my
whole body seemed terribly emaciated. I considered that I
had had quite enough of the cure, and comforted myself with
the hope that I should derive benefit from it in the future.
I accordingly left the hydropathic establishment at the end of
November. Müller was to follow me in a few days, but Karl,
wishing to be consistent, was determined to remain until he
perceived a similar result in himself to the one I had experienced or pretended I had experienced. I was much pleased
with the way in which Minna had arranged our new little flat
in Zürich. She had bought a large and luxurious divan, several carpets for the floor and various dainty little luxuries, and
in the back room my writing-table of common deal was covered with a green tablecloth and draped with soft green silk
curtains, all of which my friends admired immensely. This
table, at which I worked continually, travelled with me to
Paris, and when I left that city I presented it to Blandine
Ollivier, Liszt's elder daughter, who had it conveyed to the
little country house at St. Tropèz, belonging to her husband,
where, I believe, it stands to this day. I was very glad to
receive my Zürich friends in my new home, which was so much
more conveniently situated than my former one; only I quite
spoilt all my hospitality for a long time by my fanatical agitation for a water diet and my polemics against the evils of wine
and other intoxicating drinks. I adopted what seemed almost
a new kind of religion: when I was driven into a corner by
Sulzer and Herwegh, the latter of whom prided himself on his
knowledge of chemistry and physiology, about the absurdity
of Rausse's theory of the poisonous qualities contained in wine,
I found refuge in the moral and æsthetic motive which made
me regard the enjoyment of wine as an evil and barbarous substitute for the ecstatic state of mind which love alone should
produce. I maintained that wine, even if not taken in excess,
contained qualities producing a state of intoxication which a
man sought in order to raise his spirits, but that only he who

experienced the intoxication of love could raise his spirits in the noblest sense of the word. This led to a discussion on the modern relations of the sexes, whereupon I commented on the almost brutal manner in which men kept aloof from women in Switzerland. Sulzer said he would not at all object to the intoxication resulting from intercourse with women, but in his opinion the difficulty lay in procuring this by fair means. Herwegh was inclined to agree with my paradox, but remarked that wine had nothing whatever to do with it, that it was simply an excellent and strengthening food, which, according to Anacreon, agreed very well with the ecstasy of love. As my friends studied me and my condition more closely, they felt they had reason to be very anxious about my foolish and obstinate extravagances. I looked terribly pale and thin; I hardly slept at all, and in everything I did I betrayed a strange excitement. Although eventually sleep almost entirely forsook me, I still pretended that I had never been so well or so cheerful in my life, and I continued on the coldest winter mornings to take my cold baths, and plagued my wife to death by making her show me my way out with a lantern for the prescribed early morning walk.

I was in this state when the printed copies of *Oper und Drama* reached me, and I devoured rather than read them with an eccentric joy. I think that the delightful consciousness of now being able to say to myself, and prove to the satisfaction of everybody, and even of Minna, that I had at last completely freed myself from my hateful career as conductor and opera composer, brought about this immoderate excitement. Nobody had a right to make the demands upon me which two years ago had made me so miserable. The income which the Ritters had assured me for life, and the object of which was to give me an absolutely free hand, also contributed to my present state of mind, and made me feel confidence in everything I undertook. Although my plans for the present seemed to exclude all possibility of being realised, thanks to the indifference of an inartistic public, still I could not help inwardly cherishing the idea that I should not be for ever addressing only the paper on which I wrote. I anticipated that before long a great reaction would set in with regard to the public and everything

connected with our social life, and I believed that in my boldly
planned work there lay just the right material to supply the
changed conditions and real needs of the new public whose
relation to art would be completely altered with what was required. As these bold expectations had arisen in my mind
in consequence of my observations of the state of society in
general, I naturally could not say much about them to my
friends. I had not mistaken the significance of the general
collapse of the political movements, but felt that their real
weakness lay in the inadequate though sincere expression of
their cause, and that the social movement, so far from losing
ground by its political defeat, had, on the contrary, gained in
energy and expansion. I based my opinion upon the experience
I had had during my last visit to Paris, when I had attended,
among other things, a political meeting of the so-called social
democratic party. Their general behaviour made a great impression upon me; the meeting took place in a temporary hall
called Salle de la Fraternité in the Faubourg St. Denis; six
thousand men were present, and their conduct, far from being
noisy and tumultuous, filled me with a sense of the concentrated
energy and hope of this new party. The speeches of the principal orators of the extreme left of the Assemblée Nationale
astonished me by their oratorical flights as well as by their
evident confidence in the future. As this extreme party was
gradually strengthening itself against everything that was being
done by the reactionary party then in power, and all the old
liberals had joined these social democrats publicly and had
adopted their electioneering programme, it was easy to see that
in Paris, at all events, they would have a decided majority at
the impending elections for the year 1852, and especially in
the nomination of the President of the Republic. My own
opinions about this were shared by the whole of France, and it
seemed that the year 1852 was destined to witness a very
important reaction which was naturally dreaded by the other
party, who looked forward with great apprehension to the
approaching catastrophe. The condition of the other European
states, who suppressed every laudable impulse with brutal stupidity, convinced me that elsewhere too this state of affairs
would not continue long, and every one seemed to look for-

ward with great expectations to the decision of the following year.

I had discussed the general situation with my friend Uhlig, as well as the efficacy of the water-cure system; he had just come home fresh from orchestral rehearsals at the Dresden theatre, and found it very difficult to agree to a drastic change in human affairs or to have any faith in it. He assured me that I could not conceive how miserable and mean people were in general, but I managed to delude him into the belief that the year 1852 would be pregnant with great and important events. Our opinions on this subject were expressed in the correspondence which was once more diligently forwarded by *Figaro*.

Whenever we had to complain of any meanness or untoward circumstance, I always reminded him of this year, so great with fate and hope, and at the same time I hinted that we had better look forward quite calmly to the time when the great 'upheaval' should take place, as only then, when no one else knew what to do, could we step in and make a start.

I can hardly express how deeply and firmly this hope had taken possession of me, and I can only attribute all my confident opinions and declarations to the increased excitement of my nerves. The news of the *coup d'état* of the 2nd of December in Paris seemed to me absolutely incredible, and I thought the world was surely coming to an end. When the news was confirmed, and events which no one believed could ever happen had apparently occurred and seemed likely to be permanent, I gave the whole thing up like a riddle which it was beneath me to unravel, and turned away in disgust from the contemplation of this puzzling world. As a playful reminiscence of our hopes of the year 1852, I suggested to Uhlig that in our correspondence during that year we should ignore its existence and should date our letters December '51, in consequence of which this said month of December seemed of eternal duration.

Soon afterwards I was overpowered by an extraordinary depression in which, somehow, the disappointment about the turn of political events and the reaction created by my exaggerated water cure, almost ruined my health. I perceived the triumphant return of all the disappointing signs of reaction which excluded every high ideal from intellectual life, and from which I had hoped the shocks and fermentations of the past few years had freed us for ever. I prophesied that the time was approaching when intellectually we should be such paupers that the appearance of a new book from the pen of Heinrich Heine would create quite a sensation. When, a short time afterwards, the *Romancero* appeared from the pen of this poet who had fallen into almost complete neglect, and was very well reviewed by the newspaper critics, I laughed aloud; as a matter of fact, I suppose I am among the very few Germans who have never even looked at this book, which, by the way, is said to possess great merit.

I was now compelled to pay a great deal of attention to my physical condition, as it gave me much cause for anxiety and necessitated a complete change in my methods. I introduced this change very gradually and with the co-operation of my friends. My circle of acquaintances had widened considerably this winter, although Karl Ritter, who had escaped from Albisbrunnen a week after my own departure and had tried to settle in our neighbourhood, ran off to Dresden, as he found Zürich much too slow for his youthful spirits. A certain family of the name of Wesendonck, who had settled in Zürich a short time before, sought my acquaintance, and took up their abode in the same quarters in the Hintern Escherhäuser where I had lived when I first came to Zürich. They had taken the flat there on the recommendation of the famous Marschall von Bieberstein, who moved in after me in consequence of the revolution in Dresden. I remember, on the evening of a party there, that I displayed uncontrolled excitement in a discussion with Professor Osenbrück. I tormented him with my persistent paradoxes all through supper to such an extent that he positively loathed me, and ever afterwards carefully avoided coming into contact with me.

The acquaintance with the Wesendoncks was the means of giving me the entrée to a delightful home, which in point of comfort was a great contrast to the usual run of houses in Zürich. Herr Otto Wesendonck, who was a few years younger than I was, had amassed a considerable fortune through a partnership in a silk business in New York, and seemed to make all his plans subservient to the wishes of the young wife whom he had married a few years before. They both came from the Lower Rhine country, and, like all the inhabitants of those parts, were fair haired. As he was obliged to take up his abode in some part of Europe which was convenient for the furtherance of his business in New York, he chose Zürich, presumably because of its German character, in preference to Lyons. During the previous winter they had both attended the performance of a symphony of Beethoven under my conductorship, and knowing what a sensation this performance had aroused in Zürich, they thought it would be desirable to include me in their circle of friends.

About this time I was persuaded to undertake the directorship of the augmented orchestra in view of the performance of some musical masterpieces at three concerts to be given early in the new year under the auspices of the Société Musicale on conditions arranged in advance.

It gave me infinite pleasure on one of these occasions to conduct an excellent performance of Beethoven's music to *Egmont*. As Herwegh was so anxious to hear some of my own music I gave the *Tannhäuser* Overture, as I told him, entirely to please him, and I prepared a descriptive programme as a guide. I also succeeded in giving an excellent rendering of the *Coriolanus* Overture, to which I had also written an explanatory programme. All this was taken up with so much sympathy and enthusiasm by my friends that I was induced to accede to the request of Löwe, who was at that time manager of the theatre, and implored me to give a performance of the *Fliegender Holländer*. For the sake of my friends I agreed to enter into negotiations with the opera company, an undertaking which, though it only lasted a very short time, was exceedingly objectionable. It is true that humane considerations animated me as well, as the performance was for the benefit of Schöneck, a young conductor, whose real talent for his art had completely won me over to him.

The efforts which this unaccustomed excursion into the regions of opera rehearsals, etc., cost me, greatly contributed to the overwrought state of my nerves, and I was obliged, in spite of all my rooted prejudices against doctors, to break faith with myself and, in accordance with the Wesendonck's special recommendation, to place myself in the hands of Dr. Rahn-

Escher, who, by his gentle manner and soothing ways, succeeded after a time in bringing me into a healthier condition.

I longed to get well enough to be able to take in hand the completion of my combined *Nibelungen* poem. Before I could summon up the courage to begin, I thought I would wait for the spring, and in the meanwhile I occupied myself with a few trifles, amongst other things a letter to Liszt on the founding of a Goethe Institution (*Goethe Stiftung*), stating my ideas on the necessity of founding a German National Theatre, as also a second letter to Franz Brendel about the line of thought which in my opinion should be taken up in founding a new musical journal.

I recollect a visit from Henri Vieuxtemps at this time, who came to Zürich with Belloni to give an evening concert, and he again delighted me and my friends with his violin playing.

With the approach of spring I was agreeably surprised by a visit from Hermann Franck, with whom I had an interesting conversation about the general course of events since I had lost sight of him.

In his quiet way he expressed his astonishment at the enthusiastic manner in which I had got mixed up in the Dresden revolution. As I quite misunderstood his remark, he explained that he thought me capable of enthusiasm in everything, but he could hardly credit me with having taken a serious part in anything so foolish as trivial matters of that kind. I now learned for the first time what the prevalent opinion was about these much-maligned occurrences in Germany, and I was in a position to defend my poor friend Röckel, who had been branded as a coward, and to put not only his conduct but also my own in a different light to that in which it had been regarded hitherto even by Hermann Franck, who afterwards expressed his sincere regret that he had so misunderstood us.

With Röckel himself, whose sentence had by royal mercy been commuted to lifelong imprisonment, I carried on at this time a correspondence, the character of which soon showed that his life was more cheerful and happy in his enforced captivity than mine with its hopelessness, in spite of the freedom I enjoyed.

At last the month of May arrived, and I felt I needed change

of air in the country in order to strengthen my weakened nerves
and carry out my plans in regard to poetry. We found a fairly
comfortable *pied-à-terre* on the Rinderknecht estate. This was
situated halfway up the Zürich Berg, and we were able to enjoy
an alfresco meal on the 22nd of May — my thirty-ninth birthday — with a lovely view of the lake and the distant Alps. Unfortunately a period of incessant rain set in which scarcely
stopped throughout the whole summer, so that I had the greatest struggle to resist its depressing influence. However, I soon
got to work, and as I had begun to carry out my great plan
by beginning at the end and going backwards, I continued on
the same lines with the beginning as my goal. Consequently,
after I had completed the *Siegfrieds Tod* and *Junger Siegfried*, I next attacked one of the principal subjects, the *Walküre*,
which was to follow the introductory prelude of the *Rheingold*.
In this way I completed the poem of the *Walküre* by the end of
June. At the same time I wrote the dedication of the score
of my *Lohengrin* to Liszt, as well as a rhymed snub to an un-
provoked attack on my *Fliegender Holländer* in a Swiss newspaper. A very disagreeable incident in connection with Herwegh pursued me to my retreat in the country. One day a certain Herr Haug, who described himself as an ex-Roman general
of Mazzini's time, introduced himself to me with a view of forming a sort of conspiracy against him, on behalf, as he said, of
the deeply offended family of the ' unfortunate lyric poet ';
however, he did not succeed in getting any assistance from me.
A much pleasanter incident was a long visit from Julia, the
eldest daughter of my revered friend Frau Ritter, who had
married Kummer, the young Dresden chamber musician, whose
health seemed so entirely undermined that they were going to
consult a celebrated hydropathic doctor who practised only a few
miles from Zürich. I now had a good opportunity of abusing
this water cure about which my young friends were so eager,
and had always believed that I was perfectly mad on it also.
But we left the chamber musician to his fate, and rejoiced at the
long and pleasant visit of our amiable and charming young
friend.

As I was quite satisfied with the success of my work, and the
weather was exceptionally cold and rainy, we made up our

minds to return to our cosy winter residence in Zürich at the
end of June. I was resolved to stay there until the appearance of some real summer weather, when I intended to take a
walking tour over the Alps, which I felt would be of great
advantage to my health. Herwegh had promised to accompany me, but as he was apparently prevented from doing so, I
started alone in the middle of July, after arranging with my
travelling companion to meet me in Valais. I began my walking tour at Alpnach, on the Lake of Lucerne, and my plan was
to wander by unfrequented paths to the principal points of
the Bernese Oberland. I worked pretty hard, paying a visit,
for instance, to the Faulhorn, which at that time was considered a very difficult mountain to climb. When I reached
the hospice on the Grimsel by the Hasli Thal, I asked the host,
a fine, stately-looking man, about the ascent of the Siedelhorn.
He recommended me one of his servants as a guide, a rough,
sinister-looking man, who, instead of taking the usual zig-zag
paths up the mountain, led me up in a bee line, and I rather
suspected he intended to tire me out. At the top of the Siedelhorn I was delighted to catch a glimpse, on one side, of the
centre of the Alps, whose giant backs alone were turned to us;
and on the other side, a sudden panorama of the Italian Alps,
with Mont Blanc and Monte Rosa. I had been careful to take
a small bottle of champagne with me, following the example of
Prince Pückler when he made the ascent of Snowdon; unfortunately, I could not think of anybody whose health I could
drink. We now descended vast snow-fields, over which my
guide slid with mad haste on his alpenstock; I contented myself with leaning carefully on the iron point of mine, and
coming down at a moderate pace.

I arrived at Obergestelen dead tired, and stayed there two
days, to rest and await the arrival of Herwegh. Instead of
coming himself, however, a letter arrived from him which
dragged me down from my lofty communings with the Alps
to the humdrum consideration of the unpleasant situation in
which my unhappy friend found himself as a result of the
incident I have already described. He feared that I had
allowed myself to be taken in by his adversary, and had consequently formed an unfavourable opinion of him. I told him

to make his mind easy on that score, and to meet me again, if possible, in Italian Switzerland. So I set out for the ascent of the Gries glacier, and the climb across the pass to the southern side of the Alps, in the company of my sinister guide alone. During the ascent an extremely sad sight kept meeting my eyes; an epidemic of foot-rot had broken out among cows in the Upper Alps, and several herds passed me in single file on their way to the valley, where they were going to be doctored. The cows had become so lean that they looked like skeletons, and dragged themselves pitiably down the slopes, and the smiling country with the fat meadow-land seemed to take a savage delight in gazing on this sad pilgrimage. At the foot of the glacier, which stood out sheer and steep before me, I felt so depressed, and my nerves were so overwrought, that I said I wished to turn back. I was thereupon met by the coarse sarcasm of my guide, who seemed to scoff at my weakness. My consequent anger braced up my nerves, and I prepared myself at once to climb the steep walls of ice as quickly as possible, so that this time it was he who found difficulty in keeping up with me. We accomplished the walk over the back of the glacier, which lasted nearly two hours, under difficulties which caused even this native of Grimsel anxiety, at least on his own account. Fresh snow had fallen, which partially concealed the crevasses, and prevented one from recognising the dangerous spots. The guide, of course, had to precede me here, to examine the path. We arrived at last at the opening of the upper valley which gives on to the Formazza valley, to which a steep cutting, covered with snow and ice, led. Here my guide again began his dangerous game of conducting me straight over the steepest slopes instead of going in a safe zig-zag; in this way we reached a precipitous moraine, where I saw such unavoidable danger ahead, that I insisted upon my guide going back with me some distance, until we struck a path that I had noticed which was not so steep. He was obliged to give in, much against the grain. I was deeply impressed by the first signs of cultivation that we saw in our descent from the desolate wilds. The first scanty meadow-land accessible to cattle was called the Bettel-Matt, and the first person we met was a marmot hunter. The wild scenery was soon enlivened by the marvellous swirl and headlong rush of a mountain river called the Tosa, which at one spot breaks into a superb waterfall with three distinct branches. After the moss and reeds had, in the course of our continuous descent, given place to grass and meadows, and the shrubs had been replaced by pine trees, we at last arrived at the goal of our day's journey, the village of Pommath, called Formazza by the Italian population, which is situated in a charming valley. Here, for the first time in my life, I had to eat roast marmot. After having paid my guide, and sent him on his homeward journey, I started alone on the following morning on my further descent of the valley, although I had only partially recovered from my fatigue, owing to lack of sleep. It was not until the November of this year, when the whole of Switzerland was thrown into a state of consternation by the news that the Grimsel inn had been set fire to by the host himself, who hoped by this means to obtain the renewal of the lease from the authorities, that I learned my life had been in danger under the guidance of this man. As soon as his crime was discovered, the host drowned himself in the little lake, on the borders of which the inn is situated. The serving-man, however, whom he had bribed to arrange the fire, was caught and punished. I knew by the name that he was the same man that the worthy innkeeper had given me as companion on my solitary journey across the glacier pass, and I heard at the same time that two travellers from Frankfort had perished on the same pass a short time before my own journey. I consequently realised that I had in a really remarkable manner escaped a fatal danger which had threatened me.

I shall never forget my impressions of my journey through the continually descending valley. I was particularly astonished at the southern vegetation which suddenly spreads out before one on climbing down from a steep and narrow rocky pass by which the Tosa is confined. I arrived at Domodossola in the afternoon in a blaze of sunshine, and I was reminded here of a charming comedy by an author whose name I have forgotten, which I had once seen performed with a refinement worthy of Platen, and to which my attention had been drawn by Eduard Devrient in Dresden. The scene of the play was laid in Domodossola, and described exactly the impressions

I myself received on coming down from the Northern Alps into Italy, which suddenly burst upon one's gaze. I shall also never forget my first simple, but extremely well-served, Italian dinner. Although I was too tired to walk any further that day, I was very impatient to get to the borders of Lake Maggiore, and I accordingly arranged to drive in a one-horse chaise, which was to take me on the same evening as far as Baveno. I felt so contented while bowling along in my little vehicle that I reproached myself for want of consideration in having rudely declined the offer of company which an officer passing through the Vetturino made me by means of the driver. I admired the daintiness of the house decorations and the pleasant faces of the people in the pretty villages I passed through. A young mother, strolling along and singing as she spun the flax, with her baby in her arms, also made a never-to-be-forgotten impression on me. Soon after sunset I caught sight of the Borromean Islands rising gracefully out of Lake Maggiore, and again I could not sleep for excitement at the thought of what I might see on the following day. The next morning the visit to the islands themselves delighted me so much that I could not understand how I had managed to come upon anything so charming, and wondered what would result from it. After stopping only one day, I left the place with the feeling that I had now to flee from something to which I did not belong, and went round Lake Maggiore, up past Socarno, to Bellinzona, where I was once again on Swiss soil; from there I proceeded to Lugano, intending, if I followed out my original plan of travel, to stay there some time. But I soon suffered from the intense heat; even bathing in the sun-scorched lake was not refreshing. Apart from the dirty furniture, which included the *Denksopha* ('thinking sofa') from the *Clouds* by Aristophanes, I was sumptuously lodged in a palatial building, which in the winter served as the government house of the canton of Tessin, but in the summer was used as a hotel. However, I soon fell again into the condition that had troubled me so long, and prevented me from taking any rest, owing to my extreme nervous strain and excitement, whenever I felt disposed to idle pleasantly. I had taken a good many books with me, and proposed to entertain myself with Byron. Unfortunately it required a great effort on my part to take any pleasure in his works, and the difficulty of doing so increased when I began to read his *Don Juan*. After a few days' time I began to wonder why I had come, and what I wanted to do here, when suddenly Herwegh wrote saying that he and several friends intended to join me at this place. A mysterious instinct made me telegraph to my wife to come also. She obeyed my call with surprising alacrity, and arrived unexpectedly in the middle of the night, after travelling by post-chaise across the St. Gotthard Pass. She was so fatigued that she at once fell into a sound sleep on the *Denksopha*, from which the fiercest storm that I ever remember failed to awaken her. On the following day my Zürich friends arrived.

Herwegh's chief companion was Dr. François Wille. I had learned to know him some time before at Herwegh's house: his chief characteristics were a face much scarred in students' duels, and a great tendency to witty and outspoken remarks. He had recently been staying near Meilen on the Lake of Zürich, and he often asked me to visit him there with Herwegh. Here we saw something of the habits and customs of a Hamburg household, which was kept up in a fairly prosperous style by his wife, the daughter of Herr Sloman, a wealthy shipowner. Although in reality he remained a student all his life, he had made himself a position and formed a large circle of acquaintances by editing a Hamburg political newspaper. He was a brilliant conversationalist, and was considered good company. He seemed to have taken up with Herwegh with the object of overcoming the latter's antipathy to Alpine climbing, and his consequent reluctance to undertake it. He himself had made preparations to walk over the Gotthard Pass with a Professor Eichelberger, and this had made Herwegh furious, as he declared that walking tours were only permissible where it was impossible to drive, and not on these broad highways. After making an excursion into the neighbourhood of Lugano, during which I got heartily sick of the childish sound of the church bells, so common in Italy, I persuaded my friends to go with me to the Borromean Islands, which I was longing to see again. During the steamer trip on Lake Maggiore, we met a delicate-looking man with a long cavalry moustache, whom in private was humourously dubbed General Haynau, and the distrust with which we affected to treat him was a source of some amusement to us.

We soon found that he was an extremely good-natured Hanoverian nobleman, who had been travelling about Italy for some time for pleasure, and who was able to give us very useful information concerning intercourse with the Italians. His advice was of great service when we were visiting the Borromean Islands, where my acquaintances parted from my wife and myself to travel back by the nearest route, whereas we intended proceeding further across the Simplon and through Le Valais to Chamounix.

From the fatigue my tour had so far occasioned me, I felt that it would be some time before I started on a similar one again. I was therefore eager to see what was best worth seeing in Switzerland as thoroughly as possible now that I had the chance. Moreover, I was just then, and indeed had been for some time, in that impressionable humour from which I might anticipate important results to myself from novel scenery, and I did not like to miss Mont Blanc. A view of it was attended with great difficulties, amongst which may be mentioned our arrival by night at Martigny, where, owing to the crowded state of the hotels, we were everywhere refused accommodation, and it was only on account of a little intrigue between a postillion and a maidservant that we found clandestine shelter for the night in a private house from which the owners were absent.

We dutifully visited the so-called Mer de Glace in the Val de Chamounix and the Flégère, from which I obtained a most impressive view of Mont Blanc. However, my imagination was less busied with the ascent of that peak than with the spectacle I beheld when crossing the Col des Géants, as the great elevation that we attained did not appeal to me so much as the unbroken and sublime wildness of the latter. For some time I cherished the intention of undertaking just one more venture of the kind. While descending the Flégère, Minna had a fall and sprained her ankle; the consequence of this was so painful as to deter us from any further adventures. We therefore saw ourselves forced to hasten on our journey home via Geneva.

But even from this more important and grander expedition, and almost the only one I had ever undertaken purely for recreation, I returned with a strangely unsatisfied feeling, and I could not resist the longing for something decisive in the distance, that would give a fresh direction to my life.

On reaching home I found announcements of a new and quite different turn in my destiny. These consisted of inquiries and commissions from various German theatres anxious to produce *Tannhäuser*. The first to apply was the Schwerin Court Theatre. Röckel's youngest sister, who afterwards married the actor Moritz (whom I had known from my earliest youth), had now come to Germany as a youthful singer from England, where she had been educated. She had given such an enthusiastic account of the impression produced upon her by *Tannhäuser* at Weimar, to an official at the theatre there named Stocks, who held the position of treasurer, that he had studied the opera most assiduously, and had now induced the management to undertake to produce it. The theatres at Breslau, Prague, and Wiesbaden soon followed; at the last of these my old friend Louis Schindelmeisser was acting as conductor. In a short time other theatres followed suit; but I was most astonished when the Berlin Court Theatre made inquiries through its new manager, Herr von Hülsen. From this last incident I felt justified in assuming that the Crown Princess of Prussia, who had always had a friendly feeling towards me, fostered by my faithful friend Alwine Frommann, had again been intensely interested by the performance of *Tannhäuser* at Weimar, and had given the impetus to these unexpected developments.

Whilst I was rejoicing over commissions from the smaller theatres, those of the largest German stage were a source of anxiety. I knew that at the former there were zealous conductors, devoted to me, who had certainly been roused by the desire of having the opera performed; in Berlin, on the other hand, matters were quite different. The only other conductor besides Taubert, whom I had known previously as a man devoid of talent, and at the same time very conceited, was Heinrich Dorn, of whom I retained most unpleasant recollections from my earliest years and from our joint stay in Riga. I felt

little drawn towards either of these, nor did I perceive any
possibility of undertaking the direction of my own work; and
from my knowledge of their capabilities as well as of their ill-
will, I had every reason to question any successful rendering of
my opera under their conductorship. Being an exile, I was
unable to go to Berlin in person in order to supervise my work,
so I immediately begged Listz's permission to nominate him
as my representative and *alter ego,* to which he willingly agreed.
When I afterwards made Liszt's appointment one of my conditions, objection was raised on the part of the general manager
at Berlin on the score that the nomination of a Weimar
conductor would be regarded as a gross insult to the Prussian
court conductors, and I must consequently desist from demanding it. Thereupon prolonged negotiations ensued with a view
to compromising the matter, which resulted in the production
of *Tannhäuser* at Berlin being considerably delayed.

However, while *Tannhäuser* was now rapidly spreading to
the middle-class German theatres, I became a prey to great
uneasiness as to the quality of these performances, and could
never get a very clear idea of them. As my presence was prohibited everywhere, I had recourse to a very detailed pamphlet
which was to serve as a guide to the production of my work,
and convey a correct idea of my purpose. I had this somewhat
voluminous work printed at my own expense and tastefully
bound, and to every theatre that had given an order for the
operatic score I sent a number of copies of it, with the understanding that they were to be given to the conductor, stage
manager, and principal performers for perusal and guidance.
But from that time I have never heard of a single person who
had either read this pamphlet or taken any notice of it. In the
year 1864, when all my own copies had been exhausted, owing
to my painstaking distribution of them, I found to my great
delight, among the theatrical archives, several copies that had
been sent to the Munich Court Theatre, quite intact and uncut.
I was therefore in the agreeable position of being able to procure
copies of the missing pamphlet for the King of Bavaria, who
wished to see it, as well as for myself and some friends.

It was a singular coincidence that the news of the diffusion
of my opera through the German theatres should synchronise

with my resolve to compose a work in the conception of which I had been so decidedly influenced by the necessity of being absolutely indifferent to our own theatres; yet this unexpected turn of events in no wise affected my treatment of my design. On the contrary, by keeping to my plan, I gained confidence and let things take their own course, without attempting in any way to promote the performances of my operas. I just let people do as they liked, and looked on surprised, while continual accounts reached my ears of remarkable successes; none of them, however, induced me to alter my verdict on our theatres in general or on the opera in particular. I remained unshaken in my resolve to produce my *Nibelungen* dramas just as though the present operatic stage did not exist, since the ideal theatre of my dreams must of necessity come sooner or later. I therefore composed the libretto of the *Rheingold* in the October and November of that year, and with that I brought the whole cycle of the Nibelungen myth as I had evolved it to a conclusion. At the same time I was rewriting *Junger Siegfried* and *Siegfrieds Tod*, especially the latter, in such a way as to bring them into proper relation with the whole; and by so doing, important amplifications were made in *Siegfrieds Tod* which were in harmony with the now recognised and obvious purpose of the whole work. I was accordingly obliged to find for this last piece a new title suited to the part it plays in the complete cycle. I entitled it *Götterdämmerung*, and I changed the name *Junger Siegfried* to *Siegfried*, as it no longer dealt with an isolated episode in the life of the hero, but had assumed its proper place among the other prominent figures in the framework of the whole.

The prospect of having to leave this lengthy poem for some time entirely unknown to those whom I might expect to be interested in it was a source of great grief to me. As the theatres now and then surprised me by sending me the usual royalties on *Tannhäuser*, I devoted a part of my profits to having a number of copies of my poem neatly printed for my own use. I arranged that only fifty copies of this *édition de luxe* should be struck off. But a great sorrow overtook me before I had completed this agreeable task. It is true, I met on all sides with indications of sympathetic interest in the completion of my great lyric work, although most of my acquaintances regarded the whole thing as a chimera, or possibly a bold caprice. The only one who entered into it with any heartiness or real enthusiasm was Herwegh, with whom I frequently discussed it, and to whom I generally read aloud such portions as were completed. Sulzer was much annoyed at the remodelling of *Siegfrieds Tod*, as he regarded it as a fine and original work, and thought it would be deprived of that quality if I decided to alter it to any extent. He therefore begged me to let him have the manuscript of the earlier version to keep as a remembrance; otherwise it would have been entirely lost. In order to get an idea of the effect of the whole poem when rendered in complete sequence, I decided, only a few days after the work was completed in the middle of December, to pay a short visit to the Wille family at their country seat, so as to read it aloud to the little company there. Besides Herwegh, who accompanied me, the party there consisted of Frau Wille and her sister, Frau von Bissing. I had often entertained these ladies with music in my own peculiar fashion during my pleasant visits to Mariafeld, about two hours' walk from Zürich. In them I had secured a devoted and enthusiastic audience, somewhat to Herr Wille's annoyance, as he often admitted that he had a horror of music; nevertheless, he ended in his jovial way by taking the matter good humouredly.

I arrived towards evening, and we attacked *Rheingold* at once, and as it did not seem very late, and I was supposed to be capable of any amount of exertion, I went on with the *Walküre* until midnight. The next morning after breakfast it was *Siegfried's* turn, and in the evening I finished off with *Götterdämmerung*. I thought I had every reason to be satisfied with the result, and the ladies in particular were so much moved that they ventured no comment. Unfortunately the effort left me in a state of almost painful excitement; I could not sleep, and the next morning I was so disinclined for conversation that I left my hurried departure unexplained. Herwegh, who accompanied me back alone, appeared to divine my state of mind, and shared it by maintaining a similar silence.

However, I now wished to have the pleasure of confiding the whole completed work to my friend Uhlig at Dresden.

I carried on a regular correspondence with him, and he had
followed the development of my plan, and was thoroughly
acquainted with every phase of it. I did not want to send
him the *Walküre* before the *Rheingold* was ready, as the latter
should come first, and even then I did not want him to see the
whole thing until I could send him a handsomely printed copy.
But at the beginning of the autumn I discerned in Uhlig's
letters grounds for feeling a growing anxiety as to the state
of his health. He complained of the increase in his serious
paroxysms of coughing, and eventually of complete hoarseness.
He thought all this was merely weakness, which he hoped to
overcome by invigorating his system with the cold-water treatment and long walks. He found the violin work at the theatre
very exhausting, but if he took a sharp seven hours' walk into
the country he invariably felt much better. However, he could
not rid himself of his chest attacks or of his hoarseness, and
had a difficulty in making himself heard even when speaking
to a person quite near him. Up to that time I had been
unwilling to alarm the poor fellow, and always hoped that his
condition would necessitate his consulting a doctor, who would
naturally prescribe rational treatment. Now, however, as I
was continually hearing nothing from him but assurances of
his confidence in the principles of the water cure, I could
contain myself no longer, and I entreated him to give up this
madness and place himself in the hands of a sensible doctor,
for in his condition what he most needed was, not strength, but
very careful attention. The poor man was extremely alarmed
at this, as he gathered from my remarks that I feared he was
already in an advanced stage of consumption. 'What is to
become of my poor wife and children,' he wrote, 'if that is
really the case?' Unhappily, it was too late; with the last
strength that was left him he tried to write to me again, and
finally my old friend Fischer, the chorus-master, carried out
Uhlig's instructions, and when these were no longer audible
he had to bend down close to his lips. The news of his death
followed with frightful rapidity. It took place on the 3rd of
January, 1853. Thus, in addition to Lehrs, another of my
really devoted friends was carried off by consumption. The
handsome copy of the *Ring des Nibelungen* I had intended for

him lay uncut before me, and I sent it to his youngest boy, whom he had christened Siegfried. I asked his widow to let me have any pamphlets of a theoretical nature he might have left behind, and I came into possession of several important ones, among them the longer essay on ' Theme-Structure.' Although the publication of these works would involve a great deal of trouble, owing to the necessity of revising them, I asked Härtel of Leipzig if he would pay the widow a fair sum for a volume of Uhlig's writings. The publisher declared he could not undertake to bring it out without payment, as works of that nature were quite unremunerative. It was obvious to me, even at that time, how thoroughly every musician who had taken a keen interest in me had made himself disliked in certain circles.

Uhlig's melancholy death gave my home-circle the whip-hand over me with regard to my theories on the subject of water cures. Herwegh impressed upon my wife that she must insist upon my taking a glass of good wine after all the exertion I underwent at the rehearsals and concerts which I was attending throughout that winter. By degrees, also, I again accustomed myself to enjoy such mild stimulants as tea and coffee, my friends meanwhile perceiving to their joy that I was once more becoming a man amongst men. Dr. Rahn-Escher now became a welcome and comforting friend and visitor, who for many years thoroughly understood the management of my health, and especially the misgivings arising from the overwrought state of my nerves. He soon verified the wisdom of his treatment, when in the middle of February I had undertaken to read my tetralogy aloud on four consecutive evenings before a larger audience. I had caught a severe cold after the first evening, and on the morning of the day for the second reading I awoke suffering from severe hoarseness. I at once informed the doctor that my failure to give the reading would be a serious matter to me, and asked him what he advised me to do to get rid of the hoarseness as speedily as possible. He recommended me to keep quiet all day, and in the evening to be taken well wrapped up to the place where the readings were to be held. When I got there I was to take two or three cups of weak tea, and I should be all right; whereas if I worried over the failure to keep my engagement I might become seriously worse. And, indeed, the reading of this stirring work went off capitally, and I was, moreover, able to continue the readings on the third and fourth evenings, and felt perfectly well. I had secured a large and handsome room for these meetings in the Hôtel Baur au lac, and had the gratifying experience of seeing it fuller and fuller each evening, in spite of having invited only a small number of acquaintances, giving them the option of bringing any friends who they thought would take a genuine interest in the subject and not come out of mere curiosity. Here, too, the verdict seemed altogether favourable, and it was from the most serious university men and government officials that I received assurances of the greatest appreciation as well as kindly remarks, showing that my poem and the artistic ideas connected with it had been fully understood. From the peculiar earnestness with which they gave vent to their opinions, which in this case were so confidently unanimous, the idea occurred to me to try how far this favourable impression might be utilized to serve the higher aims of art. In accordance with the superficial views generally prevailing on the subject, every one seemed to think I might be induced to make terms with the theatre. I tried to think out how it would be possible to convert the ill-equipped Zürich theatre into a highly developed one by adopting sound principles, and I laid my views before the public in a pamphlet entitled ' A Theatre in Zürich.' The edition, consisting of about a hundred copies, was sold, yet I never noticed the least indication of any result from the publication; the only outcome was, that at a banquet of the Musical Society my excellent friend, Herr Ott-Imhoff, expressed his entire disagreement with the statements uttered by various people, that these ideas of mine were all very grand, but unfortunately quite impracticable. Nevertheless, my propositions lacked the one thing that would have made them valuable in his eyes, namely my consent to take over the management of the theatre in person, as he would not entrust the carrying out of my ideas to anyone but myself. However, as I was obliged to declare then and there that I would not have anything to do with such a scheme, the matter dropped, and in my inmost heart I could not help thinking that the good people were quite right.

Meanwhile, the sympathetic interest in my works was increasing. As I now had to refuse firmly to yield to my friends' wishes for a performance of my principal works at the theatre, I begged to be allowed to arrange a selection of characteristic pieces, which could easily be produced at concerts, so soon as I could obtain the requisite support. A subscription list was accordingly circulated, and it had the satisfactory result of inducing several well-known art patrons to put their names down to guarantee expenses. I had to undertake to engage an orchestra to suit my requirements. Skilled musicians from far and near were summoned, and after interminable efforts I began to feel that something really satisfactory would be achieved.

I had made arrangements that the performers should stay at Zürich a whole week from Sunday to Sunday. Half of this time was allotted exclusively to rehearsals. The performance was to take place on Wednesday evening, and on Friday and Sunday evenings there were to be repetitions of it. The dates were the 18th, 20th, and 22nd of May, my fortieth birthday falling on the last-named date. I had the joy of seing all my directions accurately carried out. From Mayence, Wiesbaden, Frankfort, and Stuttgart, and on the other side, from Geneva, Lausanne, Bâle, Berne, and the chief towns in Switzerland, picked musicians arrived punctually on Sunday afternoon. They were at once directed to the theatre, where they had to arrange their exact places in the orchestral stand I had previously designed at Dresden — and which proved excellent here too — so as to begin rehearsing the first thing next morning without delay or interruption. As these people were at my disposal in the early morning and in the evening, I made them learn a selection of pieces from the *Fliegender Holländer, Tannhäuser,* and *Lohengrin.* I had greater trouble in trying to train them for a chorus, but this too turned out very satisfactorily. There was nothing in the way of solo-singing, except the Ballad of Senta from the *Holländer,* which was sung by the wife of the conductor Heim in a good though untrained voice, and with an amount of spirit that left nothing to be desired. As a matter of fact, the performances could hardly be called public concerts, but were rather of the nature of family entertainments. I felt

I was fulfilling a sincere desire on the part of a larger circle of acquaintances by introducing them to the true nature of my music, rendered as intelligibly as circumstances permitted. As, at the same time, it was desirable that they should have some knowledge of the poetical basis of it, I invited those who intended to be present at my concerts to come for three evenings to the Musical Society's concert-hall to hear me read aloud the libretto of the three operas, portions of which they were about to hear. This invitation met with an enthusiastic response, and I was now able to hope that my audience would come better prepared to listen to the selections from my operas than had ever been the case before. The fact that pleased me most in the performances on these three evenings was that I was able for the first time to produce something from *Lohengrin* myself, and could thus get an idea of the effect of my combination of the instrumental parts in the overture to that work.

Between the performances there was a banquet which, with the exception of a subsequent one at Pesth, was the only function of the sort ever held in my honour. I was sincerely and deeply affected by the speech of the aged President of the Musical Society, Herr Ott-Usteri. He drew the attention of all those musicians who had come together from so many places to the significance of their meeting, and its objects and results, and recommended as a trustworthy guide to them on their homeward journey the conviction they had all doubtless arrived at, that they had come into close and genuine touch with a wonderful new creation in the realm of art.

The sensation produced by these evening concerts spread through the whole of Switzerland in ever-widening circles. Invitations and requests for further repetitions of them poured in from distant towns. I was assured that I might well repeat the three performances in the following week without any fear of seeing a diminution in the audience. When this project was discussed, and I pleaded my own fatigue, and also expressed the desire to retain for these concerts their unique character by not allowing them to become commonplace, I was very glad to have the powerful and intelligent support of my friend Hagenbuch, who on this occasion was indefatigable. The festival was concluded, and the guests were dismissed at the appointed time.

I had hoped to be able to welcome Liszt among the visitors, as he had celebrated a ' Wagner week ' at Weimar in the previous March by performing three operas of which I had only given portions here. Unfortunately he was unable to leave just then, but by way of amends he promised me a visit at the beginning of July. Of my German friends, only the faithful Mme. Julie Kummer and Mme. Emilie Ritter arrived in time. As these two ladies had gone on to Interlaken at the beginning of June, and I also began to feel in great need of a change, I started with my wife, towards the end of the month, for a short holiday. The visit was spoilt in the most dismal fashion by continuous rain; and on the 1st of July, as we were starting in desperation on our homeward journey to Zürich with our lady friends, magnificent summer weather set in, which lasted a considerable time. With affectionate enthusiasm we at once attributed this change to Liszt, as he arrived in Switzerland in the best of spirits immediately after we had returned to Zürich. Thereupon followed one of those delightful weeks, during which every hour of the day becomes a treasured memory. I had already taken more roomy apartments on the second floor in the so-called Vorderen Escher Häusern, in which I had before occupied a flat that was much too small on the ground floor. Frau Stockar-Escher, who was part owner of the house, was enthusiastically devoted to me. She was full of artistic talent herself, being an excellent amateur painter in water-colours, and had taken great pains to rearrange the new dwelling as luxuriously as possible. The unexpected improvement in my circumstances brought about by the continued demands for my operas, allowed me to indulge my desire for comfortable domestic arrangements, which had been reawakened since my stay at the hydropathic establishment, and which, after being repressed, had become quite a passionate longing.

I had the flat so charmingly furnished with carpets and decorative furniture that Liszt himself was surprised into admiration as he entered my *petite élégance,* as he called it. Now for the first time I enjoyed the delight of getting to know

my friend better as a fellow-composer. In addition to many
of his celebrated pianoforte pieces, which he had only recently
written, we went through several new symphonies with great
ardour, and especially his *Faust* Symphony. Later on, I had
the opportunity of describing in detail the impressions I received
at this time in a letter which I wrote to Marie von Wittgenstein,
which was afterwards published. My delight over everything
I heard by Liszt was as deep as it was sincere, and, above all,
extraordinary stimulating. I even thought of beginning to
compose again after the long interval that had elapsed. What
could be more full of promise and more momentous to me than
this long-desired meeting with the friend who had been engaged
all his life in his masterly practice of music, and had also devoted
himself so absolutely to my own works, and to diffusing the
proper comprehension of them. Those almost bewilderingly
delightful days, with the inevitable rush of friends and acquaintances, were interrupted by an excursion to the Lake of Lucerne,
accompanied only by Herwegh, to whom Liszt had the charming
idea of offering a ' draught of fellowship ' with himself and me
from the three springs of the Grütli.

After this my friend took leave of us, after having arranged
for another meeting with me in the autumn.

Although I felt quite disconsolate after Liszt's departure, the
officials of Zürich took good care that I should soon have some
diversion, of a kind to which I had hitherto been a stranger. It
took the form of the presentation of a masterpiece of calligraphy
in the shape of a ' Diploma of Honour,' awarded me by the
Zürich Choral Society, which was ready at last. This was to
be awarded to me with the accompaniment of an imposing
torchlight procession, in which the various elements of the
Zürich population, who, either as individuals or members of
societies, were favourably disposed to me, were to take part.
So it came to pass that one fine summer evening a large company of torchbearers approached the Zeltweg, to the accompaniment of loud music. They presented a spectacle such as
I had never seen before, and made a unique impression on my
mind. After the singing, the voice of the President of the
Choral Society could be heard rising from the street. I was
so much affected by the incident that my unconquerable

optimism quickly overpowered every other sensation. In my speech of acknowledgment I indicated plainly that I saw no reason why Zürich itself should not be the chosen place to give an impetus to the fulfilment of the aspirations I cherished for my artistic ideals, and that it might do so on proper civic lines. I believe this was taken to refer to a special development of the men's choral societies, and they were quite gratified at my bold forecasts. Apart from this confusion, for which I was responsible, that evening's ceremony and its effects on me were very cheerful and beneficial.

But I still felt the peculiar disinclination and fear of taking up composing again that I had previously experienced after protracted pauses in musical production. I also felt very much exhausted by all I had done and gone through, and the ever-recurring longing to break completely with everything in the past, that had unfortunately haunted me since my departure from Dresden, as well as the desire and yearning for new and untried surroundings, fostered by that anxiety, now acquired fresh and tormenting vigour. I felt that before entering on such a gigantic task as the music to my drama of the *Nibelungen,* I must positively make one final effort to see whether I could not, in some new environment, attain an existence more in harmony with my feelings than I could possibly aspire to after so many compromises. I planned a journey to Italy, or such parts of it as were open to me as a political refugee. The means for carrying out my wish were readily placed at my disposal through the kindness of my friend Wesendonck, who has ever since that time been devoted to me. However, I knew it was inadvisable to take that journey before the autumn, and as my doctor had recommended some special treatment for strengthening my nerves — even if only to enjoy Italy — I decided first of all to go to St. Moritz Bad in the Engadine. I started in the latter half of July, accompanied by Herwegh. Strangely enough, I have often found that what other people could note in their diaries merely as an ordinary visit or a trivial expedition, assumed me the character of an adventure. This occurred on our journey to the Bad, when, owing to the coaches being crowded, we were detained at Chur in an incessant downpour of rain. We were obliged to pass the time in reading at a most uncomfortable inn. I got hold of Goethe's *West-östlichen Divan,* for the reading of which I had been prepared by Daumer's adaptation of *Hafiz.* To this day I never think of Goethe's words in elucidating these poems without recalling that wretched delay in our journey to the Engadine. We did not get on much better at St. Moritz; the present convenient Kurhaus was not then in existence, and we had to put up with the roughest accommodation; this was particularly annoying to me on Herwegh's account, as he had not gone there for health, but simply for enjoyment. However, we were soon cheered by the lovely views of the grand valleys, which were quite bare but for the Alpine pastures, that met our eyes on our way down the steep slopes into the Italian valleys. After we had secured the schoolmaster at Samaden as a guide to the Rosetch glacier, we embarked on more serious expeditions. We had confidently looked forward to exceptional enjoyment in thus penetrating beyond the precipices of the great Mont Bernina, to which we gave the palm for beauty above Mont Blanc itself. Unfortunately the effect was lost on my friend, owing to the tremendous exertions by which the ascent and crossing of the glacier were attended. Once again, but this time to an even greater degree, I felt the sublime impression of the sacredness of that desolate spot, and the almost benumbing calm which the disappearance of all vegetation produces on the pulsating life of the human organism. After we had been wandering for two hours, deep in the glacier path, we partook of a meal we had brought with us, and champagne, iced in the fissures, to strengthen us for our wearisome return. I had to cover the distance nearly twice over, as, to my astonishment, Herwegh was in such a nervous condition that I had repeatedly to go backwards and forwards, showing him the way up and down before he would decide to follow. I then realised the peculiarly exhausting nature of the air in those regions, as on our way back we stopped at the first herdsman's cottage, and were refreshed with some delicious milk. I swallowed such quantities of it that we were both perfectly amazed, but I experienced no discomfort whatever in consequence.

The waters, whether for internal or external use, are known

to be powerfully impregnated with iron, and in taking them I
had the same experience as on previous occasions. With my
extremely excitable nervous system, they were a source of
more trouble than relief to me. The leisure hours were filled
up by reading Goethe's *Wahlverwandtschaften,* which I had not
read since I was quite young. This time I absolutely devoured
the book from beginning to end, and it also became a source of
heated discussions between Herwegh and myself. As Herwegh
possessed an extensive knowledge of the characteristics of our
great poetic literature, he felt it incumbent on him to defend
the character of Charlotte against my attacks. My vehemence
on the subject showed what a strange creature I still was at
over forty, and in my heart of hearts I had to admit that
Herwegh judged Gothe's poem objectively more correctly than
I did, as I always felt depressed by a kind of moral bondage,
to which Herwegh, if he had ever experienced it at all, submitted placidly, owing to his peculiar relations with his strong-
minded wife. When the time came to an end, and I realised
that I had not much to hope for from the treatment, we returned
to Zürich. This was about the middle of August, and I now
began to look forward impatiently to my tour in Italy. At
last, in the month of September, which I had been told was
quite suitable for visiting Italy, I set off on the journey via
Geneva, full of indescribable ideas of what was before me, and
of what I might see as the outcome of my search. Once again
amid all sorts of strange adventures, I reached Turin by special
mail-coach over Mont Cenis. Finding nothing to detain me
there more than a couple of days, I hurried on to Genoa.
There, at any rate, the longed-for marvels seemed to be within
reach. The grand impression produced on me by that city
overcomes, even to this day, any longing to visit the rest of
Italy. For a few days I was in a dream of delight; but my
extreme loneliness amidst these impressions soon made me feel
that I was a stranger in that world, and that I should never
be at home in it. Absolutely inexperienced as I was in searching
out the treasures of art on a systematic plan, I gave myself up
in this new world to a peculiar state of mind that might be
described as a musical one, and my main idea was to find some
turning-point that might induce me to remain there in quiet

enjoyment. My only object still was to find a refuge where I might enjoy the congenial peace suited to some new artistic creation. In consequence, however, of thoughtlessly indulging in ices, I soon got an attack of dysentery, which produced the most depressing lassitude after my previous exaltation. I wanted to flee from the tremendous noise of the harbour, near which I was staying, and seek for the most absolute calm; and thinking a trip to Spezia would benefit me, I went there by steamer a week later. Even this excursion, which lasted only one night, was turned into a trying adventure, thanks to a violent head-wind. The dysentery became worse, owing to sea-sickness, and in the most utterly exhausted condition, scarcely able to drag myself another step, I made for the best hotel in Spezia, which, to my horror, was situated in a noisy, narrow street.

After a night spent in fever and sleeplessness, I forced myself to take a long tramp the next day through the hilly country, which was covered with pine woods. It all looked dreary and desolate, and I could not think what I should do there. Returning in the afternoon, I stretched myself, dead tired, on a hard couch, awaiting the long-desired hour of sleep. It did not come; but I fell into a kind of somnolent state, in which I suddenly felt as though I were sinking in swiftly flowing water. The rushing sound formed itself in my brain into a musical sound, the chord of E flat major, which continually re-echoed in broken forms; these broken chords seemed to be melodic passages of increasing motion, yet the pure triad of E flat major never changed, but seemed by its continuance to impart infinite significance to the element in which I was sinking. I awoke in sudden terror from my doze, feeling as though the waves were rushing high above my head. I at once recognised that the orchestral overture to the *Rheingold,* which must long have lain latent within me, though it had been unable to find definite form, had at last been revealed to me. I then quickly realised my own nature; the stream of life was not to flow to me from without, but from within. I decided to return to Zürich immediately, and begin the composition of my great poem. I telegraphed to my wife to let her know my decision, and to have my study in readiness.

The same evening I took my place on the coach going to Genoa along the Riviera di Levante. I again had the opportunity of getting exquisite impressions of the country during this journey, which lasted over the whole of the following day. It was, above all, the colouring of the wonders that presented themselves to my eyes which gave me such delight — the redness of the rocks, the blue of the sky and the sea, the pale green of the pines; even the dazzling white of a herd of cattle worked upon me so powerfully that I murmured to myself with a sigh, ' How sad it is that I cannot remain to enjoy all this, and thus gratify my sensuous nature.'

At Genoa I again felt so agreeably stimulated that I suddenly thought I had only yielded to some foolish weakness, and resolved to carry out my original plan. I was already making arrangements for travelling to Nice along the celebrated Riviera di Ponente, of which I had heard so much, but I had scarcely decided on my former plans, when I realised that the fact which refreshed and invigorated me was not the renewal of my delight over Italy, but the resolve to take up my work again. And indeed, as soon as I made up my mind to alter this plan, the old condition set in once more, with all the symptoms of dysentery. I thereupon understood myself, and giving up the journey to Nice, I returned direct by the nearest route via Alessandria and Novara.

This time I passed the Borromean Islands with supreme indifference, and got back to Zürich over the St. Gotthard.

When I had once returned, the only thing that could have made me happy would have been to start at once on my great work. For the present, however, I saw that it would be seriously interrupted by my appointment with Liszt, who was to be in Bâle at the beginning of October. I was restless and annoyed at being so unsettled, and spent the time in visiting my wife, who, thinking that I would be away longer, was taking the waters at Baden am Stein. As I was easily prevailed upon to try any experiment of this kind if only the person who recommended it were sufficiently sanguine, I allowed myself to be persuaded into taking a course of hot baths, and the process heightened my excitment considerably.

At last the time for the meeting in Bâle arrived. At the invita-

tion of the Grand Duke of Baden, Liszt had arranged and
conducted a musical festival in Karlsruhe, the aim of which
was to give the public an adequate interpretation of our
respective works. As I was not yet allowed to enter the territory of the German confederation, Liszt had chosen Bâle as
the place nearest to the Baden frontier, and had brought with
him some young men who had been his devoted admirers in
Karlsruhe, to give me a hearty welcome.

I was the first to arrive, and in the evening, while sitting
alone in the dining-room of the hotel, ' Zu den drei Königen,'
the air of the trumpet fanfare (from *Lohengrin*) announcing
the King's arrival, sung by a strong though not numerous chorus
of men's voices, reached me from the adjacent vestibule. The
door opened and Liszt entered at the head of his joyful little
band, whom he introduced to me. I also saw Bülow again, for
the first time since his adventurous winter visit to Zürich and
St. Gall, and with him Joachim, Peter Cornelius, Richard
Pohl, and Dionys Pruckner.

Liszt told me that he was expecting a visit from his friend
Caroline von Wittgenstein and her young daughter Marie the
next day. The bright and merry spirit which prevailed at
that gathering (which, like everything that Liszt promoted,
in spite of its intimate nature, was characterised by magnificent
unconventionality) grew to a pitch of almost eccentric hilarity
as the night wore on. In the midst of our wild mood I suddenly
missed Pohl. I knew him to be a champion of our cause
through having read his articles under the pseudonym of
' Hoplit.' I stole away and found him in bed suffering from a
splitting headache. My sympathy had such an effect upon
him that he declared himself suddenly cured. Jumping out of
bed, he allowed me to help him dress hurriedly, and again joining our friends we sat up till the night was far advanced and
enjoyed ourselves thoroughly. On the following day our hap-
pinesss was complete when the ladies arrived, who for the next
few days formed the centre of our little party. In those days
it was impossible for any one coming into contact with Princess
Caroline not to be fascinated by her bright manner and the
charming way in which she entered into all our little plans.

She was as much interested in the more important questions

that affected us as in the accidental details of our life in relation to society, and she had the magnetic power of extracting the very best out of those with whom she associated. Her daughter gave one quite a different impression. She was barely fifteen and had a rather dreamy look on her young face, and was at the stage 'in which womanhood and childhood meet,' thus allowing me to pay her the compliment of calling her 'the child.' During our lively discussions and outbursts of merriment, her dark pensive eyes would gaze at us so calmly that we unconsciously felt that in her innocence she unwittingly understood the cause of our gaiety. In those days I suffered from the vanity of wishing to recite my poems aloud (a proceeding which, by the bye, annoyed Herwegh very much), and consequently it was no difficult task to induce me to read out my *Nibelungen* drama. As the time of our parting was drawing near, I decided I would read *Siegfried* only.

When Liszt was obliged to leave for Paris on a visit to his children, we all accompanied him as far as Strasburg. I had decided to follow him to Paris, but the Princess intended going on from Strasburg to Weimar with her daughter.

During the few spare hours of our short stay in Strasburg I was asked to read some of my work to the ladies, but could not find a suitable opportunity. However, on the morning of our intended parting, Liszt came to my room to tell me that the ladies had, after all, decided to accompany us to Paris, and added, laughing, that Marie had induced her mother to change her plans, as she wished to hear the rest of the *Nibelungen* poems. The prolonging of our journey, with all its delightful incidents, was quite in accordance with my taste.

We were very sorry to part from our younger friends. Bülow told me that Joachim, who had been holding himself rather aloof, could not forget my tremendous article on 'Judaism,' and that he consequently felt shy and awkward in my presence. He also said that when Joachim had asked him (Bülow) to read one of his compositions, he had inquired with a certain gentle diffidence, whether I should be able to trace 'anything Jewish' in it.

This touching trait in Joachim's character induced me to say a few particularly friendly words to him at parting and to embrace him warmly. I never saw him again,[1] and heard to my astonishment that he had taken up a hostile attitude to both Liszt and myself, almost immediately after we had left. The other young men were the victims, on their return to Germany, of a very funny although unpleasant experience, that of coming into contact with the police at Baden. They had entered the town singing the same bright tune of the fanfare from *Lohengrin,* and they had a good deal of difficulty in giving a satisfactory account of themselves to the inhabitants.

Our journey to Paris and our stay there were full of important incidents, and left indelible traces of our exceptionally devoted friendship. After great difficulty we found rooms for the ladies in the Hôtel des Princes, and Liszt then suggested that we should go for a stroll on the boulevards, which at that hour were deserted. I presume that our feelings on this occasion must have differed as much as our reminiscences. When I entered the sitting-room the next morning, Liszt remarked, with his characteristic little smile, that the Princess Marie was already in a great state of excitement at the thought of further readings. Paris did not offer much attraction to me, and as Princess Caroline desired to arouse as little attention as possible, and Liszt was frequently called away on private business, we took up our reading, where we had left it off in Bâle, on the very first morning of our stay in Paris, even before we had been outside the hotel. I was not allowed to stop reading on the following days until the *Ring des Nibelungen* was quite finished. Finally Paris claimed our attention, but while the ladies were visiting the museums I was unfortunately obliged to stay in my room, tortured by continually recurring nervous headaches. Liszt, however, induced me occasionally to join them in their excursions. At the beginning of our stay he had engaged a box for a performance of *Robert le Diable,* because he wanted the ladies to see the great opera house under the most favourable conditions. I believe that my friends shared the terrible depression from which I was suffering on this occasion. Liszt, however, must have had other motives for going. He had asked me to wear evening dress, and seemed very pleased I had done so when at the interval he invited me to go for a stroll

---

[1] This was written in 1869.

with him through the foyer. I could see he was under the influence of certain reminiscences of delightful evenings spent in this selfsame foyer, and that the dismal performance of this night must have cast a gloom over him. We stole quietly back to our friends, hardly knowing why we had started on this monotonous expedition. One of the artistic pleasures I enjoyed most was a concert given by the Morin-Chevillard Quartette Society, at which they played Beethoven's Quartettes in E flat major and C sharp minor; the excellent rendering of this work impressed me in very much the same way as the performance of the Ninth Symphony by the Conservatoire orchestra had once done. I had again the opportunity of admiring the great artistic zeal with which the French master these treasures of music, which even to this day are so coarsely handled by the Germans.

This was the first time that I really became intimately acquainted with the C sharp minor quartette, because I had never before grasped its melody. If, therefore, I had nothing else to remind me of my stay in Paris, this would have been an unfading memory. I also carried away with me other equally significant impressions. One day Liszt invited me to spend an evening with him and his children, who were living very quietly in the care of a governess in Paris.

It was quite a novelty to me to see Liszt with these young girls, and to watch him in his intercourse with his son, then a growing lad. Liszt himself seemed to feel strange in his fatherly position, which for several years had only brought him cares, without any of the attendant pleasures.

On this occasion we again resumed our reading of the last act of *Götterdämmerung*, which brought us to the longed-for end of the tetralogy. Berlioz, who looked us up during that time, endured these readings with quite admirable patience. We had lunch with him one morning before his departure, and he had already packed his music for his concert tour through Germany. Liszt played different selections from his *Benvenuto Cellini*, while Berlioz sang to them in his peculiarly monotonous style. I also met the journalist, Jules Janin, who was quite a celebrity in Paris, although it took me a long time to realise this; the only thing that impressed me about him was his colloquial Parisian French, which was quite unintelligible to me.

A dinner, followed by a musical evening at the house of the celebrated pianoforte manufacturer, Erard, also remains in my memory. At this house, as well as at a dinner-party given by Liszt at the Palais Royal, I again met his children. Daniel, the youngest of them, particularly attracted me by his brightness and his striking resemblance to his father, but the girls were very shy. I must not forget to mention an evening spent at the house of Mme. Kalergis, a woman of exceptional individuality, whom I met here for the first time since the early performance of *Tannhäuser* in Dresden. When at dinner she asked me a question about Louis Napoleon, I forgot myself so far in my excitement and resentment as to put an end to all further conversation by saying that I could not understand how anybody could possibly expect great things from a man whom no woman could really love. After dinner, when Liszt sat down at the piano, young Marie Wittgenstein noticed that I had withdrawn silently and rather sadly from the rest of the company; this was due partly to my headache, and partly to the feeling of isolation that came over me in these surroundings. I was touched by her sympathy and evident wish to divert me.

After a very fatiguing week my friends left Paris. As I had again been prevented from starting on my work, I now decided not to leave Paris until I had restored my nerves to that state of calm which was indispensable to the fulfilment of my great project. I had invited my wife to meet me on our way back to Zürich, to give her the opportunity of seeing Paris again, where we had both suffered so much. After her arrival, Kietz and Anders turned up regularly for dinner, and a young Pole, the son of my old and beloved friend, Count Vincenz Tyszkiewicz, also came to see us very often.

This young man (who had been born since the early days of my friendship with his father) had devoted himself passionately to music, as so many do nowadays. He had made quite a stir in Paris after a performance of *Freischütz* at the Grand Opera, by declaring that the many cuts and alterations which had been made were a fraud on the initiated public, and he had sued the management of the theatre for the return of the entrance money, which he regretted ever having paid. He also had an idea of publishing a paper with the view of drawing attention to the slovenly conduct of musical affairs in Paris, which in his opinion was an insult to public taste.

Prince Eugen von Wittgenstein-Sayn, a young amateur painter who had belonged to Liszt's circle of intimate friends, painted a miniature of me, for which I had to give him several sittings; it was done under Kietz's guidance, and turned out pretty well.

I had an important consultation with a young doctor named Lindemann, a friend of Kietz's; he strongly advised me to give up the water cure, and tried to convert me to the toxic theory. He had attracted the attention of Parisian society by inoculating himself with various poisons in the hospital before witnesses, in order to show their effects upon the system, an experiment which he carried out in an accurate and thoroughly effective manner. With regard to my own case, he stated that it could be easily remedied if we ascertained by careful experiments what metallic substance would specifically influence my nervous system. He unhesitatingly recommended me, in case of very violent attacks, to take laudanum, and in default of that poison he seemed to consider valerian an excellent remedy.

Tired out, restless and exceedingly unstrung, I left Paris with Minna towards the end of October, without in the least understanding why I had spent so much money there. Hoping counterbalance this by pushing my operas in Germany, I calmly retired to the seclusion of my Zürich lodgings, fully decided not to leave them again until some parts, at least, of my *Nibelungen* dramas were set to music.

In the beginning of November I started on this long-postponed work. For five and a half years (since the end of March, 1848) I had held aloof from all musical composition, and as I very soon found myself in the right mood for composing, this return to my work can best be compared to a reincarnation of my soul after it had been wandering in other spheres. As far as the technique was concerned, I soon found myself in a difficulty when I started to write down the orchestral overture, conceived in Spezia in a kind of half-dream, in my usual way

of sketching it out on two lines. I was compelled to resort to
the complete score-formula; this tempted me to try a new way
of sketching, which was a very hasty and superficial one, from
which I immediately wrote out the complete score.

This process often led to difficulties, as the slightest interruption in my work made me lose the thread of my rough draft,
and I had to start from the beginning before I could recall it
to my memory.

I did not let this occur in regard to *Rheingold*. The whole
of this composition had been finished in outline on the 16th of
January, 1854, and consequently the plan for the musical structure of this work in four parts had been drawn in all its
thematic proportions, as it was in this great prelude that these
thematic foundations of the whole had to be laid.

I remember how much my health improved during the
writing of this work; and my surroundings during that time
consequently left very little impression on my mind.

During the first months of the new year I also conducted a
few orchestral concerts. To please my friend Sulzer, I produced, amongst other works, the overture to Gluck's *Iphigenia
in Aulis,* after having written a new finale to it. The necessity
for altering the finale by Mozart induced me to write an article
for the Brendel musical journal on this artistic problem. These
occupations did not, however, prevent me from working at the
Rheingold score, which I quickly dotted down in pencil on a
few single sheets. On the 28th May I finished the instrumentation of the *Rheingold*. There had been very little change in
my life at home; things had remained the same during the
last few years, and everything went smoothly. Only my
financial position was rather precarious, owing to the past
year's expenses for furniture, etc., and also to the more luxurious
mode of living I had adopted, on the strength of my belief that
my operas, which were now better known, would bring me in a
larger income.

The most important theatres, however, still held back, and
to my mortification all my efforts at negotiation with Berlin
and Vienna proved fruitless. In consequence of these disappointments I suffered great worries and cares during the greater
part of that year. I tried to counteract these by new work,

and instead of writing out the score of *Rheingold* I began the
composition of the *Walküre*. Towards the end of July I had
finished the first scene, but had to interrupt my work on account
of a journey to the south of Switzerland.

I had received an invitation from the ' Eidgenossische Musikgesellschaft ' to conduct their musical festival at Sion that year.
I had refused, but at the same time promised that if possible I
would conduct Beethoven's Symphony in A major at one of
the gala concerts. I intended on the way to call on Karl
Ritter, who had gone to live with his young wife at Montreux
on the Lake of Geneva. The week I spent with this young
couple gave me ample opportunities for doubting whether their
happiness would be of long duration.

Karl and I left shortly afterwards for the musical festival in
Valais. On our way we were joined at Martigny by an extraordinary young man, Robert von Hornstein, who had been
introduced to me on the occasion of my great musical festival
the year before as an enthusiast and a musician. This quaint
mortal was regarded as a very welcome addition to our party,
particularly by young Ritter, and both young people looked
forward with great enthusiasm to the treat in store for them;
Hornstein had come all the way from Swabia to hear me conduct the festival in the canton of Valais. We arrived in the
midst of the musical festivities, and I was terribly disappointed
to find how very badly and inartistically the preliminary arrangements had been made. I was so taken aback, after having
received the worst possible impression of the sound of the very
scanty orchestra in a small church, which served as church and
concert-hall combined, and was so furious at the thought of
having been dragged into such an affair, that I merely wrote
a few lines to Methfessel, the organising director of the festival,
who had come from Berne, and took my leave, without further
ceremony. I escaped by the next post-chaise that was just
on the point of leaving, and I did this so expeditiously that
even my young friends were unaware of my departure. I
purposely kept the fact of my sudden flight from them; I
had my own reasons for doing so, and as they were rather
interesting from a psychological point of view, I have never
forgotten them.

On coming back to dinner that day feeling miserable and depressed after the disappointing impression I had just received, my annoyance was treated with foolish and almost insulting roars of laughter by my young friends. I presumed that their merriment was the result of remarks made at my expense before I came in, as neither my admonitions nor even my anger could induce them to behave differently. I quitted the dining-room in disgust, paid my bill and left, without giving them any opportunity of noticing my departure. I spent a few days in Geneva and Lausanne, and decided to call on Frau Ritter on my way back; and there I again met the two young people. Evidently they also had given up the wretched festival, and been completely taken aback at my sudden departure, had almost immediately left for Montreux, in the hope of hearing news of me.

I made no mention of their rude conduct, and as Karl cordially invited me to stay with them a few days longer I accepted, principally because I was very much interested in a poetical work he had only just finished. This poem was a comedy called *Alkibiades,* which he had really treated with exceptional refinement and freedom of form. He had already told me at Albisbrunnen about the sketch of this work, and had shown me an elegant dagger into the blade of which the syllables *Alki* had been burnt.

He explained that his friend, a young actor whom he had left in Stuttgart, possessed a similar weapon, the blade of which bore the syllables *Biades.* It seemed that Karl, even without the symbolic help of the daggers, had again found the complement of his own ' Alkibiadesian ' individuality, this time in the young booby Hornstein, and it is very probable that the two, whilst in Sion, had imagined they were acting an ' Alkibiadesian ' scene before Socrates. His comedy showed me that his artistic talent was fortunately far better than his society manners. To this day I regret that this decidedly difficult play has never been produced.

Hornstein now behaved properly and desired to go to Lausanne via Vevey. We did part of the journey together on foot, and his quaint appearance with his knapsack on his back was most amusing.

I continued my journey alone from Berne to Lucerne, taking the shortest possible route to Selisberg on the Lake of Lucerne, where my wife was staying for a sour-milk cure.

The symptoms of heart disease, which I had already noticed some time previously, had increased, and this place had been recommended to her as specially invigorating and beneficial. With great patience I endured several weeks of life at a Swiss *pension,* but my wife, who had quite adapted herself to the ways of the house and seemed very comfortable, looked upon me as a disturbing element.

I found this a great trial, although the beautiful air and my daily excursions into the mountains did me a great deal of good. I even went so far as to choose a very wild spot, where, in imagination, I ordered a little house to be built in which I should be able to work in absolute peace.

Towards the end of July we went back to Zürich. I returned to my *Walküre* and finished the first act in the month of August. I was terribly depressed by my worries just at this time, and as it was more than ever necessary for me to have absolute quiet for my work, I at once agreed to my wife's departure, when she told me of her intended visit to her relations and friends in Dresden and Zwickau. She left me at the beginning of September, and wrote to me about her stay in Weimar, where the Princess Wittgenstein had received her with the greatest hospitality at Altenburg Castle. There she met Röckel's wife, who was being cared for in the most self-sacrificing way by her husband's brother. It showed a spirited and original trait in Minna's character that she decided to visit Röckel in his prison at Waldheim, solely that she might give his wife news of him, although she disliked the man intensely.

She told me of this visit, saying sarcastically that Röckel looked quite happy and bright, and that life in prison did not seem to suit him badly.

Meanwhile I plunged with renewed zeal into my work, and had finished a fair copy of the *Rheingold* score by the 26th of September. In the peaceful quietness of my house at this time I first came across a book which was destined to be of great importance to me. This was Arthur Schopenhauer's *Die Welt als Wille und Vorstellung.*

Herwegh recommended this work to me, and told me that strangely enough it had only been recently discovered, although it had been published over thirty years. In a pamphlet on this subject a certain Herr Frauenstädt had drawn the attention of the public to the book, to which I immediately felt attracted, and I at once began to study it. For a long time I had wanted to understand the real value of philosophy. My conversations with Lehrs in Paris in my very young days had awakened my longing for this branch of knowledge, upon which I had first launched when I attended the lectures of several Leipzig professors and in later years by reading Schelling and Hegel. I seemed to understand the reason of their failure to satisfy me from the writings of Feuerbach, which I studied at the same time. What fascinated me so enormously about Schopenhauer's work was not only its extraordinary fate, but the clearness and manly precision with which the most difficult metaphysical problems were treated from the very beginning.

I had been greatly drawn towards the work on learning the opinion of an English critic, who candidly confessed that he respected German philosophy because of its complete in-comprehensibility, as instanced by Hegel's doctrines, until the study of Schopenhauer had made it clear to him that Hegel's lack of lucidity was due not so much to his own incapacity as to the intentionally bombastic style in which this philosopher had clothed his problems. Like every man who is passionately thrilled with life, I too sought first for the conclusions of Schopenhauer's system. With its æsthetic side I was perfectly content, and was especially astonished at his noble conception of music. But, on the other hand, the final summing-up regard-ing morals alarmed me, as, indeed, it would have startled any one in my mood; for here the annihilation of the will and complete abnegation are represented as the sole true and final deliverance from those bonds of individual limitation in estimat-ing and facing the world, which are now clearly felt for the first time. For those who hoped to find some philosophical justi-fication for political and social agitation on behalf of so-called ' individual freedom ' there was certainly no support to be found here, where all that was demanded was absolute renunciation of all such methods of satisfying the claims of personality. At first

I naturally found his ideas by no means palatable, and felt I could not readily abandon that so-called 'cheerful' Greek aspect of the world, with which I had looked out upon life in my *Kunstwerk der Zukunft*. As a matter of fact, it was Herwegh who at last, by a well-timed explanation, brought me to a calmer frame of mind about my own sensitive feelings. It is from this perception of the nullity of the visible world — so he said — that all tragedy is derived, and such a perception must necessarily have dwelt as an intuition in every great poet, and even in every great man. On looking afresh into my *Nibelungen* poem I recognised with surprise that the very things that now so embarrassed me theoretically had long been familiar to me in my own poetical conception. Now at last I could understand my *Wotan,* and I returned with chastened mind to the renewed study of Schopenhauer's book. I had learned to recognise that my first essential task was to understand the first part, namely, the exposition and enlarging of Kant's doctrine of the ideality of that world which has hitherto seemed to us so solidly founded in time and space, and I believed I had taken the first step towards such an understanding by recognising its enormous difficulty. For many years afterwards that book never left me, and by the summer of the following year I had already studied the whole of it for the fourth time. The effect thus gradually wrought upon me was extraordinary, and certainly exerted a decisive influence on the whole course of my life. In forming my judgment upon all those matters which I had hitherto acquired solely through the senses, I had gained pretty much the same power as I had formerly won in music — after abandoning the teaching of my old master Weinlich — by an exhaustive study of counterpoint. If, therefore, in later years I again expressed opinions in my casual writings on matters pertaining to that art which so particularly interested me, it is certain that traces of what I learned from my study of Schopenhauer's philosophy were clearly perceptible.

Just then I was prompted to send the venerated philosopher a copy of my *Nibelungen* poem. To its title I merely added by hand the words, 'With Reverence,' but without writing a single word to Schopenhauer himself.

This I did partly from a feeling of great shyness in addressing him, and partly because I felt that if the perusal of my poem did not enlighten Schopenhauer about the man with whom he was dealing, a letter from me, no matter how explicit, would not help him much. I also renounced by this means the vain wish to be honoured by an autograph letter from his hand. I learned later, however, from Karl Ritter, and also from Dr. Wille, both of whom visited Schopenhauer in Frankfort, that he spoke impressively and favourably of my poetry. In addition to these studies, I continued writing the music to the *Walküre*. I was living in great retirement at this time, my sole relaxation being to take long walks in the neighbourhood, and, as usual with me when hard at work at my music, I felt the longing to express myself in poetry. This must have been partly due to the serious mood created by Schopenhauer, which was trying to find ecstatic expression. It was some such mood that inspired the conception of a *Tristan und Isolde*.

Karl Ritter had just laid before me a sketch for the dramatic treatment of this subject (with which I was thoroughly acquainted through my Dresden studies), and had thereby drawn my attention to the material for this poem. I had already expressed my views to my young friend about the faultiness of his sketch. He had, in fact, made a point of giving prominence to the lighter phases of the romance, whereas it was its all-pervading tragedy that impressed me so deeply that I felt convinced it should stand out in bold relief, regardless of minor details. On my return from one of my walks I jotted down the incidents of the three acts in a concise form, with the intention of working them out more elaborately later on. In the last act I introduced an episode, which, however, I did not develop eventually, namely, the visit to Tristan's deathbed by Parsifal during his search for the Holy Grail. The picture of Tristan languishing, yet unable to die of his wound, identified itself in my mind with Amfortas in the Romance of the Grail.

For the moment I forced myself to leave this poem on one side, and to allow nothing to interrupt my great musical work. Meanwhile, through the help of friends, I succeeded in bringing about a satisfactory change in my financial position. My prospects with regard to the German theatres also seemed brighter. Minna had been in Berlin, and through the influence of our old friend, Alwine Frommann, had had an interview with Herr von Hülsen, the manager of the court theatre. After losing two years in fruitless efforts, I at last felt more certain of seeing *Tannhäuser* produced there without further obstacle, as it had become so popular with all the theatres that its failure in Berlin could not injure its reputation; it could only reflect disadvantageously on the Berlin management.

In the beginning of November Minna returned from her journey, and acting on the news she gave me about the production of *Tannhäuser* in Berlin, I allowed matters to take their course, a decision which afterwards caused me great annoyance, as the rendering of my work was simply wretched. I got some compensation, however, in the royalties, which were an important and continuous source of income to me.

The Zürich Musical Society now again enlisted my interest for their winter concerts. I promised to conduct, but only on condition that they would give serious consideration to improving the orchestra. I had already twice proposed the formation of a decent orchestra, and I now sent in a third plan to the committee, in which I described in detail how they might achieve this object at a comparatively slight outlay by co-operation with the theatre. I told them that this winter would be the last time that I should interest myself in their concerts unless they entertained this very reasonable proposition. Apart from this work, I took in hand a quartette society, made up of the soloists of the orchestra, who were anxious to study the right interpretation of the various quartettes I had recommended.

It was a great pleasure to me to see how soon the public patronised the efforts of these artists, who, by the way, thus added a little extra to their incomes for a considerable time. As far as their artistic achievements went, the work was rather slow; the mere fact of their being able to play their respective instruments well did not make them at once understand the art of playing together, for which so much more is needed than mere dynamic proportions and accents, attainable only by the individual development of a higher artistic taste in the treatment of the instrument by its exponent.

I was too ambitious about them, and actually taught them Beethoven's Quartette in C sharp minor, which meant endless trouble and rehearsing. I wrote some analytical annotations for the better appreciation of this extraordinary work, and had them printed on the programme. Whether I made any impression on the audience, or whether they liked the performance, I was never able to find out. When I say that I completed the sketch of the whole of the music to the *Walküre* by the 30th of December of that year, it will suffice to prove my strenuous and active life at that time, as well as to show that I did not allow any outside distraction to disturb my rigorous plan of work.

In January, 1855, I began the instrumentation of the *Walküre*, but I was compelled to interrupt it, owing to a promise I made to some of my friends to give them a chance of hearing the overture to *Faust*, which I had written in Paris fifteen years before. I had another look at this composition, which had been the means of so important a change in my musical ideas. Liszt had produced the work in Weimar a little while before, and had written to me in very favourable terms about it, at the same time expressing his wish that I should rewrite more elaborately some parts that were only faintly indicated. So I immediately set to work to rewrite the overture, conscientiously adopting my dear friend's delicate suggestions, and I finished it as it was afterwards published by Härtel. I taught our orchestra this overture, and did not think the performance at all bad. My wife, however, did not like it; she said it seemed to her ' as if nothing good could be made out of it,' and she begged me not to have it produced in London when I went there that year. At this time I had an extraordinary application, such as I have never received again. In January the London Philharmonic Society wrote asking me if I would be willing to conduct their concerts for the season. I did not answer immediately, as I wanted to obtain some particulars first, and was very much surprised one day to receive a visit from a certain Mr. Anderson, a member of the committee of the celebrated society, who had come to Zürich on purpose to ensure my acceptance.

I was expected to go to London for four months to give eight concerts for the Philharmonic Society, for which I was to receive in all £200. I did not quite know what to do, as, from a business point of view, it was of no advantage to me, and, as far as the conducting went, it was not much in my line, unless I could rely on at least a few high-class artistic productions.

One thing only struck me as favourable, and that was the prospect of again handling a large and excellent orchestra, after having been denied one for so long, while the fact that I had attracted the attention of that remote world of music fascinated me exceedingly. I felt as if fate were calling me, and at last I accepted the invitation of this simple and amiable-looking Englishman, Mr. Anderson, who, fully satisfied with the result of his mission, immediately left for England wrapped in a big fur coat, whose real owner I only got to know later on. Before following him to England, I had to free myself from a calamity which I had brought upon myself through being too kind-hearted. The managing director of the Zürich theatre for that year, an obtrusive and over-zealous person, had at last made me accede to his wish to produce *Tannhäuser,* on the plea that as this work was now performed at every opera house, it would be a very bad thing for the Zürich theatre if it were the only one to be deprived of the privilege, merely because I happened to live in the town. Besides this, my wife interfered in the matter, and the singers who played Tannhäuser and Wolfram at once put themselves under her wing. She really succeeded, too, in working on my humanitarian feelings with regard to one of her protégés, a poor tenor who had been badly bullied by the conductor till then. I took these people through their parts a few times, and in consequence found myself obliged to attend the stage rehearsals to superintend their performances. What it all came to in the end was that I was driven to interfere again and again, until I found myself at the conductor's desk, and eventually conducted the first performance myself. I have a particularly vivid recollection of the singer who played Elizabeth on that occasion. She had originally taken soubrette parts, and went through her rôle in white kid gloves, dangling a fan. This time I had really had enough of such concessions, and when at the close the audience called me before the curtain, I stood there and told my friends with great frankness that this was the last time they would get me to do anything of the sort.

I advised them in future to look to the state of their theatre, as they had just had a most convincing proof of its faulty construction — at which they were all much astonished. I made a similar announcement to the ' Musikgesellschaft,' where I also conducted once more — really for the last time — before my departure. Unfortunately, they put down my protests to my sense of humour, and were not in the least spurred to exert themselves, with the result that I had to be very stern and almost rude the following winter, to deter them, once and for all, from making further demands upon me. I thus left my former patrons in Zürich somewhat nonplussed when I started for London on 26th February.

I travelled through Paris and spent some days there, during which time I saw only Kietz and his friend Lindemann, whom he regarded as a quack doctor. Arriving in London on 2nd March I first went to see Ferdinand Präger. In his youth he had been a friend of the Röckel brothers, who had given me a very favourable account of him. He proved to be an unusually good-natured fellow, though of an excitability insufficiently balanced by his standard of culture. After spending the first night at his home, I installed myself the following day with his help in a house in Portland Terrace, in the neighbourhood of Regent's Park, of which I had agreeable recollections from former visits. I promised myself a pleasant stay there in the coming spring, if only on account of its close proximity to that part of the park where beautiful copper beeches overshadowed the path. But though I spent four months in London, it seemed to me that spring never came, the foggy climate so overclouded all the impressions I received. Präger was only too eager to escort me when I went to pay the customary visits, including one to Costa. I was thus introduced to the director of the Italian Opera, who was at the same time the real leader of music in London; for he was also director of the Sacred-Music Society, which gave almost regular weekly performances of Händel and Mendelssohn.

Präger also took me to see his friend Sainton, the leader of the London orchestra. After giving me a very hearty reception he told me the remarkable history of my invitation to London. Sainton, a southern Frenchman from Toulouse, of naïve and fiery temperament, was living with a full-blooded German musician from Hamburg, named Lüders, the son of a bandsman, of a brusque but friendly disposition. I was much affected when I heard, later on, of the incident which had made these two men inseparable friends. Sainton had been making a concert tour by way of St. Petersburg, and found himself stranded at Helsingfors in Finland, unable to get any further, pursued as he was by the demon of ill-luck. At this moment the curious figure of the modest Hamburg bandsman's son had accosted him on the staircase of the hotel, asking whether he would be inclined to accept his offer of friendship and take half of his available cash, as he (Lüders) had of course noticed the awkwardness of the other's position. From that moment the two became inseparable friends, made concert tours in Sweden and Denmark, found their way back in the strangest fashion to Havre, Paris, and Toulouse, by way of Hamburg, and finally settled down in London — Sainton to take an important post in the orchestra, while Lüders got along as best he could by the drudgery of giving lessons. Now I found them living together in a pretty house like a married couple, each tenderly concerned for his friend's welfare. Lüders had read my essays on art, and my *Oper und Drama* in particular moved him to exclaim, ' *Donnerwetter*, there 's something in that! ' Sainton pricked up his ears at this, and when the conductor of the Philharmonic concerts (the great Mr. Costa himself), for some unknown reason, quarrelled with the society before the season began and refused to conduct their concerts any longer, Sainton, to whom Mr. Anderson, the treasurer, had gone for advice in this awkward predicament, recommended them, at Lüders' instigation, to engage me. I now heard that they had not acted upon this suggestion at once. Only when Sainton happened to remark casually that he had seen me conduct in Dresden did Mr. Anderson decide to make the journey to Zürich to see me (in the fur coat lent by Sainton for the purpose), as a result of which visit I was now here. I soon discovered, too, that Sainton had in this case acted with the rashness characteristic of his nation. It had never occurred to Costa that he would be taken seriously in his statement to the Philharmonic Society, and he was thoroughly disgusted at my appointment. As he was at the head of the same orchestra which was at my disposal for the Philharmonic concerts, he was able to foster an attitude of hostility to the undertakings for which I was responsible, and even my friend Sainton had to suffer from his animosity without actually realising the source of the annoyance.

As time went on I saw this more plainly, while there was abundant material for unpleasantness of every description in other quarters. In the first place Mr. Davison, the musical critic of the *Times,* adopted a most hostile attitude, and it was from this that I first realised, clearly and definitely, the effect of my essay entitled ' Judaism in Music.' Präger had further informed me that Davison's extremely powerful position on the *Times* had accustomed him to expect every one who came to England on business connected with music to propitiate him by all sorts of delicate attentions. Jenny Lind was one whose submission to these pretensions did much to ensure her popular success; whereas Sontag considered that her rank as Countess Rossi elevated her above such considerations. As I had been completely absorbed in the delight of handling a good, full orchestra, with which I hoped to give some fine performances, it was a great blow to learn that I had no control whatever over the number of rehearsals I thought necessary for the concerts. For each concert, which included two symphonies and several minor pieces as well, the society's economical arrangements allowed me only one rehearsal. Still I went on hoping that the impression produced by the performances I conducted might even here justify the demand for a special effort. It proved absolutely impossible, however, to depart in any way from the beaten track, and, realising this, I at once felt that the fulfilment of the task I had undertaken was a terrible burden. At the first concert we played Beethoven's *Eroica,* and my success as a conductor seemed so marked that the committee of the society were evidently prepared to make a special effort for the second. They demanded selections from my own compositions as well as Beethoven's Ninth Symphony, and conceded me two rehearsals as an exceptional favour. This concert went off quite passably. I had drawn up an explanatory programme for my *Lohengrin* Overture, but the words 'Holy Grail' and 'God' were struck out with great solemnity, as that sort of thing was not allowed at secular concerts. I had to content myself with the chorus from the Italian Opera for the symphony, besides putting up with a baritone whose English phlegm and Italian training drove me to despair at the rehearsal. All I understood of the English version of the text was, 'Hail thee joy' for *Freude. schöner Götterfunken*. The Philharmonic Society appeared to have staked everything on the success of this concert, which, in fact, left nothing to be desired. They were accordingly horrified when the *Times* reporter fell on this performance, too, with furious contempt and disparagement. They appealed to Präger to persuade me to offer Mr. Davison some attentions, or at least to agree to meet that gentleman and be properly introduced to him at a banquet to be arranged by Mr. Anderson. But Präger now knew me well enough to dash their hopes of obtaining any concession of that sort from me. The banquet fell through, and, as I saw later, the society began from that time forward to regret my appointment, realising that they had an entirely intractable and pig-headed person to deal with.

As the Easter holidays began after the second concert, thereby involving a long pause, I asked my friend's advice as to whether it would not be more sensible to give up the whole thing — this conductorship of the Philharmonic concerts which I had so soon discovered to be a foolish and fruitless undertaking — and go quietly back to Zürich. Präger assured me that the execution of this resolve would in no wise be regarded as a reflection on the situation, but simply as a deplorable piece of rudeness on my part, and that the principal sufferers would be my friends. This decided me, and I stayed — without, it is true, any hope of giving a fresh impetus to musical life in London. The only stimulating incident occurred on the occasion of the seventh concert, which was the evening chosen by the Queen for her annual visit to these functions. She expressed a wish through her husband, Prince Albert, to hear the *Tannhäuser* Overture. The presence of the court certainly lent a pleasing air of ceremony to the evening, and I had, too, the pleasure of a fairly animated conversation with Queen Victoria and her Consort in response to their command. The question arose of putting my operas on the stage, and Prince Albert objected that Italian singers would never be able to interpret my music. I was amused when the Queen met this objection by saying that, after all, a great many Italian singers were really Germans. All this made a good impression and, it was obvious, served as a demonstration in my favour, without, however, influencing the real situation to any appreciable extent. The leading papers still announced, as before, that every concert I conducted was a fiasco. Ferdinand Hiller actually thought himself justified in proclaiming, for the consolation of his friends, that my day in London was coming to an end, and that my banishment was practically a certainty. This was on the occasion of the Rhenish Musical Festival, which was held at that time. As a set-off against this I reaped great satisfaction from a scene which took place at the close of the eighth and last concert which I conducted — one of those strange scenes which now and again result from the long-suppressed emotion of those concerned. The members of the orchestra had at once realised, after my successes, the advisability of avoiding any expression of sympathy with me if they wished to keep in good odour with their real though unacknowledged chief, Mr. Costa, and save themselves from a possible speedy dismissal at his hands. This was the explanation given me when the signs of appreciation, which I had become accustomed to receive from the players in the course of our work together, suddenly ceased. Now, however, at the end of the series their suppressed feelings burst forth, and they crowded round me on all sides with deafening cheers, while the audience, who usually left the hall noisily before the end, likewise formed up in enthusiastic groups and surrounded me, cheering warmly and pressing my hand. Thus both players and listeners combined to make my farewell a scene of cordiality which could hardly be surpassed.

But it was the personal relations which grew out of my stay in London that provided the strangest aspect of my life there.

Immediately after my arrival, Karl Klindworth, a young pupil of Liszt, who had been recommended to me as particularly gifted, came to see me. He became a faithful and intimate friend, not only during my stay in London, but ever after. Young as he was, the short time he had spent in London had sufficed to give him an opinion of English musical life, the justice of which I was soon compelled to admit, terrible though it was. Incapable of adapting himself to the curiously organised English musical cliques, he at once lost all reasonable prospect or hope of meeting with the recognition due to his talent. He resigned himself to making his way through the dreary wastes of English musical life solely by giving lessons like a day-labourer, being too proud to pay the smallest attentions to the ruling critics, who had fallen on him immediately as a pupil of Liszt. He was really an excellent musician, and in addition a distinguished pianist. He immediately approached me with the request to be allowed to make a pianoforte arrangement of the score of *Rheingold,* for the use only of virtuosi of the first rank. Unfortunately, he was overtaken by a tedious illness, which robbed me for a long time of the desired intercourse with him.

Although Präger and his wife stood by me with great constancy, my real centre of intimacy was the original Sainton-Lüders' household. I had a standing invitation to dine with them, and I found occasion, with few exceptions, to take my meals with these friends, whose devotion surpassed that of all the others. It was here that I generally found relaxation from the unpleasantness of my business relations in London. Präger was often present, and we frequently took an evening stroll through the foggy streets. On such occasions Lüders would fortify us against the inclemency of the London climate by an excellent punch which he could prepare under any conditions. Only once did we get separated, and that was in the terrific crowd that accompanied the Emperor Napoleon from St. James's Palace to Covent Garden Theatre one evening. He had come over to London with his Consort, on a visit to Queen Victoria, during the critical stage of the Crimean War, and the Londoners gaped at him as he passed no less greedily than other nations are apt to do under similar circumstances. It so befell that I was taken for a pushing sightseer, and proportionately punished by blows in the ribs when I was crossing the road to try and get into Regent Street from the Haymarket.

This caused me much amusement, on account of the obvious misunderstanding.

The grave annoyances which arose, partly from the peculiarly momentous quarrel between Sainton and Mr. Anderson (instigated by Costa), and which deprived me of every possibility of obtaining any influence over the society, were productive, on the other hand, of some amusing experiences. Anderson had, it seemed, succeeded in elevating himself to the post of conductor of the Queen's band, through the influence of the Queen's private coachman. As he possessed absolutely no knowledge of music, the annual court concert which he had to conduct became a very feast of absurdity to the unruly Sainton, and I heard some very funny stories about it. Another thing brought to light in the course of these imbroglios was that Mrs. Anderson, whom I had christened Charlemagne on account of her great corpulency, had appropriated to herself, among other things, the office and salary of a court trumpeter. I soon arrived at the conviction, from these and other similar reports, that my lively friend would be beaten by this snug little clique in the war of disclosures, and was able subsequently to see the decision go against him at the point when either he or Anderson had to give way. This confirmed my idea that in this free country of England things were managed in much the same way as elsewhere.

The arrival of Berlioz made a very important addition to our little company. He, too, had been brought over to London, to conduct two of the New Philharmonic Society's concerts. The society had appointed as ordinary conductor, by whose recommendation I could never discover, a certain Dr. Wilde, a typical chubby-faced Englishman, remarkably good-natured, but ludicrously incompetent. He had taken some special lessons in conducting from the Stuttgart conductor, Lindpaintner, who had trained him up to the point of at least attempting to catch up the orchestra with his beat, the orchestra itself going its own way entirely. I heard a Beethoven symphony performed in this fashion, and was surprised to hear the audience break into precisely the same applause with which it greeted one of my own strictly accurate and really fiery performances. To lend distinction to these concerts, however, they had, as I said,

invited Berlioz over for some of them. I thus heard him conduct some classical works, such as a Mozart symphony, and
was amazed to find a conductor, who was so energetic in
the interpretation of his own compositions, sink into the
commonest rut of the vulgar time-beater. Certain of his own
compositions, such as the more effective fragments from the
Romeo and Juliet Symphony, again made a particular impression on me, it is true; but I was now more consciously
awake to the curious weaknesses which disfigure even the finest
conceptions of this extraordinary musician than on those earlier
occasions, when I only had a sense of general discomfort adequate to the magnitude of the impression.

I felt much stimulated, however, on the two or three occasions when Sainton invited me to dine with Berlioz. I was now
brought face to face with this strangely gifted person, tormented
and even blunted in some respects as he then was. When
I saw him, a man considerably my senior, coming here merely
in the hope of earning a few guineas, I could deem myself
perfectly happy, and almost floating on air, by contrast; for
my own coming had been brought about rather by a desire
for distraction, a craving for outward inspiration. His whole
being expressed weariness and despair, and I was suddenly
seized with deep sympathy for this man whose talent so far
surpassed that of his rivals — for this was clear as daylight to
me. Berlioz seemed to be pleasantly affected by the attitude
of gay spontaneity I adopted with him. His usual short,
almost reserved, manner thawed visibly during the friendly
hours we passed together. He told me many comical things
about Meyerbeer, and the impossibility of escaping from his
flattery, which was dictated by his insatiable thirst for laudatory
articles. The first performance of his *Prophet* had been preceded by the customary *diner de la veille,* and when Berlioz
excused himself for staying away, Meyerbeer first reproached
him tenderly, then challenged him to make good the great
injustice he had done him, by writing ' a real nice article '
about his opera. Berlioz declared it was impossible to get anything detrimental to Meyerbeer inserted in a Paris paper.

I found it less easy to discuss with him matters of a more profound artistic nature, as I invariably came up against the real

Frenchman then, who, fluent and glib of tongue, was so sure of himself that it never occurred to him to doubt whether he had understood his companions aright. Once, in a pleasant glow of inspiration (having suddenly mastered the French language, to my own great surprise), I tried to express to him my idea of the 'artistic conception.' I endeavoured to describe the powerful effect of vital impressions on the temperament, how they hold us captive, as it were, until we rid ourselves of them by the unique development of our inmost spiritual visions, which are not called forth by these impressions, but only roused by them from their deep slumber. The artistic structure, therefore, appears to us as in no wise a result of, but, on the contrary, a liberation from, the vital impressions. At this point Berlioz smiled in a patronising, comprehensive way, and said: ' *Nous appelons cela: digérer.* ' My amazement at this prompt summing-up of my laboured communications was further justified by my new friend's outward behaviour. I invited him to be present at my last concert, and also at a small farewell feast which I was giving at home to my few friends after it. He soon left the table, saying that he felt unwell, but the friends who were left made no secret to me of their belief that Berlioz had been put out of humour by the exceedingly enthusiastic farewell with which the audience had parted from me.

The total harvest, however, of acquaintances I made in London was not particularly profitable. I took pleasure in the society of Mr. Ellerton, a dignified, agreeable man, the brother-in-law of Lord Brougham — a poet, a music-lover, and, alas! a composer. He asked to be introduced to me at one of the Philharmonic concerts, and did not hesitate to tell me that he welcomed me to London because it seemed likely that I was destined to check the exaggerated Mendelssohn worship. He was also the only Englishman who honoured me by any hospitality, and by entertaining myself and my friends at the University Club, gave me an opportunity of realising the munificence of such an establishment in London. After we had spent a very agreeable time there, I had a glimpse of the weaker side of English hospitalities of this order, though the incident was friendly enough. My host had to be taken home by two men, one holding each arm, quite as a matter of course, as it was obvious that he would not have got far across the road without this help.

I made the acquaintance, too, of a curious man, an old-fashioned but very friendly composer named Potter. I had to play a symphony of his, which entertained me by its modest dimensions and its neat development of counterpoint, the more so as the composer, a friendly elderly recluse, clung to me with almost distressing humility. I had positively to force him into accepting the right *tempo* for the *Andante* in his symphony, thus proving to him that it was really pretty and interesting. He had so little faith in his work, that he considered the only way to avoid the danger of boring people with it was to rattle through it at a disgraceful speed. He really beamed with delight and gratitude when I secured him great applause by taking this very *Andante* at my own time.

I got on less well with a Mr. MacFarrinc, a pompous, melancholy Scotsman, whose compositions, I was assured, were held in high esteem by the committee of the Philharmonic Society. He seemed too proud to discuss the interpretation of any of his works with me, and I was therefore relieved when a symphony of his, which did not appeal to me, was laid aside, the substitute chosen being an overture entitled the *Steeple-chase,* which I enjoyed playing, on account of its peculiarly wild, passionate character.

My acquaintance with Beneke (a merchant) and his family was attended by much awkwardness. Wesendonck had given me a letter of recommendation to them, so that I should at least have one 'house' to go to in London. I had to travel a full German mile to Camberwell in response to their invitations, only to discover that I had dropped into the very family whose house Mendelssohn had made his home when in London. The good people did not know what to do with me, apart from congratulating me on the excellence of my Mendelssohn performances, and rewarding me with descriptions of the generous character of the deceased.

Howard, the secretary of the Philharmonic Society, a worthy and agreeable old man, was another person (the only one, he believed) in the circle of my English acquaintances who took the trouble to entertain me. I had to go once or twice to the Italian Opera at Covent Garden with **his** daughter. There I heard *Fidelio,* given in rather grotesque fashion by unclean Germans and voiceless Italians, and with recitatives. I conse-quently managed to evade paying frequent visits to this theatre. When I went to say good-bye to Mr. Howard on leaving London, I was surprised to meet Meyerbeer at his house. He had just arrived in London to conduct his *Nordstern.* As I saw him come in it occurred to me immediately that Howard, whom I had only known as the secretary of the Philharmonic Society, was also the musical critic of the *Illustrated London News;* it was in the latter capacity that the great operatic composer had called upon him. Meyerbeer was absolutely paralysed when he saw me, and this put me into such a frame of mind that we found it impossible to exchange a word. Mr. Howard, who had felt sure that we were acquainted, was much surprised at this, and asked me as I was leaving whether I did not know Meyerbeer. I answered that he had better ask Meyerbeer. On meeting Howard again that evening, I was assured that Meyer-beer had spoken of me in terms of the highest praise. I then suggested his reading certain numbers of the Paris *Gazette musicale,* in which Fétis had, some time before, given a less favourable interpretation of Meyerbeer's views about me. Howard shook his head, and could not understand how two such *great composers* could meet in so strange a manner.

A visit from my old friend Hermann Franck was a pleasant surprise. He was then staying at Brighton, and had come up to London for a few days. We conversed a great deal, and I had to make a considerable effort to put him right in his ideas about me, as he had heard the most wonderful reports from German musicians during the last few years in which our inter-course had been broken off. He was astonished, in the first place, to find me in London, where he considered it impossible for me ever to find a suitable field for my musical tendencies. I did not understand what he meant by my ' tendencies,' but I told him quite simply how I came to accept the invitation of the Philharmonic Society, and that I proposed to fulfil my contract for this year's concerts, and then to go back to my work at Zürich without further ceremony. This sounded quite different to the state of things he had imagined, for he had felt bound to conclude that I proposed to create a stronghold in London from which to conduct a war of extermination against the whole race of German musicians. This was the unanimous explanation of my intentions which he had heard in Germany. Nothing could be more astounding, he said, than the surprising incongruity between the fictitious form in which I appeared to these people, and my real nature, which he had recognised at once on seeing me again. We joked about this, and came to a closer understanding. I was glad to see that he valued as much as I did the works of Schopenhauer, which had become known in the last few years. He expressed his opinion of them with singular decision; he considered that German intellect was destined, either to complete deterioration, in conjunction with the national political situation, or else to an equally complete regeneration, in which Schopenhauer would play his part. He left me — soon to meet his terrible and not less inexplicable fate. Only a few months later, after my return home, I heard of his mysterious death. He was staying, as I said, at Brighton, for the purpose of putting his son, a boy of about sixteen, into the English navy. I had noticed that the son's obstinate determination to serve in this force was repugnant to his father. On the morning of the day on which the ship was to sail, the father's body was found shattered in the street, as the result of a fall from the window, while the son was found lifeless — apparently strangled — on his bed. The mother had died some years previously, and there was no one left to give information as to the terrible occurrence, which, so far as I know, has never to this day been cleared up. Franck had, out of forgetfulness, left a map of London behind on his visit to me; this I kept, as I did not know his address, and it is still in my possession.

I have pleasanter, though not entirely unclouded, recollections of my relations with Semper, whom I also met in London, where he had been settled for some time with his family. He had always seemed to me so violent and morose when in Dresden that I was surprised and moved to admiration by the comparatively calm and resigned spirit with which he bore the terrible interruption to his professional career, and by his

readiness to adapt his talent (which was of an unusually productive order) to the circumstances in which he was placed.
Commissions for large buildings were out of the question for
him in England, but he set his hopes, to a certain extent, on
the patronage accorded him by Prince Albert, as this gave him
some prospects for the future. For the time being he contented
himself with commissions to design decorations for interiors
and luxurious furniture, for which he was well paid. He took
to this work as seriously, from an artistic point of view, as if
it had been a large building. We often met, and I also spent
a few evenings at his house in Kensington, when we invariably
dropped into the old vein of strange, serious humour that helped
us to forget the seamy side of life. The report I was able
to give of Semper after my return home did much to influence
Sulzer in his successful attempt to get him over to Zürich
to build the new Polytechnic.

On various occasions I also visited some not uninteresting
theatres in London, strictly avoiding opera-houses, of course.
I was most attracted by the little Adelphi Theatre in the
Strand, and I frequently made Präger and Lüders go with me.
They acted some dramatised fairy-tales there under the title
of *Christmas*. One of the performances interested me particularly, because it consisted of a subtly connected conglomeration
of the most familiar tales, played straight through, with no
break at the end of the acts. It began with ' The Goose that
laid the Golden Eggs,' and was transformed into ' The Three
Wishes '; this passed into ' Red Riding Hood ' (with the wolf
changed into a cannibal who sang a very comical little couplet),
and finished as ' Cinderella,' varied with other ingredients.
These pieces were in every respect excellently mounted and
played, and I gained a very good notion there of the imaginative
fare in which the English people can find amusement. I found
the performances at the Olympic Theatre less simple and
innocent. Besides witty drawing-room pieces in the French
style, which were very well played there, they acted fairy-
tales such as the *Yellow Dwarf,* in which Robson, an uncommonly popular actor, took the grotesque title-rôle. I saw the
same actor again in a little comedy called *Garrick Fever,* in
which he ends by representing a drunken man who, when people

insisted on taking him for Garrick, undertook the part of Hamlet in this condition. I was greatly astonished by many audacities in his acting on this occasion.

A small out-of-the-way theatre in Marylebone was just then trying to attract the public by Shakespeare's plays. I attended a performance of the *Merry Wives* there, which really amazed me by its correctness and precision. Even a performance of *Romeo and Juliet* at the Haymarket Theatre impressed me favourably, in spite of the great inferiority of the company, on account of its accuracy and of the scenic arrangements, which were no doubt an inheritance from the Garrick tradition. But I still remember a curious illusion in connection with this: after the first act I told Lüders, who was with me, how surprised I was at their giving the part of Romeo to an old man, whose age must at least be sixty, and who seemed anxious to retrieve his long-lost youth by laboriously adopting a sickly-sweet, feminine air. Lüders looked at the programme again, and cried, '*Donnerwetter,* it's a woman!' It was the once famous American, Miss Cushman.

In spite of every effort, I found it impossible to obtain a seat for *Henry VIII.* at the Princess's Theatre. This play had been organised according to the new stage realism, and enjoyed an incredible vogue as a gorgeous spectacular piece, mounted with unusual care.

In the province of music, with which I was more concerned, I have still to mention several of the Sacred-Music Society's concerts, which I attended in the large room at Exeter Hall. The oratorios given there nearly every week have, it must be admitted, the advantage of the great confidence which arises from frequent repetition. Neither could I refuse to recognise the great precision of the chorus of seven hundred voices, which reached quite a respectable standard on a few occasions, particularly in Händel's *Messiah.* It was here that I came to understand the true spirit of English musical culture, which is bound up with the spirit of English Protestantism. This accounts for the fact that an oratorio attracts the public far more than an opera. A further advantage is secured by the feeling among the audience that an evening spent in listening to an oratorio may be regarded as a sort of service, and is almost

as good as going to church.   Every one in the audience holds
a Händel piano score in the same way as one holds a prayer-
book in church.   These scores are sold at the box-office in shilling
editions, and are followed most diligently — out of anxiety, it
seemed to me, not to miss certain points solemnly enjoyed by
the whole audience.   For instance, at the beginning of the
'Hallelujah Chorus' it is considered proper for every one to
rise from his seat.   This movement, which probably originated
in an expression of enthusiasm, is now carried out at each performance of the *Messiah* with painful precision.

All these recollections, however, are merged in the all-
absorbing memory of almost uninterrupted ill-health, caused
primarily, no doubt, by the state of the London climate at
that season of the year, which is notorious all over the world.
I had a perpetual cold, and I therefore followed the advice of
my friends to take a heavy English diet by way of resisting the
effect of the air, but this did not improve matters in the least.
For one thing, I could not get my home sufficiently warmed
through, and the work that I had brought with me was the
first thing to suffer.   The instrumentation of the *Walküre,* which
I had hoped to finish off here, only advanced a paltry hundred
pages.   I was hindered in this principally by the circumstance
that the sketches from which I had to work on the instrumentation had been written down without considering the extent
to which a prolonged interruption of my working humour might
affect the coherence of the sketch.   How often did I sit before
those pencilled pages as if they had been unfamiliar hieroglyphics which I was incapable of deciphering!   In absolute
despair I plunged into Dante, making for the first time a serious
effort to read him.   The *Inferno,* indeed, became a never-to-be-
forgotten reality in that London atmosphere.

But at last came the hour of deliverance from even those
evils which I had brought upon myself by my last assumption
that I might be accepted, not to say wanted, in the great world.
The sole consolation I had was in the deep emotion of my new
friends when I took leave of them.   I hurried home by way of
Paris, which was clothed in its summer glory, and saw people
really promenading again, instead of pushing through the streets
on business.   And so I returned to Zürich, full of cheerful im-

pressions, on the 30th of June, my net profits being exactly one thousand francs.

My wife had an idea of taking up her sour-milk cure again on the Selisberg by Lake Lucerne, and as I thought mountain air would be good for my impaired health also, we decided to move there at once. Our project suffered a brief delay through the fatal illness of my dog Peps. As the result of old age in his thirteenth year, he suddenly exhibited such weakness that we became apprehensive of taking him up the Selisberg, for he could not have borne the fatigue of the ascent. In a few days his agony became alarmingly acute. He grew stupid, and had frequent convulsions, his only conscious act being to get up often from his bed (which was in my wife's room, as he was usually under her care) and stumble as far as my writing-table, where he sank down again in exhaustion. The veterinary surgeon said he could do no more, and as the convulsions gradually became terribly acute, I was advised to shorten the poor animal's cruel agony and free him from his pain by a little prussic acid. We delayed our departure on his account until I at last convinced myself that a quick death would be charity to the poor suffering creature, who was quite past all hope. I hired a boat, and took an hour's row across the lake to visit a young doctor of my acquaintance named Obrist, who had, I knew, come into possession of a village apothecary's stock, which included various poisons. From him I obtained a deadly dose, which I carried home across the lake in my solitary skiff on an exquisite summer evening. I was determined only to resort to this last expedient in case the poor brute were in extremity. He slept that last night as usual in his basket by my bedside, his invariable habit being to wake me with his paws in the morning. I was suddenly roused by his groans, caused by a particularly violent attack of convulsions; he then sank back without a sound; and I was so strangely moved by the significance of the moment that I immediately looked at my watch to impress on my memory the hour at which my extraordinarily devoted little friend died; it was ten minutes past one on the 10th of July. We devoted the next day to his burial, and shed bitter tears over him. Frau Stockar-Escher, our landlady, made over to us a pretty little plot in her garden, and there we buried him, with his basket and cushions. His grave was shown me many years after, but the last time I went to look at the little garden I found that everything had undergone an elegant transformation, and there were no longer any signs of Pep's grave.

At last we really started for the Selisberg, accompanied this time only by the new parrot — a substitute for good old Papo — from the Kreutzberg menagerie, which I had bought for my wife the year before. This one was a very good and intelligent bird also, but I left him entirely to Minna, treating him with invariable kindness, but never making a friend of him. Fortunately for us, our stay in the glorious air of this summer resort, of which we had grown very fond, was favoured by continuous fine weather. I devoted all my leisure, apart from my lonely walks, to making a fair copy of that part of the *Walküre* which was fully scored, and also took up my favourite reading again — the study of Schopenhauer. I had the pleasure of receiving a charming letter from Berlioz, together with *Les Soirées de l'Orchestre,* his new book, which I found inspiriting to read, although the author's taste for the grotesque was as foreign to me here as in his compositions. Here, too, I met young Robert von Hornstein again, who proved himself a pleasant and intelligent companion. I was particularly interested in his quick and evidently successful plunge into the study of Schopenhauer. He informed me that he proposed to settle for some time in Zürich, where Karl Ritter, too, had decided to take permanent winter quarters for his young wife and himself.

In the middle of August we returned to Zürich ourselves, and I was able to devote myself steadily to completing the instrumentation of the *Walküre,* while my relations with former acquaintances remained much the same. From outside I received news of the steady persistence with which my *Tannhäuser* was, little by little, being propagated in German theatres. *Lohengrin,* too, followed in its steps, though without a first meeting with an entirely favourable reception. Franz Dingelstedt, who was at the time manager of the court theatre at Munich, undertook to introduce *Tannhäuser* there, although, thanks to Lachner, the place was not prepossessed in my favour. He seemed to have managed it fairly well; its success, however, according to him, was not so great as to allow of my promised fee being punctually paid. But my income, owing to the conscientious stewardship of my friend Sulzer, was now sufficient to permit me to work without anxiety on that account. But I met with a new vexation when colder weather set in. I suffered from innumerable attacks of erysipelas during the whole winter, each fresh attack (in consequence of some tiny error of diet, or of the least cold) being attended by violent pain. It was obviously the result of the ill effects of the London climate. What pained me most was the frequent interruption of my work on this account. The most I could do was to read when the illness was taking its course. Burnouff's *Introduction à l'Histoire du Bouddhisme* interested me most among my books, and I found material in it for a dramatic poem, which has stayed in my mind ever since, though only vaguely sketched. I may still perhaps work it out. I gave it the title of *Die Sieger*. It was founded on the simple legend of a Tschantala girl, who is received into the dignified order of beggars known as *Clakyamouni,* and, through her exceedingly passionate and purified love for Ananda, the chief disciple of Buddha, herself gains merit. Besides the underlying beauty of this simple material, a curious relation between it and the subsequent development of my musical experience influenced my selection. For to the mind of Buddha the past life (in a former incarnation) of every being who appears before him stands revealed as plainly as the present; and this simple story has its significance, as showing that the past life of the suffering hero and heroine is bound up with the immediate present in this life. I saw at once that the continuous reminiscence in the music of this double existence might perfectly well be presented to the emotions, and I decided accordingly to keep in prospect the working out of this poem as a particularly congenial task.

I had thus two new subjects stamped on my imagination, *Tristan* and *Die Sieger;* with these I was constantly occupied from this time onwards, together with my great work, the *Nibelungen,* the unfinished portion of which was still of gigantic dimensions. The more these projects absorbed me, the more did I writhe with impatience at the perpetual interruptions of my work by these loathsome attacks of illness. About this time Liszt proposed to pay me a visit that had been postponed in the summer, but I had to ask him not to come, as I could not be certain, after my late experiences, of not being tied to a sick-bed during the few days he would be able to give me. Thus I spent the winter, calm and resigned in my productive moments, but moody and irritable towards the outside world, and consequently a source of some anxiety to my friends. I was glad, however, when Karl Ritter's arrival in Zürich allowed him to become more intimate with me again. By his selecting Zürich as a settled home, for the winter months, at any rate, he showed his devotion to me in a way that did me good, and wiped out more than one bad impression. Hornstein had actually managed to come too, but could not stay. He declared he was so nervous that he could not touch a note of the piano, and made no attempt to deny that the fact of his mother's having died insane made him very much afraid of going mad himself. Although this in a way made him interesting, his intellectual gifts were marred by such weakness of character, that we were soon reduced to thinking him fairly hopeless, and we were not inconsolable when he suddenly left Zürich.

My circle had gained considerably of late by the addition of a new acquaintance, Gottfried Keller, a native of Zürich, who had just returned to the welcoming arms of his affectionate fellow-townsmen from Germany, where his writings had brought him some fame. Several of his works — in particular, a longish novel, *Der Grüne Heinrich* — had been recommended to me in favourable though not exaggerated terms by Sulzer. I was therefore surprised to find him a person of extraordinarily shy and awkward demeanour. Every one felt anxious about his prospects on first becoming acquainted with him, and it was indeed this question of his future that was the difficulty. Although everything he wrote showed great original talent, it was obvious at once that they were merely efforts in the direction of artistic development, and the inevitable inquiry arose as to what was to follow and really establish his fame. I kept continually asking him what he was going to do next. In reply he would mention all sorts of fully matured schemes, which would none of them hold water on closer acquaintance. Luckily a government post was eventually found for him (from patriotic considerations, it seemed), where he no doubt did good service, although his literary activity seemed to lie fallow after his early efforts.

Herwegh, another friend of longer standing, was less fortunate. I had worried myself for a long time about him too, trying to think that his previous efforts were merely introductions to really serious artistic achievements. He admitted himself that he felt his best was still to come. It seemed to him that he had all the material — crowds of ' ideas ' — in reserve for a great poetical work; there was nothing wanting but the ' frame ' in which he could paint it all, and this is what he hoped, from day to day, to find. As I grew tired of waiting for it, I set about trying to find the longed-for frame for him myself. He evidently wished to evolve an epic poem on a large scale, in which to embody the views he had acquired. As he had once alluded to Dante's luck in finding a subject like the pilgrimage through hell and purgatory into paradise, it occurred to me to suggest, for the desired frame, the Brahman myth of *Metempsychosis*, which in Plato's version comes within reach of our classical education. He did not think it a bad idea, and I accordingly took some trouble to define the form such a poem would take. He was to decide upon three acts, each containing three songs, which would make nine songs in all. The first act would show his hero in the Asiatic country of his birth; the second, his reincarnation in Greece and Rome; the third, his reincarnation in the Middle Ages and in modern times. All this pleased him very much, and he thought it might come to something. Not so my cynical friend, Dr. Wille, who had an estate in the country where we often met in the bosom of his family. He was of opinion that we expected far too much of Herwegh. Viewed at close quarters he was, after all, only a young Swabian who had received a far larger share of honour and glory than his abilities warranted, through the Jewish halo thrown around him by his wife. In the end I had to shrug my shoulders in silent acquiescence with these hopelessly unkind remarks, as I could, of course, see poor

Herwegh sinking into deeper apathy every year, until in the end he seemed incapable of doing anything.

Semper's arrival in Zürich, which had at last taken place, enlivened our circle considerably. The Federal authorities had asked me to use my influence with Semper to induce him to accept a post as teacher at the Federal Polytechnic. Semper came over at once to have a look at the establishment first, and was favourably impressed with everything. He even found cause for delight, when out walking, in the unclipped trees, ' where one might light upon a caterpillar again,' he said, and decided definitely to migrate to Zürich, and thus brought himself and his family permanently into my circle of acquaintance. True, he had small prospect of commissions for large buildings, and considered himself doomed to play the schoolmaster for ever. He was, however, in the throes of writing a great work on art, which, after various mishaps and a change of publisher, he brought out later under the title, *Der Styl*. I often found him engaged with the drawings for illustrating this book; he drew them himself very neatly on stone, and grew so fond of the work that he declared the smallest detail in his drawing interested him far more than the big clumsy architectural jobs.

From this time forward, in accordance with my manifesto, I would have nothing whatever to do with the ' Musikgesellschaft,' neither did I ever conduct a public performance in Zürich again. The members of this society could not at first be brought to believe that I was in earnest, and I was obliged to bring it home to them by a categorical explanation, in which I dwelt on their slackness and their disregard of my urgent proposals for the establishment of a decent orchestra. The excuse I invariably received was, that although there was money enough among the musical public, yet every one fought shy of heading the subscription list with a definite sum, because of the tiresome notoriety they would win among the townspeople. My old friend, Herr Ott-Imhof, assured me that it would not embarrass him in the least to pay ten thousand francs a year to a cause of that sort, but that from that moment every one would demand why he was spending his income in that way. It would rouse such a commotion that he might easily be brought to account about the administration of his property. This called to my mind Goethe's exclamation at the beginning of his *Erste Schweizer Briefe.*[1] So my musical activities at Zürich ceased definitely from that time.

On the other hand, I occasionally had music at home. Neat and precious copies of Klindworth's pianoforte score of *Rheingold*, as well as of some acts of the *Walküre*, lay ready to hand, and Baumgartner was the first who was set down to see what he could make of the atrociously difficult arrangement. Later on we found that Theodor Kirchner, a musician who had settled at Winterthur and frequently visited Zürich, was better able to play certain bits of the pianoforte score. The wife of Heim, the head of the Glee Society, with whom we were both on friendly terms, was pressed into the service to sing the parts for female voices when I attempted to play some of the vocal parts. She had a really fine voice and a warm tone, and had been the only soloist at the big performances in 1853; only she was thoroughly unmusical, and I had hard work to make her keep in tune, and it was even more difficult to get the time right. Still, we achieved something, and my friends had an occasional foretaste of my *Nibelungen* music.

But I had to exercise great moderation here too, as every excitement threatened to bring on a return of erysipelas. A little party of us were at Karl Ritter's one evening, when I hit upon the idea of reading aloud Hoffmann's *Der Goldene Topf.* I did not notice that the room was getting gradually cooler, but before I had finished my reading I found myself, to every one's horror, with a swollen, red nose, and had to trail laboriously home to tend the malady, which exhausted me terribly

---

[1] This doubtless refers to the following passage: 'And the Swiss call themselves free! These smug bourgeois shut up in their little towns, these poor devils on their precipices and rocks, call themselves free! Is there any limit at all to what one can make people believe and cherish, provided that one preserves the old fable of "Freedom" in spirits of wine for them? Once upon a time they rid themselves of a tyrant and thought themselves free. Then, thanks to the glorious sun, a singular transformation occurred, and out of the corpse of their late oppressor a host of minor tyrants arose. Now they continue to relate the old fable; on all sides it is drummed into one's ears *ad nauseam* — they have thrown off the yoke of the despot and have remained free. And there they are, ensconsed behind their walls and imprisoned in their customs, their laws, the opinion of their neighbours, and their Philistine suburbanism' (*Goethe's Werke, Briefe aus der Schweiz, Erste Abteilung.*) — EDITOR.

every time. During these periods of suffering I became more
and more absorbed in developing the libretto of *Tristan*, whereas
my intervals of convalescence were devoted to the score of the
Walküre, at which I toiled diligently but laboriously, completing the fair copy in March of that year (1856). But my
illness and the strain of work had reduced me to a state of
unusual irritability, and I can remember how extremely bad-
tempered I was when our friends the Wesendoncks came in
that evening to pay a sort of congratulatory visit on the completion of my score. I expressed my opinion of this way of
sympathising with my work with such extraordinary bitterness that the poor insulted visitors departed abruptly in great
consternation, and it took many explanations, which I had
great difficulty in making, to atone for the insult as the days
went on. My wife came out splendidly on this occasion in
her efforts to smooth things over. A special tie between her
and our friends had been formed by the introduction of a very
friendly little dog into our house, which had been obtained
by the Wesendoncks as a successor to my good old Peps. He
proved such a good and ingratiating animal that he soon gained
my wife's tender affection, while I, too, always felt very kindly
towards him. This time I left the choice of a name to my
wife, however, and she invented, apparently as a pendant to
Peps, the name Fips, which I was quite willing for him to
have. But he was always more my wife's friend, as, despite
my great sense of justice, which made me recognise the excellence of these animals, I never was able to become so attached
to them as to Peps and Papo.

About the time of my birthday I had a visit from my old
friend Tichatschek of Dresden, who remained faithful to his
devotion and enthusiasm for me — as far as so uncultured a
person was capable of such emotions. On the morning of my
birthday I was awakened in a touching way by the strains of
my beloved *Adagio* from Beethoven's E minor Quartette. My
wife had invited the musicians in whom I took a special interest
for this occasion, and they had, with subtle delicacy, chosen
the very piece of which I had once spoken with such great
emotion. At our party in the evening Tichatschek sang several things from *Lohengrin*, and really amazed us all by the

brilliancy of voice he still preserved. He had also succeeded, by perseverance, in overcoming the irresolution of the Dresden management, due to their subserviency to the court, with regard to further performances of my operas. They were now being given there again, with great success and to full houses. I took a slight cold on an excursion which we made with our visitor to Brunnen on Lake Lucerne, and thus brought on my thirteenth attack of erysipelas. One of the terrible southern gales, which make it impossible to heat the rooms at Brunnen, made my sufferings this time more acute, added to the fact that I went through with the excursion, in spite of my painful condition, rather than spoil our guest's pleasure by turning back sooner. I was still in bed when Tichatschek left, and I decided at least to try a change of air in the south, because this dreadful malady seemed to me to haunt the locality of Zürich. I chose the Lake of Geneva, and decided to look out for a well-situated country resort in the neighbourhood of Geneva or thereabouts, where I could start on a cure which my Zürich doctor had prescribed. I therefore started for Geneva in the beginning of June. Fips, who was to accompany me into my rural retreat, caused me great anxiety on the journey; I nearly changed my destination, on account of an attempt to dislodge him from my carriage in the train for part of the journey. It was thanks to the energetic way in which I carried my point that I started my cure at Geneva, as I should otherwise probably have gone in a different direction.

In Geneva I put up first at the familiar old Hôtel de l'Écu de Genève, which called up various reminiscences to my mind. Here I consulted Dr. Coindet, who sent me to Mornex on Mont Salève, for the sake of its good air, and recommended me a *pension*. My first thought on arrival was to find a place where I should be undisturbed, and I persuaded the lady who kept the *pension* to make over to me an isolated pavilion in the garden which consisted of one large reception-room. Much persuasion was needed, as all the boarders — precisely the people I wished to avoid — were indignant at having the room originally intended for their social gatherings taken away. But at last I secured my object, though I had to bind myself to vacate my drawing-room on Sunday mornings, because it was then stocked with benches and arranged for a service, which seemed to mean a good deal to the Calvinists among the boarders. I fell in with this quite happily, and made my sacrifice honourably the very first Sunday by betaking myself to Geneva to read the papers. The next day, however, my hostess informed me that the boarders were very annoyed at only being able to hold the service, and not the week-day games in my drawing-room. I was given notice, and looked round for other quarters, which I found in the house of a neighbour.

This neighbour was a Dr. Vaillant, who had taken an equally fine site on which to erect a hydropathic institute. I first made inquiries about warm baths, as my Zürich doctor had advised the use of these with sulphur, but there was no prospect of obtaining any such thing. Dr. Vaillant's whole manner pleased me so much, however, that I told him my troubles. When I asked him which of two things I should drink: hot sulphur bath-water or a certain stinking mineral water, he smiled and said: ' *Monsieur, vous n'êtes que nerveux.* All this will only excite you more; you merely need calming. If you will entrust yourself to me, I promise that you will have so far recovered by the end of two months as never to have erysipelas again.' And he kept his word.

I certainly formed a very different opinion of hydrotherapic methods through this excellent doctor from any I could have acquired from the ' Water Jew ' of Albisbrunnen and other raw amateurs. Vaillant had been famous as a doctor in Paris itself (Lablache and Rossini had consulted him), but he had the misfortune of becoming paralysed in both legs, and after four years of helpless misery, during which he lost his whole practice and sank into utter misery, he came across the original Silesian hydrotherapeutist, Priessnitz, to whom he was conveyed, with the result that he recovered completely. There he learned the method that had proved so effective, refined it from all the brutalities of its inventor, and tried to recommend himself to the Parisians by building a hydro at Meudon. But he met with no encouragement. His former patients, whom he tried to persuade into visiting his institution, merely asked whether there was dancing there in the evening. He found it impossible to keep it up, and it is to this circumstance that I owe my meeting with him there, near Geneva, where he was once more trying to exploit his cure in a practical way. He laid claim to attention, if only by the fact that he strictly limited the number of patients he took into his house, insisting that a doctor could only be responsible for the right application and success of his treatment by being in a position to observe his patients minutely at all hours of the day. The advantage of his system, which benefited me so wonderfully, was the thoroughly calming effect of the treatment, which consisted in the most ingenious use of water at a moderate temperature.

Besides this, Vaillant took a special pleasure in satisfying my wants, particularly in procuring me rest and quiet. For instance, my presence at the common breakfast, which I found exciting and inconvenient, was excused, and I was allowed to make tea in my own room instead. This was an unaccustomed treat for me, and I indulged in it, under cover of secrecy, to excess, usually drinking tea behind closed doors for two hours, while I read Walter Scott's novels, after the fatiguing exertions of my morning cure. I had found some cheap and good French translations of these novels in Geneva, and had brought a whole pile of them to Mornex. They were admirably suited to my routine, which prohibited serious study or work; but, apart from that, I now fully endorsed Schopenhauer's high opinion of this poet's value, of which I had till then been doubtful. On my solitary strolls, it is true, I generally took a volume of Byron with me, because I possessed a miniature edition, to read on some mountain height with a view of Mont Blanc, but I soon left it at home, for I realised that I hardly ever drew it from my pocket.

The only work I permitted myself was the sketching of plans for building myself a house. These, in the end, I tried to work out correctly with all the materials of an architect's draughtsman. I had risen to this bold idea after negotiations on which I entered about that time with Härtel, the music publishers at Leipzig, for the sale of my *Nibelungen* compositions. I demanded forty thousand francs on the spot for the four works, of which half was to be paid me when the building of the house began. The publishers really seemed so far favourably inclined towards my proposals as to make my undertaking possible.

Very soon, however, their opinion of the market value of my works underwent an unhappy change. I could never make out whether this was the result of their having only just examined my poem carefully and decided that it was impracticable, or whether influence had been brought to bear on them from the same quarter to which the opposition directed against most of my undertakings could be traced, and which grew more and more evident as time wore on. Be that as it may, the hope of earning capital for my house-building forsook me; but my architectural studies took their course, and I made it my aim to obtain means to fulfil them.

As the two months I had destined to Dr. Vaillant's treatment were up on the 15th of August, I left the resort which had proved so beneficial, and went straight off on a visit to Karl Ritter, who, with his wife, had taken a lovely and very unassuming little house near Lausanne for the summer months. Both of them had visited me at Mornex, but when I tried to induce Karl to have some cold-water treatment, he declared, after one trial, that even the most soothing method excited him. On the whole, though, we found a good number of agreeable topics to discuss, and he told me he would return to Zürich in the autumn.

I returned home in a fairly good humour with Fips, on whose account I travelled by mail-coach to avoid the obnoxious railway journey. My wife, too, had returned home from her sour-milk cure on the Selisberg, and in addition I found my sister Clara installed, the only one of my relatives who had visited me in my Swiss retreat. We at once made an excursion with her to my favourite spot, Brunnen on Lake Lucerne, and spent an exquisite evening there enjoying the glorious sunset and other beautiful effects of the Alpine landscape. At nightfall, when the moon rose full over the lake, it turned out that a very pretty and effective ovation had been arranged for me (I had been a frequent visitor there) by our enthusiastic and attentive host, Colonel Auf-der-Mauer. Two boats, illuminated by coloured lanterns, came up to the beach facing our hotel, bearing the Brunnen brass band, which was formed entirely of amateurs from the countryside. With Federal staunchness, and without any attempts at punctilious unison, they proceeded to play some of my compositions in a loud and irrefutable manner. They then paid me homage in a little speech, and I replied heartily, after which there was much gripping of all sorts of horny hands on my part, as we drank a few bottles of wine on the beach. For years afterwards I never passed this beach on very frequent visits without receiving a friendly handshake or a greeting. I was generally in doubt as to what the particular boatman wanted of me, but it always turned out that I was dealing with one of the brass bandsmen whose good intentions had been manifested on that pleasant evening.

My sister Clara's lengthy stay with us at Zürich enlivened our family circle very pleasantly. She was the musical one among my brothers and sisters, and I enjoyed her society very much. It was also a relief to me when her presence acted as a damper upon the various household scenes brought on by Minna, who, as a result of the steady development of her heart trouble, grew more and more suspicious, vehement and obstinate.

In October I expected a visit from Liszt, who proposed to make a fairly long stay at Zürich, accompanied by various people of note. I could not wait so long, however, before beginning the composition of *Siegfried,* and I began to sketch the overture on the 22nd of September.

A tinker had established himself opposite our house, and stunned my ears all day long with his incessant hammering. In my disgust at never being able to find a detached house protected from every kind of noise, I was on the point of deciding to give up composing altogether until the time when this indispensable condition should be fulfilled. But it was precisely my rage over the tinker that, in a moment of agitation, gave me the theme for Siegfried's furious outburst against the bungling Mime. I played over the childishly quarrelsome Polter theme in G minor to my sister, furiously singing the words at the same time, which made us all laugh so much that I decided to make one more effort. This resulted in my writing down a good part of the first scene by the time Liszt arrived on 13th October.

Liszt came by himself, and my house at once became a

musical centre. He had finished his *Faust* and *Dante* Symphonies since I had seen him, and it was nothing short of marvellous to hear him play them to me on the piano from the score. As I felt sure that Liszt must be convinced of the great impression his compositions made on me, I felt no scruples in persuading him to alter the mistaken ending of the *Dante* Symphony. If anything had convinced me of the man's masterly and poetical powers of conception, it was the original ending of the *Faust* Symphony, in which the delicate fragrance of a last reminiscence of Gretchen overpowers everything, without arresting the attention by a violent disturbance. The ending of the *Dante* Symphony seemed to me to be quite on the same lines, for the delicately introduced Magnificat in the same way only gives a hint of a soft, shimmering Paradise. I was the more startled to hear this beautiful suggestion suddenly interrupted in an alarming way by a pompous, plagal cadence which, as I was told, was supposed to represent Domenico.

'No!' I exclaimed loudly, 'not that! Away with it! No majestic Deity! Leave us the fine soft shimmer.'

'You are right,' said Liszt. 'I said so too; it was the Princess who persuaded me differently. But it shall be as you wish.'

All well and good — but all the greater was my distress to learn later that not only had this ending of the *Dante* Symphony been preserved, but even the delicate ending of the *Faust* Symphony, which had appealed to me so particularly, had been changed, in a manner better calculated to produce an effect, by the introduction of a chorus. And this was exactly typical of my relations to Liszt and to his friend Caroline Wittgenstein!

This woman, with her daughter Marie, was soon to arrive on a visit too, and the necessary preparations were made for her reception. But before these ladies arrived, a most painful incident occurred between Liszt and Karl Ritter at my house. Ritter's looks alone, and still more, a certain abrupt contradictoriness in his way of speaking, seemed to put Liszt into a state in which he was easily irritated. One evening Liszt was speaking in an impressive tone of the merits of the Jesuits, and

Ritter's inopportune smiles appeared to offend him. At table the conversation turned on the Emperor of the French, Louis Napoleon, whose merits Liszt rather summarily insisted that we should acknowledge, whereas we were, on the whole, anything but enthusiastic about the general state of affairs in France. When Liszt, in an attempt to make clear the important influence of France on European culture, mentioned as an instance the French *Académie*, Karl again indulged in his fatal smile. This exasperated Liszt beyond all bounds, and in his reply he included some such phrase as this: ' If we are not prepared to admit this, what do we prove ourselves to be? Baboons! ' I laughed, but again Karl only smiled — this time, with deadly embarrassment. I discovered afterwards through Bülow that in some youthful squabble he had had the word ' Baboon-face ' hurled at him. It soon became impossible to hide the fact that Ritter felt himself grossly insulted by ' the doctor,' as he called him, and he left my house foaming with rage, not to set foot in it again for years. After a few days I received a letter in which he demanded, first, a complete apology from Liszt, as soon as he came to see me again, and if this were unobtainable, Liszt's exclusion from my house. It distressed me greatly to receive, soon after this, a letter from Ritter's mother, whom I respected very much, reproaching me for my unjust treatment of her son in not having obtained satisfaction for an insult offered him in my house. For a long time my relations with this family, intimate as they had been, were painfully strained, as I found it impossible to make them see the incident in the right light. When Liszt, after a time, heard of it, he regretted the disturbance too, and with praiseworthy magnanimity made the first advance towards a reconciliation by paying Ritter a friendly visit. There was nothing said about the incident, and Ritter's return visit was made, not to Liszt, but to the Princess, who had arrived in the meantime. After this Liszt decided that he could do nothing further; Ritter, therefore, withdrew from our society from this time forward, and changed his winter quarters from Zürich to Lausanne, where he settled permanently.

Not only my own modest residence, but the whole of Zürich seemed full of life when Princess Caroline and her daughter took up their abode at the Hôtel Baur for a time. The curious spell of excitement which this lady immediately threw over every one she succeeded in drawing into her circle amounted, in the case of my good sister Clara (who was still with us at the time), almost to intoxication. It was as if Zürich had suddenly become a metropolis. Carriages drove hither and thither, footmen ushered one in and out, dinners and suppers poured in upon us, and we found ourselves suddenly surrounded by an increasing number of interesting people, whose existence at Zürich we had never even suspected, though they now undoubtedly cropped up everywhere. A musician named Winterberger, who felt it incumbent on him on certain occasions to behave eccentrically, had been brought there by Liszt; Kirchner, the Schumann enthusiast from Winterthur, was practically always there, attracted by the new life, and he too did not fail to play the wag. But it was principally the professors of Zürich University whom Princess Caroline coaxed out of their hole-and-corner Zürich habits. She would have them, one at a time, for herself, and again serve them up *en masse* for us. If I looked in for a moment from my regular midday walk, the lady would be dining alone, now with Semper, now with Professor Köchly, then with Moleschott, and so on. Even my very peculiar friend Sulzer was drawn in, and, as he could not deny, in a manner intoxicated. But a really refreshing sense of freedom and spontaneity pervaded everything, and the unceremonious evenings at my house in particular were really remarkably free and easy. On these occasions the Princess, with Polish patriarchal friendliness, would help the mistress of the house in serving. Once, after we had had some music, I had to give the substance of my two newly conceived poems, *Tristan und Isolde* and *Die Sieger,* to a group which, half sitting, half lying before me, was certainly not without charm.

The crown of our festivities was, however, Liszt's birthday, on the 22nd October, which the Princess celebrated with due pomp at her own house. Every one who was some one at Zürich was there. A poem by Hoffmann von Fallersleben was telegraphed from Weimar, and at the Princess's request was solemnly read aloud by Herwegh in a strangely altered voice. I

then gave a performance, with Frau Heim, of the first act, and a
scene from the second, of the *Walküre,* Liszt accompanying. I
was able to obtain a favourable idea of the effect of our performance by the wish expressed by Dr. Wille to hear these
things badly done, so that he could form a correct judgment, as
he feared he might be seduced by the excellence of our execution. Besides these, Liszt's *Symphonic Poems* were played on
two grand pianos. At the feast, a dispute arose about Heinrich
Heine, with respect to whom Liszt made all sorts of insidious
remarks. Frau Wesendonck responded by asking if he did
not think Heine's name as a poet would, nevertheless, be
inscribed in the temple of immortality.

'Yes, but in mud,' answered Liszt quickly, creating, as may
be conceived, a great sensation.

Unfortunately, our circle was soon to suffer a great loss by
Liszt's illness — a skin eruption — which confined him to his
bed for a considerable period. As soon as he was a little better,
we quickly went to the piano again to try over by ourselves
my two finished scores of *Rheingold* and the *Walküre.* Princess
Marie listened carefully, and was even able to make intelligent
suggestions in connection with a few difficult passages in the
poem.

Princess Caroline, too, seemed to set extraordinary store
on being quite clear as to the actual intrigue concerning the
fate of the gods in my *Nibelungen.* She took me in hand one
day, quite like one of the Zürich professors, *en particulier,* to
clear up this point to her satisfaction. I must confess it was
irrefutably brought home to me that she was anxious to understand the most delicate and mysterious features of the intrigue,
though in rather too precise and matter-of-fact a spirit. In
the end I felt as though I had explained a French society play
to her. Her high spirits in all such things were as marked as
the curious amiability of her nature in other respects; for
when I one day explained to her, in illustration of the first of
these two qualities, that four weeks of uninterrupted companionship with her would have been the death of me, she
laughed heartily. I had reason for sadness in the changes
which I realised had taken place in her daughter Marie; in
the three years since I had first seen her she had faded to an

extraordinary extent. If I then called her a 'child,' I could not now properly describe her as a 'young woman.' Some disastrous experience seemed to have made her prematurely old. It was only when she was excited, especially in the evening when she was with friends, that the attractive and radiant side of her nature asserted itself to a marked extent. I remember one fine evening at Herwegh's, when Liszt was moved to the same state of enthusiasm by a grand-piano abominably out of tune, as by the disgusting cigars to which at that time he was more passionately devoted than to the finer brands. We were all compelled to exchange our belief in magic for a belief in actual witchcraft as we listened to his wonderful phantasies on this pianoforte. To my great horror, Liszt still gave evidence on more than one occasion of an irritability which was thoroughly bad-tempered and even quarrelsome, such as had already manifested itself in the unfortunate scene with young Ritter. For instance, it was dangerous, especially in the presence of Princess Caroline, to praise Goethe. Even Liszt and myself had nearly quarrelled (for which he seemed to be very eager) over the character of Egmont, which he thought it his duty to depreciate because the man allows himself to be taken in by Alba. I had been warned, and had the presence of mind to confine myself to observing the peculiar physiology of my friend on this occasion, and turning my attention to his condition, much more than to the subject of our dispute. We never actually came to blows; but from this time forward I retained throughout my life a vague feeling that we might one day come to such an encounter, in which case it would not fail to be terrific. Perhaps it was just this feeling that acted as a check on me whenever any opportunity arose for heated argument. Goodness knows that I myself had a bad enough reputation with my friends for my own irritability and sudden outbursts of temper!

After I had made a stay of more than six weeks, we had a final opportunity for coming together again before my return from this visit that had meant so much for me. We had agreed to spend a week at St. Gall, where we had an invitation from Schadrowsky, a young musical director, to give our support to a society concert in that district.

We stayed together at the Hecht inn, and the Princess entertained us as if she had been in her own house. She gave me
and my wife a room next her own private apartment. Unfortunately a most trying night was in store for us. Princess
Caroline had one of her severe nervous attacks, and in order
to preclude the approach of the painful hallucination by which
she was tormented at such times, her daughter Marie was
obliged to read to her all through the night in a voice deliberately raised a good deal above its natural pitch. I got fear-
fully excited, especially at what appeared to be an inexplicable
disregard for the peace of one's neighbour implied by such
conduct. At two o'clock in the morning I leaped out of bed,
rang the bell continuously until the waiter awoke, and asked
him to take me to a bedroom in one of the remotest parts of
the inn. We moved there and then, not without attracting the
attention of our neighbours, upon whom, however, the circumstance made no impression. The next morning I was much
astonished to see Marie appear as usual, quite unembarrassed,
and without showing the least traces of anything exceptional
having occurred. I now learned that everybody connected
with the Princess was thoroughly accustomed to such disturbances. Here, too, the house soon filled with all sorts of guests:
Herwegh and his wife came, Dr. Wille and his wife, Kirchner,
and several others, and before long our life in the Hecht
yielded nothing, in point of activity, to our life in the Hôtel
Baur. The excuse for all this, as I have said, was the society
concert of the musical club of St. Gall. At the rehearsal, to
my genuine delight, Liszt impressed two of his compositions,
Orpheus and the *Prelude,* upon the orchestra with complete
success, in spite of the limited resources at his command. The
performance turned out to be a really fine one, and full of
spirit. I was especially delighted with the *Orpheus* and with
the finely proportioned orchestral work, to which I had always
assigned a high place of honour among Liszt's compositions.
On the other hand, the special favour of the public was awarded
to the *Prelude,* of which the greater part was encored. I
conducted the *Eroica* Symphony of Beethoven under very
painful conditions, as I always caught cold on such occasions,
and generally became feverish afterwards. My conception and

rendering of Beethoven's work made a powerful impression upon Liszt, whose opinion was the only one which had any real weight with me. We watched each other over our work with a closeness and sympathy that was genuinely instructive. At night we had to take part in a little supper in our honour, which was the occasion for expressing the noble and deep sentiments of the worthy citizens of St. Gall concerning the significance of our visit. As I was regaled with a most complimentary panegyric by a poet, it was necessary for me to respond with equal seriousness and eloquence. In his dithyrambic enthusiasm, Liszt went so far as to suggest a general clinking of glasses, signifying approval of his suggestion that the new theatre of St. Gall should be opened with a model performance of *Lohengrin*. No one offered any objection. The next day, the 24th of November, we all met, for various festivities, in the house of an ardent lover of music, Herr Bourit, a rich merchant of St. Gall. Here we had some pianoforte music, and Liszt played to us, among other things, the great Sonata of Beethoven in B flat major, at the close of which Kirchner dryly and candidly remarked, ' Now we can truly say that we have witnessed the impossible, for I shall always regard what I have just heard as an impossibility.' On this occasion, attention was called to the twentieth anniversary of my marriage with Minna, which fell on this day, and after the wedding music of *Lohengrin* had been played, we formed a charming procession *à la Polonaise* through the various rooms.

In spite of all these pleasant experiences, I should have been well content to see the end of the business and return to the peace of my home in Zürich. The indisposition of the Princess, however, retarded the departure of my friends for Germany for several days, and we found ourselves compelled to remain together in a state of nervous tension and aimlessness for some time, until at last, on the 27th November, I escorted my visitors to Rorschach, and took my leave of them there on the steamer. Since then I have never seen the Princess or her daughter, nor I think it likely I shall ever meet them again.

It was not without some misgiving that I took leave of my friends, for the Princess was really ill, and Liszt seemed to be much exhausted. I recommended their immediate return to

Weimar, and told them to take care of themselves. Great was my surprise, therefore, when before long I received the news that they were making a sojourn of some duration in Munich. This followed immediately upon their departure, and was also attended with much noisy festivity and occasional artistic gatherings. I was thus led to the conclusion that it was foolish of me to recommend people with such constitutions either to do a thing or to abstain from doing it. I, for my part, returned home to Zürich very much exhausted, unable to sleep, and tormented by the frosty weather at this cold season of the year. I was afraid that I had by my recent method of life subjected myself to a fresh attack of erysipelas. I was very pleased when I awoke the next morning to discover no trace of what I feared, and from that day I continued to sing the praises of my excellent Dr. Vaillant wherever I went. By the beginning of December I had so far recovered as to be able to resume the composition of *Siegfried.* Thus I again entered upon my orderly method of life, with all its insignificance as far as outward things were concerned: work, long walks, the perusal of books, evenings spent with some friend or other of the domestic circle. The only thing that worried me was the regret I still felt for my quarrel with Ritter, in consequence of the unhappy *contre-temps* with Liszt. I now lost touch entirely with this young friend, who in so many ways had endeared himself to me. Before the close of the winter he left Zürich without seeing me again.

During the months of January and February (1857) I completed the first act of *Siegfried,* writing down the composition in full to take the place of the earlier rough pencil draft, and immediately set to work on the orchestration; but I probably carried out Vaillant's instructions with too much zeal. Pursued by the fear of a possible return of erysipelas, I sought to ward it off by a repeated and regular process of sweating once a week, wrapped up in towels, on the hydropathic system. By this means I certainly escaped the dreaded evil, but the effort exhausted me very much, and I longed for the return of the warm weather, when I should be relieved from the severities of this treatment.

It was now that the tortures inflicted upon me by noisy and

musical neighbours began to increase in intensity. Apart from
the tinker, whom I hated with a deadly hatred, and with whom
I had a terrible scene about once a week, the number of pianos
in the house where I lived was augmented. The climax came
with the arrival of a certain Herr Stockar, who played the flute
in the room under mine every Sunday, whereupon I gave up
all hope of composing any more. One day my friends the
Wesendoncks, who had returned from wintering in Paris, unfolded to me a most welcome prospect of the fulfilment of my
ardent wishes in regard to my future place of abode. Wesendonck had already had an idea of having a small house built
for me on a site I was to select for myself. My own plans,
elaborated with a deceptive skill, had been already submitted
to an architect. But the acquisition of a suitable plot of land
was and still remained a great difficulty. In my walks I had
long had my eye on a little winter residence in the district of
Enge, on the ridge of the hill that separates the Lake of Zürich
from Sihlthal. It was called Lavater Cottage, as it had belonged
to that famous phrenologist, and he had been in the habit of
staying there regularly. I had enlisted the services of my
friend Hagenbuch, the Cantonal Secretary, to use all his influence to secure me a few acres of land at this spot as cheaply as
possible. But herein lay the great difficulty. The piece of land
I required consisted of various lots attached to larger estates,
and it turned out that in order to acquire my one plot it would
have been necessary to buy out a large number of different
owners. I put the difficulties of my case before Wesendonck,
and gradually created in him a desire to purchase this wide
tract of land, and lay out a fine site containing a large villa
for his own family. The idea was that I should also have a
plot there. However, the demands made upon my friend in
regard to the preliminaries and to the building of his house,
which was to be on a scale both generous and dignified, were too
many, and he also thought the enclosure of two families within
the same confines might lead in time to inconveniences on both
sides. There happened to be an unpretentious little country
house with a garden which I had admired, and which was
only separated from his estate by a narrow carriage drive; and
this Wesendonck decided to buy for me. I rejoiced beyond

measure when I heard of his intention. The shock experienced by the over-cautious buyer was consequently all the greater when one day he discovered that the present owner, with whom he had negotiated in too timid a fashion, had just sold his piece of land to somebody else. Luckily it turned out that the buyer was a mental specialist, whose sole intention in making the purchase was to instal himself with his lunatic asylum by the side of my friend. This information awakened the most terrible anticipations in Wesendonck, and put the utmost strain upon his energy. He now gave instructions that this piece of land must be acquired at any price from the unfortunate specialist. Thus, after many vexatious vicissitudes, it came into the possession of my friend, who had to pay pretty heavily for it. He allowed me to come into possession at Easter of this year, charging me the same rent as I had paid for my lodging in the Zeltweg, that is to say, eight hundred francs a year.

Our installation in this house, which occupied me heart and soul at the beginning of the spring, was not achieved without many a disappointment. The cottage, which had only been designed for use in summer, had to be made habitable for the winter by putting in heating apparatus and various other necessaries. It is true, that most of the essentials in this respect were carried out by the proprietor; but no end of difficulties remained to be solved. There was not a single thing upon which my wife and I did not constantly differ, and my position as an ordinary middle-class man without a brass farthing of my own made matters no easier. With regard to my finances, however, events took place from time to time which were well calculated to inspire a sanguine temperament with trustful confidence in the future. In spite of the bad performances of my operas, *Tannhäuser* brought me unexpectedly good royalties from Berlin. From Vienna, too, I obtained the wherewithal to give me breathing-space in a most curious way. I was still excluded from the Royal Opera, and I had been assured that so long as there was an imperial court, I was not to dream of a performance of my seditious works in Vienna. This strange state of affairs inspired my old director, Hoffmann of Riga, now director of the Josephstadt Theatre, to venture on the production of *Tannhäuser* with a special

opera company, in a summer theatre built by himself on the
Lerchenfeld outside the boundary of Vienna. He offered me
for every performance which I would license a royalty of a
hundred francs. When Liszt, whom I informed of the matter,
thought this offer was suspicious, I wrote and told him that I
proposed to follow Mirabeau's example with regard to it.
Mirabeau, when he failed to be elected by his peers to the
assembly of Notables, addressed himself to the electors of
Marseilles in the capacity of a linendraper. This pleased Liszt;
and, indeed, I now made my way, by means of the summer
theatre on the Lerchenfeld, into the capital of the Austrian
empire. Of the performance itself the most wonderful accounts
reached me. Sulzer, who on one of his journeys had passed
through Vienna and had witnessed a performance, had complained principally of the darkness of the house, which did not
allow him to read a single word of the libretto, also of its
having rained hard right into the middle of the audience.
Another story was told me some years later by the son-in-law
of Mme. Hérold, the widow of the composer of that name. He
had been in Vienna at that period on his wedding tour, and
had heard this Lerchenfeld performance. The young man assured me that, in spite of all superficial deficiencies, the production there had given him genuine pleasure, and had been
more deeply impressive than the performance in the Berlin
Court Theatre, which he had seen afterwards, and found immeasurably inferior. The energy of my old Riga Theatre
director in Vienna brought me in two thousand francs for
twenty performances of *Tannhäuser*. After such a curious
experience, offering clear proof of my popularity, I may perhaps be excused for having felt confident about the future,
and having relied on incalculable results from my works, even
with regard to actual gain.

While I was thus occupied in arranging the little country
house for which I had longed so much, and working on the
orchestration of the first act of *Siegfried,* I plunged anew
into the philosophy of Schopenhauer and into Scott's novels,
to which I was drawn with a particular affection. I also busied
myself with elucidating my impressions of Liszt's compositions. For this purpose I adopted the form of a letter to

Marie Wittgenstein, which was published in Brendel's musical journal.

When we moved to what I intended to be my permanent refuge for life, I again set myself to consider the means of obtaining a basis for the supply of the necessities of that life. Once again I took up the threads of my negotiations with Härtel about the *Nibelungen,* but I was obliged to put them down as unfruitful, and little calculated to end in any success for this work. I complained of this to Liszt, and openly told him how glad I should be if he would bring this to the ears of the Grand Duke of Weimar (who, from what my friend told me, wished himself still to be regarded as the patron of my *Nibelungen* enterprise), so that he might realise the difficulties I was encountering in the matter. I added that if one could not expect a common bookseller to assume the responsibility of such an extraordinary undertaking, one might well hope that the Prince, whose idea was to make it a point of honour, should take a share, and a serious share, in the necessary preliminaries, among which the development of the work itself must very properly be included. My meaning was, that the Grand Duke should take the place of Härtel, should purchase the work from me, and pay by instalments as the score neared completion; he would thus become the owner, and, later on, could if he liked cover his expenses through a publisher. Liszt understood me very well, but could not refrain from dissuading me from taking up such an attitude towards his Royal Highness.

My whole attention was now directed to the young Grand Duchess of Baden. Several years had passed since Eduard Devrient had been transferred to Karlsruhe by the Grand Duke to be manager of the court theatre there. Since my departure from Dresden I had always kept in touch with Devrient, though our meetings were rare. Moreover, he had written the most enthusiastic letters in appreciation of my pamphlets, *Das Kunstwerk der Zukunft* and *Oper und Drama.* He maintained that the Karlsruhe Theatre was so poorly equipped, that he thought he could not well entertain the idea of a performance of my operas in that house. All these conditions were suddenly changed when the Grand Duke married.

and the Crown Princess's young daughter, who had been turned into a champion of mine by my old friend Alwine Frommann, thus secured a position of independence in Karlsruhe, and was eager in her demand for the performance of my works. My operas were now being produced there also, and Devrient in his turn had the pleasure of informing me of the great interest shown in them by the young Princess, who even frequently attended the rehearsals. This made a very agreeable impression upon me. On my own initiative I expressed my gratitude in an address which I directed to the Grand Duchess herself, enclosing ' Wotan's Abschied ' from the finale of the *Walküre* as a souvenir for her album.

The 20th April was now drawing near, the day on which I was to leave my lodging in the Zeltweg (which had already been let), although I could not occupy the cottage, where the arrangements were not yet complete. The bad weather had given us colds in the course of our frequent visits to the little house, in which masons and carpenters had made themselves at home. In the worst of tempers we spent a week in the inn, and I began to wonder whether it was worth while occupying this new piece of land at all, for I had a sudden foreboding that it would be my fate to wander further afield. Eventually we moved in at the end of April, in spite of everything. It was cold and damp, the new heating apparatus did not provide any warmth, and we were both ill, and could hardly leave our beds. Then came a good omen: the first letter that reached me was one of reconciliation and love from Frau Julie Ritter, in which she told me that the quarrel, brought about by her son's conduct, was at last ended. Beautiful spring weather now set in; on Good Friday I awoke to find the sun shining brightly for the first time in this house: the little garden was radiant with green, the birds sang, and at last I could sit on the roof and enjoy the long-yearned-for peace with its message of promise. Full of this sentiment, I suddenly remembered that the day was Good Friday, and I called to mind the significance this omen had already once assumed for me when I was reading Wolfram's *Parsifal*. Since the sojourn in Marienbad, where I had conceived the *Meistersinger* and *Lohengrin,* I had never occupied myself again with that poem;

now its noble possibilities struck me with overwhelming force, and out of my thoughts about Good Friday I rapidly conceived a whole drama, of which I made a rough sketch with a few dashes of the pen, dividing the whole into three acts.

In the midst of arranging the house, a never-ending task, at which I set to work with all my might, I felt an inner compulsion to work: I took up *Siegfried* again, and began to compose the second act. I had not made up my mind what name to give to my new place of refuge. As the introductory part of this act turned out very well, thanks to my favourable frame of mind, I burst out laughing at the thought that I ought to call my new home ' Fafner's Ruhe,' to correspond with the first piece of work done in it. It was not destined to be so, however. The property continued to be called simply ' Asyl,' and I have designated it under this title in the chart of dates to my works.

The miscarriage of my prospects of support for the *Nibelungen* from the Grand Duke of Weimar fostered in me a continued depression of spirits; for I saw before me a burden of which I knew not how to rid myself. At the same time a romantic message was conveyed to me: a man who rejoiced in the name of Ferreiro introduced himself to me as the Brazilian consul in Leipzig, and told me that the Emperor of Brazil was greatly attracted by my music. The man was an adept in meeting my doubts about this strange phenomenon in the letters which he wrote; the Emperor loved everything German, and wanted me very much to come to him in Rio Janeiro, so that I might conduct my operas in person. As only Italian was sung in that country, it would be necessary to translate my libretto, which the Emperor regarded as a very easy matter, and actually an improvement to the libretto itself. Strange to say, these proposals exercised a very agreeable influence on me. I felt I could easily produce a passionate musical poem which would turn out quite excellent in Italian, and I turned my thoughts once more, with an ever-reviving preference, towards *Tristan und Isolde*. In order in some way to test the intensity of that generous affection for my works protested by the Emperor of Brazil, I promptly sent to Señor Ferreiro the expensively bound volumes containing the pianoforte versions of my three earlier

operas, and for a long time I indulged in the hope of some
very handsome return from their gracious and splendid reception in Rio Janeiro. But of these pianoforte versions, and the
Emperor of Brazil and his consul Ferreiro, I never heard a
single syllable again as long as I lived. Semper, it is true,
involved himself in an architectonic entanglement with this
tropical country: a competition was invited for the building
of a new opera house in Rio; Semper had announced that he
would take part in it, and completed some splendid plans which
afforded us great entertainment, and appeared to be of special
interest, among others, to Dr. Wille, who thought that it must
be a new problem for an architect to sketch an opera house
for a black public. I have not learned whether the results of
Semper's negotiations with Brazil were much more satisfactory than mine; at all events, I know that he did not build
the theatre.

A violent cold threw me for a few days into a state of high
fever; when I recovered from it, my birthday had come. As
I was sitting once more in the evening on my roof, I was surprised at hearing one of the songs of the Three Rhine Maidens,
from the finale of *Rheingold,* which floated to my ears from the
near distance across the gardens. Frau Pollert, whose troubles
with her husband had once stood in the way of a second performance in Magdeburg of my *Liebesverbot* (in itself a very difficult production), had again appeared last winter as a singer,
and also as the mother of two daughters, in the theatrical
firmament of Zürich. As she still had a fine voice, and was full
of goodwill towards me, I allowed her to practise the last act
of *Walküre* for herself, and the Rhine Maidens scenes from the
Rheingold with her two daughters, and frequently in the course
of the winter we had managed to give short performances of
this music for our friends. On the evening of my birthday
the song of my devoted lady friends surprised me in a very
touching way, and I suddenly experienced a strange revulsion
of feeling, which made me disinclined to continue the composition of the *Nibelungen,* and all the more anxious to take up
Tristan again. I determined to yield to this desire, which I
had long nourished in secret, and to set to work at once on
this new task, which I had wished to regard only as a short

interruption to the great one. However, in order to prove to myself that I was not being scared away from the older work by any feeling of aversion, I determined, at all events, to complete the composition of the second act of *Siegfried,* which had only just been begun. This I did with a right good will, and gradually the music of *Tristan* dawned more and more clearly on my mind.

To some extent external motives, which seemed to me both attractive and advantageous to the execution of my task, acted as incentives to make me set to work on *Tristan.* These motives became fully defined when Eduard Devrient came on a visit to me at the beginning of July and stayed with me for three days. He told me of the good reception accorded to my despatch by the Grand Duchess of Baden, and I gathered that he had been commissioned to come to an understanding with me about some enterprise or other; I informed him that I had decided to interrupt my work on the *Nibelungen* by composing an opera, which was bound by its contents and requirements to put me once more into relation with the theatres, however inferior they might be. I should do myself an injustice if I said that this external motive alone inspired the conception of *Tristan,* and made me determine to have it produced. Nevertheless, I must confess that a perceptible change had come over the frame of mind in which, several years ago, I had contemplated the completion of the greater work. At the same time I had come fresh from my writings upon art, in which I had attempted to explain the reasons for the decay of our public art, and especially of the theatre, by seeking to establish some connection between these reasons and the prevailing condition of culture. It would have been impossible for me at that time to have devoted myself to a work which compelled me to study its immediate production at one of our existing theatres. It was only an utter disregard of these theatres, as I have taken occasion to observe before, that could determine me to take up my artistic work again. With regard to the *Nibelungen* dramas, I was compelled to adhere without flinching to the one essential stipulation that it could only be produced under quite exceptional conditions, such as those I afterwards described in the preface to the printed edition of the poem. Nevertheless, the successful popularisation of my earlier operas had so far influenced my frame of mind that, as I approached the completion of more than half of my great work, I felt I could look forward with growing confidence to the possibility that this too might be produced.   Up to this point Liszt had been the only person to nourish the secret hope of my heart, as he was confident that the Grand Duke of Weimar would do something for me, but to judge from my latest experience these prospects amounted to nothing, while I had grounds for hoping that a new work of similar design to *Tannhäuser* or *Lohengrin* would be taken up everywhere with considerable alacrity.   The manner in which I finally executed the plan of *Tristan* shows clearly how little I was thinking of our operatic theatres and the scope of their capabilities.   Nevertheless, I had still to fight a continuous battle for the necessaries of life, and I succeeded in deceiving myself so far as to persuade myself that in interrupting the composition of the *Nibelungen* and taking up *Tristan,* I was acting in the practical spirit of a man who carefully weighs the issues at stake.   Devrient was much pleased to hear that I was undertaking a work that could be regarded as practical.   He asked me at which theatre I contemplated producing my new work.   I answered that naturally I could only have in view a theatre in which it would be possible for me to superintend the task of production in person.   My idea was that this would either be in Brazil or, as I was excluded from the territory of the German Confederation, in one of the towns lying near the German frontiers, which I presumed would be able to place an operatic company at my disposal.   The place I had in my mind was Strasburg, but Devrient had many practical reasons for being wholly opposed to such an undertaking; he was of opinion that a performance in Karlsruhe could be arranged more easily and would meet with greater success.   My only objection to this was, that in that town I should be debarred from taking a personal share in the study and production of my work.   Devrient, however, thought that, as far as this was concerned, I might feel justified in entertaining some hope, as the Grand Duke of Baden was so well disposed towards me, and took an active interest in my work.   I was highly delighted to learn this.   Devrient also spoke with great

sympathy of the young tenor Schnorr, who, besides possessing
admirable gifts, was keenly attracted by my operas. I was
now in the best of tempers, and acted the host to Devrient
for all I was worth. One morning I played and sang to him
the whole of the *Rheingold,* which seemed to give him great
pleasure. Half seriously, and half in joke, I told him that I
had written the character of Mime especially for him, and that
if, when the work was ready, it was not too late, he might have
the pleasure of taking the part. As Devrient was with me, he
had, of course, to do his share of reciting. I invited all the
friends in our circle, including Semper and Herwegh, and
Devrient read us the Mark Antony scenes from Shakespeare's
Julius Cæsar. So happy was his interpretation of the part,
that even Herwegh, who had approached the recitation from
its outset in a spirit of ridicule, freely acknowledged the success
of the practised actor's skilful manipulation. Devrient wrote
a letter from my house to the Grand Duke of Baden, telling him
his impressions about me and what he had found me like. Soon
after his departure I received an autograph letter from the
Grand Duke, couched in very amiable terms, in which he first
thanked me most profusely for the souvenir I had presented
to his wife for her album, and at the same time declared his
intention of championing my cause, and, above all, of securing
my return to Germany.

From this time forward my resolve to produce *Tristan* had
to be seriously entertained, as it was written in plain letters
in my book of fate. To all these circumstances I was indebted
for the continuation of the favourable mood in which I now
brough the second act of *Siegfried* to a close. My daily walks
were directed on bright summer afternoons to the peaceful
Sihlthal, in whose wooded surroundings I listened long and
attentively to the song of the forest birds, and I was astonished
to make the acquaintance of entirely new melodies, sung by
singers whose forms I could not see and whose names I did not
know. In the forest scene of *Siegfried* I put down, in artistic
imitation of nature, as much as I could remember of these airs.
At the beginning of August I had carefully sketched the composition of the second act. I was glad I had reserved the third
act with the awakening of Brünhilda for the time when I

should again be able to go on with the opera, for it seemed to me that all the problems in my work were now happily solved, and that all that remained was to get pure joy out of it.

As I firmly believed in the wisdom of husbanding my artistic power, I now prepared to write out *Tristan*. A certain strain was put upon my patience at this point by the arrival of the excellent Ferdinand Präger from London. His visit, in other respects, was a source of genuine pleasure to me, for I was bound to recognise in him a faithful and life-long friend. The only difficulty was, that he laboured under the delusion that he was exceptionally nervous, and that he was persecuted by fate. This was a source of considerable annoyance to me, as with the best will in the world, I could not muster up any sympathy for him. We helped ourselves out of the dilemma by an excursion to Schaffhausen, where I paid my first visit to the famous Rhine Falls, which did not fail to impress me duly.

About this time the Wesendoncks moved into their villa, which had now been embellished by stucco-workers and upholsterers from Paris. At this point a new phase began in my relations with this family, which was not really important, but nevertheless exercised considerable influence on the outward conduct of my life. We had become so intimate, through being such near neighbours in a country place, that it was impossible to avoid a marked increase in our intimacy if only through meeting one another daily. I had often noticed that Wesendonck, in his straightforward open manner, had shown uneasiness at the way in which I made myself at home in his house. In many things, in the matter of heating and lighting the rooms, and also in the hours appointed for meals, consideration was shown me which seemed to encroach upon his rights as master of the house. It needed a few confidential discussions on the subject to establish an agreement which was half implied and half expressed. This understanding had a tendency, as time wore on, to assume a doubtful significance in the eyes of other people, and necessitated a certain measure of precaution in an intimacy which had now become exceedingly close. These precautions were occasionally the source of great amusement to the two parties who were in the secret. Curiously enough, this closer association with my neighbour coincided with the time when I began to work out my libretto, *Tristan und Isolde*.

Robert Franz now arrived in Zürich on a visit. I was delighted by his agreeable personality, and his visit reassured me that no deep significance need be attached to the somewhat strained relations which had sprung up between us since the time when he took up the cudgels for me on the occasion of the production of *Lohengrin*. The misunderstanding had been chiefly due to the intermeddling of his brother-in-law Heinrich (who had written a pamphlet about me). We played and sang together; he accompanied me in some of his songs, and my compositions for the *Nibelungen* seemed to please him. But one day, when the Wesendoncks asked him to dinner to meet me, he begged that he might be alone with the family without any other guests, because if I were there he would not attain the importance by which he set so much store. We laughed over this, and I did so the more heartily because I was sometimes quite grateful to be saved the trouble of talking to people so curiously uncommunicative as I found Franz to be. After he left us, he never sent us a word of himself or his doings again.

When I had almost finished the first act of *Tristan*, a newly married couple arrived in Zürich, who certainly had a prominent claim on my interest. It was about the beginning of September that Hans von Bülow arrived with his young wife Cosima (a daughter of Liszt's) at the Raben Hotel. I invited them to my little house, so that they might spend the whole time of their stay in Zürich with me, as their visit was mainly on my account.

We spent the month of September together most pleasantly. In the meanwhile I completed the libretto of *Tristan und Isolde*, and at the some time Hans made me a fair copy of each act. I read it over, act by act, to my two friends, until at last I was able to get them all together for a private reading, which made a deep impression on the few intimate friends who composed the audience. As Frau Wesendonck appeared to be particularly moved by the last act, I said consolingly that one ought not to grieve over it, as, under any circumstances, in a matter so grave things generally turned out in this way, and Cosima heartily agreed. We also had a good deal of music together, as in Bülow I had at last found the right man to play Klind-worth's atrocious arrangement of my *Nibelungen* scores. But the two acts of *Siegfried,* which had only been written down as rough drafts, were mastered by Hans with such consummate skill that he could play them as if they had really been arranged for the piano. As usual, I took all the singing parts; some-times we had a few listeners, amongst whom Mme. Wille was the most promising. Cosima listened silently with her head bowed; if pressed for an expression of opinion, she began to cry.

Towards the end of September my young friends left me to travel back to their destination in Berlin, and begin their married life like good citizens.

For the time being we had sounded a sort of funeral peal over the *Nibelungen* by playing so much of it, and it was now completely laid aside. The consequence was, that when later on we took it out of its folio for similar gatherings, it wore a lack-lustre look, and grew ever fainter, as if to remind us of the past. At the beginning of October, however, I at once began to compose *Tristan,* finishing the first act by the new year, when I was already engaged in orchestrating the prelude. During that time I developed a dreamy, timorous passion for retirement. Work, long walks in all winds and weathers, evenings spent in reading Calderon — such was my mode of life, and if it was disturbed, I was thrown into the deepest state of irritation. My connection with the world confined itself almost entirely to my negotiations with the music-seller Härtel about the publication of *Tristan.* As I had told this man that, by way of contrast to the immense undertaking of the *Nibelungen,* I had in my mind a practicable work, which, in its demands upon the producer, confined itself, to all intents and purposes, to the engagement of a few good singers, he showed such keenness to take up my offer that I ventured to ask four hundred louis d'or. Thereupon Härtel answered that I was to read his counter offer, made, in a sealed letter which he enclosed, only on condition that I at once agreed to waive my own demands entirely, as he did not think the work I pro-posed to write was one which could be produced without diffi-culties. In the sealed enclosure I found that he offered me only one hundred louis d'or, but he undertook, after a period of five years, to give me a half-share in the proceeds, with the alternative of buying out my rights for another hundred louis d'or. With these terms I had to comply, and soon set to work to orchestrate the first act, so as to let the engraver have one batch of sheets at a time.

Besides this, I was interested at that time in the expected crisis of the American money market in the month of November, the consequences of which, during a few fatal weeks, threatened to endanger the whole of my friend Wesendonck's fortune. I remember that the impending catastrophe was borne with great dignity by those who were likely to be its victims; still the possibility of having to sell their house, their grounds, and their horses cast an unavoidable gloom over our evening meetings; and, after a while, Wesendonck went away to make arrangements with various foreign bankers.

During that time I spent the mornings in my house composing *Tristan,* and every evening we used to read Calderon, which made a deep and permanent impression upon me, for I had become fairly familiar with Spanish dramatic literature, thanks to Schack. At last the dreaded American crisis happily blew over, and it was soon apparent that Wesendonck's fortune had considerably increased. Again, during the winter evenings, I read *Tristan* aloud to a wider circle of friends. Gottfried Keller was pleased with the compact form of the whole, which really contained only three full scenes. Semper, however, was very angry about it: he objected that I took everything too seriously, and said that the charm in the artistic construction of such material consisted in the fact that the tragic element was broken up in such a way that one could extract enjoyment even from its most affecting parts. That was just what pleased him in Mozart's *Don Juan,* one met the tragic types there, as if at a masquerade, where even the domino was preferable to the plain character. I admitted that I should get on much more comfortably if I took life more seriously and art more lightly, but for the present I intended to let the opposite relations prevail.

As a matter of fact people shook their heads. After I

had sketched the first act of the composition, and had developed the character of my musical production more precisely. I thought with a peculiar smile of my first idea of writing this work as a sort of Italian opera, and I became less anxious at the absence of news from Brazil. On the other hand, my attention was particularly drawn at the end of this year to what was going on in Paris in regard to my operas. A young author from that city wrote asking me to entrust him with the translation of my *Tannhäuser,* as the manager of the Théâtre Lyrique, M. Carvalho, was taking steps to produce that opera in Paris. I was alarmed at this, as I was afraid that the copyright of my works had not been secured in France, and that they might dispose of them there at their own sweet will. To this I most strongly objected. I was well aware how this undertaking would be carried out, from an account I had read a short time before of the performance of Weber's *Euryanthe* at that very Théâtre Lyrique, and of the objectionable elaborations or rather mutilations which had been effected for the purposes of production. As Liszt's elder daughter Blandine had recently married the famous lawyer E. Ollivier, and I could consequently rely on substantial help from them, I made up my mind to go to Paris for a week, and look after the matter about which I had been approached, and, at any rate, secure my author's rights legally. In addition to this I was in a very melancholy state of mind, to which overwork and constant occupation on the kind of task that Semper had, perhaps with justice, denounced as being too serious, had contributed by reason of the strain on my mental powers.

If I remember rightly, I gave evidence of this state of mind (which curiously enough led me to despise all worldly cares) in a letter I wrote to my old friend Alwine Frommann on New Year's Eve 1857.

With the beginning of the new year 1858 the necessity for a break in my work became so manifest, that I positively dreaded beginning the instrumentation of the first act of *Tristan und Isolde,* until I had allowed myself the trip for which I longed. For at that moment, unfortunately, neither Zürich, nor my home, nor the company of my friends afforded me any relaxation.

Even the agreeable and immediate proximity of the Wesendonck family increased my discomfort, for it was really intolerable to me to devote all my evenings to conversations and entertainments in which my kind friend Otto Wesendonck felt obliged to take as much part as myself and the rest of us. His apprehension that everything in his house would very soon follow my lead instead of his, gave him that peculiar aggressiveness with which a man who believes himself neglected interpolates himself like an extinguisher into every conversation carried on in his presence.

All this soon became oppressive and irksome to me, and no one who did not realise my condition, and show signs of sympathising with it, could excite my interest, and even then it was a very languid one. So I made up my mind in the middle of the severe winter weather, and notwithstanding the fact that for the present I was quite unprovided with the necessary means, and was consequently obliged to take all sorts of tiresome precautions, to carry out my excursion to Paris. I felt a growing presentiment that I was going away never to return. I reached Strasburg on the 15th of January, too much upset to travel any further just then. From there I wrote to Eduard Devrient at Karlsruhe, asking him to request the Grand Duke to send an adjutant to meet me at Kehl on my return from Paris, to accompany me on a visit to Karlsruhe, as I particularly wanted to become acquainted with the artists who were to sing in *Tristan*. A little later I was taken to task by Eduard Devrient for my impertinence in expecting to have grand-ducal adjutants at my disposal, from which I gathered that he had attributed my request to a desire for some mark of honour, whereas my idea had been that that was the only possible way in which I, a political outlaw, could venture to visit Karlsruhe, though my object was a purely professional one. I could not help smiling at this strange misconception, but I was also startled at this proof of shallowness in my old friend, and began to wonder what he might do next.

I was trudging wearily along in the twilight through the public promenade of Strasburg, to restore my overwrought nerves, when I was suddenly taken aback by seeing on a theatre poster the word *TANNHÄUSER*.

Looking at the bill more closely, I saw that it was the Overture to *Tannhäuser* that was to be given as a prelude to a French play. The exact meaning of this I did not quite understand, but of course I took my seat in the theatre, which was very empty. The orchestra, looking all the larger from contrast with the empty house, was assembled in a huge space and was a very strong one. The rendering given of my overture under the conductor's baton was really a very good one.

As I was sitting rather near the front in the stalls, I was recognised by the man who was playing the kettledrum, as he had taken part in my Zürich performances in 1853. The news of my presence spread like wildfire through the whole orchestra until it reached the ears of the conductor, and led to great excitement. The small audience, who had evidently put in appearance simply on account of the French play, and who were not at all inclined to pay any particular attention to the overture, were very much astonished when, at the conclusion of the overture, the conductor and the whole orchestra turned round in the direction of my stall, and gave vent to enthusiastic applause, which I had to acknowledge with a bow. All eyes followed me eagerly as I left the hall after this scene, to pay my respects to the conductor. It was Herr Hasselmann, a native of Strasburg, and apparently a very good-natured, amiable fellow. He accompanied me to my hotel and, amongst other things, told me the circumstances connected with the performance of my overture. These somewhat surprised me. According to the terms of a legacy left by a wealthy citizen of Strasburg, a great lover of music, who had already contributed very largely to the building of the theatre, the orchestra, whose flourishing condition was due to his beneficence, had to give, during the usual theatrical performances, one of the greater instrumental works with a full band once a week. This time, as it happened, it was the turn for the overture to *Tannhäuser*. The feeling that was uppermost in my mind was one of envy that Strasburg should have produced a citizen whose like had never seen the light of day in any of the towns in which I had been connected with music, and more particularly Zürich.

Whilst I was discussing the state of music in Strasburg with Conductor Hasselmann, Orsini's famous attempt on the life of the Emperor took place in Paris. I heard some vague rumours of it on my journey the following morning, but it was not until the 17th, on my arrival in Paris, that I heard the full details of it from the waiter in my hotel. I looked upon this event as a malicious stroke of fate, aimed at me personally. Even at breakfast on the following morning, I feared I should see my old acquaintance, the agent of the Ministry of the Interior, walk in and demand my instant departure from Paris as a political refugee. I presumed that as a visitor at the Grand Hôtel du Louvre, then newly opened, I should be regarded by the police with greater respect, than at the little hotel at the corner of the Rue des Filles St. Thomas, where I had once stayed for the sake of economy. I had originally intended to take up my quarters at an hotel I knew in the Rue le Pelletier, but the outrage had been perpetrated just at that spot, and the principal criminals had been pursued and arrested there. It was a strange coincidence! Supposing I had arrived in Paris just two days earlier, and had gone there!!!

After thus apostrophising the demon of my fate, I hunted up M. Ollivier and his young wife. In the former I soon found a very taking and active friend, who at once resolutely took in hand the matter which was my chief object in Paris. One day we called on a notary who was a friend of his, and who seemed to be under an obligation to him. I there gave Ollivier a formal and carefully considered power of attorney, to represent my proprietary rights as author, and in spite of many official formalities in the way of stamps I was treated with perfect hospitality, so that I felt I was well sheltered under my friend's protection. In the course of my walks with my friend Ollivier in the Palais de Justice and in the Salle des pas perdus, I was introduced to the most celebrated lawyers in the world strolling about there in their berrettas and robes, and I was soon on such intimate terms with them that they formed a circle around me, and made me explain the subject of *Tannhäuser*. This pleased me greatly. I was no less delighted by my conversation with Ollivier regarding his political views and position. He still believed in the Republic which would come to stay after the inevitable overthrow of the Napoleonic rule. He and his friends did not intend to provoke a revolution, but they held themselves in readiness for the moment when it should come, as it necessarily must, and fully resolved this time not to give it up again to the plunder of base conspirators. In principle he agreed with the logical conclusions of socialism; he knew and respected Proudhon, but not as a politician; he thought nothing could be founded on a durable basis except through the initiative of political organisation. By means of simple legislation, which had already passed several enactments protecting the public good against the abuses of private privilege, even the boldest demands for a commonwealth based on equal rights for all would gradually be met.

I now noticed with great satisfaction that I had made considerable progress in the development of my character, as I could listen to and discuss these and other topics without getting into a state of excitement, as I used formally to do in similar discussions.

Blandine impressed me at the same time most favourably with her gentleness, her cheerfulness, and a certain quiet wit added to a quick mental perception. We very soon understood each other; the slightest suggestion sufficed to create a mutual understanding on any subject in which we were interested.

Sunday arrived, and with it a concert at the Conservatoire. As I had hitherto been present only at rehearsals, and had never got so far as the performances, my friends succeeded in procuring a seat for me in the box of Mme. Hérold, the widow of the composer, a woman of sympathetic disposition, who at once declared herself warmly in favour of my music. It is true her knowledge of it was slight, but she had been won over to it by the enthusiasm of her daughter and son-in-law, who, as I have previously mentioned, had heard *Tannhäuser* during their honeymoon in Vienna and Berlin. This was really a pleasant surprise. Added to this, I now heard for the first time in my life a performance of Haydn's *Seasons*, which the audience enjoyed immensely, as they thought the steady florid vocal cadences, which are so rare in modern music, but which so frequently occur at the conclusion of the musical phrases in Haydn's music, very original and charming. The rest of the day was spent very pleasantly in the bosom of the Hérold family. Towards the end of the evening a man came in whose appearance was hailed with marked attention. This was Herr Scudo, who, I found out afterwards, was the famous musical editor of the *Revue des deux Mondes*. His influence with other journals was considerable, but so far it had certainly not been in my favour. The kind hostess wished me to make his acquaintance, so that he might have a good impression of me, but I told her such an object could not be attained through the medium of a drawing-room conversation, and later on I was confirmed in my opinion that the reasons why a gentleman of this type, who possesses no knowledge of the subject, declares himself hostile to an artist, having nothing whatever to do with his convictions or even with his approval or disapproval. On a subsequent occasion these good people had to suffer for having interested themselves in me, as, in a report of my concerts by Herr Scudo, they were held up to ridicule as a family of strong democratic tendencies.

I now looked up my friend Berlioz, whose acquaintance I had recently renewed in London, and on the whole I found him kindly disposed.

I informed him that I had only just come to Paris on a short pleasure trip. He was at that time busy composing a grand opera, *Die Trojaner*. In order to get an impression of the work, I was particularly anxious to hear the libretto Berlioz had written himself, and he spent an evening reading it out to me. I was disappointed in it, not only as far as it was concerned, but also by his singularly dry and theatrical delivery. I fancied that in the latter I could see the character of the music to which he had set his words, and I sank into utter despair about it, as I could see that he regarded this as his masterpiece, and was looking forward to its production as the great object of his life.

I also received an invitation with the Olliviers from the Erard family, at whose house I again met my old friend the widow of Spontini. We spent a rather charming evening

there, during which, strange to say, I had to be responsible
for the musical entertainment at the piano. They declared
they had thoroughly entered into the spirit of the various
selections I had played from my operas in my now characteristic fashion, and that they had enjoyed them immensely.
At any rate, such intimate heartfelt playing had never before
been heard in that gorgeous drawing-room. Apart from this, I
made one great acquisition, through the friendly courtesy of
Mme. Erard and her brother-in-law Schäffer, who since
the death of her husband had carried on the business, in
the shape of a promise of one of the celebrated grand-pianos
of their manufacture. With this the gloom of my excursion
to Paris seemed to be turned into light, for I was so rejoiced
at it, that I looked upon every other result as chimerical,
and upon this as the only reality.

After that I left Paris on the 2nd of February in a more
cheerful frame of mind, and on my homeward journey went to
look up my old friend Kietz in Epernay, where M. Paul
Chandon, who had known Kietz since boyhood, had interested
himself in the ruined painter by taking him into his house, and
giving him a number of commissions for portraits. As soon as I
arrived I was irresistibly drawn into Chandon's hospitable
house, and could not refuse to remain there for a couple of
days. I found in Chandon a passionate admirer of my operas,
particularly of *Rienzi,* the first performance of which he had
witnessed during his Dresden days. I also visited the marvellous wine vaults at Champagne, which extended for miles into
the heart of the rocky ground. Kietz was painting a portrait
in oils, and the opinion entertained by every one that it would
very soon be finished rather amused me.

After much superfluous entertainment I at last freed myself
from this unexpected hospitality and returned to Zürich on
the 5th of February, where I had arranged by letter for an
evening party immediately after my arrival, as I thought I
had much to relate which I could tell them all collectively
instead of by means of long and wearisome communications
to individual friends. Semper, who was one of the company,
was annoyed that he had stayed in Zürich whilst I had
been in Paris, and he became quite furious over my cheerful

adventures and declared I was an impudent child of fortune, while he looked upon it as the greatest calamity that he should be chained to that wretched hole Zürich. How I smiled inwardly at his envy of my fortune!

My affairs were making but little progress, as my operas had been sold to almost every theatre and I had very little left out of the proceeds. I now heard nothing about all these performances except that they were yielding very little money. I resigned myself to the fact of bringing out *Rienzi*, as it was just suited to our inferior class of theatre. Before offering it for sale, it was desirable to have it performed again in Dresden; but this, it was said, was impossible on account of the impression created by the Orsini outrage. So I worked on at the instrumentation of the first act of *Tristan*, and during that time I could not help feeling that most probably other objections, besides those of political captiousness, would be raised against the spread of this work. I therefore continued my work vaguely and somewhat hopelessly.

In the month of March Frau Wesendonck informed me that she thought of having a kind of musical entertainment in her house to celebrate her husband's birthday. She had a predilection for a little serenade music, which, with the help of eight instrumentalists from Zürich, I had arranged during the winter for the occasion of her own birthday. The pride of the Wesendonck villa was a spacious hall which had been very elegantly decorated by Parisian stucco-workers, and I had once remarked that music would not sound at all badly there. We had tested it on a small scale, but now it was to be tried on a larger one. I offered to bring together a respectable orchestra to perform fragments of the Beethoven symphonies, consisting mainly of the brighter parts, for the entertainment of the company. The necessary preparations required a good deal of time, and the date of the birthday had to be overstepped. As it was, we had nearly reached Easter, and our concert took place almost at the end of March. The musical At Home was most successful. A full orchestra for the Beethoven pieces played with the greatest éclat under my conductorship, to the assembly of guests scattered about in the surrounding rooms, selections from the symphonies. Such an unprecedented home

concert seemed to throw every one into a great state of excitement.

The young daughter of the house presented me at the beginning of the performance with an ivory baton, carved from a
design by Semper, the first and only complimentary one I
ever received. There was no lack of flowers and ornamental
trees, under which I stood when conducting, and when to suit
my taste for musical effect we concluded, not with a loud, but
with a deeply soothing piece, like the *Adagio* from the Ninth
Symphony, we felt that Zürich society had indeed witnessed
something quite unique, and my friends on whom I had
bestowed this mark of distinction were deeply touched by it.

This festival left on me the most melancholy impressions;
I felt as though I had reached the meridian of my life, that I
had in fact passed it, and that the string of the bow was over-
stretched. Mme. Wille told me afterwards that she had been
overcome by similar feelings on that evening. On the 3rd of
April I sent the manuscript of the score of the first act of
Tristan und Isolde to Leipzig to be engraved; I had already
promised to give Frau Wesendonck the pencil-sketch for the
instrumentation of the prelude, and I sent this to her accompanied by a note in which I explained to her seriously and
calmly the feelings that animated me at the time. My wife
had for some time been anxious as to her relations with our
neighbour; she complained with increasing bitterness that she
was not treated by her with the attention due to the wife of a
man whom Frau Wesendonck was so pleased to welcome in
her house, and that when we did meet, it was rather by reason
of that lady's visits to me than to her. So far she had not
really expressed any jealousy. As she happened to be in the
garden that morning, she met the servant carrying the packet
for Frau Wesendonck, took it from him and opened the letter.
As she was quite incapable of understanding the state of mind
I had described in the letter, she readily gave a vulgar interpretation to my words, and accordingly felt herself justified in
bursting into my room and attacking me with the most extraordinary reproaches about the terrible discovery she had made.
She afterwards admitted that nothing had vexed her so much
as the extreme calmness and apparent indifference with which

I treated her foolish conduct. As a matter of fact I never said a word; I hardly moved, but simply allowed her to depart. I could not help realising that this was henceforth to be the intolerable character of the conjugal relations I had resumed eight years before. I told her peremptorily to keep quiet and not be guilty of any blunder either in judgment or in act, and tried to make her realise to what a serious state of affairs this foolish occurrence had brought us. She really seemed to understand what I meant, and promised to keep quiet and not to give way to her absurd jealousy. Unfortunately the poor creature was already suffering from a serious development of heart disease, which affected her temper; she could not throw off the peculiar depression and terrible restlessness which enlargement of the heart causes, and only a few days after she felt that she must relieve her feelings, and the only possible way in which she could think of doing so was by warning our neighbour, Frau Wesendonck, with an emphasis she thought was well meant, against the consequences of any imprudent intimacy with me.

As I was returning from a walk I met Herr Wesendonck and his wife in their carriage just starting for a drive. I noticed her troubled demeanour in contrast to the peculiarly smiling and contented expression of her husband. I realised the position clearly when I afterwards met my wife looking wonderfully cheerful. She held out her hand to me with great generosity, assuring me of her renewed affection. In answer to my question, whether she had by any chance broken her promise, she said confidently that like a wise woman she had been obliged to put things into proper order. I told her she would very probably experience some very unpleasant consequences through breaking her word. In the first place, I thought it essential she should take steps to improve her health as we had previously arranged, and told her she had better go as soon as possible to the health resort she had been recommended at Brestenberg on the Hallwyler Lake. We had heard wonderful accounts of the cures of heart disease which the doctor there had effected, and Minna was quite prepared to submit to his treatment. A few days later, therefore, I took her and her parrot to the pleasantly situated and well-appointed watering-place which was about three hours distant. Meantime, I avoided asking any questions as to what had taken place in regard to our neighbours. When I left her at Brestenberg and took my leave she quite seemed to realise the painful seriousness of our position. I could say very little to comfort her, except that I would try, in the interests of our future life together, to mitigate the dreaded consequences of her having broken her word.

On my return home I experienced the unpleasant effects of my wife's conduct towards our neighbour. In Minna's utter misconstruction of my purely friendly relations with the young wife, whose only interest in me consisted in her solicitude for my peace of mind and well-being, she had gone so far as to threaten to inform the lady's husband. Frau Wesendonck felt so deeply insulted at this, as she was perfectly unconscious of having done any wrong, that she was absolutely astounded at me, and said she could not conceive how I could have led my wife into such a misunderstanding. The outcome of this disturbance was that, thanks to the discreet mediation of our mutual friend Mme. Wille, I was absolved from any responsibility for my wife's conduct; still, I was given to understand that henceforth it would be impossible for the injured lady to enter my house again, or indeed to continue to have any intercourse with my wife. They did not seem to realise, and would not admit, that this would entail the giving up of my home and my removal from Zürich. I hoped that although my relations with these good friends had been disturbed, they were not really destroyed, and that time would smooth things over. I felt that I must look forward to an improvement in my wife's health, when she would admit her folly, and thus be able to resume her intercourse with our neighbours in a reasonable manner.

Some time elapsed, during which the Wesendonck family took a pleasure trip of several weeks to Northern Italy.

The arrival of the promised Erard grand-piano made me painfully conscious of what a tin kettle my old grand-piano from Breitkopf und Härtel had been, and I forthwith banished it to the lower regions, where my wife begged she might keep it as a souvenir ' of old times.' She afterwards took it with her

to Saxony, where she sold it for three hundred marks. The new
piano appealed to my musical sense immensely, and whilst I
was improvising I seemed to drift quite naturally into the soft
nocturnal sounds of the second act of *Tristan*, the composition
of which I now began to sketch out. This was at the beginning
of May. My work was unexpectedly interrupted by the command of the Grand Duke of Weimar to meet him on a certain
day in Lucerne, where he was staying after his return from
Italy. I availed myself of this opportunity to have a lengthy
interview at the hotel in Chamberlain von Beaulieu's room, with
my former nominal patron whose acquaintance I had made at
the time of my flight.

From this interview with Karl Alexander I gathered that my
attitude towards the Grand Duke of Baden, in regard to the
performance of *Tristan*, in Karlsruhe, had made an impression
on the Weimar court, for while he made particular mention of
that matter, I gathered from what he said that he was also
anxious about my *Nibelungen* work, in which he declared he
had always taken the liveliest interest, and wanted my assurance
that this composition would be produced at Weimar. I had no
serious objection to that. Moreover, I was vastly entertained
by the personality of this free-and-easy good-natured Prince,
who, though he sat chatting next to me on a narrow sofa, was
evidently anxious by his singularly choice language to impress
me as a man of culture. I was much struck to find that his
dignified bearing was not in the least disturbed when Herr von
Beaulieu, with the object of amusing us, made some rather
clumsy remarks which were meant to be witty. After the
Grand Duke had asked me in the most guarded way my opinion
of Liszt's compositions, I was surprised to notice by his general
bearing that he was not at all uncomfortable when the chamberlain expressed the most contemptuous opinions about the Grand
Duke's famous friend, saying that Liszt's composing was a
mere mania on his part. This gave me a strange insight into this
royal friendship, and I had some difficulty in keeping serious
during the interview. I had to pay the Grand Duke another
visit on the following morning, but on that occasion I saw
him without his chamberlain, whose absence certainly had a
favourable effect on the Prince's remarks about his friend

Liszt, whose inspiring conversation and advice he loudly asserted that he could not praise enough. I was surprised to see the Grand Duchess walk in upon us, and was received by her with a most condescending bow, the formality of which I have never forgotten. I looked upon my meeting with these exalted personages as an exceedingly amusing adventure in my travels. I have never heard from them since.[1] Later on, when I called on Liszt at Weimar, just before he left there, he could not even induce the Grand Duke to receive me!

A short time after my return from that expedition Karl Tausig called with a letter of introduction from Liszt; he was then sixteen years of age, and astonished everybody by his dainty appearance and his unusual precocity of understanding and demeanour. He had already been greeted in Vienna, on his public appearance as a pianist, as a future Liszt. He gave himself all the airs of a Liszt, and already smoked the strongest cigars to such an extent that I felt a perfect horror of them. Otherwise I was very glad he had made up his mind to spend some time in the neighbourhood, all the more so as I could appreciate to the utmost his amusing, half-childish, though very intelligent and knowing personality, and, above all, his exceptionally finished piano-playing and quick musical faculty. He played the most complicated pieces at sight, and knew how to use his astonishing facility in the most extravagant tricks for my entertainment. He afterwards came to live quite near us; he was my daily guest at all meals, and accompanied me on my usual walks to the Sihlthal. He soon tried to wriggle out of these, however. He also went with me on a visit to Minna at Brestenberg. As I had to repeat these expeditions regularly every week, being anxious to watch the result of the treatment, Tausig endeavoured to escape from these also, as neither Brestenberg nor Minna's conversation seemed to appeal to him. However, he could not avoid meeting her when, feeling obliged to interrupt her cure for a few days to look after her household affairs, she returned at the end of May. I noticed by her manner that she no longer attached any importance to the recent domestic upheaval; the view she took of the matter was that there had been a little ' love affair '

---

[1] This was dictated in 1869.

which she had put straight. As she referred to this with a
certain amount of unpleasant levity, I was obliged, though I
would willingly have spared her on account of the state of her
health, to explain clearly and firmly, that in consequence of
her disobedience and her foolish conduct towards our neighbour,
the possibility of our remaining on the estate, where we had only
just settled with so much difficulty, was a matter of the most
serious doubt, and I felt bound to warn her that we must be
prepared for the necessity of a separation, as I was fully determined that if this dreaded event took place, I would not agree
to live under similar domestic conditions elsewhere. The
earnestness with which I dwelt on the character of our past
life together, on that occasion, so impressed and shocked her
that, fully realising it was through her fault that the home it
had cost us so much pain to build up had been destroyed, she
broke into a low wail of lamentation for the first time in our
lives. This was the first and only occasion on which she gave
me any token of loving humility, when late at night she kissed
my hand as I withdrew. I was deeply touched at this, and the
idea flashed across my mind that possibly a great and decided
change might take place in the character of the poor woman,
and this determined me to renew my hope of the possibility of
continuing the life we had resumed.

Everything contributed to the maintenance of this hope:
my wife returned to Brestenberg to complete the second part
of her cure; the most glorious summer weather favoured my
disposition to work at the second act of *Tristan;* the evenings
with Tausig cheered me up, and my relations with my neighbours, who had never borne me any ill-will, seemed to me to
favour the possibility of a dignified and desirable understanding in the future. It was quite probable that if my wife went on
a visit to her friends in Saxony after her cure, time would
eventually cover the past with oblivion, and her own future
conduct as well as the changed attitude of our deeply offended
neighbour, would make it possible to renew our mutual intercourse in a dignified way.

I was still further cheered by the prospect of the arrival
of an agreeable visitor, as well as by some satisfactory
negotiations with two of the most important German theatres.

In June the Berlin manager approached me about *Lohengrin,* and we soon came to an agreement. In Vienna, too, the forced intrusion of *Tannhäuser* had produced its effect on the attitude of the management of the court theatre. Just recently the well-known conductor, Karl Eckert, had been entrusted with the technical management of the Opera. He seized the happy opportunity afforded by the possession of a very good company of singers, and by the closing of the theatre for much needed restoration, to give the company time to study *Lohengrin,* with the object of securing the acceptance of this new and difficult work by the court authorities. He thereupon made me his offers. I wanted to insist on the author's rights on the same terms as those granted in Berlin, but he would not agree to this, because the takings of the house were very small, owing to the lack of space in the old theatre. On the other hand, Conductor Esser called on me one day; he had come from Vienna to make all arrangements, and in the name of the management he offered me about two thousand marks, cash down, for the first twenty performances of *Lohengrin,* and promised me a further sum of two thousand marks on their completion. The frank and genial manner of the worthy musician won me over, and I closed with him at once. The result was that Esser went through the score of *Lohengrin* with me there and then, with great conscientiousness and zeal, and paid special attention to all my wishes. With every confidence in a favourable result I bid him farewell, and he hurried back to Vienna to set to work at once.

I then completed the composition sketches for the second act of *Tristan* in excellent spirits, and began the more detailed execution of it, but I did not get quite through the first scene, as I was exposed to continual interruptions. Tichatschek came to pay me another visit, and took up his abode in my little spare room, to recover, as he said, from the effects of his recent exertions. He boasted that he had again introduced my operas, which had been repeatedly forbidden, into the repertoire of the Dresden theatre, and had also taken part in them himself with great success.

Lohengrin was also to be produced there. Although this was very gratifying, I did not in the least know what to do with

the good man at such close quarters. Fortunately I was able
to hand him over to Tausig, who understood my embarrassment, and kept Tichatschek to himself pretty well the whole
day, by playing cards with him. The young tenor Niemann,
of whose great talent I had heard so much, soon arrived with
his bride, the famous actress Seebach, and owing to his almost
gigantic frame, he struck me as being just the man for
Siegfried. The fact of having two famous tenors with me
at the same time gave rise to the annoyance that neither of
them would sing anything to me, as they were ill at ease in
each other's presence. I quite believed, however, that Niemann's
voice must be on a par with his imposing personality. About
that time (15th July) I fetched my wife from Brestenberg.
During my absence my servant, who was a cunning Saxon,
had thought fit to erect a kind of triumphal arch to celebrate
the return of the mistress of the house. This led to
great complications, as, much to her delight, Minna was convinced that this flower-bedecked triumphal arch would greatly
attract the attention of our neighbours, and thought this would
be sufficient to prevent them from regarding her return home
as a humiliating one. She insisted with triumphant joy upon
the decorations remaining up for several days. About the same
time the Bülows, true to their promise, paid another visit.
The unfortunate Tichatschek again put off his departure, and
consequently continued to occupy our one small spare
room, so I was obliged to let my friends stay at the
hotel several days longer. However, the visits they paid to
the Wesendoncks as well as to me soon afforded me an opportunity of hearing, much to my surprise, of the effect the
triumphal arch had produced on our neighbour's young
wife, who was still nursing her injured feelings. When I
heard of her passionate protests I realised to what a pass things
had come, and immediately gave up all hope of putting
a peaceful end to the discordant situation. Those were days
of terrible anxiety. I wished myself in the most distant desert,
and yet was in the awkward position of having to keep my
house open to a succession of visitors. At last Tichatschek
took his departure, and I could at least devote the remainder
of my stay to the pleasant duty of entertaining favourite

guests. The Bülows really seemed to me to have been providentially sent for the purpose of quelling the horrible excitement that prevailed in the house. Hans made the best of things when, on the day of his arrival, he caught me in the midst of a terrific scene with Minna, as I had just told her plainly that from what I could see of the present position of affairs, our stay here was no longer possible, and that I was only deferring my departure until after the visit of our young friends. This time, however, I had to admit that she was not altogether to blame.

We spent another whole month together in the cottage, which, by the way, I had unconsciously christened Asyl. It was an extremely trying period, and the experiences I went through every day only confirmed me in my decision to give up the house. Under the circumstances my young guests also had to suffer, as my worry communicated itself to all who were in sympathy with me. Klindworth, who was coming on a visit from London, to add to the gloom of this extraordinary ménage, soon joined us. So the house was suddenly filled, and the table surrounded by sad, mysteriously depressed guests, whose wants were ministered to by one who was shortly to leave her home for ever.

It seemed to me that there must be one human being in existence specially qualified to bring light and reconciliation, or at least tolerable order, into the gloom and trouble by which we were all surrounded. Liszt had promised me a visit, but he was so happily situated beyond the reach of these harassing conditions, he had had such experience of the world, and possessed that innate *aplomb* to such an extraordinary degree, that he did not seem to me to be very likely to approach these misunderstandings in a rational spirit. I almost felt inclined to make my final decision dependent on the effect of his expected visit. It was in vain that we begged of him to hasten his journey; he offered to meet me at the Lake of Geneva a month later! Then my courage failed. Intercourse with my friends now afforded me no satisfaction, for although they could not understand why I should be turned out of a home that suited me so well, yet it was apparent to every one that I could not remain under these conditions. We still had music every now and then, but it was in a half-hearted and absent-minded fashion. To make matters worse, we had a national vocal festival inflicted upon us, during which I was obliged to face all kinds of demands; matters did not always pass off without unpleasantness, as amongst others I had to decline to see Franz Lachner, who had been specially engaged for the festival, and did not return his call. Tausig certainly delighted us by carolling Lachner's ' Old German Battle Song' in the upper octave, which, thanks to his boyish falsetto, was within his reach; however, even his pranks were no longer able to cheer us. Everything, which under other circumstances would have made this summer month one of the most stimulating in my life, now contributed to my discomfort, as did also the stay of the Countess d'Agoult, who, having come on a visit to her daughter and son-in-law, attached herself to our party for the time being. By way of filling up the house, Karl Ritter also came after much grumbling and sulking, and once again proved himself to be very interesting and original.

As the time for the general leave-taking at last drew near, I had arranged all the details connected with the breaking up of my home. I settled the necessary business part by a personal visit to Herr Wesendonck, and in the presence of Bülow I took leave of Frau Wesendonck, who, in spite of her ever-recurring misconceptions on the matter, eventually reproached herself bitterly when she saw that these misunderstandings had ended by breaking up my home. My friends were much distressed at parting from me, whilst I could only meet their expressions of sorrow with apathy. On the 16th August the Bülows also left; Hans was bathed in tears and his wife Cosima was gloomy and silent. I had arranged with Minna that she should remain there for about a week to clear up and dispose of our little belongings as she thought best. I had advised her to entrust these unpleasant duties to some one else, as I hardly thought it possible that she would be fitted for such a wretched task, which, under the circumstances, would be very trying to her. She replied reproachfully that ' it would be a fine thing if, with all our misfortunes, we neglected our property. Order there must be.' I afterwards learned to my disgust that she carried out the removal and her own departure with such formality, by advertising in the daily papers that the effects would be sold cheaply owing to sudden departure, and thereby exciting much curiosity, that perplexed rumours were spread about giving the whole affair a scandalous signification, which afterwards caused much unpleasantness both to me and the Wesendonck family.

On the 17th August, the day after the departure of the Bülows (whose stay had been the only reason for detaining me), I got up at early dawn after a sleepless night, and went down into the dining-room, where Minna was already expecting me to breakfast, as I intended to start by the five o'clock train. She was calm; it was only when accompanying me in the carriage to the station that she was overpowered by her emotion under the trying circumstances. It was the most brilliant summer day with a bright, cloudless sky; I remember that I never once looked back, or shed a tear on taking leave of her, and this almost terrified me. As I travelled along in the train I could not conceal from myself an increasing feeling of comfort; it was obvious that the absolutely useless worries of the past weeks could not have been endured any longer, and that my life's ambition demanded a complete severance from them. On the evening of the same day I arrived in Geneva; here I wished to rest a little and pull myself together, so as to arrange my plan of life calmly. As I had an idea of making another attempt to settle in Italy, I proposed, after my former experience, to wait till the cooler autumn weather, so as not to expose myself again to the malignant influence of the sudden change of climate. I arranged to stay for a month at the Maison Fazy, deluding myself into the idea that a lengthy stay there would be very pleasant. I told Karl Ritter, who was at Lausanne, of my intention of going to Italy, and to my surprise he wrote saying that he also intended to give up his home and go to Italy alone, as his wife was going to Saxony for the winter on account of family affairs. He offered himself as my travelling companion. This suited me excellently, and as Ritter also assured me that he knew, from a previous visit, that the climate of Venice was quite agreeable at this season, I was induced to make a hasty departure. I had, however, to ar-

range about my passport. I expected that the embassies in
Berne would corroborate the fact that as a political refugee
I should have nothing to fear in Venice, which, although belonging to Austria, did not form part of the German Confederation. Liszt, to whom I also applied for information on
this point, advised me on no account to go to Venice; on
the other hand, the report that some of my friends in Berne
obtained from the Austrian ambassador pronounced it as quite
safe; so, after barely a week's stay in Geneva, I informed
Karl Ritter of my readiness to start, and called for him at
his villa in Lausanne, so that we might begin the journey
together.

We did not talk much on the way, but gave ourselves up
silently to our impressions. The route was over the Simplon
to Lake Maggiore, where I again visited the Borromean Islands
from Baveno. There, on the terrace garden of Isola Bella,
I spent a wonderful late summer morning in the company
of my young friend, who was never obtrusive, but, on the
contrary, inclined to be too silent. For the first time I felt
my mind entirely at rest, and filled with the hope of a new
and harmonious future. We continued our journey by coach
through Sesto Calende to Milan; and Karl was filled with such
a longing for his beloved Venice, that he could barely grant me
time to admire the famous Duomo; but I had no objection
to being hurried with this object in view. As we were looking
from the railway dike at Venice rising before us from the
mirror of water, Karl lost his hat out of the carriage owing
to an enthusiastic movement of delight; I thought that I
must follow suit, so I too threw my hat out; consequently
we arrived in Venice bareheaded, and immediately got into a
gondola to go down the Grand Canal as far as the Piazzetta
near San Marco. The weather had suddenly become gloomy,
and the aspect of the gondolas quite shocked me; for, in spite
of what I had heard about these peculiar vessels draped in
black, the sight of one was an unpleasant surprise: when I
had to go under the black awning, I could not help remembering the cholera-scare some time earlier. I certainly felt I
was taking part in a funeral procession during a pestilence.
Karl assured me that every one felt the same at first, but that

one soon got accustomed to it. Next came the long sail through the twists and turns of the Grand Canal. The impression that everything made on me here did not tend to dispel my melancholy frame of mind. Where Karl, on looking at the ruined walls, only saw the Cà d'Oro of Fanny Elser or some other famous palace, my doleful glances were completely absorbed by the crumbling ruins between these interesting buildings. At last I became silent, and allowed myself to be put down at the world-famous Piazzetta, and to be shown the palace of the Doges, though I reserved to myself the right of admiring it until I had freed myself from the extremely melancholy mood into which my arrival in Venice had thrown me.

Starting on the following morning from the Hôtel Danieli, where we had found only a gloomy lodging, I began by looking for a residence that would suit me for my prolonged stay. I heard that one of the three Giustiniani palaces, situated not far from the Palazzo Foscari, was at present very little patronised by visitors, on account of its situation, which in the winter is somewhat unfavourable. I found some very spacious and imposing apartments there, all of which they told me would remain uninhabited. I here engaged a large stately room with a spacious bedroom adjoining. I had my luggage quickly transferred there, and on the evening of 30th August I said to myself, 'At last I am living in Venice.' My leading idea was that I could work here undisturbed. I immediately wrote to Zürich asking for my Erard 'Grand' and my bed to be sent on to me, as, with regard to the latter, I felt that I should find out what cold meant in Venice. In addition to this, the grey-washed walls of my large room soon annoyed me, as they were so little suited to the ceiling, which was covered with a fresco which I thought was rather tasteful. I decided to have the walls of the large room covered with hangings of a dark-red shade, even if they were of quite common quality. This immediately caused much trouble; but it seemed to me that it was well worth surmounting, when I gazed down from my balcony with growing satisfaction on the wonderful canal, and said to myself that here I would complete *Tristan*. I also had a little more decorating done;

I arranged to have dark-red portières, even if they were of
the cheapest material, to cover the common doors which the
Hungarian landlord had had put into the ruined palace in place
of the original valuable ones, which had probably been sold.
In addition, the host had contrived to get some showy furniture,
such as a few gilded chairs, covered with common cotton plush;
but the most prominent article was a finely carved gilded table-
pedestal, on which was placed a vulgar pinewood top which
I had to cover with a plain red cloth. Finally the Erard
arrived; it was placed in the middle of the large room, and
now wonderful Venice was to be attacked by music.

However, the dysentery I had previously suffered from in
Genoa laid hold of me again, and rendered me incapable of
any intellectual activity for weeks. I had already learned to
appreciate the matchless beauty of Venice, and I was full of
hope that my joy in it would give me back my power to satisfy
my reviving artistic yearnings. On one of my first promenades
on the Riva I was accosted by two strangers, one of whom
introduced himself as Count Edmund Zichy, the other as
Prince Dolgoroukow. They had both left Vienna barely a
week before, where they had been present at the first performances of my *Lohengrin;* they gave me the most satisfactory
reports about the result of it, and by their enthusiasm I could
see that their impressions were very favourable. Count Zichy
left Venice soon afterwards, but Prince Dolgoroukow decided
to stay on for the winter. Although I certainly intended to
avoid company, this Russian, who was about fifty years of age,
soon managed to make me yield to his persuasions. He had
an earnest and extremely expressive face (he prided himself
on being of direct Caucasian descent), and showed remarkable
culture in every respect, a wide knowledge of the world, and
above all a taste for music, in the literature of which he was
also so well versed that it amounted to a passion. I had at
first explained to him that owing to the state of my health I
was bound to renounce all society, and that I needed quiet
more than anything. Apart from the difficulty of avoiding
him altogether on the limited walks in Venice, the restaurant
at Albergo San Marco where I joined Ritter every day for
meals led to inevitable meetings with this stranger, to whom I

eventually became sincerely attached. He had taken up his abode in that hotel, and I could not prevent him from taking his meals there. During my stay in Venice we met almost daily, and continued to be on very friendly terms. On the other hand I had a great surprise, on returning to my apartments one evening, to be informed that Liszt had just arrived. I rushed eagerly to the room pointed out to me as his, and there, to my horror, saw Winterberger the pianist, who had introduced himself to my host as a mutual friend of myself and of Liszt, and in the confusion of the moment the host had concluded that the new arrival was Liszt himself. As a matter of fact I had recently got to know this young man as a follower of Liszt during his comparatively long stay in Zürich; he was considered an excellent organist, and was also called into requisition as second at the piano when there were arrangements for two pianofortes. Except for some foolish behaviour on his part I had not noticed anything particular about him. I was surprised, however, that he should have selected my address as his lodging in Venice. He told me that he was merely the precursor of a certain Princess Galitzin, for whom he had to arrange winter quarters in Venice; that he knew nobody there, but having heard in Vienna that I was staying here, it was very natural he should apply first at my hotel. I argued with him that this was not an hotel, and announced that if his Russian Princess thought of taking up her abode next to me, I should move out at once. He then reassured me, by telling me that he had only wanted to make a good impression on the host by mentioning the Princess, as he thought she had already engaged rooms elsewhere. As I again asked what he thought of doing in this palace, and drew his attention to the fact that it was very expensive, and that I put up with the large outlay simply because it was most essential that I should be undisturbed, and have no neighbours, and hear no piano, he tried to pacify me by the assurance that he would certainly not be a burden to me, and that I could make my mind easy about his presence in the same house until he could arrange to move elsewhere. His next attempt was to work his way into the good graces of Karl Ritter; they both discovered a living-room in the palace at a sufficient distance from mine to be out of earshot. In this way I consented to put up with his proximity, although it was a long time before I allowed Ritter to bring him to me of an evening.

A Venetian piano-teacher, Tessarin by name, was more successful than Winterberger in winning favour with me. He was a typical handsome Venetian, with a curious impediment in his speech; he had a passion for German music, and was well acquainted with Liszt's new compositions, and also with my own operas. He admitted that having regard to his surroundings he was a 'white raven' in matters musical. He also succeeded in approaching me through Ritter, who seemed to be devoting himself in Venice to the study of human nature rather than to work. He had taken a small and extremely modest dwelling on the Riva dei Schiavoni, which, being in a sunny position, required no artificial heating. This was in reality less for himself than for his scanty luggage, as he was hardly ever at home, but was running about in the daytime after pictures and collections; in the evening, however, he studied human nature in the cafés on the Piazza San Marco. He was the only person I saw regularly every day; otherwise I rigorously avoided any other society or acquaintance. I was repeatedly asked by the Princess Galitzin's private physician to call upon that lady, who came to Venice very shortly and appeared to be living in grand style. Once, when I wanted the piano scores of *Tannhäuser* and *Lohengrin*, and had heard that the Princess was the only person in Venice who possessed them, I was bold enough to ask her for them, but I did not feel it incumbent on me to call on her for that purpose. On only one occasion did any stranger succeed in interrupting my seclusion, and then it was because his appearance had pleased me when I had met him in the Albergo San Marco; this was Rahl the painter, from Vienna. I once went so far as to arrange a sort of soirée for him, Prince Dolgoroukow, and Tessarin the pianoforte teacher, at which a few of my pieces were played. It was then that Winterberger made his début.

All my social experiences during the seven months I spent in Venice were limited to these few attempts at friendly intercourse, and apart from these my days were planned out with the utmost regularity during the whole time. I worked till two o'clock, then I got into the gondola that was always in waiting, and was taken along the solemn Grand Canal to the bright Piazzetta, the peculiar charm of which always had a cheerful effect on me. After this I made for my restaurant in the Piazza San Marco, and when I had finished my meal I walked alone or with Karl along the Riva to the Giardino Pubblico, the only pleasure-ground in Venice where there are any trees, and at nightfall I came back in the gondola down the canal, then more sombre and silent, till I reached the spot where I could see my solitary lamp shining from the night-shrouded façade of the old Palazzo Giustiniani. After I had worked a little longer Karl, heralded by the swish of the gondola, would come in regularly at eight o'clock for a few hours' chat over our tea. Very rarely did I vary this routine by a visit to one of the theatres. When I did, I preferred the performances at the Camploi Theatre, where Goldoni's pieces were very well played; but I seldom went to the opera, and when I did go it was merely out of curiosity. More frequently, when bad weather deprived us of our walk, we patronised the popular drama at the Malibran Theatre, where the performances were given in the daytime. The admission cost us six kreuzers. The audiences were excellent, the majority being in their shirtsleeves, and the pieces given were generally of the ultra-melodramatic type. However, one day to my great astonishment and intense delight I saw there *Le Baruffe Chioggiote*, the grotesque comedy that had appealed so strongly to Goethe in his day, at this very theatre. So true to nature was this performance that it surpassed anything of the kind I have ever witnessed.

There was little else that attracted my attention in the oppressed and degenerate life of the Venetian people, and the only impression I derived from the exquisite ruin of this wonderful city as far as human interest is concerned was that of a watering-place kept up for the benefit of visitors. Strangely enough, it was the thoroughly German element of good military music, to which so much attention is paid in the Austrian army, that brought me into touch with public life in Venice. The conductors in the two Austrian regiments quartered there began playing overtures of mine, *Rienzi* and *Tannhäuser* for instance, and invited me to attend their practices in their barracks. There I also met the whole staff of officers, and was treated by them with great respect. These bands played on alternate evenings amid brilliant illuminations in the middle of the Piazza San Marco, whose acoustic properties for this class of production were really excellent. I was often suddenly startled towards the end of my meal by the sound of my own overtures; then, as I sat at the restaurant window giving myself up to impressions of the music, I did not know which dazzled me most, the incomparable piazza magnificently illuminated and filled with countless numbers of moving people, or the music that seemed to be borne away in rustling glory to the winds. Only one thing was wanting that might certainly have been expected from an Italian audience: the people were gathered round the band in thousands listening most intently, but no two hands ever forgot themselves so far as to applaud, as the least sign of approbation of Austrian military music would have been looked upon as treason to the Italian Fatherland. All public life in Venice also suffered by this extraordinary rift between the general public and the authorities; this was peculiarly apparent in the relations of the population to the Austrian officers, who floated about publicly in Venice like oil on water. The populace, too, behaved with no less reserve, or one might even say hostility, to the clergy, who were for the most part of Italian origin. I saw a procession of clerics in their vestments passing along the Piazza San Marco accompanied by the people with unconcealed derision.

It was very difficult for Ritter to induce me to interrupt my daily arrangements even to visit a gallery or a church, though, whenever we had to pass through the town, the exceedingly varied architectonic peculiarities and beauties always delighted me afresh. But the frequent gondola trips towards the Lido constituted my chief enjoyment during practically the whole of my stay in Venice. It was more especially on our homeward journeys at sunset that I was always overpowered by unique impressions. During the first part of our stay in the September of that year we saw on one of these occasions the marvellous apparition of the great comet, which at that time was at its highest brilliancy, and was generally

said to portend an imminent catastrophe. The singing of a
popular choral society, trained by an official of the Venetian arsenal, seemed like a real lagoon idyll. They generally sang only three-part naturally harmonised folk-songs. It
was new to me not to hear the higher voice rise above the
compass of the alto, that is to say, without touching the
soprano, thereby imparting to the sound of the chorus a
manly youthfulness hitherto unknown to me. On fine evenings they glided down the Grand Canal in a large illuminated gondola, stopping before a few palaces as if to serenade
(when requested and paid for so doing, be it understood),
and generally attracted a number of other gondolas in their
wake. During one sleepless night, when I felt impelled to
go out on to my balcony in the small hours, I heard for the
first time the famous old folk-song of the *gondolieri*. I
seemed to hear the first call, in the stillness of the night, proceeding from the Rialto about a mile away like a rough
lament, and answered in the same tone from a yet further
distance in another direction. This melancholy dialogue, which
was repeated at longer intervals, affected me so much that
I could not fix the very simple musical component parts
in my memory. However, on a subsequent occasion I was
told that this folk-song was of great poetic interest. As I
was returning home late one night on the gloomy canal, the
moon appeared suddenly and illuminated the marvellous
palaces and the tall figure of my gondolier towering above
the stern of the gondola, slowly moving his huge sweep. Suddenly he uttered a deep wail, not unlike the cry of an animal; the cry gradually gained in strength, and formed itself,
after a long-drawn ' Oh! ' into the simple musical exclamation ' Venezia! ' This was followed by other sounds of which
I have no distinct recollection, as I was so much moved at
the time. Such were the impressions that to me appeared
the most characteristic of Venice during my stay there, and
they remained with me until the completion of the second
act of *Tristan*, and possibly even suggested to me the long-
drawn wail of the shepherd's horn at the beginning of the
third act.

These sensations, however, did not manifest themselves

very easily or consecutively. Bodily sufferings and my usual cares, that never quite left me, often considerably hindered and disturbed my work. I had scarcely settled down comfortably in my rooms, the northerly aspect of which exposed them to frequent gusts of wind (from which I had practically no protection in the form of heating appliances), and had barely got over the demoralising effect of dysentery, when I fell a victim to a specific Venetian complaint, namely a carbuncle on my leg, as the result of the extreme change of climate and of air. This happened just when I was intending to resume the second act, that had been so cruelly interrupted. The malady, which I had first regarded as slight, soon increased and became exceedingly painful, and I was obliged to call in a doctor, who had to treat me carefully for nearly four weeks. It was in the late autumn, towards the end of November, that Ritter left me to pay a visit to his relations and friends in Dresden and Berlin; I therefore remained quite alone during this long illness, with no other society than that of the servants of the house. Incapable of work, I amused myself by reading the *History of Venice* by Count Daru, in which I became much interested, as I was on the spot. Through it I lost some of my popular prejudices against the tyrannical mode of government in ancient Venice. The ill-famed Council of Ten and the State Inquisition appeared to me in a peculiar, although certainly horrible, light; the open admission that in the secrecy of its methods lay the guarantee of the power of the state, seemed to me so decidedly in the interests of each and every member of the marvellous republic, that the suppression of all knowledge was very wisely considered a republican duty. Actual hypocrisy was entirely foreign to this state constitution; moreover the clerical element, however respectfully treated by the government, never exercised an unworthy influence on the development of the character of the citizens as in other parts of Italy. The terrible selfish calculations of state reasons were turned into maxims of quite an ancient heathen character, not really evil in themselves, but reminiscent of similar maxims among the Athenians, which, as we read in Thucydides, were adopted by them in all simplicity, as the foundations of human morality.

In addition to this I once more took up, by way of a restorative, as I had often done before, a volume of Schopenhauer, with whom I became on intimate terms, and I experienced a sensation of relief when I found that I was now able to explain the tormenting gaps in his system by the aids which he himself provided.

My few associations with the outer world now became calmer, but one day I was distressed by a letter from Wesendonck in which he informed me of the death of his son Guido, who was about four years old; it depressed me to think that I had refused to stand godfather to him, on the pretext that I might bring him bad luck. This event touched me deeply, and as I was longing for a thorough rest, I mapped out for myself a short journey across the Alps, with the idea that I might spend Christmas with my old friends, and offer them my condolences. I informed Mme. Wille of this idea, and in reply received, strange to say, from her husband instead of from herself, some quite unexpected particulars regarding the extremely unpleasant curiosity which my sudden departure from Zürich had caused, especially in reference to the part my wife had played in it, and at which the Wesendonck family had been so much annoyed. As I also heard how skilfully Wesendonck had treated the matter, some agreeable communications followed couched in conciliatory terms. It was much to Minna's credit that in her relations towards me she had by her letters proved herself wise and considerate, and while staying in Dresden, where she met her old friends, she lived quietly, and I always provided for her amicably. By so doing she strengthened the impression she had made on me at the time of that touching nocturnal scene, and I willingly put before her the possibility of a domestic reunion, provided that we could establish a home that promised to be a permanent one, which at that time I could only picture to myself as feasible in Germany, and if possible in Dresden. To obtain some idea as to whether it was possible to carry out such an arrangement, I lost no time in applying to Lüttichau, as I had received favourable reports from Minna about his kindly feeling and warm attachment to me. I really went so far as to write to him cordially and in detail. It was another lesson

for me when in return I received occasionally a few dry lines
in a businesslike tone, in which he pointed out that at that
moment nothing could be done with respect to my desired return to Saxony. On the other hand, I learned through the
police authorities in Venice, that the Saxon ambassador in
Vienna ardently wished to drive me even out of Venice. This
proved unsuccessful, however, as I was sufficiently protected
by a Swiss passport, which to my great delight the Austrian
authorities duly respected. The only hope I had with regard
to my longed-for return to Germany was based on the friendly
efforts of the Grand Duke of Baden. Eduard Devrient, to
whom I also applied for more definite information respecting
our project of a first performance of *Tristan*, informed me that
the Grand Duke looked upon my presence at the performance
as an understood thing; whether he was taking any steps on
his own account against the League, in case his direct efforts
to obtain the King of Saxony's permission should be fruitless,
or whether he intended to accomplish it in some other way,
he did not know. Consequently I realised that I could not
count on the possibility of an early settlement in Germany.

A great deal of my time was taken up in correspondence with
the object of procuring the necessary means of subsistence,
which at that time, owing to the divided household, made no
small calls upon my purse. Fortunately a few of the larger
theatres had not yet come to terms about my operas, so I
might still expect some fees from them, whereas those from
the more active theatres had already been spent. The Stuttgart Court Theatre was the last to apply for *Tannhäuser*. At
that time I had a particular affection for Stuttgart, owing to
the reasons I have already mentioned; this was also true of
Vienna, which had been the first place to produce *Lohengrin*,
and, in consequence of its success, thought it necessary to secure
Tannhäuser. My negotiations with Eckert, who was director
at that time, quickly led to satisfactory results.

All this happened during the course of the winter and early
spring of 1859. Otherwise I lived very quietly and with great
regularity, as I have described. After recovering the use of
my leg, I was able in December to begin my regular gondola
trips to the Piazzetta again and the return journeys in the

evening, and also to give myself up for some time uninterruptedly to my musical work. I spent Christmas and New
Year's Eve quite alone, but in my dreams at night I often found
myself in society, which had a very disturbing effect on my rest.

At the beginning of 1859 Karl Ritter suddenly turned up
again at my rooms for his usual evening visits. His anxiety
about the performance of a dramatic piece he had written had
taken him to the shores of the Baltic. This was a work he had
completed a short time before *Armida*, much of which again
showed his great talent. The tendency of the whole play is to
show terrible glimpses of the poet's soul, and these prevent one
from passing a favourable judgment on some parts of the
piece, but other parts, notably the meeting of Rinaldo with
Armida, and the violent birth of their love, are depicted by the
author with real poetic fire. As is the case with all such works,
which are in reality always hampered by the superficiality of
the dilettante, much should have been altered and rewritten for
stage effect. Karl would not hear of this; on the contrary, he
thought he had discovered, in an intelligent theatrical manager
in Stettin, the very man who would lay aside any such considerations as were peculiar to me. He had, however, been
disappointed in this hope, and had come back to Venice intending to carry out his fond desire of living aimlessly. To wander
through Rome clad in the garb of a capuchin, studying the
treasures of art from hour to hour, was the kind of existence
he would have preferred to any other.

He would not hear of a remodelled version of *Armida*, but
declared his intention to set to work on some new dramatic
material which he had taken from Machiavelli's *Florentine
Histories*. He would not specify what this material was more
definitely, lest I should dissuade him from using it, inasmuch as
it contained only situations, and absolutely no indication of any
purpose. He seemed no longer to have any desire to give himself up to musical work, although even in this respect the
young man showed himself to me in a thoroughly interesting
light by a fantasy for the piano which he had written soon after
his arrival in Venice. Nevertheless he displayed a more highly
intelligent appreciation than before of the development of the
second act of *Tristan*, in which I had at last made regular prog-

ress. In the evening I frequently played to him, Winterberger
and Tessarin, the portions I had completed during the day, and
they were always deeply moved. During the previous interruption in my work, which had lasted rather a long time, Härtel
had engraved the first act of the score, and Bülow had arranged
it for the piano. Thus a portion of the opera lay before me in
monumental completeness, while I was still in a fruitful state
of excitement with regard to the execution of the whole. And
now in the early months of the year the orchestration of this
act, which I continued to send in groups of sheets to the publisher to be engraved, also neared completion. By the middle
of March I was able to send off the last sheets to Leipzig.

It was now necessary to make new decisions for my plan of
life. The question presented itself as to where I was going to
compose the third act; for I wished to begin it only in a place
where I had a prospect of finishing it undisturbed. It seemed
as if this was not destined to be the case in Venice. My work
would have occupied me until late into the summer, and on
account of my health I did not think I dared spend the hot
weather in Venice. Its climate about this time of the year did
not commend itself to me. Already I had found great disadvantages and anything but favourable results from the fact
that it was not possible to enjoy the invigorating recreation of
rambling about in this place. Once in the winter, when I
wanted a good walk, I had gone by train to Viterbo to take my
fill of exercise by tramping inland for several miles towards the
mountains. Inhospitable weather had opposed my progress,
and this, added to other unfavourable circumstances, resulted
in my bringing away from my excursion nothing more valuable
than a favourable opinion of the city of lagoons, to which I
fled as to a place of refuge against the dust of the streets and
the spectacle of horses being cruelly used. Moreover, it now
turned out that my further stay in Venice no longer depended
wholly on my own will. I had been recently cited (very
politely) before a commissioner of police, who informed me,
without mincing the matter, that there had been an incessant
agitation on the part of the Saxon embassy in Vienna against
my remaining in what was a part of the Austrian Empire.
When I explained that I only wished to extend my stay to the

beginning of spring, I was advised to obtain permission to do so from the Archduke Maximilian, who as viceroy resided in Milan, preferring my request on the ground of ill-health as alleged by a doctor's certificate. I did this, and the Archduke issued immediate instructions by telegram to the Administrative Government of Venice, to leave me in peace.

But soon it became clear to me that the political situation, which was putting Austrian Italy into a state of ferment, might develop into an occasion for renewing active precautionary measures against strangers. The outbreak of war with Piedmont and France became more and more imminent, and the evidence of deep agitation in the Italian population grew more unmistakable every moment. One day, when I was sauntering up and down the Riva with Tessarin, we came upon a fairly large crowd of strangers, who, with a mixture of respect and curiosity, were watching the Archduke Maximilian and his wife as they were taking the air during a short visit to Venice. The situation was rapidly conveyed to me by my Venetian pianist, who nudged me violently and sought to drag me away from the spot by my arm: in order that, as he explained, I might be spared the necessity of raising my hat to the Archduke. Seeing the stately and very attractive figure of the young Prince passing along, I slipped by my friend with a laugh, and took honest pleasure in being able by my greeting to thank him for his protection, although, of course, he did not know who I was.

Soon, however, everything began to assume a more serious aspect, and to look gloomy and depressing. Day by day the Riva was so crowded with troops newly disembarked, that it became quite unavailable for a promenade. The officers of these troops, on the whole, made a very favourable impression on me, and their homely German tongue, as they chatted harmlessly with one another, reminded me pleasantly of home. In the rank and file, on the other hand, I could not possibly feel any confidence, for in them I saw chiefly the dull servile features of certain leading Slav races in the Austrian monarchy. One could not fail to recognise in them a certain brute force, but it was no less clear that they were entirely devoid of that naïve intelligence which is such an attractive characteristic of the

Italian people. I could not but grudge the former race their victory over the latter. The facial expression of these troops recurred forcibly to my memory in the autumn of this year in Paris, when I could not avoid comparing the picked French troops, the Chasseurs de Vincennes and the Zouaves, with these Austrian soldiers; and without any scientific knowledge of strategy, I understood in a flash the battles of Magenta and Solferino. For the present I learned that Milan was already in a state of seige and was almost completely barred to foreigners. As I had determined to seek my summer refuge in Switzerland on the Lake of Lucerne, this news accelerated my departure; for I did not want to have my retreat cut off by the exigencies of war. So I packed up my things, sent the Erard once more over the Gotthard, and prepared to take leave of my few acquaintances. Ritter had resolved to remain in Italy; he intended to go to Florence and Rome, whither Winterberger, with whom he had struck up a friendship, had hurried in advance. Winterberger declared that he was provided by a brother with money enough to enjoy Italy — an experience which he declared necessary for his recreation and recovery, from what disease I do not know. Ritter therefore counted upon leaving Venice within a very short time. My leave-taking with the worthy Dolgoroukow, whom I left in great suffering, was very sincere, and I embraced Karl at the station, probably for the last time, for from that moment I was left without any direct news of him, and have not seen him to this day.

On the 24th of March, after some adventures caused by the military control of strangers, I reached Milan, where I allowed myself to stay three days to see the sights. Without any official guide to help me, I contented myself with following up the simplest directions I could obtain to the Brera, the Ambrosian Library, the ' Last Supper ' of Leonardo da Vinci, and the cathedral. I climbed the various roofs and towers of this cathedral at all points. Finding, as I always did, that my first impressions were the liveliest, I confined my attention in the Brera chiefly to two pictures which confronted me as soon as I entered; they were Van Dyck's ' Saint Anthony before the Infant Jesus ' and Crespi's ' Martyrdom of Saint Stephen.' I realised on this occasion that I was not a good judge of pictures, because when once the subject has made a clear and sympathetic appeal to me, it settles my view, and nothing else counts. A strange light, however, was shed on the effect made by the purely artistic significance of a masterpiece, when I stood before Leonardo da Vinci's ' Last Supper ' and had the same experience as every one else. This work of art, although it is almost entirely destroyed as a picture, produces such an extraordinary effect on the mind of the spectator, that even after a close examination of the copies hanging beside it representing it in a restored state, when he turns to the ruined picture the fact is suddenly revealed to the eye of his soul that the contents of the original are absolutely inimitable. In the evening I made all haste to get to the Italian comedy again. I grew very fond of it, and found it had installed itself here in the tiny *Teatro Re* for the benefit of a small audience of the lower orders. The Italians of to-day unfortunately despise it heartily. Here, too, the comedies of Goldoni were played with, as it seemed to me, considerable and ingenious skill. On the other hand, it was my fate to be present at a performance in the Scala Theatre, where, in a setting of an external magnificence that was extraordinary, it was proved true that Italian taste was degenerating sadly. Before the most brilliant and enthusiastic audience one could wish for, gathered together in that immense theatre, an incredibly worthless fake of an opera by a modern composer, whose name I have forgotten, was performed. The same evening I learned, however, that although the Italian public was passionately fond of song, it was the ballet which they regarded as the main item; for, obviously, the dreary opera at the beginning was only intended to prepare the way for a great choregraphic performance on a subject no less pretentious than that of Antony and Cleopatra. In this ballet I saw even the cold politician Octavianus, who until now had not so far lost his dignity as to appear as a character in any Italian opera, acting in pantomime and contriving fairly successfully to maintain an attitude of diplomatic reserve. The climax, however, was reached in the scene of Cleopatra's funeral. This afforded the immense staff of the ballet an opportunity for displaying the most varied picturesque effects in highly characteristic costumes.

After receiving these impressions all by myself, I travelled to Lucerne one brilliant spring day by way of Como, where everything was in full blossom, through Lugano, which I knew already, and the Gotthard, which I had to cross in small open sledges along towering walls of snow. When I reached Lucerne the weather was bitterly cold, in contrast with the genial spring I had enjoyed in Italy. The allowance of money I had made for my stay in Lucerne was based on the assumption that the big Hôtel Schweizerhof was quite empty from about this time until the summer season began, and that without further preliminaries I should be able to find a lodging there both spacious and free from noise. This hope had not been entertained in vain. The courteous manager of the hotel, Colonel Segesser, allotted to me a whole floor in the annexe on the left, to occupy at my pleasure. I could make myself quite comfortable here in the larger rooms at a moderate price. As the hotel at this time of the year had only a very small staff of servants, it was left to me to make arrangements for some one to wait upon me For this purpose I found a careful woman well suited to look after my comfort. Many years afterwards, remembering the good services she had rendered me, especially later on when the number of guests had increased, I engaged her as my housekeeper.

Soon my things arrived from Venice. The Erard had been obliged to cross the Alps again when the snow was on the ground. When it was set up in my spacious drawing-room, I said to myself that all this trouble and expense had been incurred to enable me at last to complete the third act of *Tristan und Isolde*. There were times when this seemed to me to be an extravagant ambition; for the difficulties in the way of finishing my work seemed to make it impossible. I compared myself to Leto who, in order to find a place in which to give birth to Apollo and Artemis, was hunted about the world and could find no resting-place until Poseidon, taking compassion on her, caused the island of Delos to rise from the sea.

I wished to regard Lucerne as this Delos. But the terrible influence of the weather, which was intensely cold and continuously wet, weighed upon my spirits in a most unfriendly fashion until the end of May. As such great sacrifice had been made to find this new place of refuge, I thought every day had been uselessly frittered away which had not contributed something to my work of composing. For the greater part of my third act I was occupied with a subject sad beyond words; it came to such a pass that it is only with a shudder that I can recall the first few months of this emigration to Lucerne.

A few days after my arrival I had already visited the Wesendoncks in Zürich. Our meeting was melancholy, but in no way embarrassed. I spent some days in my friends' house, where I saw my old Zürich acquaintances again, and felt as though I were passing from one dream to another. In fact, everything assumed an air of unsubstantiality for me. Several times in the course of my stay in Lucerne I repeated this visit, which was twice returned to me, once on the occasion of my birthday.

Besides the work on which I was now somewhat gloriously engaged, I was also heavy with cares about keeping myself and my wife alive. Of my own accord and out of necessary respect for the circumstances in which my friends the Ritters were placed, I had already in Venice felt myself for the future obliged to decline their voluntary support. I was beginning to exhaust the little that I could contrive to extract with difficulty from those of my operas which up to this period it had been possible to produce. It was settled that I should take up the *Nibelungen* work when Tristan was finished, and I thought it my duty to find out some way of making my future existence easier. This *Nibelungen* work spurred me to the attempt. The Grand Duke of Weimar still kept up his interest in it, to judge from the communications I had received from him during the previous year. I therefore wrote to Liszt and repeated my request that he would make a serious proposal to the Grand Duke to buy the copyright of the work and arrange for its publication, with the right of disposing of it to a publisher on his own terms. I enclosed my former negotiations with Härtel, which had been broken off, and which were now intended to serve as a fair basis for what may be called the business arrangement that Liszt was to enter into with the Grand Duke. Liszt soon gave me an embarrassed hint that his Royal Highness was not really keen on it. This was quite enough for me.

On the other hand, I was driven by circumstances to come to an agreement with Meser in Dresden about the unfortunate copyright of my three earlier operas. The actor Kriete, one of my principal creditors, was making piteous demands for the return of his capital. Schmidt, a Dresden lawyer, offered to put the matter right, and after a long and heated correspondence it was arranged that a certain H. Müller, successor to Meser, who had died a short time before, should enter into possession of the copyright of these publications. On this occasion I heard of nothing but of the costs and expenditure to which my former agent had been put; but it was impossible to get any clear account of the receipts he had taken from my works beyond the fact that the lawyer admitted to me that the late Meser must have put aside some thousands of thalers, which, however, it would not be possible to lay hands on, as he had not left his heirs any funds at all.

In order to pacify the woeful Kriete, I was eventually obliged to agree to sell my rights in the works Meser had published for nine thousand marks, which represented the exact sum I owed to Kriete and another creditor who held a smaller share. With regard to the arrears of interest still owing on the money at compound rate, I remained Kriete's personal debtor; the joint sum amounted in the year 1864 to five thousand four hundred marks, which were duly claimed of me about this time with all the pressure of the law. In the interests of Pusinelli, my chief creditor, who could only be provided under this arrangement with inadequate payment, I reserved to myself the French copyright of these three operas, in the event of this music being produced in France through my efforts at finding a publisher to purchase it in that country.

According to the contents of a letter from the lawyer Schmidt, this reservation of mine had been accepted by the present publisher in Dresden. Pusinelli in a friendly spirit forbore to take advantage of the benefits accruing to him from this arrangement, in regard to the capital he had formerly lent me. He assured me he would never claim it. Thus one possibility remained open to me for the future: that if my operas could make their way into France, although there would be no question of any profit coming to me through those works of mine, I should be reimbursed for the capital I had spent on them and for that which I had been obliged to guarantee. When, later on, my Paris publisher Flaxland and I came to make out an agreement, Meser's successor in Dresden announced himself as absolute proprietor of my operas, and actually succeeded in putting so many obstacles in Flaxland's way in the conduct of his French business, that the latter was compelled to purchase peace at the price of six thousand francs. The natural result of this was that Flaxland was placed in the position of being able to deny that it was I who owned the French copyright of my work. Upon this I made repeated appeals to Adolph Schmidt, the lawyer, to give evidence in my favour, asking nothing more of him than that he should forward to me a copy of the correspondence referring to the rights I had reserved, which had become valid in the Lucerne transaction. To all the letters addressed to him on this subject, however, he obstinately refused an answer, and I learned later on from a Viennese lawyer that I must give up hoping to get this kind of evidence, as I had no legal means in my possession to force the advocate to give it, if he were not so inclined.

While, owing to this, I had little opportunity of improving my prospects for the future, I had at least the satisfaction of seeing the score of *Tannhäuser* engraved at last. As the stock of my earlier autograph copies had come to an end, chiefly through the wasteful management of Meser, I had already persuaded Härtel when I was in Venice to have the score engraved. Meser's successor had acquired the complete rights of this work, and therefore regarded it as a point of honour not to give up the score to another publisher; consequently he took over the task of producing it at his own cost. Unluckily fate demanded that just a year later I had to revise and reconstruct the first two scenes completely. To this day it is a subject of regret to me not to have been able to introduce this fresh piece of work into the engraved score.

The Härtels, never faltering in their assumption that *Tristan* might provide good food for the theatre, set their men busily to work upon engraving the score of the second act, while I was at work on the third. The process of registering corrections, while I was in the throes of composing the third act — one long ecstasy — wielded over me a strange, almost uncanny influence; for in the first scenes of this act it was made clear to me that in this opera (which had been most unwarrantably assumed to be an easy one to produce), I had embodied the most daring and most exotic conception in all my writings. While I was at work on the great scene of *Tristan,* I found myself often asking whether I was not mad to want to give such work to a publisher to print for the theatre. And yet I could not have parted with a single accent in that tale of pain, although the whole thing tortured me to the last degree.

I tried to overcome my gastric troubles by using (among other things) Kissingen water in moderate doses. As I was fatigued and made incapable of work by the early walks I had to take during this treatment, it occurred to me to take a short ride instead. For this purpose the hotel manager lent me a horse, aged twenty-five, named Lise. On this animal I rode every morning as long as it would carry me. It never conveyed me very far, but turned back regularly at certain spots without taking the slightest notice of my directions.

Thus passed the months of April, May, and the greater part of June, without my completing even half of my composition for the third act, and all the while I was contending with a mood of the deepest melancholy. At last came the season for the visitors to arrive; the hotel with its annexes began to fill, and it was no longer possible to think of maintaining my exceptional privilege with regard to the use of such choice quarters. It was proposed to move me to the second storey of the main building, where only travellers who spent the night on their way to other places in Switzerland were put up, whereas in the annexes people were lodged who came to make a long stay, and who used their rooms day and night. As a matter of fact, this arrangement answered admirably. From this time forward I was completely undisturbed during the hours of my work in my little sitting-room with its adjoining bedchamber, as the rooms engaged for the night by strangers in this storey were perfectly empty in the daytime.

Really splendid summer weather set in eventually, lasting a good two months with a continuously cloudless sky. I enjoyed the curious charm of protecting myself against the extremes of the sun's heat by carefully keeping my room cool and dark, and going out on to my balcony only in the evening to surrender myself to the influence of the summer air. Two good horn-players gave me great pleasure by providing a performance of simple folk-songs almost regularly in a skiff on the lake. In my work, too, I had now luckily passed the critical point, and in spite of its sorrowful character, the more subdued mood of that part of my poem which I had still to master, threw me into a sincere spiritual ecstasy, during which I completed the composition of the whole work by the beginning of August, fragments only remaining to be orchestrated.

Lonely as was my life, the exciting events of the Italian war provided me plenty of interest. I followed this struggle, as unexpected as it was significant, through the thrilling course of its successes and reverses. Still I did not remain entirely without company. In July, Felix Dräsecke, whom I had not known before, came to Lucerne for a lengthy visit. After hearing a performance of the prelude to *Tristan und Isolde* conducted by Liszt, he had almost immediately determined to make himself personally acquainted with me. I was completely terrified by his arrival, and was at a loss to know what to do with him. Moreover, as his talk was in a certain facetious vein, overflowing with stories of persons and circumstances for which I was gradually losing all appreciation, he soon began to bore me, a fact which astonished him, and which he recognised so clearly that he thought he had better leave after a few days. This made me in my turn embarrassed, and I now took special care to deprive him of the bad opinion he had formed of me. I soon learned to like him, and for a considerable time, until shortly before his departure from Lucerne, he was my daily companion, from whose intercourse I derived much pleasure, as he was a highly gifted musician and by no means a prig. But Dräsecke was not my only visitor.

Wilhelm Baumgartner, my old Zürich acquaintance, came to spend a few weeks in Lucerne out of kindness to me. And lastly Alexander Séroff from St. Petersburg came to stay some time in the neighbourhood. He was a remarkable man, of great intelligence, and openly prepossessed in favour of Liszt and myself. He had heard my *Lohengrin* in Dresden and wanted to know more of me — an ambition I was obliged to satisfy by playing *Tristan* to him in the rough-and-ready fashion which was peculiar to me. I went up Mount Pilatus with Dräsecke, and again had to look after a companion who suffered from giddiness. To celebrate his departure I invited him to take an excursion to Brunnen and the Grütli. After this we took leave of each other for the time being, as his moderate resources did not permit him to remain any longer, and I too was seriously thinking of taking my departure.

The question now arose as to where I was to go. I had addressed letters, first through Eduard Devrient, and finally direct to the Grand Duke of Baden, asking the latter for a guarantee that I might settle, if not in Karlsruhe itself, at least in some small place in the neighbourhood. This would suffice to set at rest a craving, which could no longer be suppressed, for intercourse now and then with an orchestra and a company of singers, if only to hear them play. I learned later that the Grand Duke had really bestirred himself in the matter by writing to the King of Saxony. But the view still prevailed in that quarter that I could not be granted an amnesty, but could only hope to receive an act of grace; it being assumed, of course, that I would first have to report myself to a magistrate for examination. Thus the fulfilment of my wish remained impossible, and I shrank in dismay before the problem of how to secure a performance of my *Tristan* which I could superintend in person, as I had determined to do. I was assured that the Grand Duke would know what measures to resort to in order to meet the situation. But the question was, where was I to turn for a place in which to settle with some prospect of being able to remain there. I longed for a permanent home again. After due consideration I decided that Paris was the only place where I could make sure of now and then hearing a good orchestra and a first-class quartette. Without these stimulating influences Zürich at last became unbearable, and in no other city but Paris, where I could stay undisturbed, could I safely reckon on being able to obtain artistic recreation of a sufficiently high standard.

At last I had to bestir myself to come to a decision about my wife. We had now been apart from each other for a whole year. After the hard lessons she had received from me, and which, according to her letters, had left a deep impression upon her, I was justified in assuming that the renewal of our life in common might be made tolerable; especially as it would remove the grave difficulty of her maintenance. I therefore agreed with her that she should join me late in the autumn in Paris. In the meantime I was willing to look for a possible abode there, and undertook to arrange for the removal of our furniture and household goods to the French capital. In order to carry out this plan financial assistance was imperative, as the means at my disposal were quite inadequate. I then made to Wesendonck the same offer in regard to my *Nibelungen* that I had made to the Grand Duke of Weimar, that is to say, I proposed that he should buy the copyright for publishing the work. Wesendonck acceded to my wishes without demur, and was ready to buy out each of the completed portions of my work in turn for about the same sum as it was reasonable to suppose a publisher would pay for it later on. I was not able to fix my departure, which took place on the 7th of September, when I went for a three days' visit to my friends in Zürich. I spent these days at the Wesendonck's, where I was well looked after and saw my former acquaintances, Herwegh, Semper, and Gottfried Keller. One of the evenings I spent with them was marked by an animated dispute with Semper over the political events of the time. Semper professed to recognise, in the recent defeat of Austria, the defeat of the German nationality; in the Romance element represented by Louis Napoleon, he recognised a sort of Assyrian despotism which he hated both in art and politics. He expressed himself with such emphasis that Keller, who was generally so silent, was provoked into a lively debate. Semper in his turn was so aggravated at this, that at last in a fit of desperation he blamed me for luring him into the enemy's camp, by being the cause of his invitation to the Wesendonck's. We made it up before we parted that night, and met again on several occasions after this, when we took care never again to let our discussions become so passionate. From Zürich I went to Winterthur to visit Sulzer. I did not see my friend himself, but only his wife and the boy she had borne to him since my last visit; the mother and child made a very touching and friendly impression on me, particularly when I realised that I must now regard my old friend in the light of a happy father.

On the 15th of September I reached Paris. I had intended to fix my abode somewhere in the neighbourhood of the Champs Élysées, and with this object in view at once looked out for temporary lodgings in that district, which I found eventually in the Avenue de Matignon. My main object was to discover my desired peaceful place of refuge in some small house remote from the thoroughfares. I at once bestirred myself to find this, and thought it my duty to make use of every acquaintance I could call to mind. The Olliviers were not in Paris at the time; Countess d'Agoult was ill, and was also busy arranging her departure for Italy, and unable to receive me. She referred me to her daughter the Countess Charnacé, upon whom I called, but without being able to explain to her the purpose I had in view. I also looked up the Hérold family, who had received me in such a friendly way on my last visit to Paris; but I found Mme. Hérold in a strange and morbidly excitable state of mind, the result of ill-health, so that instead of discussing my views with her, my only thought was to keep her calm and avoid upsetting her by even the slightest appeal for help. In my passionate longing to find a home I decided to get no further information, but set about the matter myself. At last I discovered in the Rue Newton near the Barrière de l'Étoile, a side street off the Champs Élysées, not yet completed in accordance with a former plan of Paris, a nice little villa with a small garden. I took this on a three-years' agreement at a rent of four thousand francs a year. Here, at all events, I might look for complete quiet and total isolation from the noise of the streets. This fact alone prepossessed me very much in taking the little house, the late occupier of which had been the well-known author Octave Feuillet, who was at that time under the patronage of the imperial court. But I was puzzled that the building, in spite of my being unable to detect anything old in its structure, had been so neglected

inside. The proprietor could in no way be induced to do anything to restore the place and make it habitable, even if I
had consented to pay a higher rent. The reason of this I discovered some time afterwards: the estate itself was doomed
in consequence of the plans for the rebuilding of Paris; but
the time had not yet come to make the official announcement
of the government's intentions to the proprietors, because, had
this been done, their claims to compensation would have become valid at once. I consequently laboured under the pleasant delusion that whatever I was obliged to spend on interior
decoration and on restoring the property would, in the course
of years, prove to be money well invested. I therefore proceeded to give the necessary instructions for the work without hesitating, and ordered my furniture to be sent from
Zürich, thinking that as fate had driven me to my choice, I
could regard myself as a resident of Paris for the rest of my
life.

While the house was being prepared, I tried to get my bearings as to what could be extracted for my future existence
out of the popularity of my artistic works. The first thing
I did was to look up M. de Charnal and to get information
from him about the translation of the libretto of my *Rienzi*
with which he had been entrusted. It turned out that M.
Carvalho, the director of the Théâtre Lyrique, would hear of
absolutely nothing but *Tannhäuser*. I prevailed upon Carvalho
to visit me to talk the matter over. He declared that he was
most certainly inclined to produce one of my operas, only it
must be *Tannhäuser*, because, as he explained, this opera was
identified with me among the Parisians, who would think it
ridiculous to produce any other work under the name of
'Wagner.' As to my choice of a translator for the poem of
this opera he seemed to entertain grave doubts: he asked
whether I had not made a mistake, whereupon I tried to get
more definite information about the capabilities of M. de
Charnal, and discovered to my horror that this charming young
man, who boasted that he had collaborated in a melodrama
called *Schinderhannes*, which he thought was a German romantic
subject, had not had the slightest conception of the character
of the work he was handling.

As his enthusiasm moved me, I tried to shape some verses
with him and make them practicable for musical purposes;
but I failed utterly, and all my trouble was in vain. Bülow
had once drawn my attention to Auguste de Gaspérini, a young
doctor who had ceased to practise, and whose acquaintance he
had made in Baden-Baden, where he discovered that he was
extraordinarily fond of my music. I called upon him without
loss of time, and as he was not in Paris, I wrote to him. This
man sent his friend Leroy to me with a letter of recommendation.
He was a well-educated Parisian music-master, who won my
esteem by his attractive personality. My confidence in him
was aroused, because he at once dissuaded me from associating
myself with an obscure journalist on a theatrical newspaper
(in which character M. de Charnal finally disclosed himself),
and advised me to go to Roger, a highly gifted and experienced operatic singer, who had been a favourite with the
Parisian public and was master of the German language. This
lifted a load from my heart: I accepted the invitation which
Leroy arranged for me through another friend, who took me
down to Roger's country place one day to meet him. I have
forgotten the name of this large estate which was occupied by
the Paris tenor, whose fame had been so celebrated up to that
time; the château had once belonged to a marquis, and was
built in a very sumptuous style and surrounded by extensive
hunting-grounds. It was the desire to handle a gun and make
use of these grounds (which he loved) that, only a short time
before, had landed this charming singer in a terrible disaster
which had shattered his right arm.

I found Roger, some months after the accident, completely
recovered; but the forearm had had to be amputated. The
question now was whether a famous mechanician, who had
promised to make him a perfect substitute for the lost limb
even in the matter of free gesticulation, would be able to carry
out his task. He succeeded fairly well, as I saw with my own
eyes some time later, when I witnessed Roger act in a benefit
performance which the Grand Opera had given him, and use his
arm so ingeniously that he received great applause for this
reason alone. In spite of this he had to accept the fact that
he was regarded as ' disabled,' and that his career at the Grand

Opera in Paris had come to a close. For the time being he seemed to be glad to secure for himself some sort of literary occupation, and accepted with much pleasure my proposal that he should make a translation of *Tannhäuser* for practical use. He sang to me the French text of some of the main themes which he had already translated, and they seemed to me good. After I had spent a day and a night with the singer, who had once been such a popular favourite, and was now condemned to look forward to a sad decline, I felt in very good spirits and full of hope, more especially as his intelligent way of approaching my opera gave me a pleasing idea of the extent to which it was possible to cultivate the French mind. In spite of this I had soon to give up the notion of Roger's working for me, as for a long time he was entirely absorbed in trying to make secure the position into which he had fallen through his terrible accident. He was so busy with his own affairs that he could hardly give me an answer to my inquiries, and for the time being I lost sight of him altogether.

I had come to this arrangement with Roger more by chance than out of necessity, as I continued to adhere firmly to my plan simply to seek a suitable *pied-à-terre* in Paris. My serious artistic enterprises, on the other hand, were still directed to Germany, from which, from another point of view, I was an enforced exile. Soon, however, the whole aspect of affairs changed: the proposed performance of *Tristan* in Karlsruhe, on which I had continued to keep an eye, was finally announced as abandoned. I had to remain uncertain as to the precise reason why this undertaking had been given up, which at an earlier stage had apparently been pursued with so much zeal. Devrient pointed out to me that all his attempts to secure an appropriate representation of the rôle of Isolde had been shattered by my deciding against the singer Garrigues (who had already married young Schnorr), and that he felt his incapacity to offer advice on the rest of the business all the more keenly because Schnorr, the tenor, whose devotion to me was so great, had himself despaired of being able to execute the last portion of the task assigned to him. I realised at once that this was an obstacle which I should have been able to overcome, together with all its disastrous consequences, if I had been permitted, even for a brief space of time, to visit Karlsruhe. But the mere expression of this wish seemed, as soon as it was reiterated, to arouse the bitterest feelings against me. Devrient expressed his opinion on the matter with so much violence and brutality that I could not help seeing that what kept me from Karlsruhe was mainly his personal disinclination to have me there, or to be interfered with in the conduct of his theatre.

A less potent factor in the situation I found in the painful feeling now aroused in the Grand Duke at the prospect of not being able to fulfil the promise he had once held out to me, that I should visit him in Karlsruhe, where he was in residence; if the main object for the visit were to subside under pressure of other considerations, he could only regard this circumstance in the light of an almost desirable event. At the same time I received from Bülow, who had gone several times to Karlsruhe, fairly broad hints as to what Devrient was aiming at. Full light was shed on the affair at a later stage; for the present it was a matter of the utmost importance for me to face the fact that I was entirely cut off from Germany, and must think of a fresh field for the production of *Tristan*, which lay so near my heart. I rapidly sketched a plan for starting a German theatre in Paris itself, such as had existed in bygone years with the co-operation of Schröder-Devrient. I thought I could safely rely on the possibility of doing so, as the most eminent singers of the German theatre were known to me, and would gladly follow me if I were to summon them to Paris on such a mission. I received messages of ready acceptance, in the event of my succeeding in founding a German opera season in Paris on a solid basis, from Tichatschek, Mitterwurzer, Niemann the tenor, and also Luise Meyer in Vienna. My immediate and besetting care was then to discover in Paris a suitable man for the task, who would undertake the execution of my plan at his own risk. My object was to secure the Salle Ventadour for a spring season of two months after the close of the Italian opera. There would then be performances of my operas, *Tannhäuser, Lohengrin*, and finally *Tristan*, by a chosen company and chorus of German singers, for the benefit of the Parisian public in general and myself in particular.

With this purpose in mind, my anxieties and endeavours now

took a totally different direction from that towards which they had tended when I first settled again in Paris; to cultivate acquaintances, especially among those who had influence, was now of the utmost importance to me. For this reason I was glad to hear that Gaspérini had arrived in Paris for good. Although I had only known him very slightly before, I now immediately communicated my plans to him, and was introduced in the friendliest way to a rich man who was well disposed towards him, a M. Lucy, who, so I was told, was not without influence, and was at that time Receiver-General in Marseilles. Our deliberations convinced us that the most necessary, and indeed indispensable, thing was to find some one to come forward and finance our enterprise. My friend Gaspérini could not but agree that, on the strength of the opinions he had himself advanced, it was natural I should look upon M. Lucy as the very man we wanted; but he thought it advisable to put our wishes before his friend with some caution, for though Lucy had much *chaleur de cœur*, he was principally a man of business and understood but little of music. Above all, it was necessary that my compositions should become well known in Paris, so that further enterprises might be founded on the results thus obtained. With this object in view I decided to arrange a few important concerts. To effect this I had to welcome my old friend Belloni, Liszt's former secretary, into the circle of my closer acquaintances. He immediately enlisted a companion of his in our cause, a highly intelligent man called Giacomelli, whom I never knew to be anything but good-natured. He was the editor of a theatrical journal and was cordially recommended to me by Belloni, as much for his excellent French as for his exceptional capabilities in other respects. My new protector's strange editorial office became from this time one of my most important places of rendezvous, which I frequented almost daily, and where I met all the curious creatures with whom, for the purpose of theatrical and similar matters, one is obliged to mix in Paris. The next thing to be considered was how to obtain the most suitable hall for my intended concerts. It was evident that I should appear to greatest advantage before the Parisian public if I could secure the theatre and orchestra of the Grand Opera.

For this I had to address myself to the Emperor Napoleon, which I did in a concise letter composed for me by Gaspérini. The hostility of Fould, who was at that time the Minister of the Household to Napoleon, would probably have to be reckoned with, on account of his friendly relations to Meyerbeer. The injurious and dreaded influence of this personage we hoped to counteract by that of M. Mocquard, Napoleon's secretary, who, as Ollivier declared, composed all the imperial speeches. In an *élan* of fiery generosity Lucy decided to appeal to the friend of his youth, for as such he regarded Mocquard, in a letter of recommendation to him on my behalf. As even this communication received no answer from the Tuileries, I and my more practical friends, Belloni and Giacomelli, with whom I held consultations, grew more doubtful every day of our own power as opposed to that of the Minister of the Household, and we therefore entered into negotiations with Calzado, the director of the Italian Opera, instead. We met with a direct refusal in this quarter, whereupon I finally decided to seek a personal interview with the man. By a power of persuasion which astonished even myself, and, above all, by holding out the prospect of my *Tristan* at the Italian Opera possibly proving a huge success, I actually succeeded in at last obtaining his consent to let the Salle Ventadour for three evenings with a week's interval between each. But even my passionate eloquence, which Giacomelli extolled on our way home, could not persuade him to lower the rent, which he fixed at four thousand francs an evening, merely for the hire and lighting of the hall.

After this the most important point was to get a first-class orchestra for my concerts, and my two agents had, for the time being, more than enough to do in this respect. In consequence of their endeavours on my behalf I now began to notice the first signs of a hostile, and hitherto unsuspected, attitude towards me and my undertaking on the part of my old friend Berlioz. Full of the favourable impression he had made upon me when we met in London in 1855, which was strengthened by a friendly correspondence he had kept up for a time, I had called at his house as soon as I arrived in Paris. As he was not in I turned back into the street, where I met him on his way home, and noticed that the sight of me occasioned a convulsive movement of fright, which showed itself in his whole physiognomy and bearing in a way which was almost gruesome. I saw at a glance how matters stood between us, but concealed my own uneasiness under an appearance of natural concern about his state of health, which he immediately assured me was one of torture, and that he could only bear up against the most violent attacks of neuralgia with the help of electric treatment, from which he was just returning. In order to allay his suffering I offered to leave him immediately, but this made him so far ashamed of his attitude that he pressed me to return with him to his house. Here I succeeded in making him feel somewhat more friendly towards me by disclosing my real intentions in Paris: even the concerts I proposed giving were merely to serve the purpose of so far attracting public attention as to make it possible to establish German opera here, so that when I wished to do so I could superintend the representation of such of my own works I had not yet heard; while, on the other hand, I completely renounced the idea of a French production of *Tannhäuser*, such as the manager Carvalho had seemed to contemplate. In consequence of these explanations I was apparently for a time on quite a friendly footing with Berlioz. I consequently thought that, with regard to the engagement of musicians for the proposed concerts, I could not on this occasion do better than refer my agents to this experienced friend, whose advice would certainly prove invaluable. They afterwards informed me that Berlioz had at first shown himself sympathetically inclined, but his manner had suddenly changed one day when Mme. Berlioz entered the room where they were discussing matters, and exclaimed in a tone of angry surprise, ' *Comment, je crois que vous donnez des conseils pour les concerts de M. Wagner?* ' Belloni then discovered that this lady had just accepted a valuable bracelet sent her by Meyerbeer. Being a man of the world he said to me, ' Do not count upon Berlioz,' and there the whole matter ended.

From this time forward Belloni's bright face was clouded over with an expression of the deepest anxiety. He thought he had discovered that the whole Parisian press was exceedingly

hostile towards me, which he had not the slightest doubt was due
to the tremendous agitation Meyerbeer had set on foot from
Berlin. He discovered that an urgent correspondence had been
carried on from there with the editors of the principal Paris
journals, and that amongst others the famous *Fiorentino* had
already taken advantage of Meyerbeer's alarm at my Parisian
enterprise, to threaten him with praise of my music, thus
naturally exciting Meyerbeer to further bribery. This increased
Belloni's anxiety, and he advised me, above all, to try and find
financial support for my plans, or if I had no prospect of this,
to rely on the imperial power alone. He pointed out that it
was absolutely impossible for me to carry out the concerts
entirely on my own responsibility without financial support,
and his arguments had the effect of making me decide to be
careful; for what with my journey to Paris and my installation
there, my funds were thoroughly exhausted. So I was again
forced to enter into negotiations with the Tuileries about the
letting of the Opera House and its orchestra free of charge.
Ollivier now came forward with judicious advice and introductions, which brought me into touch with all kinds of people,
and, amongst others, with Camille Doucet (a leading member of
Fould's ministry and also a dramatic author). By this means I
hoped to penetrate into the presence of Meyerbeer's admirer,
the unapproachable and terrible Minister of State. One result
of these introductions, however, was that I formed a lasting
friendship with Jules Ferry, though our acquaintance proved
quite useless to the immediate purpose in hand. The Emperor
and his secretary remained obstinately silent, and this even
after I had obtained the Grand Duke of Baden's consent to
the intercession of his ambassador in Paris on my behalf, and
also that of the Swiss ambassador, Dr. Kern, whose combined
forces were to try and enlighten me, and possibly also the
Emperor, about Fould's manœuvres. But it was useless — all
remained silent as before.

Under these circumstances I regarded it as a freak of fate
that Minna should announce her readiness to join me in Paris,
and that I should have to expect her arrival shortly. In the
selection as well as in the arrangement of the little house in
the Rue Newton I had had particular regard to our future

existence together. My living-room was separated from hers
by a staircase, and I had taken care that the part of the house
to be occupied by her should not be wanting in comfort. But,
above all, the affection which had been revived by our last
reunion in Zürich had prompted me to furnish and decorate
the rooms with special care, so that they might have a friendly
appearance and make life in common with this woman, who
was becoming quite a stranger to me, more possible to bear.
On account of this I was afterwards reproached with a love of
luxury. There was also a possibility of arranging a drawing-
room in our house, and though I had not intended to be extravagant, I finally discovered that, in addition to the trouble
of negotiations with unreliable Parisian workmen, I was drawn
into expenses I had not counted upon. But I comforted myself with the reflection that, as it could not be helped now,
Minna would at least be pleased when she entered the house
she was henceforth to manage. I also thought it necessary
to get a maid for her, and a particularly suitable person was
recommended me by Mme. Hérold. I had also engaged a man-
servant as soon as I arrived, and although he was rather a
thick-headed Swiss from Valais, who had at one time belonged
to the Pope's bodyguard, he soon became quite devoted to me.
In addition to these two servants there was my wife's former
cook, whom she had taken with her from Zürich, and by whom
she was accompanied when at last I was able to go and meet
her at the station on the 17th of November. Here Minna
immediately handed me the parrot and her dog Fips, which involuntarily reminded me of her arrival in the harbour of Rorschach ten years ago. Just as she had done on that occasion
also, she now immediately gave me to understand that she did
not come to me out of need, and that if I treated her badly
she knew quite well where to go. Moreover, there was no denying that since then a not unimportant change had taken place
in her; she owned that she was filled with a similar anxiety
and fear like a person feels who is about to enter a new situation, and did not know whether she would be able to stand it.
Here I sought to divert her thoughts by acquainting her with
my public position, which as my wife she would naturally
share. Unfortunately she could not understand this at all,

and it failed to make any appeal to her, while her attention was immediately absorbed by the interior arrangement of our house. The fact of my having taken a man-servant merely filled her with scorn; but that, under the title of lady's maid, I should have provided her with what I had really considered a very necessary attendant, made her furious. This person, whom Mme. Hérold had recommended to me with the assurance that she had shown angelic patience in the care of her sick and aged mother, speedily became so demoralised by Minna's treatment of her that, at the end of a very short time, I of my own accord hurriedly dismissed her, and in doing so was violently reproached by my wife for giving the woman a small tip. To an even greater extent did she succeed in spoiling my man-servant, who finally refused to obey her orders, and when I found fault with him became so impertinent towards me also that I had to send him away at the shortest notice. He left a very good complete set of livery behind, which I had just bought at great expense, and which remained on my hands, as I felt no inclination ever to have a man-servant again. On the other hand, I cannot but bear the highest testimony in favour of the Swabian Therese, who from this time forward performed the entire service of the household alone during the whole of my sojourn in Paris. This woman, who was gifted with unusual penetration, at once grasped my painful position towards her mistress, and understanding my wife's faults, succeeded by her indefatigable activity in turning matters to the best advantage for me as well as for the household, and thus neutralising their bad effect.

So in this last reunion with Minna I once more entered upon a state of existence which I had repeatedly lived through before, and which it seemed was now to start afresh. This time it was almost a blessing that there could be no question of quiet retirement, but that, on the contrary, it was necessary to enter upon an endless succession of worldly relations and activities, to which I was again driven by fate entirely against my choice and inclination.

With the opening of the year 1860 a very unexpected turn of affairs made it seem possible that I should succeed in carrying out my plans. The musical director Esser in Vienna informed me that Schott, the music publisher of Mayence, wished to obtain a new opera by me for publication. I had nothing to offer at present but the *Rheingold;* the peculiar composition of this work, meant only as a prelude to the *Nibelungen* trilogy I meant to write, made it difficult for me to offer it as an opera without adding any further explanation. However, Schott's eagerness, at all costs, to have a work of mine to add to his catalogue of publications was so great that I no longer hesitated, and, without concealing from him the fact that he would have great difficulty in propagating this work, I offered to place it at his disposal for the sum of ten thousand francs, promising him at the same time the option of purchasing the three main operas which were to follow at the same price for each. In the event of Schott accepting my offer, I immediately formed a plan of spending the sum thus unexpectedly acquired for the furthering of my Paris undertaking.

Tired out with the obstinate silence maintained by the imperial cabinet, I now commissioned my agents to close with Signor Calzado for three concerts to be given at the Italian Opera, as well as to obtain the necessary orchestra and singers. When the arrangements for this had been set in motion, I was again made anxious by Schott's tardy offers of lower terms; in order not to alienate him, however, I wrote to the musical director Schmidt in Frankfort commissioning him to continue the negotiations with Schott on considerably reduced terms, to which I gave my consent. I had scarcely sent off this letter when an answer from Schott reached me, in which he at last expressed his willingness to pay me the sum of ten thousand francs for which I had asked. I thereupon sent a telegram to Schmidt promptly cancelling the commission with which I had just charged him.

With renewed courage I and my agents now followed up our plans, and the necessary preparations for the concerts engaged my whole attention. I had to look out for a choir, and for this I thought it necessary to reinforce the expensively paid company of the Italian Opera by a German society of singers who had been recommended to me and who were under the direction of a certain Herr Ehmant. In order to ingratiate myself with its members, I had one evening to visit their meeting-place in the

Rue du Temple, and cheerfully accommodate myself to the smell
of beer and the fumes of tobacco with which the atmosphere
was laden, and in the midst of which sturdy German artists
were to reveal their capabilities to me. I was also brought
into contact with a M. Chevé, the teacher and director of a
French national choral society, whose rehearsals took place in
the École de Médecine. I there met an odd enthusiast, who,
by his method of teaching people to sing without notes, hoped
to bring about the regeneration of the French people's genius.
But the worst trouble was occasioned by the necessity of my
having the different orchestral parts of the selections I was
going to have played copied out for me. For this task I hired
several poor German musicians, who remained at my house from
morning till night, in order to make the necessary arrangements,
which were often rather difficult, under my direction.

In the midst of these absorbing occupations Hans von Bülow
looked me up. He had come to Paris for some length of time,
as it turned out, more to assist me in my undertaking than to
follow his own pursuit as a concert virtuoso. He was staying
with Liszt's mother, but spent the greater part of the day with
me, in order to give help wherever it was needed, as, for instance,
with the immediate preparation of the copies. His activity
in all directions was extraordinary, but he seemed, above all,
to have set himself the task of making certain social connections,
that he and his wife had formed during their visit to Paris the
year before, useful to my undertaking. The result of this was
felt in due course, but for the present he helped me to arrange
the concerts, the rehearsals for which had begun.

The first of these took place in the Herz Hall, and led to such
an agitation on the part of the musicians against me that it
was almost as bad as a riot. I had continually to remonstrate
with them about habits on their part, which I on my side
felt unable to overlook, and tried to prove, on common-sense
grounds, how impossible it was to give way to them. My $\frac{6}{8}$
time, which I took as $\frac{4}{4}$ time, particularly incensed them, and
with tumultuous protestations they declared it should be taken
alla-breva. In consequence of a sharp call to order and an
allusion on my part to the discipline of a well-drilled orchestra,
they declared they were not ' Prussian soldiers,' but free men.

At last I saw that one of the chief mistakes had lain in the faulty setting up of the orchestra, and I now formed my plan for the next rehearsal. After a consultation with my friends I went to the concert-room on the next occasion the first thing in the morning and superintended the arranging of the desks myself, and ordered a plentiful lunch for the musicians to which, at the beginning of the rehearsal, I invited them in the following manner. I told them that on the result of our meeting of that day depended the possibility of my giving my concerts; that we must not leave the concert-room till we were quite clear about it. I therefore requested the members to rehearse for two hours, then to partake of a frugal lunch prepared for them in the adjoining salon, whereupon we would immediately hold a second rehearsal for which I would pay them. The effect of this proposal was miraculous: the advantageous arrangement of the orchestra contributed to the maintenance of the general good-humour, and the favourable impression made upon every one by the prelude to *Lohengrin*, which was then played, rose to enthusiasm, so that at the conclusion of the first rehearsal both players and audience, amongst whom was Gaspérini, were delighted with me. This friendly disposition was most agreeably displayed at the principal rehearsal, which took place on the stage of the Italian Opera House. I had now gained sufficient control to allow me to dismiss a careless cornet-player from the orchestra with a severe reproof, without incurring any difficulties owing to their *esprit de corps*.

At last the first concert took place on the 25th of January (1860); all the pieces which I had chosen from my various operas, including *Tristan und Isolde*, met with an entirely favourable, nay enthusiastic, reception from the public, and I even had the experience of one of my pieces, the march from *Tannhäuser*, being interrupted by storms of applause. The pleasure thus expressed was aroused, it seems, because the audience was surprised to find that my music, of which there had been so many contradictory reports, contained such long phrases of connected melody. Well satisfied as I was, both with the way in which the concert had been carried out and its enthusiastic reception, I had on the following days to overcome contrary impressions caused by the papers giving vent to their feelings against me. It was now clear that Belloni had been quite right in supposing that they were hostile to me, and his foresight, which had led us to omit inviting the press, had merely roused our opponents to greater fury. As the whole undertaking had been arranged more for the stimulation of friends than to excite praise, I was not so much disturbed by the blustering of these gentlemen as by the absence of any sign from the former. What caused me most anxiety was that the apparently well-filled house should not have brought us better returns than was found to be the case. We had made from five to six thousand francs, but the expenses amounted to eleven thousand francs. This might be partially covered if, in the case of the two less expensive concerts still to come, we could rely on considerably higher returns. Belloni and Giacomelli shook their heads, however; they thought it better not to close their eyes to the fact that concerts were not suited to the taste of the French people, who demanded the dramatic element as well, that is to say, costumes, scenery, the ballet, etc., in order to feel satisfied. The small number of tickets sold for the second concert, which was given on the 1st of February, actually put my agents to the necessity of filling the room artificially, so as at least to save appearances. I had to allow them to do as they thought best in this matter, and was afterwards astonished to learn how they had managed to fill the first places in this aristocratic theatre in such a way as to deceive even our enemies. The real receipts amounted to little over two thousand francs, and it now required all my determination and my contempt for the miseries that might result not to cancel the third concert to be given on the 8th of February. My fees from Schott, a part of which, it is true, I had to devote to the household expenses of my troubled domestic existence, were all spent, and I had to look round for futher subsidies. These I obtained with great difficulty, through Gaspérini's mediation, from the very man to win whose assistance in a much wider sense had been the whole object of the concerts. In short, we had to have recourse to M. Lucy, the Receiver-General of Marseilles, who was to come to Paris at the time my concerts were being given, and upon whom my friend Gaspérini had assumed that an important Parisian success would have the

effect of making him declare his readiness to finance my project
of establishing German opera in Paris. M. Lucy, on the
contrary, did not appear at the first concert at all, and was only
present at a part of the second, during which he fell asleep.
The fact that he was now called upon to advance several
thousands of francs for the third concert naturally seemed to
him to protect him against any further demands on our part, and
he felt a certain satisfaction at being exempt from all further
participation in my plans, at the price of this loan. Although,
as a matter of fact, this concert now seemed useless, it nevertheless gave me great pleasure, as much through the spirited
performance itself as on account of its favourable reception by
the audience, which, it is true, my agents had again to supplement in order to give the appearance of a full hall, but which,
nevertheless, showed a marked increase in the number of tickets
paid for.

The realisation of the deep impression I had made on certain
people had more effect upon me at this time than the dejection
I felt at having to all outward appearances failed in this enterprise. It was undeniable that the sensation I had produced
had directly, as the comments of the press had indirectly,
aroused extraordinary interest in me. My omission to invite
any journalists seemed to be regarded on all sides as a wonderful
piece of audacity on my part. I had foreseen the attitude likely
to be adopted by the majority of reporters, but I was sorry that
even such men as M. Franc-Marie, the critic of the *Patrie,*
who at the end of the concert had come forward to thank me
with deep emotion, should have found themselves forced to
follow the lead of the others, without compromising, and even
to go so far as to deny their true opinion of me. Berlioz aroused
a universal feeling of anger amongst my adherents, by an article
which began in a roundabout way, but ended with an open
attack on me which he published in the *Journal des Débats.*
As he had once been an old friend, I was determined not to
overlook this treatment, and answered his onslaught in a letter
which, with the greatest difficulty, I managed to get translated
into good French, and succeeded, not without trouble, in having
it inserted in the *Journal des Débats.* It so happened that this
very letter had the effect of drawing those on whom my concerts

had already made an impression more enthusiastically towards me. Amongst others a M. Perrin introduced himself to me; he had formerly been director of the Opéra Comique, and was now a well-to-do *bel esprit* and painter, and later became director of the Grand Opera. He had heard *Lohengrin* and *Tannhäuser* performed in Germany, and expressed himself in such a way as led me to suppose that he would make it a point of honour to bring these operas to France should he at any time be in a position to do so. A certain Count Foucher de Careil had also become acquainted with my operas in the same way, through seeing them performed in Germany, and he too became one of my distinguished and lasting friends. He had made a name by various publications on German philosophy, and more especially through a book on Leibnitz, and it could not but prove interesting to me to be brought through him into touch with a form of the French genius as yet unknown to me.

It is impossible to record all the passing acquaintances with whom I was brought in contact at this time, amongst whom a Russian Count Tolstoi was conspicuously kind; but I must here mention the excellent impression made upon me by the novelist Champfleury's amiable pamphlet, of which I and my concerts formed the subject. In a series of light and airy aphorisms he displayed such a comprehension of my music, and even of my personality, that I had never again met with such a suggestive and masterly appreciation, and had only come across its equal once before in Liszt's lucubrations on *Lohengrin* and *Tannhäuser*. My personal acquaintance with Champfleury, which followed, brought me face to face with a very simple and in a certain sense easy-tempered individual, such as one seldom meets, and belonging to a type of Frenchman fast becoming extinct.

The advances made me by the poet Baudelaire were in their way still more significant. My acquaintance with him began with a letter in which he told me his impressions of my music and the effect it had produced upon him, in spite of his having thought till then that he possessed an artistic sense for colouring, but none for sound. His opinions on the matter, which he expressed in the most fantastic terms and with audacious self-assurance, proved him, to say the least, a man of extra-

ordinary understanding, who with impetuous energy followed
the impressions he received from my music to their ultimate
consequences. He explained that he did not put his address
to his letter in order that I might not be led to think that he
wanted something from me. Needless to say, I knew how to
find him, and had soon included him among the acquaintances
to whom I announced my intention of being at home every
Wednesday evening.

I had been told by my older Parisian friends, amongst whom
I continued to count the faithful Gaspérini, that this was the
right thing to do in Paris; and so it came about that, in accordance with the fashion, I used to hold a *salon* in my small house
in the Rue Newton, which made Minna feel that she occupied
a very dignified position, though she only knew a few scraps of
French, with which she could barely help herself out. This
salon, which the Olliviers also attended in a friendly way, was
crowded for a time by an ever-growing circle. Here an old
acquaintance of mine, Malwida von Meysenbug, again came
across me, and from that time forth became a close friend for
life. I had only met her once before; this was during my
visit to London in 1855, when she had made herself known to
me by a letter in which she enthusiastically expressed her agreement with the opinions contained in my book *Das Kunstwerk
der Zukunft*. The occasion on which we had met in London
had been at an evening party at the house of a family called
Althaus, when I found her full of the desires and projects
for the future perfection of the human race to which I had
given expression in my book, but from which, under the influence of Schopenhauer and a profound realisation of the
intense tragedy of life and the emptiness of its phenomena, I
had turned away with almost a feeling of irritation. I found
it very painful in discussing the question, not to be understood
by this enthusiastic friend and to have to appear to her in the
light of a renegade from a noble cause. We parted in London
on very bad terms with one another. It was almost a shock to
me to meet Malwida again in Paris. Very soon, however, all
unpleasant recollections of our discussion in London were
wiped out, as she at once explained to me, that our dispute had
had the effect of making her decide to read Schopenhauer at

once. When, by earnest study, she had made herself acquainted with his philosophy, she came to the conclusion that the opinions she had at that time expressed and eagerly maintained concerning the happiness of the world must have vexed me on account of their shallowness. She then declared herself to be one of my most zealous followers in the sense that she, from now, became a true friend who was ever anxious for my welfare. When the laws of propriety compelled me to introduce her as a friend of mine to my wife, she could not help noticing at the first glance the misery of our merely nominal life in common, and realising the discomfort resulting from it, made it her business to interpose with affectionate solicitude. She also quickly saw the difficult position in which I was placed in Paris with my almost purposeless enterprises and the absence of all material security. The tremendous expenses I had incurred in giving the three concerts had not remained a secret from any of those concerned about me. Malwida also soon guessed the difficulties in which I found myself, since no prospect was opened on any side which could be looked upon as a practical result of my enterprise and a compensation for the sacrifices I had made. Entirely of her own accord she felt it her duty to try and obtain help for me, which she endeavoured to get from a certain Mme. Schwabe, the widow of a rich English tradesman, in whose house she had found shelter as governess to the eldest daughter, and whom she now proposed to introduce to me. She did not conceal from herself or from me what a disagreeable task the cultivation of this acquaintance might be to me; nevertheless she relied on the kindness she thought this somewhat grotesque woman possessed, as well as on her vanity, which would prompt her to repay me for the distinction she obtained by frequenting my *salon*. As a matter of fact I was entirely at the end of my resources, and I only found courage to deny my poverty-stricken condition in public on account of the horror I felt when I learned that a collection was being made for me amongst the Germans in Paris to indemnify me for the expense I had incurred in giving the three concerts. When the news of this reached me I immediately interfered with the declaration that the idea that I was in distress in consequence of the losses I had sustained was founded on a false report, and that I should be obliged to refuse all efforts made on my behalf. On this supposition Mme. Schwabe, who regularly attended my soirées and as regularly fell asleep while any music was going on, was however induced, through the solicitations of Malwida, to offer me her personal assistance. She gave me about three thousand francs, of which at this moment I was certainly in the greatest need; as I did not wish to accept this money as a gift, I gave the lady, who in no way exacted it, a written agreement of my own accord, by which I undertook to return this sum at the end of a year. She good-naturedly accepted this, not as a security but merely in order to satisfy my feelings. When, at the end of this time, I found it impossible to meet my obligation, I turned to Malwida, who was still in Paris, and asked her to tell Mme. Schwabe, who had left, how matters stood, and to obtain her consent to the renewal of the agreement for another year. Malwida earnestly assured me I need not take the trouble to ask for a renewal, as Mme. Schwabe had never looked upon the sum given me as anything but a contribution towards my undertaking, in which she flattered herself that she took great interest. We shall see later on how the case really stood.

During this stirring time I was deeply moved and surprised to receive a present from an admirer in Dresden called Richard Weiland; it was an artistic silver ornament representing a sheet of music surrounded by a crown of laurels; upon the sheet were engraved the first bars from the principal themes of my various operas up to *Rheingold* and *Tristan*. The modest fellow once paid me a visit afterwards and told me that he had gone regularly to different places in order to see the productions of my operas, which had given him the opportunity of comparing the representation of *Tannhäuser* in Prague, in which the overture had lasted twenty minutes, with the one in Dresden, which, under my direction, had only taken twelve minutes.

My acquaintance with Rossini also proved agreeably stimulating to me in another way; a comic writer had attributed an anecdote to him according to which, when his friend Caraffa declared himself an admirer of my music, he had served him his fish without sauce at dinner, and explained in so doing that his friend liked music without melody. Rossini openly protested against this in an article in which he designated the story as a *mauvaise blague* and at the same time declared that he would never allow himself such a jest at the expense of a man who was trying to extend his influence in the artistic world. When I heard of this, I did not for a moment hesitate to pay Rossini a visit, and was received by him in the friendliest manner, which I afterwards described in a memorandum devoted to reminiscences of him. I was also glad to hear that my old acquaintance Halévy, during the controversy occasioned by my music, had taken my part in a kindly way, and I have already described my visit to him and our conversation on that occasion.

In spite of all these pleasant and stimulating events, nothing occurred to make my position less uncertain. I was still kept in doubt as to whether I should receive an answer from the Emperor Napoleon to my request for the use of the Opera House for the repetition of my concerts. Only by obtaining this, and having no preliminary expenses in consequence, could I gain the benefit which was becoming more and more necessary to me. It remained an understood thing that the Minister Fould was assiduously using his influence to turn the Emperor against me. As, on the other hand, I had made the surprising discovery that Marshal Magnan had been present at all three of my concerts, I hoped to enlist this gentleman's sympathy, which might be turned to good account, as the Emperor was particularly indebted to him since the events of the 2nd of December. I was anxious to circumvent Fould's intrigues, as the man had become most obnoxious to me, and I consequently introduced myself to the Marshal, and was one day surprised to see a hussar ride up to my door, who got down from his horse, rang the bell, and handed my astonished man-servant a letter from Magnan, in which he summoned me to his presence.

I was therefore duly received at the Commandant's residence by this military man, whose bearing struck me as stately, almost to the point of rudeness. He chatted very intelligently with me, frankly confessing his delight in my music, and listening very attentively to the report of my flagrantly futile addresses to the Emperor, as well as to my expressions of suspicion regarding Fould. I was told later that he spoke very plainly to Fould that very evening at the Tuileries on my behalf.

This much at least is certain, that from that moment I noticed that my affairs took a more favourable turn in that quarter. Yet the deciding factor was found at last in a movement on my behalf from a source I had hitherto entirely disregarded. Bülow, arrested by his interest in the outcome of these matters, continued to prolong his stay in Paris. He had come with letters of introduction from the Princess-Regent of Prussia to the Ambassador, Count Pourtalès. His hope that the latter might eventually express a desire to have me presented to him had so far remained unfulfilled. In order, therefore, to compel him to make my acquaintance, he finally adopted the plan of inviting the Prussian Ambassador and his attaché, Count Paul Hatzfeld, to lunch at Vachette's, a first-class restaurant, where I was to accompany him. The result of this meeting was certainly everything that could be desired. Not only did Count Pourtalès charm me with the simplicity and undisguised warmth of his conversation and attitude towards me, but from this time forward Count Hatzfeld used to visit me and also frequented my Wednesday evening At Homes, and at last brought me the news that there was a distinct movement in my favour at the Tuileries. Finally, one day he requested me to go with him to call on the Emperor's military chamberlain, Count Bacciochi, and from this official I received the first hints of a reply to my earlier application to his Imperial Majesty, who now expressed a wish to know why I wanted to give a concert in the Grand Opera House. No one, he said, took any serious interest in such enterprises, and it could do me no good. He thought it might perhaps be better if he were to persuade M. Alphonse Royer, the director of this imperial institution, to come to some understanding with me respecting the composition of an opera written on purpose for Paris. As I would not agree to his suggestion, this and other subsequent interviews remained for the time being without result. On one of these occasions Bülow accompanied me, and we were both struck by a ridiculous habit peculiar to this singular old man, whom Belloni said he had known in his youth as a box-office clerk at the Scala Theatre in Milan. He suffered from involuntary spasmodic movements of the hands, the result of certain not very creditable physical infirmities, and probably to conceal these he continually toyed with a small stick, which he tossed to and fro with seeming affectation. But even after I had at last succeeded in gaining access to the imperial officials, it seemed as though next to nothing would be done on my behalf, when suddenly one morning Count Hatzfeld overwhelmed me with news that on the preceding evening the Emperor had given orders for a performance of my *Tannhäuser*. The decisive word had been spoken by Princess Metternich. As I happened to be the subject of conversation near the Emperor, she had joined the circle, and on being asked for her opinion, she said she had heard *Tannhäuser* in Dresden, and spoke in such enthusiastic terms in favour of it that the Emperor at once promised to give orders for its production. It is true that Fould, on receiving the imperial command the same evening, broke out into a furious rage, but the Emperor told him he could not go back upon his promise, as he had pledged his word to Princess Metternich. I was now once more taken to Bacciochi, who this time received me very seriously, but first of all made the singular inquiry as to what was the subject of my opera. This I had to outline for him, and when I had finished, he exclaimed with satisfaction, ' *Ah! le Pape ne vient pas en scène? C'est bon! On nous avait dit que vous aviez fait paraître le Saint Père, et ceci, vous comprenez, n'aurait pas pu passer. Du reste, monsieur, on sait à présent que vous avez énormément de génie; l'Empereur a donné l'ordre de représenter votre opéra.*' He moreover assured me that every facility should be placed at my disposal for the fulfilment of my wishes, and that henceforth I must make my arrangements direct with the manager Royer.

This new turn of affairs put me into a state of vague agitation, for at first my inner conviction could only make me feel that singular misunderstandings would be sure to arise. For one thing, all hope of being able to carry out my original plan of producing my work in Paris with a picked German company was now at an end, and I could not conceal from myself that I had been launched upon an adventure which might turn out well or badly. A few interviews with the manager Royer sufficed to enlighten me as to the character of the enterprise entrusted to me. His chief anxiety was to convince me of the necessity of rearranging my second act, because according to

him it was absolutely necessary for a grand ballet to be introduced at this point. To this and similar suggestions I hardly
deigned to reply, and as I went home asked myself what I
should do next, in case I decided to refuse to produce my
Tannhäuser at the Grand Opera.

Meanwhile other cares, more immediately connected with
my personal affairs, pressed heavily upon me, and compelled me
to devote every effort to their removal. With this object in
view I decided at once to carry out an undertaking suggested
to me by Giacomelli, namely, a repetition of my concerts in
Brussels. A contract had been made with the Théâtre de la
Monnaie there for three concerts, half the proceeds of which,
after the deduction of all expenses, was to be mine. Accompanied by my agent, I started on 19th March for the Belgian
capital, to see whether I could not manage to recoup the money
lost on my Paris concerts. Under the guidance of my mentor
I found myself compelled to call upon all sorts of newspaper
editors and, among other Belgian worthies, a certain M. Fétis
père. All I knew about him was that, years before, he had
allowed himself to be bribed by Meyerbeer to write articles
against me, and I now found it amusing to enter into conversation with this man, who, although he assumed great airs
of authority, yet in the end declared himself entirely of my
opinion.

Here also I made the acquaintance of a very remarkable man,
the Councillor of State Klindworth, whose daughter, or, as
some said, his wife, had been recommended to me by Liszt
when I was in London. But I had not seen her on that occasion,
and I now had the pleasant surprise of being invited to call upon
her in Brussels. While she, on her part, showed the greatest
cordiality towards me, M. Klindworth provided me with inexhaustible entertainment by the narrative of his wonderful
career as a diplomatist in numerous transactions of which I
had hitherto known nothing. I dined with them several times,
and met Count and Countess Condenhoven, the latter being a
daughter of my old friend Mme. Kalergis. M. Klindworth
showed a keen and lasting interest in me, which even prompted
him to give me a letter of recommendation to Prince Metternich,
with whose father he said he had been on very familiar terms.

He had a strange habit of interlarding his otherwise frivolous
conversation with continual references to an omnipotent
Providence, and when, during one of our later interviews, I
once hazarded a risky retort, he quite lost his temper, and I
fancied he was going to break off our connection. Fortunately
this fear was not realised, either at that time or afterwards.

But except for these interesting acquaintances, I gained
nothing in Brussels but anxiety and fruitless exertion. The
first concert, for which season-tickets were suspended, drew a
large audience. But, owing to my misconception of a clause
in our agreement, the cost of musical accompaniment, which
was put down to me alone, was reckoned at so high a figure by
the managers, that next to nothing was left over by way of
profit. This deficiency was to be recouped from the second
concert, to which, however, season-ticket holders were admitted
free. But beyond these persons, who, I was told, almost filled
the house, there were few single-ticket holders, so that there
was not enough left to pay my travelling and hotel expenses,
which had been increased by the inclusion of my agent and
servant. I consequently gave up the idea of having a third
concert, and set off once more for Paris in a not very cheerful
frame of mind, but with the gift of a vase of Bohemian glass
from Mme. Street, Klindworth's daughter whom I have already
mentioned. Nevertheless, my stay in Brussels, including a
short trip from there to Antwerp, had served to distract my
thoughts a little. As I did not at that moment feel at all
inclined to devote my precious time to looking at works of art,
I contented myself in Antwerp with a cursory glance at its
outward aspect, which I found less rich in antiquities than I
had anticipated. The situation of its famous citadel proved
peculiarly disappointing. In view of the first act of my
Lohengrin I had presumed that this citadel, which I imagined
as the ancient keep of Antwerp, would from the opposite side
of the Scheldt be a prominent object to the eye. Instead of
which, nothing whatever was to be seen but a monotonous
plain, with fortifications sunk into the earth. After this,
whenever I saw *Lohengrin* again, I could not restrain a smile
at the scene-painter's castle, perched aloft in the background
on its stately mountain.

On returning to Paris at the end of March my sole anxiety was how to repair my impecunious and therefore hopeless position. The pressure of these monetary cares seemed all the more incongruous from the fact that the notoriety of my position had made my house, where, of course, I allowed no signs of poverty to appear, exceedingly popular. My Wednesday receptions became more brilliant than ever. Interesting strangers sought me out, in the hope that they, too, might attain to equal fortune through knowing me. Fräulein Ingeborg Stark, who afterwards married young Hans von Bronsart, put in an appearance among us, a vision of bewitching elegance, and played the piano, in which she was modestly assisted by Fräulein Aline Hund of Weimar. A highly gifted young French musician, Camille Saint-Saëns, also played a very agreeable part in our musical entertainments; a noteworthy addition to my other French acquaintances was made in the person of M. Frédéric Villot. He was Conservateur des Tableaux du Louvre, an exceedingly polished and cultured man, whom I met for the first time in Flaxland's music-shop, where I did a good deal of business. To my surprise I happened to overhear him asking about the score of *Tristan*, which he had ordered. On being introduced to him I learned, in reply to my inquiry, that he already possessed the scores of my earlier operas; and when I then asked whether he thought it possible for me to make my dramatic compositions pay, as I could not understand how he, without any knowledge of the German language, could rightly appreciate the music, which was so closely allied to the sense of the poetry, he answered wittily that it was precisely my music which afforded him the best guidance to a comprehension of the poem itself. This reply strongly attracted me to the man, and from that time I found great pleasure in keeping up an active correspondence with him. For this reason, when I brought out a translation of my operatic poems, I felt that its very detailed preface could not be dedicated to any worthier man. As he was not able to play the scores of my operas himself, he had them performed for him by Saint-Saëns, whom he apparently patronised. I thus learned to appreciate the skill and talent of this young musician, which was simply amazing. With an unparalleled sureness and rapidity of glance with regard to even the most complicated orchestral score, this young man combined a not less marvellous memory. He was not only able to play my scores, including *Tristan*, by heart, but could also reproduce their several parts, whether they were leading or minor themes. And this he did with such precision that one might easily have thought that he had the actual music before his eyes. I afterwards learned that this stupendous receptivity for all the technical material of a work was not accompanied by any corresponding intensity of productive power; so that when he tried to set up as a composer I quite lost sight of him in the course of time.

I now had to enter into closer communication with the manager of the Opera House, M. Royer, with regard to the production of *Tannhäuser*, which he had been commissioned to prepare. Two months passed before I was able to make up my mind whether to say yes or no to the business. At no single interview did this man fail to press for the introduction of a ballet into the second act. I might bewilder him, but with all the eloquence at my command I could never convince him on the point. At last, however, I could no longer refuse to consider the advisability of preparing a suitable translation of the poem.

Arrangements for this work had so far progressed very slowly. As I have already said, I had found M. de Charnal altogether incompetent, Roger had permanently disappeared from my sight, and Gaspérini showed no real desire for the work. At last a certain Herr Lindau came to see me, who protested that with the aid of young Edmond Roche he could produce a faithful translation of *Tannhäuser*. This man Lindau was a native of Magdeburg, who had fled to escape the Prussian military service. He had first been introduced to me by Giacomelli on an occasion when the French singer engaged by him to sing ' L'Étoile du Soir ' at one of my concerts had disappointed us, and he had recommended Lindau as a very efficient substitute. This man promptly declared his readiness to undertake this song, with which he was quite familiar, without any rehearsal, an offer which led me to regard him as a genius sent down from heaven on purpose for me. Nothing could, therefore, equal my amazement at the unbounded impudence of the man; for on the evening of the concert he executed his task with the most amateurish timidity; he did not enunciate a single note of the song clearly, and nothing but astonishment at so unprecedented a performance appeared to restrain the audience from breaking out into marked disapproval. Yet, in spite of this, Lindau, who had all sorts of explanations and excuses to offer for his short-comings, contrived to insinuate himself into my house, if not as a successful singer, at least as a sympathetic friend. There, thanks to Minna's partiality, he soon became an almost daily guest. In spite of a certain inward repugnance towards him, I treated him with tolerant good-nature, not so much because of the ' enormous connection' he said he could influence, but because he really showed himself to be a most obliging fellow on all sorts of occasions.

But the fact that finally induced me to grant him a share in the translation of *Tannhäuser* was his suggestion that young Roche should also participate in the work.

I had become acquainted with Roche immediately after my arrival in Paris (in the September of the previous year), and this in a somewhat remarkable and flattering way. In order to receive my furniture on its arrival from Zürich I had to go to the Custom House, where I was referred to a pale, seedy-looking young man, who appeared full of life, however, with whom I had to settle my business. When I wished to give him my name, he enthusiastically interrupted me with the exclamation, ' O, je connais bien Monsieur Richard Wagner, puisque j'ai son portrait suspendu au-dessus de mon piano.' Much astonished, I asked what he knew about me, and learned that by careful study of my pianoforte arrangements he had become one of my most fervent admirers. After he had helped me with self-sacrificing attentions to complete my tiresome business with the Custom House, I made him promise to pay me a visit. This he did, and I was able to obtain a clearer insight into the necessitous position of the poor fellow, who, so far as I was able to judge, showed signs of possessing great poetic talent. He further informed me that he had tried to eke out a precarious living as a violinist in the orchestras of the smaller vaudeville theatres, but that being a married man he would, for the sake of his family, much prefer a situation in some office with a fixed salary and prospects of promotion. I soon found that he thoroughly understood my music, which, he assured me, gave him the only pleasure he had in his hard life. As regards his power of poetical composition, I could only gather from Gaspérini and other competent judges that he could, at any rate, turn out very good verse. I had already thought of him as a translator for *Tannhäuser*, and now that the only obstacle to his doing the work, his ignorance of the German language, was removed by Lindau's proffered collaboration, the possibility of such an arrangement at once decided me to accept the latter's offer.

The first thing on which we agreed was that a fair prose translation of the whole subject should be taken in hand, and this task I naturally entrusted to Lindau alone. A serious delay, however, intervened before this was delivered to me, which was subsequently explained by the fact that Lindau was quite unable to provide even this dry version, and had pressed the work on another man, a Frenchman who knew German, and whom he induced to undertake it by holding out hopes of a fee, to be squeezed out of me later on. At the same time Roche turned a few of the leading stanzas of my poem into verse, with which I was well contented. As I was thus satisfied about the ability of my two helpers, I visited Royer in order to make my position secure by obtaining his authority for a contract with the two men. He did not seem to like my placing the work in the hands of two perfectly unknown people; but I insisted that they should at least have a fair trial. As I was obstinately resolved not to withdraw the work from Roche, but soon realised Lindau's complete inefficiency, I joined in the task myself at a cost of much exertion. We frequently spent four hours together in my room in translating a few verses, during which time I often felt tempted to kick Lindau out, for although he did not even understand the German text, he was always ready with the most impudent suggestions. It was only because I could not think of any other way of keeping poor Roche in the business that I endured such an absurd association.

This irritating and laborious work lasted for several months, during which I had to enter into fuller negotiations with Royer respecting his preparations for the production of *Tannhäuser*, and particularly with regard to the cast and distribution of the parts. It struck me as odd that hardly any of the leading singers of the Opera were suggested by him. As a matter of fact none of them aroused my sympathy, with the sole exception of Mme. Gueymard, whom I would gladly have secured for Venus, but who, for reasons I never clearly understood, was refused me. In order to form an honest opinion of the company at my disposal, I now had to attend several performances of such operas as *La Favorita, Il Trovatore,* and *Semiramis,* on which occasions my inner conviction told me so clearly that I was being hopelessly led astray, that each time I reached home I felt I must renounce the whole enterprise. On the other hand, I found continual encouragement in the generous way in which M. Royer, in obedience to authority, now offered to secure me any singer I might choose to designate. The most important item was a tenor for the title-rôle. I could think of no one but Niemann of Hanover, whose fame reached me from every quarter. Even Frenchmen such as Foucher de Careil and Perrin, who had heard him in my operas, confirmed the report of his great talent. The manager also regarded such an acquisition as highly desirable for his theatre, and Niemann was accordingly invited to come to Paris with a view of being engaged. Besides him, M. Royer wished me to agree to his securing a certain Mme. Tedesco, a tragedienne, who, on account of her beauty, would be a very valuable addition to the repertoire of his theatre, protesting that he could think of no woman better fitted for the part of Venus. Without knowing the lady I gave my consent to this excellent proposal, and moreover agreed to the engagement of a Mlle. Sax, a still unspoiled young singer with a very beautiful voice, as well as of an Italian baritone, Morelli, whose sonorous tones, as contrasted with the sickly French singers of this class, had greatly pleased me during my visits to the Opera. When these arrangements were concluded, I thought I had done all that was really necessary, though I did not cherish any very firm conviction on the matter.

Amid these labours I passed my forty-seventh birthday in a far from happy frame of mind, to which, however, on the evening of this day, the peculiarly bright glow of Jupiter gave me an omen of better things to come. The beautiful weather, suitable to the time of year, which in Paris is never favourable to the conduct of business, had only tended to increase the stringency of my needs. I was and still continued to be without any prospect of meeting my household expenses, which had now become very heavy. As I was ever anxious, amid all my other discomforts, to find some relief from this burden, I had made an agreement with the music-dealer Flaxland for the sale of all my French rights in the *Fliegender Holländer, Tannhäuser,* and *Lohengrin* for whatever they would fetch. Our contract stipulated that for each of these three operas he was to pay me a sum of one thousand francs down, and further payments on their being performed in a Paris theatre, namely, one thousand francs after the first ten performances, and the same amount for the following performances up to the twentieth. I at once notified my friend Pusinelli of this contract, having made this condition in his favour when selling my operas to Meser's successors. This I did by way of guaranteeing him the repayment of the capital advanced for their publication. I begged him, however, to allow me to retain Flaxland's first instalment on account, as otherwise I should be stranded in Paris without the means of bringing my operas to the point of being profitable. My friend agreed to all my suggestions. The Dresden publisher, on the contrary, was just as disagreeable, and complained at once that I was infringing his rights in France, and so worried Flaxland that the latter felt justified in raising all sorts of difficulties against me.

I had almost become involved in fresh complications in consequence, when one day Count Paul Hatzfeld appeared at my house with a request that I would visit Mme. Kalergis, who had just arrived in Paris, to receive certain communications from her. I now saw the lady again for the first time since my stay in Paris with Liszt in 1853. She greeted me by declaring how much she regretted not having been present at my concerts in the preceding winter, as she had thereby missed the chance of helping me in a time of great stress. She had heard that I had suffered great losses, the account of which she had been told ran to ten thousand francs, and she now begged me to accept that sum from her hand. Although I had thought it right to deny these losses to Count Hatzfeld, when an application was made to the Prussian embassy on behalf of the odious subscription-list, yet I had now no reason whatever for hiding the truth from this noble-hearted woman. I felt as though something were now being fulfilled which I had always been entitled to expect, and my only impulse was an immediate desire to show my gratitude to this rare lady by at least doing something for her. All the friction which disturbed our later intercourse sprang solely from my inability to fulfil this desire, in which I felt ever more and more confirmed by her singular character and restless, unsettled life. For the present I endeavoured to do something for her which should prove the reality of my feeling of obligation. I improvised a special performance of the second act of my *Tristan*, in which Mme. Viardot was to share the singing parts with myself, and on which occasion my friendship for the latter received a considerable impetus; while for the pianoforte accompaniment I summoned Klindworth at my own expense from London. This exceedingly select performence took place in Mme. Viardot's house. Besides Mme. Kalergis, in whose honour alone it was given, Berlioz was the only person present. Mme. Viardot had specially charged herself with securing his presence, apparently with the avowed object of easing the strained relations between Berlioz and myself. I was never clear as to the effect produced upon both performers and listeners by the presentation under such circumstances of this extraordinary selection. Mme. Kalergis remained dumb. Berlioz merely expressed himself warmly on the *chaleur* of my delivery, which may very well have afforded a strong contrast to that of my partner in the work, who rendered most of her part in low tones. Klindworth seemed particularly stirred to anger at the result. His own share was admirably executed; but he declared that he had been consumed with indignation at observing Viardot's lukewarm execution of her part, in which she was probably determined by the presence of Berlioz. By way of set-off to this, we were very pleased by the performance, on another evening, of the first act of the *Walküre*, at which, in addition to Mme. Kalergis, the singer Niemann was present.

This man had now arrived in Paris, at the request of the manager Royer, to arrange a contract. I confess I was astounded at the pose he assumed, and the airs with which he presented himself at my door with the question, ' Well, do you want me or do you not? ' Nevertheless, when we went to the manager's office he pulled himself together, so as to make a good effect. In this he succeeded admirably, for every one was amazed to meet a tenor of such extraordinary physical endowments. Nevertheless, he had to submit to a nominal trial performance, for which he chose the description of the pilgrimage in *Tannhäuser*, acting and singing it upon the stage of the Grand Opera House. Mme. Kalergis and Princess Metternich, who were secretly present at this performance, were both enthusiastically prepossessed in Niemann's favour, as were also all the members of the management. He was engaged for eight months at a monthly salary of ten thousand francs. His contract referred solely to *Tannhäuser*, as I felt obliged to protest against the singer appearing before this in other operas.

The conclusion of this agreement, and the remarkable circumstances under which it had been brought about, filled me with a hitherto unknown consciousness of the power thus suddenly placed in my hands. I had also been drawn into closer contact with Princess Metternich, who was undoubtedly the good fairy of the whole enterprise, and I was now also received with flattering cordiality by her husband and by the whole diplomatic circle to which they belonged. To the Princess, in particular, people attributed an almost omnipotent influence at the French Imperial Court, where Fould, the otherwise influential Minister of State, could effect nothing against her in matters pertaining to myself. She instructed me to apply only to her for the fulfilment of all my wishes, and said she would know how to find ways and means of attaining the success of the project, on which she had now evidently set her heart, all the more firmly because she saw that I still had no real faith in the enterprise.

Under these more hopeful auspices I spent the months from summer to autumn, when rehearsals were to begin. It was a great boon to me that I was just then able to make provision for Minna's health, as the doctors had urgently prescribed her a visit to the baths of Soden, near Frankfort. . She accordingly set off at the beginning of July, when I promised myself the pleasure of fetching her on the completion of her cure, as it happened that I myself had occasion to visit the Rhine at that time.

It was just at this moment that an improvement took place in my relations with the King of Saxony, who had hitherto obstinately opposed to grant me an amnesty. I owed this to the growing interest now taken in me by the other German embassies, especially those of Austria and Prussia. Herr von Seebach, the Saxon Ambassador, who was married to a cousin of my magnanimous friend, Mme. Kalergis, had shown great kindness to me, and at last he seemed to grow tired of being continually taunted by his colleagues about my objectionable position as a ' political refugee,' and consequently felt it his duty to make representations to his court on my behalf. In this action he appears to have been generously assisted by the Princess-Regent of Prussia — once more through the intervention of Count Pourtalès. I heard that on the occasion of a meeting between the German princes and the Emperor Napoleon in Baden she used her influence on my behalf with the King of Saxony. The result was that, after settling several ridiculous objections, all of which Herr von Seebach had to repeat to me, the latter was able to report that, although King John would not pardon me, nor permit my return to the kingdom of Saxony, yet he would raise no obstacle to my staying in any other state in the German Confederation which I might have to visit in pursuit of my artistic aims, provided such a state made no objection to my presence. Herr von Seebach added the further hint, that it would be advisable for me to present myself to the Princess-Regent on the occasion of my next visit to the Rhineland, in order to express my thanks for her kindly intercession, a courtesy which he gave me to understand the King of Saxony himself appeared to desire.

But before this project could be realised I had still to endure the most harassing torments with my translators of *Tannhäuser*. Amid these anxieties, and indeed throughout all my previous worries, I was again suffering from my old malady, which now seemed to have settled in my abdomen. As a remedy I was advised to take horse exercise. The painter Czermak, a friendly young man, whom Fräulein Meysenburg had introduced to me, offered his help for the necessary riding lessons. In return for a subscription for a fixed period, a man from a livery stables brought round his quietest horses, for which we had specially bargained, for the use of myself and comrade, upon which we ventured forth with the utmost caution for a ride in the Bois de Boulogne. We chose the morning hours for this exercise, so as not to meet the elegant cavaliers of the fashionable world. As I placed implicit reliance on Czermak's experience, I was naturally astonished to find that I far excelled him, if not in horsemanship, at least in courage, for I was able to endure the exceedingly disagreeable trot of my horse, whereas he loudly protested against every repetition of the experience. As I grew bolder I resolved one day to ride out alone. The groom who brought me the horse prudently kept an eye on me as far as the Barrière de l'Étoile, as he was doubtful of my ability to take my horse beyond this point. And, in fact, as I drew near to the Avenue de l'Impératrice my steed obstinately refused to go any further: he curveted sideways and backwards and frequently stood stock-still. In this he persisted until at last I decided to return, in which the prudent foresight of the groom luckily came to my rescue. He helped me down from my beast in the open street and led it home smiling. With this experience my last effort to become a horseman came to an inglorious end, and I lost ten rides, the vouchers for which remained unused in my desk.

By way of compensation I found abundant refreshment and regular exercise in solitary walks in the Bois de Boulogne, gaily accompanied by my little dog Fips, during which I learned once more to appreciate the sylvan beauty of this artificial pleasure-ground. Life also had become quieter, as is usually the case at this season in Paris. Bülow, after hearing that his déjeûner at Vachette's had produced the extraordinary result of an imperial command for the production of *Tannhäuser,* had long since gone back to Germany; and in August I also set out on my carefully planned excursion to the German Rhine districts. There I first turned my steps, via Cologne, to Coblenz, where I expected to find Princess Augusta of Prussia. Learning, however, that she was in Baden, I made my way towards Soden, whence I fetched Minna for a further tour, accompanied by her recently acquired friend, Mathilde Schiffner. We touched at Frankfort, where I met my brother Albert for the first time since leaving Dresden, as he also happened to be passing through this city.

When I was there it occurred to me that this was the residence of Schopenhauer, but a singular timidity restrained me from calling upon him. My temper just then seemed too distraught and too far removed from all that which might have formed a subject for conversation with Schopenhauer, even if I had felt strongly attracted towards him, and which alone could have furnished a reason for intruding myself upon him, in spite of such disinclination. As with so many other things in my life, I again deferred one of its most precious opportunities until that fervently expected ' more favourable season,' which I presumed was sure to come some day. When, a year after this flying visit, I again stayed some time in Frankfort to superintend the production of my *Meistersinger*, I imagined that at last this more favourable opportunity for seeing Schopenhauer had come. But, alas! he died that very year, a fact which led me to many bitter reflections on the uncertainty of fate.

During this earlier visit another fondly cherished hope also came to nothing. I had reckoned on being able to induce Liszt to meet me in Frankfort, but instead found only a letter declaring it impossible to grant the fulfilment of my wish.

From this town we went straight to Baden-Baden. Here I abandoned Minna and her friend to the seductions of the roulette-table, while I availed myself of a letter of introduction from Count Pourtalès to Countess Hacke, a lady-in-waiting on her Royal Highness, through whom I hoped to be presented to her exalted patroness. After a little delay I duly received an invitation to meet her in the Trinkhalle at five o'clock in the afternoon. It was a wet, cold day, and at that hour the whole surroundings of the place seemed absolutely devoid of life as I approached my momentous rendezvous. I found Augusta pacing to and fro with Countess Hacke, and as I approached she graciously stopped. Her conversation consisted almost entirely of assurances that she was completely powerless in every respect, in reponse to which I imprudently cited the hint received from the King of Saxony that I should offer her my personal thanks for previous intervention on my behalf. This she seemed evidently to resent, and dismissed me with an air of indifference meant to show that she took very little interest in my concerns. My old friend Alwine Frommann told me later that she did not know what there was about me that displeased the Princess, but thought it might possibly be my Saxon accent.

This time I left the much-praised paradise of Baden without carrying away any very friendly impression, and at Mannheim boarded a steamer, accompanied only by Minna, on which for the first time I was borne along the famous Rhine. It struck me as very strange that I should so often have crossed the Rhine without having once made the acquaintance of this most characteristic historical thoroughfare of mediæval Germany. A hasty return to Cologne concluded this excursion, which had lasted only a week, and from which I returned to face once more the solution of the problems of my Parisian enterprise, now opening out painfully before me.

One factor which seemed likely greatly to relieve the difficulties confronting me was to be found in the friendly relationship into which the young banker, Emil Erlanger, was pleased to enter towards me. This I owed, in the first place, to an extraordinary man named Albert Beckmann, a former Hanoverian revolutionary, and afterwards private librarian to Louis Napoleon, who was at this time a press agent for several interests, respecting which I was never quite clear. This man succeeded in making my acquaintance as an open admirer, in which capacity he showed himself remarkably obliging. He now informed me that M. Erlanger, by whom he was also employed in connection with the press, would be pleased to know me. I was on the point of bluntly declining the honour, saying that I wanted to know nothing about any banker except with regard to his money, when he answered my jest by telling me in all seriousness that it was precisely in this way that M. Erlanger desired to serve me. As a result of this invitation I made the acquaintance of a genuinely agreeable man, who, having often heard my music in Germany, had become inspired by a sympathetic interest in my person. He frankly expressed a desire that I should commit the management of my financial business entirely to his hands, which meant, in fact, nothing less than that he would permanently hold himself responsible for any needful subsidies, in return for which I was to assign to him all the eventual proceeds of my Paris undertakings. This offer was distinctly novel, and moreover exactly fell in with the needs of my peculiar situation. And, in fact, so far as my subsequent financial security was concerned, I had no further difficulties to encounter until my position in Paris was fully decided. And although my later intercourse with M. Erlanger was accompanied by many circumstances which no man's kindly courtesy could have relieved, yet I ever found in him a truly devoted friend, who earnestly studied both my own personal welfare and the success of my enterprises.

This eminently satisfactory turn of events was calculated to inspire me with high courage had the circumstances been somewhat different. As it was, it had no power to excite in me even the slightest enthusiasm for an undertaking of which the hollowness and unsuitability for me personally were clearly revealed every time I approached it. It was with a feeling of ill-humour that I met every demand made by this venture, and yet it represented the foundation of the confidence reposed in me. My mind was subjected, however, to a certain refreshing uncertainty as to the character of my scheme by a new acquaintance who was introduced to me in connection with it. M. Royer informed me that he could not 'pass' the translation which I had taken infinite pains to conjure into existence through the two men who had volunteered to help me. He most earnestly recommended a thorough revision by M. Charles Truinet, whose pseudonym was Nuitter. This man was still young and extraordinarily attractive, with something friendly and open in his manner. He had called on me a few months ago to offer his co-operation in the translation of my operas, on the introduction of Ollivier, his colleague at the Paris bar. Proud of my connection with Lindau, however, I had refused his help; but the time had now come when, in consequence of M. Royer's strictures, Truinet's renewed offer of his services had to be taken into consideration. He understood no German, but maintained that as far as this was concerned he could place sufficient reliance upon his old father, who had travelled for a long time in Germany and had acquired the essentials of our language. As a matter of fact, there was no need for special knowledge in this respect, as the sole problem seemed to be to make the French verses less stiff and stilted which poor Roche had constructed under the shameful control of Lindau, who used to make out that he knew everything better than any one else. The inexhaustible patience with which Truinet proceeded from one change to another in order to satisfy my requirements, even with regard to the musical fitness of the version, won my sympathy for this last collaborator. From this time forward we had to keep Lindau away from the slightest interference in this new modelling of the 'book.' He had been recognised as quite incompetent. Roche, on the other hand, was retained, in so far as his work served as a basis for the new versification. As it was difficult for him to leave his custom office, he was excused from troubling about the remaining part of the work, as Truinet was quite free and could keep in daily touch with me. I now saw that Truinet's law degree was merely ornamental, and that he never had any thought of conducting a case. His chief interests lay in the administration of the Grand Opera, to which he was attached as keeper of the archives. First with one collaborator and then with another he had also worked at little plays for the vaudeville and theatres of a lower order, and even for the Bouffes Parisiens; but he was ashamed of these productions and always knew how to evade talking about this sphere of activity. I was greatly obliged to him for the final arrangement of a text to my *Tannhäuser* which could be sung and which was regarded on all sides as 'acceptable.' But I cannot remember ever having been attracted by anything poetic or even æsthetic in his nature. His value, however, as an experienced, warm-hearted, staunchly devoted friend at all times, especially in periods of the greatest distress, made itself more and more clearly felt. I can hardly remember ever meeting a man of such sound judgment on the most difficult points, or one so actively ready when occasion arose to uphold the view I advocated.

We had first of all to join forces in promoting an entirely new piece of work. In obedience to a need I had always felt, I had seized the occasion of this carefully prepared production of *Tannhäuser* to expand and considerably fill out the first Venus scene. For this purpose I wrote the text in loosely constructed German verses, so as to leave the translator quite free to work them out in a suitable French form: people told me that Truinet's verses were not at all bad; and with these as a basis I composed the extra music for the scene, and only fitted a German text to it afterwards. My annoying discussions with the management on the subject of a big ballet had determined me to make extensive additions to the scene of the 'Venusberg.' I thought that this would give the staff of the ballet a chorographic task of so magnificent a character that there would no longer be any occasion to grumble at me for my obstinacy in this matter. The musical composition of the two scenes occupied most of my time during the month of September, and at the same time I began the pianoforte rehearsals of *Tannhäuser* in the foyer of the Grand Opera.

The company, part of which had been freshly engaged for this purpose, were now assembled, and I was interested in learning the way in which a new work is studied at the French Opera.

The characteristic features of the system in Paris may be described simply as extreme frigidity and extraordinary accuracy. M. Vauthrot, the chorus-master, excelled in both these qualities. He was a man whom I could not help regarding as hostile to me, because I had never been able to win from him a single expression of enthusiasm. On the other hand, he proved to me by the most punctilious solicitude how conscientious he really was about his work. He insisted on considerable alterations in the text, so as to obtain a favourable medium for singing. My knowledge of the scores of Auber and Boieldieu had misled me into assuming that the French people were entirely indifferent as to whether the mute syllables in poetry and singing were to be sounded or not. Vauthrot maintained that this was only the case with composers, but not with good singers. He was always feeling misgivings about the length of my work, which I met with the observation that I could not understand how he could be afraid of boring the public with any opera after they had been accustomed to find pleasure in

Rossini's *Semiramis*, which was often produced. Upon this he paused to reflect,. and agreed with me so far as the monotony of action and of music in that work was concerned. He told me not to forget, however, that the public neither cared for action nor music, but that their whole attention was directed to the brilliancy of the singers. *Tannhäuser* gave little scope for brilliancy, and, as a matter of fact, I had none of that quality at my disposal. The only singer in my company who had any claim to such a distinction was Mme. Tedesco, a rather grotesque but voluptuous type of Jewess who had returned from Portugal and Spain after having had great triumphs in Italian operas. She did not conceal her satisfaction at having secured an, engagement at the Paris Opera through my unwilling choice of her for the part of Venus. She gave herself no end of trouble to solve the problem to the best of her ability — a problem which was entirely beyond her and which was suited only to a genuine tragedy actress. For a certain time her efforts appeared to be crowned with success, and several special rehearsals with Niemann led to a lively affinity between Tannhäuser and Venus. As Niemann mastered the French pronunciation with considerable skill, these rehearsals, in which Fräulein Sax also proved delightful, made genuine and encouraging progress. Up to this point these rehearsals were undisturbed, as my acquaintance with M. Dietzsch was as yet very slight. According to the rules of the Opera House, Dietzsch had hitherto only been present at the pianoforte rehearsals as *chef d'orchestre* and future conductor of the opera, so as to make himself accurately acquainted with the intentions of the singers. Still less was I disturbed by M. Cormon, the stage manager, who was also present at the rehearsals, and with a lively skill, characteristic of the French people, conducted the numerous so-called 'property' rehearsals, at which the way each scene was to be played was determined. Even when M. Cormon or others did not understand me, they were always ready to subordinate themselves to my decisions; for I continued to be regarded as all-powerful, and everybody thought that I could enforce what I wanted through Princess Metternich, a belief which, indeed, was not without foundation. For instance, I had learned that Prince Poniatowsky was threatening

to place a serious obstacle in the way of continuing our rehearsals by reviving one of his own operas, the production of
which had fallen through. The undaunted Princess met my
complaints on this subject by obtaining an immediate order
that the Prince's opera should be laid aside. Naturally this
did not tend to ingratiate me with the Prince, and he did not
fail to make me feel his displeasure when I called upon him.
In the midst of all this work I was afforded some recreation
by a visit from my sister Louise with part of her family. To
entertain her in my own home presented the greatest difficulties
owing to the strange fact that it was now becoming absolutely
dangerous to approach my house. When I first took it, the
proprietor gave me a fairly long lease, but would not undertake
any repairs. I now discovered the reason of this was that it
had just been decided by the Paris Committee of Reconstruction
to clear the Rue Newton with all its side streets to facilitate the
opening up of a broad boulevard from one of the bridges to the
Barrière de l'Étoile. But up to the last moment this plan was
officially denied, so as to avoid for as long as possible the
liability of paying compensation for the land that was to be
expropriated. To my astonishment I noticed that excavations
were being made close to my front door; these increased in
width, so that at first no carriages could pass my door, and
finally my house was unapproachable even on foot. Under
these circumstances the proprietor had no objection to make
to my leaving the house. His sole stipulation was that I should
sue him for damages, as that was the only way by which he in
his turn could sue the government. About this time my friend
Ollivier was debarred for three months on account of a parlia-
mentary misdemeanour; he therefore recommended me for
the conduct of my case to his friend Picard, who, as I saw
later on from the legal proceedings, acquitted himself of his
task with much humour. Nevertheless, there was no chance of
damages for me (whether the proprietor obtained any, I cannot
say); but, at all events, I had to content myself with being
released from my agreement. I also obtained leave to look
about for another house, and instituted my search in a neighbourhood less remote from the Opera. I found a poor cheerless
spot in the Rue d'Aumale. Late in the autumn in stormy

weather we completed the arduous task of moving, in which
Louisa's daughter, my niece Ottilie, proved a capable and willing
child. Unfortunately I caught a violent cold in the course of
moving and took few precautions to check it. I again exposed
myself to the growing excitement of the rehearsals, and eventually I was struck down by typhoid fever.

We had reached the month of November. My relations had
to go home, leaving me behind in a state of unconsciousness,
in which I was consigned to the care of my friend Gaspérini.
In my fits of fever I insisted on their calling in all imaginable
medical aid, and, as a matter of fact, Count Hatzfeld did
bring in the doctor attached to the Prussian embassy. The
injustice thus done to my friend, who took the greatest care of
me, was due to no mistrust of him, but to feverish hallucinations
which filled my brain with the most outrageous and luxuriant
fancies. In this condition, not only did I imagine that Princess Metternich and Mme. Kalergis were arranging a complete
court for me, to which I invited the Emperor Napoleon, but
I actually requested that Emil Erlanger should place a villa
near Paris at my disposal, and that I should be removed to
it, as it was impossible for me to recover in the dark hole
where I was. At last I insisted on being taken to Naples,
where I promised myself a speedy recovery in free intercourse
with Garibaldi. Gaspérini held bravely out against all this
madness, and he and Minna had to use force in order to apply
the necessary mustard-plasters to the soles of my feet. During
bad nights later on in life similar vain and extravagant fancies
used to return to me, and on waking I have realised with horror
that they were the offspring of that period of fever. After five
days we mastered the fever; but I seemed to be threatened
with blindness, and my weakness was extreme. At last the
injury to my sight passed away, and after a few weeks I again
trusted myself to steal along the few streets between my house
and the Opera, to satisfy my anxiety for the continuation of the
rehearsals.

People here had indulged in the oddest ideas, and seemed to
have assumed that I was as good as dead. I learned that
the rehearsals had been needlessly suspended, and moreover
gathered from one indication after another that the affair had

practically collapsed, although in my intense desire for recovery
I tried my utmost to conceal this from myself. But I was
much elated and pleased to see that the translation of the four
operatic librettos which had so far appeared had been published.
I had written a very exhaustive preface to them addressed to
M. Frédéric Villot. The translation of all this had been arranged for me by M. Challemel Lacour, a man with whom I had
become acquainted at Herwegh's house in days gone by when
he was a political refugee. He was a highly intelligent translator, and had now done me such admirable service that every
one recognised the value of his work. I had given J. J.
Weber, the bookseller in Leipzig, the German original of the
preface to publish under the title of *Zukunftsmusik*. This
pamphlet also reached me now, and pleased me, as it probably
represented the only result of my whole Paris undertaking,
which looked so brilliant on the surface.

At the same time I was now in a position to complete the new
composition for *Tannhäuser*, of which the great dance scene in
the Venusberg was still incomplete. I finished it at three
o'clock one morning after staying up all night, just as Minna
returned home from a great ball at the Hôtel de Ville to which
she had been with a friend. I had given her some handsome
presents for Christmas, but as far as I myself was concerned I
continued, on the advice of my doctor, to assist the slow process
of recovery by a beefsteak in the morning and a glass of Bavarian beer before going to bed. We did not watch the old year
out; on the contrary, I retired to bed and slept calmly into 1861.

1861. — The slackness with which the rehearsals of *Tannhäuser* were being conducted when I fell ill changed at the beginning of the new year into a more decided handling of all the
details connected with the intended performance. But I could
not fail to notice at the same time that the attitude of all those
who took part was substantially altered. The rehearsals, which
were more numerous than might be expected, gave me the
impression that the management was adhering to the strict
execution of a command, but were not fired by any hope of
successful results. Certainly I now obtained a clearer insight
into the actual state of affairs. From the press, which was
entirely in the hands of Meyerbeer, I knew long ago what I had

to expect. The management of the Opera, probably after repeated efforts to make the chief leaders in the press tractable,
were now likewise convinced that my *Tannhäuser* venture
would only meet with a hostile reception from that quarter.
This view was shared even in the highest circles, and it seemed
as if an attempt was being made to discover some means
whereby to win over to my side that part of the operatic public
which could turn the scales. Prince Metternich sent me an invitation one day to meet the new cabinet minister, Count Walewsky. An air of ceremony pervaded the introduction, and made it
particularly significant when the Count in a persuasive speech
endeavoured to convince me that they entertained every wish
for my good fortune and desired to help me to a brilliant success.
He added in conclusion that the power to effect this was in my
own hands, if I would only consent to introduce a ballet into
the second act of my opera; the most celebrated ballet-dancers
from St. Petersburg and London had been proposed to me,
and I had only to make my selection; their engagement would
be concluded as soon as I had entrusted the success of my
work to their co-operation. In declining these proposals I
think I was no less eloquent than he in making them. My
complete failure, however, was due to the fact that I did not
appear to understand the worthy minister when he informed
me that the ballet in the first act counted for nothing, because
those devotees of the theatre who only cared for the ballet
on an opera night were accustomed, according to the new
fashion, not to dine until eight o'clock, and so did not reach the
theatre until ten o'clock, when about half the performance was
over. I replied that I could not undertake myself to oblige these
gentlemen, but might well hope duly to impress another part
of the public. But with his imperturbable air of ceremony he
met me with the objection that these gentlemen's support could
alone be counted upon to produce a successful result, inasmuch
as they were powerful enough even to defy the hostile attitude
of the press. This precaution awakened no response in me, and
I offered to withdraw my work altogether, whereupon I was
assured with the greatest earnestness that, according to the
Emperor's command, which had to be universally respected,
I was master of the situation, and my wishes would be followed

in everything. The Count had only thought it his duty to give me a friendly piece of advice.

The consequences of this conversation soon became evident in many ways. I threw myself enthusiastically into the work of carrying out the great dance scenes of the first act, and tried to win Petitpas, the ballet-master, to my side. I asked for unheard-of combinations quite different from those generally employed in the ballet. I drew attention to the dances of the Mænads and Bacchantes, and astounded Petitpas with the mere proposition that he would be able to accomplish something of the kind with his graceful pupils, as it was well within his powers. He explained to me that by placing my ballet at the beginning of the first act I had myself renounced all claim to the step-dancers attached to the Opera, and all he could do was to offer to engage three Hungarian dancers, who had formerly danced in the fairy scenes at the Porte St. Martin, to fill the parts of the three graces. As I was quite content to dispense with the distinguished dancers belonging to the Opera, I insisted all the more that the rank and file of the ballet should be actively coached. I wanted to know that the male staff was present in full force, but I learned that it was impossible to bring it up to my requirements, unless some tailors were engaged who, for a monthly salary of fifty francs, figured in a vague way in the wings during the performances of the solo dancers. Finally I tried to produce my effects by means of the costumes, and asked for considerable funds for that purpose, only to learn, after I had been wearied by one subterfuge after another, that the management was determined not to expend a halfpenny on my ballet, which they regarded as completely wasted. Such was the substance of what my trusty friend Truinet conveyed to me. This was the first sign out of many which soon revealed to me the fact, that even in the circles of the operatic administration itself *Tannhäuser* was already regarded as labour lost and sheer waste of trouble.

The atmosphere created by this conviction now weighed with increasing pressure upon everything which was undertaken for the preparation of a performance which was postponed time after time. With the beginning of the year the rehearsals had reached the stage at which the scenes were arranged and the orchestral practices begun. Everything was conducted with a care which impressed me very agreeably at the beginning, until finally I was bored by it, because I saw that the powers of the performers were being relaxed by eternal repetition, and it was now evident that I must trust to my own ability to pull the matter quickly through as I thought best. But it was not the fatigue due to this system that finally made Niemann, the main prop in my work, recoil from the task which at the start he had undertaken with an energy full of promise. He had been informed that there was a conspiracy to ruin my work. From this time forward he was a victim to a despondency to which, in his relations with me, he sought to lend a sort of diabolical character. He maintained that so far he could only see the matter in a black light, and he brought forward some arguments that sounded very sensible; he criticised the whole Opera as an institution and the public attached to it, and also our staff of singers, of whom he maintained that not a single one understood his part as I intended it; and he exposed all the disadvantages of the undertaking, which I myself could not fail to see as soon as I came to deal with the *chef du chant,* the *régisseur,* the ballet-master, the conductor of the chorus, but, particularly, with the *chef d'orchestre.* Above all, Niemann (who at the beginning, with a full knowledge of what it involved, had imposed upon himself the task of playing his part without curtailments of any sort) insisted upon cutting down the score. He met my expression of astonishment with the remark, that I must not suppose that the sacrifice of this or that passage mattered, but that we were in the throes of an undertaking which could not be got through too quickly.

Under circumstances from which so little encouragement could be derived, the study of *Tannhäuser* dragged itself along to the brink of the so-called ' dress ' rehearsals. From all sides the friends of my past life gathered together in Paris to be present at the apotheosis of the first performance. Among these were Otto Wesendonck, Ferdinand Präger, the unfortunate Kietz, for whom I had to pay the costs of his journey and of his stay in Paris; luckily M. Chandon from Epernay came, too, with a hamper of ' Fleur du Jardin,' the finest of all his champagne brands. This was to be drunk to the success of *Tann-*

häuser. Bülow also came, depressed and saddened by the burdens of his own life, and hoping to be able to gather courage and renewed vitality from the success of my undertaking. I did not dare to tell him in so many words of the miserable state of affairs; on the contrary, seeing him so depressed, I made the best of a bad matter. At the first rehearsal, however, at which Bülow was present, he did not fail to grasp how matters stood. I no longer concealed anything from him; and we continued to indulge in sorrowful intercourse till the night of the performance, which was again and again postponed, and it was only his untiring efforts to be of use to me that gave some life to our companionship. From whatever side we regarded our grotesque undertaking, we encountered unsuitability and incompetence. For instance, it was impossible in the whole of Paris to find the twelve French horns which in Dresden had so bravely sounded the hunting call in the first act. In connection with this matter I had to deal with the terrible man Sax, the celebrated instrument-maker. He had to help me out with all kinds of substitutes in the shape of saxophones and saxhorns; moreover, he was officially appointed to conduct the music behind the scenes. It was an impossibility ever to get this music properly played.

The main grievance, however, lay in the incompetence of M. Dietzsch, the conductor, which had now reached a pitch hitherto unsuspected. In the numerous orchestral rehearsals which had been held hitherto, I had accustomed myself to use this man like a machine. From my habitual position on the stage near his desk I had conducted both conductor and orchestra. In this way I had maintained my *tempi* in such a way that I felt no doubt that on my removal all my points would remain firmly established. I found, on the contrary, that no sooner was Dietzsch left to his own resources than everything began to waver; not one *tempo,* not one *nuance* was conscientiously and strictly preserved. I then realised the extreme danger in which we were placed. Granted that no one singer was suited to his task, or qualified to achieve it so as to produce a genuine effect; granted that the ballet, and even the sumptuous mounting and vitality of the Parisian performances of the day, could contribute nothing on this occasion,

or at most but little; granted that the whole spirit of the
libretto, and that indefinable *something* which even in the worst
performances of *Tannhäuser* in Germany roused a feeling of
home, was likely here to strike an alien or at best an unfamiliar note; yet in spite of all this the character of the
orchestral music, which if rendered with emphasis was full of
suggestive expression, led one to hope that it would make an
impression even upon a Parisian audience. But it was precisely
in this particular that I saw everything submerged in a colourless
chaos, with every line of the drawing obliterated; moreover, the
singers became more and more uncertain in their work; even
the poor ballet-girls were no longer able to keep time in their
trivial steps; so that at last I thought myself obliged to interpose
with the declaration that the opera required a different conductor, and that in case of necessity I myself was ready to take
his place. This declaration brought to a climax the confusion
that had grown up around me. Even the members of the
orchestra, who had long recognised and openly ridiculed their
conductor's incompetence, took sides against me now that the
matter concerned their notorious chief. The press lashed itself
into fury over my ' arrogance,' and in the face of all the agitation caused by the affair, Napoleon III. could send me no
better advice than to forgo my requests, as in adhering to
them I should only be exposing the chances of my work to the
greatest risks. On the other hand, I was allowed to start fresh
rehearsals and have them repeated until I was satisfied.

This way out of the difficulty could lead to nothing but an
increase of fatigue for me and for the whole staff actively engaged in the undertaking, and the fact still remained that M.
Dietzsch could not be depended upon for the *tempo*. Finally, by
sheer force of will rather than of conviction, I tried to imagine
I was doing a service by holding out for the correct interpretation of a performance which, after all, had to be got through;
whereupon for the first time the impetuous musicians broke out
into rebellion against the excessive rehearsals. At this stage
I noticed that the guarantee of my practical control given by
the general management was not altogether made in good faith,
and in the face of the growing complaint on all sides against
being overfatigued I decided ' to demand the return of my

score,' as they called it; that is to say, to dispense with the production of the opera. I addressed an express request to this effect to the cabinet minister Walewsky, but received the answer that it was impossible to comply with my wishes, more particularly on account of the heavy expenses which had already been incurred in its preparation. I refused to abide by his decision, and called a conference of those friends of mine who were more closely interested in me, among whom were Count Hatzfeld and Emil Erlanger. I took counsel with them as to the means at my disposal for forbidding *Tannhäuser* to be performed at the Opera House. It happened that Otto Wesendonck was present at this conference; he was still waiting in Paris hoping to have the pleasure of attending the first performance, but he was now thoroughly convinced that the situation was hopeless, and promptly fled back to Zürich. Präger had already done likewise. Kietz alone held out faithfully, and he busied himself in trying to make some money in Paris to provide for his future, in which attempt he was hampered by many difficulties that stood in the way of his desire. This conference resulted in fresh representations being made to the Emperor Napoleon, which, however, met with the same gracious reply as before, and I was authorised to institute a fresh course of rehearsals. At last, weary to the depths of my soul, completely disillusioned, and absolutely decided in my pessimistic view of the matter, I determined to abandon it to its fate.

Having at last, in this frame of mind, given my consent to fix the date of the first performance of my opera, I was now plagued in another direction in the most astonishing way. Every one of my friends and partisans demanded a good seat for the first night; but the management pointed out that the occupation of the house on such occasions was entirely in the hands of the court and those dependent on it, and I was soon to realise clearly enough to whom these seats were to be allotted. At present I had to suffer the annoyance of being unable to serve many of my friends as I should have liked. Some of them were very quick to resent what they supposed to be my neglect of them. Champfleury in a letter complained of this flagrant breach of friendship; Gaspérini started an open quarrel because

I had not reserved one of the best boxes for his patron and my creditor Lucy, the Receiver-General of Marseilles. Even Blandine, who had been filled with the most generous enthusiasm for my work at the rehearsals she had attended, could not suppress a suspicion that I was guilty of neglecting my best friends when I was unable to offer her and her husband Ollivier anything better than a couple of stalls. It needed all Emil's *sang-froid* to obtain from this deeply offended friend a just appreciation of the honest assurance that I was in an impossible position, in which I was exposed to betrayal on all sides. Poor Bülow alone understood everything; he suffered with me, and shirked no trouble to be of use to me in all these difficulties. The first performance on the 13th of March put an end to all these complications; my friends now understood that it was to no celebration of my triumphs, as they supposed, to which they should have been invited.

I have already said enough elsewhere of the way in which this evening passed off. I was justified in flattering myself that in the end a favourable view of my opera prevailed, inasmuch as the intention of my opponents had been to break up this performance completely, and this they had found it impossible to do. But I was grieved the next day to receive nothing but reproaches from my friends, with Gaspérini at the head of them, because I had allowed the occupation of the house at the first performance to be completely wrested out of my hands. Meyerbeer, they urged, knew how to work such things differently; had he not, ever since he first appeared in Paris, refused to allow the production of a single one of his operas to take place without a guarantee that he himself should fill the auditorium, to the remotest corner? As I had not looked after my best friends, such as M. Lucy, was not the ill-success of that evening to be ascribed to my own conduct? Confronted with these and similar arguments, I had to spend the whole day in writing letters and in devoting myself to the most urgent efforts at propitiation. Above all, I was besieged with advice as to how I might recover the lost ground at the subsequent performances. As the management placed a very small number of free seats at my disposal, money had to be found for the purchase of tickets. In the pursuit of this object, which my

friends were so warmly advocating and which involved much
that was disagreeable, I shrank from approaching Emil Erlanger
or anybody else. Giacomelli, however, had found out that
Aufmordt, the merchant, a business friend of Wesendonck, had
offered to help to the extent of five hundred francs. I now
allowed these champions of my welfare to act according to their
own ideas, and was curious to see what assistance I should derive
from these resources which I had previously neglected and now
utilised.

The second performance took place on the 18th of March,
and, indeed, the first act promised well. The overture was
loudly applauded without a note of opposition. Mme. Tedesco,
who had eventually been completely won over to her part of
Venus by a wig powdered with gold dust, called out triumphantly
to me in the manager's box, when the 'septuor' of the finale
of the first act was again vigorously applauded, that everything
was now all right and that we had won the victory. But when
shrill whistling was suddenly heard in the second act, Royer
the manager turned to me with an air of complete resignation
and said, '*Ce sont les Jockeys; nous sommes perdus.*' Apparently at the bidding of the Emperor, extensive negotiations
had been entered into with these members of the Jockey Club
as to the fate of my opera. They had been requested to allow
three performances to take place, after which they had been
promised that it should be so curtailed as to admit of its
presentation only as a curtain-raiser to introduce a ballet which
was to follow. But these gentlemen had not agreed to the terms.
In the first place, my attitude during the first performance
(which had been such a bone of contention) had been observed
to be utterly unlike that of a man who would consent to the
proposed line of conduct; this being so, it was to be feared
that if two more performances were allowed to take place
without interruption, we might hope to win so many adherents
that the friends of the ballet would be treated to repetitions of
this work thirty times running. To guard against this they
determined to protest in time. The fact that these gentlemen
meant business was now realised by the excellent M. Royer;
and from that time he gave up all attempt to resist them, in
spite of the support granted to our party by the Emperor and

his Consort, who stoically kept their seats through the uproars of their own courtiers.

The impression made by this scene had a disastrous effect upon my friends. After the performance Bülow broke out into sobs as he embraced Minna, who had not been spared the insults of those next to her when they recognised her as the wife of the composer. Our trusty servant Therese, a Swabian girl, had been sneered at by a crazy hooligan, but when she realised that he understood German, she succeeded in quieting him for a time by calling him *Schweinhund* at the top of her voice. Poor Kietz was struck dumb with disappointment, and Chandon's 'Fleur du Jardin' was growing sour in the storeroom.

Hearing that in spite of everything a third performance was fixed, I was confronted with only two possible solutions of the difficulty. One was, to try once more to withdraw my score; the other, to demand that my opera should be given on a Sunday, that is to say, on a non-subscriber's day. I assumed that such a performance could not be regarded by the usual ticket-holders as a provocation, for they were quite accustomed on such days to surrender their boxes to any of the general public who chanced to come and buy them. My strategical proposal seemed to please the management and the Tuileries, and was accepted. Only they refused to conform to my wish to announce this as the third and *last* performance. Both Minna and I stayed away from this, as it was just as embarrassing for me to know that my wife was insulted as to see the singers on the stage subjected to such behaviour. I was really sorry for Morelli and Mlle. Sax, who had proved their genuine devotion to me. As soon as the first performance was over, I met Mlle. Sax in the corridor on her way home, and chaffed her about being whistled off the stage. With proud dignity she replied, '*Je le supporterai cent fois comme aujourd' hui. Ah, les misérables!*' Morelli found himself strangely perplexed when he had to weather the onslaught of the hooligans. I had explained to him in the minutest detail how to act his part from the time when Elizabeth disappears in the third act, until the beginning of his song to the evening star. He was not to move an inch from his rocky ledge, and from this position, half turning to the audience, he was to address his farewell to the departing lady. It had been a difficult task for him to obey my instructions, as he maintained that it was against all operatic custom for the singer not to address such an important passage straight to the public from the footlights. When in the course of the performance he seized his harp to begin the song, there was a cry from the audience, '*Ah! il prend encore sa harpe,*' upon which there was a universal outburst of laughter followed by fresh whistling, so prolonged, that at last Morelli decided boldly to lay aside his harp and step forward to the proscenium in the usual way. Here he resolutely sang his evening carol entirely unaccompanied, as Dietzsch only found his place at the tenth bar. Peace was then restored, and at last the public listened breathlessly to the song, and at its close covered the singer with applause.

As the vocalists showed a courageous determination to encounter fresh onslaughts, I could not protest. At the same time I could not endure to be in the position of a passive spectator suffering at the infliction of such unworthy methods, and as the third performance was also likely to be attended with doubtful consequences, I stayed at home. After the various acts messages reached us informing us that after the first act Truinet at once came round to my opinion that the score should be withdrawn; it was found that the 'Jockeys' had not stayed away, as was their custom, from this Sunday performance; on the contrary, they had purposely taken their seats from the beginning, so as not to allow a single scene to pass without a row. I was assured that in the first act the performance had been twice suspended by fights lasting a quarter of an hour each. By far the greater part of the public obstinately took my part against the childish conduct of the rowdies, without intending by their action to express any opinion of my work. But in opposing their assailants they were at a great disadvantage. When everybody on my side was utterly wearied out with clapping and shouting applause and calling 'Order,' and it looked as if peace were about to reign once more, the 'Jockeys' returned afresh to their task and began cheerfully whistling their hunting-tunes and playing their flageolets, so that they were always bound to have the last word. In an interval between the acts one of these gentlemen entered the box of a certain great lady, who in the excess of her anger introduced him to one of her friends with the words, ' *C'est un de ces misérables, mon cousin.*' The young man, completely unabashed, answered, ' *Que voulez-vous?* I am beginning to like the music myself. But, you see, a man must keep his word. If you will excuse me, I will return to my work again.' He thereupon took his leave. The next day I met Herr von Seebach, the friendly Saxon Ambassador, who was as hoarse as he could be, as he and all his friends had completely lost their voices through the uproar of the previous night. Princess Metternich had remained at home, as she had already had to endure the coarse insults and ridicule of our opponents at the first two performances.

She indicated the height to which this fury had risen by mentioning some of her best friends, with whom she had engaged in so virulent a controversy that she had ended by saying: ' Away with your free France! In Vienna, where at least there is a genuine aristocracy, it would be unthinkable for a Prince Liechtenstein or Schwarzenberg to scream from his box for a ballet in *Fidelio*. I believe she also spoke to the Emperor in the same strain, so that he seriously debated whether by police intervention some check could not be put upon the unmannerly conduct of these gentlemen, most of whom, unfortunately, belonged to the Imperial Household. Some rumour of this got abroad, so that my friends believed they had really gained the day when, at the third performance, they found the corridors of the theatre occupied by a strong body of police. But it turned out later on that these precautions had only been taken to ensure the safety of the ' Jockeys,' as it was feared they might be attacked from the pit as a punishment for their insolence. It seems that the performance, which was again carried through to the end, was accompanied from start to finish by an endless tumult. After the second act the wife of von Szemere, the Hungarian revolutionary minister, joined us in a state of complete collapse, declaring that the row in the theatre was more than she could bear. No one seemed able to tell me exactly how the third act had been got through. As far as I could make out, it resembled the turmoil of a battle thick with the smoke of gunpowder.

I invited my friend Truinet to visit me the next morning, so that with his help I might compose a letter to the management withdrawing my work and, as author, forbidding any further performance of the same, as I did not wish to see my singers abused instead of myself by a section of the public from whom the Imperial administration seemed unable to protect them. The astonishing thing about the whole matter was that in thus interfering I was guilty of no bravado, for a fourth and fifth performance of the opera had been already arranged, and the management protested that they were under obligations to the public, who still continued to crowd to this opera. But through Truinet I contrived to have my letter published the next day in the *Journal des Débats*, so that at last, though with great reluctance, the management gave their consent to my withdrawal of the piece.

Thereupon the legal action taken on my behalf by Ollivier against Lindau also came to an end. The latter had put in a claim on my author's rights in the libretto, in which he said he was entitled to a share as one of the three collaborators. His counsel, Maître Marie, based his plea on a principle which I was said to have established myself, namely that the point of chief importance was not the melody, but the correct declamation of the words of the libretto, which obviously neither Roche nor Truinet could have ensured, seeing that neither of them understood German. Ollivier's argument for the defence was so energetic that he was almost on the point of proving the purely musical essence of my melody by singing the 'Abendstern.' Completely carried away by this, the judges rejected the plaintiff's claim, but requested me to pay him a small sum by way of compensation, as he seemed really to have taken some part in the work at the beginning. In any case, however, I could not have paid this out of the proceeds of the Paris performances of *Tannhäuser*, as I had decided with Truinet, on withdrawing the opera, to hand over the whole of the proceeds from my author's rights, both for libretto and music, to poor Roche, to whom the failure of my work meant the ruin of all his hopes for the amelioration of his position.

Various other connections were also dissolved by this outcome of affairs. During the past few months I had busied

myself with an artistic club which had been founded, chiefly
through the influence of the German embassies, among an
aristocratic connection for the production of good music apart
from the theatres, and to stimulate interest in this branch of
art among the upper classes. Unfortunately, in the circular
it had published it had illustrated its endeavours to produce
good music by comparing them to those of the Jockey Club
to improve the breed of horses. Their object was to enrol all
who had won a name in the musical world, and I was obliged
to become a member at a yearly subscription of two hundred
francs. Together with M. Gounod and other Parisian celebrities, I was nominated one of an artistic committee, of which
Auber was elected president. The society often held its meetings at the house of a certain Count Osmond, a lively young
man, who had lost an arm in a duel, and posed as a musical
dilettante. In this way I also learned to know a young Prince
Polignac, who interested me particularly on account of his
brother, to whom we were indebted for a complete translation
of *Faust*. I went to lunch with him one morning, when he
revealed to me the fact that he composed musical fantasies.
He was very anxious to convince me of the correctness of his
interpretation of Beethoven's Symphony in A major, in the
last movement of which he declared he could clearly demon-
strate all the phases of a shipwreck. Our earlier general meetings were chiefly occupied with arrangements and preparations
for a great classical concert, for which I also was to compose
something. These meetings were enlivened solely by Gounod's
pedantic zeal, who with unflagging and nauseating garrulity
executed his duties as secretary, while Auber continually interrupted, rather than assisted the proceedings, with trifling
and not always very delicate anecdotes and puns, all evidently
intended to urge us to end the discussions. Even after the
decisive failure of *Tannhäuser* I received summonses to the
meetings of this committee, but never attended it any more,
and sent in my resignation to the president of the society, stating that I should probably soon be returning to Germany.

With Gounod alone did I still continue on friendly terms,
and I heard that he energetically championed my cause in
society. He is said on one occasion to have exclaimed: ' *Que*

Dieu me donne une pareille chute! ' As an acknowledgment of this advocacy I presented him with the score of *Tristan und Isolde,* being all the more gratified by his behaviour because no feeling of friendship had ever been able to induce me to hear his *Faust.*

I now came into touch with energetic protagonists of my cause at every turn. I was particularly honoured in the columns of those smaller journals of which Meyerbeer had as yet taken no account, and several good criticisms now appeared. In one of these I read that my *Tannhäuser* was *la symphonie chantée.* Baudelaire distinguished himself by an exceedingly witty and aptly turned pamphlet on this topic; and finally Jules Janin himself astonished me by an article in the *Journal des Débats,* in which, with burning indignation, he gave a somewhat exaggerated report, in his own peculiar style, of the whole episode. Even parodies of *Tannhäuser* were given in the theatres for the delectation of the public; and Musard could find no better means of attracting audiences to his concerts than the daily announcement, in enormous letters, of the Overture to *Tannhäuser.* Pasdeloup also frequently produced some of my pieces by way of showing his sentiments. And lastly, Countess Löwenthal, the wife of the Austrian military plenipotentiary, gave a great matinée, at which Mme. Viardot sang various items from *Tannhäuser,* for which she received five hundred francs.

By some singular coincidence people managed to confound my fate with that of a certain M. de la Vaquerie, who had also made a dismal failure with a drama, *Les Funérailles de l'Honneur.* His friends gave a banquet, to which I was invited, and we were both enthusiastically acclaimed. Fiery speeches were made about the *encanaillement* of the public, containing references to politics, which were easily explained by the fact that my partner in the festivity was related to Victor Hugo. Unfortunately particular supporters had provided a small piano, on which I was literally compelled to play favourite passages from *Tannhäuser.* Whereupon the evening became a festival in my honour alone.

But a much more important result than these was that people began to recognise the reality of my popularity, and

began to plan yet greater undertakings. The manager of the
Théâtre Lyrique sought everywhere for a tenor suitable for
Tannhäuser, and only his inability to find one compelled him
to renounce his intention of producing my opera at once. M. de
Beaumont, the manager of the Opéra Comique, who was on
the verge of bankruptcy, hoped to save himself with *Tannhäuser,* with which intention he approached me with the most
urgent proposals. True, he hoped at the same time to enlist
Princess Metternich's intervention on his behalf with the
Emperor, who was to help him out of his embarrassments. He
reproached me with coldness when I failed to fall in with his
glowing dreams, in which I could find no pleasure. But I was
interested to learn that Roger, who now had a post at the
Opéra Comique, had included part of the last act of *Tannhäuser* in the programme of a performance given for his own
benefit, whereby he drew down upon his head the fury of the
more influential press, but won a good reception from the
public. Schemes now began to multiply. A. M. Chabrol, whose
journalistic name was Lorbach, visited me on behalf of a company, whose director was an enormously wealthy man, with a
plan for founding a Théâtre Wagner, of which I refused to
hear anything until it could secure an experienced man of
first-class reputation as manager. Eventually M. Perrin was
selected for the post. This man had lived for years in the firm
conviction that he would be some day appointed manager of
the Grand Opera, and thought, therefore, that he ought not
to compromise himself. It is true, he ascribed the failure of
Tannhäuser entirely to Royer's incapacity, who ought to have
made it his business to win over the press to his side. Nevertheless he was strongly tempted to share in the attempt because
of the opportunity it afforded him of proving that, if he took
the matter in hand, everything would at once wear a different
aspect, and *Tannhäuser* become a great success. But as he
was an exceedingly cold and cautious man, he thought he had
discovered serious flaws in M. Lorbach's proposals, and when
the latter began to stipulate for certain commissions, Perrin
immediately fancied that he detected a not quite blameless
savour of speculation in the whole business, and declared that
if he wanted to found a Wagner Theatre, he would manage to

procure the necessary funds in his own way. As a matter of fact, he did actually entertain the notion of securing a large café, the 'Alcazar,' and after that the 'Bazar de la Bonne Nouvelle,' for the purposes of such a theatre. It also seemed possible that the requisite capitalists would be found for his enterprise. M. Erlanger believed he could succeed in getting ten bankers to guarantee fifty thousand francs, thus placing a sum of five hundred thousand francs at M. Perrin's disposal. But the latter soon lost courage when he found that the gentlemen thus approached were willing to risk their money on a theatre for their own amusement, but not for the serious purpose of acclimatising my music in Paris.

With this disappointing experience M. Erlanger now withdrew from all further participation in my fate. From a business point of view he regarded the arrangement made with me as a sort of deal, in which he had not succeeded. The settlement of my financial position seemed likely now to be undertaken by other friends, and with this object in view the German embassies approached me with great delicacy, commissioning Count Hatzfeld to inquire into my necessities. My own view of the situation was simply that, in obedience to the Emperor's command for the production of my opera, I had wasted my time over an enterprise the failure of which had not been my fault. With perfect justice my friends pointed out how careless I had been not to secure from the first certain stipulations about compensations, a demand which the Frenchman's practical mind would at once have recognised as reasonable and obvious. As matters stood, I had demanded no return for my time and labour beyond certain author's rights in case of success. Feeling how impossible it was for me to approach either the management or the Emperor to retrieve this omission, I was content to leave Princess Metternich to intercede on my behalf. Count Pourtalès had stayed on in Berlin to try and persuade the Prince Regent to order a performance of *Tannhäuser* for my benefit. Unfortunately, the latter had been unable to secure the execution of his order owing to the opposition of his manager, Herr von Hülsen, who was hostile to me. As I had no other prospect for a long time to come but one of complete helplessness, I had no option but to leave the representation of my claim for compensation to the kindly care of my royal patroness. All these events had taken place within the short space of a month after the production of *Tannhäuser*, and now, on the 15th April, I went for a short trip to Germany, to try and find some solid ground for my future in that country.

The only person who really understood my deepest needs had already set out on the same road, away from the chaos of Parisian theatrical life. Bülow had just sent me news from Karlsruhe that the grand-ducal family were favourably disposed towards me, and I promptly formed the plan of immediately setting to work seriously on the production there of my *Tristan*, which had been so fatally deferred. Accordingly I went to Karlsruhe, and if anything could have decided me to execute my hastily formed plan, it would certainly have been the exceptionally cordial welcome I now received at the hands of the Grand Duke of Baden. This exalted personage seemed really desirous of awakening my sincerest confidence in himself. During an exceedingly intimate interview, at which his young wife was also present, the Grand Duke took pains to convince me that his profound sympathy for me was less as a composer of operas, whose excellence he neither wished nor was able to appreciate, than as the man who had suffered so much for his patriotic and independent opinions. As I naturally could not attach much value to the political importance of my past career, he imagined this arose from suspicious reticence, and encouraged me by the assurance that, although great mistakes and even offences might have been committed in this respect, these only affected those who, while they had remained in Germany, had not been made happy, and had thereby certainly atoned for their misdeeds by inward suffering. On the other hand, it was now the duty of all these guilty ones to repair the wrongs they had done to those who had been driven into exile. He gladly placed his theatre at my disposal, and gave the necessary orders to the manager. This was my old 'friend' Eduard Devrient, and the painful embarrassment he betrayed on my arrival fully justified all that Bülow had said about the complete worthlessness of those sentiments of sincere sympathy for me which he had hitherto affected. But in the happy atmosphere created by the Grand Duke's gracious reception I was soon able to bring Devrient — in appearance at least — to do as I wished, and he was compelled to assent to the proposed production of *Tristan*. As he was unable to deny that, especially since Schnorr's departure for Dresden, he did not possess the requisite singers for my work, he referred me to Vienna, expressing at the same time his astonishment that I did not try to have my operas produced there, where everything required was ready to hand. It cost me some trouble to make him understand why I preferred a few exceptionally fine performances of my works in Karlsruhe to the mere chance of having them inscribed on the repertoire of the Vienna Opera House. I obtained permission to secure Schnorr, who of course would be engaged only for the special performances at Karlsruhe, and was also allowed to choose in Vienna the other singers for our intended 'model performance.'

I was thus left to rely on Vienna, and had meanwhile to return to Paris, so as to settle my affairs there in such a way as to suit the execution of my latest project. I arrived there, after an absence of only six days, and my sole occupation was to provide money for the needs of the moment. Under these circumstances I could only feel indifferent to the many sympathetic advances and assurances which reached me with ever-growing cordiality, although at the same time they filled me with apprehension. In the meantime, the operations undertaken on a larger scale by Princess Metternich to secure me some compensation dragged along with mysterious slowness, and it was to a merchant named Stürmer, whom I had previously known in Zürich, that I owed my deliverance from my present troubles. He had constantly interested himself in my welfare while in Paris, and now by his help I was enabled, first to set my household affairs in order, and then to set off for Vienna.

Liszt had announced that he was coming to Paris some time before, and during the recent disastrous time I had longed for his presence, as I thought that, with his recognised position in the higher circles of Parisian society, he would have been able to exert a very helpful influence upon my hopelessly involved situation. A mysterious epistolary ' shrug of the shoulders ' had been the only answer I had received to my various inquiries as to the cause of his delay. It seemed like irony on the part of Fate that, just as I had arranged everything for my journey to Vienna, news should come that Liszt would reach Paris in a few days. But I could only yield to the pressure of my necessities which sternly demanded that I should pick up new threads for my plan of life, and I quitted Paris about the middle of May, without awaiting my old friend's arrival.

I stopped first of all at Karlsruhe for another interview with the Grand Duke, who received me as kindly as ever, and granted me permission to engage in Vienna any singers I liked for a really fine performance of *Tristan* in his theatre. Armed with this command I went on to Vienna, where I stayed at the 'Erzherzog Karl,' and there waited for Conductor Esser to fulfil the promises he had made by letter to allow me to see a few performances of my operas. It was here that for the first time I saw my own *Lohengrin*. Although the opera had already been played very frequently, the entire company was present at the full rehearsal, as I desired. The orchestra played the prelude with such delightful warmth, the voices of the singers and many of their good qualities were so conspicuously and surprisingly pleasing, that I was too much overcome by the sensation created by them to have any desire to criticise the general performance. My profound emotion seemed to attract attention, and Dr. Hanslick probably thought this was a suitable moment for being introduced to me in a friendly way as I sat listening on the stage. I greeted him shortly, like a perfectly unknown person; whereupon the tenor, Ander, presented him a second time with the remark that Dr. Hanslick was an old acquaintance. I answered briefly that I remembered Dr. Hanslick very well, and once more turned my attention to the stage. It seems that exactly the same now happened with my Vienna friends as once before in the case of my London acquaintances, when the latter found me disinclined to respond to their efforts to make me conciliate the dreaded critics. This man, who as a budding young student had been present at the earliest performances of *Tannhäuser* in Dresden, and had written glowing reports on my work, had since become one of my most vicious antagonists, as was proved on the production of my operas in Vienna. The members of the opera company, who were all well disposed towards me, seemed to have devoted their whole attention to reconciling me, as best they could, with this critic. As they failed to do so, those who ascribe, to the enmity thus aroused, the subsequent failure of every attempt to launch my enterprise in Vienna, may be right in their opinion.

But for the present it seemed as though the flood of enthusiasm would bear down all opposition. The performance of *Lohengrin*, which I attended, was made the occasion of a frantic ovation, such as I have only experienced from the Viennese public. I was urged to have both my other operas presented also, but felt a sort of shyness at the thought of a repetition of that evening's occurrences. As I had now fully realised the serious weaknesses in the performance of *Tannhäuser*, I only agreed to a revival of the *Fliegender Holländer*, for the reason that I wished to hear the singer Beck, who excelled in that opera. On this occasion also the public indulged in similar manifestations of delight, so that, backed up by universal favour, I could begin to consider the main business on which I had come. The students of the University offered me the honour of a torchlight procession, which I declined, thereby winning the hearty approval of Esser, who, together with the chief officials of the Opera, asked me how these triumphs could be turned to account. I then presented myself to Count Lanckoronski, the Controller of the Emperor's household, who had been described to me as a peculiar person, totally ignorant of art and all its requirements. When I unfolded to him my request that he would graciously grant leave of obsence for a fairly long period to the chief singers of his Opera, namely, Frau Dustmann (*née* Luise Meyer), Herr Beck, and probably also Herr Ander, for the proposed performance of *Tristan* in Karlsruhe, the old gentleman dryly answered that it was quite impossible. He thought it much more reasonable, seeing I was satisfied with his company, that I should produce my new work in Vienna, and the courage necessary to refuse this proposition melted completely away.

As I descended the steps of the Hofburg, lost in meditation over this new turn of affairs, a stately gentleman of unusually sympathetic mien came to meet me at the door, and offered to accompany me in the carriage to my hotel. This was Joseph

Standhartner, a famous physician, who was exceedingly popular in high circles, an earnest devotee of music, thenceforth destined to be a faithful friend to me all my life.

Karl Tausig had also sought me out, and was now devoting his energies to Vienna, with the express determination of conquering this field for Liszt's compositions, and had opened his campaign there during the previous winter with a series of orchestral concerts, started and conducted by himself. He introduced me to Peter Cornelius, who had also been drawn to Vienna, and whom I only knew from our meeting in Bâle in 1853. They both raved about the recently published pianoforte arrangement of *Tristan*, which Bülow had prepared. In my room at the hotel, whither Tausig had transported a Bösendorff grand-piano, a musical orgy was soon in full swing. They would have liked me to have started rehearsing *Tristan* at once; and, in any case, I was now so bent on securing the acceptance of the proposal that my work should first be performed here, that I finally quitted Vienna with a promise to return in a few months, in order to start the preliminary study at once.

I felt no little embarrassment at the prospect of communicating my change of plan to the Grand Duke, and therefore readily yielded to the impulse of only visiting Karlsruhe after a long detour. As my birthday fell just at the time of this return journey, I resolved to celebrate it at Zürich. I reached Winterthur, via Munich, without delay, and hoped to meet my friend Sulzer there. Unfortunately he was away, and I only saw his wife, who had a pathetic interest for me, and also their little son, a lively and attractive boy. Sulzer himself, I learned, was expected back the next day, the 22nd of the month, and I accordingly spent most of the day in a small room at the inn. I had brought Goethe's *Wilhelm Meister's Wanderjahre* with me, and now for the first time was enraptured by fuller comprehension of this wonderful production. The spirit of the poet attracted me most profoundly to his work by the impression left on my mind by his lively description of the breaking-up of the players' company, in which the action almost becomes a furious lyric. Next morning at early dawn I returned to Zürich. The wonderfully clear air decided me to try the long and circuitous path through the familiar haunts of the Sihlthal to Wesendonck's estate. Here I arrived quite unannounced; and when I inquired what the habits of the household were, I learned that about this time Wesendonck usually came down to his dining-room to breakfast alone. There I accordingly seated myself in a corner, where I awaited the tall, good-tempered man, who, on entering quietly for his morning coffee, broke out into joyous astonishment on beholding me. The day passed most sociably; Sulzer, Semper, Herwegh, and Gottfried Keller were all sent for, and I thoroughly enjoyed the satisfaction of a well-contrived surprise, under such strange circumstances, as my recent fate had only just been forming the daily topic of animated discussion among these friends.

The next day I hurried back to Karlsruhe, where my announcement was received by the Grand Duke with kindly acquiescence. I could truly state that my request for leave of absence for the singers had been refused, and the projected performance in Karlsruhe thereby rendered impossible. Without any grief, but, on the contrary, with undisguised satisfaction, Eduard Devrient yielded to this fresh turn of affairs, and prophesied a splendid future for me in Vienna. Here Tausig overtook me, having already decided in Vienna to pay a visit to Paris, where he wished to see Liszt; and we accordingly continued our journey from Karlsruhe together by way of Strasburg.

When I reached Paris, I found my household on the point of breaking up. My only anxiety with regard to this was to procure means for getting away from the city, and for the prompt settlement of a future which seemed hopeless. Meanwhile Minna found an opportunity for exhibiting her talents as a housewife. Liszt had already fallen back into his old current of life, and even his own daughter, Blandine, could only manage to get a word with him in his carriage, as he drove from one visit to another. Nevertheless, impelled by his goodness of heart, he found time once to accept an invitation to 'beef-steaks' at my house. He even managed to spare me a whole evening, for which he kindly placed himself at my disposal for the settlement of my small obligations. In the presence of a few friends, who had remained true after the recent days of trouble, he played the piano to us on this occasion, during which a curious coincidence occurred. The day before poor Tausig had filled up a spare hour by playing Liszt's ' Fantaisie ' on the name of Bach,[1] and now when Liszt chanced to play us the same piece, he literally collapsed with amazement before this wonderful prodigy of a man.

Another day we met for lunch at Gounod's, when we had a very dull time, which was only enlivened by poor Baudelaire, who indulged in the most outrageous witticisms. This man, *criblé de dettes,* as he told me, and daily compelled to adopt the most extravagant methods for a bare subsistence, had repeatedly approached me with adventurous schemes for the exploitation of my notorious fiasco. I could not on any account consent to adopt any of these, and was glad to find this really capable man safe under the eagle-wing of Liszt's ' ascendency.' Liszt took him everywhere where there was a possibility of a fortune being found. Whether this helped him into anything or not, I never knew. I only heard that he died a short time afterwards, certainly not from an excess of good fortune.

In addition to this festive morning, I met Liszt again at a dinner at the Austrian embassy, on which occasion he once more showed his kindly sympathy by playing several passages from my *Lohengrin* on the piano to Princess Metternich. He was also summoned to a dinner at the Tuileries, to which, however, it was not thought necessary to invite me to accompany him. With regard to this he related a conversation, which was very much to the point, with the Emperor Napoleon about the episode of my *Tannhäuser* performances in Paris, the upshot of which appears to have been that I was not in my right place at the Grand Opera House. Whether Liszt ever discussed these matters with Lamartine I do not know, I only heard that my old friend several times addressed him, to try and arrange a meeting with him, for which I was very anxious. Tausig, who at first had taken refuge chiefly with me, fell back later into his natural dependence upon his master, so that in the end he quite vanished from my sight, when he went with Liszt to visit Mme. Street in Brussels.

[1] The notes B, A, C, H, are equivalent to our English B flat, A, C, B. — EDITOR.

I was now longing to leave Paris. I had fortunately managed to get rid of my house in the Rue d'Aumale by sub-letting it, a transaction in which I was helped by a present of a hundred francs to the concierge, and was now merely waiting for news from my protectors. As I did not wish to press them, my situation became most painfully prolonged, though it was not altogether devoid of pleasant but tantalising incidents. For instance, I had won the special favour of Mlle. Eberty, Meyerbeer's elderly niece. She had been an almost rabid partisan of my cause during the painful episode of the *Tannhäuser* performances, and now seemed earnestly desirous of doing something to brighten my cheerless situation. With this object she arranged a really charming dinner in a first-class restaurant in the Bois de Boulogne, to which we and Kietz, of whom we were not yet rid, were invited, and which took place in lovely spring weather. The Flaxland family also, with whom I had had some differences over the publication of *Tannhäuser,* now exerted themselves in every possible way to show me kindness, but I could only wish that they had had no reason for doing so.

It was now settled that we must at all costs leave Paris soon. It was proposed that Minna should resume her treatment at the Soden baths and also revisit her old friends in Dresden, while I was to wait until it was time for me to return to Vienna for the preliminary study of my *Tristan.* We decided to deposit all our household belongings, well packed, with a forwarding-agent in Paris. While thus occupied with thoughts of our painfully delayed departure, we also discussed the difficulty of transporting our little dog Fips by rail. One day, the 22nd of June, my wife returned from a walk, bringing the animal back with her, in some mysterious way dangerously ill. According to Minna's account, we could only think that the dog had swallowed some virulent poison spread in the street. His condition was pitiable. Though he showed no marks of outward injury, yet his breathing was so convulsive that we thought his lungs must be seriously damaged. In his first frantic pangs he had bitten Minna violently in the mouth, so that I had sent for a doctor immediately, who, however, soon relieved our fears that she had been bitten by a mad dog.

But we could get no relief for the poor animal. He lay quietly curled up, and his breathing grew steadily shorter and more violent. Towards eleven o'clock at night he seemed to have fallen asleep under Minna's bed, but when I drew him out he was dead. The effect of this melancholy event upon Minna and myself was never expressed in words. In our childless life together the influence of domestic pets had been very important. The sudden death of this lively and lovable animal acted as the final rift in a union which had long become impossible. For the moment I had no more urgent care than to rescue the body from the usual fate of dead dogs in Paris, that of being flung out into the street for the scavengers to carry off in the morning. My friend Stürmer had a small garden behind his house in the Rue de la Tour des Dames, where I wished to bury Fips the next day. But it cost me a rare expenditure of persuasion to induce the absent owner's housekeeper to give me permission to do so. At last, however, with the help of the concierge of our house, I dug a small grave, as deep as possible, among the bushes of the garden, for the reception of our poor little pet. When the sad ceremony was completed, I covered up the grave with the utmost care and tried to make the spot as indistinguishable as possible, as I had a suspicion that Herr Stürmer might object to harbouring the dog's body, and have it removed, a misfortune which I strove to prevent.

At last Count Hatzfeld announced in the kindliest possible manner that some friends of my art, who wished to remain unknown, sympathising with my unmerited condition, had united to offer me the means of relieving my burdensome position. I considered it fitting to express my thanks for this happy consummation only to my patroness, Princess Metternich, and now set about making arrangements for the final dissolution of my Paris establishment. My first care, after concluding all these necessary labours, was to see that Minna set out at once for Germany to begin her treatment; while, as for myself, I had no better object there for the present than to pay a visit to Liszt in Weimar, where in August a German-music festival was to be celebrated with farewell performances of Liszt's compositions. Moreover Flaxland, who had now taken courage to issue my other operas in French, wished to retain me in Paris until, in collaboration with Truinet, I had completed the translation of the *Fliegender Holländer*. For this work I needed several weeks, which it was impossible for me to spend in our apartments, now entirely stripped of furniture. Count Pourtalès, hearing of this, invited me to take up my abode for this period in the Prussian embassy, a remarkable and indeed in its way unprecedented act of kindness which I accepted with a gratitude full of foreboding. On the 12th of July I saw Minna off to Soden, and the same day went to reside at the embassy, where they assigned me a pleasant little room looking out upon the garden, with a view of the Tuileries in the distance. In a pool in the garden there were two black swans, to which, in a dreamy sort of way, I felt strangely attracted. When young Hatzfeld looked me up in my room, to make inquiries about my needs in the name of my well-wishers, a strong emotion overwhelmed me for the first time in many years, and I felt a profound sense of well-being in the midst of a condition of complete impecuniosity and detachment from everything usually considered as necessary for permanent existence.

I asked permission to have my Erard brought to my room for the period of my stay, as it had not been packed away with the rest of my furniture, whereupon a handsome room was given up to me on the first floor. Here I worked every morning at the translation of my *Fliegender Holländer,* and also composed two musical album pieces, one of which, intended for Princess Metternich, contained a pretty theme which had long floated in my mind, and was afterwards published, while a similar one, for Frau Pourtalès, got somehow mislaid.

My intercourse with the family of my friend and host had not only a soothing influence upon my spirit, but also filled me with calm content. We dined together daily, and the midday meal often developed into the well-known ' diplomatic dinner.' I here made acquaintance with the former Prussian minister, Bethmann-Hollweg, the father of Countess Pourtalès, with whom I discussed in detail my ideas respecting the relations between art and the state. When at last I had succeeded in making them clear to the minister, our conversation closed with the fatal assertion that such an understanding with the supreme head of the state would always remain an impossibility, seeing that in his eyes art belonged merely to the realm of amusement.

In addition to Count Hatzfeld, the two other attachés, Prince Reuss and Count Dönhoff, often shared these domestic gatherings. The former seemed to be the politician of the company, and was particularly commended to me on account of the great and able efforts he had made on my behalf at the Imperial Court, while the latter simply appealed to me by his looks and by his attractive and open-hearted friendliness. Here, too, I was again frequently brought into social contact with Prince and Princess Metternich, but I could not help noticing that a certain embarrassment marked our demeanour. Owing to her energetic complicity in the fate of *Tannhäuser,* Princess Pauline had not only been subjected to the coarsest handling by the press, but had also suffered the most ungallant and ill-natured treatment at the hands of so-called higher society. Her husband seems to have borne all this very well, though doubtless he experienced many a bitter moment. It was difficult for me now to understand what compensation the Princess could have found in a genuine sympathy for my art for all she had been obliged to endure.

Thus I frequently spent the evenings in familiar intercourse with my amiable hosts, and was even seduced into trying to instruct them about Schopenhauer. On one occasion a larger evening assembly led to almost intoxicating excitement. Selections from several of my works were vivaciously played in a circle of friends all very much prepossessed in my favour. Saint-Saëns took the piano, and I had the unusual experience of hearing the final scene of *Isolde* rendered by the Neapolitan Princess Campo-Reale, who, to that excellent musician's accompaniment, sang it with a beautiful German accent and an astounding faithfulness of intonation.

I thus passed three weeks in peace and quiet. Meanwhile, Count Pourtalès had procured me a superior Prussian ministerial passport for my projected visit to Germany, his attempt to get me a Saxon passport having failed, owing to the nervousness of Herr von Seebach.

This time, before taking leave of Paris — for ever, as I sup-

posed — I felt impelled to bid an intimate farewell to the few
French friends who had stood by me loyally in the difficulties
I had overcome.   We met at a café in Rue Lafitte — Gaspérini,
Champfleury, Truinet and I — and talked until late in the night.
When I was about to start on my homeward way to the Fau-
bourg St. Germain, Champfleury, who lived on the heights of
Montmartre, declared that he must take me home, because we
did not know whether we should ever see each other again.
I enjoyed the exquisite effect of the bright moonlight on the
deserted Paris streets ; only the huge business firms, whose
premises extend to the uppermost floors, seemed to have turned
night into day in a picturesque fashion, particularly those houses
which have been pressed into the service of trade in the Rue
Richelieu.   Champfleury smoked his short pipe and discussed
with me the prospects of French politics.   His father was, he
told me, an old Bonapartist of the first water, but had been
moved to exclaim, a short time before, after reading the papers
day after day, ' *Pourtant, avant de mourir je voudrais voir
autre chose.*'   We parted very affectionately at the door of the
embassy.

I took leave in equally friendly fashion of a young Parisian
friend, who has not yet been mentioned — Gustave Doré — who
had been sent to me by Ollivier at the very outset of my Paris
venture.   He had proposed to make a fantastic drawing of me
in the act of conducting, without, it is true, ever realising his
intention.   I do not know why, except, perhaps, that I did
not show any particular inclination for it.   Doré remained
loyal to me, however, and was one of those who made a point
of demonstrating their friendship just now in their extreme
indignation at the outrage inflicted on me.   This extraordinarily prolific artist proposed to include the *Nibelungen* among his
many subjects for illustration, and I wished first to make him
acquainted with my interpretation of this cycle of legends.
This was undoubtedly difficult, but as he assured me he had
a friend well versed in the German language and German
literature, I gave myself the pleasure of presenting him with
the recently published pianoforte score of *Rheingold,* the text
of which would give him the clearest idea of the plan on which
I had moulded the material.   I thus returned the compliment

of his having sent me a copy of his illustrations to Dante, which had just appeared.

Full of pleasant and agreeable impressions, which formed the only actual gain of real worth that I reaped from my Paris enterprise, I left the generous asylum offered by my Prussian friends the first week in August to go, first, to Soden by way of Cologne. Here I found Minna in the society of Mathilde Schiffner, who seemed to have become indispensable to her as an easy victim for her tyranny. I spent two extremely painful days there in trying to make the poor woman understand that she was to establish herself at Dresden (where I was not at present allowed to stay), while I looked about me in Germany — in Vienna first — for a new centre of operations. She glanced at her friend with peculiar satisfaction on hearing my proposal and my promise to remember, under any circumstances, to provide her with three thousand marks a year. This bargain set the standard of my relation to her for the rest of her life. She went with me as far as Frankfort, where I parted from her to go, for the time being, to Weimar — the town where Schopenhauer had died a short time before.

PART IV

1861-1864

AND so I again crossed Thuringia, passing the Wartburg which, whether I visited it or merely saw it in the distance, seemed so strangely bound up with my departures from Germany or my return thither. I reached Weimar at two in the morning, and was conducted later in the day to the rooms which Liszt had arranged for my use at the Altenburg. They were, as he took good care to inform me, Princess Marie's rooms. This time, however, there were no women to entertain us. Princess Caroline was already in Rome, and her daughter had married Prince Constantin Hohenlohe and gone to Vienna. There was only Miss Anderson, Princess Marie's governess, left to help Liszt entertain his guests. Indeed, I found the Altenburg was about to be closed, and that Liszt's youthful uncle Eduard had come from Vienna for this purpose, and also to make an inventory of all its contents. But at the same time there reigned an unusual stir of conviviality in connection with the Society of Musical Artists, as Liszt was putting up a considerable number of musicians himself, first and foremost among his guests being Bülow and Cornelius. Every one, including Liszt himself, was wearing a travelling cap, and this strange choice of head-dress seemed to me typical of the lack of ceremony attending this rural festival at Weimar. On the top floor of the house Franz Brendel and his wife were installed with some splendour, and a swarm of musicians soon filled the place, among them my old acquaintance Dräsecke and a certain young man called Weisheimer, whom Liszt had once sent to see me at Zürich. Tausig put in an appearance too, but excluded himself from most of our free and easy gatherings to carry on a love-affair with a young lady. Liszt gave me Emilie Genast as a companion on one or two short excursions, an arrangement with which I found no fault, as she was witty and very intelligent. I made the acquaintance of Damrosch too, a violinist and a musician. It was a great pleasure to see my old friend Alwine Frommann, who had come in spite of her somewhat strained relations with Liszt; and when Blandine and Ollivier arrived from Paris and became my neighbours on the Altenburg, the days which were lively before to begin with, now became boisterously merry. Bülow, who had been chosen to conduct Liszt's *Faust* Symphony, seemed to me the wildest of all. His activity was extraordinary. He had learned the entire score by heart, and gave us an unusually precise, intelligent, and spirited performance with an orchestra composed of anything but the pick of German players. After this symphony the *Prometheus* music had the greatest success, while I was particularly affected by Emilie Genast's singing of a song-cycle, composed by Bülow, called *Die Entsagende*. There was little else that was enjoyable at the festival concert with the exception of a cantata, *Das Grab im Busento* by Weisheimer, and a regular scandal arose in connection with Dräsecke's ' German March.' For some obscure reason Liszt adopted a challenging and protecting attitude towards this strange composition, written apparently in mockery by a man of great talent in other directions. Liszt insisted on Bülow's conducting the march, and ultimately Hans made a success of it, even doing it by heart; but the whole thing ended in the following incredible scene. The jubilant reception of Liszt's own works had not once induced him to show himself to the audience, but when Dräsecke's march, which concluded the programme, was at last rejected by the audience in an irresistible wave of illhumour, Liszt came into the stage-box and, stretching out his hands, clapped vigorously and shouted ' Bravos.' A real battle set in between Liszt, whose face was red with anger, and the audience. Blandine, who was sitting next to me, was, like me, beside herself at this outrageously provocative behaviour on the part of her father, and it was a long time before we could compose ourselves after the incident. There was little in the way of explanation to be got out of Liszt. We only heard him refer a few times, in terms of furious contempt, to the audience, ' for whom the march was far and away too good.' I heard from another quarter that this was a form of revenge on the regular Weimar public, but it was a strange way of wreaking it, as they were not represented on this occasion. Liszt thought it was a good opportunity to avenge Cornelius, whose opera *The Barber of Bagdad* had been hissed by the Weimar public when Liszt had conducted it in person some time previously. Besides this, I could of course see that Liszt had much to bear in other directions. He admitted to me that he had been trying to induce the Grand Duke of Weimar to show me some particular mark of distinction. He first wanted him to invite me, with himself, to dine at court, but as the Duke had qualms about entertaining a person who was still exiled from the kingdom of Saxony as a political refugee, Liszt thought he could at least get me the Order of the White Falcon. This too was refused him, and as his exertions at court had been so fruitless, he was bent on making the townsmen of the Residency do their part in celebrating my presence. A torchlight procession was accordingly arranged, but when I heard of it I took all possible pains to thwart the plan — and succeeded. But I was not to get off without any ovation at all. One afternoon *Justizrath* Gille of Jena and six students grouped themselves under my window, and sang a nice little choral society song, for which attention I thanked them most warmly. A contrast to this was presented by the great banquet attended by all the musical artists. I sat between Blandine and Ollivier, and the feast developed into a really hearty ovation for the composer of *Tannhäuser* and *Lohengrin*, whom they now ' welcomed back to Germany after he had won their love and esteem during his banishment.' Liszt's speech was short but vigorous, and I had to respond in greater detail to another speaker. Very pleasant were the select gatherings which on several occasions met round Liszt's own dinner-table, and I thought of the absent hostess of Altenburg at one of them. Once we had our meal in the garden, and I had the pleasure of seeing my good friend Alwine Frommann there conversing intelligently with Ollivier, as a reconciliation with Liszt had taken place.

The day for parting was drawing near for us all, after a week of very varied and exciting experiences. A happy chance enabled me to make the greater part of my prearranged journey

to Vienna in the company of Blandine and Ollivier, who had
decided to visit Cosima at Reichenhall, where she was staying
for a ' cure.' As we were all saying good-bye to Liszt on the
railway platform, we thought of Bülow, who had distinguished
himself so remarkably in the past few days. He had started a
day in advance, and we exhausted ourselves in singing his
praises, though I added with jesting familiarity, ' There was no
necessity for him to marry Cosima.' And Liszt added, bowing
slightly, ' That was a luxury.'

We travellers — Blandine and I, that is — soon fell into a
frivolous mood which was much intensified by Ollivier's query,
repeated after each burst of laughter, ' Qu'est-ce qu'il dit?'
He had to submit good-humouredly to our continuous joking in
German, though we always responded in French to his frequent
demands for tonique or jambon cru, which seemed to form the
staple of his diet. It was long after midnight when we reached
Nuremberg, where we were obliged to halt for the night. We got
ourselves conveyed to an inn by dint of much effort, and were
kept waiting there some time before the door opened. A fat
and elderly innkeeper acceded to our entreaties to give us
rooms, late as it was, but to accomplish this he found it necessary — after much anxious reflection — to leave us in the hall
for a good long time while he vanished down a back passage.
There he stood outside a bedroom door, and we heard him
calling ' Margarethe ' in bashful and friendly tones. He
repeated the name several times with the information that
visitors had arrived, and a woman answered him with oaths.
After much pressing entreaty on the innkeeper's part Margarethe
at last appeared, in négligé, and showed us, after various
mysterious confabulations with the host, the rooms selected for
us. The odd part of the incident was that the immoderate
laughter in which we all three indulged seemed to be noticed
neither by the innkeeper nor by his chambermaid. The next
day we went to see some of the sights of the town, last of all the
Germanisches Museum, which was in such a wretched condition
at that time as to earn the contempt of my French companion
particularly. The large collection of instruments of torture,
which included a box studded with nails, filled Blandine with
sympathetic horror.

We reached Munich that evening, and inspected it the next day (after *tonique* and ham had again been obtained) with great satisfaction, particularly on the part of Ollivier, who thought that the ' antique ' style in which King Ludwig I. had had the museums built contrasted most favourably with the buildings with which, much to his indignation, it had pleased Louis Napoleon to fill Paris. I here ran across an old acquaintance, young Hornstein, whom I introduced to my friends as ' the baron.' His comical figure and clumsy behaviour gave them food for mirth, which degenerated into a positive orgy of merriment when ' the baron ' thought it necessary, before we started on our night journey to Reichenhall, to take us to a *Bier-Brauerei* some distance away, so that we should see that side of Munich life. It was pitch dark and there was no light provided, except a stump of a candle to light ' the baron,' who had to go down himself to fetch the beer from the cellar. The beer certainly tasted particularly good, and Hornstein repeated his descent into the cellar several times. When, being obliged to hurry, we set off on our perilous journey across fields and ditches to the station, we found that the unwonted refreshment had somewhat dazed us. Blandine fell fast asleep as soon as she got into the carriage, only waking at daybreak when we arrived at Reichenhall. Here Cosima met us, and took us to the rooms that had been prepared for us.

We were first of all rejoiced to find Cosima's state of health much less alarming than we — I in particular — had known it to be before. She had been ordered a sour-milk cure, and we went to look on the next morning when she took her walk to the institution. Cosima appeared to lay less stress on the actual milk-drinking, however, than on the walks and the sojourn in the splendid, bracing, mountain air. Ollivier and I were generally excluded from the merriment which here too immediately set in, as the two sisters, to secure more privacy for their talks — they laughed so incessantly that they could be heard a long way off — usually shut themselves away from us in their bedrooms, and almost my only resource was to converse in French with my political friend. I succeeded in gaining admission to the sisters once or twice, to announce to them amongst other things my intention of adopting them, as their father took no

more notice of them — a proposition received with more mirth
than confidence.   I once deplored Cosima's wild ways to
Blandine, who seemed unable to understand me, until she had
persuaded herself that I meant *timidité d'un sauvage* by my
expression.   After a few days I had really to think of continu--
ing my journey, which had been so pleasantly interrupted.   I
said good-bye in the hall, and caught a glimpse of almost timid
inquiry from Cosima.

I first drove down the valley to Salzburg in a one-horse
carriage.   On the Austrian frontier I had an adventure with the
custom-house.   Liszt had given me at Weimar a box of the
most costly cigars — a present to him from Baron Sina.   As I
knew from my visit to Venice what incredible formalities make
it exceedingly difficult to introduce these articles into Austria,
I hit upon the plan of hiding the cigars singly among my dirty
linen and in the pockets of my clothes.   The officer, who was an
old soldier, seemed to be prepared for precautionary measures
of this sort, and drew forth the *corpora delicta* skilfully from all
the folds of my little trunk.   I tried to bribe him with a tip,
which he actually accepted, and I was all the more indignant
when, in spite of this, he denounced me to the authorities.   I
was made to pay a heavy fine, but received permission to buy
back the cigars.   This I furiously declined to do.   With the
receipt of the fine I had paid, however, I was also given back
the Prussian thaler which the old soldier had quietly tucked
away before, and when I got into my carriage to continue the
journey I saw the same officer sitting placidly before his beer
and bread and cheese.   He bowed very politely, and I offered to
give him his thaler back, but this time he refused it.   I have
often been angry with myself since for not asking the man's
name, as I clung to the notion that he must be a particularly
faithful servant, in which capacity I should like to have engaged
him myself later on.

I touched at Salzburg, arriving soaked through by floods of
rain, and spent the night there, and on the following day at
last reached my place of destination — Vienna.   I proposed to
accept the hospitality of Kolatschek, with whom I had been
friendly in Switzerland.   He had long since been granted an
amnesty by Austria, and had, on my last visit to Vienna,

called on me and offered me the use of his house, to avoid the unpleasantness of an inn, in the event of my returning for a longer stay. For reasons of economy alone — and these at the time were very urgent — I had willingly accepted this offer, and now drove direct with my hand luggage to the house described. To my surprise I at once discovered that I was in an exceedingly remote suburb, practically cut off from Vienna itself. The house was quite deserted, Kolatschek and his family having gone to a summer resort at Hütteldorf. With some difficulty I unearthed an old servant, who seemed to think she had been warned of my arrival by her master. She showed me a small room in which I could sleep if I liked, but was apparently unable to provide either linen or service of any kind. Greatly discomfited by this disappointment, I first drove back into town to wait for Kolatschek at a certain café in Stephan's Platz, which, according to the servant, he was likely to visit at a particular time. I had been sitting there a good while, making repeated inquiries for the man I expected to see, when suddenly I saw Standhartner come in. His extreme surprise at finding me there was intensified, as he told me, by the fact that he had never in his life entered this café. It had been quite a special coincidence that had brought him there on that day and at that time. On being made aware of my situation he at once became furious at the idea of my living in the most deserted part of Vienna when I had such pressing business in the city, and promptly offered me his own house for temporary quarters, as he and all his family would be away for six weeks. A pretty niece, who, with her mother and sister, lived in the same house, was to see to all my wants, including breakfast, etc., and I should be able to make use of the whole place with the greatest freedom. He took me triumphantly home with him at once to a deserted dwelling, as the family had already gone to their summer resort at Salzburg. I let Kolatschek know, had my luggage brought in, and for a few days had the pleasure of Standhartner's society and easy hospitality. I realised, however, from information given me by my friend, that my path was beset with new difficulties. The rehearsals for *Tristan und Isolde*, which had been planned in the spring to take place about this time (I had arrived in Vienna on 14th August), had been postponed indefinitely as Ander, the tenor, had sent word that he had injured his voice. On hearing this I at once concluded that my stay in Vienna would be useless; but I knew that no one would be able to suggest any other place where I could employ myself profitably.

My situation was, as I now saw plainly, quite hopeless, for every one seemed to have deserted me. A few years back I might, in a similar case, have flattered myself that Liszt would be pleased to have me at Weimar during the period of waiting, but if I returned to Germany just now I should only have to look on at the dismantling of the house — to which I have already alluded. My chief concern, then, was to find a friendly shelter somewhere. It was with this sole end in view that I turned to the Grand Duke of Baden, who had shortly before greeted me with such kindness and sympathy. I wrote him a beseeching letter, urging him to consider my necessitous condition. I pointed out that what I wanted, above all, was an asylum, however modest, and implored him to provide me with one in or near Karlsruhe, by securing me a pension of two thousand four hundred marks. Judge of my surprise on receiving a reply, not in the Grand Duke's own hand, but only signed by him, to the effect that if my request were granted, it would probably mean that I would interfere with the management of the theatre, and, as a very natural result, discussions would ensue with the director (my old friend E. Devrient, who was now doing splendidly). As the Grand Duke would in any such case feel obliged to act in the interests of justice, ' possibly to my disadvantage,' as he put it, he must, after mature consideration, regretfully decline to accede to my request.

Princess Metternich, who had suspected my embarrassment on that score also when I left Paris, had given me a warm recommendation to Count Nako and his family in Vienna, referring me with particular emphasis to his wife. Now I had made the acquaintance through Standhartner, during the short time before he left me, of young Prince Rudolph Liechtenstein — known to his friends as Rudi. His doctor, with whom he was very intimate, had spoken of him to me in the most flattering way as being a passionate admirer of my music. I often met him at meal times at the ' Erzherzog Karl,' after Standhartner had joined his family, and we planned a visit to Count Nako on his estate at Schwarzau, some distance away. The journey was made in the most comfortable fashion, partly by rail, in the company of the Prince's young wife. They introduced me to the Nakos at Schwarzau. The Count proved to be a particularly handsome man, while his wife was more of a cultured gipsy, whose talent for painting was evidenced in striking fashion by the gigantic copies of Van Dyck resplendent on the walls. It was more painful to hear her amuse herself at the piano, where she gave faithful renderings of gipsy music, which, she said, Liszt failed to do. The music to *Lohengrin* seemed to have prepossessed them all very much in my favour, and this appreciation was confirmed by other magnates who were visiting there, among them being Count Edmund Zichy, whom I had known in Venice. I was thus able to observe the character of unconstrained Hungarian hospitality, without being much edified by the subjects of conversation, and I had soon, alas! to face the question as to what I was to get from these people. I was given a decent room for the night, and on the following day took an early opportunity of looking round the beautifully kept precincts of the majestic castle, wondering in which part of the building there might be found room for me in case of a longer visit. But my remarks in praise of the size of the building were met at breakfast with the assurance that it really was hardly big enough for the family, as the young Countess in particular lived in great style with her suite. It was a cold morning in September, and we spent it out of doors. My friend Rudi seemed to be out of humour. I felt cold, and very soon took leave of the great man's board with the consciousness of having rarely found myself in the company of such nice people without discovering the smallest subject in common. This consciousness grew into a positive feeling of disgust when I was driving with several of the *cavalieri* to the station at Mödling, for I was reduced to absolute silence during the hour's drive, as they had literally only the one topic of conversation, by that time so terribly familiar to me! — namely horses.

I got out at Mödling to call on Ander the tenor, having

invited myself for that day with the intention of going through *Tristan*. It was still very early on a bright morning, and the day was gradually growing warmer. I decided to take a walk in the lovely Brühl before looking up Ander. There I ordered a lunch in the garden of the beautifully situated inn, and enjoyed an extremely refreshing hour of complete solitude. The wild birds had already ceased singing, but I shared my meal with an army of sparrows, which assumed alarming proportions. As I fed them with bread-crumbs, they finally became so tame that they settled in swarms on the table in front of me to seize their booty. I was reminded of the morning in the tavern with the landlord Homo in Montmorency. Here again, after shedding many a tear, I laughed aloud, and set off to Ander's summer residence. Unfortunately his condition confirmed the statement that the injury to his voice was not merely an excuse; but in any case I soon saw that this helpless person could never under any circumstances be equal to the task of playing Tristan, demi-god as he was, in Vienna. All the same I did my best, as I was there, to show him the whole of *Tristan* in my own interpretation of the part (which always excited me very much), after which he declared that it might have been written for him. I had arranged for Tausig and Cornelius, whom I had again met in Vienna, to come out to Ander's house that day, and I returned with them in the evening.

I spent a good deal of time with these two, who were sincerely concerned about me and did their best to cheer me. Tausig, it is true, was rather more reserved, as he had aspirations in high quarters at that time. But he, too, accepted Frau Dustmann's invitations to the three of us. She was then at Hietzing for the summer, and there dinners were given more than once, and also a few vocal rehearsals for Isolde, for which part her voice seemed to possess some of the spiritual susceptibility required. There, too, I read through the poem of *Tristan* again, still thinking the prospect of its performance possible with the exercise of patience and enthusiasm. For the present patience was the quality most needed; certainly nothing was to be obtained by enthusiasm. Ander's voice still failed him and did not improve, and no doctor was prepared to fix a limit to his malady.

I got through the time as best I could, and hit upon the idea of translating back into German the new scene to *Tannhäuser*, written to a French text for the performance in Paris. Cornelius had first to copy it from the original score for me, as this was in a very defective condition. I accepted his copy without inquiring further about the original left in his hands, and we shall see the result of this later on.

A musician named Winterberger also joined our party. He was an old acquaintance, and I found him in a position I much envied. Countess Banfy, an old friend of Liszt's, had taken him into her very pleasant house at Hietzing, and he was thus in excellent quarters, living at ease, and with nothing to trouble about, as the kind lady thought it her duty to keep this fellow — in other respects so undeserving — supplied with everything. Through him I again had news of Karl Ritter, and was told that he was now at Naples, where he lived in the house of a piano-maker, whose children he had to teach in return for board and lodging. It seems that Winterberger, after running through everything, had on the strength of some of Liszt's introductions started off to seek his fortune in Hungary. But things did not fall out to his satisfaction, and he was now enjoying compensation in the house of the worthy Countess. I met an excellent harpist there — also one of the family — Fräulein Mössner. By the Countess's orders she was made to betake herself and her harp to the garden, where, either at or with her harp, she had a most pert air and looked quite delightful, so that I gained an impression which lingered pleasantly in my mind. Unfortunately I became involved in a quarrel with the young lady because I would not compose a solo for her instrument. From the time when I definitely refused to humour her ambitions she took no more notice of me.

The poet Hebbel must be mentioned among the special acquaintances I made in Vienna during this difficult epoch. As it seemed not unlikely that I should have to make Vienna the scene of my labours for some time, I thought it desirable to become better acquainted with the literary celebrities living there. I prepared myself for meeting Hebbel by taking considerable trouble to read his dramatic pieces beforehand, doing my best to think that they were good and that a closer acquaintance with the author was desirable. I was not to be deterred from my purpose by my consciousness of the great weakness of his poems, although I realised the unnaturalness of his conceptions and the invariably affected and frequently vulgar form of expression. I only visited him once, and did not have a particularly long talk with him even then. I did not find any expression in the poet's personality of the eccentric force which threatens to explode in the figures of his dramas. When I heard, some years later, that Hebbel had died of softening of the bones, I understood why he had affected me so unpleasantly. He talked about the theatrical world in Vienna with the air of an amateur who feels himself neglected but continues to work in a businesslike fashion. I felt no particular desire to repeat my visit, especially after his return call in my absence, when he left a card announcing himself as ' *Hebbel, chevalier de plusieurs ordres!* '

My old friend Heinrich Laube had now long been established as director of the Royal and Imperial Court Theatre. He had felt it his duty on my previous visit to Vienna to introduce me to the literary celebrities, among whom, being of a practical turn, he counted chiefly journalists and critics. He invited Dr. Hanslick to a big dinner-party, thinking I should be particularly interested in meeting him, and was surprised that I had not a word to say to him. The conclusions Laube drew from this led him to prophesy that I should find it hard to get on in Vienna if I really hoped to make it the sphere of my artistic labours. On my return this time he welcomed me simply as an old friend, and begged me to dine with him as often as I cared to come. He was a passionate sportsman, and was able to provide the luxury of fresh game for his table. I did not avail myself very often of this invitation, however, as the conversation, which was inspired solely by the dull business routine of the stage, did not attract me. After dinner a few actors and literary men would come in for coffee and cigars, sitting at a large table where Laube's wife generally held her court, while Laube himself enjoyed his rest and his cigar in silence. Frau Laube had consented to become *Theatre Directrice* solely to please her husband, and now thought herself obliged to make long and careful speeches about things of which she had no understanding whatever. The only pleasure I had was in renewed glimpses of the good-nature which I had admired in her of old; for instance, when none of the company dared to oppose her, and I intervened with some frank criticism, she usually accepted it with unreserved merriment. To her and her husband I probably seemed a good-natured sort of fool and nothing more, for my conversation was generally in a joking strain, as I was utterly indifferent to their earnestness. In fact, when I gave my concerts in Vienna later on, Frau Laube remarked with the most friendly air of surprise that I was quite a good conductor, contrary to what she had expected after reading some newspaper report or other.

For one thing, Laube's practical knowledge was not without importance, as he could tell me all about the character of the chief inspectors of the Royal and Imperial Court Theatre. It now transpired that the Imperial Councillor, von Raymond, was a most important personage, and the aged Count Lanckoronski, the Lord High Marshall, who in other respects was extremely tenacious of his authority, could not trust himself to come to any decision in matters of finance without consulting this exceedingly competent man.

Raymond himself, whom I soon got to know and regard as a model of ignorance, took fright and felt bound to withhold his consent to my performance of *Tristan,* mainly on account of the Vienna papers, which always ran me down and scoffed at my proposal. Officially I was referred to the actual manager of the Opera, Herr Salvi, who had formerly been the singing-master of a lady-in-waiting to the Grand Duchess Sophia. He was an absolutely incapable and ignorant man, who was obliged to pretend in front of me that, according to the command of the supreme authorities, nothing lay so near his heart as the furtherance of the performance of *Tristan.* Accordingly he tried by perpetual expressions of zeal and goodwill to conceal the increasing spirit of doubt and hesitation with which even the staff was imbued.

I found out the state of affairs one day when a company of our singers was invited with me to the country house of a certain Herr Dumba, who was introduced to me as a most enthusiastic well-wisher. Herr Ander had taken the score of

Tristan with him, as if to show that he could not part with it
for a single day. Frau Dustmann grew very angry about it,
and accused Ander of trying to impose upon me by playing the
hypocrite; for he knew as well as any one else that he would
never sing that part, and that the management was only awaiting a chance of preventing the performance of *Tristan* in some
way or other, and then laying the blame on her shoulders.
Salvi tried most zealously to interfere in these extremely awkward revelations. He recommended me to choose the tenor
Walter, and as I objected on the ground of my antipathy to
the man, he next referred me to certain foreign singers whom
he was quite ready to approach.

As a matter of fact, we tried a few outside players of whom
the most promising was a certain Signor Morini, and I really
felt so depressed and so desirous of furthering my work at any
price that I attended a performance of *Luzia* by Donizetti with
my friend Cornelius to see if I could extract from him a favourable judgment of the singer. Cornelius, who was apparently
absorbed in listening, whilst I attentively watched him, suddenly started up in a passion and exclaimed, ' Horrible! horrible! ' which made us both laugh so heartily that we soon left
the theatre in quite a cheerful frame of mind.

At last I carried on my negotiations with the conductor
Heinrich Esser alone, as he was apparently the only honest man
in the management. Although he found *Tristan* very difficult,
yet he worked at it with great earnestness, and never really
gave up the hope of making a performance possible, if only I
would accept Walter as the tenor; but, in spite of my persistent
refusal to make use of such help, we always remained good
friends. As he, like myself, was a keen walker, we often
explored the neighbourhood of Vienna, and our conversations
during these expeditions were enthusiastic on my part and
thoroughly honest and serious on his.

Whilst these *Tristan* matters were running their weary
course like a chronic disease, whose outcome it is impossible
to foresee, Standhartner returned at the end of September with
his family. Consequently the next thing I had to do was to
look out for a residence, which I chose in the Hôtel Kaiserin
Elizabeth.

Through my cordial intercourse with the family of this friend I became quite intimate not only with his wife, but also with her three sons and a daughter by her first marriage, and a younger daughter by the second marriage with Standhartner. On looking back upon my former residence in my friend's house, I greatly missed the presence and kindly care bestowed upon me by his niece Seraphine, whom I have already mentioned, as well as her untiring thoughtfulness and pleasant, amusing companionship. On account of her natty figure and hair carefully curled à l'enfant, I had given her the name of ' The Doll.' Now I had to look after myself in the dull room of the hotel, and the expense of my living increased considerably. I remember at that time that I had only received twenty-five or thirty louis d'or for *Tannhäuser* from Brunswick. On the other hand, Minna sent me from Dresden a few leaves of the silver-spangled wreath presented by some of her friends as a souvenir of her silver wedding-day, which she had celebrated on the 24th of November. I could hardly wonder that there was no lack of bitter reproach on her part when sending me this gift; however, I tried to inspire her with the hope of having a golden wedding. For the present, seeing that I was staying without any object in an expensive Viennese hotel, I did my utmost to secure a chance of performing *Tristan*. First I turned to Tichatschek in Dresden, but obtained no promise from him. I then had recourse to Schnorr, with a similar result, and I was at last obliged to acknowledge that my affairs were in a bad way. Of this I made no secret in my occasional communications to the Wesendoncks, who, apparently to cheer me up, invited me to meet them in Venice, where they were just going for a pleasure trip. Heaven knows what my intention was as I started off in a casual sort of way by train, first to Trieste and then by steamer (which did not agree with me at all) to Venice, where I again put up in my little room at the Hôtel Danieli.

My friends, whom I found in very flourishing circumstances, seemed to be revelling in the pictures, and fully expected that a participation in their enjoyment would drive away my ' blues.' They seemed to have no desire to realise my position in Vienna. Indeed, after the ill-success of my Paris undertaking, entered upon with such glorious anticipations, I had learned to recognise among most of my friends a tacitly submissive abandonment of all hope for my future success.

Wesendonck, who always went about armed with huge fieldglasses, and was ever ready for sight-seeing, only once took me with him to see the Academy of Arts, a building which on my former visit to Venice I had only known from the outside. In spite of all my indifference, I must confess that the ' Assumption of the Virgin ' by Titian exercised a most sublime influence over me, so that, as soon as I realised its conception, my old powers revived within me, as though by a sudden flash of inspiration.

I determined at once on the composition of the *Meistersinger*.

After a frugal dinner with my old acquaintances Tessarin and the Wesendoncks, whom I invited to the Albergo San Marco, and once more exchanging friendly greetings with Luigia, my former attendant at the Palazzo Giustiniani, to the astonishment of my friends I suddenly left Venice. I had spent four dreary days there, and now started by train on my dull journey to Vienna, following the roundabout overland route. It was during this journey that the music of the *Meistersinger* first dawned on my mind, in which I still retained the libretto as I had originally conceived it. With the utmost distinctness I at once composed the principal part of the Overture in C major.

Under the influence of these last impressions I arrived in Vienna in a very cheerful frame of mind. I at once announced my return to Cornelius by sending him a small Venetian gondola, which I had bought for him in Venice, and to which I added a canzona written with nonsensical Italian words. The communication of my plan for the immediate composition of the *Meistersinger* made him almost frantic with delight, and until my departure from Vienna he remained in a state of delirious excitement.

I urged my friend to procure me material for mastering the subject of the *Meistersinger*. My first idea was to make a thorough study of Grimm's controversy on the *Song of the Meistersinger;* and the next question was how to get hold of old Wagenseil's *Nuremberg Chronicle.* Cornelius accompanied me to the Imperial Library, but in order to obtain a loan of this book, which we were fortunate enough to find, my friend was obliged to visit Baron Münch-Bellinghausen (Halm), a visit which he described to me as very disagreeable. I remained at my hotel, eagerly making extracts of portions of the *Chronicle,* which to the astonishment of the ignorant I appropriated for my libretto.

But my most urgent task was to secure some means of livelihood during the composition of my work. I applied first to the music publisher Schott at Mayence, to whom I offered the *Meistersinger* if he would make me the necessary advance. Being animated by the desire to provide myself with money for as long a time as possible, I offered him not only the literary rights, but also the rights of performance for my work, for the sum of twenty thousand francs. A telegram from Schott containing an absolute refusal at once destroyed all hope. As I was now obliged to think of other means, I decided to turn to Berlin. Bülow, who was always kindly exerting himself on my behalf, had hinted at the possibility of being able to raise a considerable sum of money there by means of a concert, which I should conduct; and as I was at the same time longing to find a home amongst friends, Berlin seemed to beckon me as a last refuge. At noon, just before the evening of my intended departure, a letter came from Schott, following on his telegram of refusal, which certainly held out some more consoling prospect. He offered to undertake the publication of the pianoforte edition of the *Walküre* at once and to advance me three thousand marks to be deducted from a future account. The joy of Cornelius at what he called the salvation of the *Meistersinger* knew no bounds. From Berlin Bülow, in great indignation and evident low spirits, wrote to me of his dreadful experiences in attempting to organise my concert. Herr von Hülsen declared that he would not countenance my visit to Berlin, while as to giving a concert at the great Kroll Restaurant, Bülow found after much deliberation that it would be quite impracticable.

Whilst I was busily engaged on a detailed scenic sketch of the *Meistersinger,* the arrival of Prince and Princess Metternich in Vienna seemed to create a favourable diversion on my behalf.

The concern expressed by my Paris patrons about me and my position was undoubtedly real; therefore, in order to show myself gratefully disposed towards them, I induced the management of the Opera to allow me to invite their splendid orchestra for a few hours one morning to play some selections from *Tristan* in the theatre by way of rehearsal. Both the orchestra and Frau Dustmann were quite ready to grant my request in the most friendly manner, and Princess Metternich, with some of her acquaintances, was invited to this rehearsal. With the orchestra we played through two of the principal selections, namely, the prelude to the first act, and the beginning of the second act, as far as the middle, while the singing part was sustained by Frau Dustmann, the whole being so brilliantly executed that I felt fully justified in believing I had created a most excellent impression Herr Ander, too, had appeared on the scene, but without knowing a single note of the music or attempting to sing it. Both my princely friends, as well as Fräulein Couqui, the *première danseuse,* who singularly enough had attended the rehearsal on the sly, overwhelmed me with enthusiastic marks of admiration. Hearing of my ardent desire for retirement in order to go on with the composition of a new work, the Metternichs one day suggested that they were in a position to offer me just such a quiet retreat in Paris. The Prince, who had now completely arranged his spacious embassy, could place at my disposal a pleasant suite of rooms looking on to a quiet garden, just like the one I had found in the Prussian embassy. My Erard was still in Paris, and if I could arrange to go there at the end of the year, I should find everything ready for me to begin my work. With unconcealed joy I most gratefully accepted this kind invitation, and my only care now was so to arrange my affairs that I could take my departure from Vienna and effect my removal to Paris in a proper manner. The arrangement that had been made through Standhartner's mediation, that the management should pay me a part of the stipulated fee for *Tristan,* would be a great help in this. But as I was only to get one thousand marks, and even this was to be subject to so many clauses and conditions as to suggest a desire to renounce the whole transaction, I at once rejected the offer. This fact, however, did not prevent the press, which was always in touch with the theatrical management, from publishing that I had accepted an indemnity for the non-performance of *Tristan*. Fortunately I was able to protest against this calumny by producing proof of what I had actually done in the matter. Meanwhile, the negotiations with Schott dragged out to some length, because I would not agree at present to his suggestions about the *Walküre*. I adhered to my first offer of a new opera, the *Meistersinger*, and at last received three thousand marks as an instalment on this work. As soon as I had received the cheque, I packed up my things, when a telegram from Princess Metternich reached me, in which she begged of me to put off my departure until the 1st of January. I decided not give up my plan, being anxious to get away from Vienna, so I determined to go straight to Mayence to pursue further negotiations with Schott. My leavetaking at the station was made particularly gay by Cornelius, who whispered to me with mysterious enthusiasm a stanza of ' Sachs ' which I had communicated to him. This was the verse:

> ' *Der Vogel der heut' sang,*
> *Dem war der Schnabel hold gewachsen;*
> *Ward auch den Meistern dabei bang,*
> *Gar wohl gefiel er doch Hans Sachsen.*' [1]

In Mayence I got to know the Schott family, with whom I had only had a casual acquaintance in Paris, more intimately. The young musician Weisheimer, who was just then beginning his career as musical director at the local theatre, was a daily visitor at their house. At one of our dinners another young man, Städl, a lawyer, proposed a remarkable toast in my honour in a most eloquent and astonishing speech. Notwithstanding all this I had to recognise that in Franz Schott I was dealing with a very singular man, and our negotiations proceeded with extraordinary difficulty. I insisted emphatically on carrying out my first proposal, namely, that he should provide

[1]   ' The bird who sang this morn
         From Nature's self had learned his singing ;
         Masters that song may scorn,
         For aye Hans Sachs will hear it singing.'
(Translation of the *Meistersinger*, by Frederick Jameson.) — EDITOR.

me for two successive years with funds necessary for the undisturbed execution of my work. He excused his unwillingness
to do this by pretending it was painful to his feelings to drive
a bargain with a man like myself by purchasing my work for a
certain sum of money, including also the profits of my author's
rights in the theatrical performances; that, in a word, he was
a music publisher, and did not want to be anything else. I
represented to him that he need only advance me the necessary
amount in proper form, and that I would guarantee him the
repayment of that proportion of it which might be considered
due payment for the literary property, out of my future theatrical takings, which would thus be his security.

After a long time he agreed to make advances on ' musical
compositions still to be delivered,' and to this suggestion I
gladly acceded, insisting, however, that I must be able to depend
on a total gradual payment of twenty thousand francs. As,
after settling my Vienna hotel bill, I was in immediate want of
money, Schott gave me a draft on Paris. From that city I
now received a letter from Princess Metternich, which mystified
me, inasmuch as it merely announced the sudden death of her
mother, Countess Sandor, and the consequent change in her
family circumstances. Once more I deliberated whether it would
not be better, after all, to take at random a modest lodging in
or near Karlsruhe, which in time might develop into a peaceful
and permanent dwelling. Owing to my difficulty in providing
Minna's allowance, which according to our agreement was three
thousand marks a year, it struck me as more reasonable and
certainly more economical to ask my wife to share my home.
But a letter which just then reached me from her, and the
main contents of which were nothing less than an attempt
to incite me against my own friends, scared me away from
any thought of reunion with her, and determined me to adhere to my Paris plans and keep as far away from her as
possible.

So towards the middle of December I started for Paris, where
I alighted at the dingy-looking Hôtel Voltaire, situated on the
quay of the same name, and took a very modest room with a
pleasant outlook. Here I wished to remain unrecognised (preparing myself meanwhile for my work) until I could present

myself to Princess Metternich at the beginning of the new year, according to her wish. In order not to embarrass the Metternich's friends, Pourtalès and Hatzfeld, I pretended that I was not in Paris, and looked up only those of my old acquaintances who did not know these gentlemen, such as Truinet, Gaspérini, Flaxland, and the painter Czermak. I met Truinet and his father regularly at supper time in the Taverne Anglaise, to which I used to make my way unobserved through the streets at dusk. One day, on opening one of the papers there I read the news of the death of Count Pourtalès. My grief was great, and I felt particularly sorry that, out of my singular regard for the Metternichs, I had neglected to visit this man who had been a real friend to me. I at once called on Count Hatzfeld, who confirmed the sad news and told me the circumstances of the sudden death, which was the result of heart disease, the existence of which the doctor had not discovered till the very last moment. At the same time I learned the true significance of the events which had taken place at the Hôtel Metternich. The death of Countess Sandor, of which Princess Pauline had informed me, had produced the following developments: the Count, who was the famous Hungarian madman, had up to that time, in the general interest of the family, been strictly guarded by his wife as an invalid. At her death the family lived in fear of the most terrible disturbances from her husband, now no longer under control, and the Metternichs therefore thought it necessary to take him at once to Paris, and keep him there under proper supervision. For that purpose the Princess found that the only suitable suite of apartments at her command was the one previously offered to me. I at once saw it was useless to think any more of taking up my residence at the Austrian embassy, and I was left to reflect on the strange freak of fortune that had again cast me adrift in this ill-omened Paris.

At first the only course open to me was to stay in my inexpensive lodging in the Hôtel Voltaire until I had finished the libretto of the *Meistersinger,* and meanwhile set to work to find the refuge so earnestly sought for the completion of my new work. It was not an easy matter; my name and person, which everybody involuntarily regarded in the doubtful light of my Paris failure, seemed surrounded by a cloud of mist, which

made me unrecognisable even to my old friends. The Olliviers
also appeared to receive me with an air of distrust; at any
rate, they thought it very strange to see me again so soon in
Paris. I was obliged to explain the extraordinary circumstances
that had brought me back, and told them that I did not contemplate a long stay. Apart from this probably deceptive
impression, I soon noticed the great change that had taken
place in the home life of the family. The grandmother was
laid up with a broken leg, which at her age was incurable.
Ollivier had taken her into his very small flat for more efficient
nursing and care, and we all met for dinner at her bedside in
the tiny room. Blandine had greatly changed since the previous
summer, and wore a sad and serious expression, and I fancied
that she was *enceinte*. Émile, although dry and superficial,
was the only one who gave me any sound advice. When the
fellow Lindau sent me a letter through his lawyer demanding
the compensation awarded him by the law for his imaginary
co-operation in the translation of *Tannhäuser*, all that Émile
said on reading the letter was, ' *Ne répondez pas,*' and his
advice proved as useful as it was easy to follow, for I never
heard anything more of the matter. I sorrowfully made up my
mind not to trouble Ollivier any more, and it was with an inex-
pressibly sad look that Blandine and I parted.

With Czermak, on the other hand, I entered into almost
daily intercourse. I used to join him and the Truinet family
of an evening at the Taverne Anglaise, or some other equally
cheap restaurants which we hunted out. Afterwards we generally went to one of the smaller theatres, which, owing to
pressure of work, I had not troubled about on my former
visits. The best of them all was the Gymnase, where all the
pieces were good and played by an excellent company. Of
these pieces a particularly tender and touching one-act play
called *Je dîne chez ma Mère* remains in my memory. In the
Théâtre du Palais Royal, where things were not now so refined
as formerly, and also in the Théâtre Déjazet, I recognised the
prototypes of all the jokes with which, in spite of poor elaboration and unsuitable localisation, the German public is being
entertained all the year round. Besides this I occasionally
dined with the Flaxland family, who still refused to despair

of my eventual success with the Parisians. For the present my Paris publisher continued to issue the *Fliegender Holländer* as well as *Rienzi*, for which he paid me fifteen hundred francs as a small fee, which I had not bargained for on the first edition.

The cause of the almost cheerful complacency with which I managed to regard my adverse situation in Paris, and which enabled me afterwards to look back on it as a pleasant memory, was that my libretto of the *Meistersinger* daily increased its swelling volume of rhyme. How could I help being filled with facetious thoughts, when on raising my eyes from the paper, after meditating upon the quaint verses and sayings of my Nuremberg Meistersinger, I gazed from the third-floor window of my hotel on the tremendous crowds passing along the quays and over the numerous bridges, and enjoyed a prospect embracing the Tuileries, the Louvre, and even the Hôtel de Ville!

I had already got far on into the first act when the momentous New Year's Day of 1862 arrived, and I paid my long-delayed visit to Princess Metternich. I found her very naturally embarrassed, but I quite cheerfully accepted her assurances of regret at being obliged to withdraw her invitation owing to circumstances with which I was already acquainted, and I did my utmost to reassure her. I also begged Count Hatzfeld to inform me when Countess Pourtalès would feel equal to receiving me.

Thus through the whole month of January I continued working on the *Meistersinger* libretto, and completed it in exactly thirty days. The melody for the fragment of Sachs's poem on the Reformation, with which I make my characters in the last act greet their beloved master, occurred to me on the way to the Taverne Anglaise, whilst strolling through the galleries of the Palais Royal. There I found Truinet already waiting for me, and asked him to give me a scrap of paper and a pencil to jot down my melody, which I quietly hummed over to him at the time. I usually accompanied him and his father along the boulevards to his flat in the Faubourg St. Honoré, and on that evening he could do nothing but exclaim, ' *Mais, quelle gaîté d'esprit, cher maître!* '

The nearer my work approached its termination, the more earnestly had I to think about a place of abode. I still imagined

that something similar to what I had lost by Liszt's abandonment of the Altenburg was in store for me. I now remembered
that in the previous year I had received a most pressing invitation from Mme. Street, to pay her and her father a long visit in
Brussels; on the strength of which I wrote to the lady and asked
if she could put me up for a time without any ceremony. She
was *en désolation* at being obliged to deny my wish. I next
turned to Cosima, who was in Berlin, with a similar request,
at which she seemed to be quite alarmed, but I quite understood
the reason of this when, on visiting Berlin later on, I saw the
style of Bülow's quarters. It struck me as very strange, on
the other hand, that my brother-in-law Avenarius, who, I heard,
was very comfortably settled in Berlin, begged me most earnestly
to go to him, and judge for myself whether I could not pay him
a long visit. My sister Cecilia, however, forbade me to take
Minna there, although she thought she could find her a lodging
in the immediate neighbourhood if she wanted to visit Berlin.
Unfortunately for herself, poor Minna could find nothing better
to do than to write me a furious letter about my sister's cruel
behaviour to her, so the possibility of a renewal of our old
squabbles deterred me at once from accepting my brother-in-
law's proposal. At last I bethought me of looking out for a
quiet retreat in the neighbourhood of Mayence, under the
financial protection of Schott. He had spoken to me about a
pretty estate there belonging to the young Baron von Hornstein.
I thought I was conferring an honour upon the latter when I
wrote to him at Munich asking permission to take up my abode
for a time at his place in the Rhine district, and was therefore
greatly perplexed when I received an answer expressing terror
at my suggestion. I now determined to go at once to Mayence,
and ordered all our furniture and household goods, which had
been stored in Paris for nearly a year, to be sent there. Before
leaving Paris, after coming to this decision, I had the consolation
of receiving a sublime exhortation to face everything with
resignation. I had previously informed Frau Wesendonck of
my situation and the chief source of my trouble, though of
course only as one writes to a sympathetic friend; she answered
by sending me a small letter-weight of cast-iron which she had
bought for me in Venice. It represented the lion of San Marco

with his paw on the book, and was intended to admonish me to imitate this lion in all things. On the other hand, Countess Pourtalès granted me the privilege of another visit to her house. In spite of her mourning, this lady did not wish to leave her sincere interest in me unexpressed on account of her sad bereavement; and when I told her what I was then doing, she asked to see my libretto. On my assuring her that in her present frame of mind she could not enter into the lively character of my *Meistersinger,* she kindly expressed a great wish to hear me read it, and invited me to spend an evening with her. She was the first person to whom I had the opportunity of reading my now completed work, and it made such a lively impression upon us both, that we were many times compelled to burst out into fits of hearty laughter.

On the evening of my departure on the first of February, I invited my friends Gaspérini, Czermak, and the Truinets to a farewell meal in my hotel. All were in capital spirits, and my good-humour enhanced the general cheerfulness, although no one quite understood what connection it could have with the subject on which I had just completed a libretto, and from the performance of which I anticipated so much.

In my anxiety to choose a suitable residence, which was now so necessary to me, I directed my steps once more to Karlsruhe. I was again received in the kindest manner by the Grand Duke and Duchess, who inquired about my future plans. It turned out, however, that the residence I so earnestly desired could not be provided for me in Karlsruhe. I was much struck by the sympathetic concern of the Grand Duke as to how I could meet the cost of my arduous life, or even my travelling expenses. I cheerfully endeavoured to set his mind at rest by telling him of the contract I had made with Schott, who had bound himself to provide me with the necessary funds in the form of advances on my *Meistersinger.* This seemed to reassure him. Later on I heard from Alwine Frommann that the Grand Duke had once said that I had been somewhat cold towards him, considering that he had been kind enough to place his purse at my disposal. But I was certainly not conscious of his having done so. The only point raised in our discussion had been whether I should go to Karlsruhe again to rehearse one of my operas there, possibly *Lohengrin,* and conduct it in person.

At any rate I started for Mayence, which I reached on the 4th February, and found the whole place flooded. Owing to the early breaking up of the ice, the Rhine had overflowed its banks to an unusual extent, and I only reached Schott's house at some considerable risk. Nevertheless, I had already arranged to read the *Meistersinger* on the evening of the 5th of that month, and had even made Cornelius promise to come from Vienna, and had sent him a hundred francs from Paris for that purpose. I had not received any answer from him, and as I now learned that the floods had spread to all the river districts of Germany, and impeded the railway traffic, I had already ceased to count upon him. I waited until the last moment and — in fact, just as the clock struck seven — Cornelius appeared. He had met with all sorts of adventures, had even lost his overcoat on the way, and reached his sister's house in a half-frozen condition only a few hours before. The reading of my libretto put us all into excellent humour, but I was very sorry I could not shake Cornelius's determination to start on his return journey the next day. He wished me to understand that his sole object in coming to Mayence was for this one reading of the *Meistersinger,* and as a matter of fact, in spite of floods and floating ice, he left for Vienna on the following day.

As we had already arranged, I began in company with Schott to search for a residence on the opposite bank of the Rhine. We had had Biebrich in our mind's eye; but as nothing suitable seemed to present itself there, we thought of Wiesbaden. At last I decided to stay at the ' Europäischer Hof ' at Biebrich, and continue my search from there. As I had always been most particular to keep aloof as far as possible from the noise of music, I decided to rent a small but very suitable flat in a large summer residence newly built by the architect Frickhöfer, and situated close to the Rhine. I was obliged to await the arrival of my furniture and household effects from Paris before I could get it in order. At last they came, and at endless trouble and expense were duly unloaded at the Biebrich custom-house, where I took possession only of those things which I required most.

I kept only what was absolutely necessary in Biebrich, intending to send the greater part to my wife in Dresden. I had already informed Minna of this, whereupon she immediately assumed that with my clumsy unpacking I should lose half the things or ruin them all. About a week after I had fairly settled down with my newly arrived Erard grand, Minna suddenly appeared in Biebrich. At first I felt nothing but sincere pleasure at her healthy appearance and untiring energy in the practical management of affairs, and even thought the best thing I could do was to let her remain with me. Unfortunately my good resolutions did not last long, as the old scenes were soon renewed. When we went to the custom-house, intending to separate her things from mine, she could not contain her anger that I had not waited for her arrival before removing on my own account the articles I required for myself. Nevertheless, she thought it only proper that I should be provided with certain household effects, and gave me four sets of knives, forks and spoons, a few cups and saucers, with plates to match. She then superintended the packing of the remainder, which was not inconsiderable, and, after arranging everything to her satisfaction, took her departure to Dresden a week later.

She now flattered herself that her establishment there would be sufficiently furnished to receive me, as she hoped, very shortly. With this idea she had taken the necessary steps with regard to the superior government officials, and these latter had been successful in obtaining a declaration from the minister that I might now send in a formal petition to the King to grant me an amnesty, and that nothing would then stand in the way of my return to Dresden.

I deliberated with considerable hesitation as to what I should do in this matter. Minna's presence had greatly increased the mental discord arising from my recent anxieties. Rough weather, defective stoves, my badly managed household, and my unexpectedly heavy expenses, particularly for Minna's establishment, all combined to mar the pleasure I had taken in pursuing the work I had started at the Hôtel Voltaire. Presumably to distract my thoughts, the Schott family invited me to witness a performance of *Rienzi* at Darmstadt, with

Niemann in the title-rôle. The ex-minister, Herr von Dalwigk, fearing that a demonstration at the theatre in my favour in the presence of the Grand Duke, might wound the latter's susceptibilities, introduced himself to me at the station and accompanied me to his own box, where he cleverly thought he could play the part of presenting me to the public on behalf of the Grand Duke. Thus everything went off pleasantly. The performance itself, in which Niemann played one of his best parts, interested me greatly; I also noticed that they cut out as much of the opera as they could, presumably in deference to the tastes of the Grand Duke, so as to extend the ballet as much as possible by repeating the lighter parts of it.

From this excursion I had again to return home through the floating ice on the Rhine. As I was still in very low spirits, I tried to introduce a few comforts into my home, and for this purpose engaged a maid-servant to prepare my breakfast; my other meals I took at the ' Europäischer Hof.'

When I found, however, that I could not recover my working mood, and feeling somewhat restless, I offered to redeem my promise and pay another visit to the Grand Duke of Baden, suggesting that I should give him a reading of the *Meistersinger*. The Grand Duke replied by a very kind telegram signed by himself, in response to which I went to Karlsruhe on the 7th March and read my manuscript to him and his wife. A drawing-room had been specially selected for this reading, in which hung a great historical picture by my old friend Pecht, portraying Goethe as a young man reading the first fragments of his *Faust* before the Grand Duke's ancestors. My work received very kind attention, and at the conclusion of the reading I was exceedingly pleased to hear the Grand Duchess recommend me particularly to find a suitable musical setting for the excellent part of Pogner, which was a friendly admission of regret that a citizen should be more zealous in the interests of art than many a prince. A performance of *Lohengrin*, under my conductorship, was once more discussed, and I was advised to make fresh terms with Eduard Devrient. Unfortunately the latter made a terrible impression on me by his production of *Tannhäuser* at the theatre. I was obliged to witness this performance seated by his side, and was astonished to realise that this ' Dramaturge,' whom I had hitherto so highly recommended, had now sunk to the most vulgar practices of the theatrical profession. To my amazement at the monstrous mistakes made in the performance, he replied, with great surprise and a certain haughty indignation, that he could not understand why I made so much fuss about such trifles, as I must know very well that in theatres it was impossible to do otherwise. Nevertheless, a model performance of *Lohengrin* was arranged for the following summer, with the co-operation of Herr Schnorr and his wife.

A much pleasanter impression was made upon me by a play I saw at the Frankfort theatre, where, in passing through that town, I saw a pretty comedy, in which the delicate and tender acting of Friederike Meyer, the sister of my Vienna singer, Mme. Dustmann, impressed me more than any German acting had ever done. I now began to calculate on the possibility of making suitable friends in the neighbourhood of Biebrich, so as not to be entirely dependent on the Schott family or on my hotel-keeper for society. I had already looked up the Raff family in Wiesbaden, where Frau Raff had an engagement at the court theatre. She was a sister of Emilie Genast, with whom I had been on friendly terms during my stay in Weimar. One excellent piece of information I heard about her was that by extraordinary thrift and good management she had succeeded in raising her husband's position of careless wastefulness to a flourishing and prosperous one. Raff himself, who by his own accounts of his dissipated life under Liszt's patronage, had led me to regard him as an eccentric genius, at once disabused me of this idea when, on a closer acquaintance, I found him an uncommonly uninteresting and insipid man, full of self-conceit, but without any power of taking a wide outlook on the world.

Taking advantage of the prosperous condition to which he had attained, thanks to his wife, he considered he was entitled to patronise me by giving me some friendly advice in regard to my position at the time. He thought it advisable to tell me that I ought in my dramatic compositions to pay more attention to the reality of things, and to illustrate his meaning he pointed to my score of *Tristan* as an abortion of idealistic extravagances.

In the course of my rambles on foot to Wiesbaden I sometimes liked to call on Raff's wife, a rather insignificant woman, but Raff himself was a person to whom I soon became perfectly indifferent. Still, when he came to know me a little better, he lowered the tone of his sagelike maxims, and even appeared to be rather afraid of my chaffing humour, against the shafts of which he knew he was defenceless.

Wendelin Weisheimer, whom I had known slightly before, often called on me in Biebrich. He was the son of a rich peasant of Osthofen, and to the astonishment of his father refused to give up the musical profession. He was particularly anxious to introduce me to his parent, that I might influence the old man's mind in favour of his son's choice of an artistic career. This involved me in excursions into their district, and I had an opportunity of witnessing young Weisheimer's talent as an orchestral conductor at a performance of Offenbach's *Orpheus* in the theatre at Mayence, where he had hitherto occupied a subordinate position. I was horrified that my sympathy for this young man should make me descend so low as to be present at such an abomination, and for a long time I could not refrain from letting Weisheimer see the annoyance I felt.

In my search for a more dignified entertainment I wrote to Friedericke Meyer in Frankfort and asked her to let me know when the performance of Calderon's comedy, *Das öffentliche Geheimniss,* would be repeated, as the last time I had seen an announcement of it, I had been too late. She was much pleased at my sympathetic inquiry, and informed me that the comedy was not likely to be revived in the immediate future, but that there was a prospect of Calderon's *Don Gutierre* being produced. I again paid a visit to Frankfort to see this play, and made the personal acquaintance of this interesting actress for the first time. I had every reason to be highly satisfied with the performance of Calderon's tragedy, although the talented actress who played the leading part was thoroughly successful only in the tenderer passages, her resources being insufficient to depict the more passionate scenes. She told me she very often visited some friends of hers in Mayence, and I followed up this communication by expressing a wish that when doing so she would look me up at Biebrich, to which she replied that

I might hope on some future occasion for the fulfilment of my wish.

A grand soirée given by the Schotts to their Mayence acquaintances was the occasion of my making friends with Mathilde Maier, whom Frau Schott, at least so she informed me, had specially selected for her ' cleverness ' to be my companion at the supper table; her highly intelligent, sincere manner and her peculiar Mayence dialect distinguished her favourably from the rest of the company; nor was this distinction accompanied by anything *outré*. I promised to visit her, and thus became acquainted with an idyllic home such as I had never met before. This Mathilde, who was the daughter of a lawyer who had died leaving only a small fortune behind, lived with her mother, two aunts and a sister in a neat little house, while her brother, who was learning business in Paris, was a continual source of trouble to her. Mathilde, with her practical common-sense, attended to the affairs of the whole family, apparently to every one's complete satisfaction. I was received among them with remarkable warmth whenever, in the pursuit of my business, I chanced to come to Mayence. This happened about once a week, and on each occasion I was made to accept their hospitality. But as Mathilde had a large circle of acquaintances, among others an old gentleman in Mayence who had been Schopenhauer's only friend, I frequently met her in other people's houses, as for instance at the Raffs in Wiesbaden. From there she and her old friend Luise Wagner would often accompany me on my way home, and I would sometimes go with them further on the way to Mayence.

These meetings were full of agreeable impressions, to which frequent walks in the beautiful park of Biebrich Castle contributed. The fair season of the year was now approaching, and I was once more seized with a desire for work. As from the balcony of my flat, in a sunset of great splendour, I gazed upon the magnificent spectacle of ' Golden ' Mayence, with the majestic Rhine pouring along its outskirts in a glory of light, the prelude to my *Meistersinger* again suddenly made its presence closely and distinctly felt in my soul. Once before had I seen it rise before me out of a lake of sorrow, like some distant mirage. I proceeded to write down the prelude exactly as it appears to-day in the score, that is, containing the clear outlines of the leading themes of the whole drama. I proceeded at once to continue the composition, intending to allow the remaining scenes to follow in due succession. As I was feeling in a good temper I thought I would like to pay a visit to the Duke of Nassau. He was my neighbour, and I had so often met him on my lonely walks in the park, that I considered it polite to call on him. Unfortunately there was not much to be got out of the interview which took place. He was a very narrow-minded but amiable man, who excused himself for continuing to smoke his cigar in my presence because he could not get on without it, and he thereupon proceeded to describe to me his preference for Italian opera, which I was quite content he should retain. But I had an ulterior motive in trying to prepossess him in my favour. At the back of his park stood a tiny castle of ancient appearance on the borders of a lake. It had grown into a sort of picturesque ruin, and at the time served as a studio for a sculptor. I was filled with a bold desire to acquire this small, half-tumbledown building for the rest of my life; for I had already become a prey to alarming anxiety as to whether I should be able to hold out in the quarters I had so far tenanted, as the greater part of the storey, on which I occupied only two small rooms, had been let to a family for the approaching summer, and I heard that they would enter into possession, armed with a piano. I was soon dissuaded, however, from further attempts to induce the Duke of Nassau to favour my views, for he told me that this little castle, on account of its damp situation, would be thoroughly unhealthy.

Nevertheless, I did not allow myself to be deterred from setting to work to find some lonely little house with a garden, for which I still longed. In the excursions I repeatedly undertook for this purpose I was frequently accompanied not only by Weisheimer but also by Dr. Städl, the young lawyer who at Schott's house had proposed the charming toast which I have already mentioned. He was an extraordinary man, and I could only explain his very excitable nature by the fact that he was a passionate gambler at the roulette tables in Wiesbaden. He it was who had introduced me to another friend, a practised musician, Dr. Schüler from Wiesbaden. With both these gentlemen I now weighed all the possibilities of acquiring, or at least of discovering, my little castle for the future. On one occasion we visited Bingen with this object, and ascended the celebrated old tower there in which the Emperor Henry IV. was imprisoned long ago. After going for some distance up the rock on which the tower was built, we reached a room on the fourth storey occupying the entire square of the building, with a single projecting window looking out upon the Rhine.

I recognised this room as the ideal of everything I had imagined in the way of a residence for myself. I thought I could arrange for the necessary smaller apartments in the flat by means of curtains, and thus prepare for myself a splendid place of refuge for ever. Städl and Schüler thought it possible they might help me in the fulfilment of my wishes, as they were both acquainted with the proprietor of this ruin. Shortly afterwards, in fact, they informed me that the owner had no objection to letting me this large room at a low rent, but at the same time they pointed out the utter impracticability of carrying out my plan; nobody, they said, would be either able or willing to act as my servant there, for, amongst other things, there was no well, and the only water obtainable was from a cistern lying at a frightful depth down in the keep, and even this was not good. Under such circumstances it did not require more than one such obstacle to deter me from the pursuit of such an extravagant scheme. I had a similar experience with a property in Rheingau belonging to Count Schönborn. My attention had been drawn to it, because it was unoccupied by the proprietor. Here I certainly found a number of empty rooms, out of which I should have been able to arrange something suitable for my purpose. After obtaining further details from the land agent, who wrote on my behalf to Count Schönborn, I had to content myself with a refusal.

A strange incident that occurred about this time seriously threatened to interrupt me to some extent in the work I had begun. Friederike Meyer kept her promise and called on me one afternoon on her return from her usual excursion to Mayence. She was accompanied by a lady friend. Shortly after her arrival she was suddenly overwhelmed with fear, and to the terror of all present declared she was afraid she had caught scarlet fever. Her condition soon became alarming, and she had to find accommodation immediately in the 'Europäischer Hof' hotel and send for a doctor. The certainty with which she had immediately recognised the symptoms of a disease, which in most cases can only be caught from children, could not fail to impress me strangely. But my amazement was increased when on the following morning, at a very early hour, Herr von Guaita, the manager of the Frankfort theatre, who had heard of her illness, paid a visit to the patient and expressed for her an anxiety, the intensity of which it was impossible to ascribe entirely to his interest as a theatrical manager. He took Friederike at once under his protection, and treated her with the greatest care, thus relieving me from the pangs of anxiety aroused by this strange case. I spent some time with Herr von Guaita, talking with him about the possibility of producing one of my operas in Frankfort. On the second day I was present when the sick lady was conveyed to the railway station by Guaita, who evinced towards her what appeared to me the most tender paternal solicitude. Soon after this, Herr Bürde (the husband of Madame Ney, a famous singer), who was at that time an actor at the Frankfort theatre, paid me a call. This gentleman, with whom amongst other things I discussed Friederike Meyer's talents, informed me that she was supposed to be the mistress of Herr von Guaita, a man who was held in great respect in the town on account of his noble rank, and that he had presented her with a house in which she was now living. As Herr von Guaita had not made an agreeable impression upon me, but on the contrary had struck me as a strange creature, this news filled me with a certain uneasiness. My other acquaintances who lived near my place of refuge in Biebrich were kind and friendly when, on the evening of my birthday on the 22nd of May, I entertained this little company in my flat. Mathilde Maier with her sister and her lady friend were very clever in utilising my small stock of crockery, and in a certain sense she did the honours as mistress of the house.

But my peace of mind was soon disturbed by an interchange of letters with Minna, which grew more and more unsatisfactory. I had settled her in Dresden, but wanted to spare her the humiliation of a permanent separation from me. In pursuance of this idea I had at last found myself compelled to adopt the plan she had initiated, by communicating with the Saxon Minister of Justice; and I finally petitioned for a complete amnesty from the government, and received permission to settle in Dresden. Minna now thought herself authorised to take a large flat, in which it would be easy to arrange the furniture allotted to her, assuming that after a little while I would share the abode with her, at least periodically. I had to try to meet cheerfully her demands for the wherewithal to carry out her wishes, and especially to procure the two thousand seven hundred marks she required for the purpose. The more calmly I acted in this matter, the more deeply she seemed to be offended by the quiet frigidity of my letters. Reproaches for supposed injuries in the past and recriminations of every kind now poured in from her faster than ever. At last I turned to my old friend Pusinelli. Out of affection for me he had always been a loyal helper of my intractable spouse. Through his mediation I now prescribed the strong medicine which my sister Clara a short while ago had recommended as the best remedy for the patient, and asked him to impress upon Minna the necessity for a legal separation. It seemed to be no easy task for my poor friend to carry out this proposal in earnest, but he had been asked to do it, and obeyed. He informed me that she was very much alarmed, but that she definitely refused to discuss an amicable separation, and, as my sister had foreseen, Minna's conduct now changed in a very striking manner; she ceased to annoy me and seemed to realise her position and abide by it. To relieve her heart trouble, Pusinelli had prescribed for her a cure at Reichenhall. I obtained the money for this, and apparently she spent the summer in tolerable spirits in the very place in which a year ago I had met Cosima undergoing a cure.

Once more I turned to my work, to which I always had recourse as the best means of raising my spirits so soon as interruptions were removed. One night I was disturbed by a strange event. The evening had been pleasant, and I had sketched out the pretty theme for Pogner's *Anrede,* ' Das schöne Fest Johannistag,' etc., when, while I was dozing off and still

had this tune floating in my mind, I was suddenly awakened
to full consciousness by an unrestrained outburst of a woman's
laughter above my room. This laughter, growing madder and
madder, at last turned into a horrible whimpering and frightful
howling. I sprang out of bed in a terrified condition, to
discover that the sound proceeded from my servant Lieschen,
who had been attacked with hysterical convulsions as she lay
in bed in the room overhead. My host's maid went to help
her, and a doctor was summoned. While I was horrified at
the thought that the girl would soon die, I could not help wondering at the curious tranquillity of the others who were present.
I was told that such fits were of common occurrence in young
girls, especially after dances. Without heeding this, I was
riveted to the spot for a long time by the spectacle, with the
horrible symptoms it presented. Several times I saw what
resembled a childish fit of merriment pass, like the ebb and
flow of the tide, through all the different stages, up to the most
impudent laughter, and then to what seemed like the screams
of the damned in torture. When the disturbance had somewhat subsided, I went to bed again, and once more Pogner's
'Johannistag' rose to my memory, and gradually banished the
fearful impressions that I had undergone.

One day, when I was watching young Städl at the gambling-
table in Wiesbaden, I thought he was rather like the poor
servant-girl. I had taken coffee with him and Weisheimer in
the Kur garden, and we had enjoyed one another's company,
when Städl disappeared for a time. Weisheimer led me to the
gambling-table to find him. Seldom have I witnessed a more
horrible change of expression than that now stamped on the
man who was a prey to the gambling mania. As a demon had
possessed poor Lieschen, so now a demon possessed this man.
As folk say, the devils ' pursued their evil lusts in him.' No
appeal, no humiliating admonitions could prevail upon the man
tortured by his losses in the game to summon up his moral
powers. As I remembered my own experiences of the gambling
passion, to which I had succumbed for a time when I was a
youth, I spoke to young Weisheimer on the subject, and offered
to show him how I was not afraid to make a stake on pure
chance, but that I had no belief in my luck. When a new

round of roulette began, I said to him in a voice of quiet certainty, ' Number 11 will win '; and it did. I added fuel to the fire of his astonishment at this stroke of good luck by predicting Number 27 for the next round. Certainly I remember being overcome by a spell as I spoke, and my number was in fact again victorious. My young friend was now in a state of such astonishment, that he vehemently urged me to stake something on the numbers which I foretold. Again I cannot but call to mind the curious, quiet feeling of being spellbound which possessed me as I said, ' As soon as I introduce my own personal interests into the game, my gift of prophecy will disappear at once.' I then drew him away from the gambling-table, and we took our way back to Biebrich in a fine sunset.

I now came into very painful relations with poor Friederike Meyer. She wrote and told me of her recovery and requested me to visit her, because she felt it her duty to apologise to me for the trouble in which she had involved me. As the short drive to Frankfort often helped to entertain me and distract my thoughts, I gladly fulfilled her wishes, and found her in a state of convalescence but still weak, and obviously preoccupied with the effort to fortify my mind against all disagreeable surmises about herself. She said that Herr von Guaita was like an anxious, almost hypersensitive father to her. She told me that she was very young when she left her family, and that with her sister Luise in particular she had severed all connection. She had thus come quite friendless to Frankfort, where the chance protection of Herr von Guaita, a man of mature age, had been very welcome to her. Unfortunately she had to suffer much that was painful under this arrangement, for she was most bitterly persecuted, chiefly on the score of her reputation, by her patron's family, who feared he might want to marry her. As she told me this, I could not refrain from drawing her attention to some of the consequences of the antagonism I had noticed, and I went so far as to speak of the house which people said had been given her as a present. This seemed to produce an extraordinary effect upon Friederike, who was still an invalid. She expressed the greatest annoyance at these rumours, although, as she admitted, she had long been obliged to suspect that slander of this kind would be disseminated about her; more than once she had considered the advisability of giving up the Frankfort stage, and now she was more determined than ever to do so. I saw nothing in her demeanour to shake my confidence in the truth of her story; moreover, as Herr von Guaita became more and more unintelligible to me both as a man and in the light of his incredible conduct on the occasion of Friederike's illness, my attitude towards this highly gifted girl was henceforth unconditionally on the side of her interests, which were being prejudiced by an obvious injustice. To facilitate her recovery I advised her, without delay, to take a long holiday for a tour on the Rhine.

In accordance with the instructions conveyed to him by the Grand Duke, Eduard Devrient now addressed me in reference to the appointed performance of *Lohengrin* in Karlsruhe under my superintendence. The angry and arrogant disgust expressed in his letter at my desire to see that *Lohengrin* was produced without ' cuts,' served admirably to expose to me the profound antipathy of this man whom I had once so blindly overestimated. He wrote that one of the first things he had done was to have a copy of the score made for the orchestra with the ' cuts ' introduced by Conductor Rietz for the Leipzig performance, and that it would consequently be a tiresome business to put back all the passages which I wished to have restored. He regarded my request in this particular as merely malicious. I now remembered that the only performance of *Lohengrin,* which had been taken off almost immediately on account of its complete failure, was the one in Leipzig produced by Conductor Rietz. Devrient, regarding Rietz as Mendelssohn's successor and the most solid musician of ' modern times,' had concluded that this mutilation of my work was a suitable one for production in Karlsruhe. But I shuddered at the misguided light in which I had so long persisted in regarding this man. I informed him briefly of my indignation and of my decision to have nothing to do with *Lohengrin* in Karlsruhe. I also expressed my intention to make my excuses to the Grand Duke at a suitable time. Soon after this I heard that *Lohengrin* was, after all, to be produced in Karlsruhe in the usual way, and that the newly wedded Schnorrs had been specially

engaged for it. A great longing at last filled me to make the
acquaintance of Schnorr and his achievements. Without announcing my intentions, I travelled to Karlsruhe, obtained a
ticket through Kaliwoda, and heedless of all else went to the
performance. In my published *Memoirs* I have described more
accurately the impressions I received on this occasion, more particularly of Schnorr. I fell in love with him at once, and after
the performance I sent him a message to come and see me in
my room at the hotel and have a little chat. I had heard so
much of his delicate state of health that I was genuinely
delighted to see him enter the room with a lively step and a
look of joy in his eyes. Although it was late at night, and he
had undergone a considerable strain, he met my anxiety to
avoid all dissipation out of regard to his welfare, by willingly
accepting my offer to celebrate our new acquaintance with a
bottle of champagne. We spent the greater part of the night
in the best of spirits, and among our discussions those on
Devrient's character were especially instructive to me. I undertook to stay another day, so as to avail myself of an invitation
to lunch with Schnorr and his wife. As by this lengthy stay
in Karlsruhe I knew my presence would become known to
the Grand Duke, I took advantage on the following day to inform him of my arrival, and he made an appointment to meet
me in the afternoon. After talking at lunch to Frau Schnorr,
in whom I had recognised a great and well-developed theatrical
talent, and after making the most astonishing discoveries about
Devrient's behaviour in the *Tristan* affair, I had my interview
at the ducal palace. It was marked by uneasiness on both
sides. I openly stated my reasons for withdrawing my promise
with regard to the *Lohengrin* performance, and also my unalter-
able conviction that a conspiracy to interfere with the production of *Tristan* originally proposed had been the work of
Devrient. As Devrient, by his ingenious attitude, had led the
Grand Duke to believe in his profound and genuinely solicitous
friendship for me, my communications obviously pained the
Grand Duke a great deal. Still, he seemed eager to assume
that the matter turned on artistic differences of opinion between
me and his theatrical manager, and in bidding me good-bye he
expressed the hope of seeing these apparent misunderstandings

give way to a satisfactory explanation. I replied with in-difference that I did not think it likely I should ever come to an agreement with Devrient. The Grand Duke now gave vent to genuine indignation; he had not thought, he said, that I could so easily treat an old friend with such ingratitude. To meet the keenness of this reproach I could at first only tender my apologies for not having expressed my decision with the emphasis he had a right to expect, but as the Grand Duke had taken this matter so seriously and had thereby seemed to justify me in expressing my real opinion of this supposed friend with equal seriousness, I was bound, with all the earnestness at my command, to assure him that I did not wish to have any-thing more to do with Devrient. At this the Grand Duke told me, with renewed gentleness, that he declined to regard my assurance as irrevocable, for it lay in his power to propitiate me by other means. I took my departure with an expression of serious regret that I could not help regarding as fruitless any effort made in the direction contemplated by my patron. Later on I ascertained that Devrient, who, of course, was informed by the Grand Duke of what had taken place, looked upon my behaviour as an attempt on my part to ruin and supplant him. The Grand Duke had not abandoned his desire to arrange for the performance of a concert consisting of selections from my most recent works. Devrient had after-wards to write to me again in his official capacity on this subject. In his letter he took occasion to make it clear that he regarded himself as victorious over the intrigues I had practised against him, assuring me at the same time that his distinguished patron nevertheless wished to carry out the concert in ques-tion, as from his lofty point of view he knew very well how to distinguish ' the art from the artist.' My answer was a simple refusal.

I had many a conversation with the Schnorrs over the episode, and I made an arrangement with them to visit me soon in Biebrich. I returned there now, to be in time for Bülow's visit, of which I had already been informed. He arrived at the beginning of July to look for lodgings for himself and Cosima, who followed two days later. We were immensely pleased to meet again, and utilised the occasion to make

excursions of all sorts for the benefit of our health in the
pleasant Rheingau country. We took our meals together
regularly in the public dining-room of the ' Europäischer Hof '
(where the Schnorrs also came to stay), and we were generally
as merry as possible. In the evening we had music in my
rooms. Alwine Frommann, on her way through Biebrich, also
came to the reading of the *Meistersinger*. All present seemed
to be struck with surprise on hearing my latest libretto, and
especially by the vernacular gaiety of the style, of which until
now I had not availed myself. Frau Dustmann also, who
had a special engagement for a performance at Wiesbaden, paid
me a visit. Unfortunately I noticed in her a lively antipathy
to her sister Friederike, a fact which, among others, strengthened my conviction that it was high time for Friederike to dis-
sociate herself from all ties in Frankfort. After I had been
enabled, with Bülow's support, to play my friends the completed
parts of the composition of the *Meistersinger,* I went through
most of *Tristan,* and in this process the Schnorrs had an opportunity of showing the extent to which they had already made
themselves acquainted with their task. I found that both were
a good deal lacking in clearness of enunciation.

The summer now brought more visitors into our neighbourhood, and amongst them several of my acquaintances. David,
the Leipzig concert director, called on me with his young pupil,
August Wilhelmj, the son of a Wiesbaden lawyer. We now
had music in the true sense of the word, and Conductor Alois
Schmitt from Schwerin contributed an odd share by performing
what he called a worthless old composition of his. One evening we had a crowded party, the Schotts joining the rest of my
friends, and both the Schnorrs delighted us keenly with a
performance of the so-called love-scene in the third act of
Lohengrin. We were all deeply moved by the sudden apparition of Röckel in our common dining-room at the hotel. He
had been released from Waldheimer prison after thirteen years.
I was astounded to find absolutely no radical change in the
appearance of my old acquaintance, except for the faded colour
of his hair. He himself explained this to me by observing
that he had stepped out of something like a shell in which he
had been ensconced for his own preservation. As we were

deliberating about the field of activity on which he ought now to enter, I advised him to seek some useful employment in the service of a benevolent and liberal-minded man like the Grand Duke of Baden. He did not think he would succeed in any ministerial capacity, owing to his want of legal knowledge; on the other hand, he was eminently qualified to undertake the supervision of a house of correction, as he had obtained not only the most accurate information on this subject, but at the same time had noted what reforms were necessary. He went off to the German shooting competition taking place at Frankfort. There, in recognition of his martyrdom and his unwavering conduct, he was accorded a flattering ovation, and he stayed in Frankfort and its neighbourhool for some time.

Cäsar Willig, a painter who had received a commission from Otto Wesendonck to paint my portrait at his expense, worried me and my intimate friends at this time. Unfortunately the painter was utterly unsuccessful in his attempt to make a good likeness of me. Although Cosima was present at nearly all the sittings, and tried her utmost to put the artist on the right track, the end of it was that I had to sit for a sharp profile, to enable him to produce anything that could be in the least recognisable as a likeness. After he had performed this task to his satisfaction, he painted another copy for me out of gratitude. I sent this at once to Minna in Dresden, through whom it ultimately went to my sister Louisa. It was a horrible picture, and I was confronted with it once afterwards when it was exhibited by the artist in Frankfort.

I made a pleasant excursion with the Bülows and the Schnorrs to Bingen one evening, and availed myself of the opportunity to cross over to Rüdesheim to bring back Friederike Meyer, who had been enjoying her holiday there. I introduced her to my friends, and Cosima especially took a friendly interest in this uncommonly gifted woman. Our gaiety as we sat over a glass of wine in the open air was heightened by our being unexpectedly accosted by a traveller who approached us respectfully from a distant table; he held his glass filled, and at once greeted me politely and with the utmost warmth. He was a native of Berlin and a great enthusiast of my work. He spoke not only for himself, but also on behalf of two of his friends, who joined us at our table; and our good-humour led us ultimately to champagne. A splendid evening with a wonderful moon-rise shed its influence over the gladness of our spirits as we returned home late in the evening after this delightful excursion. When we visited Schlangenbad (where Alwine Frommann was staying) in equally high spirits, our reckless humour beguiled us into making an even longer excursion to Rolandseck. We made our first halt at Remagen, where we visited the handsome church, in which a young monk was preaching to an immense crowd, and we afterwards lunched in a garden on the bank of the Rhine. We remained that night in Rolandseck, and next morning we went up the Drachenfels. In connection with this ascent, an adventure happened which had a merry sequel. On the return journey, after getting out of the train at the railway station and crossing the Rhine, I missed my letter-case containing a note for two hundred marks; it had slipped out of my overcoat pocket. Two gentlemen who had joined us on the way from the Drachenfels immediately offered to retrace their steps, a somewhat arduous undertaking, to hunt for the lost object. After a few hours they returned, and handed me the letter-case with its contents intact. Two stone-cutters at work on the summit of the mountain had found it. They restored it at once, and the honest fellows were presented with a handsome reward. The happy issue to this adventure had, of course, to be celebrated by a good dinner with the best wine. The story was not completed for me until a long time afterwards. In 1873, on my entering a restaurant in Cologne, the host introduced himself to me as the man who, eleven years previously, had catered for us at the inn on the Rhine, and had changed that very two-hundred-mark note for me. He then told me what had happened to that note. An Englishman, to whom he had related the adventure of the note on the same day, offered to buy it from him for double its value. The host declined any such transaction, but allowed the Englishman to have the note on the promise of the latter to stand champagne to all those present at the time. The promise was fulfilled to the letter.

An invitation to Osthofen from the Weisheimer family was the origin of a less satisfactory excursion than the one

described above. We put up there for one night after being
compelled on the previous day to take part at all hours in
the frolics of a peasant wedding-feast which was simply interminable. Cosima was the only one who managed to keep in
a good temper throughout the proceedings. I supported her
to the best of my abilities. But Bülow's depression, which
had increased during the preceding days, grew deeper and
deeper, was aggravated by every possible incident, until at last
it developed into an outbreak of fury. We tried to console
ourselves with the reflection that a similar infliction could never
again fall to our lot. The following day, while I was preparing
for my departure, and brooding over other sources of dissatisfaction at my position, Cosima induced Hans to continue the
journey as far as Worms in the hope of finding something
refreshing and cheering in a visit to the ancient cathedral there,
and from that place they followed me later to Biebrich.

One little adventure we had at the gaming-table at Wiesbaden still lingers in my memory. Within the last few days
I had received a royalty of twenty louis d'or from the theatre
for an opera. Not knowing what to do with so small a sum
(as my situation, on the whole, was growing worse and worse), I
ventured to ask Cosima to risk half the sum at roulette in our
joint interest. I observed with astonishment how, without
even the smallest knowledge of the game, she staked one gold
piece after another on the table, throwing it down so that it
never definitely covered any particular number or colour. In
this way it gradually disappeared behind the croupier's rake.
I grew alarmed, and hurriedly went to another table in the
hope of counteracting the effect of Cosima's unguided and
misguided efforts. In this very economical pursuit luck
befriended me so substantially, that I at once recovered the
ten louis d'or which my fair friend had lost at the other table.
This soon put us into a very merry mood. Less cheering than
this adventure was our visit to a performance of *Lohengrin* in
Wiesbaden. After we had been pretty well satisfied and put
into a fairly good humour by the first act, the representation
turned, as it proceeded, into a current of maddening mis-
representation such as I should never have believed possible.
In a fury I left the theatre before the end, while Hans, urged

by Cosima's reminder of the proprieties (though they were both as much infuriated as I was), endured the martyrdom of witnessing the performance to a close.

On another occasion I heard that the Metternichs had arrived at their Castle Johannisberg. Still preoccupied with my main anxiety to obtain a peaceful domicile in which to conclude the *Meistersinger,* I kept an eye on this castle, which was generally unoccupied, and announced my intention of calling on the Prince. An invitation soon followed, and the Bülows accompanied me to the railway station. I could not fail to be satisfied with the friendly reception accorded to me by my patrons. They, too, had been considering the question of finding a temporary resting-place for me in the Johannisberg Castle, and found they could give me a small flat in the house of the keeper of the castle for my sole use, only they drew my attention to the difficulty of obtaining my board. The Prince, however, had busied himself more actively with another matter, that of creating a permanent position for me in Vienna. He said that on his next stay in Vienna he would have a discussion about my affairs with Schmerling the minister, whom he thought it was most suitable to consult on such a matter. He was a man who would understand me, and perhaps be able to discover a proper position for me in the higher sense of the word, and arouse the Emperor's interest in me. If I went to Vienna again, I was simply to call on Schmerling, and he would receive me as a matter of course on account of the Prince's introduction. As the result of an invitation to the ducal court, the Metternichs had repaired without loss of time to Wiesbaden, to which city I accompanied them, and again fell in with the Bülows.

Schnorr had left us after a fortnight's stay, and now the time had also come for the Bülows to depart. I accompanied them as far as Frankfort, where we spent two more days together to see a performance of Goethe's *Tasso.* Liszt's symphonic poem *Tasso* was to precede the play. It was with odd feelings that we witnessed this performance. Friederike Meyer as the Princess and Herr Schneider as Tasso appealed to us greatly, but Hans could not get over the shameful execution of Liszt's work by the conductor, Ignaz Lachner. Before going to the theatre Friedrike gave us a luncheon at the

restaurant in the Botanical Gardens.   In the end the mysterious
Herr von Guaita also joined us there.   We now noticed with
astonishment that all further conversation was carried on
between them as a duologue which was quite unintelligible to us.
All that we could make out was the furious jealousy of Herr
von Guaita and Friederike's witty, scornful defence.   But the
excited man became more composed when he suggested I
should arrange for a performance of *Lohengrin* in Frankfort
under my own direction.   I was favourably disposed to the
suggestion, as I saw in it an opportunity for another meeting
with the Bülows and the Schnorrs.   The Bülows promised
to come, and I invited the Schnorrs to be in the cast.   This
time we could take leave of one another cheerfully, although
the increasing and often excessive ill-humour of poor Hans had
drawn many an involuntary sigh from me.   He seemed to be
in perpetual torment.   On the other hand, Cosima appeared
to have lost the shyness she had evinced towards me when I
visited Reichenhall in the previous year, and a very friendly
manner had taken its place.   While I was singing ' Wotan's
Abschied ' to my friends I noticed the same expression on
Cosima's face as I had seen on it, to my astonishment, in Zürich
on a similar occasion, only the ecstasy of it was transfigured
into something higher.   Everything connected with this was
shrouded in silence and mystery, but the belief that she belonged
to me grew to such certainty in my mind, that when I was
under the influence of more than ordinary excitement my
conduct betrayed the most reckless gaiety.   As I was accompanying Cosima to the hotel across a public square, I suddenly
suggested she should sit in an empty wheelbarrow which stood
in the street, so that I might wheel her to the hotel.   She
assented in an instant.   My astonishment was so great that I
felt all my courage desert me, and was unable to carry out my
mad project.

On returning to Biebrich I was at once confronted with grave
difficulties, for Schott, after keeping me some time in suspense,
now definitely refused to pay me any further subsidies.   The
advances I had already received from my publisher had, it is
true, until quite recently, served to defray all my expenses
since leaving Vienna, including my wife's removal to Dresden

and my own migration to Biebrich by way of Paris, where I had to satisfy more than one lurking creditor. But in spite of these initial difficulties, which, I suppose, took about half the money I was to have for the *Meistersinger* by agreement, I had counted upon finishing my work in peace with the remainder of the sum stipulated. But since then Schott had put me off with vain promises about a fixed date for balancing accounts with the bookseller. I had already been put to great straits, and now everything seemed to depend on my being able to hand over a complete act of the *Meistersinger* to Schott quickly. I had got as far as the scene where Pogner is about to introduce Walther von Stolzing to the meistersingers, when — about the middle of August, while Bülow was still there — an accident occurred which, though slight in itself, made me incapable of writing for two whole months.

My surly host kept a bulldog named Leo chained up, and neglected him so cruelly that it excited my constant sympathy. I therefore tried one day to have him freed from vermin, and held his head myself, so that the servant who was doing it should not be frightened. Although the dog had learned to trust me thoroughly, he snapped at me once involuntarily and bit me — apparently very slightly — in the upper joint of my right-hand thumb. There was no wound visible, but it was soon evident that the periosteum had become inflamed from the contusion. As the pain increased more and more with the use of the thumb, I was ordered to do no writing until my hand was quite healed. If my plight was not quite so terrible as the newspapers — which announced that I had been bitten by a mad dog — made out, it was still conducive to serious reflection on human frailty. To complete my task, therefore, I needed, not only a sound mind and good ideas, irrespective of any required skill, but also a healthy thumb to write with, as my work was not a libretto I could dictate, but music which no one but myself could write down.

On the advice of Raff, who considered a volume of my songs to be worth one thousand francs, I decided to offer my publisher, by way of temporary compensation, five poems by my friend Frau Wesendonck which I had set to music (consisting chiefly of studies for *Tristan* with which I was occupied at the time),

so that he should at least have something on the market. The
songs were accepted and published, but they seemed to have
produced no softening effect on Schott's mood. I was obliged
to conclude that he was acting on some one else's instigation,
and I betook myself to Kissingen (where he was staying for
his 'cure') in order to get to the bottom of it and shape my
next moves accordingly. An interview with him was obstinately
denied me, and Frau Schott, who was posted outside his door
in the rôle of guardian angel, informed me that a bad liver
attack prevented him from seeing me. I now realised my
position with regard to him. For the moment I drew on young
Weisheimer for some money, which he gave me most willingly,
supported as he was by a wealthy father, and then set to work
to consider what I could do next. I could no longer count
on Schott, and had in consequence lost all prospect of an
unopposed performance of the *Meistersinger*.

At this juncture I was much surprised to receive a renewed
official invitation to Vienna for the performance of *Tristan* at
the Opera, where I was informed all obstacles had been removed, as Ander had completely recovered his voice. I was
genuinely astonished to hear this, and on further inquiry
arrived at the following elucidation of the transactions that had
been taking place on my behalf in Vienna during the interval.
Before I left there the last time Frau Luise Dustmann, who
seemed to take a real pleasure in the part of Isolde, had tried
to clear away the real impediment to my undertaking by
persuading me to go to an evening party, where she intended
to introduce me again to Dr. Hanslick. She knew that unless
this gentleman could be brought round to my side nothing
could be accomplished in Vienna. As I was in a good temper
that evening I found it easy to treat Hanslick as a superficial
acquaintance, until he drew me aside for an intimate talk, and
with sobs and tears assured me he could not bear to be misunderstood by me any longer. The blame for anything that might
have been extraordinary in his judgment of me was to be laid,
not on any malicious intention, but solely on the narrow-
mindedness of an individual who desired nothing more ardently
than to learn from me how to widen the boundaries of his
knowledge. All this was said in such a burst of emotion that I

could do nothing but soothe his grief and promise him my unreserved sympathy with his work in future. Just before leaving Vienna I actually heard that Hanslick had launched forth into unmeasured praise of myself and my amiability. This change had so affected both the singers at the Opera and also Councillor Raymond (the Lord High Steward's adviser) that at last, working from high circles downwards, it came to be regarded as a point of honour with the Viennese to have *Tristan* performed in their city. Hence my summons!

I heard at the same time from young Weisheimer, who had betaken himself to Leipzig, that he was sure he could arrange a good concert there if I could assist him by conducting my new prelude to the *Meistersinger* as well as the *Tannhäuser* Overture. He believed it would make so great a sensation that the probable sale of all the tickets would enable him to place a not inconsiderable sum at my disposal after the bare expenses had been deducted. In addition to this, I could hardly go back on my promise to Herr von Guaita with respect to a performance of *Lohengrin* at Frankfort, although the Schnorrs had been obliged to decline to take part in it. After weighing all these offers I decided to put the *Meistersinger* aside, and try to earn enough by enterprises abroad to enable me in the following spring to take up and finish my interrupted work on the spot, unaffected by Schott's humours. I therefore decided at all costs to keep on the house at Biebrich, which I really liked. Minna, on the other hand, had been pressing me to send some of the furniture which I had kept, to complete her own establishment at Dresden, namely, my bed and a few other things to which I was accustomed, ' so that when I went to see her,' she said, ' I should find everything in proper order.' I did not want to act contrary to the established fiction which was to make the parting from me easier for her ; I therefore sent her what she wanted, and bought new furniture for my home on the Rhine with the assistance of a Wiesbaden manu- facturer, who allowed me fairly long credit.

At the end of September I went to Frankfort for a week to take over the rehearsals of *Lohengrin*. Here again I went through the same experience as I had so often done before. I no sooner came into contact with the members of the opera company than I felt a desire to throw up the undertaking on the spot; then the general consternation and the entreaties that I would persevere caused a reaction, under the influence of which I held out until I at last became interested in certain things for their own sake, and quite apart from any consideration of the wretched singers. The things that pleased me were the effect of an uncurtailed performance, and the employment of correct *tempi* and correct staging. Yet I suppose Friederike Meyer was the only one who completely realised these effects. The usual ' animation ' of the audience was not lacking, but I was told later on that the subsequent performances fell off, so that the opera had to be curtailed in the old way to keep it going. (They were conducted by Herr Ignaz Lachner of Frankfort, a smart, sleek man, but a wretchedly bad, muddle-headed conductor.)

I was the more prostrated by the effect of all this because even the Bülows had failed to pay me their expected visit. Cosima, as I was now informed, had passed me by in haste on her way to Paris to offer her support for a short time to her grandmother, who was suffering from a tedious illness, and had now received a most painful blow by the news of the death of Blandine after her confinement, which had taken place at St. Tropèz.

I now shut myself up for some time in my house at Biebrich, the weather having suddenly turned cold, and prevailed on my thumb to prove itself capable of writing down the instrumentation of some extracts for immediate concert purposes from the *Meistersinger,* which was now complete. I sent the prelude to Weisheimer at once to be copied at Leipzig, and also set the *Versammlung der Meistersinger* and Pogner's *Anrede* for orchestra.

By the end of October I was at last ready to start on my journey to Leipzig, in the course of which I was induced in a strange way to enter the Wartburg once more. I had alighted for a few minutes at Eisenach, and the train had just begun to move as I was hurriedly trying to catch it. I ran after the vanishing train involuntarily with a sharp cry to the guard, but naturally without being able to stop it. A considerable crowd, which had gathered on the station to watch the de-

parture of a prince, thereupon broke into loud outbursts of
laughter, and when I said to them, 'I suppose you are glad
that this happened to me ?' they replied, 'Yes, it was very
funny.' On this incident I based my axiom that you can
please the German public by your misfortunes if by nothing
else. As there was no other train to Leipzig for five hours I
telegraphed to my brother-in-law, Hermann Brockhaus (whom
I had asked to put me up), telling him of my delay, and allowed
a man who introduced himself as a guide to persuade me to
visit the Wartburg. There I saw the partial restoration made
by the Grand Duke, and also the hall containing Schwind's
pictures, to all of which I was quite indifferent. I then turned
into the restaurant of this show-place of Eisenach, and found
several women there engaged in knitting stockings. The
Grand Duke of Weimar assured me some time afterwards that
Tannhäuser enjoyed great popularity throughout the whole of
Thuringia down to the lowest peasant boy, but neither the
host nor my guide seemed to know anything about it. However, I signed the visitors' book with my full name, and described in it the pleasant greeting I had received at the station,
though I have never heard that any one noticed it.

Hermann Brockhaus, who had aged rather and grown stout,
gave me a most cheerful reception when I arrived, late at
night, at Leipzig. He took me to his house, where I found
Ottilie and her family, and was installed in comfort. We had
much to talk about, and my brother-in-law's remarkably good-
natured way of entering into our conversation often kept us
up fascinated until all hours of the morning. My connection
with Weisheimer, a young and quite unknown composer,
aroused some misgivings. His concert programme was in fact
filled with a great number of his own compositions, including
a symphonic poem, just completed, entitled *Der Ritter Toggenburg.* I should probably have raised a protest against carrying out this programme in its entirety had I attended the
rehearsals in an undisturbed frame of mind, but it so happened
that the hours I spent in the concert-room proved to be among
the most intimate and pleasant recollections of my life, for
there I met the Bülows again. Hans seemed to have felt it
his duty to join me in celebrating Weisheimer's début, his

contribution being a new pianoforte concerto by Liszt. To enter the old familiar hall of the Gewandhaus at Leipzig was enough in itself to cause me an uneasy feeling of depression, which was increased by my reception by the members of the orchestra — of whose estrangement I was keenly conscious — and to whom I had to introduce myself as an entire stranger. But I felt myself suddenly transported when I discovered Cosima sitting in a corner of the hall, in deep mourning and very pale, but smiling cheerfully at me. She had returned shortly before from Paris — where her grandmother now lay hopelessly bedridden — filled with grief at the inexplicably sudden death of her sister, and she now seemed, even to my eyes, to be leaving another world to approach me. Our emotions were so genuinely deep and sincere that only an unconditional surrender to the enjoyment of meeting again could bridge the chasm. All the incidents of the rehearsal affected us like a magic-lantern show of peculiarly enlivening character, at which we looked on like merry children. Hans, who was in an equally happy mood — for we all seemed to each other to be embarked on some Quixotic adventure — called my attention to Brendel, who was sitting not far from us, and seemed to be expecting me to recognise him. I found it entertaining to prolong this suspense thus occasioned, by pretending not to know him, whereat, as it appears, the poor man was much offended. Recalling my unjust behaviour on this occasion, I therefore made a point of alluding specially to Brendel's services when speaking in public some time afterwards on *Judaism in Music,* by way of atonement, as it were, to this man, who had died in the meantime. The arrival of Alexander Ritter with my niece Franziska helped to enliven us. My niece, indeed, found constant entertainment and excitement in the enormity of Weisheimer's compositions, while Ritter, who was acquainted with the text of my *Meistersinger,* described a highly unintelligible melody given to the basses in *Ritter Toggenburg* as 'the lonely gormandiser mode.' [1] Our good-humour might have failed us in the end, however, had we not been refreshed and uplifted by the happy effect which the prelude to the *Meistersinger* (which had at last been success-

---

[1] *Meistersinger* (English version), Act 1, scene ii.

fully rehearsed) and Bülow's glorious rendering of Liszt's new work produced. The actual concert itself gave a final ghostly touch to an adventure to which we had looked forward so contentedly till then. To Weisheimer's horror the Leipzig public stayed away *en masse,* in response apparently to a sign from the leaders of the regular subscription concerts. I have never seen any place so empty on an occasion of this sort; besides the members of my family — among whom my sister Ottilie was conspicuous in a very eccentric cap — there was no one to be seen but a few visitors, who had come into town for the occasion, occupying one or two benches. I noticed in particular my Weimar friends, Conductor Lassen, Councillor Franz Müller, the never-failing Richard Pohl, and *Justizrath* Gille, who had all nobly put in an appearance. I also recognised with a shock of surprise old Councillor Küstner, the former manager of the Court Theatre in Berlin, and I had to respond amiably to his greeting and his astonishment at the incomprehensible emptiness of the hall. The people of Leipzig were represented solely by special friends of my family, who never went to a concert in the ordinary way, among them being my devoted friend, Dr. Lothar Müller, the son of Dr. Moritz Müller, an allopath whom I had known very well in my earliest youth. In the middle of the hall there were only the concert-giver's *fiancée* and her mother. At a little distance away, and facing this lady, I took a seat next to Cosima while the concert was in progress. My family, observing us from a distance, were offended by the almost incessant laughter which possessed us, as they themselves were in the depths of depression.

As regards the prelude to the *Meistersinger,* its successful performance affected the few friends who formed the audience so favourably that we had to repeat it there and then — to the satisfaction even of the orchestra. Indeed, their artificially nurtured distrust of me, which had been like a coating of ice, now seemed to have melted, for when I brought the concert to a close with the *Tannhäuser* Overture the orchestra celebrated my recall with a tremendous flourish of instruments. This delighted my sister Ottilie beyond measure, as she maintained that such an honour had never

been accorded before except to Jenny Lind. My friend
Weisheimer, who had really tired every one's patience in the
most inconsiderate way, afterwards developed a feeling of
dissatisfaction towards me which dated from this period. He
felt bound to confess to himself that he would have done much
better without my brilliant orchestral pieces, in which case he
might have offered the public a concert at a cheaper rate,
consisting exclusively of his own works. As it was, he had to
bear the costs — to his father's great disappointment — and also
to overcome the unnecessary humiliation of being unable to
give me any profits.

My brother-in-law was not to be deterred by these painful
impressions from carrying out the household festivities, which
had been arranged beforehand in celebration of my expected
triumphs. The Bülows were also invited to one of the banquets,
and there was an evening party at which I read the *Meistersinger*
to an imposing array of professors, and met with much appreciation. I renewed my acquaintance with Professor Weiss, too,
who interested me very much, for I remembered him from my
young days as a friend of my uncle's. He expressed himself as
particularly surprised by my skill in reading aloud.

The Bülows had now unfortunately returned to Berlin.
We had met once more on a very cold day in the street (under
unpleasant conditions, for they were paying duty calls), but
the general depression which had settled on us seemed more
noticeable, during our short leave-taking, than the fleeting
good-humour of the last few days. My friends were well aware
of the terrible and utterly forlorn condition in which I found
myself. I had been idiotic enough to count on the proceeds
from the Leipzig concert to provide at least the needs of the
moment, and I was, in the first place, put into the awkward
position of being unable to pay my landlord punctually (the
house rent at Biebrich being now due). But I was ready to
stake everything on keeping this asylum for another year, and
I had to deal with an obstinate, bad-tempered creature whom
I thought it necessary to pay in advance for the sake of securing
the place. As I had just then to supply Minna with her
quarterly allowance also, the money which *Regierungsrath*
Müller forwarded to me from the Grand Duke seemed, indeed,

a heaven-sent windfall. For after giving up Schott entirely I had, in my distress, turned to this old acquaintance and begged him to explain my situation to the Grand Duke and induce him to send me some help — to be regarded possibly as payment in advance for my new operas. In response to this I received the startling and unexpected sum of fifteen hundred marks through Müller's instrumentality. It was not until some time after that I accounted for this generosity by the supposition that the Grand Duke's amiable behaviour towards me had been a deliberate attempt to make an impression upon his friend Liszt, whom he wished to entice back to Weimar at all costs. He was certainly not mistaken in counting on the excellent effect his binding generosity to me would have on our common friend.

I was therefore in a position to go to Dresden for a few days at once, to renew my provision for Minna, and at the same time to honour her with one of the visits deemed necessary to support her in her difficult situation. Minna conducted me from the station to the flat which she had taken and furnished in Walpurgisstrasse, a street which had not been built at the time I left Dresden. She had as usual arranged her home very tastefully, and with the aim evidently of making me comfortable. I was greeted on the threshold by a little mat embroidered with the word *Salve,* and I recognised our Paris drawing-room at once in the red silk curtains and the furniture. I was to have a majestic bedroom, an exceedingly comfortable study on the other side, as well as the drawing-room at my entire disposal, while she installed herself in one little room with recesses looking on to the yard. The study was adorned by the magnificent mahogany bureau which had originally been made for my house when I was conductor at Dresden. It had been bought in by the Ritter family, after my flight from that city, and presented to Kummer, the son-in-law, from whom Minna had hired it temporarily, leaving me the option of buying it back for one hundred and eighty marks. As I showed no desire to do so her mood became gloomier. Oppressed by the fearful embarrassment which she experienced on being alone with me, she had invited my sister Clara to come on a visit from Chemnitz, and was now sharing the small room at her disposal with her. Clara proved herself extraordinarily wise and sympathetic on this as on former occasions. She pitied Minna of course, and was anxious to help her at this difficult period, though always with a view to strengthening her in the conviction that our parting was unavoidable. An exact knowledge of my extremely awkward position now seemed called for. My financial difficulties were so crushing that the only excuse for telling Minna was to silence her uneasy suspicions about me. I did, however, succeed in avoiding all explanations with her — the more easily as my meetings with Fritz Brockhaus and his family (including the married daughter Clara Kessinger), the Pusinellis, old Heine, and lastly the two Schnorrs, provided a pretext for our spending most of the time in the society of others.

I filled the mornings by making calls, and it was when I set out to pay my respects and thanks to Minister Bär for my amnesty that I trod the familiar streets of Dresden again. My first impression was one of extraordinary boredom and emptiness, for I had last seen them filled with barricades, in which fantastic condition they had looked so unusually interesting. I did not see a single familiar face on the way. Even the glover, whom I had always patronised and whose shop I now had occasion to revisit, did not seem to know me, until an oldish man rushed across the street to me and greeted me with great excitement and tears in his eyes. It turned out to be Karl Kummer of the court orchestra (looking much older), the most inspired oboist I ever met. I had taken him almost tenderly to my heart on account of his playing, and we embraced joyfully. I asked whether he still played his instrument as beautifully as before, whereupon he assured me that since I had left his oboe had failed to give real satisfaction, and it was now a long time since he had had himself pensioned off. He told me in response to my inquiries that all my old military bandsmen — including Dietz, the tall double-bass player — were either dead or pensioned off. Our manager Lüttichau and Conductor Reissiger were among those who had died, Lipinsky had returned to Poland long before, Schubert, the leader, was unfit for work, and everything seemed to me sad and strange. Minister Bär expressed to me the grave qualms he still felt about the amnesty granted me. True, he had ventured to sign it himself, but was still troubled to think that my great popularity as a composer of opera would make it easy for me to raise annoying demonstrations. I comforted him at once by promising only to remain a few days and to refrain from visiting the theatre, upon which he dismissed me with a deep sigh and an exceedingly grave face.

Very different was my reception from Herr von Beust, who with smiling elegance of manner implied by his conversation that I was perhaps not so innocent after all as I now seemed to think myself. He drew my attention to a letter of mine which had been found in Röckel's pocket at the time. This was new to me, and I willingly gave him to understand that I felt myself bound to look on the amnesty accorded me as a pardon for my incautious behaviour in the past, and we parted with the liveliest manifestations of friendship.

We invited some friends one evening in Minna's drawing-room, where I read out the *Meistersinger* once more to the people who did not know it. After Minna had been provided with enough money to last some time, she accompanied me back to the station on the fourth day; but she was filled with such fearful presentiments of never seeing me again that her farewell was made in positive anguish.

At Leipzig I put up at an inn for one day. There I met Alexander Ritter, and we spent a pleasant evening together over our punch. The reason that had induced me to make this short stay was the assurance given me that if I gave a concert of my own it would not be one of the regular series. I had weighed this information with reference to the much-needed money it might bring in, but I now realised that the undertaking rested on no security. I returned in haste to Biebrich, where I had to get my household affairs into order. To my great annoyance I found my landlord in a more impossible temper than ever. He seemed unable to forget my having blamed him for his treatment of the dog, and also of my servant, whom I had been obliged to protect against him when she had had a love-affair with a tailor. In spite of receiving payment and promises he remained peevish, and insisted that he would have to move into my part of the house on account of his health in the coming spring. So while I forced him, by paying advance, to leave my household goods untouched until Easter at least, I went about trying to find a suitable house for the following year, visiting various places in the Rheingau under the guidance of Dr. Schüler and Mathilde Maier. I had no success, however, the time being so short, but my friends promised to search untiringly for what I wanted.

At Mayence I met Friederike Meyer again. Her situation in Frankfort seemed to have grown more and more difficult. When she heard that I had turned away Herr von Guaita's manager, who had been sent to Biebrich with instructions to pay me fifteen louis d'or for conducting *Lohengrin*, she upheld my action strongly. As for herself, she had broken with that gentleman entirely, insisting on being released from her contract, and was now about to enter upon a special engagement at the Burgtheater. She won my sympathy once more by her conduct and determination, which I had to consider as a powerful refutation of the calumnies brought up against her. As I too was in the act of starting for Vienna, she was glad to be able to make part of the journey in my company. She proposed to stop a day at Nuremberg, where I could pick her up for the next stage of the journey. This we did and arrived in Vienna together, where my friend went to Hôtel Munsch, while I chose the Kaiserin Elizabeth, where I now felt at home. This was on the 15th of November. I went to see Conductor Esser at once, and heard from him that *Tristan* was really being studied vigorously. With Frau Dustmann, on the other hand, I became immediately involved in very unpleasant disagreements through my relation to her sister Friederike, which it was easy to misunderstand. It was impossible to make her see how things really stood. In her eyes her sister was involved in a *liaison*, and had been cast off by her family, so that her arrival in Vienna was compromising to them. In addition to this Friederike's own condition soon caused me the greatest anxiety. She had made an engagement to appear three times at the Burgtheater without considering that just then she was not likely to make a good appearance on the stage, particularly before the Viennese public. Her serious illness, the recovery from which had been attended by

the most exciting circumstances, had disfigured her and made
her very thin. She had also gone almost entirely bald, but
nevertheless persisted in her great objection to wearing a wig.
Her sister's hostility had estranged her colleagues at the theatre,
and as a result of all this, and also on account of her unfortunate
choice of a rôle, her appearance was a failure. There could be
no question of her being taken on at that theatre. Although
her weakness increased, and she suffered from constant in-
somnia, she still tried, in her magnanimity and her shame, to
hide from me the awkwardness of her situation. She went
to a cheaper inn, the ' Stadt Frankfurt,' where she intended to
wait and see the result of sparing her nerves as far as possible.
She seemed to be in no embarrassment as far as money was
concerned, but at my request consulted Standhartner, who did
not seem to know how to help her much. As open-air exercise had been strongly recommended, and as the weather was
at present bitterly cold (from the end of November to the beginning of December), I hit on the idea of advising her to
go to Venice for a prolonged stay. Once again there seemed
no lack of means, and she followed my advice. One icy morning I accompanied her to the station, and there for the present
I left her, as I hoped, to a kinder fate. She had a faithful maid
with her, and I soon had the satisfaction of receiving reassuring accounts — of her health especially — from Venice.

While my relations with her had brought me troublesome
complications, I still kept up my old Viennese acquaintances.
A curious incident occurred at the very beginning of my visit.
I had to read the *Meistersinger* aloud to the Standhartner
family, as I had done everywhere else. As Dr. Hanslick was
now supposed to be well disposed towards me, it was considered
the right thing to invite him too. We noticed that as the reading proceeded the dangerous critic became more and more pale
and depressed, and it was remarked by everyone that it was
impossible to persuade him to stay on at the close, but that
he took his leave there and then in an unmistakably vexed
manner. My friends all agreed in thinking that Hanslick
looked on the whole libretto as a lampoon aimed at himself,
and had felt an invitation to the reading to be an insult. And
undoubtedly the critic's attitude towards me underwent a very

remarkable change from that evening. He became uncompromisingly hostile, with results that were obvious to us at once.

Cornelius and Tausig had again been to see me, but I had to work off my resentment against them both for the fit of real ill-humour their behaviour had caused me in the previous summer. This had happened when I expected the Bülows and the Schnorrs to stay with me together at Biebrich, and my warm interest in these two young friends, Cornelius and Tausig, led me to invite them too. I received Cornelius's acceptance immediately, and was the more surprised to get a letter from Geneva, whither Tausig (who appeared to have funds at his disposal all of a sudden) had carried him off on a summer excursion — no doubt of a more important and pleasanter nature. Without the least mention of any regret at not being able to meet me that summer, they simply announced to me that ' a glorious cigar had just been smoked to my health.' And now, when I met them again in Vienna, I found it impossible to refrain from pointing out to them the insulting nature of their behaviour; but they seemed unable to understand how I could object to their preferring the beautiful tour into French Switzerland to paying me a visit at Biebrich. I was obviously a tyrant to them. Besides this, I thought Tausig's curious conduct at my hotel suspicious. I was told that he took his meals in the downstairs restaurant, after which he climbed up past my floor to the fourth storey, to pay long visits to Countess Krockow. When I asked him about it, and learned that the lady in question was also a friend of Cosima's, I expressed my surprise at his not introducing me. He continued to evade this suggestion with singularly vague phrases, and when I ventured to tease him by the supposition of a love-affair, he said there could be no question of such a thing, as the lady was old. So I let him alone, but the amazement which his peculiar behaviour then caused me was intensified some years later when I at last learned to know Countess Krockow very well, and was assured of her deep interest in me. It seemed that she had desired nothing more than to make my acquaintance also at that time, but that Tausig had always refused to find an opportunity, and had made the excuse that I did not care about women's society.

But we eventually resumed our lively and sociable habits when I began seriously to carry out my project of giving concerts in Vienna. Although the piano rehearsals for the principal solo parts of *Tristan* had been put in hand diligently — I had left them to Conductor Esser, who took them zealously in hand — my mistrust as to the real success of these studies was unshaken, and the point which I doubted most was not so much the capabilities of the singers as their goodwill. Moreover, Frau Dustmann's absurd behaviour disgusted me on my frequent attendance at the rehearsals. On the other hand, I now set my hopes on making a good impression, on the score of novelty alone, by performing selections from my own works still unknown to the Viennese public. In this way I could show my secret enemies that there were other means open to me of bringing my more recent compositions before the public than by the medium of the stage, where they could so easily stop me. For all the practical details of the performance Tausig now proved himself particularly useful. We agreed to hire the Theatre on the Wien for three evenings, the idea being to give one concert at the end of December and to repeat the experiment twice after a week's interval. The first thing was to copy out the orchestral parts from the sections which I cut out from my scores for the concert. There were two selections from *Rheingold* and two from the *Walküre* and the *Meistersinger*, but I kept back the prelude to *Tristan* for the present, so as not to clash with the performance of the whole work at the Opera which was still being advertised. Cornelius and Tausig, with some assistant copyists, now started on the work, which could only be carried out by experienced score-readers if it was to be done correctly. They were joined by Weisheimer, who had arrived in Vienna, having in the end decided to come to the concert. Tausig also mentioned Brahms to me, recommending him as a ' very good fellow,' who, although he was so famous himself, would willingly take over a part of their work, and a selection from the *Meistersinger* was accordingly allotted to him. And, indeed, Brahms's behaviour proved unassuming and good-natured, but he showed little vivacity and was often hardly noticed at our gatherings. I also came across Friedrich Uhl again, an old acquaintance who was now editing a political paper called *Der Botschafter* with Julius Fröbel under Schmerling's auspices. He placed his journal at my disposal, and made me give him the first act of the libretto of *Meistersinger* for his *feuilleton*. Whereupon my friends chose to think that Hanslick grew more and more venomous.

While I and my companions were overwhelmed by the preparations for the concert, there came in one day a certain Herr Moritz, whom Bülow had introduced to me in Paris as a ridiculous person. His clumsy and importunate behaviour and the idiotic messages — evidently of his own invention — which he brought me from Bülow drove me in the end to show him the door with great emphasis, for I too was carried away by Tausig's lively annoyance at this very officious intruder. He reported on this to Cosima in a manner so insulting to Bülow that she in return found it necessary to express to me in writing her intense indignation at my inconsiderate behaviour towards my best friends. I was really so surprised and dumbfounded by this strange and inexplicable event that I handed Cosima's letter to Tausig without comment, merely asking him what could be done in the face of such nonsense. He at once undertook to show Cosima the incident in a correct light and clear up the misunderstanding, and I soon had the pleasure of hearing that he had met with success.

We had now come to the point of rehearsing for the concert. The Royal Opera had supplied me with the singers needed for the selections from *Rheingold*, the *Walküre*, and *Siegfried* ' Schmiede-Lieder '), and also for *Pogner's Anrede* from the *Meistersinger*. I had only to fall back on amateurs for the three Rhine maidens. The concert director Hellmesberger was a great help to me in this matter as in every other way, and his fine playing and enthusiastic demonstrations when leading the orchestra never failed in any circumstances. After the deafening preliminary rehearsals in a small music-room in the opera house, which had perplexed Cornelius by the great noise they made, we arrived at the stage itself. In addition to the expense of hiring the place, I had to bear the cost of the requisite extension of the orchestra. The room, which was lined all round with theatrical scenery, was still extraordinarily unfavourable for sound. I hardly felt like running the risk of providing an acoustic wall and ceiling on my own account, however. Although the first performance on 26th December drew a large audience, it brought me in nothing but outrageously heavy expenses and great distress at the dismal effect of the orchestra owing to the bad acoustics. In spite of the dark outlook I decided to bear the cost of building a sound-screen, in order to enhance the effect of the two following concerts, when I flattered myself I might count on the success of the efforts that were being made to arouse interest in the highest circles.

My friend Prince Liechtenstein thought this was by no means impossible, and believed he might manage to interest the Imperial Court through Countess Zamoïska, one of the ladies-in-waiting, and he one day accompanied me through the interminable corridors of the Imperial Castle on a visit to this lady. I afterwards learned that Mme. Kalergis had also been at work here on my behalf, but she had apparently only succeeded in winning over the young Empress, for she alone was present at the performance, and without any retinue. But at the second concert I had to endure all kinds of disillusionment. In spite of all warnings to the contrary, I had fixed it for the New Year's Day of 1863. The hall was exceedingly badly filled, and my sole satisfaction was to know that by improving the acoustic properties of the place the orchestra sounded extremely well. In consequence of this the reception of the various pieces was so favourable that at the third concert, on 8th January, I was able to perform before an overflowing house, and thus obtained very gratifying testimony to the fine musical taste of the Viennese public. The by no means startling prelude to Pogner's *Anrede* from the *Meistersinger* was enthusiastically encored, in spite of the fact that the singer had already risen to his feet for the next part. At this moment I chanced to see in one of the boxes a most comforting omen for my present position; for I recognised Mme. Kalergis, who had just arrived for a prolonged stay in Vienna, to which I fondly imagined she was prompted by some idea of helping me here also. As she too was on friendly terms with Standhartner, she at once entered into consultation with him as to how I could be helped out of the critical situation in which I was once more placed by the expenses of my concerts. She confessed

to our mutual friend that she had no means at her disposal,
and would only be able to meet our extraordinary expenditure by contracting fresh debts.   It was therefore necessary
to secure wealthier patrons, among whom she mentioned Baroness
von Stockhausen, the wife of the Hanoverian ambassador.
This lady, who was a great friend of Standhartner's, was most
kind to me, and won me the sympathy of Lady Bloomfield
and her husband, the English ambassador.   A soirée was given
in the house of the latter, and at Frau von Stockhausen's there
were also several evening assemblies.   One day Standhartner
brought me a thousand marks as an instalment towards my
expenses, saying that they came from an anonymous donor.
Meanwhile Mme. Kalergis had managed to procure two thousand marks, which were also placed at my disposal, through
Standhartner, for further needs.   But all her efforts to interest
the court on my behalf remained entirely fruitless, in spite
of her intimacy with Countess Zamoïska; for unfortunately
a member of that Könneritz family from Saxony, which was
everywhere turning up for my discomfiture, had now appeared
as ambassador here also.   He succeeded in suppressing any
inclination the all-powerful Archduchess Sophie might have
had towards me, by pretending that during his time I had
burnt down the King of Saxony's castle.

But my patroness, undaunted still, endeavoured to help me
in every conceivable way demanded by my necessities.   In
order to gratify my most earnest longing for a peaceful home
where I could stay for a while, she managed to secure the house
of the English attaché, a son of the famous Bulwer Lytton,
who had been called away, but was keeping up his establishment for some time longer.   Thus through her I was introduced to this exceedingly amiable young man.   I dined with
him one evening, together with Cornelius and Mme. Kalergis,
and after dinner began to read them my *Götterdämmerung*.   I
did not seem to have secured a very attentive audience, however, and when I noticed this I stopped and withdrew with
Cornelius.   We found it very cold as we went home, and
Bulwer's rooms seem also to have been insufficiently heated,
so that we took refuge in a restaurant to drink a glass of hot
punch.   The incident has remained fixed in my memory

because here for the first time I saw Cornelius in an ungovernably eccentric humour. While we thus took our pleasure, Mme. Kalergis used her influence—so I was afterwards informed —as an exceedingly powerful and irresistible female advocate to inspire Bulwer with a definite interest in my fate. In this she so far succeeded, that he unconditionally placed his house at my disposal for nine months. On considering the matter more deeply, however, I did not see what advantage this would be to me, seeing that I had no further prospect of earning any income in Vienna for my sustenance.

On the other hand, my plans were decided for me by an offer which reached me from St. Petersburg to conduct two concerts there in the month of March for the Philharmonic Society for a fee of two thousand silver roubles. For this also I had to thank Mme. Kalergis, who urgently counselled me to accept the invitation, holding out at the same time a prospect of further increasing my receipts by giving an additional concert on my own account, from which very important material results might be expected. The only thing which could have induced me to decline this invitation would have been an assurance that my *Tristan* would be staged in Vienna during the next few months; but a fresh indisposition on the part of the tenor Ander had once more brought our preparations to a standstill, and moreover I had completely lost all faith in those promises which had lured me again to Vienna. To this the effect of my visit to the minister Schmerling immediately on my return to Vienna had certainly contributed. This man had been much astonished at my referring to a recommendation by Prince Metternich, for the latter, so the minister declared, had never spoken a word to him about me. Nevertheless, he very politely assured me that it needed no such recommendation to interest him in a man of my merit. When, therefore, I mentioned the idea suggested by Prince Metternich's kindness that the Emperor might assign me some special position in Vienna, he hastened at once to inform me that he was completely powerless to influence any of the Emperor's decisions. This admission on the part of Herr von Schmerling certainly helped to explain Prince Metternich's behaviour, and I concluded that the latter had preferred an attempt to win the

Chief Chamberlain for a serious revival of *Tristan* to a fruitless effort with the minister.

As these prospects were therefore thrust into the uncertain future, I now agreed to the St. Petersburg proposal, but first of all sought about for means to provide the necessary funds. For these I relied on a concert which Heinrich Porges had already arranged for me in Prague. Consequently early in February I set out for that city, and had every reason to be satisfied with my reception there. Young Porges, an out-and-out partisan of Liszt and myself, pleased me greatly, not only personally, but by his obvious enthusiasm. The concert took place at the hall on the Sophia Island, and was crowned with great success. Besides one of Beethoven's symphonies, several selections from my newer works were given, and when next day Porges paid me about two thousand marks, with the reservation of a few smaller supplementary payments, I laughingly assured him that this was the first money I had ever earned by my own exertions. He also gave me some very pleasant introductions to several exceedingly devoted and intelligent young people, belonging both to the German and Czech parties, and among them to a teacher of mathematics called Lieblein, and an author whose name was Musiol. It was with a certain pathetic interest that, after so many years, I here discovered a friend of my earliest youth, named Marie Löwe, who had given up singing and taken to the harp instead, and was now engaged to play this instrument in the orchestra, in which capacity she assisted at my concert. On the occasion of the first performance of *Tannhäuser* in Prague, she had sent me a most enthusiastic report about it. Her admiration was now intensified, and for many years afterwards she remained tenderly attached to me. Well satisfied then, and filled with newly awakened hope, I hurried back to Vienna again in order to put the arrangement for *Tristan* on as firm a basis as possible. It was found feasible to arrange another pianoforte rehearsal in my presence of the two first acts, and I was astonished at the really passable performance of the tenor, while from Frau Dustmann I could not withhold my sincerest congratulations on her admirable execution of her difficult part. It was therefore decided that my work should be produced a little after Easter, which would fit in very well with the expected date of my return from Russia.

The hope of being now able to count on earning a large income decided me to revive my former idea of settling for good in the peace and quiet of Biebrich. As there was still time before I had to start for Russia, I returned to the Rhine to arrange matters there as rapidly as possible. Once more I lodged in Frickhöfer's house, and in the company of Mathilde Maier and her friend Luise Wagner once more hunted through the Rheingau in search of a suitable house. Not finding what I wanted, I finally entered into treaty with Frickhöfer for the erection of a small cottage on a plot of land I proposed to buy near his villa. Dr. Schüler, the man who had been introduced to me by young Städl, was to take the matter in hand, as he had both legal and business experience. Estimates were prepared, and it now depended entirely on the amount of my Russian receipts as to whether the undertaking could be begun in the following spring or not. As in any case I had to give up my rooms in Frickhöfer's house at Easter, I removed all my furniture and sent it packed to the furniture-dealer in Wiesbaden, to whom I was still indebted for the greater part of it.

Thus in the best of spirits I went first to Berlin, where I called at once on Bülow. Cosima, who was expecting an early confinement, seemed delighted to see me again, and insisted on accompanying me at once to the music-school, where we should find Hans. I entered a long room, at one end of which Bülow was giving a music-lesson. As I stood for some time in silence in the doorway, he gave an exclamation of anger at being disturbed, only to burst out into joyful laughter on recognising who it was. Our midday meal together was lively, and in excellent humour I set out with Cosima alone for a drive in a fine carriage (belonging to the Hôtel de Russie), whose grey satin lining and cushions provided us with endless fun. Bülow seemed troubled that I should see his wife in a condition of advanced pregnancy, as I had once expressed my aversion from such a sight when speaking of another woman of our acquaintance. It put us into a good-humour to be able to set his mind at rest in this case, for nothing could possibly put me out of sympathy with Cosima. So, sharing my hopes and heartily rejoicing in the turn of my fortune, these two friends accompanied me to the Königsburg railway station and saw me off on my long night journey.

In Königsburg I had to wait half a day and a night. As I had no desire to revisit my haunts in a place which had once been so fatal to me, I spent the time quietly in the room of an hotel, the position of which I did not even try to fix, and early in the morning continued my journey towards the Russian frontier. With certain uneasy memories of my former illegal passage of this frontier, I carefully scanned the faces of my fellow-passengers during the long hours of travel. Among these I was especially struck by one, a Livland nobleman of German descent, who, in the haughtiest German Tory tone, proclaimed his disgust at the Tsar's emancipation of the serfs. He wished me clearly to understand that any efforts on the part of the Russians to obtain their freedom would receive but scant support from the German nobles settled in their midst. But as we approached St. Petersburg I was genuinely frightened to find our train suddenly stopped and examined by the police. They were apparently searching for various persons suspected of complicity in the latest Polish insurrection, which had just broken out. Not far from the capital itself the empty seats in our carriage were filled by several people, whose high Russian fur caps aroused my suspicions, which were not allayed by the attention which their wearers bestowed upon me in particular. But suddenly the face of one of them brightened up, and he impulsively turned towards me and saluted me as the man whom he and several other musicians of the Imperial orchestra had come out on purpose to meet. They were all Germans, and on our arrival at the St. Petersburg railway station they joyfully introduced me to a further large contingent from the orchestra, headed by the committee of the Philharmonic Society. I had been recommended to a German boarding-house on the Newsky Prospect as a suitable residence. There I was very graciously and flatteringly received by Frau Kunst, the wife of a German merchant, in a drawing-room whose windows commanded a view of the wide and busy street, and where I was very well served. I dined in common with the other boarders and visitors, and often invited Alexander Séroff, whom I had formerly known in Lucerne, to be my guest at table. He had called on me immediately on my arrival, and I learned that he held a very poor appointment as censor of German newspapers. His person bore signs of much neglect and ill-health, and proved that he had had a hard struggle for existence; but he speedily won my respect by the great independence and truthfulness of his opinions, whereby, combined with an excellent understanding, I soon learned that he had won himself a reputation as a most influential and much-dreaded critic. I appreciated this better later on when advances were made to me from high quarters to use my influence with Séroff to assuage the bitterness of his persecution of Anton Rubinstein, who just at that time was being somewhat offensively patronised. On my mentioning the matter to him, he explained his reasons for believing Rubinstein's influence in Russia to be pernicious, whereupon I begged him, for my sake at least, to hold his hand a little, as I did not wish, during my brief stay in St. Petersburg, to pose as Rubinstein's rival. To this he replied with all the violence of a sickly man, ' I hate him, and cannot make any concessions.' With me, on the contrary, he entered into the most intimate understanding, as he had so perfect an appreciation of me and my art that our intercourse became almost one of mere pleasantry, for on all serious points we were in entire agreement. Nothing could equal the care with which he sought to help me at every opportunity. He provided the necessary translation into Russian, both of the songs contained in the selections taken from my operas and of my explanatory programme for the concerts. He also displayed the utmost judgment in choosing the most suitable singers for me, and for this he appeared to find abundant recompense in attending the rehearsals and performances. His radiant face beamed everywhere upon me with encouragement and fresh inspiration. I was eminently satisfied with the orchestra which I managed to gather around me in the large and handsome hall of the Society of Nobles. It contained one hundred and twenty picked players from the Imperial orchestras, who were for the most part excellent musicians, usually employed in accompanying Italian opera and ballets. They now seemed delighted to be allowed to breathe more freely in thus occupying themselves with nobler music under a method of conducting which I had made peculiarly my own.

After the great success of my first concert advances were made to me from those circles to which, as I could very well understand, I had been secretly but influentially recommended by Mme. Kalergis. With great circumspection my unseen protectress had prepared the way for my presentation to the Grand Duchess Helène. I was instructed, in the first place, to make use of a recommendation from Standhartner to Dr. Arneth, the Grand Duchess's private physician, whom he had known in Vienna, in order through him to be introduced to Fräulein von Rhaden, her most confidential lady-in-waiting. I should have been well content with the acquaintance of this lady alone, for in her I learned to know a woman of wide culture, great intelligence, and noble bearing, whose ever-growing interest in me I perceived to be mingled with a certain timidity, apparently concerned chiefly with the Grand Duchess. She gave me the impression that she felt something more important ought to happen for me than, from the spirit and character of her mistress, she could expect. I was, however, not taken to pay my respects to the Grand Duchess at once, but received first of all an invitation to an evening party in the apartments of the lady-in-waiting, at which, among others, the Grand Duchess herself was to be present. Here Anton Rubinstein did the musical honours, and after the hostess had introduced me to him, she ventured to present me to the Grand Duchess herself. The ceremony went off fairly well, and, as a result, I shortly afterwards received a direct invitation to a friendly evening tea-party at the Grand Duchess's house. Here, in addition to Fräulein von Rhaden, I met the lady next to her in rank, Fräulein von Stahl, as well as a genial old gentleman, who was introduced to me as General von Brebern, for many years one of the Grand Duchess's closest friends. Fräulein von Rhaden appeared to have made extraordinary efforts on my behalf, which for the present resulted in the Grand Duchess expressing a wish that I should make her better acquainted with the text of my *Nibelungen Ring*. As I had no copy of the work with me, although Weber of Leipzig ought by this time to have finished printing it, they insisted that I should at once telegraph to him in Leipzig to send the finished sheets with the utmost despatch to the Grand Duchess's address. Meanwhile my patrons had to be content with hearing me read the *Meistersinger.* To this reading the Grand Duchess Marie was also induced to come — a very stately and still beautiful daughter of the Tsar Nicholas, who was notorious for the passion she had shown throughout her life. As to the impression made upon this lady by my poem, Fräulein von Rhaden only told me that she had been seriously alarmed lest Hans Sachs might end by marrying Eva.

In the course of a few days the loose proof-sheets of my *Nibelungen* work duly arrived, and the Grand Duchess's intimates met at four tea-parties to hear me read it, and listened with sympathetic attention. General von Brebern was present at them all, but only, as Fräulein von Rhaden said, ' to blush like the rose ' in profoundest slumber, a habit which always afforded a subject for merriment to Fräulein von Stahl, a very lively and beautiful woman, when each night I accompanied the two court ladies from the spacious salons along endless corridors and staircases to their distant apartments.

The only other person in the great world whom I learned to know here was Count Wilohorsky, who occupied a high position of trust at the Imperial court, and was chiefly esteemed as a patron of music, and considered himself a distinguished violoncello-player. The old gentleman appeared well disposed towards me, and altogether satisfied with my musical performances. Indeed, he assured me that he had first learned to understand Beethoven's Eighth Symphony (in F major) through my interpretation. He also considered that he had fully grasped my overture to the *Meistersinger,* and said the Grand Duchess Marie was affected because she had found this piece incomprehensible, but had expressed herself enraptured by the overture to *Tristan,* which he himself only managed to understand by the exertion of all his musical knowledge. When I told Séroff of this, he exclaimed enthusiastically, ' Ah, that beast of a Count! That woman knows what love is! '

The Count arranged a splendid dinner in my honour, at which both Anton Rubinstein and Mme. Abaza were present. As I begged Rubinstein to play something after dinner, Mme. Abaza insisted on singing his Persian songs, which seemed greatly to annoy the composer, as he knew very well that he had produced much finer work. Nevertheless both the composition and its execution gave me a very favourable opinion of the talents of both artists. Through this singer, who had originally had a professional engagement in the Grand Duchess's household, and was now married to a wealthy and cultured Russian gentleman of rank, I obtained an entry into the house of M. Abaza, who received me with great ceremony. About the same time a certain Baron Vittinghof had also made himself known to me as an enthusiastic lover of music, and honoured me with an invitation to his house, where I met once more with Ingeborg Stark, the beautiful Swedish pianist and composer of sonatas, whom I had formerly known in Paris. She amazed me by the impertinent outburst of laughter with which she accompanied the performance of one of the Baron's compositions. On the other hand, she assumed a more serious air when she informed me that she was engaged to Hans von Bronsart.

Rubinstein, with whom I exchanged friendly visits, behaved very creditably, although, as I had expected, he felt himself somewhat injured by me. He told me that he was thinking of resigning his position in St. Petersburg, as it had been made difficult by Séroff's antagonism. It was also thought advisable to introduce me to the commercial circles of St. Petersburg, with a view to my coming benefit concert, and a visit was consequently arranged to a concert in the hall of the Merchants' Guild. Here I was met on the staircase by a drunken Russian, who announced himself as the conductor. With a small selection of Imperial musicians and others he conducted the overtures of Rossini's *Tell* and Weber's *Oberon,* in which the kettledrums were replaced by a small military drum, which produced a wonderful effect, especially in the lovely transfiguration part of the *Oberon* Overture.

Although I was admirably equipped for my own concerts as far as the orchestra was concerned, yet I had much trouble in procuring the requisite singers. The soprano was very passably represented by Mlle. Bianchi; but for the tenor parts I had to make shift with a M. Setoff, who, although possessing plenty of courage, had very little voice. But he managed to help me through the ' Schmiede-Lieder ' in *Siegfried,* for his presence at least gave an appearance of song, while the orchestra alone undertook the effective reality. On the conclusion of my two concerts for the Philharmonic Society, I set seriously to work on my own concert, which was to be held in the Imperial Opera House, in the material arrangements for which I was helped by a retired musician. This man often spent hours with Séroff in my well-heated rooms without laying aside his enormous fur coat, and as his incapacity gave us a great deal of trouble, we agreed that he was like ' the sheep in wolf's clothing.' The concert, however, succeeded beyond all my expectations, and I do not think I was ever so enthusiastically received by any audience as on this occasion. Indeed, their greeting when I first appeared was so loudly prolonged that I felt quite touched, a rare occurrence with me. To this wild abandonment on the part of the audience the ardent devotion of my orchestra naturally contributed, as my one hundred and twenty musicians renewed the frantic acclamations again and again, a procedure which appeared to be quite novel in St. Petersburg. From some of them I heard such exclamations as, ' We must admit we have never known what music is till now.'

Conductor Schuberth, who, with a certain amount of condescension, had helped me with advice on business matters, now utilised this favourable turn of affairs to ask for my co-operation at a concert to be given shortly for his own benefit. Although I was fully aware that by this means he reckoned on conjuring a handsome profit out of my pocket into his own, yet on the advice of my friends I thought it best to comply with his request, albeit much against the grain. So a week later I repeated the most popular items of my programme before an equally numerous audience and with the same success, but this time the handsome receipts of three thousand roubles were destined for an invalid man, who as a retribution for this encroachment on my rights was suddenly summoned to another world in the same year.

To balance this, I now had a prospect of further artistic and material successes from a contract concluded with General Lwoff, the manager of the Moscow theatre. I was to give

three concerts in the Grand Theatre, of which I was to have
half the receipts, guaranteed in each case at a minimum of
one thousand roubles. I arrived there suffering from a cold,
miserable and ill at ease, in weather which was a mixture of
frost and thaw, and put up at a badly situated German boarding-house. My preliminary arrangements were made with the
manager, who, in spite of the orders hanging from his neck,
looked a very insignificant person, and the difficult selection of
the vocal items had to be arranged with a Russian tenor and a
superannuated Italian lady-singer. Having settled these, I
entered upon the task of orchestral rehearsals. It was here
that I first met the younger Rubinstein, Anton's brother
Nicholas, who, as director of the Russian Musical Society, was
the leading authority in his profession in Moscow; his demeanour towards me was characterised throughout by modesty and
consideration. The orchestra consisted of the hundred musicians who provided the Imperial household with Italian opera
and ballet. It was, on the whole, far inferior to that of
St. Petersburg, yet among them I found a small number of
excellent quartette players, all devotedly attached to me.
Among these was one of my old Riga acquaintances, the
'cellist von Lutzau, who in those days had a great reputation as a wag. But I was particularly pleased with a certain
Herr Albrecht, a violinist, a brother of the Albrecht who was
one of the party whose Russian fur caps had so scared me on
my way to St. Petersburg. But even these men could not dispel
my feeling that in dealing with this Moscow orchestra I had
descended in the artistic scale. I gave myself a great deal of
trouble without deriving any compensating satisfaction, and my
bile was not a little stirred by the Russian tenor, who came to
rehearsal in a red shirt, to show his patriotic aversion from my
music, and sang the 'Schmiede-Lieder' of *Siegfried* in the insipid
style acquired from the Italians. On the very morning of the
first concert I was obliged to cancel it, and declare myself
on the sick-list, with a bad, feverish cold. In the slush and
snow which inundated the streets of Moscow it seems to have
been impossible to announce this fact to the public, and I heard
that angry disturbances resulted when many splendid equipages
arrived on a fruitless errand and had to be turned away. After

three days' rest I insisted on giving the three concerts I had
contracted for within six days, an exertion to which I was
spurred by a desire to have done with an undertaking I felt
was not worthy of me. Although the Grand Theatre was filled
on each occasion with a brilliant audience such as I had never
before seen, yet, according to the calculations of the Imperial
manager, the receipts did not exceed the amount of the guarantee. With this, however, I was content, considering the
magnificent reception accorded to my efforts, and above all
the fervid enthusiasm of the orchestra, which was expressed
here as it had been in St. Petersburg. A deputation of members
of the orchestra begged me to give a fourth concert, and on
my refusal, they tried to persuade me to remain for another
' rehearsal,' but this too I was compelled to decline with a
smile. However, the orchestra honoured me with a banquet,
at which, after N. Rubinstein had made a very enthusiastic
and appropriate speech, which was greeted with hearty and
tumultuous applause, one of the company hoisted me on to his
shoulders and carried me round the hall; whereupon there
was a great outcry, and every one wanted to render me the same
kindly service. I was presented on this occasion with a gold
snuff-box from the members of the orchestra, on which was
engraved the words ' Doch Einer kam,' from Siegmund's song
in the Walküre. I returned the compliment by presenting to
the orchestra a large photograph of myself, on which I wrote
the words ' Keiner ging,' from the same song.

In addition to these musical circles I also became acquainted
with Prince Odoiewsky, as the result of an introduction and
strong recommendation by Mme. Kalergis. She had told me
that in the Prince I should meet one of the noblest of men, who
would fully understand me. After a most arduous drive of
many hours, I reached his modest dwelling, and was received
with patriarchal simplicity at his family mid-day dinner, but
I found it exceedingly difficult to convey to him any particulars
as to myself and my plans. With regard to any impressions
I might be expected to gather respecting himself, he seemed
to rely on the effect produced by the contemplation of a large
instrument resembling an organ, which he had had designed
and erected in one of his principal rooms. Unluckily there

was no one there who could play it; but I could not help thinking it must have been intended for some specially devised form
of divine worship, which he held there on Sundays for the
benefit of his household, relatives and acquaintances. Ever
mindful of my kindly patroness, I attempted to give the genial
Prince some idea of my position and my aspirations. With
apparent emotion he exclaimed, '*J'ai ce qu'il vous faut;
parlez à Wolffsohn.*' On further inquiry I learned that the
guardian spirit thus commended to me was not a banker, but a
Russian Jew who wrote romances.

All these events seemed to justify the conclusion that my
receipts, especially if I included what I might still derive from
St. Petersburg, would amply suffice to carry out my project
of building a house at Biebrich. I therefore sent a telegram
about it to my authorised agent in Wiesbaden from Moscow,
and left there after a stay of only ten days. I also forwarded
one thousand roubles to Minna, who was complaining that her
expenses for settling down in Dresden were very heavy.

But, unfortunately, on reaching St. Petersburg I met with
serious disappointments. Every one advised me to relinquish
the idea of giving my second concert on Easter Monday, the
date I had fixed, as it was the general custom in Russian society
to reserve that day for private gatherings. On the other hand,
I could not well refuse to give a concert, on the third day after
the date announced for my own, on behalf of those imprisoned
for debt in St. Petersburg, seeing that this was to be given at
the urgent request of the Grand Duchess Helène herself. In this
latter function all St. Petersburg was already interested for the
sake of their own credit, as it was under the most distinguished
patronage; so that, while every seat was sold in advance for
this function, I had to be content with a very empty house at
the Nobles' Casino, and with proceeds which luckily did at least
cover expenses. By way of contrast, the debtors' concert went
off with the greatest success, and General Suwarof, the governor
of the city, a strikingly handsome man, handed me a very beautifully wrought silver drinking-horn as a thank-offering from
the imprisoned debtors.

I now set about paying my farewell calls, one of which was
on Fräulein von Rhaden, who distinguished herself by the

warmth of her sympathy and interest. By way of compensating me for the loss of the receipts I had reckoned upon,
the Grand Duchess sent me through this lady the sum of one
thousand roubles, coupled with a promise that, until my
circumstances improved, she would repeat the gift annually.
On discovering this friendly interest, I could not help regretting
that the connection thus formed was not likely to have more
stable and profitable results. I addressed a petition through
Fräulein von Rhaden to the Grand Duchess, praying that she
would permit me to come to St. Petersburg for a few months
every year, to place my talents at her disposal, both for concerts
and theatrical performances, in return for which she would
only have to pay me a suitable yearly salary. To this I received an evasive reply. On the day before my departure I
informed my amiable guardian of my plan for settling at
Biebrich, and in doing so I made no secret of my fear that after
spending the money I had earned here in carrying out my
building plan, my condition might be very much the same as
of yore, a fear which made me wonder whether it would not
be better to abandon it altogether. Whereupon I received the
spirited reply: ' Build and hope! ' At the last moment before
starting I gratefully answered her in the same manner, and said
that I now knew what to do. Thus at the end of April I departed, carrying with me the hearty good wishes of Séroff and
the enthusiastic members of the orchestra, and steamed away
across the Russian wilderness without calling at Riga, where
I had been invited to give a concert. The long and weary
road brought me at last to the frontier station of Wirballen,
where I received a telegram from Fräulein von Rhaden: ' Not
too rash.' This was in reference to a few lines I had left
behind for her, and it conveyed quite enough to revive my
doubts as to the wisdom of carrying out my house-building
plans.

I reached Berlin without further delay, and at once made for
Bülow's house. During the last few months I had heard no
news of Cosima's condition, and it was, therefore, with some
trepidation that I stood at the door, through which the maid
did not seem disposed to let me pass, saying that ' her mistress
was not well.' ' Is she seriously ill ? ' I asked, and receiving

a smilingly evasive reply, at once realised to my joy the true situation, and hastened in to greet Cosima. She had been some time delivered of her daughter Blandine, and was now on the highroad to complete recovery. It was only from casual callers that she remained secluded. Everything seemed well, and Hans was quite gay, the more so that he now thought me freed from all care for some time to come, owing to the success of my Russian trip. But I could not regard this assumption as justified, unless my wish to be invited for some months every year to St. Petersburg for renewed activity there met with a ready response. On this point I was enlightened in a more detailed letter from Fräulein von Rhaden following the above telegram, in which she told me on no account to rely upon this invitation. This distinct statement compelled me to reckon up the balance of my Russian receipts very seriously, and after deducting hotel and travelling expenses, the money sent to Minna, and certain payments to the furniture dealer at Wiesbaden, I found I had very little more than twelve thousand marks left. So the scheme of buying land and building a house had to be relinquished. But Cosima's excellent health and high spirits dispelled all anxious thought for the present. We drove out again in a splendid carriage, and in the most extravagant of good humours, through the avenues of the Tiergarten, dined to our hearts' content at the Hôtel de Russie, and made up our minds that bad times had fled for ever.

For the immediate present my plans were directed towards Vienna. I had recently heard that *Tristan* had once more been abandoned, this time owing to the indisposition of Frau Dustmann. In order to have this important matter more directly under my own supervision, and also because I had formed no such intimate artistic ties with any other German city as with Vienna, I clung to this as the most suitable place in which to settle. Tausig, whom I now met there in excellent health and spirits, entirely confirmed me in this opinion, and still further strengthened it by undertaking to find me precisely the pleasant and quiet dwelling in the neighbourhood of Vienna that I had set my mind upon, and through his own landlord he succeeded in getting something exactly to my taste. In what had been the pleasant abode of old Baron von Rackowitz at Penzing, I was offered the most delightful accommodation for a yearly rent of two thousand four hundred marks. I could have the entire upper part of the house and the exclusive use of a shady and fairly large garden. In the housekeeper, Franz Mrazek, I found a very obliging man, whom I at once took into my service, together with his wife Anna, an exceedingly gifted and obliging woman. For many years, amid ever-changing fortunes, this couple remained faithful to me. I now had to begin spending money in order to make my long-desired asylum fit and cosy both for rest and work. The remnant of my household belongings, including my Erard grand, was sent on from Biebrich, as well as the new furniture I had found it necessary to buy. On the 12th of May, in lovely spring weather, I took possession of my pleasant home, and for a while wasted much time over the exciting cares connected with the fitting up of my comfortable apartments. It was at this period that my connection with Phillip Haas and Sons was first established, which was destined with the lapse of time to give me some cause for anxiety. For the moment every exertion expended on a domicile associated with so many hopes only helped to put me into the best of spirits. The grand-piano arrived in due course, and with the addition of various engravings after Raphael, which had fallen to my lot in the Biebrich division, my music-room was completely furnished in readiness for the 22nd of May, when I celebrated my fiftieth birthday. In honour of the occasion the Merchants' Choral Society gave me an evening serenade with Chinese-lantern illuminations, in which a deputation of students also joined and greeted me with an enthusiastic oration. I had laid in a supply of wine, and everything passed off excellently. The Mrazeks looked after my housekeeping fairly well, and thanks to the culinary arts of Anna, I was able to invite Tausig and Cornelius to dine with me pretty frequently.

But I was soon in great trouble again, on account of Minna, who bitterly reproached me for everything I did. Having made up my mind never to answer her again, I wrote this time to her daughter Nathalie — who was still in ignorance of the relationship between them — referring her to my decision of the previous year.

On the other hand, the fact that I sadly stood in need just now of some womanly attentions and care in the management of the household became abundantly clear to me when I expressed to Mathilde Maier of Mayence the ingenuous wish that she would come and supply the deficiency.

I had certainly thought that my good friend was sensible enough to interpret my meaning correctly without feeling put to the blush, and I was very likely right, but I had not made sufficient allowance for her mother and her bourgeois surroundings generally. She appears to have been thrown into the greatest excitement by my proposal, while her friend Louise Wagner was in the end so powerfully influenced that she frankly advised me, with homely shrewdness and precision, to obtain a legal separation from my wife first of all, after which everything else would be easily arranged. Grievously shocked, I at once withdrew my offer, as having been made without due deliberation, and strove as far as possible to allay the excitement thus produced. On the other hand, Friederike Meyer's inexplicable fate still caused me much involuntary anxiety. After she had spent several months of the previous winter in Venice, apparently to her benefit, I had written to her from St. Petersburg suggesting that she should meet me at the Bülows' in Berlin. I had taken into mature consideration the kindly interest which Cosima had conceived for her, with a view to discussing what steps we could take to bring order into our friend's flagrantly disorganised circumstances. She did not appear, however, but wrote instead to inform me that she had taken up her abode with a lady friend at Coburg, as her very delicate state of health seriously interfered with her theatrical career, and was endeavouring to maintain herself by occasional appearances at the small theatre there. It was obvious that for many reasons I could not send her an invitation such as that sent to Mathilde Maier, though she expressed a violent desire to see me once more for a short time, assuring me that afterwards she would for ever leave me in peace. I could only regard it as purposeless and risky to accede to this wish just then, though I kept the idea in reserve for the future. During the course of the summer she repeated the same request from several places, until, as I was engaged late in the autumn for a concert at Karlsruhe, I at last appointed that time and place for the desired meeting. From that time forth I never received the slightest communication from this most singular and attractive friend of mine, and as, moreover, I did not know where she was, I looked upon our connection as severed. Not until many years later was the secret of her position — certainly a very difficult one — revealed to me, and from the facts then stated I could only conclude that she shrank from telling me the truth concerning her connection with Herr von Guaita. It appeared that this man had much more serious claims upon her than I had suspected, and she had apparently been compelled by the necessities of her situation to accept his protection, as he was the only friend left to her, while his devotion was undeniably genuine. I heard that she was then living in complete retirement both from the stage and from society on a tiny estate on the Rhine with her two children, being, it was believed, secretly married to Herr von Guaita.

But my careful and elaborate preparations for a quiet spell of work had not yet been successful. A burglary in the house, which robbed me of the golden snuff-box presented by the Moscow musicians, renewed my old longing to have a dog. My kind old landlord consequently handed over to me an old and somewhat neglected hound named Pohl, one of the most affectionate and excellent animals that ever attached itself to me. In his company I daily undertook long excursions on foot, for which the very pleasant neighbourhood afforded admirable opportunities. Nevertheless I was still rather lonely, as Tausig was confined to bed for a long time by severe illness, while Cornelius was suffering from an injured foot, the result of a careless descent from an omnibus when visiting Penzing. Meanwhile I was in constant friendly intercourse with Standhartner and his family. Fritz, the younger brother of Heinrich Porges, had also begun to visit me. He was a doctor who had just set up practice, a really nice fellow, whose acquaintance with me dated from the serenade of the Merchants' Glee Club, of which he had been the originator.

I was now convinced that there was no longer any chance of having *Tristan* produced at the Opera, as I had found out that Frau Dustmann's indisposition was merely a feint, Herr

Ander's complete loss of voice having been the real cause of the last interruption. Good old Conductor Esser tried hard to persuade me to assign the part of Tristan to another tenor of the theatre named Walter, but the very idea of him was so odious to me that I could not even bring myself to hear him in *Lohengrin*. I therefore let the matter sink into oblivion, and concentrated myself exclusively on getting into touch with the *Meistersinger* again. I first set to work on the instrumentation of the completed portion of the first act, of which I had only arranged detached fragments as yet. But as summer approached, the old anxiety as to my future subsistence began to pervade all my thoughts and sensations in the present. It was clear that, if I were to fulfil all my responsibilities, particularly with regard to Minna, I should soon have to think of undertaking some lucrative enterprise again.

It was therefore most opportune when a quite unexpected invitation from the management of the National Theatre in Buda-Pesth reached me to give two concerts there, in compliance with which I went at the end of July to the Hungarian capital, and was received by the manager Radnodfay. There I met a really very talented violinist named Réményi, who at one time had been a protégé of Liszt, and showed boundless admiration for me, even declaring that the invitation to me had been given entirely on his initiative. Although there was no prospect of large earnings here, as I had professed myself content to accept a thousand marks for each of the two concerts, I had reason to be pleased both with their success and with the great interest manifested by the audience. In this city, where the Magyar opposition to Austria was still at its strongest, I made the acquaintance of some exceedingly gifted and distinguished-looking young men, among them Herr Rosti, of whom I have a pleasant recollection. They organised a truly idyllic festivity for me, in the form of a feast, held by a few intimates on an island in the Danube, where we gathered under an ancient oak tree, as though for a patriarchal ceremony. A young lawyer, whose name I have unfortunately forgotten, had undertaken to propose the toast of the evening, and filled me with amazement and deep emotion, not only by the fire of his delivery, but also by the truly noble earnestness of his ideas, which he

based upon a perfect knowledge of all my works and undertakings. We returned home down the Danube in the small
boats of the Rowing Club, of which my hosts were members,
and on our way had to face a hurricane, which lashed the
mighty stream into the wildest tumult. There was only one
lady in our party, Countess Bethlen-Gabor, who was seated
with me in a narrow boat. Rosti and a friend of his who had
the oars were concerned solely with the fear that our boat
would be shivered against one of the timber-rafts, towards
which the flood was carrying us, and therefore exerted themselves to the utmost to avoid them; whereas I could see no
other way of escape, especially for the lady sitting beside me,
than by boarding one of these very rafts. In order to effect
this (against the wish of our two oarsmen) I seized with one
hand a projecting peg on a raft we were passing and held our
little vessel fast, and, while the two rowers screamed that the
Ellida would be lost, quickly hoisted the lady out of the skiff
on to the raft, across which we walked to the shore, calmly
leaving our friends to save the *Ellida* as best they could. We
two then continued our way along the bank through a terrific
storm of rain, but yet on safe and sure ground, towards the city.
My conduct in presence of this danger did not fail to increase
the respect in which my friends held me, as was proved by a
banquet given in a public garden at which a great number
of my admirers were present. Here they treated me quite
in Hungarian style. An enormous band of gipsy musicians
was drawn up, and greeted me with the *Rakoczy* March as I
approached, while the assembled guests joined in with impetuous shouts of '*Eljen!*' There were also fiery orations with
appreciative allusions to myself and my influence which extended far and wide throughout Germany. The introductory
parts of these speeches were always in Hungarian, and were
meant to excuse the fact that the main oration would be
delivered in German for the sake of their guest. Here I
noticed that they never spoke of me as ' Richard Wagner,' but
as ' Wagner Richard.'
   Even the highest military officials were not behindhand in
offering me their homage, through the medium of Field-Marshal
Coronini. The Count invited me to a performance by the

military bands in the castle at Ofen, where I was graciously received by him and his family, treated to ices, and then conducted to a balcony whence I listened to a concert given by the massed bands. The effect of all these demonstrations was exceedingly refreshing, and I almost regretted having to leave the rejuvenating atmosphere of Buda-Pesth, and return to my dull and musty Viennese asylum.

On the homeward journey, in the beginning of August, I travelled part of the way with Herr von Seebach, the amiable Saxon Ambassador, whom I had known in Paris. He complained of the enormous losses he had incurred through the difficulty of administering the South Russian estates he had acquired by marriage, and from which he was just returning. On the other hand, I was able to reassure him as to my own position, which seemed to give him genuine pleasure.

The small receipts from my Buda-Pesth concerts, of which, moreover, I had only been able to carry away half, were not calculated to afford me any effectual relief as to the future. Having now staked my all on what I trusted might be a permanent establishment, the first question was how best to secure a salary, which should at least be certain though not necessarily over-large. Meanwhile I did not consider myself bound to abandon my St. Petersburg connection, nor the plans I had founded upon it. Nor did I entirely disbelieve the assurances of Réményi, who boasted that he had great influence with the Magyar magnates, and assured me it would be no great matter to obtain a pension in Buda-Pesth, such as I had thought of securing in St. Petersburg and involving similar obligations. He did, in fact, visit me soon after my return to Penzing, accompanied by his adopted son, young Plotenyi, whose extraordinary good looks and amiability made a very favourable impression on me. As for the father himself, although he won my warm approbation by his brilliant performance of the *Rakoczy* March on the violin, yet I quickly perceived that his glowing promises had been meant rather to create an immediate impression on me than to ensure any permanent result. In accordance with his own desire, I very soon afterwards lost sight of him altogether.

While still obliged to busy myself with plans for concert tours,

I was able meantime to enjoy the pleasant shade of my garden
during the intense heat, and I used to go for long rambles
every evening with my faithful dog Pohl, the most refreshing
of these being by way of the dairy-farm at St. Veit, where
delicious milk was available. My small social circle was still
restricted to Cornelius and Tausig, who was at last restored to
health, although he disappeared from my sight for some time
owing to his intercourse with wealthy Austrian officers. But
I was frequently joined on my excursions by the younger
Porges, and for a time by the elder also. My niece Ottilie
Brockhaus too, who was living with the family of her mother's
friend Heinrich Laube, occasionally delighted me with a visit.

But whenever I settled down seriously to work, I was goaded
afresh by an uneasy apprehension as to the means of subsistence. As another journey to Russia was out of the question
until the following Easter, only German towns could serve my
purpose for the present. From many quarters, as for instance
from Darmstadt, I received unfavourable replies; and from
Karlsruhe, where I had applied direct to the Grand Duke, the
answer was indefinite. But the severest blow to my confidence
was a direct refusal which came in response to the application
I had at last made to St. Petersburg, the acceptance of which
would have ensured a regular salary. This time the excuse
made was that the Polish revolution of that summer had
paralysed the spirit of artistic enterprise.

Pleasanter news, however, came from Moscow, where they
held out prospects of some good concerts for the coming year.
I next bethought me of a very sound suggestion about Kieff
made to me by Setoff the singer, who thought there was a
prospect of a highly profitable engagement there. I entered
into correspondence on the matter, and was again put off until
the following Easter, when all the smaller Russian nobility
congregated at Kieff. These were all plans for the future
which, if I then had considered them in detail at that time,
would have been enough to rob me of all peace of mind for my
work. In any case there was a long interval during which I
must provide, not only for myself, but also for Minna. Any
prospect of a position in Vienna had to be handled most warily,
so that, with the approach of autumn, there was nothing left

me but to raise money on loan, a business in which Tausig was
able to help me, as he possessed extraordinary experience in
such matters.

I could not help wondering whether I should have to give
up my Penzing establishment, but, on the other hand, what
alternative was open to me? Every time I was seized with the
desire to compose, these cares obtruded themselves on my
mind, until, seeing that it was only a question of putting things
off from day to day, I was driven to take up the study of
Dunker's *Geschichte des Alterthums*. In the end my correspondence about concerts swallowed up the whole of my time.
I first asked Heinrich Porges to see what he could arrange in
Prague. He also held out a reasonable prospect of a concert
at Löwenberg, relying upon the favourable disposition of the
Prince of Hohenzollern, who lived there. I was also advised
to apply to Hans von Bronsart, who at this time was conductor
to a private orchestral society in Dresden. He responded
loyally to my proposition, and between us we settled the date
and programme of a concert to be conducted by me in Dresden.
As the Grand Duke of Baden had also placed his theatre at
Karlsruhe at my disposal for a concert to be given in November,
I thought I had now done enough in this direction to be entitled
to take up something different. I therefore wrote a fairly long
article for Uhl-Fröbel's paper *Der Botschafter* on the Imperial
Grand Opera House in Vienna, in which I made suggestions
for a thorough reform of this very badly managed institution.
The excellence of this article was at once acknowledged on all
sides, even by the press; and I appear to have made some
impression in the highest administrative circles, for I shortly
afterwards heard from my friend Rudolf Liechtenstein, that
tentative advances had been made to him with a view to his
accepting the position of manager, associated with which there
was certainly an idea of asking me to become conductor of the
Grand Opera. Among the reasons which caused this proposal
to fall through was the fear, Liechtenstein informed me, that
under his direction people would hear nothing but ' Wagner
operas.'

In the end it was a relief to escape from the anxieties of my
position by starting on my concert tour. First I went to

Prague, in the beginning of November, to try my luck again in the matter of big receipts. Unfortunately Heinrich Porges had not been able to take the arrangements in hand this time, and his deputies, who were very busy schoolmasters, were not at all his equals for the task. Expenses were increased, while receipts diminished, for they had not ventured to ask such high prices as before. I wished to repair this deficiency by a second concert a few days later, and insisted on the point, although my friends urgently dissuaded me, and, as the event proved, they were quite right. This time the receipts hardly covered the costs, and as I had been obliged to send away the proceeds of the first concert to redeem an old bill in Vienna, I had no other means of paying my hotel expenses and my fare home than by accepting the offer of a banker, who posed as a patron, to help me out of my embarrassment.

In the chastened mood induced by these occurrences I pursued my journey to Karlsruhe, via Nuremberg and Stuttgart, under wretched conditions of severe cold and constant delays. At Karlsruhe I was at once surrounded by various friends, who had come there on hearing of my project. Richard Pohl from Baden, who never failed me, Mathilde Maier, Frau Betty Schott, the wife of my publisher; even Raff from Wiesbaden and Emilie Genast were there, as well as Karl Eckert, who had recently been appointed conductor at Stuttgart. Trouble began at once with the vocalists for my first concert, fixed for 14th November, as the baritone, Hauser, who was to sing ' Wotan's Farewell ' and Hans Sachs's ' Cobbler Song,' was ill and had to be replaced by a voiceless though well-drilled vaudeville singer. In Eduard Devrient's opinion this made no difference. My relations with him were strictly official, but he certainly carried out my instructions for the arrangement of the orchestra very correctly. From an orchestral point of view the concert went off so well that the Grand Duke, who received me very graciously in his box, desired a repetition in a week's time. To this proposal I raised serious objections, having learned by experience that the large attendances at such concerts, particularly at special prices, were mainly accounted for by the curiosity of the hearers, who often came from long distances; whereas the number of genuine students of art,

whose interest was chiefly in the music, was but small. But
the Grand Duke insisted, as he wished to give his mother-in-
law, Queen Augusta, whose arrival was expected within a few
days, the pleasure of hearing my production. I should have
found it dreadfully wearisome to have to spend the intervening
time in the solitude of my Karlsruhe hotel, but I received a
kind invitation to Baden-Baden from Mme. Kalergis, who had
just become Mme. Moukhanoff, and had gone to live there.
She had, to my delight, been one of those who came over for
the concert, and was now on the station to meet me when I
arrived. I felt I ought to decline her proffered escort into
the town, not considering myself sufficiently smart in my
'brigand-hat,' but with the assurance, 'We all wear these
brigand-hats here,' she took my arm, and thus we reached
Pauline Viardot's villa, where we were to dine, as my friend's
own house was not yet quite ready. Seated by my old acquaintance, I was now introduced to the Russian poet Tur-
genieff. Mme. Moukhanoff presented me to her husband with
some hesitation, wondering what I should think of her marriage. Supported by her companions, who were all society
people, she exerted herself to maintain a fairly lively conversation during the time we were together. Well satisfied by
the admirable intention of my friend and benefactress, I again
left Baden to fill up my time by a little trip to Zürich, where
I again tried to get a few days' rest in the house of the Wesendonck family. The idea of assisting me did not seem even to
dawn on these friends of mine, although I frankly informed
them of my position. I therefore returned to Karlsruhe, where,
on the 22nd of November, as I had foreseen, I gave my second
concert to a poorly filled house. But, in the opinion of the
Grand Duke and his wife, Queen Augusta's appreciation should
have dispelled any unpleasant impressions I might have received. I was again summoned to the royal box, where I
found all the court gathered round the Queen, who wore a blue
rose on her forehead as an ornament. The few complimentary
observations she had to offer were listened to by the members
of the court with breathless attention; but when the royal
lady had made a few general remarks, and was about to enter
into details, she left all further demonstration to her daughter,

who, as she said, knew more about it. The next day I received my share of the takings, half the net profits, which amounted to two hundred marks, and with this I at once bought myself a fur coat. The sum asked for it was two hundred and twenty marks, but when I explained that my receipts had only been two hundred marks, I managed to get the extra twenty knocked off the price. There was still the Grand Duke's private gift, consisting of a gold snuff-box with fifteen louis d'or, for which I, of course, returned my thanks in writing. I next had to face the question whether, after the toilsome fatigue of the past weeks, I would add to my disappointments by attempting to give the proposed concert in Dresden. Many considerations, practically everything indeed that I had to weigh in connection with a visit to Dresden, moved me to have the courage to write and tell Hans von Bronsart at the last moment to cancel all arrangements and not expect me there, a decision which, although it must have caused him much inconvenience after all the preparations he had kindly made, he accepted with a very good grace.

I still wanted to see what I could do with the firm of Schott, and travelled by night to Mayence, where Mathilde Maier's family insisted on my spending the day at their little house, where I was entertained in a simple and friendly fashion. During the day and night I spent here in the narrow Karthäuser-gasse, I was waited upon with the greatest care, and from this outpost I assaulted the publishing house of Schott, though without securing much booty. This was because I refused my consent to a separate issue of the various selections from my new works which had been picked out and prepared for concert use.

As my only remaining source of profit now seemed to be the concert at Löwenberg, I turned my face thither; but, in order to avoid passing Dresden, I made a short détour by way of Berlin, where, after travelling all night, I arrived, very tired, early on the 28th of November. In compliance with my request the Bülows took me in, and at once began urging me to break my intended journey to Silesia by giving them a day in Berlin. Hans was particularly anxious for me to be present at a concert to be given that evening under his direction, a fact which finally decided me to remain. In defiance of the cold, raw and gloomy weather, we discussed as cheerfully as we could my unfortunate position. By way of increasing my capital, it was resolved to hand over the Grand Duke of Baden's gold snuff-box to our good old friend Weitzmann for sale. The sum of two hundred and seventy marks realised by this was brought to me at the Hôtel Brandenburg, where I was dining with the Bülows, and was an addition to my reserves that furnished us with many a jest. As Bülow had to complete the preparations for his concert, I drove out alone with Cosima on the promenade, as before, in a fine carriage. This time all our jocularity died away into silence. We gazed speechless into each other's eyes; an intense longing for an avowal of the truth mastered us and led to a confession — which needed no words — of the boundless unhappiness which oppressed us. The experience brought relief to us both, and the profound tranquillity which ensued enabled us to attend the concert in a cheerful, unembarrassed mood. I was actually able to fix my attention clearly on an exquisitely refined and elevated performance of Beethoven's smaller Concert Overture (in C major), and likewise on Hans's very clever arrangement of Gluck's overture to *Paris and Helen.* We noticed Alwine Frommann in the audience, and during the interval met her on the grand staircase of the concert-hall. After the second part had begun and the stairs were empty, we sat for some time on one of the steps chatting gaily with our old friend. After the concert we were due at my friend Weitzmann's for supper, the length and abundance of which reduced us, whose hearts yearned for profound peace, to almost frantic despair. But the day came to an end at last, and after a night spent under Bülow's roof, I continued my journey. Our farewell reminded me so vividly of that first exquisitely pathetic parting from Cosima at Zürich, that all the intervening years vanished like a dream of desolation separating two days of lifelong moment and decision. If on the first occasion our presentiment of something mysterious and inexplicable had compelled silence, it was now no less impossible to give words to that which we silently acknowledged.

I was met at one of the stations in Silesia by Conductor Seifriz, who accompanied me in one of the Prince's carriages to

Löwenberg. The old Prince of Hohenzollern-Hechingen was already very well disposed towards me on account of his great friendship for Liszt, and had, moreover, been fully informed of my position by Heinrich Porges, who had been engaged by him for a short time. He had invited me to give a concert in his small castle to an audience composed exclusively of invited guests. I was very comfortably accommodated in apartments on the ground floor of his house, whither he frequently came on his wheeled chair from his own rooms directly opposite. Here I could not only feel at ease, but be to some extent hopeful. I at once began rehearsing the pieces I had chosen from my operas with the Prince's by no means ill-equipped private orchestra, during which my host was invariably present and seemed well satisfied. Meals were all taken very sociably in common; but on the day of the concert there was a kind of gala-dinner, at which I was astonished to meet Henriette von Bissing, the sister of Mme. Wille of Marienbad, with whom I had been intimate at Zürich. As she had an estate near Löwenberg, she had also been invited by the Prince, and now gave me proof of her faithful and enthusiastic devotion. Being both intelligent and witty, she at once became my favourite companion. After the concert had passed off with reasonable success, I had to fulfil another wish of the Prince's next day, by privately playing to him Beethoven's Symphony in C minor, when Frau von Bissing was also present. She had now been for some time a widow. She promised to come to Breslau, when I gave my concert there. Before my departure Conductor Seifriz brought me a fee of four thousand two hundred marks from the Prince, with an expression of regret that for the present it was impossible for him to be more liberal. After all my previous experiences I was truly astonished and contented, and it was with pleasure I returned the gallant Prince my heartfelt thanks with all the eloquence at my command.

Thence I travelled to Breslau, where the concert director, Damrosch, had arranged a concert for me. I had made his acquaintance on my last visit to Weimar, and had also heard of him through Liszt. Unfortunately the conditions here struck me as extraordinarily dismal and desperate. The whole affair had been planned on the meanest scale, as indeed

I might have expected. A perfectly horrible concert-room, which usually served as a beer-restaurant, had been engaged. At the rear of this, and separated from it by a dreadfully vulgar curtain, was a small 'Tivoli' theatre, for which I was obliged to procure an elevated plank-floor for the orchestra, and the whole concern so disgusted me that my first impulse was to dismiss the seedy-looking musicians on the spot. My friend Damrosch, who was very much upset, had to promise me that at least he would have the horrible reek of tobacco in the place neutralised. As he could offer no guarantee as to the amount of the receipts, I was only induced in the end to go on with the enterprise by my desire not to compromise him too severely. To my amazement I found almost the entire room, at all events the front seats, filled with Jews, and in fact I owed such success as I obtained to the interest excited in this section of the population, as I learned the next day, when I attended a mid-day dinner arranged in my honour by Damrosch, at which again only Jews were present.

It was like a ray of light from a better world when, on leaving the concert-hall, I perceived Fräulein Marie von Buch, who had hurried hither with her grandmother from the Hatzfeld estate to be present at my concert, and was waiting in a boarded compartment dignified by the name of box, for me to come out after the audience had left; the young lady came up to me once more in travelling costume after Damrosch's dinner and attempted by kindly and sympathetic assurances somewhat to assuage my evident anxiety respecting the future. I thanked her once more by letter for her sympathy after my return to Vienna, to which she replied by a request for a contribution to her album. In memory of the emotions which had convulsed me on leaving Berlin, and also as an indication of my mental mood to one worthy of the confidence, I added Calderon's words, 'Things impossible to conceal, yet impossible of utterance.' By this I felt I had conveyed to a kindly disposed person, though with a happy vagueness, some idea of the secret knowledge which was my sole inspiration.

But the results of my meeting with Henriette von Bissing in Breslau were very different. She had followed me thither, and put up at the same hotel. Influenced, no doubt, by my sickly appearance, she seemed to give her sympathy for myself and my situation full play. I placed the latter before her without reserve, telling her how, ever since the upset following on my departure from Zürich in 1858, I had been unable to secure the regular income necessary for the steady pursuit of my calling; and also of my invariably vain attempts to bring my affairs into any settled and definite order. My friend did not shrink from attributing some blame to the relationship between Frau Wesendonck and my wife, and declared that she felt it her mission to conciliate them. She approved my settling down at Penzing, and only hoped that I might not spoil its beneficial effect upon me by distant enterprises. She would not listen to my plan of touring in Russia, in the coming winter, in order to earn money for my absolute necessities, and herself undertook to provide from her own very considerable fortune the not unimportant sum requisite to maintain me in independence for some time to come. But she explained to me that for a short while longer I was to try and get along through thick and thin, as she would have some difficulty — possibly a good deal — in placing the promised money at my disposal.

Greatly cheered by the impressions of this meeting I returned to Vienna on the 9th December. At Löwenberg I had been obliged to remit to Vienna the greater portion of the Prince's gift, part of it for Minna, and part for the payment of debts. Though I had but little cash I felt thoroughly sanguine; I could now greet my few friends with tolerable good-humour, and among them Peter Cornelius, who looked in on me every evening. As Heinrich Porges and Gustav Schönaich sometimes joined us, we founded an intimate little circle and met regularly. On Christmas Eve I invited them all to my house, where I had the Christmas tree lighted up, and gave each one an appropriate trifle. Some work also came my way again, for Tausig asked me to help him with a concert which he was to give in the great Redouten-Saal. In addition to a few selections from my new operas, I also conducted the *Freischütz* Overture, for my own particular satisfaction and entirely according to my own interpretation. Its effect, even upon the orchestra, was truly startling.

But there did not seem the slightest prospect of any official recognition of my abilities; I was, and continued to be, ignored by the great. Frau von Bissing's communications revealed by degrees the difficulties which she had encountered in the fulfilment of her promise; but as they were still hopeful in tone, I was able to spend New Year's Eve at the Standhartner's in good spirits, and to enjoy a poem specially written by Cornelius for the occasion, which was as humorous as it was solemnly appropriate.

The new year 1864 assumed for me an aspect of gravity which soon became intensified. I fell ill with a painful and increasing malady due to a chill, which often made demands on Standhartner's care. But I was yet more seriously threatened by the turn of Frau von Bissing's communications. It seemed she could only raise the promised money with the help of her family, the Slomans, who were shipowners in Hamburg, and from them she was meeting with violent opposition, mingled, as it seemed, with slanderous charges against me. These circumstances upset me so much that I wished I could renounce all help from this friend, and I began once more to turn my serious attention to Russia. Fräulein von Rhaden, to whom I again applied, felt she must vigorously dissuade me from any attempt to visit St. Petersburg, in the first place because, owing to the military disturbances in the Polish provinces, I should find the route blocked, and secondly because, roughly speaking, I should attract no notice in the Russian capital. On the other hand, a visit to Kieff, with a chance of five thousand roubles profit, was represented as undoubtedly feasible. Keeping my thoughts fixed on this, I arranged with Cornelius, who was to accompany me, a plan for crossing the Black Sea to Odessa, and going from there to Kieff, with a view to which we both resolved to procure the indispensable fur coats at once. Meanwhile, the only course open to me was to see about raising money by fresh bills at short dates, wherewith to pay all my other bills, which were also short-dated. Thus I became launched upon a business system which, leading, as it did, to obvious and inevitable ruin, could only be finally resolved by the acceptance of prompt and effectual help. In these straits I was at last compelled to request a clear declaration from my friend, not as to whether she *could* help me at once, but whether she really *wished* to help me at all, as I could no longer stave off ruin. She must have been in the highest degree wounded by some notion or other, of which I was ignorant, before bringing herself to reply in the following tone: ' You wish to know finally whether I *will* or not? Well, then, in God's name, *No!* ' Not long after this I received from her sister, Mme. Wille, a very surprising explanation of her conduct, which seemed at the time perfectly inexplicable, and only to be accounted for by the weakness of her not very reliable character.

Amid all these vacillations the month of February had run to an end, and while Cornelius and I were busy on our Russian plans, I received news from Kieff and Odessa that it would be unwise to attempt any artistic enterprises there during the present year. By this time it had become clear that, under the conditions thus developed, I could no longer reckon on maintaining my position in Vienna, or my establishment at Penzing. Not only did there seem no prospect of even a temporary nature of earning money, but my debts had mounted up, in the usual style of such usury, to so great a sum, and assumed so threatening an aspect, that, failing some extraordinary relief, my very person was in danger. In this perplexity I addressed myself with perfect frankness — at first only for advice — to the judge of the Imperial Provincial Court, Eduard Liszt, the youthful uncle of my old friend Franz. During my first stay in Vienna this man had shown himself a warmly devoted friend, always ready to help me. For the discharge of my bill-debts he could naturally suggest no other method than the intervention of some wealthy patron, who should settle with my creditors. For some time he believed that a certain Mme. Schöller, the wife of a rich merchant and one of my admirers, not only possessed the means, but was willing to use them on my behalf. Standhartner also, with whom I made no pretence of secrecy, thought he could do something for me in this way. Thus my position was for some weeks again most uncertain, until at last it became clear that all my friends could procure me was the means for flight to Switzerland — which was now deemed absolutely necessary — where, having saved my skin so far, I should have to raise money for my bills. To the lawyer, Eduard Liszt, this way of escape seemed specially

desirable, because he would then be in a position to punish the
outrageous usury practised against me.

During the anxious time of the last few months, through
which, nevertheless, there had run an undercurrent of indefinite
hope, I had kept up a lively intercourse with my few friends.
Cornelius turned up regularly every evening, and was joined
by O. Bach, little Count Laurencin, and, on one occasion, by
Rudolph Liechtenstein. With Cornelius alone I began reading
the *Iliad*. When we reached the catalogue of ships I wished to
skip it; but Peter protested, and offered to read it out himself; but whether we ever came to the end of it I forget. My
reading by myself consisted of Chateaubriand's *La Vie de Rancé*,
which Tausig had brought me. Meanwhile, he himself vanished
without leaving any trace, until after some time he reappeared
engaged to a Hungarian pianist. During the whole of this
time I was very ill and suffered exceedingly from a violent
catarrh. The thought of death took such hold on me that I
at last lost all desire to shake it off, and even set about bequeath-
ing my books and manuscripts, of which a portion fell to the lot
of Cornelius.

I had taken the precaution some time before of commending
into Standhartner's keeping my remaining — and now, alas!
exceedingly doubtful — assets which were in the house at Penzing. As my friends were most positive in recommending preparation for immediate flight, I had written to Otto Wesendonck
requesting to be taken into his house, as Switzerland was to
be my destination. He refused point-blank, and I could not
resist sending him a reply to prove the injustice of this. The
next thing was to make my absence from home a short one and
to count upon a speedy return. Standhartner made me go and
dine at his house in his great anxiety to cover up my departure,
and my servant Franz Mrazek brought my trunk there too.
My farewell to Standhartner, his wife Anna, and the good
dog Pohl was very depressing. Standhartner's stepson Karl
Schönaich and Cornelius accompanied me to the station, the
one in grief and tears, the other inclining to a frivolous mood.
It was on the afternoon of 23rd March that I left for Munich,
my first stopping-place, where I hoped to rest for two days
after the terrible disturbances I had gone through, without

attracting any notice. I stayed at the 'Bayerischer Hof' and took a few walks through the city at my leisure. It was Good Friday and the weather was bitterly cold. The mood proper to the day seemed to possess the whole population, whom I saw going from one church to another dressed in deepest mourning. King Maximilian II. — of whom the Bavarians had become so fond — had died a few days before, leaving as heir to the throne a son aged eighteen and a half, whose extreme youth was no bar to his accession. I saw a portrait of the young king, Ludwig II., in a shop window, and experienced the peculiar emotion which is aroused by the sight of youth and beauty placed in a position presumed to be unusually trying. After writing a humorous epitaph for myself, I crossed Lake Constance unmolested and reached Zürich — once more a refugee in need of an asylum — where I at once betook myself to Dr. Wille's estate at Mariafeld.

I had already written to my friend's wife to ask her to put me up for a few days, which she very kindly agreed to do. I had got to know her very well during my last stay at Zürich, while my friendship with him had somewhat cooled. I wanted to have time to find what seemed suitable quarters in one of the places bordering on Lake Zürich. Dr. Wille himself was not there, as he had gone to Constantinople on a pleasure trip. I had no difficulty in making my friend understand my situation, which I found her most willing to relieve. First of all she cleared one or two living rooms in Frau von Bissing's old house next door, from which, however, the fairly comfortable furniture had been removed. I wanted to cater for myself, but had to yield to her request to take over that responsibility. Only furniture was lacking, and for this she ventured to apply to Frau Wesendonck, who immediately sent all she could spare of her household goods, as well as a cottage piano. The good woman was also anxious that I should visit my old friends at Zürich to avoid any appearance of unpleasantness, but I was prevented from doing so by serious indisposition, which was increased by the badly heated rooms, and finally Otto and Mathilde Wesendonck came over to us at Mariafeld. The very uncertain and strained attitude apparent in these two was not entirely incomprehensible to me, but I behaved as if

I did not notice it. My cold, which rendered me incapable of looking about for a house in the neighbouring districts, was continually aggravated by the bad weather and my own deep depression. I spent these dreadful days sitting huddled in my Karlsruhe fur coat from morning till night, and addled my brain with reading one after another of the volumes which Mme. Wille sent me in my seclusion. I read Jean Paul's *Siebenkäs,* Frederick the Great's *Tagebuch,* Tauser, George Sand's novels and Walter Scott's, and finally *Felicitas,* a work from my sympathetic hostess's own pen. Nothing reached me from the outside world except a passionate lament from Mathilde Maier, and a most pleasant surprise in the shape of royalties (seventy-five francs), which Truinet sent from Paris. This led to a conversation with Mme. Wille, half in anger and half with condemned-cell cynicism, as to what I could do to obtain complete release from my wretched situation. Among other things we touched upon the necessity of obtaining a divorce from my wife in order to contract a rich marriage. As everything seemed right and nothing inexpedient in my eyes, I actually wrote and asked my sister Luise Brockhaus whether she could not, by talking sensibly to Minna, persuade her to depend on her settled yearly allowance without making any claims on my person in future. In reply I received a deeply pathetic letter advising me first to think of establishing my reputation and to create for myself an unassailable position by some new work. In this way I might very probably reap some benefit without taking any foolish step; and in any case I should do well to apply for the post of conductor which was now vacant in Darmstadt.

I had very bad news from Vienna. Standhartner, to make sure of the furniture I had left in the house, sold it to a Viennese agent, with the option of re-purchase. I wrote back in great indignation, particularly as I realised the prejudicial effect of this on my landlord, to whom I had to pay rent within the next few days. Through Mme. Wille I succeeded in getting placed at my disposal the money required for the rent, which I forwarded at once to Baron Rackowitz. Unfortunately, however, I found that Standhartner had already cleared up everything with Eduard Liszt, paying the rent with the proceeds from the furniture, and thereby cutting off my return to Vienna, which they both considered would be positive ruin to me. But when I heard at the same time from Cornelius that Tausig, who was then in Hungary and who had added his signature to one of the bills of exchange, felt himself prevented by me from returning to Vienna as he desired, I was so sensibly wounded that I decided to go back on the spot, however great the danger might be. I announced my intention to my friends there immediately, but decided first to try and provide myself with enough money to be in a position to suggest a composition with my creditors. To this end I had written most urgently to Schott at Mayence, and did not refrain from reproaching him bitterly for his behaviour to me. I now decided to leave Mariafeld for Stuttgart to await the result of these efforts, and to prosecute them from a nearer vantage-ground. But I was also, as will be seen, moved to carry out this change by other motives.

Dr. Wille had returned, and I could see at once that my stay at Mariafeld alarmed him. He probably feared I might rely on his help also. In some confusion, occasioned by the attitude I had adopted in consequence, he made this confession to me in a moment of agitation. He was, he said, overpowered by a sentiment with regard to me which amounted to this — that a man wanted, after all, to be something more than a cipher in his own house, where, if anywhere, it is not pleasant to serve as a mere foil to some one else. This sentiment was merely excusable, he thought, in a man who, though he might reasonably suppose himself of some account among his fellows, had been brought into close contact with another to whom he felt himself in the strangest manner subordinate. Mme. Wille, foreseeing her husband's frame of mind, had come to an agreement with the Wesendonck family by which they were to provide me with one hundred francs a month during my stay at Mariafeld. When this came to my knowledge, I could do nothing but announce to Frau Wesendonck my immediate departure from Switzerland, and request her in the kindest possible way to consider herself relieved of all anxiety about me, as I had arranged my affairs quite in accordance with my wishes. I heard later that she had returned this letter — which, possibly, she considered compromising — to Mme. Wille unopened.

My next move was to go to Stuttgart on 30th April. I knew
that Karl Eckert had been settled there some time as conductor
at the Royal Court Theatre, and I had reason to believe the
good-natured fellow to be unprejudiced and well disposed
towards me, judging by his admirable behaviour when he had
been director of the opera in Vienna, and also by the enthusiasm he exhibited in coming to my concert at Karlsruhe the
year before. I expected nothing further of him than a little
assistance in looking for a quiet lodging for the coming summer
at Cannstadt or some such place near Stuttgart. I wanted,
above all, to finish the first act of the *Meistersinger* with all
possible despatch, so as to send Schott part of the manuscript
at last. I had told him that I was going to send it to him almost
immediately when I attacked him about the advances which had
so long been withheld from me. I then intended to collect
the means wherewith to meet my obligations in Vienna, while
living in complete retirement and, as I hoped, in concealment.
Eckert welcomed me most kindly. His wife — one of the
greatest beauties in Vienna — had, in her fantastic desire to
marry an artist, given up a very profitable post, but was still
rich enough for the conductor to live comfortably and show
hospitality, and the impression I now received was very pleasant. Eckert felt himself absolutely bound to take me to see
Baron von Gall, the manager of the court theatre, who alluded
sensibly and kindly to my difficult position in Germany, where
everything was likely to remain closed to me as long as the
Saxon ambassadors and agents — who were scattered everywhere — were allowed to attempt to injure me by all kinds
of suspicions. After getting to know me better, he considered himself authorised to act on my behalf through the
medium of the court of Würtemberg. As I was talking over
these matters rather late on the evening of 3rd May at the
Eckerts', a gentleman's card with the inscription ' Secretary
to the King of Bavaria ' was handed to me. I was disagreeably
surprised that my presence in Stuttgart should be known to
passing travellers, and sent word that I was not there, after
which I retired to my hotel, only to be again informed by the
landlord that a gentleman from Munich desired to see me on
urgent business. I made an appointment for the morning at

ten o'clock, and passed a disturbed night in my constant anticipation of misfortune. I received Herr Pfistermeister, the
private secretary of H.M. the King of Bavaria, in my room.
He first expressed great pleasure at having found me at last,
thanks to receiving some happy directions, after vainly seeking
me in Vienna and even at Mariafeld on Lake Zürich. He was
charged with a note for me from the young King of Bavaria,
together with a portrait and a ring as a present. In words
which, though few, penetrated to the very core of my being,
the youthful monarch confessed his great partiality for my
work, and announced his firm resolve to keep me near him as
his friend, so that I might escape any malignant stroke of fate.
Herr Pfistermeister informed me at the same time that he was
instructed to conduct me to Munich at once to see the King,
and begged my permission to inform his master by telegram
that I would come on the following day. I was invited to dine
with the Eckerts, but Herr Pfistermeister was obliged to decline
to accompany me. My friends, who had been joined by young
Weisheimer from Osthofen, were very naturally amazed and
delighted at the news I brought them. While we were at
table Eckert was informed by telegram of Meyerbeer's death
in Paris, and Weisheimer burst out in boorish laughter to think
that the master of opera, who had done me so much harm, had
by a strange coincidence not lived to see this day. Herr von
Gall also made his appearance, and had to admit in friendly
surprise that I certainly did not need his good services any
more. He had already given the order for *Lohengrin*, and
now paid me the stipulated sum on the spot. At five o'clock
that afternoon I met Herr Pfistermeister at the station to travel
with him to Munich, where my visit to the King was announced
for the following morning.

On the same day I had received the most urgent warnings
against returning to Vienna. But my life was to have no more
of these alarms; the dangerous road along which fate beckoned
me to such great ends was not destined to be clear of troubles
and anxieties of a kind unknown to me heretofore, but I was
never again to feel the weight of the everyday hardships of
existence under the protection of my exalted friend.

INDEX

906 INDEX

Königsberg, 169; domestic quarrels, 170, 171; Minna's flight, 172; Minna returns, 174; conductorship at Riga, 174; a peaceful summer, 176-7; close sympathy with his sister Ottilie, 176; arrives at Riga, 177; comic opera, 179, 180; composes Russian national hymn, 180; his news of Minna's illness, 180; his reconciliation with Minna, 181; domestic happiness renewed, 182-3; composes music to Rienzi, 185, 186, 194; isolation in Riga, 187-8; discovers the cause of Holtei's enmity, 188-9; loses the conductorship at Riga, 188 sqq.; misplaced confidence, 190; in communication with Paris, 193; preparations for journey to, 194-5; perilous journey to Paris, 195-208; secret flight from Riga, 195-7; visit to London, 203-7; visit to the House of Lords, 206; calls on Meyerbeer, 207-8; first impressions of Paris, 208; discouraging time in Paris, 211 sqq.; composition of songs, 212; impression made by Ninth Symphony renewed, 214-15; has recourse to the 'Mont de Piété,' 217; makes Kietz's acquaintance, 218, 219; loses his dog Robber, 218; renews friendship with Laube, 220; moves into a flat, 221-2; obtains means of livelihood for six months, 221; returns to his love for classical music, 223; composition of Rienzi, 224; lets some of his rooms, 225; loses score of Rule Britannia Overture, 225; writes articles for the Gazette Musicale, 227-9; attempts to write method for Cornet à pistons, 229; commissioned to arrange La Favorita for piano, etc., 232 sqq.; and Berlioz, 233 sqq.; writes successful short stories, 233-4; Heine's criticism of his story, 233; a disastrous performance of Columbus Overture, 235-6; a New Year's party, 237-8; enforced economies, 237; Vieuxtemps pays him a visit, 238; goes to Meudon, 239; contributes Paris letters to Dresden Abendzeitung, 240 sqq.; increasing journalistic work, 242 sqq.; sells French rights to plot of Fliegender Holländer, 243-4, 246; composes music to Fliegender

Holländer, 246-7, 249, 250; obtains assistance from Kietz, 250; contempt for Parisian musical taste, 241, 242, 252; turns to philosophy and history, 256 sqq.; attracted by German history, 257; first conceives his idea of Tannhäuser, 260, 265; the ground-work of his Lohengrin, 260; hopeful news from Germany, 262; leaves Paris for Dresden, 264 sqq.; revisits Leipzig, 266; offer of help from Hermann Brockhaus, 268; goes to Dresden, 268, 269; preparations for staging of Rienzi, 270; a summer visit to Töplitz, 272; visit to the Bohemian mountains, 273; meets Schröder-Devrient again, 274; enthusiasm over the rehearsals of Rienzi, 277 sqq.; his talent as a librettist, 277; first performance of Rienzi, 280 sqq.; unqualified success of Rienzi, 282 sqq.; jealousy follows on success, 284; negotiations for the performance of Der Fliegender Holländer in Dresden, 286; his impressions of Mendelssohn, 287, 288; meets Liszt, 289, 290, 291; performance of Fliegender Holländer, 292 sqq.; failure of Der Fliegender Holländer, 294; his reflections on causes of success of Rienzi, 295 sqq.; made conductor to the court at Dresden, 297 sqq.; performance of Der Fliegender Holländer at Cassel and Riga, 301; enmity of the press, 302 sqq., 320; conducts his operas in person, 303 sqq.; hostility of his colleagues, 304 sqq.; friendship with August Röckel, 306 sqq.; friendship with Anton Pusinelli, 308 sqq.; introduction into aristocratic society, 309; influence exercised by Frau von Lüttichau over, 309 sqq.; composes Liebesmahl der Apostel, 311 sqq.; receives gold snuff-box, 312; summer holiday in Töplitz, 313; Tannhäuser libretto, 313; an unsuccessful cure, 313-14; composition of music to Tannhäuser, 314, 316; influence of Grimm's work on, 314; a settled home in Dresden, 315, 316; his library, 316; performance of Fliegender Holländer in Berlin, 317 sqq.; a midnight visitor, 320, 321, 326; performance of Rienzi at Hamburg, 321 sqq.; undertakes

545; guarantor for Karl Ritter, 548, 549; conducting at Zürich, 551, 552, 553; meeting of friends, 554, 555; refuses Duke of Coburg's offer to arrange instrumentation of an opera, 561; offered payment for *Siegfrieds Tod*, 561; ill-health, 562, 580; settles in Karl Ritter's old quarters, 563; enters into contract with Weimar management, 563; friendship with Uhlig, 564, 568; 'Judaism in Music,' 565; visits Rorschach, 566; visit to Karl Ritter, 566; influenced by Rausse's book, 569; excursion through Switzerland with Uhlig, 579; goes to Albisbrunnen for cure, 572, 573; loan from Ritter, 574; received income from Laussot and Ritter families, 574; political view of, 577 *sqq.*; illness of, 579; friends in Zürich, 579; conducts *Egmont*, 580; undertakes directorship of orchestra for musical society, 580; goes to Rinderknecht estate, 582; walking tour in Switzerland, 583 *sqq.*; applications for productions of *Tannhäuser*, 589; prints copies of his *Ring des Nibelungen*, 591–2; reads his tetralogy, 594, 595; increasing interest in Zürich in his works, 596; influence of Liszt on, 599; goes to St. Moritz Bad, 600 *sqq.*; composes Overture to *Rheingold*, 603; writes new finale to *Iphigenia* Overture, 611; influence of Schopenhauer on, 614 *sqq.*; sends a copy of his *Nibelungen* to Schopenhauer, 616–617; invitation from London Philharmonic Society, 619; goes to London to conduct for Philharmonic Society, 621 *sqq.*; encounters hostility in London, 623 *sqq.*; London acquaintances, 626 *sqq.*; his intercourse with Berlioz, 628; visits the London theatres, 633, 634; returns to Zürich, 635; death of his dog Peps, 636; a visit to Selisberg, 637; frequent illness of, 638, 643; goes to Geneva for a cure, 644 *sqq.*; relations with the Ritter family, 650; conducts *Eroica* Symphony at St. Gall, 654–5; symphony between Liszt and, 655; composition of music to *Siegfried*, 656, 659, 664, 666; Wesendonck procures him a house, 657 *sqq.*; noisy

neighbours, 657; royalites from Berlin, 658; sketches out libretto to *Parsifal*, 662; writes libretto of *Tristan und Isolde*, 667, 668; his relations with the Wesendonck family, 667, 668, 672, 678, 686, 687, 688; composes music to *Tristan und Isolde*, 669, 670, 671, 678, 684, 685; a state of melancholy, 671; goes to Paris, 674 *sqq.*; his intercourse with Berlioz, 676 *sqq.*; is promised an Erard grand-piano, 677; Minna's jealousy, 680 *sqq.*; the Erard grand-piano arrives, 681; interview with Grand Duke of Weimar, 682; forced to give up his house, 688; parting from Minna, 689; goes to Italy, 689; visit to Maison Fazy, 689; visit to Venice, 690; journeys to Venice with Karl Ritter, 690, 691; sends to Zürich for his Erard 'Grand,' 691; settles at Giustiniani palace, Venice, 691; impressions of Venice, 691, 692; ill-health of, 692, 710, 747, 748, 860; friendship with Prince Dolgoroukow, 692; life in Venice, 692 *sqq.*; illness of, 698, 880; relations with Minna Planer, 699; effect of Leonardo da Vinci's 'Last Supper' on, 704, 705; criticism of Italian drama, 705; goes to Lucerne in order to complete third act of *Tristan und Isolde*, 706; declines voluntary support of the Ritters, 707; offers copyright of *Nibelungen* to Grand Duke of Weimar, 707; reserves French copyright of operas, 708; forced to an agreement with Meser, 708; legal difficulties over French copyright, 709; enmity of Saxons against, 700, 702; leaves Venice, 704; sends Erard back, 704; visit to and impressions of Milan, 704, 705; friendship with Dräsecke, 711; ascends Mt. Pilatus with Dräsecke, 712; reconciliation with Minna Planer, 712; addresses letter to Grand Duke of Baden for guarantee to settle at Karlsruhe, 712; meets old friends in Zürich, 713; visit to Winterthur, 714; reaches Paris, 714; takes villa in Rue Newton, 714; proposes starting German theatre in Paris, 718 *sqq.*; arranges concerts in Paris, 719; essays to obtain influential friends, 719; appeals to Napoleon to secure